501

GREAT DAYS OUT IN THE UK & IRELAND

501

GREAT DAYS OUT IN THE UK & IRELAND

Bounty
Books

Publisher: Polly Manguel

Project Editor: Emma Beare

Publishing Assistant: Frankie Pateman

Designer: Ron Callow/Design 23

Picture Researcher: Emma O'Neill

Production Manager: Neil Randles

Production Assistant: Gemma Seddon

First published in Great Britain in 2009 by
Bounty Books, a division of Octopus Publishing Group Limited
2-4 Heron Quays, London E14 4JP
www.octopusbooks.co.uk

An Hachette Livre UK Company
www.hachettelivre.co.uk

A CIP catalogue record is available from the British Library

ISBN: 978-0-753718-27-8

Printed and bound in China

Please note: The guidance sometimes given for people with mobility problems is intended only as a very rough guide and those concerned about this issue should make their own appropriate investigations before setting off on their day out.

The advice given on costs, which is based on a day out for a family of two adults and two children, is a rough indication only and excludes the cost of travel, food and drink. **Low**: £20 or less, **Reasonable**: £20 - £50 and **Expensive**: over £50*. Admission charges often change and discounts for families and for online bookings are frequently available, so always check before you set out.

or the Euro equivalents in Ireland

Contents

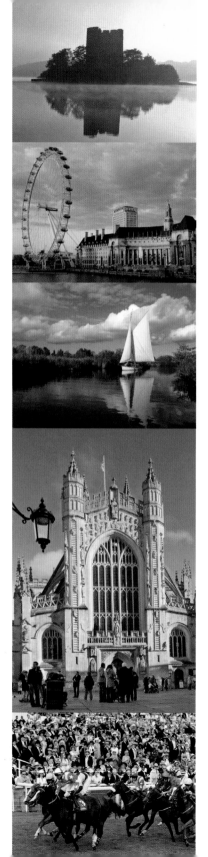

Introduction

There is such a wealth of places to see and things to do in the islands of Britain and Ireland that we really are spoilt for choice. Palaces, castles, museums, churches, stately homes and gardens are all part of the extraordinarily rich heritage that we are privileged to enjoy. Combined with the enormous variety of landscapes, seascapes, villages, towns and cities, when planning a day out we are therefore presented with thousands of choices.

This book is a collection of suggestions of where to go and what to do on a day out. Some of these will be great on cold and miserable winter days, while others can only be contemplated when the sun is shining. Yet more can be enjoyed at any time of year. Some have specific interests or age groups in mind – whilst children may adore spending a day by the seaside, they might well find an art gallery or museum rather boring. Therefore as families are, of course, often made up of people of very different ages and interests, the ideal family day out should ensure that there is something for everyone to enjoy.

There are zoos, wildlife parks and aquariums to visit, picturesque train journeys to take, caves to explore, mountains to climb and cathedrals to wonder at. Some of the suggested days out, like visiting the Tower of London, are well known traditions. Others are more unusual – like visiting an auction, going to the races, or a trip to Portmeirion, the surreal, Italianate Welsh fantasy village.

There are days out here which will help you get to know the joys of Dublin, Glasgow and Leeds and many other towns and cities, as well as London, of course; other very different days out might involve a ferry boat trip to an offshore island or a walk through an ancient forest. Many of the UK and Ireland's oldest buildings are featured, along with numerous examples of fine contemporary architecture and design – from London's

Millennium Bridge to The Lowry in Salford. Plenty of families may find such modern attractions as Legoland or Alton Towers or Cadbury World more to their taste.

Some of the days out here are very full days – and to visit everything could mean you're hurrying to complete the whole itinerary. If that's the case, then relax – and don't try to do everything. The purpose of your day out after all is to enjoy it. So if you find yourself somewhere you love, why not stay there the whole day? You can always visit the other attractions another time. Naturally, the price of your day out can be a big consideration – not just the price of entry, but of the travelling too. Some of the suggestions are relatively expensive, while others involve very little cost at all. You can mix and match at will – simply look at a map to make sure that everywhere you want to go is actually within a reasonable distance and you're ready to roll.

Do you really know your own neighbourhood and what there is to do within a few miles of your home? Why not take the opportunity to visit well-known places nearby that you've passed many times but never actually been to? Then again, perhaps you are going away for the weekend, or half term, a holiday or travelling for work in an area you have never visited before – you'll almost certainly find ideas here for interesting trips to take.

Of course, much depends on your frame of mind – do you feel like doing something cerebral or cultural, fun or madcap, sporty or peaceful? There are as many definitions of a great day out as there are people wishing to have one. Will you be on your own or with others? Perhaps you are going to be with an elderly relative or a disabled friend, or maybe you're one of a group of twenty-something-year-olds. Whatever your situation, you should be able to find just the great day out you're looking for here.

So tear yourself away from the housework or the television. Decide where you're going to go, check in advance that the places you want to visit are open and set off on your great day out.

ENGLAND

Avebury's Ancient Stones

MARLBOROUGH AND PEWSEY VALE

WHERE:
Wiltshire
BEST TIME TO GO:
Any time of year
DON'T MISS:
A close examination of 4,600 year-old Silbury Hill. Its perfectly round base covers 2.2 hectares (5 acres), and it is 40 m (130 ft) high, with a flat top 30 m (100 ft) wide. From the top you feel as if you can see forever – and you'll probably see crop circles in surrounding fields as well as a number of barrows, mounds and Avebury itself. Only intuition can explain why it is what it is – archaeology can't.
AMOUNT OF WALKING:
Moderate, unless you choose to take a walk along the downland of Pewsey Vale or Marlborough Downs.
COST:
Low
YOU SHOULD KNOW:
Wiltshire contains more than half of Britain's 260 long barrows; and Pewsey Vale alone has a large share of the crop circles that appear annually near these ancient monuments.

Wiltshire has more megalithic circles, standing stones, chambers, long barrows, and neolithic remains than any other county – and Avebury is the oldest, biggest and most complex of them all. It's not as immediately impressive as Stonehenge, but its scale makes it much more fascinating. Start out in the morning from Avebury's great circle, and in a few hours you'll see a whole variety of the most complete megalithic sites, set in some of Wiltshire's loveliest countryside and downland.

Imagining what they were for, and how they fitted together, will turn you willing detective for the day. The 18th-century 'The Barn' and 'The Stables' galleries in Avebury village – itself in the middle of the great circle of standing stones – are local museums where you can get clues about the meaning of the ancient sites. Existing stones (at least you can touch and examine them, unlike at Stonehenge) show the circle was designed with two ceremonial avenues stretching 2.5 km (1.5 mi) north and south from the village. The West Kennet Avenue survives, leading to the small stone circle of The Sanctuary on Overton Hill: was it an ancient religious representation of a serpent passing through a circle? On the way is Silbury Hill, the biggest megalithic monument in Europe, and West Kennet Long Barrow. From here, follow the lanes a little way south and east. Spread before you is the incomparable rural haven of the Vale of Pewsey. You can see for miles – and understand the suggestion that Avebury is central to a network of neolithic sacred sites aligned across southern England, along which you also find sacred centres like Glastonbury Tor and St Michael's Mount.

The drive brings you through pretty Lockeridge on the River Kennet, in a loop to the archetypal English market town of Marlborough. Here you can feast on medieval, Tudor and Georgian architecture, and a late tea.

Part of the circle of standing stones in Avebury

English Style

SAXON TO ARTS AND CRAFTS BRADFORD-ON-AVON, THE COURTS GARDEN AND LACOCK ABBEY

Bradford-on-Avon has been a crossroads for more than 2,000 years – and successive eras have bequeathed it buildings hallmarked with real distinction. A gentle stroll around its historic streets is an opportunity for the entertaining game of architectural 'I Spy'. Saxon-spotting includes the Church of St Laurence, the surviving chapel of a 7th-century monastery; the Shambles (from the Saxon word *scamel* describing a bench on which goods are displayed for sale), a crooked lane of shops between Silver and Market Streets, still with the 'face' of a medieval street; and the stunning Tithe Barn at Barton Farm – huge, authentic, and a location for the film of Chaucer's *Canterbury Tales*. You reach the Barn by way of the Norman-arched bridge over the Avon, with a two-cell built-in 'Lock-up' that used to be a chantry, and the lovely houses of 18th-century Barton Orchard. With 14th- and 15th-century Holy Trinity Church, and 18th- and 19th-century weavers' cottages terracing the hillside, Bradford is a composite gem.

Take the Melksham road to Holt for The Courts Garden. The Georgian house is not open, but the 2.8 hectares (7 acres) of terraces, arboretum, hedges, ponds, bog and kitchen gardens divided by sculptured yew trees show how the English Arts and Crafts movement can really fire your imagination – especially the irises and lilies of the water gardens. Have lunch at Sandy Lane, just to admire the amazing thatched cottages of 'Wiltshire's prettiest village'.

With a full afternoon at Lacock, head for the magnificent medieval cloisters, sacristy and chapter house of the Abbey. The picturesque 13th-century village grew around it, and will be familiar from many films. Now run by the National Trust, Lacock has been in the same family since the Reformation. That domestic authenticity, spanning English history, makes it one of the most rewarding properties in the country to ramble through.

WHERE:
Wiltshire
BEST TIME TO GO:
Mid-March to October – Lacock Abbey has shorter opening hours during the winter months.
DON'T MISS:
Having a drink at The Angel in Lacock Village, not just because sightseeing is thirsty work, but also because it's typical of the exceptionally well preserved, ancient houses there. The houses, of course, are private, so you can only see inside the five pubs, four of which have brick facades masking their real age.
AMOUNT OF WALKING:
Lots – and most of it inaccessible to wheelchairs.
COST:
The day starts free, but becomes increasingly expensive.
YOU SHOULD KNOW:
William Henry Fox Talbot (1800-77), a former owner of Lacock Abbey, invented the negative/positive photographic process. His photographic achievements are celebrated in the Fox Talbot Museum in Lacock village – and his lifelong scientific interests in the Botanic Garden of the Abbey's Victorian woodland grounds.

The cloisters at Lacock Abbey

The High Street in Castle Coombe

Castle Combe

MALMESBURY, WESTONBIRT AND TETBURY

The countryside on both sides of the M4, between junctions 17 and 18, is some of the prettiest in England. South of the motorway is Castle Combe, justly famous for the picturesque homogeneity of its ancient houses, built of Cotswold stone and bedecked with flowers. It wears its long history well – even if only earthworks remain of its British hill fort, Roman camp and Norman castle. With the river bubbling through its centre, the village prospered in the medieval wool industry; and its centuries-old charm is now preserved in a conservation area that teems with birdsong and wildlife.

It's a short, lovely drive along the edge of the Cotwolds to Malmesbury. A walled, hilltop town in the 12th century, Malmesbury's recorded history is 1,500 years old, and its importance can be gauged by the huge Abbey. Even in ruins it's a magnificent sight, with beautiful cloister gardens – and among the absorbing historic exhibits in the Parvise (a room above the porch) is a silver penny minted in Malmesbury in the reign of Edward the Confessor. In the town, the broad marketplaces are flanked by buildings that proclaim Malmesbury's significance as a weaving centre throughout the 15th, 16th and 17th centuries. The markets have sadly gone, but there are several old pubs to lunch in.

In the afternoon, take the long way round to Tetbury. You'll pass Westonbirt Arboretum as you ascend the southern Cotswolds into Gloucestershire. Westonbirt is particularly good fun for families, because besides its seasonal and heritage 'trails', it has a programme of craft workshops and children's and family events that make the most of its choices between wide, grassy avenues, meandering gravel footpaths, and the glades of trees collected from all over the world.

Tetbury shares Malmesbury's history and heritage status – but owes its sleeker veneer to the cluster of shops 'By Appointment' to locally based royalty.

WHERE:
Wiltshire and Gloucestershire
BEST TIME TO GO:
March to October
DON'T MISS:
Acer Glade at Westonbirt – lovely all year but spectacular in its autumn colours (and if you want to know more about the varieties of trees, there's a fascinating 'interpretive centre' next to the cafés).
AMOUNT OF WALKING:
Lots – but access around the villages is generally possible; and at Westonbirt, where access may be impossible, a good alternative is suggested.
COST:
Low
YOU SHOULD KNOW:
The centre of Tetbury is largely unchanged since the 16th and 17th centuries: most of the buildings in the principal street were there when Queen Elizabeth I was on the throne. NB. Shops 'By Appointment' to HRH Prince Charles display a heraldic fleur-de-lys of three feathers.

Corsham and Corsham Court

The north Wiltshire village of Corsham grew and evolved in the shadow of one of England's great houses, and even on a domestic scale, shares much of its grandeur. Walking around (visit Corsham in the morning – Corsham Court only opens in the afternoon), you get a vision of 18th-century architecture built in Cotswold stone. A closer look shows how your first impression masks more modern styles, and much older ones like the 17th-century 'Flemish Cottages' built (with a Flemish signature) for religious refugees who revived the local wool industry, which eventually paid for Corsham's 'facelift'. Corsham is full of revelatory historical surprises, and you'll see why its look and its association with Corsham Court inspired Charles Dickens in writing *Pickwick Papers*.

As a stately home, Corsham Court is *primus inter pares*. A Saxon royal manor, after William the Conqueror it passed down the monarchy, forming part of the dowry of 14th- and 15th-century queens of England (under Henry VIII, of course, both Catherine of Aragon and Katherine Parr held it in succession). Sold into private hands, the present enormous house was built in 1582, and enlarged after 1745 by Paul Methuen, whose family still live there. You will see something very special indeed. You approach the Court through a park with lake, trees and grand avenues designed by Capability Brown, and completed by Humphrey Repton. Inside the house, magnificent state rooms by Brown, John Nash, and Thomas Bellamy house 16th- and 17th-century Italian and Flemish Old Masters including Rubens and Van Dyck, and a spectacular collection of statuary, furniture and other paintings. Works by Reynolds, Romney, Chippendale, Cobb and John and Robert Adam make Corsham Court a treasure house of the rare, the unexpected, and the supremely beautiful. Get there for the 2.00 pm opening – you'll enjoy every second.

WHERE:
Wiltshire
BEST TIME TO GO:
Any time of year, but you should check opening times at Corsham Court before you go. Very much a private, family house, nevertheless there are occasional scheduled tours of the amazing Breakfast Room and Library in the private wing.
DON'T MISS:
The exquisitely refined and romantic 'gothick' Georgian Bath House, behind the walled garden – like the Picture Gallery and the Cabinet Room, unchanged since the Napoleonic era.
AMOUNT OF WALKING:
Moderate; a lot if you explore the farthest reaches of the Park and Gardens.
COST:
Reasonable
YOU SHOULD KNOW:
Lancelot 'Capability' Brown's design for the park and gardens was his most important commission after Blenheim Palace, though the work wasn't completed until forty years later. The flower gardens were created in the 1830s, and greatly enhanced by shrubs and exotica added by the Methuen family in the 1950s and 60s. The gardens as well as the house featured in the Stanley Kubrick film *Barry Lyndon*.

Corsham Court

Longleat House and Safari Park

WESTBURY WHITE HORSE

WHERE:
Wiltshire

BEST TIME TO GO:
Any time of year – but from April to October there are many more outdoor activities (especially for children) and a large number of concerts and special events in the house and Safari Park.

DON'T MISS:
The 'Animal Park Challenge' that takes place during school summer holidays. Contestants could find themselves cleaning 'priceless' works of art, howling like wolves or gibbering like monkeys – it's immense fun.

AMOUNT OF WALKING:
Lots, even if you confine yourself to the house and its collections.

COST:
Expensive – but Longleat's 'Passport Tickets' entitle you to visit the House/Gardens/ Safari Park over several days.

YOU SHOULD KNOW:
Opened in 1966, Longleat Safari Park plays a major role in international breeding programmes for rare and endangered species, some of which have been featured in BBC TV series. Children enjoy learning about these projects as much as they love playing gorillas or 'feed daddy to the lions'.

On your way to Longleat, make a short detour past Westbury village to the Iron Age hill fort of Bratton Castle, on the edge of Salisbury Plain. On the steep slope below the mound is Wiltshire's oldest White Horse. The enormous, elegant carving has been there since the early 18th century, but the exposed chalk has been concreted over since the 1950s to prevent further erosion. When locals began calling it 'the old grey mare', it was steam-cleaned. Now it is bright white and magnificent – but is it any longer the real thing?

The authenticity of Longleat House is thrilling. Not even 400 years of remodelling by the famously eccentric Thynne family (who built it and live in it) can diminish some of the best examples of high Elizabethan architecture in England. The Great Hall has a 10.6-m (35-ft) high ceiling supported by ten massive hammer beams, and a Minstrels' Gallery added in 1600. Hung with the appropriate tapestries and filled with paintings and objets of the period, it's easy to imagine it as the Elizabethan household's centre of activity. The Elizabethan Long Gallery was remodeled in 1870 as 'The Saloon', with an eye-popping ceiling based on the Palazzo Massimo in Rome; and various ghosts stalk the seven(!) libraries, which house some 40,000 books.

Longleat was the first stately home to open its doors to the public, and it has developed all kinds of fun and games to keep visitors amused. Some are children's and family 'quests' linked to the house and its upstairs/downstairs history. There's a brilliant Elizabethan Knot Maze, an Adventure Castle and a narrow-gauge railway. Most popular of all is the Safari and Animal Park, which has its own interactive displays and activities. In fact at Longleat, you have to be careful not to be spoiled for choice.

Be prepared to lose your wiper blades!

Muchelney Abbey

EAST LAMBROOK MANOR GARDENS AND BARRINGTON COURT

In a remote corner of the Somerset Levels, the faded grandeur of ancient buildings is set off to advantage by two of Britain's greatest 20th-century gardens. Muchelney Abbey was founded in the 7th century by King Ine of Wessex, even if the present remains are largely a 12th-century Norman reconstruction. External stone tracings on the Abbot's Lodging – still an imposing combination of farmhouse practicality and Tudor ecclesiastical pomp – show the craftsmanship that made this once-huge complex second only to Glastonbury in significance. Its medieval wealth is demonstrated not so much by the rich decorations on walls and tapestries, but by the thatched, two-storey monks' lavatory, unique in Britain.

Save some time to see the extraordinary works of art produced by the Leach family at the Muchelney Pottery on the edge of the village. Following his father and grandfather, John Leach is a traditional potter famous for his saggar-fired 'Black Moods' pots; and his work is in the collections of the Victoria and Albert Museum and Tate St Ives. A short drive away, East Lambrook Manor Gardens near South Petherton show a different way of applying modern aesthetics to the most traditional of crafts. Margery Fish, who created the Grade-1 listed gardens between 1938-69, was the first to incorporate modern planting ideas into the archetypal cottage garden on a domestic scale – and this is her inspirational masterpiece.

Just beyond Petherton, the National Trust garden at Barrington Court has an elegant formality inspired by Gertrude Jekyll. She created colourful garden 'rooms' like the White and the Lily gardens, and the working Kitchen garden full of apple, pear and plum trees espaliered on high stone walls. Jekyll matched the garden's sophisticated charm to the stylistic magnificence of Barrington Court. Its panelled interiors are crammed with authentic Tudor and Stuart decorative detail – but the Court is rented as a showroom for antique and reproduction furniture, so you can buy some of its historic perfection.

Barrington Court Gardens

WHERE:
Somerset
BEST TIME TO GO:
Any time of year (East Lambrook Manor Gardens and Muchelney Pottery); March to early November (Jekyll's Barrington Court Gardens); April to October (Muchelney Abbey).
DON'T MISS:
The sprung floor of Barrington Court's Elizabethan Great Hall – fitted in the 1920s for dancing during the glamorous parties that were a feature of family life for its then owners.
AMOUNT OF WALKING:
Moderate – and wheelchair access is highly restricted at best.
COST:
Expensive overall – but reasonable for the quality of each place.
YOU SHOULD KNOW:
The small, 15th-century East Lambrook Manor House with the 20th-century cottage garden is the conceptual and actual template for Britain's post-World War II gardening ideal. Known internationally as 'The Home of English Cottage Gardening', and often featured on BBC TV or Radio, it was the site of the horticultural experiments and stunningly original designs that earned Margery Fish the title of undisputed 'Leading Lady of Gardening' from the 1950s.

Salisbury

OLD SARUM, HEALE GARDEN AND STONEHENGE

WHERE:
Wiltshire
BEST TIME TO GO:
Any time of year – except Heale
Gardens, which are open between
February and October.
DON'T MISS:
The authentic Japanese Tea House in
Heale Gardens, built over a trout
stream, which then flows under a
red Nikko bridge...
AMOUNT OF WALKING:
Lots
COST:
Reasonable
YOU SHOULD KNOW:
When Old Sarum was a 13th-century
chartered burgh, it acquired the right
to two representatives in Parliament.
It retained this right for centuries
after the city was a ruin, without a
single elector – so the local landlord
could send two nominees to
Westminster, and was open to
ministerial bribery and corruption.
'Rotten Boroughs' like Old Sarum
were abolished by the Reform Act of
1832, but Old Sarum remains
synonymous with political chicanery.

Salisbury is one of England's loveliest cities. Set in water meadows and swept by trees, it wears its half-timbered alleys and Norman stone splendour with grace beneath the needle spire of Britain's finest medieval cathedral. The cathedral is itself at the heart of England's largest medieval close, a huge green sward edged with trees hiding beautiful houses from different eras. Above them, the tallest spire in the country seems to rise out of green fields. Close-to, you can see its architectural brilliance, and Europe's oldest working clock and a copy of Magna Carta, too. But the Cathedral is very much a place of worship – and to hear music performed there, as you can, is to be transformed.

The transcendent harmony of Salisbury replaced what is now just a colossal earthworks called Old Sarum, on Salisbury's northern edge. High on the windswept chalky downs, Old Sarum looks like the ancient hill fort it once was, before Romans, Saxons and Normans made it both castle and cathedral. Its ruins make a fascinating, but bleak timeline of historical suspicion and strife. Contrast it with Heale Gardens, north along the lush Woodford Valley. They are a perfect example of generations of benign and imaginative eccentricity creating pure magic from flowers, trees and shrubs. Woodland, Japanese, and Kitchen gardens are all touched by the genius of fantasy, timed to bloom in constant seasonal flux.

Drive on to the World Heritage glory of Stonehenge, a series of ceremonial earthworks, mounds and domestic remains clustered round the iconic circular stones of the Henge itself. You may have to fight your way through crowds, and await your timed entry to the actual stones – but whatever it actually is, Stonehenge is unique. It will fire your imagination.

The great stones at Stonehenge

Nadder Valley and Wilton House

The Nadder Valley, running west from Salisbury, has some of the least spoilt countryside in Wiltshire, easily missed by the hordes of motorists hurrying down the nearby A303 to the West Country. You can get a good flavour of the area with this leisurely drive around some of its pretty villages. Start your tour in Tisbury, which boasts a 15th-century tithe barn with the largest expanse of thatch in Britain. Following the course of the Nadder to the east brings you to the twin villages of Teffont Evias and Teffont Magna; in both cases a single main street is lined with picture-postcard stone cottages, many with thatched roofs, and a stream running beside the road.

Turning west you come next to Chilmark, which has given its name to the elegant stone that is such a harmonious feature of the area. Salisbury Cathedral and many other important local buildings were constructed with stone mined from the quarries that once lay south of the modern village. A left turn in the village of Fonthill Bishop takes you through an imposing gateway, which once led into the grounds of Fonthill Abbey and thence back to your starting point.

Just 16 km (10 mi) east of Tisbury stands one of the great stately homes of England, Wilton House. The extensive estate lies just south of the ancient Saxon village of Wilton and has been the family seat of the earls of Pembroke for over 450 years. The house owes its present appearance largely to the endeavours of two Earls: the fourth Earl who employed Inigo Jones, the pre-eminent architect of the day, to design a house in the Palladian style in the mid-17th century, and the eleventh Earl who commissioned the neo-Gothic cloisters from James Wyatt at the beginning of the 19th century.

WHERE:
Wiltshire
BEST TIME TO GO:
April to September
DON'T MISS:
The famous Double Cube room at Wilton, one of the finest interiors in the country.
AMOUNT OF WALKING:
Little
COST:
Reasonable
YOU SHOULD KNOW:
There is an excellent adventure playground in the grounds of Wilton, which the present Earl designed for his children.

The famous Double Cube room in Wilton House

There is plenty to do in the park, including the landscaped Play Trail.

Moors Valley Country Park

In little more than twenty years Moors Valley has become one of the most popular country parks in southern England; it is not hard to see why from the range and quality of its attractions. Lying west of Ringwood and the River Avon, which here forms the county border with Hampshire, Moors Valley Country Park offers an impressive array of facilities and activities catering for all ages. If the straightforward pleasure of a good walk takes your fancy there are miles of well-marked trails throughout the park. And as cycle hire is available on site, you do not even have to bring your own bikes to enjoy the cycling tracks as well.

The park is mostly covered in woodland and various features make the best of this environment. If your idea of a good day out involves more adrenalin-fuelled activity than walking then you might want to challenge yourself to Go Ape!, an adventure high up in the forest where, strapped into a harness, you cross from tree to tree below the canopy, negotiating scramble nets, rope bridges, slides and Tarzan swings. For younger explorers there is a landscaped play trail comprising eight pieces of artist-designed wooden play equipment hidden around the forest; names such as the Snake Pit and the Crocodile Crossing help to give rein to young imaginations. Close by is a short tree-top trail, its raised walkway giving you an unusual bird's eye view of the woods.

At the heart of the park stands a large and well-equipped visitor centre, housed in an 18th-century wooden barn. From here you can arrange other, more sedate activities such as fishing in the lake, a round on the 18-hole golf course, or a ride on the 1.6-km (1-mi) narrow-gauge steam railway.

WHERE:
Dorset
BEST TIME TO GO:
Any time of year
DON'T MISS:
The ride on the little steam railway, which gives you a good overview of the country park, as well as being a great family experience.
AMOUNT OF WALKING:
Moderate
COST:
Low (but your costs will rise if you opt for additional activities such as Go Ape!).
YOU SHOULD KNOW:
You need to be reasonably fit to go on Go Ape! – 10 is the minimum age and 1m 40cm (4ft 7in) the minimum height for this adventure.

Athelhampton House and the Abbases

The countryside immortalized in the novels of Thomas Hardy is powerfully evoked in this day out amidst the gently rolling hills of central Dorset. Athelhampton House is a well-preserved example of a Tudor English manor house and still in private hands, after over 500 years. The interior houses an outstanding collection of English furniture and has recovered well from a fire in 1992, which badly damaged the East Wing. The surrounding formal gardens were created at the end of the 19th century in an Elizabethan style that complements the house perfectly.

A short drive into the countryside north of Athelhampton brings you to the charming village of Milton Abbas, an unusual survival of a purpose-built estate village from the late 18th century. With its identical cob and thatch cottages lining a street with broad grass verges, Milton Abbas owes its existence to a capricious act of the local landowner who decided that, because the old village spoiled the view from his new mansion, he would move the entire settlement to its present site! Lord Milton's mansion is now a private school but you can visit its fine 14th-century Abbey Church.

Watchful eyes and a good map are needed for the drive some 16 km (10 mi) westward along country lanes to the more typical Dorset village of Cerne Abbas. Once again its name indicates its origins in a religious settlement, in this case a great Benedictine abbey founded in 987 – and some minor remains of the abbey buildings can still be seen. The village's most famous feature lies just outside, a 55-m (180-ft) high Giant cut into the chalk downland. Although its precise origins are unknown it is thought to have been a Celtic fertility symbol from pre-Roman times. The best view is from the main road north to Sherborne.

WHERE:
Dorset
BEST TIME TO GO:
Any time of year (but note that Athelhampton is only open on Sundays from November to February).
DON'T MISS:
The Great Hall at Athelhampton, with its original roof timbers and exquisite linenfold panelling.
AMOUNT OF WALKING:
Moderate
COST:
Low (children under 16 receive free entry to Athelhampton).
YOU SHOULD KNOW:
The ditches forming the striking male organ of the Cerne Giant were filled in with dirt by prudish Victorians in the 19th century!

Athelhampton House

Sherborne and Beaminster

WHERE:
Dorset
BEST TIME TO GO:
Any time of year (but note that
Sherborne New Castle and
Mapperton Gardens are only open
from April to October).
DON'T MISS:
The coin-operated meter in Sherborne
Abbey which sheds additional light on
the glorious fan vaulting.
AMOUNT OF WALKING:
Moderate
COST:
Low (children 15 years and under are
admitted free to Sherborne New
Castle).
YOU SHOULD KNOW:
Beaminster is Thomas Hardy's
'Emminster', where Angel Clare walks
to visit his family in *Tess of the
d'Urbervilles*.

Sherborne is a lively town offering plenty to interest the day visitor. A remarkable number of buildings survive from medieval times and the town's overall appearance is enhanced immeasurably by the prevailing use of Ham stone, an attractive mellow sandstone once quarried just over the county border in Somerset. Sherborne's chief glory is its 15th-century Abbey, formerly the church of a great monastery dating back to Anglo-Saxon times and the seat of a Bishopric that moved to Salisbury following the Norman Conquest. Like so many similar churches, following Henry VIII's dissolution of the monasteries the townspeople of Sherborne acquired the Abbey as their parish church, and so it has remained to this day. The fan vaulting in the ceiling is every bit as fine as its more famous counterpart at King's College, Cambridge.

Some of the former monastic buildings are now occupied by Sherborne School, founded in 1550 and one of the country's top public schools. Sherborne also boasts two castles: a medieval ruin and a stately home built in 1594 by Sir Walter Raleigh. The so-called 'New Castle' is set in beautifully landscaped parkland and is well worth a visit for its sumptuous interiors. Other buildings worth seeking out are the 15th-century almshouses and the conduit, which was once the monks' *lavatorium* (washhouse).

Sherborne can fill your day easily but if you want a change of scenery, head 32 km (20 mi) south west to the small market town of Beaminster which nestles in a quiet valley off the beaten track. Its many Tudor and Georgian buildings are evidence of its former heyday when it grew rich on the wool and cloth trades. Just outside Beaminster the stunning gardens of Mapperton House descend in three terraces down a hidden valley, giving fine views of the West Dorset countryside.

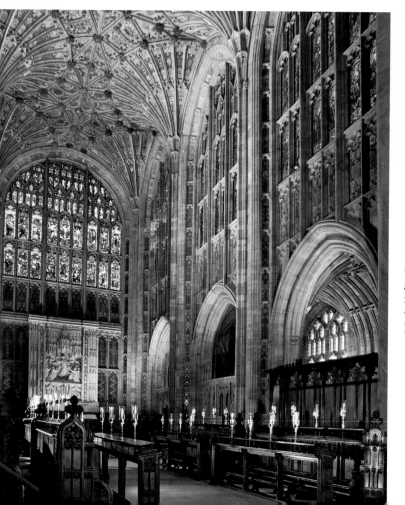

The famous fan-vaulted ceiling at Sherborne Abbey was added in the 15th century.

Wimborne Minster and Kingston Lacy

Kingston Lacy

In spite of lying close to the suburban sprawl of Bournemouth and Poole, Wimborne Minster retains the distinctive charms of a market town. There has been a settlement on this strategic site, where the River Allen meets the River Stour, since Roman times. The present town grew up around a Benedictine nunnery whose principal surviving feature is the imposing Minster itself, now the parish church. The eastern of the twin towers is the oldest part, dating from the 12th century. The interior is worth a visit to see the elaborate carving on the arches and a handsome chained library. The town's pretty Georgian streets repay some exploration and you might also want to visit the famous Model Town.

Just west of Wimborne Minster stands the grand mansion of Kingston Lacy, the home of the Bankes family for 300 years. The land was gifted to Sir Ralph Bankes by Charles II in the 1660s in appreciation of the family's loyalty to the Royalist cause during the Civil War. The original was a classical brick building in the Restoration style but the house as we see it today is the work of Sir Charles Barry, the architect of the Houses of Parliament, who carried out an extensive re-modelling in the 1830s which included encasing the outside in stone and creating elaborate new interiors, including a grand marble staircase and the visual riot that is the Spanish room, its walls covered in gilded leather and the intricately carved ceiling, reputedly hailing from a Venetian palace.

Much of the huge estate surrounding Kingston Lacy is available for you to explore. Driving west through the stupendous avenue of beech trees lining the road brings you to Badbury Rings, a well-preserved Iron Age hill-fort and a great place for flying a kite.

WHERE:
Dorset
BEST TIME TO GO:
March to October (but note that the gardens at Kingston Lacy open early in February for the wonderful displays of snowdrops).
DON'T MISS:
Kingston Lacy has one of the finest collections of Old Master paintings in any stately home in the country.
AMOUNT OF WALKING:
Moderate (although you can do a lot more walking, should you wish, on the many way-marked trails on the Kingston Lacy estate).
COST:
Low
YOU SHOULD KNOW:
The 3-km (2-mi) long Beech Avenue was a gift of William Bankes to his mother in 1835 – 731 trees were planted originally, a pair for each day of the year, plus one for a leap year!

The ferry pulls away from Brownsea Island.

Dorset Heavy Horse Centre and Brownsea Island

You take a step back in time when you visit the Heavy Horse Centre near Verwood. The Centre celebrates a key form of transport of a bygone age, when enormous shire horses pulled wagons loaded high with freshly harvested wheat and barrels of ale. The Centre is home to a number of these gentle giants and gives you the chance to admire them at close quarters. Nowadays the only load the horses draw is people; wagon rides are included in the price of your ticket. Younger children will enjoy the cart rides behind a miniature pony as well as the friendly farm animals, many of which can be petted. If you are big and brave enough you can even try your hand at driving a vintage tractor.

A short return to the transport of the present and in less than an hour you are at Sandbanks at the mouth of Poole Harbour, ready to embark on the ferry that takes you over to Brownsea Island. Easily visible from the mainland, Brownsea nevertheless feels a whole world away. With no motor vehicles and not even bicycles allowed, it is the perfect place to relax and unwind. The island has a surprising variety of habitats for its size and if you enjoy walking, you should be able to explore most of them in a few hours. If you are feeling less energetic there are plenty of good picnic spots where patience and quiet may be rewarded with the sight of a red squirrel, the undoubted star of the island's wildlife and a rare sight today on the mainland.

Isle of Purbeck

Although not an island at all the Isle of Purbeck still offers the sense of a world apart that characterizes many true island communities. For its limited area the Isle has an astonishing range of geology, including Purbeck Marble, a fine limestone with a bluish-grey sheen that was highly prized by medieval builders. Swanage is the main town on the Isle and the best starting-point for your day. A relaxed and popular seaside resort, Swanage sits in a gently curving bay with fine walks along the coast path in both directions, north to the chalk stacks of Old Harry Rocks, south to Durlston Head. A monument on the seafront commemorates a naval victory here of King Alfred over the Danes in 877 AD.

Just 10 km (6 mi) inland, and in an appropriately commanding position in the centre of the Isle, stand the picturesque ruins of Corfe Castle. The medieval castle once controlled the whole area but was destroyed, following a protracted siege by Parliamentary forces during the Civil War. The wife of Sir John Bankes, 'Brave Dame Mary', showed great fortitude in defending the castle, only yielding when she was betrayed from within. The best way to visit Corfe is to take the train from Swanage on the privately run railway drawn by vintage steam locomotives.

Back in Swanage, pick up the car and drive the short distance north to Studland Bay where you can finish your day relaxing on one of the country's finest beaches. A 5-km (3-mi) sweep of uninterrupted golden sands, Studland offers clean and safe swimming in an environment that is surprisingly unspoilt, given its location so close to Poole. The heathland behind the beach is a national nature reserve and it's a great place for spotting waders and other birds.

WHERE:
Dorset
BEST TIME TO GO:
Any time of year. The ruins of Corfe Castle look especially atmospheric in an autumn or early spring mist, but note that the Railway only runs at weekends in the winter months.
DON'T MISS:
Look out for the ravens at Corfe, now resident once again and reputed to be bringers of good fortune to the Castle.
AMOUNT OF WALKING:
Moderate (if you take your car to Corfe Castle, it's a 1-km (1/2-mi) walk from the car park).
COST:
Reasonable (there is a reduced admission charge to Corfe Castle if you use public transport to get there).
YOU SHOULD KNOW:
There is a clearly marked section for naturists at Knoll Beach on Studland Bay.

Punch and Judy are still playing to young audiences on Swanage beach.

Lulworth Cove and Dorset Beaches

WHERE:
Dorset
BEST TIME TO GO:
Any time of year (but note that the access roads and car park at Lulworth Cove can get very busy in the summer months).
DON'T MISS:
The Heritage Centre at Lulworth Cove, which tells you all you want to know about the geology of the Cove and surrounding area.
AMOUNT OF WALKING:
Moderate (although you can do longer walks along the cliffs at various points).
COST:
Low
YOU SHOULD KNOW:
The brown Lulworth Skipper is a butterfly unique to this section of the coast.

This day out exploring the dramatic coastline of East Dorset begins at Lulworth Cove, a renowned beauty spot and one of the most remarkable natural sights in the country. The unrelenting action of the sea over thousands of years has caused a breach at a weak spot in the hard limestone cliffs, and the resulting erosion of the softer rocks behind has formed a perfect oyster-shaped harbour, almost completely enclosed by cliffs that rise to 135 m (440 ft). Immediately to the west of Lulworth, at Stair Hole, you can see a new cove in the process of formation. The 1.5-km (1-mi) walk west along the cliffs to the natural limestone arch at Durdle Door is definitely worth doing; not only will you see outstanding examples of the folding rock strata so characteristic of this coast, but in the summer months you will escape the inevitable crowds that build up at Lulworth. And you will have the added satisfaction of knowing that Durdle Door itself is not accessible by road.

Lulworth Cove is part of the large Lulworth Estate, which has belonged to the same family since the 1640s. Only the exterior of the mock medieval Lulworth Castle has been restored, since being gutted by fire in 1929. If you visit during the summer holidays you will see an exciting display of medieval jousting by knights on horseback. Don't miss the very unusual family church, a Catholic shrine built to resemble a round classical temple.

Heading west from Lulworth you can explore the beaches at Ringstead Bay and Bowleaze Cove. Both are really pebble beaches, with sand exposed only at low tide. They are safe and popular bathing spots, however, and Bowleaze Cove, the more developed of the two, has several amenities including a funfair.

Lulworth Cove – a perfect oyster-shaped harbour

Thomas Hardy Country

Mention Dorset and the writer who comes instantly to mind is the great Victorian novelist and poet Thomas Hardy, who celebrated the people and landscapes of his native county in masterpieces such as *Far from the Madding Crowd*, *The Woodlanders* and *Tess of the d'Urbervilles*. Hardy was the unrivalled chronicler of a vanishing agrarian way of life, observing, with a compassionate but sternly unsentimental eye, the encroachment of the machine age on rural customs. Apart from a brief period as a young man working in London, Thomas Hardy spent the whole of his long life in Dorset and a powerful impression of the man and his milieu emerges from this day spent touring key sites.

Start your day at Higher Bockhampton, 5 km (3 mi) east of Dorchester, where you can visit the simple thatched cottage where Hardy was born in 1840. As you emerge from the woods, its isolated setting helps you appreciate the profound influence the natural world exercised upon the writer's imagination. Your next stop is Dorchester itself, the county town and an important settlement since Roman times. Housed in magnificent Victorian galleries, the Dorset County Museum features a detailed reconstruction of Hardy's study at Max Gate, the red-brick suburban mansion on the edge of town which Hardy designed himself and where he lived for the last forty years of his life.

Hardy died at Max Gate in 1928 and although public pressure led to his ashes being buried in Westminster Abbey, his heart remained literally in his beloved Dorset and was interred beside his first wife in the little churchyard at Stinsford just outside Dorchester. There is no better place to finish your day's reflection on a man for whom the transience of life was an ever-present concern.

WHERE:
Dorset
BEST TIME TO GO:
April to September, if you want to see inside the Hardy houses (but note that both are closed on Fridays and Saturdays).
DON'T MISS:
The King's Arms in Dorchester High Street, where the fictional Thomas Henchard held court as the Mayor of Casterbridge.
AMOUNT OF WALKING:
Moderate (but note that it is a 0.5-km (0.3-mi) walk from the car park to Hardy's birthplace).
COST:
Low (accompanied children gain free entry to the County Museum).
YOU SHOULD KNOW:
A persistent rumour has it that the heart buried at Stinsford is not in fact Thomas Hardy's, which was accidentally eaten by the household cat!

Thomas Hardy's Cottage at Higher Bockhampton

Shaftesbury and Stourhead

Shaftesbury is Dorset's only hilltop town and commands spectacular views of Blackmore Vale to the south. Its origins date back to Saxon times, when Alfred the Great founded a Benedictine nunnery and installed his daughter as the first Abbess. When the bones of the murdered boy-king Edward the Martyr were moved here soon after, the Abbey became a leading pilgrimage site and one of the wealthiest foundations in the land. All the more severe was Henry VIII's retribution at the Dissolution, so that only a few foundations of the abbey buildings now remain. The excellent site museum does a good job of recapturing past glories.

Shaftesbury's other must-see sight is Gold Hill, where you can be forgiven a sense of déjà vu as this must be one of the most photographed views in Britain. Dropping steeply down the hill from the Abbey gardens, Gold Hill is a charming ensemble of cobbled street, thatched cottages and part of the great medieval wall that once enclosed the Abbey. It has long been a renowned beauty spot but was propelled into superstardom in the early 1970s when it featured in a famous television commercial.

Situated 16 km (10 mi) from Shaftesbury, over the border in Wiltshire, is the Stourhead Estate. The imposing house dates from the 1720s but it is the garden, laid out a generation later by Henry Hoare II, which has sealed Stourhead's reputation as one of the world's great man-made landscapes. Hoare was at the forefront of a reaction to excessive French formality which resulted in a style of English landscape design that sought to blend in with its surroundings. By placing classical temples and other follies in strategic locations around an artificial lake, he created a series of carefully contrived vistas that are as enchanting as they are unexpected.

Gold Hill, Shaftesbury

WHERE:
Dorset and Wiltshire
BEST TIME TO GO:
Any time of year (but note that the garden at Stourhead is particularly famous for its rhododendron and azalea displays in April/May and its autumn colours).
DON'T MISS:
Climbing to the top of King Alfred's Tower, a 50-m (160-ft) high red-brick folly on the estate, for panoramic views of three counties.
AMOUNT OF WALKING:
Lots
COST:
Reasonable
YOU SHOULD KNOW:
The television advertisement (for Hovis bread) that turned Gold Hill into a household sight was made by Ridley Scott who found subsequent fame as a director of feature films such as *Alien* and *Blade Runner*.

Weymouth and Portland

Blessed with golden sands, safe bathing and a gently curving bay Weymouth is the main holiday town on Dorset's coast. The elegant Georgian terraces scattered throughout town are testament to the time when this small fishing port exploded into fashion following the visit by King George III in 1789. The King spent no fewer than fourteen holidays here, taking the sea air on his doctors' advice and attracting the cream of fashionable society in his wake. No wonder the grateful townspeople erected the unusual painted statue of the monarch in 1810 to honour the 50th anniversary of his reign.

Not content to rely on the royal seal of approval, the town fathers have been busy in recent years devising state-of-the-art attractions to complement all the traditional amenities you find in a seaside resort. Brewers Quay is an imaginatively redeveloped Victorian brewery, which offers many activities in one complex; a highlight is certainly the Timewalk, which takes you through 600 years of Weymouth's history in a series of atmospheric tableaux and streetscapes. Elsewhere, at the Deep Sea Adventure you can experience what it is like to be a deep-sea diver in black water, as you learn about the history of underwater exploration.

Extending south, the Isle of Portland is really a misnomer as it is connected to Weymouth by a causeway. Thomas Hardy called it the 'Gibraltar of Wessex, stretching out like the head of a bird into the English Channel'. There is much to see in its compact area, including Portland Castle, one of Henry VIII's finest coastal forts, the old quarrying sites for the world-famous Portland Stone, and not least the Bill, the southernmost tip of the Isle, with its lighthouse and rocks much frequented by sea birds.

WHERE:
Dorset
BEST TIME TO GO:
March to October when all the visitor attractions are open, although Portland Bill can be an exciting place to stand and watch the swell on a winter's day.
DON'T MISS:
The bathing machine used by King George when swimming in the sea, which is featured in the Timewalk.
AMOUNT OF WALKING:
Moderate
COST:
Reasonable
YOU SHOULD KNOW:
Portland Stone has been used in such famous buildings as St Paul's Cathedral and Buckingham Palace, as well as the United Nations building in New York.

Weymouth beach in the height of summer

Chesil Beach and Abbotsbury

The remarkable natural phenomenon known as Chesil Beach is in fact a vast bank of pebbles, which extends for 16 km (10 mi) along the Dorset coast from Portland to Abbotsbury. Piled up in places as high as 17 m (56 ft), the smooth pebbles get progressively larger from west to east, the result of tidal action and prevailing winds. The long, narrow body of water trapped behind the bank is known as the Fleet, a brackish lagoon that is now a nature reserve; trips are available in glass-bottomed boats to observe the wide variety of waterfowl, plants and fish. A walk along the beach is hard work but you can be guaranteed an escape from the summer crowds.

Snuggling into the hills at the western end of Chesil Beach, the little village of Abbotsbury is one of Dorset's most delightful. The thatched yellow-stone cottages, many built with stones from the Benedictine abbey that once stood here, evoke a quintessential picture of rural tranquillity. For its small size there is much to interest the visitor. Two buildings survive from the once mighty Abbey: tiny 14th-century St Catherine's Chapel, prominent on its hill-top perch and formerly a vital beacon for sailors navigating the treacherous coast; and the huge tithe barn, which once stored wool and grain for the Abbey. At 83 m (272 ft) it stood originally twice the length of today's building, making it the largest medieval barn in England.

To provide a food source during the winter months the Abbey monks established a colony of breeding swans, which is now the world-famous Swannery, home to some 600 free-flying mute swans. The colony flourished because the Fleet is rich in their favourite food. Watching massed swans being fed and seeing the newly hatched cygnets in season are very special experiences not to be missed.

WHERE:
Dorset
BEST TIME TO GO:
April to October (the best time to visit the Swannery is between the end of May and the end of June when the baby swans hatch in their hundreds).
DON'T MISS:
The views of Chesil Beach and Lyme Bay from St Catherine's Chapel.
AMOUNT OF WALKING:
Moderate (but note that walking on Chesil Beach is strenuous).
COST:
Reasonable (best value is the passport ticket in Abbotsbury, which gives entry to the Sub-Tropical Gardens and the Children's Farm as well as the Swannery).
YOU SHOULD KNOW:
Mute swans are not in fact silent but are so named because their call is less strident than that of other species.

Chesil Beach

The Jurassic Coast

The Dorset and East Devon coast is England's only natural World Heritage site. Known as the Jurassic Coast, it secured its designation owing to a high level of cliff erosion yielding a continuous exposure of geological strata. The 150 km (95 mi) of coastline is in effect one enormous open-air museum spanning 185 million years of the Earth's history. Start your day at Beer in Devon, where you can take a guided tour of the huge caves formed from centuries of quarrying. The local stone was much prized by masons for its ease of carving and elegant finish, and it was used in many of England's medieval cathedrals.

The ancient port of Lyme Regis lies 16 km (10 mi) to the east and just over the Dorset border. At the end of the 13th century the enterprising townsfolk constructed the Cobb, a great curving sea wall which offered safe anchorage from south-westerly storms to ships plying their trade along this notoriously exposed coast. For many people today the abiding image of Lyme is of the title character of *The French Lieutenant's Woman* standing alone on the wave-lashed Cobb. Its maze of narrow streets and many Georgian houses make Lyme a pleasant place to explore on foot.

Complete your day in the small seaside village of Charmouth, 5 km (3 mi) to the east. Swimming off the shingle beach here can be dangerous, but the activity everyone comes for is fossil hunting. Spend some time combing the beach with an alert eye and you might just be lucky enough to find your very own relic of a prehistoric life-form. If you do not trust your own eye, experts are on hand at the Heritage Coast Centre to give tips and to lead fossil-hunting walks.

WHERE:
Devon and Dorset
BEST TIME TO GO:
Any time of year (but note that the Beer Caves are only open from April to October).
DON'T MISS:
The views from Golden Cap, just east of Charmouth and the highest point on the south coast.
AMOUNT OF WALKING:
Lots
COST:
Low
YOU SHOULD KNOW:
Because the coastal cliffs are unstable and there is a real danger of landslips you should only search for fossils on the beach.

The Cobb at Lyme Regis

Chedworth Roman Villa

LODGE PARK AND THE SHERBORNE ESTATE

WHERE:
Gloucestershire
BEST TIME TO GO:
March to November (though the Park is open year-round and Father Christmas visits the Lodge in December).
DON'T MISS:
Just off the Foss Way/A40 crossroads is the attractive little town of Northleach with its impressive 'wool' church and market square with handsome timber-framed buildings.
AMOUNT OF WALKING:
Moderate (stout footwear recommended for the villa where some parts are inaccessible by wheelchair, and Park Estate walks. Access to the Lodge is by steps).
COST:
Reasonable (family discounts available; Sherborne Park Estate is free and children and dogs on leads can join the guided walks for nothing).
YOU SHOULD KNOW:
The Lodge stages occasional deerhound races – using lures.

In the hills just north of Chedworth village at the head of a lovely wooded valley – exactly the location a modern wealthy merchant might choose – lies Chedworth Villa, one of the largest Romano-British sites in the country. The original villa was arranged around two courtyards, and fine mosaics survive in the rooms; there are also hypocausts, bath-houses, latrines and a water shrine, as well as extensive walls. The site was originally excavated in 1864; now, in addition to the excellent museum, an audio tour is available. There is a programme of 'living history' weekends and activities for children, many on Roman themes, and nature trails in the delightful Cotswold countryside around the villa.

Foss Way runs past Chedworth, as straight as when the Romans built it. To the west, by narrow country lanes, lies Lodge Park, England's only surviving 17th-century Grandstand and Deer Course. It was built in 1634 for John 'Crump' Dutton, for gaming, banqueting and viewing the coursing. In the 19th century it was converted to a dwelling; the National Trust have restored it to its original form – a hall with a large room above and a balcony to watch the sport. It is set in impressive 18th-century landscaping (splendid for dog-walking) and hosts historical re-enactments and open air Shakespeare.

The Sherborne Park Estate was home to the Dutton family; it covers a large area of rolling Cotswold countryside on both sides of the River Windrush, where the water meadows have been restored. The Park is open to the public for walking, bird watching and themed, guided walks.

A Roman army re-enactment at Chedworth

Gloucester Cathedral

DEERHURST, TEWKESBURY ABBEY AND BREDON HILL

The honey-coloured bulk of Gloucester Cathedral – 'that great ornament of the city' (John Dorney, 1656) – is visible from miles around. Originally a monastic church dating from 1069, the great unadorned columns of the nave, its Norman heart, are surrounded by the fine lines of Perpendicular tracery, vaults, arches and chapels. The impressive early fan-vaulted cloisters will be familiar to the followers of Harry Potter films! Other features are the lively misericords, some fascinating tombs and memorials and the immense medieval stained-glass East window.

Tiny Odda's Chapel is incorporated into a medieval farmhouse in Deerhurst in the wide green valley of the Severn between Gloucester and Tewkesbury. The simple building retains its Saxon chancel arch and windows; an inscription implies that a palace once stood here, too. Close examination of the village church, St Mary's, reveals architectural details – including high, pointed windows and wolf-head carvings – that make it one of England's finest surviving Saxon churches.

The delightful town of Tewkesbury, lying between the Severn and Avon rivers, is distinguished by a medieval streetscape of narrow alleyways between fine black-and-white houses, and its enormous, beautiful and peaceful Norman Abbey. Massive pillars flanked by chantry chapels and tombs support an ornate roof whose gilded bosses are outstanding. The 17th-century Milton organ is in daily use.

Bredon Hill, isolated from the Cotswold chain in the Vale of Evesham, can be climbed on paths from the pretty encircling villages (immortalized in John Moore's 'Brensham Trilogy'); the circular climb takes at least three hours. On the summit, among remains of ancient earthworks, stands a stone tower, Parson's Folly. Emerging from ancient woods onto the open grassland, hearing the larks and seeing Houseman's 'coloured counties' all around, is unforgettable.

Tewkesbury Abbey

Typical Cotswold stone buildings in Broadway

Cotswold Drive

The Cotswold Hills extend along the east of Gloucestershire; the steep escarpment to the west gives views over the Vale of Gloucester and the Severn to the hills of Wales. To the east, the rolling hills, green valleys and hanging woods, scattered with honey-stone villages and small towns, seem to epitomize the English countryside. The wealth of the Cotswolds came from the wool trade, important since Roman times; many of the handsome manor houses and churches date from the Middle Ages, when the greatest wool fortunes were made.

Chipping Camden, with its mullioned windows, undulating roof-scapes and superb 'wool' church, retains the feel of a prosperous medieval wool town, particularly early or late when the streets are not packed with tourists and the golden stone glows in the soft light. Close by, delightful Hidcote Manor Gardens is composed of a series of small garden 'rooms', each with its own character, walled by hedges of different species. This is one of the 20th century's most inventive and influential gardens.

Busy Moreton-in-Marsh was once a coaching station. Its Market Charter was granted in 1227 and on Tuesdays its broad main street is still packed with stalls. Nearby Batsford Arboretum has a huge collection of rare trees; with its oriental atmosphere, it is wonderfully restful.

The narrow alleyways running into the square in much-visited Stow-on-the-Wold were built to funnel the sheep into the market place, now surrounded by pubs, restaurants and galleries.

The River Windrush, crossed by several attractive stone bridges, flows right through the middle of pretty Bourton-on-the-Water. There is something for everyone here, from motor museum to bird park. The Model Village is a detailed 1/9th scale model of Bourton, made of Cotswold stone in 1937, complete with a miniature flowing river and little trees.

WHERE:
Gloucestershire
BEST TIME TO GO:
Any time of year (though some attractions close, the roads and towns are quiet in the winter; the Cotswolds are very picturesque in the snow)
DON'T MISS:
Sezincote, south of Moreton: the house, with its domes and minarets, inspired the Brighton Pavilion. It is surrounded by exotic oriental water-gardens and statuary. Limited opening hours.
AMOUNT OF WALKING:
Moderate
COST:
Low to expensive (depending on how many of the attractions are visited)
YOU SHOULD KNOW:
Outside Moreton-in-Marsh stands the Four Shires Stone, marking the historic meeting point of Gloucestershire, Worcestershire, Oxfordshire and Warwickshire.

Forest of Dean
THE FAMILY CYCLE PATH

The ancient woodlands of the Forest of Dean lie between the Rivers Severn and Wye. Used for hunting since Roman times, it is now a Royal Forest, the preserve of monarchs. In Tudor times it was considered the best source of oak for shipbuilding, and fittingly it provided tall timbers for the new Globe Theatre in London. Iron and coal have been extracted here since before the Roman occupation and one of the rights of Foresters (those born in the central area) is that of 'Free Mining'. Though large-scale mining operations ceased in the 20th century, several small private mines are still worked.

The Forest of Dean, with its thick coniferous and deciduous (still largely oak) woods and rolling hills, is excellent cycling country and there is a good network of well-maintained and signed tracks. At least one of the bike-hire companies offers a range, from mountain bikes and tandems to bikes adapted for special-needs users and small children. They can give you advice on safety, clothing, the country code, etc, and their route maps mark nearby pubs!

This 19-km (12-mi) circular route runs through the heart of the Forest where, as well as woodland birds including pied-flycatchers and woodwarblers, fallow deer (resident since the 13th century) may be seen. Wild boar are making a reappearance and are welcomed by many – they break ground vegetation and clear bracken, allowing a greater diversity of plant life. They are usually very shy.

The green tranquillity of the Forest offers endless good picnic spots; official areas provide tables and sometimes (as at Beechenhurst Lodge), fixed barbecues. On Cannop Ponds, Mandarin ducks squabble over crusts and goshawks may be spotted from a panoramic viewpoint at New Fancy, an old colliery site.

Cyclists on the trail from the Pedalabikeaway Cycle Centre

WHERE:
Gloucestershire
BEST TIME TO GO:
Any time of year (daffodils are followed by bluebells and then foxgloves; the dappled shade in summer is lovely, the colours of autumn superb).
DON'T MISS:
The Forest Sculpture Trail starts at Beechenhurst; the gentle walk makes a welcome change for cyclists' legs.
AMOUNT OF WALKING:
Little
COST:
Reasonable
YOU SHOULD KNOW:
The writer Dennis Potter was born in the Forest which features in much of his work; it also appears in *Harry Potter and the Deathly Hallows* and has been used as a location for TV productions.

Forest of Dean

THE ROYAL FOREST ROUTE

This 32-km (20-mi) circuit of the heart of the Royal Forest of Dean on minor roads allows visits to a range of attractions on the route or just off it. In picturesque Soudley Valley, the Dean Heritage Centre can provide maps and information; it also has extensive exhibitions on life and natural history in the Forest and runs activities for children.

The route anti-clockwise passes the Speech House Hotel which began life as a hunting lodge for Charles II, then housed the Verderers' Court. This body was established to look after the king's interests in this Royal hunting reserve, and it still meets in the hotel. A little further west, Hopewell Colliery is a reminder of the industrial past when many such small coalmines were active; there is a museum, and part of the mine is open to the public. A few miles north of the charming, historic town of Coleford is Symonds Yat Rock, a spectacular viewpoint, high above the serpentine Wye Valley. Peregrine falcons are among the birds which nest in nearby cliffs.

Just outside Coleford, Puzzle Wood, a pre-Roman ore mine, has

been transformed into a green, leafy three-dimensional maze. Further south, Clearwell Caves have been mined since the Iron Age – powdered oxides, valued as pigments, are still extracted. Nine impressive, linked, natural caverns are open to visitors. Every December the caves are transformed into a floodlit wonderland, with a visit to Father Christmas included. The mine at Ellwood where, in 1850 the first steel in the world was manufactured, is open to visitors.

The beautiful southern part of the circuit passes Nags Head Nature Reserve and at Mallards Pike, man-made lakes offer an easy walk with fine views and a chance to see a variety of ducks, including the colourful Mandarin. The last section of the route is particularly gorgeous in autumn.

The River Wye from Symonds Yat Rock

Bristol

Despite its inland location, Bristol was, in the 17th and 18th centuries, one of the world's greatest ports. John Cabot discovered Newfoundland in 1497, and the merchants of Bristol exploited the New World – fortunes were made from sugar, rum, tobacco and slaves. Slavery was abolished, trade declined but, in the 19th century Bristol became synonymous with engineering and with Isambard Kingdom Brunel. Projects here included the Great Western Railway, two ships, the SS *Great Western* and the SS *Great Britain* and, most famously, the Clifton Suspension Bridge, now a symbol of the city.

Modern Bristol is a vibrant, attractive city. The richly varied architecture illustrates its history – fine old churches (Elizabeth I described St Mary Radcliffe as 'the finest parish church in England'); the elegant Georgian terraces and crescents of Clifton and squares in the city, once the homes of wealthy merchants; imposing Victorian public buildings and warehousing. The arts are well served, with theatres and concert halls, museums and galleries. The excellent Zoo is beautifully situated on the Downs. Annual events include an International Balloon Festival.

Bristol can be explored by sightseeing bus or on a range of guided walks, but a great way to see its maritime heritage is by water. From Brunel's magnificent Temple Meads Station a ferry runs through the city and around the harbour. Here are two contemporary arts centres and a hands-on science centre and planetarium, sculptures and boatyards. The star of the docks though is the SS *Great Britain*, the first iron hulled screw-propelled steamship to cross the Atlantic. Visitors explore the ship and its museum and enjoy a programme of activities including 'Visits from Mr Brunel'. *The Matthew*, a replica of Cabot's ship, moors alongside when in Bristol.

The balloons go up over Clifton Suspension Bridge during the annual Balloon Festival.

WHERE:
Bristol
BEST TIME TO GO:
Any time of year
DON'T MISS:
The New Room, John Wesley's Chapel and first headquarters, is the oldest Methodist building in the world. Built in 1739, this lovely, peaceful building in the centre of the city remains a place of worship. Above the chapel, with its original pews and pulpit, is a small, fascinating museum.
AMOUNT OF WALKING:
Little or moderate (Bristol is very hilly; some of the cobbled quays are uneven. SS *Great Britain* has full wheelchair access and facilities for the blind and deaf).
COST:
Low to reasonable (free returns for a year on the SS *Great Britain*; buses and ferries offer multi-stop fares).
YOU SHOULD KNOW:
Before the Corn Exchange was built, business was conducted in the street. Merchants completed money transactions on four flat-topped bronze pillars, 'nails' (still standing in Corn Street, the oldest is 16th century). This is the origin of the expression 'paying on the nail'.

Sidmouth

BRANSCOMBE AND THE SEATON TRAMWAY

Sidmouth's handsome Georgian and Regency villas (now mostly hotels) and broad Esplanade date from its days as a fashionable resort; the elegant cream and white town with its fine, long shingle beach and flanking red cliffs, remains a popular seaside destination. Heading east, it is possible to hike the spectacular Jurassic Coast all the way to Seaton, or to take the winding country lanes inland through the lovely countryside of East Devonshire.

The road passes the Norman Lockyer Observatory and the Donkey Sanctuary before descending to the wide, picturesque valley and pebble beach at Branscombe. This part of the coast is owned by the National Trust, which has restored a forge, mill and the Old Bakery in the attractive village. Branscombe is reputed to be the longest village in Britain, as well as one of East Devon's prettiest – with rows of lovely thatched cottages, two pubs, a brewery and a church that offers what is arguably the finest view in the county.

From Seaton, a seaside and harbour town, the narrow gauge electric Seaton Tramway starts from an impressive terminus, and runs inland along the beautiful Axe Valley through a nature reserve. In addition to open-top trams, closed saloons run all year. First stop is the little village of Colyford (T.E. Lawrence was a regular customer at the filling station, now a motor museum). Colyton, the terminus, is a small, ancient, unspoilt and very attractive town.

Just north, the National Trust property Shute Barton is one of the most important surviving non-fortified manor houses of the Middle Ages. Dating from 1380, it has battlemented turrets and a Tudor gatehouse.

The Seaton Tramway

WHERE:
Devon
BEST TIME TO GO:
All year round (Shute Barton opens on Wednesdays and Saturdays from April till October; Sidmouth is packed during the August Folk Week; the Seaton Tramway runs 'Santa Specials' at Christmas time).
DON'T MISS:
Colyford was made a Royal Borough in the 13th century; it has its own Mayor and holds a Goose Fair each September.
AMOUNT OF WALKING:
Moderate or lots (the South West Coast Path is steep; the cliffs near Sidmouth are subject to erosion).
COSTS:
Reasonable (the Tramway offers a range of discounts).
YOU SHOULD KNOW:
The Branscombe Vale Brewery's strongest ale is called Summa That.

Exeter Cathedral to Ottery Church

VIA EXMOUTH AND BICTON

Much of Exeter's old town was destroyed by World War II bombs, but St Peter's Cathedral survives, and it dominates the city's skyline. Its two great towers are Norman, but most of the cathedral is Gothic. The façade has weathered carvings of English kings, including Alfred and William the Conqueror. Inside, the long ceiling is decorated with painted bosses (one shows the martyrdom of St Thomas à Becket); there is a huge Bishop's Throne and early misericords are decorated with mythological figures.

The road and railway along the Exe Estuary cross an area rich in birdlife – the avocet winters here. Exmouth enjoys both sea and river frontages; a Georgian terrace above the waterfront is a reminder of its elegant past. Its long sand beach still makes it a popular seaside resort. On the edge of town, A la Ronde is a unique sixteen-sided house, built for spinster cousins; it contains a collection of 18th-century souvenirs from their Grand Tour.

North of Budleigh Salterton and the ancient village of East Budleigh in the lovely Axe Valley is Bicton Park Botanical Gardens. This superbly landscaped park contains an arboretum and several distinct garden areas; the earliest is the ornamental 18th-century Italian Garden. Victorian gardens include a Fernery (with Shell House). Among the glasshouses are an orangery and the beautiful curvilinear Palm House. There are activities for children and an interesting museum of rural life. Bicton Woodland Railway, a narrow gauge leisure line, meanders through the gardens.

The church at Ottery St Mary (a little town famous for its flaming tar-barrel processions) is huge; it was rebuilt in the 14th century as a Collegiate Church, along the lines of Exeter Cathedral. The great Ottery Clock is an astronomical clock, thought to date from the 14th century.

WHERE:
Devon
BEST TIME TO GO:
Any time of year (Bicton is open all year).
DON'T MISS:
Topsham, between Exeter and Exmouth, is delightful; a busy port in the 17th century, many of its buildings date from this period. It's an excellent place to watch the birds of the Exe estuary.
AMOUNT OF WALKING:
Moderate
COST:
Reasonable
YOU SHOULD KNOW:
East Budleigh is the birthplace of Roger Conant, founder of Salem, Massachusetts and of Sir Walter Raleigh. The vicarage, where Raleigh was educated, has a secret passageway, used in the 19th century by the Reverend Stapleton (who apparently preached great sermons) to stash contraband.

Exeter Cathedral

Lydford Gorge

TAVISTOCK AND COTEHELE ESTATE

WHERE:
Devon and Cornwall
BEST TIME TO GO:
All year round (the walk at Lydford Gorge closes in winter but access to the waterfall is year-round; the gardens at Cotehele remain open, with a winter events programme).
DON'T MISS:
The lovely ancient woodland of Lydford Gorge is a haven for wildlife; the air is full of butterflies and birds, while herons and kingfishers may be spotted near quiet stretches of water.
AMOUNT OF WALKING:
Moderate to lots (Lydford Gorge is a strenuous walk with uneven, slippery stretches, unsuitable for small children; the extensive Cotehele Estate is very steep, with loose gravel).
COST:
Reasonable (both the Gorge and Cotehele offer family discounts).
YOU SHOULD KNOW:
For Christmas at Cotehele, greenery and berries are gathered from the estate and made into an enormous garland, which is displayed in the candlelit Hall (specially opened from late November).

The little Dartmoor village of Lydford, with its ruined castle, was a defensive Saxon town. Down the hill past a stone bridge, the River Lyd rushes from the Moor and drops into the deep, tree-lined ravine, Lydford Gorge. The deep-set Gorge runs through dense deciduous woodland and alongside the water on granite slabs for 2.5 km (1.5 mi). Near the bridge, the Devil's Cauldron, a whirlpool of white foaming water battering the black rocks, is heard before it is seen; at the bottom end, the 30-m (100-ft) White Lady Waterfall plunges – an almost vertical torrent.

South of Lydford on the River Tavy, Tavistock grew up around an important Benedictine monastery, whose remains can still be seen. It was granted a Market Charter in 1105 and became a Stannary (tin-essaying and marketing) Town 200 years later, though most of its stone buildings date from the 19th century, after copper was discovered here. Still a flourishing market town with excellent independent food shops, Tavistock holds a traditional Goose Fair each October.

West of Tavistock on the Cornish side of the Tamar lies the Cotehele Estate. The house, dating from the 15th century and owned by the Edgcumbe family till 1947, is one of the least altered Tudor manor houses in the country, with fine collections of textiles, armour and furniture. The estate is criss-crossed by footpaths and scattered with old buildings including a watermill and an apple-press; the steep valley gardens contain a medieval dovecote and stewpond. Down on the Quay, a branch of the National Maritime Museum displays an exhibition on the vital role played by the Tamar in the life and economy of the area; a restored Tamar sailing barge is moored alongside.

The White Lady Waterfall in Lydford Gorge

Dartmouth to Salcombe

The sheltered harbour of Salcombe

BY THE COAST ROAD

Dartmouth has a long seafaring tradition: the Crusaders sailed from here, ships left to fight the Spanish Armada, the Pilgrim Fathers put in en route to America and a fleet sailed to the D-Day Landings. Home to the British Navy for centuries, it is now dominated by the Royal Naval College. The original wharf, Bayards Cove, is a picturesque cobbled quay lined with 18th-century houses. At the mouth of the estuary 15th-century Dartmouth Castle is reached on foot or by ferry. Fine half-timbered, overhanging buildings include the arcaded 17th-century Butterwalk, now home to the Museum.

The coast road follows the long shallow curve of Start Bay south. Lovely Blackpool Sands lies beneath pine-clad cliffs; Slapton Sands was evacuated during World War II, to allow training for Operation Overlord. At Torcross, a huge shingle bank encloses Slapton Ley, a freshwater lake rich in birdlife and rare flora. The main road turns inland to Kingsbridge, but back roads and the coast path continue to Beesands, a lonely row of cottages on an exposed beach, and Hallsands, where the whole village was engulfed by the sea in 1917. At Start Point, a lighthouse stands above perilous rocks; Prawle Point is Devon's most southerly point. From East Portlemouth village a foot-ferry crosses to Salcombe.

Built in glorious countryside on the western slopes of the Kingsbridge Estuary and blessed with a large, sheltered natural harbour, Salcombe is a very desirable place to live and the water is dotted with luxury yachts. In the 19th century, this was an important shipbuilding and port town, busy with coastal and foreign trade.

WHERE:
Devon
BEST TIME TO GO:
April to October
DON'T MISS:
Salcombe museum offers a fascinating glimpse of its shipbuilding past, when fast Salcombe schooners carried fruit from around the world.
AMOUNT OF WALKING:
Moderate
COST:
Low
YOU SHOULD KNOW:
On Slapton Sands, a Sherman Tank recovered from the seabed stands as a memorial to the US servicemen who died during Exercise Tiger in WWII. This tragedy has only recently come to light.

39

The steam railway passing Goodrington Sands.

Paignton Zoo

PAIGNTON AND DARTMOUTH STEAM RAILWAY

WHERE:
Devon
BEST TIME TO GO:
Any time of year
DON'T MISS:
The Brook Side Aviary at Paignton Zoo – one of the best, and humane, displays of wild birds in the country; and a riot of fun and colour.
AMOUNT OF WALKING:
Lots, in the morning; but access is good apart from some quite steep hills at the Zoo, and excellent at the Steam Railway.
COST:
Expensive
YOU SHOULD KNOW:
Dartmouth has a purpose-built railway station, but has never had a train in it. The bridge that should have connected it to Paignton was never built, so the railway company bought the ferry to complete the route. Dartmouth is believed to be the only place in the world with an official railway station on a pontoon.

Spread across 30 hectares (75 acres) of hillside by the ring road, Paignton Zoo is one of England's biggest and most comprehensive – so get there for opening at 9.00 am and make the most of it. As far as possible, the 300 species (about 1,200 animals) live in something like their natural habitats, recreated with native plants, trees and vegetation. You can explore the African Savannah, the Desert, Wetlands, and both Temperate and Tropical Forests. You can also get surprisingly – and scarily – close to lions, tigers, elephants, snakes, rhinos, gorillas, gibbons and whole flocks of flamingos, storks and other multi-coloured birds. The Zoo offers tours (1 to 2 hours) that take you to unexpected corners in the woods or marshes, and introduce you to rare and endangered animals and exotic plants like the Japanese raisin tree, the Chusan fan palm and the pagoda tree. The Crocodile Swamp's dripping heat holds 5 m (16 ft) saltwater killers and the very rare, very agile Cuban croc that can leap straight up from the water to snatch birds from overhead trees. Attractions include Monkey Heights, Gibbon Island, the Jungle Express miniature railway, and opportunities to hold and feed animals or birds, and talk to the Keepers. The animals will always keep you on your toes, highly entertained and often amused, too.

You can rest your feet in the afternoon on the Paignton and Dartmouth Steam Railway. It's a dedicated holiday line that puffs and whistles just behind the glorious sandy beaches of Torbay; then runs along the spectacular wooded headland and beautiful coves of the Dart estuary to Kingswear. You cross the river by ferry (it's part of your ticket) – and you can either explore historic Dartmouth (try the Butterwalk or the 14th-century buildings in Higher Street), or take an estuary boat trip towards Totnes before steaming back to Paignton for tea.

Buckfastleigh

SOUTH DEVON STEAM RAILWAY TO TOTNES

On the southern edge of Dartmoor National Park, Buckfastleigh stands at the head of the woods and meadows of the Dart Valley, itself protected as one of Devon's outstanding scenic glories. The little town repays close inspection. Higher Town reflects its 19th-century prosperity, but along Lower Town's Fore Street, you can see that the predominantly 18th- and early 19th-century facades mask much older buildings. The Valiant Soldier visitor centre (a pub for 100 years until 1965, its 1940s-50s interior is preserved in meticulous detail) is actually medieval. Climb the 196 'Wishing Steps' from Station Road to the hilltop panorama from the ruined 13th-century church, and you can see that Buckfastleigh is cloaked in 1,000 years of history.

To your north you'll see Buckfast Abbey, established in 1018 by King Cnut (Canute of tidal fame), ceded to the 12th-century Cistercians until the Dissolution of 1539, and restored to the Benedictines who rebuilt it in its medieval incarnation between 1907-38. Be amazed by the monks' magnificent achievement: the blend of early English and French styles was achieved by a handful of men with no previous experience of stonemasonry. Now the Abbey is famous for its dazzling stained glass, its 'Buckfast Tonic Wine', and produce from its disease-free bees (internationally, the late Brother Adam was the 'Nelson Mandela' of apiarists). But to understand the Abbey's raison d'être of peace and tranquility, visit the Lavender, Physic and Sensory Gardens; and perhaps listen to one of the Benedictines' nine daily plainchant Offices in the Abbey itself.

From the Abbey, take the vintage bus to the station, where the South Devon Railway brilliantly recreates the Age of Steam with a thirty-minute ride to Totnes (return by boat, bus or train!) on a former branch line. The 11 km (7 mi) of wildlife-filled riverbank are as thrilling as the splendid, gleaming trains – so many visitors do the whole thing twice.

WHERE:
Devon
BEST TIME TO GO:
April to October
DON'T MISS:
The chance to reflect for a moment, on the chamomile seat surrounded by honeysuckle and a rose-covered trellis in Buckfast Abbey's Sensory Garden – the whole of which is based on medieval designs for pleasure gardens.
AMOUNT OF WALKING:
Lots, in the morning – but access is reasonable around Buckfastleigh, very good at the Abbey, and 'all areas' (including the museum, sheds and every aspect of the trains and stations en route) of the South Devon Railway.
COST:
Free in the morning; expensive but worth it for the whole Railway experience.
YOU SHOULD KNOW:
1. Special joint tickets enable you to visit Buckfast Butterflies and the Dartmoor Otter Sanctuary, both adjacent to Buckfastleigh Station, as well as ride a steam train to Totnes.
2. The name 'Buckfastleigh' contains half the letters of the alphabet, none of them repeated. Check it out.

Buckfast Abbey in its glorious setting

Bovey Tracey to Castle Drogo

THE HEART OF DARTMOOR NATIONAL PARK

The drive from Bovey Tracey through Dartmoor National Park's eastern edge leads into the landscapes of high tor and thickly wooded river valleys that define the irresistible charm of this part of Devon. Bovey Tracey is fairly typical of the doggedly individualistic villages. Buildings that might be 1,000 years old house artists and artisans practising ancient crafts in profoundly modern ways. The Devon Guild of Craftsmen showcases work including jewellery, ceramics, sculpture, glass, textiles and furniture in Bovey Tracey's Riverside Mill, and you can see free demonstrations of glass blowing at Teign Valley Glassworks.

Drive west up to Haytor, one of the most famous local outcrops. The lanes to Widecombe pass through some of the loveliest countryside in Britain, and Widecombe, immortalized by the song 'Widdecombe Fair' featuring "Uncle Tom Cobley and All…", is one of Dartmoor's most picturesque villages. Dartmeet's charm is famous. Lush trees crowd a steep valley where the East and West Dart gurgle under a pretty 'clapper' bridge. The 13th-century 'clapper' at nearby Postbridge is the largest anywhere. In 1670 this track, now the B3357, was the only route across the Moor deemed reliable for the post; and at this spot the past is easy to conjure. Steep, narrow lanes take you to the lyric perfection of North Bovey's 18th-century thatched cottages; and the two-storey, arcaded, 15th-century almshouses and church in the old market square are just two of a dozen surprises in Moretonhampstead. Chagford is another unspoilt village. In its 15th-century church, the tinminers' badge of three conjoint rabbits marks it as an ancient stannary town.

Across the river at Drewsteignton, standing dramatically 250 m (820 ft) above the Teign Gorge, is Castle Drogo. It's an heroic folly, a country house designed in severe granite by Sir Edwin Lutyens to look like a medieval fortress. It's fascinating, completely brilliant, and very Dartmoor.

WHERE:
Devon
BEST TIME TO GO:
Any time of year, Dartmoor is impossibly beautiful; but it's warmer from April to October, and Castle Drogo is open then.
DON'T MISS:
The formal garden at Castle Drogo – inspired by Gertrude Jekyll, and in extraordinary contrast to the bent creepers of Dartmoor's ancient woodlands that border it.
AMOUNT OF WALKING:
Little, at any one time.
COST:
Low, unless something wonderful takes your fancy at the Devon Guild of Craftsmen shop.
YOU SHOULD KNOW:
Bovey Tracey gets its name from the River Bovey and from the Norman de Tracey family from Bayeux, who settled here after 1066. William de Tracey, a member of the family, is infamous as one of the four Knights who murdered Thomas a Becket in Canterbury Cathedral in 1170.

Bovey Tracey in the heart of the English countryside

Bigbury-on-Sea

Low tide from Bigbury to Burgh Island

NEWTON FERRERS, NOSS MAYO AND SALTRAM HOUSE

Writers love Devon. Devon has beautiful pockets of bucolic innocence that bring to mind works by Jane Austen, Agatha Christie, or even Enid Blyton. The broad sands of the beach at Bigbury face Burgh Island across a causeway, which you can pass on foot at low tide, or on a telescopically elevated jumbo tractor at other times. The island is famous for its Art Deco hotel, built in 1929 and the actual setting for two of Agatha Christie's detective thrillers. Tear yourself away from this idyllic beach playground, and follow the coastal lanes and creeks to the lush woods of the Yealm Estuary above Noss Mayo. With the stunning scenery of the South Devon Coastal Path on three sides, the village is perfect for a short stroll followed by lunch in a garden at the water's tranquil edge.

Across the Yealm, Newton Ferrers clusters round its stone jetty, its weathered cottages radiating up the steep hill and vanishing among the trees. It is a haven of peace. The woods along Yealm Pool are full of wildlife; swans and herons nest on its banks, and kingfishers and egrets transfix the green with flashing colours. There's no through traffic, and the 900 year-old church adds to Newton Ferrers' sense of timelessness. Even without joining the chattering knot at the quayside, it's a place where solitude is amicable.

Back in Plymouth, the classic George II mansion Saltram House stands in 202 hectares (500 acres) of rolling parkland on the banks of the Plym itself. Besides its fabulous original contents, Saltram's glory includes some of Robert Adams's finest rooms, with astonishing plasterwork ceilings and original Chinese wallpapers. It's an appropriately magnificent setting for the collections of furniture, fine art and china – and just one more reason why Saltram House starred in the film of Jane Austen's *Sense and Sensibility*.

WHERE:
Devon
BEST TIME TO GO:
March to October, when estuary life revives, and the interior of Saltram House is open.
DON'T MISS:
The 18th-century Great Kitchen in Saltram House, with its original tools and furnishings – less flamboyant than the Salon and Staterooms, but equally impressive.
AMOUNT OF WALKING:
Lots – and it's all a bit up-hill, down-dale.
COST:
Devon's lovely coast comes free; and Saltram's treasures are reasonable.
YOU SHOULD KNOW:
Both Bigbury and the woods flanking the River Yealm estuary formed the backdrop to scenes in Enid Blyton's Famous Five series of children's stories.

Cricket St Thomas Wildlife Park

The elegant manor house of Cricket St Thomas is famous as the setting for the 1970s TV sitcom 'To The Manor Born', and the estate, between Crewkerne and Chard, is recorded in the Domesday Book of 1086. Now the house is an exclusive hotel, and the estate is a wildlife park almost as celebrated for its exceptional layout as it is for its animals. As you arrive, you see Przewalski horses from the Hungarian plains in their splendid enclosure. They are emblematic of the Park, one of many severely endangered species in its breeding recovery programme. Most are in enclosures that mimic their natural environments: in Lemur Wood, four species of lemur can both root among the forest floor litter and scramble high into the 'forest' canopy. The Park's hills and hollows reveal habitats as a series of surprises. Open, green pastures are bounded by woods, lakes and low waterfalls: each and all, approximations of home for reindeer, cheetah, zebra, oryx, tapir, mongoose, camel, macaques, tamarins, meerkat, flamingo, ibis, peach-faced lovebird and many other birds, mammals, reptiles, big cats and wild African dogs. A miniature railway will take you through the heart of the enclosures for the closest possible view.

There are several opportunities to hold and/or feed animals, including reptiles; and enjoyable displays at the heavy horse centre and in the aviaries. Keen younger visitors like to become 'Keeper for a Day', joining one of the professionals at some of the noisy, messy (and sometimes smelly!) daily tasks of caring for animals. Cricket St Thomas puts on a dazzling show, but you can easily see its commitment to serious environmental and wildlife research. It's one of a handful of places in the world where you can see the Amur leopard, one of the rarest creatures on the planet.

WHERE:
Somerset
BEST TIME TO GO:
April to October. The Park is open throughout the year, but many of the facilities and programmes that make it a great family day out are not.
DON'T MISS:
The Amur leopard, of which only about 40 survive in the wild. With their dense fur (adapted to survive Siberian temperatures of –30 °C/ –22 °F), Amur leopards are particularly beautiful, and their cubs are especially cute: Cricket St Thomas has successfully bred 13, and sent offspring to Canada, Germany and the USA.
AMOUNT OF WALKING:
Lots – and on the often steep and varied pathways (asphalt, gravel, grass and woodchip), wheelchairs and buggies are tricky to handle. But there are also strategically well-placed cafés and bars.
COST:
Expensive – and very expensive indeed if you take the 3-hour 'Walk on the Wild Side' behind-the-scenes, exclusive, guided tour for a maximum of two people.
YOU SHOULD KNOW:
Guests staying at Cricket St Thomas Hotel are entitled to reduced entry rates to the Wildlife Park. From the magnificent house, you can appreciate the influence of Capability Brown on the fundamental design of the rolling parkland (including what is now the wildlife park).

The startled look of a Ruffed lemur

Haynes Motor Museum

SPARKFORD AND THE FLEET AIR ARM MUSEUM

Try to approach Sparkford from the south. From the hill just above the old market village of Queen Camel, you get a spectacular panorama of the arcadian wonderland of Somerset as your heart wants it to be, all green hill and watered dale. In this bucolic rural vision, it's a bit of a surprise to discover Britain's biggest collection of historic cars. Haynes Motor Museum holds over 340 cars and motorbikes, classified in eleven display halls to illustrate automotive history, motor sport, design classics, celebrities of speed on the circuit and speedway, and technological innovation. Besides Ferrari, Bentley and Rolls-Royce, you can see a 1900 Clement, a 1931 Duesenberg, a 1926 Bugatti and a 1917 Morris Cowley. You can watch restorers at work on historic cars, play arcade games from the 1950s and 60s, pit your skills in the ultimate race car simulator, explore the outdoor military vehicle display or sit in Michael Schumacher's F1 show car. Let the children rush off to the themed play area, the interactive displays or the Kids' (outdoor) Race Track: you can enjoy fulfilling a dozen childhood fantasies guilt-free.

Barely 8 km (5 mi) down the road at Yeovilton, the Fleet Air Arm Museum sits next to one of the Royal Navy's most important operational air bases. It houses the flying prototype Concorde 002, and some ninety aircraft illustrating the history of airborne naval warfare. Up close, you can appreciate the specialist adaptations on Fairey biplanes, Sea Harriers, the Wyvern and other folding-wing carrier craft, and a range of helicopters. But whatever you do, sign up for the Aircraft Carrier Experience. Thanks to stunning special effects and real Navy simulators, you 'fly' to Ark Royal and witness an authentic operational launch from the flight deck. Not even the professionals can get any closer to the real thing.

WHERE:
Somerset
BEST TIME TO GO:
Any time of year
DON'T MISS:
The Aircraft Carrier Experience at the Fleet Air Arm Museum. It has deservedly won many awards for plunging you into the authentic sight, touch, smell and feel of combined sea-air ops. It's a genuine, once-in-a-lifetime experience.
AMOUNT OF WALKING:
Moderate, and access is excellent.
COST:
Reasonably expensive – but you certainly get your money's worth.
YOU SHOULD KNOW:
The Carrier Experience sets you in front of a 9 m (30 ft) wide, 3-screen video programme that gives you a pilot's eye view of landing on a carrier deck at sea.

A Corsair FG-1 holds pride of place at Yeovilton.

Bath and a walk by Combe Hay

WHERE:
Somerset
BEST TIME TO GO:
Any time of year – but there's a trade-off between summer crowds in Bath and full bloom in Combe Hay.
DON'T MISS:
The early industrial relics of the disused Somerset Coal Canal in Combe Hay village. They include parts of the flight of 10 caisson locks of 1805.
AMOUNT OF WALKING:
Lots
COST:
None
YOU SHOULD KNOW:
It's particularly interesting that, though the relative placing of manor house, church, village and village industry make Combe Hay a perfect example of the social order of the era in which it developed, exactly the same set-up is now valued purely as an example of visual beauty and harmony.

The World Heritage Site of Bath is one of Britain's most beautiful cities. Treasured by the Romans, who discovered its mineral-rich springs, and Georgian society of the 18th century, whose hypochondria revived the city as a fashionable spa, Bath is a treasure house of ancient buildings with a history of inspired town planning. Royal Crescent, Pulteney Bridge and The Circus epitomize Georgian elegance, and a morning spent wandering the facades of mellow stone, and the pillared formality of the Theatre Royal and public buildings in the city's heart, can be a refreshingly civilized urban delight. If you prefer, the Mayor's 'Honorary Guides' offer free, two-hour guided walks of Bath's major historical and architectural sights – from Abbey Church Yard at 10.30 am. The only downside is Bath's popularity, but it's easy to leave the crowds and bustle. Just 3.5 km (2 mi) south of Bath is a rural enclave apparently untouched for at least two centuries.

The village of Combe Hay grows out of the countryside, its buildings interlocked around the lake and grounds of Combe Hay Manor. The Manor isn't open to the public, but you can walk round the lake, and admire the honeyed Bath stone perfection of it from close enough. The house is Grade I listed, and proclaims its rarity from every angle. Even so, it is just the centrepiece of an equally beautiful village, and a valley whose secluded landscape seems to waft in an evergreen timewarp. Wandering around Combe Hay is balm to the soul. It's a microcosm of a loved and valued aesthetic – of order on a human scale – and the same one that makes Bath so special. Today you can see both its urban and rural expressions.

The Abbey with the Pump Room to the right

Montacute House and Tintinhull

Montacute is one of the best preserved, and one of the greatest of Elizabethan houses. It's significant because it was among the very first to be built (1588-1601) solely for display. Instead of unnecessary fortifications, it has banks of windows, flooding light into splendid rooms and the biggest (52 m/172 ft) Long Gallery in England. Inside and out, you can see the exquisite detail of Renaissance influences and designs grafted onto the Gothic architectural tradition of the times. Saved by the National Trust, Montacute has wonderful Tudor and Jacobean portraits from the national collection, and some of Britain's best 17th- and 18th-century furniture and textiles. Outside, formal gardens include outstanding topiary, and designs laid out by Vita Sackville-West in dramatic empathy with the house.

Part of the Montacute estate in 1539, neighbouring Tintinhull is a small, 17th-century manor with vintage charm on a more domestic scale. With a new façade added in 1722, the building is a doll's house gem – and though you can rent it from the National Trust and play lord and lady of the manor, you can't visit it. Instead, rejoice in the glorious, formal gardens. Designed predominantly by Mrs Reiss from 1933 to 1960, and replanted by Penelope Hobhouse in the 1980s, Tintinhull's garden is divided by clipped yew hedges and walls of mellow brick into seven 'rooms'. Carefully sited seats delicately point out vistas that combine complex seasonal flowerings with perspectives of shrub and water features. The pool garden, fountain garden, white garden, traditional garden and delightful kitchen garden are each utterly distinctive, yet with the secluded lawns and linking avenues, contributors to a greater harmony. This is the genius of Tintinhull, and you won't want to leave.

The west front of Montacute House

WHERE:
Somerset
BEST TIME TO GO:
March to October (but Tintinhull's traditional English garden is at its most welcoming and colourful in June).
DON'T MISS:
The huge bed in Montacute's Crimson Bedroom, a massive oak four-poster intricately carved with acanthus leaves, James I's coat of arms, and the date 1612. This bed held Johnny Depp in scenes from the 2004 Hollywood film *The Libertine*. During filming, a National Trust restorer was positioned underneath the bed to monitor any damage to its ancient fabric.
AMOUNT OF WALKING:
Lots – and there is only partial wheelchair access at either Montacute or Tintinhull (though staff do their best).
COST:
Reasonable
YOU SHOULD KNOW:
Before she came to Tintinhull, Mrs Reiss had lived near Hidcote Manor, renowned for its classic Elizabethan garden. Her use of garden enclosures, pools and rich planting to create carefully organized vistas acknowledges her debt to Hidcote's elegant ideas.

Evening in the Saxon town of Bruton

Street

WYKE CHAMPFLOWER AND BRUTON

WHERE:
Somerset
BEST TIME TO GO:
April to October (though Clark's Shoe Museum is open all year).
DON'T MISS:
The wooden tympanum between the nave and chancel of Holy Trinity, Wyke Champflower, painted with the Royal Arms, and the arms of the then Bishop of Bath and Wells.
AMOUNT OF WALKING:
Little
COST:
None (but who can resist a factory outlet for shoes?).
YOU SHOULD KNOW:
The medieval alleys in Bruton are called 'bartons' – but the town has much older Celtic, Roman and Saxon sites which included a church in 690, an Abbey, and a royal mint. Now the town is a historical playground for students from five major schools in the vicinity, whose numbers double the resident population in term-time.

Street was an ancient but unremarkable Wessex village until it became a company town. In the 1820s it became the headquarters and factory of Clarks Shoes. Owned and run by Quakers, the company built new homes and facilities for its employees; and though the factory has now moved, the company opened a factory outlet in its place, attracting other manufacturers to do the same. Now Street has millions of visitors looking for designer bargains in a shopping centre out of all proportion to the size of the town. As you'll see, Clark's remains pre-eminent. At the company HQ there's a Shoe Museum guaranteed to captivate the most reluctant shopper or child. It tells the history of shoes since Roman times, but it includes examples from all over the world, along with the fashion magazines and advertisements that promoted them. The silk slippers! The crocodile platforms! The prices! The Shoe Museum is really good fun.

From Street head east through the villages folded into the rolling hills along the River Brue. In summer you drink in a sense of natural abundance that has existed here since before these villages were entered in Domesday; but in any season it's obvious how deeply rooted local communities are in the annual cycle. Rural churches are just one reminder how those roots transcend centuries in which only architectural style changes – and you'll come to a fine example at Wyke Champflower, near Bruton. Holy Trinity at Wyke is hidden by the much older manor house. Go round the back (you're allowed!) and you find an exquisitely simple, Jacobean church, with its original box pews dated 1624. Bruton itself is a Saxon town, with Jacobean almshouses, a medieval dovecote, riverside walk, twin-towered church and a beautiful 15th-century packhorse bridge.

Glastonbury

WELLS, NUNNEY AND MELLS

The Peat Moors Centre puts the legend and mysticism associated with Glastonbury's mythic sites in the rugged context of a real Iron Age settlement. Glastonbury Lake Village is a reconstruction of three Iron Age roundhouses in which, for most of the year, visitors can participate in craft and living history demonstrations of every aspect of life in the prehistoric Somerset wetlands. Wattle-and-daub repairs to walls is one (muddy) favourite; and the folk-history of peat cutting on the misty moors of Avalon becomes spookily mysterious round the cooking-pots on the fire.

A short drive away, Wells is testament to more worldly manifestations of warriors and bishops. Wells Cathedral glorifies God in no uncertain terms; but the Bishop's Palace, enclosed in a moated bailey, and rising with increasing magnificence to the private apartments, glorifies turbulent 13th-century bishops. You can see the private chapel, the ruined Great Hall and the gatehouse with its portcullis and drawbridge – a glimpse of the medieval splendour which for 800 years has been home to the Bishops of Bath and Wells.

Next door, the intricate Gothic carving on the Cathedral's West Front puts the Palace to shame by comparison. Wells Cathedral is one of the glories of Britain – just the fan vaulting of the Chapter House is a measure of its timeless beauty. What you see will become your benchmarks of human aspiration to the eternal. It's that good.

Take a breather to reflect, and head for Nunney Castle near Frome. It's a gentle, scenic ruin of a 14th-century castle in the French style (drum towers and a mansard-type roof), placed like a folly in a lovely village. Then on to Mells, where both Ronald Knox and Siegfried Sassoon are buried in the 15th- to 16th-century church yard of a village of astonishing beauty and tranquillity.

WHERE:
Somerset
BEST TIME TO GO:
Any time of year (but check the Peat Moors Centre, which opens to coincide with school holidays and weekends).
DON'T MISS:
Vicar's Close, the oldest complete street of 14th-century houses in Europe. Built to house Cathedral vicars, it runs off the Cathedral complex.
AMOUNT OF WALKING:
Lots, but most of it is accessible to wheelchairs, and assistance can frequently be provided.
COST:
Very reasonable, where there is any.
YOU SHOULD KNOW:
Like the church, the manor at Mells is Grade I listed. It is the home of the Asquith and Horner families (represented in the church by memorials by Alfred Munnings and Edwin Lutyens). Mells Manor was (allegedly) procured by Jack Horner when he discovered the deeds in a pie given to him to carry to London by the last Abbot of Glastonbury. Thus was born the children's rhyme about 'Little Jack Horner'.

Nunney Castle

Cheddar's Caves and Gorges

WHERE:
Somerset

BEST TIME TO GO:
Any time of year (Cheddar Gorge is never less than stunning, and the cave systems are amazing in all weathers; but Priddy Pools and Ebbor Gorge (both Sites of Special Scientific Interest) only come into their own between April and October).

DON'T MISS:
The mossy landscape of Priddy Pools, outside Priddy village. Once incorporated into a water system for lead mining, the Pools are integrated via St Cuthbert's Swallet (sink hole) into the 16-km (10-mi) Wookey Hole cave system. The peculiar ecological and geological combination supports extraordinary fauna, including newts, and the Cheddar Pink butterfly.

AMOUNT OF WALKING:
Lots. Access is inevitably restricted – but at Cheddar Gorge and Wookey Hole, for those areas where access is impossible, there is at least a virtual tour on offer.

COST:
None, to admire the dramatic scenery. Expensive, to access Cheddar Caves and Wookey Hole.

YOU SHOULD KNOW:
At Cheddar Gorge, the view from the Lookout Tower is majestic; but to reach it, you have to walk up the 274 steps of Jacob's Ladder.

Cheddar Gorge is stunning at any time of year.

Along the southern rim of the Mendip Hills, spectacular limestone formations of 100 m (328 ft) cliffs, rock pinnacles, cave systems and precipitous gorges stretch from Cheddar to Wookey Hole, just outside Wells. It is a prehistoric landscape of wild and rugged beauty, riddled with caves like huge underground cathedrals echoing to the drip of time, and of broad panoramas from the heights of the cliffs across the misty Somerset Levels spread far below. Nature is at its most dramatic at the village of Cheddar – and in both Cheddar Gorge and underground in Cheddar Caves, a variety of themed, guided tours add real theatrical value to an amazing experience. From April to September, the best way to see Cheddar Gorge is from the open-topped, double-decker bus tour. Underground, access to the most important cave complexes is by tours like 'The Crystal Quest' fantasy adventure, or 'Cheddar Man and the Cannibals', which includes evidence of Stone-Age occupation (and hazards) in the area. One recently revived custom in the caves is 'cheddaring': the process of maturing Cheddar cheese inside the limestone caves to get the original taste and consistency.

You'll see more evidence of neolithic society on the road to Priddy and Ebbor Gorge. As the cliffs of Cheddar give way to green hills, there are barrows, swallet holes, Priddy Circles, caves and rock shelters. In Priddy village, it's worth the effort to find the lane over the hill down to Ebbor. Once you've parked, you'll be in a woodland paradise of birdsong. Ebbor is a steep defile of pristine arcadia, full of nature and empty of people. Happily, nearby Wookey Hole offers vital re-entry to the human world. Wookey's system of 25 chambers is zoned and lit as a fabulous demonstration of both the natural world, and of prehistoric life within it. It's as entertaining as it is dramatic.

Clevedon

FLAX BOURTON, CHEW MAGNA AND BURRINGTON COMBE

The pier and bandstand are gentle reminders that Cleveland, on the Bristol Channel south of Portishead, was once a popular Victorian seaside resort. Its true Saxon

Clevedon Pier

origins are much better represented by 14th-century Clevedon Court on the edge of town. With a 12th-century tower and 13th-century Great Hall, Clevedon is a Grade I listed National Trust gem, with fascinating additions from every era, and especially lovely 18th-century terraced gardens and parkland. It's the perfect place to begin a mini-tour of one of Somerset's areas of outstanding natural beauty. On the way to Flax Bourton, pause just beyond Tickenham village to look on the Iron Age magnificence of Cadbury Camp. Locally associated with King Arthur's Camelot, its scale still ranks it among the great forts of Britain.

From Flax Bourton, take the path that follows the edge of the Tyntesfield Estate. You'll glimpse the enormous Gothic-Revival mansion across fields before you reach the thick woodland of Bourton Combe. When the woods form a steep promontory, sloping down away from you, pause for the immense view over sylvan Somerset, the Chew Valley. Chew Magna is regarded as the archetypal Somerset village, with watermill, stream, green, churches, pubs, cricket pitch and houses listed in the Domesday Book. Surrounded by picture-perfect fields and copses, with Chew Valley Lake and its legion of wildfowl and waders as indicators of regional good health, you just feel grateful that such lovely places still exist.

On the south side of Chew Valley, head west to Burrington Combe. The village is in a small gorge, pierced by caves and swallets typical of the Mendips' limestone features. Opposite the car park, you'll see a prominent rock sticking out of the cliff-face. Here, in 1762, an Anglican vicar called Augustus Toplady sought shelter from a storm. Musing on his 'rescue', he wrote the hymn 'Rock of Ages'.

WHERE:
Somerset
BEST TIME TO GO:
March to September
DON'T MISS:
The 'Rock of Ages' fissure in the high cliffs of Burrington Combe gorge. You can even celebrate the memory of the Reverend Toplady at the 'Rock of Ages' pub by the car park opposite.
AMOUNT OF WALKING:
Lots, or none (rural paths, often steep and wooded, make access restricted – but you can enjoy all the essentials of this beautiful region from a car).
COST:
Low (Clevedon Court), or none.
YOU SHOULD KNOW:
Chew Magna has been called 'the greenest village in Britain' because it was the first to adopt a 'zero-waste' policy with whole-hearted endorsement from its residents. Part of the policy involves reducing the local carbon-footprint by eating locally produced food – around here, you'll certainly want to help.

51

Burrow Mump is a natural hill that stands tall on the Somerset Levels.

Burrow Mump

THE WILLOWS AND WETLANDS VISITOR CENTRE AND HESTERCOMBE GARDENS

WHERE:
Somerset
BEST TIME TO GO:
Any time of year
DON'T MISS:
The Great Cascade at Hestercombe, created by Coplestone Warre Bampfylde in the 1750s when he first built his pleasure gardens, and brought to life after 125 years. The artificial waterfall expresses the scale, visual drama and spirit of Bampfylde's conception. Pure delight.
AMOUNT OF WALKING:
Lots, and most of it accessible (apart from Burrow Mump).
COST:
Low
YOU SHOULD KNOW:
Hestercombe is the scene of many and varied events throughout the year. Besides nature events concerning the gardens' wildlife and botanical issues, there are music and theatre shows, historical re-enactments and medieval banquets, exhibitions and car shows.

You can't miss Burrow Mump. It's a natural hill rising some 75 m (250 ft) above the watery flatness of the Somerset Levels, crowned with a church whose ruins were 'romanticised' in the 19th century. On a misty day, its silhouette above the Levels embodies all the mysteries and legends associated with the area; from the top in good weather, you get an unrivalled panorama of one of England's most distinctive and important wetlands. It's right next to Athelney, where King Alfred planned victory against the Danes (and burned the cakes), and to Stoke St Gregory, where the Willows and Wetlands Visitor Centre guards the cultural and commercial traditions of the area with gusto and determination. Owned and run privately by the Coate family, willow producers on the Levels since 1819, the Centre is farmer, manufacturer, distributor and guide to everything willow, including artists' charcoal, World War I fighter aircraft seats, coffins and DVD holders. They'll take you out in the waterlogged withies, feed you, show you everything, and make you feel like a million dollars (and informed about willow).

You'll be engrossed, but the lure of Hestercombe Gardens, back down the A361 close to Bishops Lydeard, is equally strong. Hestercombe is a triumph of botanical archaeology. It has three distinct gardens. The 18th-century landscape, famous in its day for its picturesque winding walks, follies and amazing waterfalls, had to be re-deciphered after centuries of neglect and overplanting. The 1.5-hectare (3.75-acre) Edwardian garden designed by Gertrude Jekyll and Edwin Lutyens had to be replanted in the 1980s following Jekyll's original design notes, found pinned up in a potting shed. The formal Victorian Terrace added a third distinct dimension to the restoration. Hestercombe's triumph is to have illuminated a fundamentally serious project with such horticultural flare. These gardens are beautiful, fascinating and fun.

Nether Stowey

EAST QUANTOXHEAD, CROWCOMBE, COMBE FLOREY, COTHAY AND WELLINGTON

Nether Stowey is a lovely old Domesday village on the edge of the Quantock Hills, and it's the capital of Coleridge country. Coleridge lived there in 1797-8, and, intoxicated with his surroundings, wrote *The Ancient Mariner* and *Kubla Khan* in a cottage in Lime Street, preserved as he might have known it. One of Coleridge's favourite walks was at East Quantoxhead, even then famed for its abundance of ammonites, nautilus and other Jurassic marine fossils. You can still find them by the dozen, but unless you're an expert, stay away from the base of the cliffs and look in the rock rubble. The medieval village (especially the 14th-century church) is worth a look while you're there.

Round the southern edge of the Quantocks is Crowcombe, another ancient village with a wonderful Grade I listed 14th-century church (believed to be the only one in England to be dedicated to the Holy Ghost), and a Grade I listed manor, early 18th-century Crowcombe Court. As you drive deeper into Taunton Vale, the pattern – of long family association with a village evolving from earlier church ministration – continues even into modern times. Combe Florey is as old and pretty as many villages, but it's famous for literary association, firstly with 19th-century wit the Reverend Sidney Smith, and in the 20th century, authors Evelyn Waugh and his son Auberon, who lived at 17th-century Combe Florey House.

The beautiful woodland valley of Combe Florey is typical of a succession you pass to reach Cothay Manor. Perhaps the finest small medieval manor in Britain, 15th-century Cothay, with original wall paintings and 17th-century paneling, is an enchanting, timeless gem reflected in the River Tone surrounding it. Afterwards, as the sun sets, you can look back across the glories of the Vale of Taunton from the nearby Wellington Monument. It's one of Somerset's finest vistas.

WHERE:
Somerset
BEST TIME TO GO:
April to September
DON'T MISS:
The magical gardens of Cothay Manor. It's not just the house that is romantic – there's a river walk to dream about, and a 200-m (650-ft) yew walk links several colourful garden 'rooms' restored to something like their original designs.
AMOUNT OF WALKING:
Moderate
COST:
Reasonable, where there is any.
YOU SHOULD KNOW:
The town of Wellington has nothing to do with the Iron Duke and victor of Waterloo. The monument to him is built on land given to his family – but he chose his title only because his brother had already used the family name 'Wellesley', and 'Wellington' seemed to him a close approximation. (Source: Wellington's letters).

Salvia Path in the magical gardens of Cothay Manor

The West Somerset Railway
BISHOPS LYDEARD TO MINEHEAD

WHERE:
Somerset
BEST TIME TO GO:
Any time of year – and the West Somerset Railway runs all kinds of special trains, like the 'Quantock Belle' Luxury Dining Trains, Christmas Carol Trains, and 'Murder Mystery', 'Cream and Steam', and 'Fish and Chip' Specials, among many others which combine a theme with the fabulous scenery and steam nostalgia.
DON'T MISS:
The Turntable at Minehead, as rare a bit of steam memorabilia as exists. It's impossible to guarantee seeing it in action, but it's a marvellous restoration of a hardcore railway engineering problem: turning an engine through 360 degrees.
AMOUNT OF WALKING:
Little, and the trains are fully accessible.
COST:
Reasonably expensive, especially on the special trains, but there are all kinds of discounts available.
YOU SHOULD KNOW:
You can of course, stop off at any station to explore, and continue your journey on a later train – but make sure you find out in advance if you have to book your onward seat. The WSR is extremely popular.

The steam train leaving Watchet.

Bishops Lydeard is a 13th-century village of sandstone and mellowed brick, with a 14th-century church and a working watermill next to the village smithy and the wheelwright's shop. It's also the southern terminus of the West Somerset Railway to Minehead, a 33-km (20-mi) long former branch line of the Great Western Railway now devoted to running a scheduled service of steam trains to some of Somerset's most popular coastal resorts.

The line was designed by Brunel himself (though he never saw it completed), and it smoothly follows the geometry of the leafy countryside, through the villages in the lee of the rolling Quantock Hills to the cliffs and beaches lining the Bristol Channel. Each station proclaims its individuality – for casual visitors as well as steam railway enthusiasts. Crowcombe is a tranquil, rural halt that featured in the Beatles' film *A Hard Day's Night*. Stogumber is cut into a hillside and surrounded by a garden and woods. Doniford has a cast-iron pagoda shelter as its only furniture on a long, long platform set in fields. Watchet is an historic harbour town, and the track reaches right to the water before turning towards Washford (decked in Southern Region colours to reflect the origins of the Somerset and Dorset Railway Trust who are based there) and the huge strand of Blue Anchor Bay. The views get even more dramatic at Dunster, a medieval village with a vast Norman castle; and if Dunster station looks familiar, it's probably because it was the model for Hornby's 4 mm scale series. The quarter-mile long station at Minehead is a fitting terminus for such a memorably scenic ride. Only steam trains make you feel like that – and if you want, the West Somerset Railway will even teach you to drive one.

Watchet, Cleeve and Dunster

Watchet is a charming resort on the Bristol Channel between the Quantock Hills and Exmoor National Park. It's been a working harbour for 2,000 years, and its Boat Museum provides an unstuffy introduction to the world of 'flatners', and 'turf', 'withy' and 'bay' boats designed for the variety of inshore tasks which gave Watchet a living. Here, and in the nearby Market House Museum, you can see displays of the fossils that abound on the foreshore and cliffs. Spectacular fossil finds by visitors are not at all unusual: Watchet is scoured by tides that are compared to those in Nova Scotia's Bay of Fundy.

The community served by Watchet's harbour trading post in its early heyday included medieval Old Cleeve, a short walk or drive along the coast. The village's 12th-century church of St Andrew is Grade I listed for its ancient beauty – and for the outstanding modern stained glass windows it has acquired since the 1890s. But make sure you also see Cleeve Abbey, nearer Washford than Old Cleeve. It's a 13th-century Cistercian monastery with the most complete set of unaltered cloister buildings in England. The gatehouse, the carved 'angel' roof in the 15th-century refectory, the great dormitory, elaborate floor mosaics and wall paintings show how complex were the aesthetics even of a minor monastic community.

If Cleeve is fascinating, the medieval Exmoor village of Dunster is idyllic. More than 200 of its buildings are listed, including the Old Yarn Market in the High Street, once the centre of Exmoor's wool and cloth industry. It helps that 11th-century Dunster Castle, perched dramatically on a wooded hill above the village, is a wildly romantic concoction of turrets, towers and crenellations looking out to sea across fabulous terraced gardens. It's the perfect place to watch a slowly setting sun.

The view along the High Street to Dunster Castle

WHERE:
Somerset
BEST TIME TO GO:
Any time of year (though Dunster Castle is only open from March to October, the park and gardens don't close during winter).
DON'T MISS:
The 'Attic and Basement' tour at Dunster Castle. If you ring ahead to arrange it, you can see parts of the castle not usually on public view.
AMOUNT OF WALKING:
Moderate – but there's lots of pottering about.
COST:
Reasonable where there's any at all.
YOU SHOULD KNOW:
The subtropical plants on Dunster Castle's sunny terraces are not the only horticultural surprise. Dunster is home to the National Collection of Strawberry Trees.

Porlock

BRENDON, LYNTON AND COMBE MARTIN

One of Exmoor's most dramatic features is its spectacular coastline. You follow it along a switchback of tiny lanes with Exmoor's combination of green valleys, wooded combes, rivers and moorland on one side, and on the other, precipitous cliffs plunging into the sea. Porlock Hill is so steep (1 in 4!) that a new toll road has been built to bypass it; but from the medieval harbour of Porlock Weir, there is an enchanting walk through rare species of whitebeam and rowan woods to Culbone Church, the smallest complete parish church in England. Its tiny perfection dates back to circa 635, and it is still in regular use, despite being inaccessible to cars. In a farmhouse just above the church, Coleridge wrote *Kubla Khan* until interrupted by the legendary 'person from Porlock', who blunted the poet's inspiration.

From Porlock, take the road up onto open moorland and to Brendon. Its thatched cottages sit in a cleft of gnarled oak trees, by a medieval bridge over the River Lyn. The wild beauty of bracken and heather reaches from Brendon to the very cliffs of Lynton, connected to its twin, Lynmouth, by a funicular railway 263-m (862-ft) long up the sheer cliff-face. Powered by water and gravity, the century-old railway was built in Lynton/Lynmouth's heyday of Victorian popularity. People flocked to see what was then a new discovery – the incredible stretch of cliffs between Lynton and Combe Martin.

These are among the highest sea-cliffs in Britain, and include the Great and Little Hangman, the headlands on either side of Combe Martin's harbour and beach. The Great Hangman is at 318 m (1043 ft) the highest point of the SW Coastal Path, with a sheer cliff face of 250 m (820 ft). Of all the pleasures on tap along the coast, it's the natural wonders like these that you will remember best.

WHERE:
Somerset and Devon
BEST TIME TO GO:
Any time of year. The narrow roads are very much busier in July and August – but resorts like Combe Martin are jumping with festivals and other family entertainments.
DON'T MISS:
The Valley of Rocks, Lynton – a stretch of exceptionally high cliffs broken into fantastic shapes and jagged outcrops hanging over the sea.
AMOUNT OF WALKING:
Lots; but if access is a problem, you can at least see all the good bits (except Culbone) from a car.
COST:
Low, if any
YOU SHOULD KNOW:
7-8,000 years ago, what is now Porlock Beach was thickly wooded hunting ground. At low tide, you can still see the stumps of trees long submerged, and preserved in the marshy conditions.

The Lynton and Lynmouth Cliff Railway

Across Exmoor

DOONE VALLEY TO DUNKERY BEACON

If you follow the beautiful cascades of Watersmeet away from Lynmouth, you quickly reach the high moorlands and rolling hills south of Brendon and Oare. This is the landscape romanticised in R.D. Blackmore's novel *Lorna Doone*, and it includes some of Exmoor's loveliest places. Doone Valley itself is a pastoral wonderland of streams and hollows, hidden in the folds of spartan uplands of gorse and heather. It encapsulates the variety of Exmoor's terrain and moods – of severity and harshness tempered by gentle tranquillity. Soak up the panoramas between Simonsbath and Exford. You'll realize that the history written into the peaceful villages is that of endurance, and the collaboration of man and nature on Exmoor is a centuries-old tradition. Most communities predate Domesday mention, and their treasures (Molland's medieval church with intact 18th century box pews; the clapper bridge over the River Barle at Tarr Steps near Hawkridge; Dulverton's winding medieval streets built on a Saxon ground plan) represent man's efforts to make a living out of a landscape better suited to wildlife than cultivation or even mining.

It's a fascinating, illuminating drive; but pause for a stroll at Tarr Steps, and again, to admire the stunning views from Winsford Hill. Where there's water, there are herons, kingfishers, kestrels and many other bird species. In the woods you might see deer. Everywhere you'll see earthworks or diggings that could be prehistoric or evidence of 18th-century mining, but are now a haven for Exmoor ponies or grazing for sheep. Winsford – a delightful village surrounded by a patchwork of fields – looks north to Dunkery Beacon. The highest point on Exmoor, Dunkery Beacon emphasizes its most fundamental characteristic: it's nature's own, brilliant playground, but humans are allowed temporary access to every one of its delights.

WHERE:
Somerset and Devon
BEST TIME TO GO:
April to October
DON'T MISS:
The wildlife – with so much history, and so many different kinds of entertainment available to distract visitors, Exmoor's importance as an unfenced natural resource is paramount.
AMOUNT OF WALKING:
Moderate, but disabled access is difficult.
COST:
None
YOU SHOULD KNOW:
The last (1815-66), paid parish clerk of St Mary's Church, Molland, had an official wooden stave with a wooden ball at one end, and a spray of feathers at the other. If a man fell asleep during a service, the clerk was required to hit him on the head with the ball; sleeping women would be tickled with the feathers.

A windswept Hawthorn tree on Exmoor

Clovelly and Rosemoor Gardens

WHERE:
Devon
BEST TIME TO GO:
Any time of year
DON'T MISS:
Walking the high cliffs to which Clovelly clings – to Gallantry Bower, a balcony set in the sheer cliff face above the sea; or along the SW coastal path as far as the (genuine) former smugglers' cove of Mouth Mill, next to spectacular Blackchurch Rock.
AMOUNT OF WALKING:
Lots. Clovelly is both cobbled and seriously steep, so don't wear high heels. Wheelchair access is limited to the Visitor Centre at the top of the village, and to the harbour area – a Land Rover ferry service will take you up or down via a back road.
COST:
Low – and what you pay at Clovelly goes solely towards maintenance of the village fabric and visitor facilities.
YOU SHOULD KNOW:
Charles Kingsley, the author of *The Water Babies*, spent his childhood in Clovelly.

Clovelly has the dramatic perfection of a fantasy smugglers' or pirates' lair. Its 16th-century fishermen's cottages tumble down a single, cobbled street, set in the thick woods cramming a ravine cut into sheer black cliffs overlooking Bideford Bay. Adorned with fuschias and geraniums that flourish in Clovelly's benign microclimate, the whitewashed houses hug a lane that falls 122 m (400 ft) in just 0.8 km (0.5 mi) to the 13th-century stone quay. The main street (called both 'Up-Along' and 'Down-Along' depending which way you're going) is too steep for wheeled traffic: donkeys and sledges do the carrying. You'll quickly realize that Clovelly, unlike any other picturesque seaside village, is not a holiday home resort. The village is wholly owned by the Clovelly Court Estate, which has maintained it as a living entity full of craftsmen, artists and genuine cottage industries. It makes a world of difference – half Clovelly's enchanting charm is that it's occupied by full-time residents. They're even happy to show you what they do, and where to go. Take your time, and look for the Fisherman's Cottage, Crazy Kate's (the oldest cottage, with the best view over the quay), and the little harbour. You'll be completely smitten by Clovelly's intrinsic beauty and by its genuinely buzzing atmosphere. It may get crowded, but you'll still feel its beating heart.

The compensation for wrenching yourself away from Clovelly's magic is Rosemoor Gardens, near Great Torrington. In 26 hectares (65 acres) overlooking the splendour of the Torridge Valley, the RHS has created formal and cottage gardens, a winding gorge of luxuriant ferns and bamboos, a bog garden leading to a lake, an arboretum, terraces planted for colour, and twin gardens in themed opposition – the 'hot' Square Garden and 'cool' Spiral Garden. Their glorious variety is inspirational!

The long, hard walk up Clovelly's main street

Cornish Coastal Drive 1

BOSCASTLE, TINTAGEL, PORT ISAAC, RUMPS CLIFF CASTLE AND PENCARROW HOUSE

The pretty harbour of Port Isaac

At over 500 km (300 mi) long, the Cornish coast is the longest of any county in England. It is a place of rocky outcrops, smugglers' coves, long sandy beaches and secluded villages. It is home to great feats of derring-do, in legend, literature and in fact.

Starting at Boscastle, a village that appears to be carved out of the very rock on which it stands, this tour takes you through the seat of King Arthur, through the villages of Cornwall's wild Atlantic coast, before heading inland to sample the Georgian elegance of Pencarrow House. Boscastle is a medieval port concealed in a precipitous valley. Strong legs are required to sample its hidden delights on foot, but the rewards are plentiful. The Chapel of St. James and Minster Church stand out amongst many historic buildings.

Heading west along the B3263, you arrive at Tintagel, a town that never let facts stand in the way of a good story. Supposedly the birthplace of King Arthur, its castle actually postdates the legend by several hundred years. That aside, Tintagel is a fun place and has a younger, more vibrant feel than many English seaside towns.

The next stop along the coast is Port Isaac, the archetypal Cornish village. Narrow alleys, lined with charming 18th-century cottages, wind down steep hillsides and fish are still landed in its harbour. It is the perfect spot to stop for lunch. Pressing on, it is now time to visit ancient Cornwall in the form of Rumps Cliff Castle, near Polzeath. Though there are many Iron Age fortifications around Britain, Rumps Cliff's location, sitting perched on a spectacular headland, makes it the most staggering. Following the path of the River Camel inland, the day can be rounded off with a visit to Pencarrow House – a commanding mansion set in 20 hectares (50 acres) of lush woodland.

WHERE:
Cornwall
BEST TIME TO GO:
The weather is best from May to October. Pencarrow House opens its doors to the public from Easter to mid-October.
DON'T MISS:
The view out to sea from the top of Boscastle – well worth the walk.
AMOUNT OF WALKING:
Moderate
COST:
Low (there is a charge to tour the house and garden at Pencarrow).
YOU SHOULD KNOW:
If you are a fan of all things Arthurian, you should sample an 'Excaliburger', a culinary delight served in the eateries of Tintagel.

Padstow

PRIDEAUX PLACE, BEDRUTHAN STEPS AND ST COLUMB MAJOR

WHERE:
Cornwall
BEST TIME TO GO:
Prideaux Place opens its doors from Easter to late September, but will open at other times for groups of 15 or more. Padstow gets frantically busy during July and August.
DON'T MISS:
The fun of walking on the beach around Bedruthan Steps. Check the times of the tides at the tourist information point before setting off, and plan your day around them.
AMOUNT OF WALKING:
Moderate – and you need to be fit to climb the stairs to 'The Steps.'
COST:
Reasonable
YOU SHOULD KNOW:
An 'ancient' legend about a giant called Bedruthan using the steps as a short cut across the bay is in fact an invention of the late 19th century. Perhaps borrowing the story from Ulster's Giant's Causeway, it was used to charm gullible tourists.

*The monolithic
Bedruthan Steps*

This excursion along the north coast of Cornwall takes in new money, old money, giant stepping-stones and an exploding church. Starting at the mouth of the Camel River, there are times when it seems only three activities take place in Padstow – the catching, the cooking and the eating of fish. Dubbed 'Knightsbridge-on-Sea', it has become a magnet for wealthy second-homers, but despite that, Padstow is an extraordinarily pretty place. Most of the activity takes place around the compact harbour, but you don't have to wander far to escape the crowds.

Nearby Prideaux Place is a bit of an oddity. An Elizabethan mansion, it has been home to the Prideaux family for fourteen generations. Each generation added something new, so what you see today is a magnificent old house with a number of Italianate and Gothic alterations in a sometimes-curious mixture of styles. The gardens are gradually being restored to their former glory.

Westwards along the coast, access to Bedruthan Steps is via a precipitous, but well maintained, staircase. Reachable only at low tide, these giant monoliths form one of the most impressive sights of the Cornish coastline. Once down at beach level you can walk around them and marvel at these huge edifices of solidified magma. Before attempting the descent, remember that you will have to come back up the same way.

The final leg of this trip takes you inland to the sturdy town of St Columb Major. Named after St Columba, an early Christian martyr, it has an imposing church at its centre. A church has occupied the site for over a thousand years, but extensive rebuilding was required after 1676, when local youths ignited a store of gunpowder. Much of the inside of the church was damaged or destroyed in the ensuing blaze, though the impressive consecration cross survived.

Dairyland Farm World

THE BLUE REEF AQUARIUM AND PERRANPORTH

A farm, an aquarium, a beach and some churches make up a perfect day out for a tri-generational family. Children can learn about food production and creatures of the deep, while all can enjoy the pleasures of the beach. Hopefully by the time the grandparents express an interest in visiting churches, the kids will be too tired to complain!

The wonderful golden sands of Perranporth Beach

It is a sad reflection on modern living that many children, and even some adults, are so divorced from production that they cannot explain where the food on their plate comes from. Dairyland, located just outside Newquay, sets out to educate and illuminate, providing a wonderfully interactive educational environment, all done with an emphasis on fun. Children can gain a close-up experience of farm life, with pony and mini-tractor rides thrown in for good measure.

Next you can swap udders for gills and head into Newquay to sample the delights of the Blue Reef Aquarium. Billed as the 'Ultimate Underwater Experience', it doesn't disappoint. Sharks, giant crabs and seahorses are all on display, but the highlight has to be the walk-through tunnel that takes you into the heart of an exotic coral reef.

It is now time to use up the last remaining energy of the little 'uns with a frolic on the beach. By heading out of town and travelling 13 km (8 mi) west, you arrive at the extensive golden sands of Perranporth beach. Framed by sand dunes and blessed with great surf, it is the perfect place to stroll, build sandcastles or simply sit and soak up the sun.

This fullest of days out can be rounded off with a tour of Perranporth's three churches. All go by the name of St Piran's and they are filled with enough iconography, interwoven with an often-grizzly history, to keep the whole family interested.

WHERE:
Newquay and environs, Cornwall
BEST TIME TO GO:
All year round (Dairyland and the Blue Reef Aquarium are mostly undercover, so are fun on even the rainiest of days).
DON'T MISS:
The milking parlour at Dairyland – for a fascinating insight into how our daily 'pinta' is produced.
AMOUNT OF WALKING:
Moderate (there is good wheelchair access to both Dairyland and the Aquarium).
COST:
Reasonable (family tickets are available for both attractions).
YOU SHOULD KNOW:
The oldest St Piran's Church, dating from the 6th century, was lost under shifting dunes until the 19th century. When it was excavated, so local legend goes, three headless skeletons were uncovered with it.

Gwennap Pit – the perfect amphitheatre

Trerice House and Truro

GWENNAP PIT

WHERE:
Cornwall
BEST TIME TO GO:
Trerice House is open from March to early November. It is best to phone ahead though as the opening hours are idiosyncratic.
DON'T MISS:
Taking a photograph of the front of Trerice House. It has a rare perfect symmetry.
AMOUNT OF WALKING:
Moderate
COST:
Low (group and family tickets are available at Trerice House).
YOU SHOULD KNOW:
Wesley claimed to have preached to over 30,000 people at Gwennap Pit in one sitting. This may have been something of an exaggeration as the pit's capacity has been estimated at 5,000.

Even though it is only 6 km (4 mi) from Newquay, such is the labyrinthine nature of the approach to Trerice House that you might begin to doubt its existence. Don't worry; you'll get there eventually and the journey is well worth it. This most hidden of 'hidden gems' was built in 1573 and the wonderfully compact structure stands as one of the finest and best-preserved Elizabethan manor houses in Britain. Surrounded by classically designed orchards, the house itself is really impressive. Behind the Dutch-style gabled frontage lie intricate plaster ceilings, elaborate fireplaces and an assortment of high quality English furniture.

The journey down to Truro takes you through pleasant rolling countryside to Britain's most southerly city. The huge Cathedral dominates the skyline, most of the cobbled streets are lined with quaint pastel-coloured buildings and Truro's pedestrianized centre is alive with buskers and street artists. If shopping isn't your thing, you can visit the Royal Cornwall Museum, a place dedicated to all things Cornish.

Travelling westwards you come to the strangely beautiful Gwennap Pit, an eerily symmetrical amphitheatre, created by slippage caused by copper mining. Its main claim to fame is that it was used by John Wesley to preach his brand of Methodism to a vast audience. Sadly the pit is little used today, but it would provide the perfect stage for an impromptu performance of *A Midsummer Night's Dream*.

St Ives

GEEVOR TIN MINE, PENDEEN, ST JUST, SENNEN COVE, PORTHCURNO, MOUSEHOLE AND NEWLYN

It is the arts that occupy us on the first leg of this whistle-stop tour of the western extremity of mainland Britain. The renowned sculptor Barbara Hepworth drew her inspiration from what she dubbed 'this remarkable pagan landscape'. While viewing all the attractions that the Tate St Ives has on offer, ample time should be given to an exploration of the museum and garden that houses many of Hepworth's works.

Industrial heritage can be found farther round the coast in the form of the Geevor Tin Mine near Pendeen. Now disused, this phenomenal mine – which in its prime stretched far out under the sea – has been turned into a wonderfully educational museum. Before leaving the area, take the short drive out to the magnificent white lighthouse at Pendeen Watch, for great views out over the Atlantic.

Now it is time to head off along the B3306 coastal road to St Just – a pleasant little town with a history that closely matches that of the whole of Cornwall. Since ancient times it has been a centre for mining, fishing and farming, and the surrounding countryside is full of relics that bear testament to St Just's longstanding importance as a centre for trade. Heading farther along the coast, you arrive at Sennen Cove. Although only a short distance from Land's End, it is less crowded and has long white sandy beaches. The next port of call is Porthcurno, a small village which has on its outskirts the petite St Levan Church and churchyard, replete with stone crosses and standing stones.

The penultimate leg of this tour takes you to Mousehole, a quintessentially Cornish hamlet, built from granite and crammed around a tiny harbour. Finally you can round off the day with a visit to Newlyn – home to many artists and galleries.

WHERE:
Cornwall
BEST TIME TO GO:
All year round – although busiest in June and July.
DON'T MISS:
The lighthouse at Pendeen Watch – a perfect place to view the rolling white horses of the Atlantic waves.
AMOUNT OF WALKING:
Little (Tate St Ives has excellent access. Geevor Tin Mine has full wheelchair access to the museum, but only partial access to the rest of the site).
COST:
Reasonable
YOU SHOULD KNOW:
The true perils of the sea were starkly revealed in 1981 when the lifeboat at Mousehole was called out in hurricane-force winds. All eight members of the *Solomon Browne* were lost to the sea.

Porthcurno Beach

The Isles of Scilly

There are three ways to reach the Isles of Scilly. You can take the ferry from Penzance or the Skybus air service from Newquay. If you really want to push the boat out (excuse the mixing of metaphors) there is also a scheduled helicopter service from Penzance. Whichever way you make the crossing, you will be glad you did. It is as if someone had taken a few square miles of the most pleasant British countryside, preserved them in amber and strewn them 45 km (28 mi) out to sea.

All three modes of transport land in or near the islands' capital, Hugh Town on St Mary's, the only place that closely resembles busy on this peaceful archipelago. Most of the activity centres on the harbour, and it is from here that you can get connecting ferry services to the other islands, but not before exploring St Mary's' main attractions. Most interesting amongst these are Star Castle, a 16th-century fortification, and Halangy Down, an Iron Age settlement.

Returning to the harbour it is time to go island hopping. Take any ferry to any island and you can't go far wrong, such is the charm of these tranquil islands. However, no visit to the Isles of Scilly would be complete without a visit to Tresco and to one of the uninhabited islands. The islands are blessed with warm summers and frost-free winters and Tresco utilises its climatic advantage to the full. The island has several wonderful gardens, the most impressive being Abbey Gardens, a subtropical paradise built around the ruins of a Benedictine priory.

Just across the water lies Samson, the largest of the uninhabited islands. Settled until the 1850's, this island is now given over to wildlife. Its gorse-covered hills are populated by hordes of black rabbits, while its shores are home to vast colonies of seabirds.

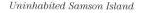

Uninhabited Samson Island

Penzance

MARAZION, ST MICHAEL'S MOUNT, MULLION COVE AND KYNANCE COVE

Tucked in at the sheltered northwest corner of Mount's Bay, Penzance marks the western terminus for the Great Western Railway and is a great place to start a tour of this beautiful corner of England. It is a town where all things seem to radiate from the magnificent silver-domed Market House and, if you ever lose your way, this shiny orb will lead you back to the centre. If you have time to visit only one street in town you should make it Chapel Street. Its elegant buildings now house mainly art galleries, but there are good cafés and bakeries where you can buy goodies for the journey.

Following the coast road eastbound for 8 km (5 mi), you arrive at Marazion, one of Cornwall's oldest towns. The town itself is charming enough, but the main reason most people visit lies just out to sea. Reachable by foot at low tide and by ferry at other times, the monument to St Michael dates back to the 5th century, when the Archangel Michael 'appeared' to local fishermen. Usurped by Celts, monks and kings over the centuries, St Michael's Mount is positively brimming with history. Even if all that is not your bag, the walk along the causeway, to and from the mount, is reason enough to make the trip.

Following the road out towards the Lizard Peninsula, at the other end of the bay you reach the protected little harbour of Mullion Cove. The village overflows with art galleries and eateries, but do make time to see the ornate oak carvings at the 15th-century church of St Mellanus. Mullion can get busy, so for a more off-the-beaten-track cove, head further along the Lizard to Kynance where little but white sands and turquoise water await you.

WHERE:
Cornwall
BEST TIME TO GO:
All year round, though November to February can be wet and windy. The castle and grounds at St Michael's are usually open from just before Easter to late October.
DON'T MISS:
Even though it is accessible by ferry at high tide, walking over to the Mount is fun, so check the tides and try to do it at least one way.
AMOUNT OF WALKING:
Moderate
COST:
Reasonable. There is a charge to enter the castle and grounds at St Michael's Mount. National Trust members get in free.
YOU SHOULD KNOW:
The National Trust owns, manages and maintains a large number of properties in Cornwall. It offers great concessions to members and their families, so even if your stay is short it might be worth considering joining. Aside from the money you save, it also means that you don't have to queue to pay.

The subtropical Trebah Garden is well worth a visit.

The National Maritime Museum

FALMOUTH AND THE VILLAGES OF DURGAN AND HELFORD

It is the water and all things nautical that occupy us in this exploration of the shores of the fabulously wide Falmouth Bay and its tributaries. In geological terms, Falmouth Harbour together with Carrick Roads, are rias –valleys formed by great ephemeral rivers that flowed at the end of the last ice age. When all the ice had melted, the sea levels rose and flooded the deep valleys. In Falmouth's case this led to the formation of the third deepest natural harbour in the world.

Overlooking Pendennis Marina, the National Maritime Museum sits well with its surroundings. Its central tower looks like a lighthouse and the long oak-panelled walls resemble those of a boatyard. This award-winning building houses galleries, boatbuilding workshops and interactive displays, as well as over a hundred boats of all shapes and sizes.

Travelling further along the bay we come to the tiny former fishing village of Durgan. Now owned and maintained by the National Trust, it is like a hamlet frozen in time. The beautiful surrounding countryside is the perfect place to take a gentle stroll, and the two subtropical gardens at nearby Glendurgan and Trebah are well worth a visit. From here it is a short walk to Helford Passage, where a passenger ferry takes you across the river to the whitewashed stone cottages of Helford village. Finally it is back to the water, but this time under you own steam. By hiring a rowing boat from the village harbour it is possible to explore at your leisure the many creeks that form offshoots of the Helford River – the best known is Fisherman's Creek, made famous by the author Daphne du Maurier.

WHERE:
Cornwall
BEST TIME TO GO:
The museum is open all year round, as are the gardens. The ferry across the Helford River operates from Easter to late September, subject to tides and weather conditions.
DON'T MISS:
The view across Falmouth Bay from the lookout at the National Maritime Museum.
AMOUNT OF WALKING:
Moderate. You can, if you want, do the whole trip on foot and by boat.
COST:
Reasonable
YOU SHOULD KNOW:
Durgan was the home of Captain George Vancouver, who charted the west coast of Canada, giving his name to two cities, one in the USA, the other in Canada, as well as to the large island that lies off the coast of British Columbia.

Cornish Coastal Drive 2

MEVAGISSEY, VERYAN, THE ROSELAND PENINSULA AND TRELISSICK GARDEN

Mevagissey is the quintessential Cornish south coast fishing village. Scores of small boats line the snug harbour and its narrow lanes are lined with cafés, galleries and artists' workshops. The only proper tourist attraction in the village is a small museum, but that is the appeal of this charming 'olde worlde' place. Leaving Mevagissey in either direction you can join the Cornish Coastal Footpath, or for those in search of a good beach, nearby Polstreath offers a chance to have a stroll or take a dip. Accessed by 200 steep steps, it is a haven of calm.

Much of the charm of this remote corner of England lies in its meandering cambered roads. The drive from Mevagissey to Veryan takes you over gently rolling hills into the heart of rural Cornwall. Once there you quickly realize that you are in a curious gem of a village. Built in the early 19th century by the wonderfully named Reverend Jeremiah Trist, all the houses in Veryan's centre are white and circular. The thinking behind this design was that the devil would have nowhere to hide.

It is now time to head for the A3078 and out onto the scenic Roseland Peninsula. A visit to either of the delightful villages of St Anthony or St Just is highly recommended, but you can't go wrong pulling up anywhere on this unspoilt cape. It has lovely beaches framed by cliffs, and enchanting hamlets, all set in picture postcard perfect countryside.

The final leg of the journey takes you alongside Carrick Roads, an arm of the Fal Estuary and over to Trelissick Garden. In an area famed for its gardens, Trelissick stands out. It is home to the National Collection of Photinias and Azaras, as well as housing a gallery dedicated to local artists. Beyond the formal gardens there is an extensive park offering magnificent views over Falmouth Bay.

WHERE:
Cornwall
BEST TIME TO GO:
The weather is best from March to October.
DON'T MISS:
The grounds around Trelissick Garden. Even if you have no interest in horticulture, these delightful grounds are a wonderful place to stretch your legs after a long day's driving.
AMOUNT OF WALKING:
Little – unless you decide to walk along the coastal path or through the park at Trelissick.
COST:
Reasonable. There is a charge to enter Trelissick Garden – with a sizeable discount for National Trust members.
YOU SHOULD KNOW:
Cornwall's roads can get very busy during the Easter and Summer school holidays. The roads are however relatively quiet around lunchtime, so you can cover more miles if you can be flexible in your eating patterns.

Traditional round houses at Veryan

The Eden Project and Luxulyan

WHERE:
Cornwall
BEST TIME TO GO:
All year round. The walk through the Luxulyan Valley is best in March or April when the bluebells and wild garlic are out.
DON'T MISS:
The aromatic garden at the Eden Project. Prepare for your olfactory senses to be bombarded.
AMOUNT OF WALKING:
Moderate. The Eden Project has excellent access and has an abundance of free wheelchairs for those who may find the going a bit tough.
COST:
Reasonable
YOU SHOULD KNOW:
Although the Eden Project has ample parking spaces, Cornwall's roads are ill equipped to handle the huge numbers who descend on the attraction in high season (Easter to September). Therefore you should allow plenty of time to enter and leave the area.

Rainforest Biome Conservatory at the Eden Project

The china clay industry has been a mixed blessing for Cornwall. In its heyday it was a huge source of revenue and employment for the region, but, since its decline due to fierce foreign competition, it has left much of the landscape scarred and infertile. However, the problem of what to do with this wasteland provided the horticultural entrepreneur, Tim Smit, with his greatest challenge. The resulting Eden Project has replaced the dying industry as the economic mainstay of the eastern corner of Cornwall, while quickly becoming one of the UK's most visited attractions.

Armed with a mandate to change disused quarries into a fertile 'Eden', the designers overcame a rocky start – the soil, composed of china clay waste, was prone to leeching – to produce a marvel of modern architecture and a true triumph of landscape gardening on the grandest of scales. At its centre lie two giant biomes, home to just about every plant on the planet, while the outside areas consist of carefully constructed tiered gardens.

It is a place to amble through at a gentle pace and to learn about and marvel at the diverse flora of planet Earth. Although visitor numbers have far outstripped expectations, the clever design of this 14-hectare (35-acre) site means that it rarely seems crowded and there are plenty of places to rest and find a bite to eat.

If the Eden Project is nature on an extensive scale, a walk through the nearby Luxulyan Woods offers you a chance to experience the best of rural Cornwall without the clamour. The Luxulyan Valley is a spectacular, thickly wooded, steep-sided ravine through which the River Par flows at its fastest. From March to June the smell of wild flowers fills the air, while the ozone of the rushing stream will blow away any remaining urban cobwebs.

China Clay Country Park

LOST GARDENS OF HELIGAN

If you were asked to name the last time you touched china clay, you could be forgiven for trying to remember when you last sipped tea from a bone china cup. It may come as a surprise to you that you are probably touching it now. Such is the flexibility of this endlessly malleable product that it is used in the production of rubber, textiles and paper, to name but a few of its literally hundreds of applications. You can learn this and much more at the wonderfully informative China Clay Country Park, located fittingly in the grounds of two former working china clay pits, just outside St Austell. The attraction provides a stimulating insight into china clay – how it was excavated, what it was used for and its place in the history of the local community.

If the morning is to be filled with industrial heritage, then the afternoon can be given over to the magic of nature. Heligan is the sleeping beauty of gardens. Tended by the Tremayne family for over four hundred years, it fell into disrepair when many of the staff were killed in the Great War. When it was rediscovered by Tim Smit, who later conceived the Eden Project, it was little more than a forest of ivy and bramble. The excavation and recovery of this working garden has been remarkable, and Heligan now has a function that far outstrips its original purpose. Among the delights on show are an Italianate garden inspired by the discoveries at Pompeii, a Sundial garden with innovative herbaceous borders and extensive kitchen gardens. Heligan is a place to come back to time and time again. It is an ever-changing environment where the displays and exhibitions are constantly being updated.

Visitors taking a stroll through the Lost Gardens.

WHERE:
Cornwall
BEST TIME TO GO:
China Clay Country Park is fully open from February to the end of September. Heligan is open every day except Christmas Eve and Christmas Day.
DON'T MISS:
The boardwalk through the vibrant colours of 'The Jungle' at Heligan.
AMOUNT OF WALKING:
Moderate. China Clay Country Park is set on a hillside so those with difficulty walking may find their enjoyment restricted. Heligan has reasonable access and will provide a detailed guide of degrees of difficulty presented by various slopes, etc.
COST:
Reasonable. Concessions and group tickets are available for both attractions and children under 5 get in free.
YOU SHOULD KNOW:
After four years of hard work, the team at Heligan have finally managed to replicate one of the most impressive (and wacky) feats of their Victorian predecessors – the production of a home-grown pineapple ripe for eating on Christmas Day.

Lanhydrock House and Garden

BODMIN MOOR AND ALTARNUN

One of the most captivating late 19th-century mansions in England, Lanhydrock is a place of exceptional beauty. Nestled amongst 180 hectares (445 acres) of superb woodland, it is surrounded by an exquisite formal garden. Fifty of its rooms are open to the public and many are jam-packed with the accoutrements of high Victorian living. Taken as a whole, they offer a wonderful insight into the upstairs-downstairs life of yesteryear and the contrast between the spartan simplicity of the maids' quarters and the ornate opulence of the Long Gallery could not be greater. Guided tours are available, but even without a guide, there is enough to occupy the inquisitive tourist for a few hours. Outside you will find one of the finest cottage gardens in Britain. At various times of the year the place is awash with the colours and smells of roses, peonies, rhododendrons, magnolias and poppies. The adjoining woodland has sufficient clearings to allow for the spreading of a blanket and the opening of a picnic hamper, if the weather is kind.

On leaving Lanhydrock, take the A38 and then the A30 Bodmin bypass, which brings you on to Bodmin Moor. Though the moor is smaller than Exmoor and Dartmoor, you are quickly transported into a wonderful wilderness landscape. There are ample pull-over places and a walk around the shores of Colliford Reservoir has much to commend it. Heading further eastwards along the A30 you arrive at Fivelanes, where a minor road takes you to the ghostly apparition of Altarnun Church, known locally as the 'Cathedral in the Moor'. Dedicated to the 6th-century St Nonna, mother of St David, this fascinating medieval building is filled with Celtic and early Christian iconography. The small pretty village of Altarnun is also worth strolling around, its granite cottages, rectory and inn have hardly changed since Victorian times.

Exquisite Lanhydrock House – fifty rooms are open to the public.

WHERE:
Cornwall
BEST TIME TO GO:
Lanhydrock House is open from March to the end of October. The garden is open all year round.
DON'T MISS:
The magnificently worked plaster ceiling portraying biblical scenes in the Long Gallery at Lanhydrock.
AMOUNT OF WALKING:
Moderate
COST:
Reasonable. A discount is given to those who arrive by bicycle or on foot at Lanhydrock.
YOU SHOULD KNOW:
The original house at Lanhydrock dates from 1630; however a fire in 1881 completely destroyed the old house, leaving only the entrance porch and the gatehouse standing.

St Neot and Cardinham Woods

The southern edge of Bodmin Moor is much more thickly wooded and green than other areas, and its prettiest village, St Neot, lies in a tree-filled river valley. The 15th-century granite church is St Neot's pride and international glory. Miraculously, it has retained much of its early 16th-century stained glass, notably the Creation Window in its south aisle; and ever since, patrons have been adding glass narratives of comparable quality. Architecturally, too, the church is magnificent. Just outside the door, the intricacy of the Celtic carvings on a 10th-century cross is typical of local masons' mastery in working granite. St Neot is also famous for the Carnglaze Slate Caverns. The former workings, in three cathedral-size caverns, now form a dazzlingly colourful underworld of rock minerals reflected in a subterranean lake; and one, a former Royal Navy rum store, is also used as a concert venue acclaimed for its slate-walled acoustics. In the bluebell woods on the hills above the caves, improbable 'Enchanted Dells' full of iridescent 'Wendy' statues make highly entertaining walks.

Between St Neot and Liskeard, there's a truly idyllic woodland marvel at Golitha Falls. On the edge of the Moor, the ancient oak and ash forest is a nature reserve, with the River Fowey tumbling in a series of cascades through its rocky heart. For pure romance, it's the loveliest place in Cornwall. For adventure in the big outdoors, it has major local challengers. Colliford Lake is a vast adventure playground, on the water, in the woods and on moorland, with plenty of supervision for children and activities like animal petting. Closer to Bodmin town, Cardinham Woods are spread over hundreds of acres, and include a complex of steep ravines and valleys. The gentler, mixed woodland is full of ability trails, play areas, and charming facilities like the café in a 17th-century woodsman's cottage.

WHERE:
Cornwall
BEST TIME TO GO:
March to October
DON'T MISS:
'Shanhara and her Friends' – in the Enchanted Dell at Carnglaze. You emerge from a terrace garden with water features onto a wooded hillside set with limited edition bronze faerie figures, giant red and white mushrooms, and a dragon. The proportionately life-sized nymphs have 'pearlized', shimmering wings, and are posed to show nature's allure at its most feminine and innocent.
AMOUNT OF WALKING:
Lots – but access is much better than you usually expect in adventure and woodland parks.
COST:
Low to reasonable – depending on what activities you sign up for at Carnglaze or Colliford.
YOU SHOULD KNOW:
For years there have been stories about 'The Beast of Bodmin Moor' – a creature consistently described as being about 3 ft long and 2 ft high. True or false, there have been several 'big cat' sightings around Colliford Lake, all of them associated with 'the beast'.

The romantic Golitha Falls

St Cleer and Launceston

WHERE:
Cornwall
BEST TIME TO GO:
Any time of year
DON'T MISS:
The Launceston Steam Railway – a narrow-gauge track between Launceston and the little village of Newmills, using late 19th century steam locomotives. Short but very sweet.
AMOUNT OF WALKING:
Lots, much of it on irregular grass or country surfaces.
COST:
Low, if any
YOU SHOULD KNOW:
Long before the chapel was built over it, the holy well at St Cleer was believed to have magical healing properties – it was used as a 'bowsening' (total immersion) pool, into which the insane were dipped in hope of being cured.

The granite spire of St Cleer's ancient church is a landmark for miles across the eastern edge of Bodmin Moor. Originally Norman, its 13th- and 15th-century additions make it appear almost 'modern' – but from the pre-medieval holy well enclosed in a 15th-century arched chapel, to the eleven female saints enshrined in Victorian stained glass immortality, the church is an oblique record of each wave of prosperity to leave its mark on St Cleer, like others in and around the village. To the north is Trethevy Quoit, a primitive, 2,000 year-old granite burial chamber, of six uprights and a single covering slab. Nearby, an intricately carved granite block is dedicated in Latin to King Doniert (Durngarth) of Cornwall, who drowned in 875. Around Caradon Hill, on the moor behind, are the ruins and remnants of the copper mining boom of 1836-90 – like the many other circles, stones and monuments in the vicinity, already acquiring the patina of timeless serenity that characterizes St Cleer.

Launceston, 18 km (11 mi) away, wears its considerable history more boldly. A medieval walled city and Royal Mint, it was Cornwall's capital for centuries. Its church tower was commissioned by the Black Prince in the 14th century; its stately Priory razed in the Dissolution of the 16th; and at the junction of the Blind Hole and Southgate Street, rows of 18th-century cottages vie with elements of 600 years of continuous change, including the old portcullis gate. Only the Keep is left of the castle, but from it you can see both Bodmin and Dartmoor – lovely countryside for a short drive to Jamaica Inn, a 1750 coaching inn on the moor itself, or to the Tamar Otter and Wildlife Centre. But if the weather fails, Launceston comes up trumps with the Trethorne leisure centre.

Launceston Castle

Coastal Villages

ST GERMANS TO LOSTWITHIEL

On high ground where the River Lynher meets the Tamar Estuary, the village of St Germans placidly contemplates its significant history – as a 9th- to 11th-century bishopric, and a successful Victorian port. It gained a massive Norman church from one era, and a lovely quayside from the other. Bypassed by traffic, St Germans makes an inspirational beginning to a drive along the Cornish coast. Cut across the neck of the Rame Peninsula to East and West Looe, twins divided by a river and united by a 19th-century bridge of seven arches. In their maze of narrow alleyways, crowded with tiny shops, you'll find the medieval guildhall, the South East Cornwall Discovery Centre, and children's crab-catching tackle (to take to the rock pools on the town beach, a paradise for sandcastles). It's a switchback along 5 km (3 mi) of narrow lanes to Polperro, one of Cornwall's most picturesque fishing villages. Whitewashed cottages are webbed together on a steep cliff above a tiny harbour cove. Once a smugglers' haven, Polperro is now a famous magnet for artists, whose work you can see and possibly, buy.

To reach Fowey without a long detour, enjoy the single-track roads that open to glorious panoramas including majestic Pencarrow Head. At Bodinnick, a huddle of elegant, balconied Victorian houses on the tree-fringed bank of the Fowey River conceals both Daphne du Maurier's house, and the quay of the most charming car-ferry on earth. Fowey, four minutes away, is an important port and lively sailing resort, with every kind of activity; but the 10 km (6 mi) approach to Lostwithiel along the meadows of the Fowey Estuary is one of Cornwall's joys. The verdant countryside is delicious, and medieval Lostwithiel emerges from the river mists – former port, Cornish capital and Stannary town. And, somehow, deeply fulfilling.

The picturesque fishing village of Polperro

WHERE:
Cornwall
BEST TIME TO GO:
Any time of year. Some enthusiasts advise visiting from October to March, because the views are better when there are no leaves on the trees. Others prefer the dimpled smile of nature's summer.
DON'T MISS:
The waterside village of Golant, a perfect gem with 13th-century church, pub and all essentials, overlooking the estuary between Fowey and Lostwithiel in an Area of Outstanding Natural Beauty. Even in winter you'll see cormorants, egrets, herons, kingfishers and swans.
AMOUNT OF WALKING:
Low to moderate
COST:
None
YOU SHOULD KNOW:
Polperro's cottages are largely 16th century, but it has been a working fishing village since the 13th. In the 18th and 19th centuries it was so notorious for smuggling, that it became the site of the first 'Water Preventative Guard Station'.

Plymouth Dockyards

RAME PENINSULA

Plymouth tells a salty story. Possessed of a fabulous natural harbour, it has witnessed some of the greatest moments in naval and marine history. The best way to enjoy them is by boat from the Mayflower Steps near the Barbican: the very steps from which the Pilgrim Fathers embarked for America in 1620, and Captain Cook took ship for his circumnavigation. Cruising Plymouth Sound you'll come to Plymouth Hoe, where Francis Drake played his imperturbable game of bowls in defiance of the Armada; see the Royal Citadel of Charles II, with its massive cannon; and look into the great Royal Navy Dockyard of Devonport, to admire the sleek grey menace of warships at berth. Devonport has refitted everything from nuclear submarines to the Royal Yacht Britannia. Now you can also see huge, luxury yachts on its slipways.

Across the busy estuary, you drive into open country on the heights of Torpoint. There's a brilliant vista in every direction, of trees framing sea and boats and the green coastline. You can't tire of it, but you can be distracted by the early 18th-century genius of Antony House, magnificently sited in thick woods with long views over the water, and enchanting grounds including a knot garden. Then potter about the steep, narrow lanes, with to-die-for views across both sides of Plymouth Sound – either to the spectacular architectural and domestic treasures of Mount Edgcumbe House, spread round the headland next to lovely old Cremyll village; or to the end of the peninsula, where the unspoiled 16th- and 17th-century fishing villages of Kingsand and Cawsand cluster in a maze of interesting streets around a deep-water harbour. From Cawsand, the short drive up to Rame Head offers a definitive panorama, and coming back along the wide sweep of Whitsand Bay, surf breaking below the cliffs, completes a beautiful day.

WHERE:
Devon and Cornwall
BEST TIME TO GO:
April to September
DON'T MISS:
The 'Zig-Zag', intricate paths carved in the cliffs of Mount Edgcumbe's Country Park, and famously known as 'The Horrors' in the 18th and 19th centuries. They are just one of dozens of follies, monuments, grottoes and amusements built to the whims of generations of the Mount Edgcumbe family in their Grade I listed Cornish Gardens.
AMOUNT OF WALKING:
Little to moderate
COST:
Low
YOU SHOULD KNOW:
The Plymouth Dome, on Plymouth Hoe, is a high-tech visitor centre with startlingly vivid interactive displays covering much of Plymouth's illustrious history under one roof. Besides Drake, the Pilgrims and Cook, there's an inspirational account of Plymouth's annihilation in the 1941 Blitz, and its subsequent regeneration – and from the Observation Deck, you can monitor harbour traffic on radar and computers.

Sitting on the Hoe, watching the warships come home.

North Oxfordshire Tour

WHERE:
Oxfordshire
BEST TIME TO GO:
Any time
DON'T MISS:
Serious shoppers should go on from
Rousham House to Bicester Village –
this massive factory-shop complex
offers top-designer-label bargains
galore.
AMOUNT OF WALKING:
Lots
COST:
Low
YOU SHOULD KNOW:
In St Kenelm's Church at Enstone
there is a stained glass window by
Arts and Crafts guru William Morris.

The medieval town of Chipping Norton is often described as 'the Gateway to the Cotswolds', but heading in the opposite direction for the North Oxfordshire countryside with its picturesque villages and classic pastoral landscapes can also be rewarding.

Chipping Norton is a great starting point. This lively market town has many interesting buildings, testifying to the wealth that shaped the place after wool production boomed in the Middle Ages – as does the town's magnificent wool church. Other evidence may be found in splendid almshouses and the large number of medieval structures that survive. Even after the wool trade declined, agriculture brought prosperity (and more fine buildings) in Georgian times.

After exploring Chipping Norton, head north through Over Norton to Little Rollright, where the Rollright Stones are located. This large megalithic monument consists of the King's Men (a stone circle), the King Stone (a single monolith) and the Whispering Knights (a Neolithic burial chamber).

Go on towards Great Rollright, but turn right at the main road. Continue until it meets the A44 then drive down to Enstone (officially Neat Enstone). Turn left for Church Enstone and pause to see the parish church and fine tithe barn dated 1382. You'll soon reach the chocolate-box village of Great Tew, often described as one of the prettiest in the land – surely everyone's idea of a perfect English village.

Continue via Ledwell to Duns Tew and Steeple Aston, where the gardens of Rousham Park House provide a satisfying way to complete the day. Bring a picnic, because the place is delightfully uncommercial (no tearoom or shop). The extensive gardens and landscaped parkland were created by William Kent in the 18th century and are virtually unaltered since. Rousham Park House also bears his stamp, but is only open to groups by prior arrangement.

The Bliss Valley Tweed Mill at Chipping Norton has been transformed into apartments.

Blenheim Palace and Woodstock

Winning the War of Spanish Succession was the easy part for John Churchill, first Duke of Marlborough. Construction of the monumental country house that was to have been his reward – Blenheim Palace – turned out to be a twenty-year saga of political infighting and intrigue, during which the Duke was exiled and died before his house was finished, his influential Duchess fell from power, the reputation of architect Sir John Vanbrugh was destroyed and the Palace's English Baroque style quickly went out of fashion.

Be that as it may, this magnificent mansion is the only country house in England to hold the title 'Palace'. Surrounded by formal gardens and parkland designed by Capability Brown, a day out at Blenheim is an unforgettable experience.

It starts with lavishly decorated and furnished Palace State Rooms, including the spectacular Great Hall, Saloon and extraordinary Long Library. It's possible to wander at leisure or take the guided tour, and there are also tours of the Private Apartments. Within the house there is an exhibition dedicated to Sir Winston Churchill near the room where he was born and the innovative 'Blenheim Palace: the Untold Story' audio-visual presentation further enhances appreciation of this extraordinary place.

Outside may be found the Churchills' Destiny Exhibition in the stables, featuring the family's two war leaders, plus a cinema showing a film of the park's creation by Lancelot 'Capability' Brown in the 1760s. There are spectacular Formal Gardens, modern Pleasure Gardens (miniature train, maze, butterfly house and adventure playground) plus a beautiful lake and extensive parkland in which to wander at will.

Oh, and be sure to spend an hour exploring Woodstock, just outside the park's back gate. This lively small town with its variety of interesting shops has many splendid buildings, including one where Geoffrey Chaucer once told tales.

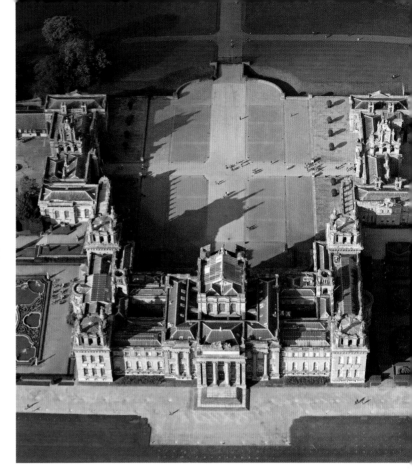

Blenheim is the only country house in England to be called a 'Palace'.

WHERE:
Oxfordshire
BEST TIME TO GO:
April to October
DON'T MISS:
The Fletcher's House in Woodstock that contains The Oxfordshire Museum featuring local history, art, archaeology, landscape and wildlife.
AMOUNT OF WALKING:
Lots
COST:
Expensive
YOU SHOULD KNOW:
The grave of Sir Winston Churchill (also those of his wife and parents) is in the graveyard at Bladon Church, within sight of Blenheim.

The Oxford skyline

Oxford

Those who have never visited Oxford may expect to find the ancient university town with dreaming spires pictured in guidebooks, but Oxford is a bustling industrial city with a serious traffic problem. Happily, that doesn't stop the historic centre retaining much original charm and some of England's finest medieval buildings.

They (with others constructed in subsequent centuries) are home to the English-speaking world's oldest university – though Oxford was a prestigious town with important religious houses and a charter from Henry II, before the first college was founded in 1249. Since then, Parliaments have been held, martyrs burned, Charles I was based here during the English Civil War and his son came during London's Great Plague in the 1660s.

The imprint of such events may be found on Oxford's historic fabric – go by train or use Park and Ride from the edge of town to enjoy exploring on foot. Look out for Christ Church Cathedral (both Cathedral and college chapel), the Radcliffe Camera (a circular Palladian library building); Wren's Sheldonian Theatre; University Church of St Mary the Virgin (13th century); Magdalen College; Tom Tower; The Bridge of Sighs; the Covered Market (opened in 1774).

Of course there's a whole lot more to discover, including all those locations for Inspector Morse's investigations, but that's the joy of the place – get a wonderful view of everything from Carfax Tower in the centre of town, all that remains of 13th-century St Martin's Church.

One unmissable highlight of an Oxford visit is the Ashmolean Museum with its eclectic collections, ranging from antiquities of Ancient Greece and Egypt to Picasso paintings. Look out for curiosities like the lantern carried by gunpowder plotter Guy Fawkes, Oliver Cromwell's death mask and Lawrence of Arabia's ceremonial Arab outfit. Surely such cultural delights are worth half a day!

Waddesdon Manor and Ascott House

England's most perfect French-style country house is Waddesdon Manor, near Aylesbury, built in the 19th century for banker Baron Ferdinand de Rothschild – a hilltop mansion that deliberately echoes those magnificent châteaux of the Loire Valley. For all that, it was constructed using the most modern methods of the day, like a steel frame, and incorporated then-luxurious features like hot-and-cold running water, central heating and electricity.

Although Waddesdon Manor is a National Trust property, it is still administered by a Rothschild Family Trust that has contributed to a major restoration, developed new attractions and further enhanced the collections within. These – beginning with Baron Ferdinand's extensive collections of Renaissance works of art, tapestries, ornate panelling, ceramics, furniture and paintings – have been enhanced by subsequent generations, and the interior is a treasure house of beautiful objects.

Outside, the landscaped grounds contain some wonderful pavilions, great statuary (including the beautiful Prosperino Fountain that once graced the Palace of the Dukes of Parma in Northern Italy) and an aviary. There are also modern features like a Children's Corner and Explorer Trails. Note that the house is closed on Mondays and Tuesdays.

If you can tear yourself away from Waddesdon with time to spare, a complete visual contrast may be found by visiting Ascott House at Wing, near Leighton Buzzard – although it, too, is a Rothschild property. Leopold de Rothschild extended this Jacobean house in the 19th century, though very much in a traditional style that reflected the half-timbered construction of the original. Ascott also contains fabulous collections – including some exceptional furniture and Chinese ceramics – and the grounds are magnificent. Opening times are complicated – every day except Monday (April), Tuesday to Thursday (May, June, July), daily except Monday (August). Make sure you arrive on an open day – Ascott is well worth it.

WHERE:
Buckinghamshire
BEST TIME TO GO:
April to August
DON'T MISS:
A perfect example of the Victorian country house cricket ground at Ascott – with any luck, there might be a match in progress, as it is still used on a regular basis.
AMOUNT OF WALKING:
Moderate
COST:
Reasonable
YOU SHOULD KNOW:
Queen Victoria visited Waddesdon Manor in 1890 and was most impressed not by the great house, nor by the fabulous gardens...but by the invention she had never seen before – electric light.

The Terrace at Waddesdon Manor

Around South Buckinghamshire

BURNHAM BEECHES, BEKONSCOT MODEL VILLAGE AND HUGHENDEN MANOR

WHERE:
Buckinghamshire
BEST TIME TO GO:
March to October
DON'T MISS:
West Wycombe Caves – known as the Hell-Fire Caves because they were extended by Sir Francis Dashwood and used for meetings of the notorious club he founded.
AMOUNT OF WALKING:
Lots
COST:
Reasonable
YOU SHOULD KNOW:
Bekonscot was the dream of Roland Callingham, a London accountant who built the model village in a meadow next to his home – and the profits from his eccentric creation have always gone to charity.

This pretty county north west of London has a variety of appealing attractions. Start with the county's most characteristic natural feature – beech woods. One of the finest examples of ancient woodland in the British Isles is Burnham Beeches, owned since the 19th century by the City of London as public open space managed for the benefit of all.

The Burnham Beeches National Nature Reserve is off the A355 road between Burnham and Beaconsfield. There is ample car parking and refreshments are available, but the real attraction is the network of paths, many surfaced, that offer the opportunity for extended walks through beautiful terrain of mature woodlands and hillsides.

For something completely different, drive to Beaconsfield and visit the world's first-ever model village – Bekonscot Model Village and Railway. This miniature kingdom is stuck in a 1930s time warp that delights adults and children alike. It features six villages in a landscape of fields and farms, woods and hills, lakes and rivers, castles and churches, windmills and cottages...and lots of tiny people enjoying a range of activities from visiting the zoo to cricket on the village green. It's all linked by a garden railway.

The next port of call has altogether more gravitas – it is the National Trust's Hughenden Manor near High Wycombe, former home of the great 19th-century statesman Benjamin Disraeli. The house contains fascinating memorabilia, personal possessions, furniture and paintings, plus interesting audio trails. There are park, river and lakeside walks, with great views of the Chiltern Hills.

If there's time, visit nearby West Wycombe Park, also owned by the National Trust. It has a flamboyant Italianate house with splendid interiors, rococo landscape gardens, an ornamental lake and rolling parkland. This was the 18th-century home of Sir Francis Dashwood, who founded the famously decadent Hell-Fire Club.

Bekonscot Model Village

Windsor Castle and Runnymede

The Long Walk at Windsor Castle

Urban folk everywhere dream of a place out of town where they can get away from it all, and some do indeed enjoy just such a bolthole – but none can match the splendour of Windsor Castle, said to be the favourite weekend retreat of Her Majesty Queen Elizabeth II. It is, after all, both the oldest and largest occupied castle in the world (rebuilt by Edward III from 1350).

Guided tours of the Castle's precincts introduce its history and modern role, and there is also an audio tour. Within the Castle, visitors see magnificent State Apartments furnished with some the finest works of art from the Royal Collection, including splendid paintings by the likes of Rubens, Rembrandt, Canaletto, van Dyck and Gainsborough. The Semi-State Rooms (George IV's private apartments) may be viewed in the winter months. St George's Chapel is a splendid example of Gothic architecture. It contains ten royal tombs including those of Henry VIII and Charles I. In St Albans Street south of the Castle there is a display of the Queen's gifts and royal carriages.

From Windsor, it's but a short hop to Eton, home of the public school and those famous playing fields. Founded in 1440, it has superb medieval buildings and guided tours feature the Cloisters, College Chapel, the school's oldest classroom and the Museum of Eton Life.

While you're in these parts, take the opportunity to see the unassuming cradle of Britain's rule of law – Runnymede, where that sly but inefficient King John was forced to sign the Magna Carta by his concerned barons. Today, the site is protected by the National Trust, and consists of beautiful water meadows, grassland and woods. Find it off the A308 road on the south bank of the River Thames, 9.5 km (6 mi) southeast of Windsor.

WHERE:
Berkshire and Surrey
BEST TIME TO GO:
Any time
DON'T MISS:
The extraordinary Queen Mary's Doll's House at Windsor Castle, designed by Sir Edwin Lutyens and completed in 1924 – artists and manufacturers queued up to produce its perfectly executed miniature contents and everything works, including the electric lights and plumbing.
AMOUNT OF WALKING:
Moderate.
COST:
Expensive.
YOU SHOULD KNOW:
Windsor Castle is a working royal residence; so opening hours and/or days may change at short notice if affairs of State intervene. St George's Chapel is closed on Sundays, except for those who wish to worship.

London in Lego

Legoland

Don't visit this major attraction at Windsor unless you have children below the age of 12 in tow. If you do, they'll be in Legoheaven and you'll have solved that 'kids are bored and fractious again' problem for a whole blissful day.

Legoland consists of Lego-themed rides, ambitious models created using Lego and Lego building workshops. The place has constantly expanded since it was opened in the 1990s and now offers an exciting all-round theme park experience.

So what will this fun-packed day hold? It begins at...The Beginning, a reception area that includes The Hill Train funicular railway and a Creation Centre that showcases the most imaginative work of Legoland's talented model makers, including the Lego Crown Jewels and famous faces. From there, visitors are indulged with some fifty attractions from which to choose.

At the heart of the park, Miniland is a fascinating recreation of well-known cityscapes – including London, Paris and Amsterdam – using around 35 million pieces of Lego. After strolling around great cities, it's action all the way with rides and activities galore for all ages.

Here's a selection, ranging from the gentle to the fairly dramatic (the names give a good idea of what's in store): Fairy Tale Brook; Ferris Wheel and Carousel; Chairoplane; Chopper Squadron; The Duplo Train for youngsters; Orient Expedition; Jungle Coaster; Climbing Wall; Sky Rider; Space Tower; The Dragon and Dragon's Apprentice; Dino Safari and Dino Dipper; Pirate Falls; Longboat Invader; Vikings' River Splash; Wave Surfer; Extreme Team Challenge; Fire Academy; Spinning Spider. There are also hands-on activities like L-Drivers, Driving School, Boating School and Digger Challenge.

It's hard to know where to begin because everything's just fantastic – but there's one immutable law in Legoland. If you enter into the spirit of things, you'll get wet.

WHERE:
Berkshire
BEST TIME TO GO:
Any time
DON'T MISS:
Legoland's Imagination Theatre – where you either join the Lego Racers or enjoy a medieval adventure where the clever Blacksmith battles against the vile Wizard and his Skeleton Army...and rescues the Princess.
AMOUNT OF WALKING:
Reasonable (every effort is made to cater for wheelchair users, but clearly many rides are excluded).
COST:
Expensive
YOU SHOULD KNOW:
The brand name LEGO was devised by founder Ole Kirk Christiansen from the Danish phrase *leg godt*, meaning 'play well'. How true!

Vale of White Horse

UFFINGTON CASTLE AND KELMSCOTT MANOR

This fine stretch of English countryside between the Berkshire Downs and the River Thames is named after the prehistoric Uffington White Horse – but more of that mysterious beast later. The ancient Ridgeway path follows one side of the Vale, but today is about a scenic drive – albeit with ample opportunity to stop and walk amidst wonderful scenery.

Begin the round trip at Botley on Oxford's western outskirts and start down the A420 road to Kingston Bagpuize, where those addicted to historic houses may find 17th-century Kingston House open on several days each month from February to September.

Take back roads to Charney Bassett (12th-century St Peter's Church and watermill), Goosey and Uffington. The latter is a charming village with thatched cottages and 'the Cathedral of the Vale' – St Mary's Church with its rare octagonal tower. But the real attractions are close by.

Uffington Castle is an Iron Age hilltop fort south of the village, and nearby Wayland's Smithy is an impressive neolithic long barrow and chamber tomb. They're worth the walk, offering fabulous Vale views. Then there's the famous White Horse itself – if indeed it is a horse. Despite the name opinions differ...make up your own mind! It is best viewed from Fernham, north of Uffington. From there, drive to Farringdon and take the A4095 to the Kelmscott turning.

Kelmscott Manor was the home of Victorian Arts and Crafts giant William Morris and this Tudor farmhouse by the Thames remains as he left it. The Manor is open every Wednesday and on eight Saturdays between April and September, but even if the house is closed the village is delightful. From Kelmscott, go back to the A4095 and turn left for waterside Thrup and Littleworth before returning along the A420 to your starting point, tired but happy.

WHERE:
Oxfordshire
BEST TIME TO GO:
Any time
DON'T MISS:
The Old School in Uffington – now a small museum dedicated to the memory of local resident Thomas Hughes, creator of *Tom Brown's Schooldays*...and the awful Flashman.
AMOUNT OF WALKING:
Lots (note that wheelchair and pushchair users should probably give Uffington Castle and Wayland's Smithy a wide berth).
COST:
Low
YOU SHOULD KNOW:
The White Horse requires frequent scouring if it is to remain visible, and until the 19th century this task was undertaken every seven years as part of a local fair held on White Horse Hill.

The ancient White Horse at Uffington

Thorpe Park

If theme parks are your thing and you've already made a meal of Legoland, Thorpe Park makes a delicious dessert. Alton Towers is the UK's top draw, but Thorpe Park near Chertsey runs it a close second, delivering an action-packed day of excitement and thrills (but hopefully no spills). It's possible to reach the park by train or coach from Central London, or by car.

The buzzword at Thorpe is 'thrill' – with Young Thrills, Extreme Thrills and Thrilling & Fun being categories into which numerous rides are divided. The range is constantly being expanded, as no theme park can ever afford to stand still...onwards and upwards is the route to success!

Stroll around the Park's zones as you decide on a ride. These are Lost City, Ranger Country, Amity Cove, Calypso Quay, Canada Creek, Neptune's Kingdom, Octopus' Garden and The Showcase. Ride names give an idea of what you're about to receive, but there are some seriously scary options (often with restrictions – usually insisting that a trembling adult accompanies the eager youngster). But there are plenty of less dramatic choices for families with smaller children.

Okay, here goes...Extreme Thrills may be had on Stealth, Colossus, Detonator, Nemesis Inferno, Quantum, Rush, Samurai, Slammer, Tidal Wave, Vortex, X:\No Way Out and Zodiac. Still in one piece? Thrilling and Fun rides are Time Voyagers, Flying Fish, Depth Charge, Logger's Leap, Mr Monkey's Banana Ride, Rumba Rapids, Rocky Express and Storm in a Teacup. The calmer waters of Young Thrill Seekers include Fantasy Fish, Galleon Race, Happy Halibuts, Neptune's Beach, Ollie Octopus, Sea Snakes and Ladders, Slippery Serpent, Swinging Seashells, Up Periscope, Miss Hippo's Fungle Safari, Chief Ranger's Carousel and The Sing Zone. No denying it – the only word for the Thorpe experience is 'awesome'!

The scary Colossus

The Royal Landscape

SAVILL GARDEN, VALLEY GARDENS AND VIRGINIA WATER

Early morning at Virginia Water

A few kilometres from kiss-me-quick Thorpe Park, the Royal Landscape provides a complete contrast. These three linked natural delights offer 400 hectares (988 acres) of landscaped gardens, woodland and lakes. They are the Savill Garden (one of Britain's greatest ornamental gardens), Valley Gardens (flowering landscaped gardens and woods) and Virginia Water (extensive woodland around a beautiful lake).

Start at the Savill Garden near Egham. Here, the newest addition to The Royal Landscape is the Savill Building, a visitor centre where a beech grove was devastated by 1987's Great Storm. It represents cutting-edge design, but merges into the landscape and serves as a wonderful entry-point to the Savill Garden in Windsor Great Park. Laid out by Sir Eric Savill in the 1930s as a place for horticulturalists to savour, it has a mix of native and exotic trees and plants with many important hybrids. Themed areas include Spring, Summer and Autumn Woods, Hidden Gardens, Summer Gardens, Glades, Azalea Walks and the New Zealand Garden.

Close by, Valley Gardens are located on the northern shores of Virginia Water, with sensational views from on high and a network of meandering pathways through the flowering forest with its array of shrubs, meadowland and a splendid assortment of trees. Detailed material on this delightful corner of Windsor Great Park may be obtained at the Savill Centre.

The third element of this rewarding outdoor day is Virginia Water itself, an artificial lake created in 1753, since which time its surrounds have been constantly planted with a variety of trees to create wonderful woodlands that can be explored at leisure. Look out for an 18th-century ornamental cascade and the Roman Temple constructed with columns and lintels 'liberated' from the ancient city of Leptis Magna in the 19th century. Take a picnic and take your time exploring the magical Royal Landscape.

WHERE:
Surrey
BEST TIME TO GO:
Any time of year
DON'T MISS:
The Queen Elizabeth Temperate House in the Savill Garden – recently revamped, this extensive glasshouse has a wonderful selection of tender species from National Plant Collections.
AMOUNT OF WALKING:
Lots
COST:
Reasonable (Valley Gardens and Virginia Water are free, but parking charges apply).
YOU SHOULD KNOW:
The towering totem pole beside Virginia Water was a gift from the Government and people of British Columbia, Canada.

Along the Thames

THE COOKHAMS, HENLEY AND GREY'S COURT

North of Maidenhead are three Cookhams – rural Cookham Dean, Cookham Rise around the railway station and Cookham itself. This village beside the River Thames retains the appearance known by its most famous resident – painter Sir Stanley Spencer – and the High Street has hardly changed over the years. The chapel where he worshipped – now the Stanley Spencer Gallery with over one hundred of his paintings and drawings – provides a wonderful starting point for the day. The village is a convenient place from which to stroll along the Thames Path, or serious walkers can climb Winter Hill for sweeping views of the Thames Valley.

From Cookham, drive to the pleasant riverside town of Marlow and admire the early 19th-century suspension bridge and adjacent All Saints Church. Continue to Henley-on-Thames, with its impressive town hall and lively market square. It, too, has a fine bridge (built in 1786) and a wonderful old church, St Mary's. The town and river, overlooked by the Chiltern Hills, are the scene of the annual Henley Royal Regatta – a fact soon confirmed by a walk along the river with its picturesque boathouses and famous rowing clubs.

From Henley, take the opportunity to see an outstanding country house – Grey's Court at Rotherfield Greys, west of town. This enchanting Tudor manor has ornamental gardens set within medieval walls and the Gentle Walk, a pleasant half-hour stroll around the estate.

Return to the Thames at Mapledurham on the northern outskirts of Reading, where the watermill in the grounds of Mapledurham House may be seen working on weekend and Bank Holiday afternoons. Make the scenic drive upriver through Goring and Wallingford to Shillingford, where the outing can end scenically at the nearby beauty spot of Wittenham Clumps, a set of small hills topped by trees.

The bridge over the Thames at Henley

WHERE:
Berkshire, Buckinghamshire and Oxfordshire
BEST TIME TO GO:
April to September
DON'T MISS:
Fabulous Stonor Park just north of Henley, one of England's oldest manor houses, in a stunning setting. But you'll have to plan the visit because this family home has limited opening times – Sundays (April to mid-September), Bank Holiday Mondays and Wednesdays (July and August).
AMOUNT OF WALKING:
Lots (optional, with Winter Hill a definite 'miss' for wheelchair users).
COST:
Reasonable
YOU SHOULD KNOW:
Stanley Spencer was born in Cookham High Street, at the cottage named Fernlea where he lived for most of his life. Cookham villagers featured in many of his later paintings.

Painshill Park and Wisley Gardens

One of Britain's finest landscape parks fell into decay after the Second World War – but happily Painshill Park (just off the A3 road at Cobham) is back from the dead, thanks to a local authority that bought most of the park and formed a trust to start an ambitious restoration programme.

Painshill Park was originally created between 1738 and 1773 by Charles Hamilton, a gifted and artistic son (but sadly not heir!) of the Earl of Abercorn. He eventually ran out of money, but not before Painshill had become an archetypal 18th-century landscape, complete with beautiful lake, artfully created views and romantic follies. Most survive, including the Abbey, Gothic Temple, Chinese Bridge, Grotto, Temple of Bacchus, Mausoleum and Turkish Tent. The planting echoes Hamilton's scheme, with particular emphasis on species he introduced from North America. It's easy to spend at least half a day here, wandering on a voyage of discovery as breathtaking new vistas and romantic follies appear at every turn. Take a picnic, or enjoy a light meal in the Park's tearoom.

To complete this garden-lover's dream day, the short drive down the A3 will take you to Wisley Gardens, beside the green space of Wisley Common. The house and its lily pond make a beautiful backdrop to the Royal Horticultural Society's flagship garden, which was an existing experimental garden acquired by donation in the early 20th century. Since then, it has been developed into a world-class horticultural facility covering some 98 hectares (242 acres). This large and diverse site includes formal and informal gardens of all sorts, model gardens that provide visitors with ideas to try at home, different cultivation techniques, glasshouses, an arboretum and extensive trial grounds where new cultivars are assessed. It's a magical place that should top every dedicated gardener's want-to-visit wish list.

WHERE:
Surrey
BEST TIME TO GO:
March to October
DON'T MISS:
The wonderful new Bicentenary Glasshouse at Wisley, containing three main planting areas that represent desert, tropical and temperate climate zones.
AMOUNT OF WALKING:
Lots
COST:
Reasonable
YOU SHOULD KNOW:
American plants at Painshill represent seeds and plants collected by natural scientist John Bartram on the northeastern seaboard of North America in the mid-1700s and sent to England – Painshill's creator Charles Hamilton got his first box of seeds in 1748 and trees grown from those seeds may still be seen in the Park.

The vineyard and folly at Painshill Park

87

Surrey Heights

LEITH HILL, POLESDEN LACEY AND BOX HILL

WHERE:
Surrey
BEST TIME TO GO:
April to October for Polesden Lacey
but any clear day for the walks and
stunning views.
DON'T MISS:
The flowering orchids on Box Hill –
expect to see at least a dozen
varieties from early June to early July.
Failing that, the autumnal leaves are
spectacular.
AMOUNT OF WALKING:
Lots
COST:
Reasonable
YOU SHOULD KNOW:
When he was still Prince Albert, Duke
of York, the future King George VI
and his bride Elizabeth
honeymooned at Polesden Lacey.

Surprisingly for a commuter county cheek-by-jowl with the great metropolis of London, the county of Surrey has some classic English countryside, as a day spent driving along the right roads (and extended walks in some superb scenic locations) will confirm.

Start the day at the South East's highest point – Leith Hill, near Coldharbour off the B2126 road south of Dorking. Heath and woodland maintained by the National Trust offers self-guided trails, assorted wildlife and colourful rhododendron displays in May and June. There is a Gothic tower at the summit that provides stunning panoramic views across London and south to the English Channel.

From Leith Hill, take the scenic drive along lanes through the pretty hamlet of Friday Street, set around a pond deep in a wooded valley. Continue to Abinger and Abinger Hammer with its quintessentially English village green – a splendid spot for a summer picnic, with luck when a cricket match is in progress.

From Abinger Hammer take the back road to Effingham, turning right for Denbies and Polesden Lacey, a National Trust property set in beautiful downland countryside with sweeping valley views. This impressive Regency house was the home of a great hostess, the Hon. Mrs Greville, and opulent Edwardian interiors reflect the high style of the early 20th century's grand house parties. The elegant gardens and landscaped park offer a variety of walks. The gardens and shop are open daily, the house from Wednesday to Sunday (mid-March to October only).

Continue via Westhumble and along the main road towards Mickleham, then follow the signs to Box Hill, an outstanding area of chalk downland and woods with interesting nature trails and exceptional views of the South Downs. There's a visitor centre and car parking at the summit for those who want those fabulous views without the effort of walking!

The beautiful Surrey
countryside as seen from
Box Hill

Farnham and the Hog's Back

With many attractive buildings from different periods – notably splendid Georgian architecture – and narrow streets or side passages that lead to interesting 'secret places' – the old-fashioned market town of Farnham on Surrey's western edge merits an extended visit (find details of the self-guided heritage trail at visitor information points). There is a Norman castle keep, St Andrew's Church

The romantic ruin of Waverley Abbey

dating from the 12th century and Britain's first Cistercian foundation, Waverley Abbey dating from 1128 – now a romantic ruin beside the River Wey (just outside town on the B3001 road).

Farnham's pride in its heritage – and determination to preserve traditional character – is emphasised by the award-winning Museum of Farnham, located in a Georgian townhouse. This well-stocked museum puts on changing exhibitions and has permanent displays that explore the town's history, significant links to the creative arts and town life over the centuries.

But the day is yet youngish, so there should be time to take the A31 road towards Guildford, following the Hog's Back. Unfortunately, it's hard to find stopping points along the busy main road, but those there are have distant views of London and a sweeping Area of Outstanding Natural Beauty to the south.

Turn right for Compton, where Victorian artist George Frederick Watts created the Watts Gallery early in the 20th century as a purpose-built showcase for his own works. It is now closed for major renovation works, but the extraordinary Watts Cemetery Chapel where he is interred is worth a visit in its own right.

End the outing at Loseley Park, near Compton. This historic manor house was built with stone from Waverley Abbey in the 1560s after Elizabeth I said the existing house was too small for a royal visit, and it has wonderful interiors and fabulous grounds, together requiring several hours of satisfying exploration.

WHERE:
Surrey
BEST TIME TO GO:
Any time (May to August for Loseley House).
DON'T MISS:
The display on John Henry Knight at the Museum of Farnham – he was the first man in Britain to build a petrol-driven car (in 1895) and for a brief period Farnham was the centre for building motor cars. Not many people know that!
AMOUNT OF WALKING:
Lots
COST:
Reasonable
YOU SHOULD KNOW:
Jane Austen was once driven across the Hog's Back in a curricle en route to her brother's house in London and described it as a perfect viewpoint over magnificent countryside.

Rochester Cathedral

Rochester

Its strategic location near the confluence of the Rivers Thames and Medway ensured Rochester's importance and prosperity from Roman times – until 1984, when the nearby Royal Dockyard at Chatham closed. This plunged the town into crisis, with a huge rise in unemployment and consequent social deprivation, with recovery taking two decades.

But Rochester's proud history makes it an interesting place in which to spend a day. England's second-oldest cathedral is here, beside a castle keep that's the tallest in the land. Rochester Cathedral was begun in 1080. The architecture is a mix of Norman, Gothic and Early Perpendicular and notable features include a crypt, medieval wall paintings and a splendid 15th-century chapter-room doorway. The Castle is one of the best examples of Norman military architecture in England – its effectiveness proved when King John failed to take the place in 1215, which only surrendered when the defenders ran out of food. It was begun in 1087 and added to in the 12th century. Though only the keep and curtain walls remain (the rest was demolished in 1610), a model of the castle in its heyday may be seen.

The Guildhall Museum has a wide range of exhibits dating from prehistoric times to the 19th century with a life-sized replica of a convict hulk once moored in the Medway forming an unusual centrepiece. Restoration House is a city mansion with fine interiors and links to Charles II, Samuel Pepys and Charles Dickens. The High Street has received a characterful Victorian makeover in tribute to Dickens.

Rochester is surrounded by two rings of fortification – the inner line of Forts Clarence, Pitt, Amherst and Gillingham, built in the Napoleonic Wars and outer 'Palmerston' forts, built in the 1860s (Borstal, Bridgewood, Luton, Hoo and Darnet, plus the Twydall Redoubts). Many of these interesting fortifications survive.

WHERE:
Kent
BEST TIME TO GO:
Any time
DON'T MISS:
Strood's Temple Manor, across the Medway from Rochester Castle – this 13th-century house with 17th-century additions once belonged to the Knights Templar, who used it as a staging post for members heading for the Crusades.
AMOUNT OF WALKING:
Moderate (partly because access to Rochester's outlying forts is not easy).
COST:
Low
YOU SHOULD KNOW:
Charles Dickens lived nearby in Gad's Hill and Rochester featured in many of his novels, including *The Pickwick Papers*, *Great Expectations* and *The Mystery of Edwin Drood*.

The Historic Dockyard

CHATHAM

Once upon a time, Britannia ruled the waves...and thereby created an Empire that spanned the globe. Many of the Royal Navy ships that made this unprecedented world domination possible were built on the River Medway at Chatham Dockyard from the 1560s, though when it finally closed in the 1980s the British Navy had become a shadow of its former self and the British Empire was history. But the heart of the Historic Dockyard survived – preserved for posterity and giving unique insight into vanished shipbuilding processes that helped to add the Great to Britain.

This compelling maritime heritage site will provide a very special day out, offering a variety of attractions. An abundance of historic buildings forms the core of the experience, and they may be appreciated with the help of guides in period costume who bring dockyard history to life. The 32-hectare (79-acre) site has over one hundred structures, mostly dating from the period 1704-1855. These include: administrative and residential buildings; dry docks and building slips; timber working and storage facilities; rope, sail and chain-making buildings; manufactories using wood, iron and steel; storage sites. The bold architecture and technically advanced buildings of their day are wonderful to behold.

The Royal Dockyard Museum unfurls 400 years of endeavour, featuring not only familiar names like Samuel Pepys and Charles Dickens but also countless thousands of workers who toiled here over the centuries. There are three warships to explore – the Victorian sloop *Gannet*, World-War-II destroyer *Cavalier* and Cold-War submarine *Ocelot*, plus exhibitions mounted in conjunction with the National Maritime Museum and Imperial War Museum.

Indeed, there's so much to see that the admission ticket allows you to return as many times as you like within twelve months, to fully appreciate this unique naval heritage site.

WHERE:
Kent
BEST TIME TO GO:
Any time
DON'T MISS:
The Royal National Lifeboat Institute's historic lifeboat collection, with 17 vessels that between them saved hundreds of lives.
AMOUNT OF WALKING:
Lots (the Dockyard is wheelchair friendly, though with some areas of restricted access).
COST:
Reasonable
YOU SHOULD KNOW:
It is said that Oliver Cromwell stood beside the mulberry tree that still grows in the Commissioner's Italianate Garden of 1640, watching Parliamentary forces take Rochester from the Royalists in the English Civil War.

Ahoy shipmates! Come aboard HMS Gannet.

Lullingstone and Knole

On the outer fringes of London (down the A225 road south of Dartford, close to Junction 3 of the M25 motorway) the peaceful village of Lullingstone has two contrasting attractions to offer – each unusual in its own way.

The Roman Villa (discovered in 1939) is one of very few excavated villas in Britain that is open to the public, and a covered facility makes it possible to undertake a unique exploration of Roman domestic life over three centuries, from 80 AD to 420 AD when the place was destroyed by fire. The highlights are fine mosaic floors, but there is much more of relevant interest on display.

The Romans attempted to conquer their known universe, and at Lullingstone Castle and World Garden (open on Fridays, Saturdays, Sundays and Bank Holidays excluding Good Friday) a young man is attempting to repeat the trick in gardening terms. The ancestral home of the eccentric Hart Dykes will be familiar to many television viewers, as will son and heir Tom's efforts to revive the family fortunes by creating his ambitious World Garden. See both the Castle and maturing result of Tom Hart Dyke's efforts before scooping up an unusual plant or two from the nursery.

There should be time to crown the day with a visit to Knole, farther down the A225 near Sevenoaks. This magnificent stately home is surrounded by a park that has changed little in four centuries – and the house itself boasts interiors that have remained largely unaltered since the 17th century. This splendid late medieval Archbishop's Palace was transformed into a great Renaissance country house in the early 17th century by Thomas Sackville, first Earl of Dorset, before his descendents added the Stuart furniture and textiles, then fine pictures, that make up the fabulous contents of Knole's State Rooms.

One of the mosaic floors at the Roman Villa in Lullingstone

Squerryes Court, Quebec House, Titsey and Toys Hill

The church at Titsey is set in beautiful countryside.

The English were particularly good at building beautiful country houses in stunning settings, and Squerryes Court is a classic example of just such a gem. This 18th-century manor has been home to the Warde family since 1731 and sits comfortably amidst extensive historic gardens that include a lake, parterres and a dovecote. The house contains some fine paintings and the garden includes woodland walks. This delightful family home is open on Wednesdays and Sundays between April and September, and may be found off the A25 road just south of the charming small town of Westerham.

In Westerham itself, it's worth visiting Quebec House, childhood home of General James Wolfe, the famous victor of the Battle of Quebec in 1759 (a victory that cost his life). This grand red-brick gabled townhouse has 16th-century origins but was extensively remodelled in the 1700s. It contains Wolfe family memorabilia and military relics, and there's a Battle of Quebec Exhibition in the old coach house.

On the same two days as Squerryes Court – Wednesdays and Sundays – nearby Titsey (just outside Limpsfield) is open. It is one of the largest historic estates in Surrey and the early 19th-century house is at the heart of a wonderful garden and rolling expanse of preserved countryside on the flank of the North Downs. There are some excellent woodland walks in the Titsey Place plantation and High Chart woodland, open all year.

A stroll through the National Trust's magical 30-hectare (74-acre) Toys Hill woodlands, south of Westerham, is a relaxing way to complete the day. There are three way-marked walks of manageable distance, starting from the car park near the Fox and Hounds pub in the village of Toys Hill. There are many viewpoints, most with seats where it's possible to relax and appreciate that wonderful outlook over the Kent Weald.

WHERE:
Kent and Surrey
BEST TIME TO GO:
April to September
DON'T MISS:
The Church of St James at Titsey, rebuilt in Gothic-Revival style in 1861 after being moved earlier from a site adjacent to the house – it has family monuments, a vaulted chapel and a splendid Victorian interior.
AMOUNT OF WALKING:
Lots
COST:
Reasonable
YOU SHOULD KNOW:
One of the first gifts to the National Trust was the terrace with a sunken well in Toys Hill village – given by one of the Trust's founders, Octavia Hill, in 1898.

Leeds Castle and the Museum of Kent Life

WHERE:
Kent
BEST TIME TO GO:
Any time (Leeds Castle), Mid-February to Early November (Museum of Kent Life).
DON'T MISS:
The wildfowl sanctuary at Leeds Castle, where black swans that have become a symbol of the Castle may be seen lording it over many other species.
AMOUNT OF WALKING:
Lots
COST:
Reasonable
YOU SHOULD KNOW:
The Royal connections of Leeds Castle are extensive – it was owned by Edward I, besieged by Edward II, housed Richard II's future wife, refurbished by Henry VIII for Catherine of Aragon and used to imprison Elizabeth I before her accession. Give it a curtsey!

There isn't a more satisfying medieval castle in England – and this one has the added bonus of royal heritage. Leeds Castle stands proudly on two islands in the wide River Len, looking just as a 12th-century fortress should, though of course it has been the subject of considerable works since first constructed around 1120. Actually, Leeds Castle was eventually refurbished with the help of American money. The last private owner was Olive, Lady Baillie – the daughter of an American heiress. She bought Leeds Castle in 1926 and sumptuously created the rich interiors we see today.

Now run by a trust and open to the public, a tour of this special place is a magical experience. The extensive grounds and park also have a lot to offer – formal gardens, woodland walks, a famous aviary, children's play area, mazes, a grotto and a unique collection of...dog collars.

Find Leeds Castle southeast of Maidstone, close to Junction 8 of the M20 motorway – it is very well signed from all directions. Any time that remains after exploring the castle and its environs may profitably be invested in a visit to the Museum of Kent Life. This, too, is near the M20 at Maidstone – use Junction 6 and find the Museum signed from there.

This wonderful open-air facility on the banks of the River Medway is a joy to those who have an interest in bygone rural life. Created around an original farmstead, the Museum has assembled a varied selection of buildings that have been rescued and re-erected. These include farmhouses, cottages, oasts and barns, with others such as a chapel, village hall and shepherds' huts. Various aspects of farming and country life are vividly recreated to bring the experience alive. An evocative journey back in time!

The annual Hot Air Balloon Festival at Leeds Castle

Hop Farm Country Park and Penshurst Place

WHERE:
Kent
BEST TIME TO GO:
April to October
DON'T MISS:
Two galleries at Penshurst Place –
the splendid Elizabethan Long Gallery
with its great collection of royal and
family portraits, and the Nether
Gallery with an impressive display of
armour and early weapons.
AMOUNT OF WALKING:
Lots
COST:
Reasonable
YOU SHOULD KNOW:
There is a regular programme of
special events at the Hop Farm
Family Park throughout the summer,
including visits from TV children's
favourites like Bob The Builder...and
grown-up activities like an annual
beer festival.

A major harvest from the Garden of England was (and still is) hops that make English beer what it is. The days when hordes of Londoners descended for the picking season are long gone, but it's still possible to enjoy the Hop Farm Family Park, located on the A228 road near Paddock Wood.

This former hop farm is now a family-orientated visitor attraction, centred on a large group of old oast houses. There are children's facilities like the Driving School, Indoor Play Barn, Outdoor Play Area and Mini Fairground. There's an Animal Farm and Pets Corner, shire horses and an all-action Pottery Centre. Extra dimensions are provided by Yesterday's Village with shops and artefacts, an interactive Hop Story Museum which brings traditional hop-picking days to life, military vehicle exhibition and waxworks collection. When hunger strikes, there is a restaurant, tea-room and café to choose from, and gift shops for those essential souvenirs.

It's possible to spend a happy family day enjoying the Hop Farm experience, but for those lacking children (or yearning for something more restful by lunchtime), a visit to Penshurst Place could be the answer. It, too, has attractions for little people (including a splendid Toy Museum and Venture Playground), but there is also an enchanting medieval house and gardens that have changed little over the centuries. The State Rooms (including the spectacular Baron's Hall) are awe-inspiring and the huge walled gardens date back to the 14th century, though they were remodelled as recently as Elizabethan times.

To find Penshurst Place from the Hop Farm, continue down the A228 to the A21 and turn right towards Tonbridge. Continue along the A21 until you reach the A26. Turn left there and almost immediately turn right onto the B2176 for Penshurst. The short journey will not be wasted.

*Penshurst Place has been the
home of the Sydney family
since 1552.*

Chiddingstone and Groombridge

A 'dinosaur' at Groombridge Place

Between Tonbridge and Edenbridge is the extraordinary village of Chiddingstone on the River Eden – extraordinary because it is entirely owned by the National Trust and frequently described as 'the most perfect Tudor village in England'. This pretty one-street settlement is typical of the Kent vernacular, with an abundance of half-timbering, gables and red-tile roofs. The majority of buildings in Chiddingstone are over two centuries old, with most dating to the 1500s and 1600s, though some are even earlier. It's a special place.

The one thing the National Trust doesn't own is Chiddingstone Castle. It was once a Tudor manor house, but it was remodelled early in the 19th century using the then popular 'castle style'. Nestling in the Kent Weald, it is surrounded by grounds that include woodland and a lake. The last occupant was passionate connoisseur Denys Eyre who devoted his life to amassing a collection of art and artefacts, notably Japanese and Egyptian antiquities. But there's much more, and exhibitions constantly change as his vast collection is rotated. The castle is open from Thursday to Sunday and on Bank Holidays.

A pleasant drive down the B2188 takes you to Groombridge, straddling the border with East Sussex. The main attraction is historic Groombridge Place. The charming 17th-century house is not open to the public, but there are extensive formal gardens to explore, created behind walls in the 1600s as superb 'outside rooms' to enhance the house. Then go through a door at the top of the estate vineyard and find the Enchanted Forest, a rustic theme park set on a hillside overlooking the house. It has many features designed to intrigue and entertain, including exciting playgrounds, huge swings, an adventure boardwalk, fantasy gardens, a dinosaur and dragon valley and canal cruise. Fun, fun, fun!

WHERE:
Kent
BEST TIME TO GO:
April to October
DON'T MISS:
The Chiding Stone from which Chiddingstone gets its name – just outside the village, this carved sandstone boulder is believed to be a Saxon boundary marker and/or a Druidical altar.
AMOUNT OF WALKING:
Moderate
COST:
Reasonable
YOU SHOULD KNOW:
Arthur Conan Doyle was a regular visitor to Groombridge Place and used it as the setting for the Sherlock Holmes mystery *The Valley of Fear*. There is a Conan Doyle Museum in a former dairy at Groombridge.

Bewl Water and National Pinetum

WHERE:
Kent and East Sussex
BEST TIME TO GO:
April to September
DON'T MISS:
The Leyland cypresses at Bedgebury, the finest examples you are likely to find anywhere – but when you look at their size, it's a stern reminder not to plant this species as garden hedging!
AMOUNT OF WALKING:
Lots (the Round Reservoir Route at Bewl is not suitable for wheelchairs or pushchairs, but there are plenty of viable options).

For those in search of a bracing outdoor day, Bewl Water is a great place to start. Set in the Weald of Kent, it is the largest and most picturesque stretch of inland water in south-eastern England. This reservoir south of Lamberhurst is of recent origin – created in the 1970s by damming a river valley – but it quickly became a major leisure facility.

Dedicated walkers will be tempted by a morning spent tackling the 20-km (12.5-mi) Round Reservoir Route through woodland, across meadows and along quiet country lanes. There are plenty of viewpoints and it's a great way to see the wildlife that abounds. For those in a hurry, mountain bikes may be hired for more speedy circumnavigation. Of course it's possible to take satisfying shorter walks or simply picnic beside the water. Non-athletic types may prefer a cruise aboard *The Swallow* or eating in the Look-Out family restaurant, with its lake vista and perfect view of Bewl's varied waterborne activities. Motor and rowing boats may be hired from the Fishing Lodge.

Across the A21 from Bewl is Bedgebury Pinetum, a 130-hectare (321-acre) park adjoining Bedgebury Forest on the B2079 Goudhurst road. It was set up jointly in 1924 by The Royal Botanic Gardens, Kew and the Forestry Commission. The Pinetum contains the National Collection – the world's most comprehensive collection of different conifers on a single site. There are children's play facilities plus an information centre and shop, with home-made refreshments also available at the Bedgebury Pantry, but this really is a place simply to enjoy the beauty and tranquillity of a unique location...and the extraordinary variety of conifers it contains. There are over 10,000 specimens, including rare, historically important and endangered trees and Bedgebury is home to over fifty vulnerable or endangered species. Truly a tree-huggers paradise!

COST:
Low
YOU SHOULD KNOW:
Confirming the argument for protecting every possible plant species, an obscure Victorian cultivar of yew – growing only at Bedgebury – has been found to have extremely high levels of the active natural chemicals needed to formulate Taxol, a leading cancer drug.

Cycling around Bewl Water.

The Pantiles at Tunbridge Wells

Royal Tunbridge Wells

AND SURROUNDING VILLAGES

The High Weald on the Kent-Sussex borders – with lovely villages, rolling hills, woodland and sunken lanes – represents classic English countryside at its best and an ideal centre for touring this captivating area is Royal Tunbridge Wells, itself deserving of an extended visit.

Tunbridge Wells rose and rose in the 17th and 18th centuries, when it went from nothing to fashionable spa town in a few decades. Surprisingly in view of the fact that royalty first took the waters in 1629, the 'Royal' was only bestowed by Edward VII in 1909. The town that grew up to service hopeful health-seekers using many iron-rich wells dug after 1606 may still be discerned at the heart of modern Tunbridge Wells, which has expanded mightily. The elegance that characterized the town in its Georgian heyday is evident, with the most striking feature being the famous Pantiles – a long promenade built in the 1680s along with fine shops to serve the leisured classes.

After appreciating the town centre, take a scenic drive around some of that wonderful local countryside and visit typically pleasing villages – a good circular route goes from Tunbridge Wells through Pembury (green and two churches), Matfield (lovely green with pond, fine Georgian houses), Brenchley (green surrounded by half-timbered houses), Horsmonden (lovely church outside the village, overlooking the river), Goudhurst (delightful hillside street tumbling from church to village pond), Cranbrook (pretty medieval town), Benenden (Church of St George) and Hawkhurst (a group of hamlets), before returning to Tunbridge Wells along the main road.

As an alternative to driving, a ride on the short but scenic Spa Valley Railway from the West Station in Tunbridge Wells via High Rocks to Groombridge lets the train take the strain. This heritage line operates standard-gauge steam locos on selected days throughout the year, mainly in summer.

WHERE:
Kent
BEST TIME TO GO:
April to September
DON'T MISS:
Tunbridge Wells Museum and Art Gallery – regular exhibitions plus collections of Tunbridge Ware, toys, natural and local history, costume and textiles, old money and fine art.
AMOUNT OF WALKING:
Moderate
COST:
Low
YOU SHOULD KNOW:
The original Chalybeate Spring in Tunbridge Wells – whose discovery in 1606 led to the establishment of a spa – may still be seen in the Pantiles.

Old Soar Manor and Ightham Mote

Just outside London's M25 orbital motorway, it's possible to get reminders of another, more ancient world. Deep in the Kentish Weald between the A21 and A26 roads may be found two fine historic houses – one an impressive ruin, the other beautifully restored. Each represents the era in which it was built, with a tangible aura of history to stimulate the imagination.

Old Soar Manor dates from 1290 and this stone house in its peaceful setting was a knight's dwelling. It has a solar chamber and chapel over a barrel-vaulted undercroft with a timber spiral staircase, and there is an interesting exhibition on the house. Find it signposted along a narrow lane near Plaxtol, just south of Borough Green. There is no entry charge but the house is closed on Fridays.

Just across the A227 near Ivy Hatch lies Ightham Mote. This 14th-century house owes its salvation as an unadulterated survivor of the Middle Ages to the fact that it was owned by squires and courtiers who couldn't afford expensive rebuilding. The house rises from its moat and the inner courtyard is reached via a bridge and castellated gatehouse. There is an abundance of half-timbering and the house has an unspoiled interior that includes a fine Great Hall, Old Chapel, Crypt and Tudor Chapel. Is there a more lovely medieval house in Britain? Maybe, but Ightham Mote must be near the top of the list. The house is closed on Tuesdays and Wednesdays but the woodland gardens are open every day.

Speaking of gardens, a gastronomic way to complete this rewarding day in North Kent is to visit Garden Organic at Yalding, just south of Maidstone. This provides a thoroughly modern opportunity to see the latest advances in sustainable organic gardening – and consume the garden's tasty produce in the café.

WHERE:
Kent
BEST TIME TO GO:
April to September
DON'T MISS:
The painted ceiling of the Ightham Mote Chapel which – in an attempt to curry favour with the monarch – was painted with scenes depicting the marriage of King Henry VIII with Catherine of Aragon, also shown on stained glass windows in the Great Hall. Oops!
AMOUNT OF WALKING:
Moderate
COST:
Reasonable
YOU SHOULD KNOW:
The importance of Ightham Mote is reflected in the fact that it has been the subject of the National Trust's largest-ever conservation project.

Ightham Mote is a typical timber-framed manor house.

Chartwell and Hever Castle

WHERE:
Kent
BEST TIME TO GO:
Any time
DON'T MISS:
The Henry VIII lock at Hever – the paranoid monarch took special locks everywhere he went and had them fastened to his bedroom door to ensure that he would not be attacked during the night.
AMOUNT OF WALKING:
Moderate
COST:
Reasonable
YOU SHOULD KNOW:
Winston Churchill was never rich and Chartwell was purchased by a group of wealthy friends in 1947, and then rented back to Sir Winston and Lady Clementine for a nominal sum, before being presented to the nation after his death.

The area around Westerham is well endowed with historic houses, including Chartwell – home of statesman and writer Sir Winston Churchill. Now owned by the National Trust, the house is in an area of great natural beauty. Winston and Clementine Churchill bought the property in 1922 and had it modernized in the style popularized by Lutyens.

The house is as the Churchills left it, containing an incomparable collection of memorabilia. Terraced hillside gardens were also remodelled to take advantage of stunning views over the Kent Weald to Sussex and include the lake Winston created, a water garden where he fed his fish and Clementine's rose garden. Many of Churchill's paintings may be seen in the garden studio.

Chartwell is off the B2026 road south of Westerham, open from Wednesday to Sunday (Tuesday, too, in July and August). Further down the same road is Edenbridge, where a left turn just after the village leads to moated Hever Castle, begun in 1270.

Billed as the childhood home of Anne Boleyn, Henry VIII's second wife did spend time here, though she was sent abroad to complete her education. After the Boleyns fell from favour (Anne and brother George losing their heads in the process), Hever Castle passed through many hands over time. It was acquired by American tycoon William Waldorf Astor in 1903, who had the place completely restored as a family home. It now offers a range of attractions that will easily fill the rest of the day. This romantic castle is furnished much as the Tudors would have known it, with artefacts that include Books of Hours signed by Anne Boleyn. There's an exhibition of weaponry and torture instruments in the gatehouse. Outside, excellent gardens include two mazes – one of traditional yew, the other a splashy water maze.

Hever Castle was the childhood home of Anne Boleyn.

Sissinghurst

KENT & EAST SUSSEX RAILWAY AND CRANBROOK MUSEUM

Off the A262 road east of Tunbridge Wells is Sissinghurst Castle, forever associated with Vita Sackville-West. A poet and novelist, The Hon Lady Nicholson (her official title) was a fringe member of the Bloomsbury Group that included Lytton Strachey and Virginia Woolf (with whom Vita had a passionate affair).

Sissinghurst Castle has magnificent gardens.

She was also a passionate gardener and horticultural writer, and the garden she created at Sissinghurst with husband Harold Nicholson is world-famous. Designed around extant portions of an Elizabethan mansion, it consists of many enclosed compartments that deliver colour through the seasons and create an intimate, romantic atmosphere. The Sissinghurst Castle Garden is closed on Wednesdays and Thursdays, but free lakeside and woodland walks are always open.

The Bloomsbury Group knew how to party, and would have appreciated the next stop – Biddenden Vineyard, along the back road from Sissinghurst to Tenterden. A flagship for the thriving English wine industry, it's possible to take a vineyard tour, sample fine Kentish wines (or strong local cider) and carry off a trophy bottle or two.

At nearby Tenterden, the Kent & East Sussex Railway is Britain's finest heritage light railway, running a 16-km (10-mi) steam service through the unspoiled Rother Valley via Northiam to Bodiam, with its magnificent castle. There is a good 'hop on, hop off' service all summer (restricted timetable in winter) and a Railway Museum at Tenterden.

To end a memorable day, drive via the pretty village of Benenden to Cranbrook, where Cranbrook Museum in a timber-framed farmhouse is full of collections illuminating town and country life, plus subjects as varied as war and birds' eggs. Compelling viewing – and the town itself is pretty good. Known as 'The Capital of the Weald', it is a pretty place with a medieval layout of streets and alleys containing many appealing old buildings.

WHERE:
Kent
BEST TIME TO GO:
Mid-March to October
DON'T MISS:
The library and study at Sissinghurst where Vita Sackville-West worked – or the long climb to the top of the Elizabethan tower.
AMOUNT OF WALKING:
Lots
COST:
Reasonable
YOU SHOULD KNOW:
The famous 'Biddenden Maids' were born in that village in 1100 – conjoined twins Mary and Eliza Chulkhurst lived for 34 years and a charity established in their name still exists today.

Around Lamberhurst

SCOTNEY CASTLE, FINCHCOCKS AND BATEMAN'S

WHERE:
Kent
BEST TIME TO GO:
Mid-March to October
DON'T MISS:
The striking Gothic-Revival church in the village of Kilndown – built in 1839, it has a wonderfully elaborate interior.
AMOUNT OF WALKING:
Moderate
COST:
Reasonable
YOU SHOULD KNOW:
It's possible to see original illustrations by the Detmold brothers for *The Jungle Book* at Bateman's.

The village of Lamberhurst has three hills – School, Spray and Town – leading up from the River Teise. This Kentish settlement in rolling countryside is a good starting point for three attractions that together make a great day out.

Just off the A21 road near Lamberhurst, the National Trust's Scotney Castle is a Victorian country house in Elizabethan style, with some rooms open for viewing. It is surrounded by a wooded estate containing one of the most romantic gardens in England. Created around the picturesque ruins of a moated castle in the 1830s, it provides fabulous displays of flowering rhododendrons, azaleas and kalmia in May and June, wisteria and roses in summer and the autumn colour of trees and ferns. There are excellent walks through the park, hop farm and woodlands with wonderful vistas at every turn.

A short distance down the A21, the turn to Kilndown will take you on to Finchcocks. This early Georgian manor house with a dramatic front elevation was built in 1725. It is surrounded by parkland, lawns, a wild-flower orchard and walled gardens. The house is magnificent, but the unique attraction is the Finchcock Collection of historic keyboard instruments – clavichords, harpsichords, pianos and organs – with many restored to working order. The house is open from Easter to the end of September on Sundays and Bank Holiday Mondays, plus Wednesdays and Thursdays in August.

Return to the A21 and drive on to Hurst Green, turning right onto the A265 for Burwash. There, Bateman's is a lovely Jacobean house that was the home of Rudyard Kipling. It is just as the jingoistic British author left it, with an interior that reflects his passionate association with the East. Gardens run down to a working watermill on the River Dudwell. Bateman's is closed on Thursdays and Fridays.

Some of the many keyboard instruments at Finchcocks

Canterbury

Situated on Watling Street, the Roman road from London to the coast, the ancient city of Canterbury is the traditional seat of the Primate of All England. The Cathedral has seen many significant historical events, not least the murder of Archbishop Thomas Becket in 1170 – an infamous event that confirmed England's most significant religious centre as a major pilgrimage site.

The first thing to see in Canterbury must therefore be its finest building. Christ Church Cathedral was begun in the 7th century, then extended and altered until the Norman era. This breathtaking combination of Perpendicular and Gothic architecture has some superb early stained glass and England's largest Norman crypt. St Augustine's Abbey with Fyndon's Gate is an extensive early ruin and St Martin's is one of the oldest churches in England still being used for worship. Together with the Cathedral they form a UNESCO World Heritage Site.

Impressive medieval town walls are largely intact (the surviving West Gate is a museum with a fine view up the High Street to the Cathedral) and the town centre is partially pedestrianized. Canterbury retains an interesting mix of historic buildings, including medieval structures like 13th-century Greyfriars Chapel spanning the River Stour, a ruined castle keep, the 14th-century Poor Priests' Hospital (now a heritage museum) plus many fine 17th- and 18th-century houses.

After exploring a town rich in static heritage, an afternoon at nearby Howletts Wild Animal Park will provide some living history. This animal conservation facility is at Bekesbourne, signed off the A2 road just south of Canterbury. Here you will find nearly a hundred rare and endangered species living in conditions as near to their natural habitats as is possible in captivity – so be aware that many of them will therefore become invisible in bad weather as they seek shelter!

A view to the West Gate along one of the many side alleys leading from the High Street.

WHERE:
Kent
BEST TIME TO GO:
Any time
DON'T MISS:
The large and entertaining group of breeding western lowland gorillas at Howletts Wild Animal Park – and then take a walk through the lemur enclosure to mingle happily with these friendly but scatter-brained animals.
AMOUNT OF WALKING:
Lots
COST:
Expensive for a family (Howletts).
YOU SHOULD KNOW:
Every cloud...post-war reconstruction after extensive bomb damage revealed many substantial remains of Durovernum Cantiacorum, the Roman town that stood on the site of Canterbury – see a host of recovered artefacts at the town's Roman Museum.

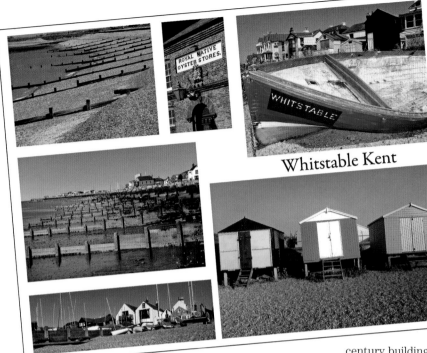

Whitstable Kent

A typical seaside postcard showing the gentle charms of Whitstable.

Whitstable

QUEX HOUSE, BIRCHINGTON

Anyone for oysters? That can only mean Whitstable, the picturesque seaside town in northeast Kent famous for its delicious bivalves since time immemorial. Full of salty character, Whitstable is criss-crossed by alleys once used by fishermen to reach the beach. Island Wall on the seafront has many 19th-century buildings and here, too, is *Favourite*, a rare surviving Whitstable Oyster Yawl. The maritime message is underlined at Starvation Point opposite the harbour – now a memorial to those lost at sea, fishermen once gathered here hoping for work.

The town is enjoying a renaissance and streets are packed with traditional shops like butchers and bakers (no candlestick makers), plus delis, galleries, craft shops and boutiques. The harbour with its sheltering walls and bobbing boats is all it should be, Tankerton Beach proudly flies a Blue Flag, and cliff-top Tankerton Slopes provide a relaxing vantage point from which to watch the nautical world go by. The Street is a shingle bank running out at right angles from the shore, revealed at low tide.

You may stay in Whitstable all day, but if you fancy cramming some more unusual sights into the outing a trip to Birchington could fit the bill – take the coast road past Herne Bay towards Margate and find it just before you get there. Why Birchington? It's home to Quex Museum, House and Gardens.

The Museum is...incredible. Assembled by a tireless Victorian hunter and collector, it features animals of the world in lifelike naturalistic settings, most of them mounted by the great taxidermist Rowland Hill. There is also a weapons collection and early porcelain display. Several rooms in the Regency Quex House are open to visitors, providing an added dimension to a Museum visit, as do inviting gardens. But it's still those glassy-eyed animals that count!

WHERE:
Kent
BEST TIME TO GO:
Off season – April to June or September to October – to avoid the crowds.
DON'T MISS:
The Three Towers Trail at Quex, a pleasant stroll around three of the estate's taller landmarks – the Round Tower, Clock Tower in the stable yard and Waterloo Tower with its extraordinary cast-iron spire.
AMOUNT OF WALKING:
Moderate
COST:
Reasonable – unless you buy a lot of oysters.
YOU SHOULD KNOW:
Beware of Squeeze Gut Alley in Whitstable, which most people have to turn sideways to get through – and some can't manage at all.

Sandwich

This charming former Cinque Port between Ramsgate and Deal has lost its once-mighty status – perhaps because it is now some way from the sea! But Sandwich still has great charm, retaining many ancient buildings within the town walls. Indeed, the conservation area is one of the best-preserved medieval quarters in England, with period houses arranged in a street plan that has changed little since the Domesday Book was written in 1086.

To get a feel for the place, follow the town wall – now mostly a raised bank that provides a walk around the historic centre with great views over a jumble of tiled roofs. Part of the route follows a dry moat, part a wet moat, and part a river. It consists of The Butts, Ropewalk, Millwall, Bulwarks and Town Wall. The Barbican and original Fisher Gate can be viewed from the Quay. It's no longer necessary to pay a toll to cross the Stour Bridge (though you may be delayed if it's swung open for river traffic). Find out about the town's history at the Elizabethan Guildhall, where it's possible to see the Mayor's Parlour and Ancient Court Room. A museum offers informative panels and artefacts dating back to the 13th century.

After seeing the town, cast the net wider. Gazen Salts Nature Reserve has woodland, waterways, reed beds and ponds adjacent to Canterbury Road. Monks Wall Nature Reserve on Ramsgate Road has a bird observatory (permit required – free from the Guildhall). There's a good riverside walk from Sandwich Quay to Sandwich Bay (an alternative route will appeal to golfers, crossing the famous Royal St Georges Course). But the best outing is a riverboat trip from the Quay to the remains of Richborough Roman Fort (daily in summer, reduced service out of season). A great way to end the day!

WHERE:
Kent
BEST TIME TO GO:
April to September
DON'T MISS:
The White Mill at Sandwich – the sole survivor of many that once worked in the town, this all-white tower mill has now been restored as a folk and heritage museum.
AMOUNT OF WALKING:
Lots (those in wheelchairs should approach the Nature Reserves with care).
COST:
Reasonable
YOU SHOULD KNOW:
A high point in the history of Sandwich was a national triumph in 1255, when the first captive elephant to arrive in Britain was landed at the port – it was a gift to Henry III from French King Louis IX and ended up in Henry's menagerie at the Tower of London.

The giant cooling towers on the bay behind Richborough Roman Fort. The Romans landed here when they conquered Britain.

Coastal Castles

DEAL, WALMER AND DOVER

WHERE:
Kent
BEST TIME TO GO:
April to September
DON'T MISS:
The guided tour of a secret labyrinth of wartime tunnels beneath Dover's White Cliffs, complete with an audio-visual commentary that explains their important strategic role in World War II (limited numbers on a daily 'first come, first served' basis).
AMOUNT OF WALKING:
Lots
COST:
Reasonable
YOU SHOULD KNOW:
A museum at Walmer Castle includes the chair in which the Duke of Wellington died in 1852 during his tenure as Lord Warden of the Cinque Ports – also an original pair of 'wellies', the Duke's Spartan campaign bed and many other personal effects.

The importance of historic ports along the Kent and Sussex coast may be judged by looking at great castles built to defend them. Despite having two, it's hard to believe that the quiet seaside community of Deal was once the country's busiest port, at the spot where Julius Caesar stepped ashore after coming and seeing, but before conquering.

The town has some quaint streets and ancient houses, but its former importance only becomes clear upon visiting Deal Castle – one of the so-called Device Forts built from 1539 to 1544 to defend against Catholic invasion after Henry VIII's spat with the Church of Rome. It's shaped like a Tudor Rose, with a low keep at the centre of six rounded bastions, the whole surrounded by a moat. Whilst there have been alterations, the massive character of the Tudor original is still awe-inspiring.

A walk along the beachfront will take you to the next link in Henry VIII's defensive chain – Walmer Castle on Deal's southern outskirts. This has been upgraded into a fine residence over the centuries, home to Lords Warden of the Cinque Ports since 1704. There is also a splendid garden (named after the Queen's mother) to enjoy after touring the impressive castle. It was also the place where the Duke of Wellington died and his rather macabre death mask is on show; this is where Queen Victoria spent her honeymoon with Albert and it has the first French window in England.

Unlike Deal, Dover hasn't become a shrinking violet over time, and its giant of a Castle atop the White Cliffs displays the fascinating evolution of Britain's shore defences right into the 20th century. No fortress in England has a longer history than Dover Castle – starting with one of Europe's best-preserved Roman lighthouses, and continuing through the 1216 siege to complex defence systems evolved during two World Wars. This 12th-century structure is massively impressive, with the dominant keep (royal accommodation on the second floor) having spectacular views over the English Channel to France. These were used to their full extent during WWII. The castle issued the first early warnings of attack from German air power and it houses extensive relics of the Second World War. The lookout points and underground communication tunnels (built deep within Dover's White Cliffs) are open to the public.

This really is the ultimate castle experience.

The great Dover Castle towers over the port of Dover and is an impressive greeting for visitors from the continent.

Romney Marsh

WHERE:
Kent
BEST TIME TO GO:
Any time (restricted winter service on the RHD Railway).
DON'T MISS:
Feeding time at Port Lympne's 'Palace of the Apes', the world's largest 'gorillarium' (12 noon and 15.00 daily).
AMOUNT OF WALKING:
Lots
COST:
Reasonable
YOU SHOULD KNOW:
Yes, Romney Marsh really was a haunt of smugglers in days gone by – and the villages of Lympne and Aldington were favourite vantage points from which to watch for prowling Excisemen.

The very name conjures up dark nights, smugglers and mysterious eddying mist – and indeed Romney Marsh is one of England's most atmospheric landscapes. This unique area south of Ashford is served by a maze of narrow roads that criss-cross flat land with few signposts and little regard for logic, connecting settlements with quaint names like Hamstreet, Botolph's Bridge and Donkey Street.

To explore this special place, drive south from Ashford to New Romney, then head for St Mary in the Marsh and look for Newchurch, Burmarsh and Dymchurch. When you get lost, enjoy the scenery and wait until you arrive somewhere you recognize on the map.

If that's Dymchurch, take the coast road towards Hythe, turning inland to find Lympne on former sea cliffs above the Marsh. The picturesque village dates back to Roman times, when it was on the sea. There is a castle (not open to the public), fine medieval church and wonderful Marsh and sea views.

Port Lympne Wild Animal Park is a 'must' for those who love

seeing exotic animals running free in areas representing natural habitat. The Park is set in 250 hectares (618 acres) that include an opulent mansion once owned by Siegfried Sassoon, with landscaped gardens that have magnificent views over the channel. You can even stay overnight! See the largest breeding herd of black rhinos outside Africa, Siberian and Indian tigers, Barbary lions and many more endangered species.

Those who prefer live steam to live animals will relish a trip on the Romney, Hythe and Dymchurch Railway. This delightful miniature railway runs on 38 cm (15 in) tracks over a distance of 22 km (13.5 mi) from the picturesque Cinque Port of Hythe to the bleak tip of Dungeness (where there is a friendly café, an anceint lighthouse and the nuclear power station looms over all) via Dymchurch, St Mary's Bay, New Romney and Romney Sands. The eleven pre-war steam locomotives are now supported by a couple of diddy diesels. Still used everyday, it's a scenic ride like no other!

At Dungeness, old fishermen's huts have been converted into trendy homes. Prospect Cottage (below) was once the home of the late filmmaker Derek Jarman and has a magical garden – part of which can be seen here with the nuclear power station in the background.

Rye

CAMBER SANDS AND CAMBER CASTLE

WHERE:
East Sussex
BEST TIME TO GO:
April to October
DON'T MISS:
The National Trust's Lamb House in West Street, a fine 18th-century residence in Rye that was once the home of American novelist Henry James – some of his possessions can be seen and there is a pleasant walled garden (open on Thursdays and Saturdays).
AMOUNT OF WALKING:
Lots (wheelchair use in the Camber sand dunes is not recommended and Camber Castle should be viewed from afar).
COST:
Low
YOU SHOULD KNOW:
When trade dried up along with the harbour, smuggling became a major activity in and around Rye – the notoriously violent 18th-century Hawkhurst Gang used to meet in the Mermaid Inn in the town, openly carrying weapons.

Often described as a Cinque Port (it wasn't actually one of the original five, though closely associated), Rye was nonetheless an important port – suffering mightily when the sea destroyed part of the town in 1375. Subsequently, the anchorage silted up leaving Rye high and very nearly dry. Today it only has a river harbour outside town for fishing boats and pleasure craft.

Perched on a hill overlooking Romney Marsh and the River Rother, this ancient town has cobbled streets, an old church and preserved buildings from medieval, Tudor and Georgian times. Almost suspended in time, it has an atmosphere that entices visitors drawn by old-fashioned charm. The Heritage Centre on Strand Quay gives an ideal introduction with its Rye Town Model, whilst the Tourist Information Centre in the Old Sail Loft suggests see-it-all town walks.

One highlight is Rye Castle Museum. The Ypres Tower built in 1250 was part of Rye's defences and contains interesting artefacts, a relief map showing coastline changes and an exhibition charting the life of a medieval soldier. It's hard to believe now, but the lofty Tower overlooks what was once one of England's busiest harbours. The East Street museum site is a storehouse of local memorabilia, including Rye's 18th-century fire engine.

When you've finished exploring the town (though perfectly formed, it's small), go down to nearby Camber Sands for beach action or a wander through scenic dunes. Then head out of Rye on towards Winchelsea and find Camber Castle. Built by Henry VIII to protect the then-vast Rye anchorage, this mighty fortress became redundant as the coast retreated, so was never updated. After a pleasant walk across flat fields, it's hard to imagine that the sea once lapped those massive walls. The interior may be visited in the afternoon on summer weekends.

A winter walk on the sands at Camber

Bodiam Castle and Great Dixter

Dozens of English castles vie for the title 'finest of its type', but Bodiam Castle definitely takes all ten points in the late-medieval-moated category. This quadrangular castle was built in 1385, more to impress Richard II than as a true defence against French invasion. It saw no action until slighted (rendered indefensible) by Parliamentary forces in the Civil War.

Bodiam Castle embodies everyone's idea of how a castle should look.

Surrounded by a wide moat, it has a massive round tower at each corner and square towers in the side walls. Within the walls may be found a range of grand (but sadly ruined) domestic buildings, including a Great Hall. The chapel is in one corner tower, the well in another and a rare original portcullis survives in the gatehouse. There are spiral staircases to climb and great views of the scenic Rother Valley from the towers. Bodiam is just south of Hawkhurst, off the B2244.

Spend the afternoon at another magical place. From Bodiam to Great Dixter is not far as the crow flies but slightly longer by road. This charming 15th-century manor house has one of England's most renowned gardens. Sir Edwin Lutyens renovated and extended the near-derelict house before World War 1 (looking at the front, everything to the right is original, everything to the left was built around 1910).

Great Dixter's extension blended seamlessly partly because much of it was based on a transplanted medieval Wealden house. Within, see the original Great Hall, the old Parlour and Solar. But (though you might never know it) the Waiting and Yeoman's Halls were Lutyens creations. The fabulous gardens, also designed by Lutyens, are largely the work of the late Christopher Lloyd; they surround the house, so that views of the old manor enhance the stunning garden experience at every turn. In a word (or three) – must be seen!

WHERE:
East Sussex
BEST TIME TO GO:
April to October
DON'T MISS:
The inscription on a beam in the Parlour at Great Dixter: JOHN HARRISON DWELT ATT DIXTERN XXXVI YEARS AN VI MONTHES. CAME YE FERST OF ELISABETHE RAIN.
AMOUNT OF WALKING:
Moderate
COST:
Reasonable
YOU SHOULD KNOW:
Look at the east front of Great Dixter from the garden's Long Border and spot the small window on a different level from others – a typical Lutyens touch, it's a floor-level nursery window that would allow a small child who could not reach a conventional window to look out.

All aboard Thomas the Tank Engine at the Bluebell Railway!

Sheffield Park and the Bluebell Railway

How the mighty are fallen – and resurrected. Sheffield Park House (off the A275 road near Haywards Heath) was a typically ambitious 18th-century creation – James Wyatt remodelled the medieval house in Gothic style and Capability Brown landscaped the park around new lakes. Subsequent owners further developed the park in the 19th and 20th centuries but World War II saw its downfall – the house was requisitioned for a Canadian armoured division and the park filled with huts. Post-war taxation finished the job, and the estate was broken up and sold in 1953.

Happily, the National Trust galloped to rescue the park, now restored as a tranquil landscape garden. Capability Brown's *pièce de résistance* remains – the landscaped garden with cascade and lakes and a profusion of year-round colour (the National Collection of Ghent azaleas is here). The actual parkland may only be seen if you take the guided tour.

Step out of the Sheffield Park Garden and onto the train – the heritage Bluebell Railway runs from Sheffield Park (as a result of originally being sponsored by the Earl of Sheffield) to Horsted Keynes and Kingscote (soon to be extended to East Grinstead and a connection to the national rail network). Despite becoming a top tourist attraction, the active volunteer-run Bluebell Railway has held true to its primary objective – the preservation for posterity of an English country branch line, complete with steam locomotives, rolling stock, signalling systems and stations.

Actually, there is a greater concentration of locos (over thirty) and rolling stock than anything a typical branch line would have ever seen, either working, awaiting restoration or on static display. There are special services like Victorian Trains, the Golden Arrow Pullman Dining Train, a Lounge Car Tea Service and various one-off events. Trains run every two hours from April to October, with a limited winter timetable.

WHERE:
East Sussex and West Sussex
BEST TIME TO GO:
April to October
DON'T MISS:
The journey through the 668-m (731-yd) Sharpthorne Tunnel on the Bluebell Line – the longest tunnel on a British heritage railway.
AMOUNT OF WALKING:
Moderate
COST:
Reasonable
YOU SHOULD KNOW:
1. Sheffield Park Garden was planted with spectacular autumn colour in mind (especially with black tupelo trees) –– and the Bluebell Line runs 'Autumn Foliage' specials.
2. Thomas the Tank Engine does not run on the Bluebell Railway all the time, so be sure to check when his next visit is to avoid disappointment.

South Downs Drive

A crowning glory of the Sussex countryside is the sparsely populated chalk uplands of the South Downs. This delightful day out is around the eastern end at Beachy Head. Start at Lewes and take the back road to Rodmell, where the Monk's House was the country home of novelist Virginia Woolf and husband Leonard. He buried her ashes in the garden after she drowned herself in 1941. The Monk's House is open on Wednesdays and Saturdays.

Continue through Newhaven and Seaford to Cuckmere Haven. The Haven's meandering river and flood plain are made for long walks – more sedentary types can simply enjoy the beach and sweeping views beneath the famous Seven Sisters white cliffs.

Drive up beside the Cuckmere River to Wilmington, pausing to admire the Long Man on the slope of Windover Hill. See also a 12th-century parish church and ruined priory. A left turn along the A27 road then takes you to Charleston Farmhouse, between Firle and Selmeston.

This mellow old house salutes the famous Bloomsbury Group. In 1916 it became home to artist Vanessa Bell (Virginia Woolf's sister), her two children, lover Duncan Grant and writer David Garnett (joined by Vanessa's husband Clive in 1939). Regular visitors included the Woolfs, Lytton Strachey, John Maynard Keynes, T.S. Eliot and E.M. Forster, and the house was exuberantly decorated by the occupants. When Grant died in 1978 a trust was formed to preserve the Bloomsbury legacy for posterity. Charleston is open from Wednesday to Sunday.

Across the main road, climb to Upper Dicker and complete the tour at Michelham Priory, on the site of a former Augustine foundation of 1229. Contained within England's longest moat, the Priory is a beautiful house with historic exhibits, beautiful gardens, art exhibitions, watermill, great barn, forge and rope museum. Open every day except Monday.

Detail of an overmantel by Duncan Grant in the Garden Room at Charlestone Farmhouse

WHERE:
East Sussex
BEST TIME TO GO:
April to October
DON'T MISS:
A short detour from Cuckmere Haven to the Countryside Centre atop Beachy Head, with stunning views and the Downland Experience, a static walk through the history of the South Downs (it's free!).
AMOUNT OF WALKING:
Moderate
COST:
Reasonable
YOU SHOULD KNOW:
It is said that when the Reverend W. de St Croix marked out the outline of the overgrown Long Man at Wilmington in 1874, he discreetly removed the genitalia that are all too apparent on England's other only chalk man, the Cerne Abbas Giant!

Brighton

The fishing village of Brighthelmstone took off as Brighton when the Prince Regent gave the thumbs up in the late 18th century, subsequently building the Royal Pavilion. This not-so-discreet bolthole was where 'Prinny' took seawater for his gout and also took Mistress Fitzherbert. The extraordinary Indian design was by John Nash.

Don't visit Brighton hoping for peace and quiet. This vibrant city lies at the heart of a sprawling coastal conurbation and is full of roistering young people, pubs, trendy shops, restaurants and entertainment facilities. Though the shingle beach gets busy when the sun shines, Brighton is the place where Londoners go for a lively seaside day out. Many of them head straight to The Lanes, once the haunt of disreputable antique dealers but now full of fashionable emporia.

There are plenty of fine Regency terraces in town, supplemented by the results of a Victorian building boom that followed the railway's arrival. Notable Victorian structures are The Grand Hotel and Brighton Pier (formerly Palace Pier before it became the one-and-only), featuring arcades, restaurants and a funfair. The West Pier burned in 2003, and plans to replace it with the futuristic i360 observation tower have been approved. The world's oldest operating electric railway is Volk's Electric Railway along the seafront from Brighton Pier to Black Rock.

Everyone should see Brighton at least once, but if an antidote to jostling city crowds is required it may be found close at hand. The South Downs crown the ribbon development along the Sussex shore, proving a peaceful contrast to the bustle below. Just up the A23 road from Brighton, a right turn will take you to Clayton and Ditchling. The attraction here is Ditchling Beacon, the highest point in East Sussex with wonderful views – the walk will soon blow away those city blues!

Brighton is one of the busiest seaside towns in Britain.

Arundel

England's leading Catholic family, the Howards (Dukes of Norfolk and Earls of Arundel) don't live in Norfolk, but above the lovely market town of Arundel on the Sussex Downs – 'above' because they occupy the massive medieval castle that dominates the place. What's more, their religion explains the town's other great structure, Arundel Cathedral. After Catholic worship again became legal in England, the 15th Duke commissioned a magnificent parish church with enough 'oomph' to counterbalance the Castle, and the resultant French Gothic masterpiece (part dedicated to St Philip Howard, canonized 20th Earl of Arundel) was more than worthy of subsequent elevation to cathedral status.

The Castle dates back to the 11th century, with modernization in the 18th and 19th centuries (the latter in anticipation of a hugely successful royal visit by Prince Albert and Queen Victoria). It's one of the most impressive treasure houses in Europe and visitors can only marvel at the stunning quality of rooms filled with great paintings and furniture, clocks and china, stained glass and tapestries, sculpture and carving, heraldry and armour. Other attractions include the keep, early Fitzalan Chapel, gardens and grounds. The Castle is not open on Mondays (except Bank Holidays).

After seeing the Castle and Cathedral and exploring the town and banks of the River Arun, allow half a day to visit the Amberley Working Museum, north of Arundel. The open-air site next to Amberley Station is dedicated to local industrial and commercial heritage, with particular emphasis on transport and communications. Among attractions too numerous to list is a large collection of operating Southdown buses and all sorts of transplanted buildings like a brewery, laundry, cobbler's shop, print shop, fire station, pump house, 1930s roadside café, village garage and rural telephone exchange.

WHERE:
West Sussex
BEST TIME TO GO:
April to October
DON'T MISS:
The working railway and railway exhibition hall at Amberley, with over 30 locomotives and some 80 pieces of rolling stock celebrating Britain's numerous industrial narrow-gauge railways.
AMOUNT OF WALKING:
Lots
COST:
Reasonable
YOU SHOULD KNOW:
A prayer book and rosary beads at Arundel Castle belonged to Mary, Queen of Scots – the Fourth Duke of Norfolk was beheaded in 1572 for not-so-secretly plotting to marry her.

Arundel Castle stands on the bank of the River Arun.

Parham and Petworth

WHERE:
West Sussex
BEST TIME TO GO:
April to September
DON'T MISS:
The Cottage Museum at 346
Petworth High Street, furnished as it
would have been in 1910 when the
occupant was Mrs Mary Cummings,
a seamstress at Petworth House –
see her cottage garden, scullery,
living room, bedroom, workroom,
attic and cellar.
AMOUNT OF WALKING:
Lots (not mandatory!)
COST:
Reasonable
YOU SHOULD KNOW:
The dappled fallow deer in the
grounds of Parham Park are direct
descendents of a herd first
mentioned in the house's records in
1628, and Petworth has Britain's
largest herd of fallow deer.

There are two splendid country houses on the South Downs, not far from each other, together offering a wonderful day out for those who appreciate that unique combination of the best of English historic architecture, contents showing refined taste over the centuries and (last but not least) impressive gardens.

Parham Park is an Elizabethan house near Storrington that has been a family home since the foundation stone was laid in 1577. A son of Viscount Cowdray purchased Parham in 1922 and embarked on an extended programme to restore this lovely house and fill it with old furniture, paintings and early textiles, whenever possible acquiring items historically associated with the house. Outside may be found an award-winning romantic walled garden, pleasure grounds and a lake, set within an ancient deer park.

Just up the road, Petworth House and Park is an altogether grander house with an even larger deer park. It was rebuilt around 1670 and altered in Victorian times, though the 13th-century undercroft and chapel of the earlier house survive. The house contains a superb collection of paintings (The National Trust's largest, augmented by family pictures and gallery loans), carvings by Grinling Gibbons, classical sculptures – plus fascinating kitchens and service rooms. Petworth has a large woodland garden known as the Pleasure Ground and a deer park landscaped by Capability Brown and made famous by appearing in numerous paintings by that great English artist J.W.M. Turner, a frequent visitor.

The house at Parham Park is open on Wednesdays, Thursdays, Sundays and Bank Holiday Mondays (plus Tuesdays and Fridays in August). The gardens are open from Tuesday to Friday, on Sunday and Bank Holiday Mondays. Petworth is open daily from mid-March to early November, with the exception of Thursdays and Fridays, and on fewer days until late December.

The Grand Staircase in Petworth House showing the mural by Louis Laguerre of the Duchess of Somerset riding in a triumphal chariot. The statue is a copy of 'Silenus nursing the infant Bacchus'.

Goodwood House and Fishbourne Palace

Not everyone has a prestigious racecourse in their front garden – well, on their estate – but that's precisely what the Earl of March can boast. In fact, the Goodwood Estate Company is a commercial enterprise with a motor-racing circuit, golf course, airfield, hotel, farm shop, restaurants, health club and sporting members' club (amongst other ventures) adjoining the racecourse.

Find Goodwood House north of Chichester. It is an unusual and striking confection – an older house sits behind the great Regency State Apartments with pepper-pot towers built by James Wyatt that make up three sides of a planned octagon which was never completed. These grand rooms are open on most Sundays and Mondays from spring to autumn (more days in August) and it would be foolish to miss out – the interiors are mouth-watering, with one of Britain's finest picture collections, superb French furniture, Sèvres porcelain and priceless Gobelin tapestries showing scenes from the Don Quixote story made for King Louis XV of France, together making for sumptuous room settings.

After all that aristocratic luxury, Fishbourne Palace is very different, despite the name – though once equally prestigious. It is located in Fishbourne village, just west of Chichester. This extensive structure was built shortly after the Roman Conquest and then extended. There were four wings with colonnaded fronts and suites of rooms around courtyards – together enclosing a large square garden – a monumental entrance, assembly hall, ceremonial reception room, state rooms, gallery and private apartments. There was under-floor heating and up to fifty mosaic floors. A modern museum encloses visible remains of the north wing that include fabulous mosaics; part of the original garden has been replanted and there is a great collection of artefacts. The story of the Palace is told with the help of models and an audio-visual programme.

The mosaics at Fishbourne Palace were discovered by workmen laying a new water main in the 1960s.

WHERE:
West Sussex
BEST TIME TO GO:
April to October
DON'T MISS:
A highlight of the Goodwood House art collection – Canaletto's classic veduta (large cityscape) entitled *The River Thames from Richmond House*.
AMOUNT OF WALKING:
Moderate
COST:
Reasonable
YOU SHOULD KNOW:
To put things into perspective, Fishbourne Roman Palace has a floor area roughly similar to a more familiar structure – Buckingham Palace.

Weald & Downland Open-Air Museum

WEST DEAN GARDENS

The medieval village at the museum

There couldn't be a better setting for some fifty historic buildings dating from the 13th to the 19th centuries. The Weald & Downland Open-Air Museum is set in fabulous rolling countryside at Singleton, north of Chichester, and the best thing is not the fabulous collection of old country buildings (special though they may be) but the fact that they still exist. All are 'rescues' that would otherwise have been destroyed, coming together to provide a romantic reminder of the rural life that people like to look back on with affection, though in truth it was often harsh and demanding for the people who lived it.

Those days are long gone, while much built heritage has remained – and some of the vernacular buildings here are simply wonderful. Wander amongst them and marvel at the variety – a timber-framed farmhouse from Kent, hall house, recreated Tudor farm, cottages, Victorian school, Hampshire market hall, medieval shop, artisans' workshops, smithy, barns, granaries and all sorts of ancillary buildings.

But this isn't merely an impressive static display. Many interiors are furnished to show their original purpose and way of life, practical gardens replicate those created by country people over the centuries to meet their needs, a Tudor kitchen is used by cooks, the watermill works, traditional farm animals abound and demonstrations of rural skills add to a living experience. It isn't all ancient – the thoroughly modern timber Downland Gridshell contains the Museum's supporting collections.

After travelling back in time at the Museum, cross the main road and call in at West Dean Gardens – the Georgian mansion houses West Dean College, an arts-and-crafts school, but the gardens around the house are open and contain glasshouses and well-preserved Victorian walled gardens. There is also an arboretum and parkland in which to roam, enjoying wonderful Downland views.

North Hampshire Tour

Hampshire has wonderful countryside, unspoiled villages and fine old houses – and this is a day to see all those things. You may not cram everything in, but the attempt will be entertaining. Begin in Odiham, near Junction 5 on the M3 motorway. It has two notable structures – a ruined castle built by King John and a historic Pest House, where locals and travellers suffering from infectious diseases could be isolated.

From Odiham, go to neighbouring Greywell, a regular winner of 'best-kept village' contests. Continue to Upton Grey, where a restored Gertrude Jekyll garden may be seen at the Manor House by prior arrangement in summer. Take back roads via Mapledurwell to Old Basing and visit the remains of 16th-century Old Basing House after a riverside walk – it was once England's largest private house with 380 rooms (open Wednesday to Sunday).

Skirt Basingstoke to Sherborne St John, where The Vyne is a 16th-century house with contents assembled over four centuries and a Tudor chapel containing stunning Renaissance stained glass. The large park is made for walks, offering gardens, lake, meadows, woodland and wetlands (house closed on Thursdays and Fridays).

Take country roads through Monk Sherborne, Ramsdell and Wolverton to Kingsclere, from whence another back road leads to Burghclere and Sandham Memorial Chapel beneath Watership Down. It contains murals considered to be among artist Stanley Spencer's finest works, inspired by World War I experiences. From there, it's a short hop to Highclere Castle (open daily in July and August apart from Fridays and Saturdays). This superb Victorian mansion has truly amazing interiors and extensive parkland. End the tour at Whitchurch Silk Mill, down the A34 road – this splendid working watermill may be found on Frog Island in the famous River Test (open daily except Mondays). Hampshire? You'll want to move there!

WHERE:
Hampshire
BEST TIME TO GO:
April to September
DON'T MISS:
The Egyptian Exhibition at Highclere – the Fifth Lord Carnarvon financed the expedition that discovered the fabulous tomb of Boy King Tutankhamun and this tells the tale, complete with fascinating artefacts. Is there a Curse of the Mummy? Risk it...
AMOUNT OF WALKING:
Moderate
COST:
Reasonable
YOU SHOULD KNOW:
The veterinary profession has its genesis in The Odiham Agricultural Society, started at The George Inn in 1783 to encourage good agricultural practice and animal care – leading to the foundation of the Royal Veterinary College in London (1791).

The Saloon at Highclere Castle

Winchester AND ITS ENVIRONS

WHERE:
Hampshire
BEST TIME TO GO:
Any time
DON'T MISS:
The Winchester City Mill in Bridge
Street – it has been restored by the
National Trust and is again grinding
corn...there's a pretty island
garden, too.
AMOUNT OF WALKING:
Moderate
COST:
Reasonable
YOU SHOULD KNOW:
King Arthur's Round Table in
Winchester Castle Museum was
actually constructed in the 13th
century – and painted with the names
of Arthur's knights by order of King
Henry VIII, who obviously bought into
the whole chivalrous legend.

The ancient city of Winchester (once capital of Wessex and then England) has many fine buildings, but Winchester Cathedral is the place to start. It was originally completed in 1079, with additions over several centuries. Europe's longest cathedral has a wonderful Close. The Deanery dates back to the 1200s, Cheyney Court is a 15th-century structure incorporating the former priory gate and porter's lodge. The Pilgrims' Hall is England's earliest hammer-beamed building.

See also Wolvesey Castle and Palace, the ruined Norman Bishop's Palace, Winchester Castle's Great Hall (13th century, now a museum of city history), Winchester College (largely unchanged since 1382) and the Hospital of St Cross (almshouses and vast Norman chapel).

Winchester offers an absorbing morning, leaving the afternoon free for two prominent Hampshire citizens of yesteryear. Take the B3047 road through Kings Worthy, Abbots Worthy, Martyr Worthy,

Itchen Abbas and New Alresford, before joining the A31 and hurrying to Chawton for a date with Jane Austen. The pleasant red-brick house where she lived towards the end of her life (and wrote *Mansfield Park*, *Emma* and *Persuasion*) is a museum dedicated to the much-loved author. Don't look for her grave in the village – it's in Winchester Cathedral.

Go south on the B3006 to Selborne – immortalized by the writings of the Reverend Gilbert White, a pioneering naturalist who studied the village's flora and fauna minutely, detailing the results in letters published as *The Natural History and Antiquities of Selborne* in 1789. His substantial house, The Wakes, is now a museum dedicated to White and Captain 'Titus' Oates (of 'I am just going outside and may be some time' fame), who died gallantly after reaching the South Pole on Captain Scott's last expedition. The house is as White would have known it, and there are gardens and woodland walks.

The magnificent vaulted ceiling of Winchester Cathedral

Hampshire River Villages

This is a day for exploring the backbone of English rural life – country villages. Hampshire has plenty of special ones and is also renowned for beautiful rivers, so this tour combines both.

Upper Clatford is south of Andover in the River Anton valley, with thatched cottages and ancient All Saints Church. Neighbouring Goodworth Clatworth is also on the Anton (both villages have charming bridges). Walkers can ascend Bury Hill for sweeping valley views, or stroll in Harewood Forest.

Take the southbound A3057 road and turn left for Wherwell, down a hill with splendid views of the Test Valley. The village is a showpiece, with cottages clustered around the River Test, a gin-clear chalk stream – stand on the wooden footbridge and spot the brown trout that anglers will pay almost anything to pursue.

Across the river is Chilbolton, a picturesque collection of cottages and farmhouses, plus a 12th-century church. Return to the A3057 and a sharp right and left will take you to Longstock. This village would be the most delightful in Hampshire if there weren't numerous other contenders. A single street is lined with timber-framed period houses in pastel colours and the divided Test has circular thatched fishing huts.

Continue to Stockbridge with its wide main street and river bridge, headquarters of the angling fraternity. Walkers will appreciate the sweeping expanse of Stockbridge Down. Just up the road, the enchanting Wallops (Nether, Middle and Over) are strung along Wallop Brook. Nether Wallop has a mill and 14th-century church, whilst Over Wallop Church has a fine early font. Drive down the Wallop Brook to Broughton and Mottisfont in the Test Valley, where the 13th-century former priory of Mottisfont Abbey is set in glorious landscaped grounds. A wonderful way to end a day that has shown the English countryside at its very best.

The gardens at Mottisfont Abbey

WHERE:
Hampshire
BEST TIME TO GO:
Any time
DON'T MISS:
The National Collection of old-fashioned roses in the walled gardens at Mottisfont Abbey (best seen in May and June). Cultural types may prefer the unusual drawing room decorated by artist Rex Whistler.
AMOUNT OF WALKING:
Lots (if you want, but wheelchairs and pushchairs should not essay Bury Hill).
COST:
Low
YOU SHOULD KNOW:
Surprisingly, the Vikings had a facility at Longstock on the River Test for building and repairing ships, fully 24 km (15 mi) inland from Southampton Water.

New Forest Drive

The New Forest is a National Park that consists of heath, pasture and woodland that William the Conqueror declared should be a royal hunting ground in 1080. Much of this unique area remains Crown land, with verderers policing the ancient rights of commoners. A network of small roads allows you to explore wonderful countryside, taking Forest walks (spot abundant wildlife and the famous ponies) and stopping at pretty villages as the mood suggests.

A good circuit starts at the busy market town of Ringwood. Take the A338 road towards Salisbury, soon turning right for Moyles Court, a true Forest hamlet. Continue north through the Gorleys, Hungerford, Frogham, Blissford and Godshill to Breamore. This largely unspoiled village has Tudor cottages and an excellent Saxon church. Here (if open) you can visit Breamore House, a magnificent Elizabethan manor noted for fine paintings, plus a 'bygone life' Countryside Museum.

Go up to Downton and down to North Charford and Fritham, where a scattering of houses seems to underline the Forest's remoteness. Continue to Cadnam with an attractive thatched inn and broad common, then on to Minstead and its unusual 13th-century church. Drive on to Lyndhurst, the 'Capital of the Forest'. This lively large village has the New Forest Museum, with galleries featuring every aspect of local life and explaining Forest history.

Head past the much-photographed row of thatched cottages to Emery Down, before finding the hamlet of Swan Green that really does seem to belong to another era – in the Forest's heart, it has thatched Tudor cottages surrounding a village green and superb woodland walks. Take the main A35 road towards Christchurch through the Forest's heart, turning right across Markway Hill to the pleasant village of Burley, from whence it's a short drive back to the starting point at Ringwood.

AMOUNT OF WALKING:
Lots (optional, and those in wheelchairs and families with small children may get into difficulty if they venture far from the beaten track).
COST:
Low
YOU SHOULD KNOW:
Two of William the Conqueror's sons died violently in the New Forest – Prince Richard (mauled and killed by a stag in 1081) and William Rufus (King of England, mysteriously killed by an arrow on a hunting trip in 1100; the Rufus Stone near Minstead marks the spot).

Portsmouth

The once 'rough 'n tough' naval and port town of Portsmouth is busy revamping its image with developments like Spinnaker Tower (great views from the top) and surrounding Gunwharf Quays – a complex of shops, entertainment facilities and luxury apartments. But even here Pompey's maritime heritage is close by. There is a modern marina and Gunwharf Quays overlook the harbour.

This is the only British city on an island (Portsea) and its long history means there's much to see. An obvious starting point is the Royal Navy's Historic Dockyard, full of wonderful old buildings. Here you will explore Nelson's flagship HMS *Victory*, see the fascinating remains of Henry VIII's ill-fated *Mary Rose* and the amazing ironclad HMS *Warrior* dating from 1860. But there's much more.

The Royal Naval Museum tells the Senior Service story and has wonderful artefacts and permanent exhibitions, including Nelson memorabilia and the amazing walk-through Trafalgar Experience. The Dockyard Apprentice Exhibition reminds us that this place was the world's greatest industrial complex during the 18th and 19th centuries and features life here when mighty Dreadnought battleships were being constructed. Harbour cruises offer informative commentary and fabulous views.

The Dockyard has supporting shops and eateries, so it's tempting to spend a happy day there. However, the city does have other attractions. The D-Day Museum on Clarence Parade contains the magnificent Overlord Embroidery, conceived as a modern counterpart to the Bayeux Tapestry. It is a staggering 83 m (272 ft) long, graphically telling the tale of the 1944 Normandy Invasion with the help of an audio commentary. There are two cathedrals, an imposing Guildhall, Victorian-era forts on Portsdown Hill, the Royal Armouries Museum at Fort Nelson, Tudor Southsea Castle and seafront defences to the Round Tower, plus the extensive leisure facilities of a modern city. Pompey may come as a nice surprise!

HMS Victory – *the Flagship of Lord Nelson*

Beaulieu, Buckler's Hard and Exbury Gardens

WHERE:
Hampshire
BEST TIME TO GO:
March to October (Beaulieu is open all year).
DON'T MISS:
Bluebird – a star National Motor Museum exhibit, it is the jet car in which Donald Campbell broke the world land-speed record in 1964.
AMOUNT OF WALKING:
Little or lots
COST:
Reasonable
YOU SHOULD KNOW:
Exbury Gardens were created by perfectionist Lionel Nathan de Rothschild, who bought the estate in 1919 – a passionate gardener, he built a water tower and laid some 35 km (22 mi) of irrigation pipes to help implement his dream.

In the south-eastern corner of the New Forest is Beaulieu. Here may be found the threefold appeal of Palace House (home of the Montague family), the National Motor Museum and historic Beaulieu Abbey.

Palace House was the 13th-century Great Gatehouse of Beaulieu Abbey and is set in immaculate grounds overlooking the Beaulieu River. The house is maintained in the style of Victorian additions, though monastic origins are still obvious. The contents have been accumulated over centuries but the house retains the friendly atmosphere of a family home.

Beaulieu Abbey was founded in 1204 and badly damaged during Henry VIII's Dissolution of the Monasteries, but it remains an impressive place. Stroll through the Cloisters and herb garden and see a film and exhibition exploring the lives of the monks who once lived here. Then explore the extensive gardens.

Next stop is the world-famous National Motor Museum, showcasing over 250 vehicles representing every era of motoring. There is a reconstructed 1930s garage, a James Bond Experience, custom car display and a journey through motoring history. This can be supplemented by a monorail ride through the grounds, a veteran bus ride and go-karting.

If all that wasn't enough, Buckler's Hard is moments away. This picturesque waterside hamlet consists of Georgian terraces running down to the Beaulieu River. Navy ships used to be built here, but now there is a marina and small nautical museum.

Continuing the transport theme, Exbury Gardens are just across the river from Buckler's Hard. This well-known woodland wonderland contains a renowned collection of rhododendrons, azaleas and camellias. There are also many rare plants and trees. A great way to see the Gardens is to hop aboard the miniature steam railway, a circular line that follows a route containing a bridge, tunnel and causeway, travelling through a series of individual gardens.

The National Motor Museum at Beaulieu

Isle of Wight Day 1

OSBORNE HOUSE AND INLAND VILLAGE TOUR

The picturesque village of Godshill

With the coming of the railways, Victorians 'discovered' the Isle of Wight, building resorts that give the place enduring appeal for lovers of 19th-century architecture. But the island has extraordinary variety, with ever-changing scenery and each town or village offering something different.

The ferries dock at Yarmouth (from Lymington), Cowes (Southampton) or Fishbourne Creek (Portsmouth). Start at East Cowes with the ultimate Victorian experience – a visit to Osborne House, purchased by Prince Albert and Queen Victoria in 1845. Built in the style of an Italian villa to Prince Albert's designs, sweeping Solent views reminded him of the Bay of Naples. Victoria's favourite retreat has changed little since she died in 1901. Highly decorative interiors are complemented by beautiful gardens and grounds, with the Swiss Cottage, a museum, Victoria Fort and Albert Barracks – all designed to create a paradise for the royal children. Allow half a day to appreciate this fabulous place properly.

Don't be seduced by all those resorts and natural wonders around the coast. Instead, spend the afternoon seeing the island's beautiful interior. Drive down to Newport, then take the A3020 road south to Godshill, a lovely village on a steep hill with a fine old church and cluster of immaculate cottages. Continue via Chale Green to Shorwell – a pretty village that Queen Victoria loved to visit, where the 12th-century church has a famous early painting of St Christopher. Take the B3399 to picturesque Brightstone (good walks over Brightstone Down) and on to Mottistone with its romantic old buildings, including the National Trust's Mottistone Manor. End the village tour at Calbourne, a showpiece village noted for low stone cottages in Winkle Street, the watermill and Norman church.

The island's landscape has been described as 'England in miniature, as once it was' – and now you know why.

WHERE:
Isle of Wight
BEST TIME TO GO:
April to September
DON'T MISS:
Chessell Pottery Barns on the road from Mottistone to Calbourne – a working pottery with café and children's facilities amidst National Trust land at the unspoiled western end of the island.
AMOUNT OF WALKING:
Moderate (with the full traverse of Brightstone Down not suitable for wheelchairs or pushchairs).
COST:
Reasonable
YOU SHOULD KNOW:
Although magnificent Appuldurcombe House just south of Godshill is yet to be fully restored, it has grounds designed by Capability Brown, which make a perfect spot for a picnic.

The Needles chair lift at Alum Bay

Isle of Wight Day 2

HERITAGE TOUR

This is the day for some natural wonders and impressive heritage sites – usually rolled into one. That's certainly the way of it at the National Trust's Needles Old Battery outside Freshwater. This impressive Victorian gun emplacement is in a spectacular cliff-top location, with a tunnel through cliffs to a magnificent outlook above the famous marine stacks of the Needles, with views to Hampshire and Dorset. A nearby chair lift leads down to Alum Bay, source of all those little tubes of multicoloured sands.

From there, drive via Freshwater and Yarmouth (see Henry VIII's blockhouse guarding the harbour) to Newtown on scenic Newtown Bay. The heritage attraction here is the 17th-century Old Town Hall, a red-brick building with local history exhibits on the edge of a marshland nature reserve. Continue along the A3054 until a right turn for Carisbrook.

Carisbrook Castle, built in the 11th century, is well preserved and contains an excellent museum featuring historic aspects of island life. The Great Hall, Great Chamber and smaller rooms are open and there's a gatehouse, chapel, well house (with working donkey wheel) and ruined domestic buildings. Those who make the 71-step climb to the top of the keep will be rewarded with a splendid view.

From the Castle, drive south via Shorwell to Chale on the coast road. Turn left and see St Catherine's Point near Niton, the island's most southerly point. On a nearby hill is St Catherine's Oratory, a lighthouse built in 1323 with views to die for. Go on towards Ventnor and Bonchurch along one of the island's most interesting stretches of coastline – the Undercliff, where tumbling ground is covered by lush, semi-tropical vegetation. Continue through Shanklin and Sandown and finish the heritage tour at Brading Roman Villa with its lovely mosaics. There is more to see, but a day is not enough!

WHERE:
Isle of Wight
BEST TIME TO GO:
April to September
DON'T MISS:
Ventnor Botanic Garden, containing a worldwide selection of trees and shrubs organized by region, encouraged by the warm microclimate.
AMOUNT OF WALKING:
Lots (note there is limited wheelchair access to upper parts of Carisbrook Castle).
COST:
Reasonable
YOU SHOULD KNOW:
King Charles I was imprisoned in Carisbrook Castle for the last year of his life, and much Carolean memorabilia remains there.

130

Isle of Wight Day 3
EAST COAST ATTRACTIONS

The local economy has depended on tourism for a century and more and the Isle of Wight offers many attractions – old and new – designed to appeal to visitors galore. At the top of the list are resorts on the East Coast with their sandy beaches and traditional seaside features – Ryde, Bembridge, Sandown and Shanklin. But there are plenty of more modern possibilities awaiting those seeking a fun day out.

At Ryde, Seaview Wildlife Encounter offers interactive contact with Flamingo Park's free-roaming wildfowl, penguins, wallabies and parrots. There are flocks of flamingos, cheeky meerkats, pets corner and a tropical house with free-flying birds – all in a stunning setting overlooking the Solent.

Close to the seafront in Sandown is something that combines both old and new – Dinosaur Isle, a modern museum housing the island's extensive fossil collection and taking visitors back to the time when dinosaurs roamed. Displays include fossils, reconstructed skeletons, life-sized models and two animated dinosaurs. Nearby, the biggest collection of tigers in the UK is at the Isle of Wight Zoo, housed in an old fort on the coast.

The Rare Breeds and Waterfowl Park near Ventnor has a large collection of endangered farm animals and exotics from around the globe, including child-appeal deals like a guinea pig village, owls, miniature horses and more. The coastal setting is fabulous.

Further round the coast is Blackgang Chine, a family theme park set in Victorian gardens atop cliffs. It has attractions for youngsters (such as Crossbones, Nurseryland, Dinosaurland, Butterfly Walk, Fantasy Land, Crooked House, Jonah's Whale, Smugglers' Ship, Sleeping Beauty's Castle) and older kids (including Pirate Fort, Giant Maze, Water Gardens, Snakes and Ladders, Rumpus Mansion, Smugglers' Cave, Frontierland Cowboy Town, Myth and Legend). And that's without mentioning the Water Force Slide and Cliff Hanger roller coaster above sheer cliffs. What a climax!

WHERE:
Isle of Wight
BEST TIME TO GO:
April to September
DON'T MISS:
The Isle of Wight steam railway through lovely countryside from Wootton through Havenstreet and Ashley to Smallbrook Junction and a connection with Island Line's electric trains from Shanklin to Ryde Pier Head. The line utilises mainly Victorian locos and carriages that have always lived on the island.
AMOUNT OF WALKING:
Moderate
COST:
Expensive (if you do everything).
YOU SHOULD KNOW:
The Isle of Wight is the smallest county in England at high tide, but not when the tide goes out (when it becomes larger than Rutland).

Crossbones, a pirate themed adventure playground at Blackgang Chine

Waterbus to London Zoo

REGENT'S PARK

WHERE:
Central London
BEST TIME TO GO:
June to September. Mid-June to enjoy
Queen Mary's Rose Garden at
its best.
DON'T MISS:
Climbing to the top of Primrose Hill,
just across the road from London
Zoo, from where there is a superb
panoramic view of London and you
can pick out the landmarks all the
way to Canary Wharf.
AMOUNT OF WALKING:
Moderate
COST:
Expensive
YOU SHOULD KNOW:
If you take the canal boat from Little
Venice rather than Camden Lock, you
will get considerably more time on
board for your money and will
experience the dank, dark thrill of
Maida Hill tunnel.

The waterbus at Little Venice

For an especially memorable outing to London Zoo, take the waterbus along the Regent's Canal. Traditional narrow boats ply the canal between Camden Lock and Little Venice, stopping at a waterside stairway that leads into the middle of the zoo. You will see London from a completely different angle – a fascinating backwater view along the green fringes of Regent's Park, of period terraced houses, white stucco mansions and historic industrial buildings, catching glimpses of the golden dome of London's Central Mosque.

The zoo was set up in 1828, initially simply for research purposes. Twenty years later it opened to the public, becoming one of London's top tourist attractions. Changing attitudes in the 1980s led to a decline in visitor numbers and the zoo only narrowly survived by re-branding itself as an eco-aware, educational conservation centre. Today it has more than 750 species housed in a remarkable collection of buildings, many of them listed. Although you may find the caged animals faintly dispiriting, children are invariably thrilled at seeing the gorillas, bears and great cats; and nobody can fail to be impressed by the Blackburn Pavilion – a simulated rainforest with fifty different species of tropical birds flying around.

Leave the zoo by the Regent's Park exit to explore one of

London's largest and most beautiful green spaces. Watch a performance of *A Midsummer Night's Dream* at the famous Open Air Theatre; row a boat around the islands in the huge lake where wildfowl breed; stroll past extravagantly planted herbaceous borders and across picturesque bridges; feed the ornamental ducks; laze on the lawns by the bandstand listening to live music; watch an amateur soccer game on one of the sports pitches; and, whatever you do, make sure you see Queen Mary's Rose Garden, one of the best rose collections you will find anywhere.

Old Bailey

ST PAUL'S CATHEDRAL AND TATE MODERN

Some of London's most famous institutions, an eclectic mix of old and new, are within easy walking distance of each other so you can see an awful lot of culture in a day without expending very much effort.

Start at the Central Criminal Court. Better known as the Old Bailey, this rather awesome neo-baroque building stands on the site of the infamous Newgate Gaol, which deteriorated into such a pestilent hellhole that it had to be demolished in 1902. Look upwards to see the famous statue of Justice – scales in one hand, sword in the other – perched on the dome. Over the main entrance are the figures of Fortitude, the Recording Angel and Truth. All major criminal trials are held here, and if you enter one of the public galleries you will soon find yourself caught up in the proceedings, a riveting theatrical charade played out between judge, clerk and barristers in which centuries' old courtroom rituals are enacted with precision.

When you've had your fill of courtroom drama, step round the corner to St Paul's. This iconic 400 year-old building, generally reckoned to be Christopher Wren's masterpiece, is remarkably imposing in the worldly rather than religious sense, its gargantuan pillared dome dwarfing everything in the vicinity. Whether it is worth paying the hefty admission charge to gain access to the beautiful mosaics and be terrified by the dizzying views from its gallery heights depends very much upon the depth of your pocket.

Cross the river by the Millennium Bridge, a post-modern steel gangplank that connects St Paul's to another outsized building – the 'cathedral of art' that was once Bankside Power Station but has now been brilliantly converted to house Tate Modern. The largest modern art museum in the world, this is a really wonderful place to while away an afternoon wandering through the airy galleries and looking out over the river.

WHERE:
City of London/Central London
BEST TIME TO GO:
Any time
DON'T MISS:
The perfect picture postcard view across the Thames of the Embankment and St Paul's from Level 7 of Tate Modern.
AMOUNT OF WALKING:
Moderate
COST:
Low if you do not buy tickets for inside St Paul's or special exhibitions at the Tate. Otherwise expensive.
YOU SHOULD KNOW:
Wren's gravestone is in St Paul's Cathedral and translated from the Latin reads: 'If you seek his memorial look about you'.

The Millennium Bridge runs from Tate Modern to St Paul's Cathedral.

'The Old Lady of Threadneedle Street' – the Bank of England

Museum of London

BANK OF ENGLAND MUSEUM AND DENNIS SEVERS' HOUSE IN FOLGATE STREET

Inconspicuously tucked away among the brutalist towers and murky underpasses of the Barbican is one of London's best museums. The Museum of London is the world's largest urban history museum with impressive displays of the city's history, from the Stone Age to the present day. Here you can see the many layers of London's past unpeeled – from the Roman walls, the Great Fire and the Blitz to the great post-modern city of today. The temporary exhibitions, displays and lectures are especially highly regarded.

Hop on the Central Line for a couple of stops and surface at Bank. Here, in the heart of the City, you will find the 'Old Lady of Threadneedle Street' otherwise known as the Bank of England, the institution responsible for ensuring the nation's financial stability. The Bank's museum is surprisingly interesting. You step straight into a reconstruction of the 18th century banking hall and, amongst fabulous collections of silver and furniture, you can see gold ingots, old banknotes, printing equipment and calculating machines as well as learn about the story of money and how inflation happens.

Number 18 Folgate Street is an extraordinary work of art created by Dennis Severs. With the minutest attention to every detail, he transformed his Georgian terraced house in Spitalfields into a period set-piece inhabited by an imaginary family. You go from room to room in silence and by candlelight, seeing signs of the inhabitants everywhere but never actually bumping into them. Each of the ten rooms is a perfect re-creation of a distinct period in the 18th and 19th centuries so that by the end of your tour you are meant to have the illusion of having travelled through time as well as space. The motto of the house is *Aut visum aut non* – Either you see it or you don't.

WHERE:
City of London/Central London
BEST TIME TO GO:
Any time
DON'T MISS:
The brilliantly gilded Lord Mayor's Coach in the Museum of London.
AMOUNT OF WALKING:
Moderate if you use the tube.
COST:
Reasonable
YOU SHOULD KNOW:
Dennis Severs' House is only open Sundays and Mondays. Check exact times before you attempt to visit. It is a serious work of art and not really suitable for children.

Tower of London

ALL HALLOWS BY THE TOWER CHURCH AND THE LONDON DUNGEON

The Tower of London stands as a monumental testament to the story of England. This magnificent World Heritage complex of perfectly intact medieval fortified buildings, still patrolled by Beefeaters and ravens, contains nearly a millennium of history within its walls. It is best known for its ghoulish history as a place of incarceration, torture and execution, but when William the Conqueror began building it in 1078, he intended it merely as a fortified royal palace and later on it was often used for this innocuous purpose, as well as being the home of the Royal Menagerie, the forerunner of London Zoo. Go up into the Bloody Tower where Edward IV's sons, 'the princes in the tower' were murdered and Walter Raleigh was imprisoned; see Traitors' Gate, where prisoners were handed over to the turnkeys, and the spot on Tower Green where executions took place; and look at the collections of weaponry and armour in the Royal Armoury, and of course the Crown Jewels.

On a hill overlooking the Tower is All Hallows Church. It was here that the decapitated corpses of Thomas More and Archbishop Laud were brought from the execution block. It is not only the oldest consecrated site in the City of London but is, unusually, a fully-functioning place of worship open throughout the day. A church has existed here since AD 675 and you can see the original Saxon doorway. All Hallows miraculously survived the Great Fire but was bombed to bits in 1940. In 1948 it was rebuilt and although the post-war reconstruction is unremarkable, the interior furnishings are impressive; and for anyone interested in brass rubbing, it's a real delight.

Follow up a morning of serious history with some light-hearted masochistic entertainment. Just across the river is the London Dungeon where you can scare yourself among waxwork torture scenes, experience a Jack the Ripper stalking and flee from the Great Fire.

WHERE:
City of London/Central London
BEST TIME TO GO:
Any time
DON'T MISS:
The 15th-century and 16th-century wooden statues of saints in All Hallows.
AMOUNT OF WALKING:
Moderate
COST:
Expensive
YOU SHOULD KNOW:
Legend has it that if the ravens ever leave the Tower of London, the monarchy will fall. The nine ravens that live here have clipped wings so they can't fly away.

The White Tower – the main Keep of the Tower of London

Monument

ACROSS TOWER BRIDGE TO SOUTHWARK CATHEDRAL AND BOROUGH MARKET

The landmark of Monument was designed by Christopher Wren and Robert Hooke to commemorate the Great Fire of London in 1666. It is the tallest free-standing column in the world, 61 m (202 ft) high, topped by an urn, sprouting spiked bronze flames. A narrow spiral staircase of 311 steps leads to the top, from where there used to be a fabulous view, sadly now partially obscured by the surrounding mega-buildings.

From here it is a very pleasant short walk to Tower Bridge. Pass the old Billingsgate Fish Market and cut down a backstreet to the riverside where you will get a great side-on view of the stupendous battle cruiser, HMS *Belfast*. Tower Bridge, completed in 1894, is a marvel of Victorian engineering with magnificent views in all directions. If you want to climb to the high level walkways you must pay an admission fee, which also entitles you to a tour of the engine room, with films and exhibits to demonstrate the technology and history behind the bridge.

From the grandeur of the City, cross the Thames to be confronted by a world of roaring traffic and grimy streets. Turn immediately right along the riverside to London Bridge and you will soon stumble upon Southwark Cathedral, a beautifully preserved 13th century Augustinian priory incongruously hemmed in between railway arches and office blocks. Its churchyard is a welcome oasis of calm and there is always something going on inside with daily services, organ recitals and art exhibitions.

In the atmospheric maze of narrow streets under the railway arches next to the Cathedral you will find Borough Market, London's oldest and most prestigious food market. Independent traders sell everything from freshly baked patisserie to Orkney kippers, and there are loads of small bars and restaurants around Crown Square and along the riverside in which to chill out.

WHERE:
City of London/Central London
BEST TIME TO GO:
Any time
DON'T MISS:
The beautiful sculpted stone in Southwark Cathedral churchyard. It symbolizes the 'paths travelled through life' and is dedicated to a Mohegan (not to be confused with Mohican) Indian Chief who sailed from America to London in 1735 to petition King George II to return native lands stolen by British settlers in New England. His mission failed, he caught smallpox and died in London in 1736. In 2006 one of the last of the Mohegan elders came to witness Queen Elizabeth II inaugurate the sculpture in his honour.
AMOUNT OF WALKING:
Moderate
COST:
Reasonable if you are prepared to miss out on the Tower Bridge Exhibition and can restrain yourself in Borough Market, otherwise it could prove expensive.
YOU SHOULD KNOW:
Borough Market is only open for retail trade on Thursdays, Fridays and Saturdays.

Tower Bridge with HMS Belfast keeping guard.

Somerset House

LONDON TRANSPORT MUSEUM

Somerset House is one of the nation's great architectural treasures, a vast 18th century Palladian mansion covering the ground between the Strand and the Thames. It occupies the site where in the 16th century Edward Seymour, Lord Protector of King Edward VI, built a palace befitting his new station in life. It was one of the royal residences for many years but eventually fell into such a state of disrepair that in 1776 George III moved his court to Buckingham Palace and had it completely rebuilt. For years it housed government administrative offices, but in the 1990s it was completely refurbished to be opened to the public as an arts, crafts and cultural venue.

The Courtauld Institute art collection is housed here and there is an incredibly varied programme of exhibitions, events, lectures and art workshops for children and adults alike. The huge central courtyard, once a car park, has been brilliantly converted into the romantic Fountain Court. During the summer an array of fifty-five fountains emits dancing jets of water, and open-air concerts and film shows are held here; in winter it becomes an ice-rink, by far the best skating venue in London.

When you have had your fill of high culture, stroll up to the piazza at Covent Garden where, among the market stalls, shops and restaurants you will find the London Transport Museum in a Victorian iron building that once housed London's flower market.

The museum has recently been given a major facelift and it really is impressive. There is an eclectic assortment of vehicles on display, ranging from a sedan chair to the ubiquitous red bus, including early examples of trams and trolleybuses. Children and adults alike will have fun seeing how the first underground worked, driving a simulated tube train and playing the 'future generator' while small children can explore London in miniature in the transport of their choice.

*Enjoying the waterjets at
Somerset House.*

St Pancras Station

BRITISH LIBRARY THROUGH BLOOMSBURY TO SIR JOHN SOANE'S MUSEUM

For years the fairytale vaults and turrets and spires of St Pancras Chambers languished on the Euston Road, a neglected phantasm of Victorian Gothic, its grimy brick and stonework façade growing increasingly derelict.

Sir John Soane's Museum in Lincoln's Inn Fields

But the new Eurostar terminal has brought one of London's most romantic landmarks back to life. The famous Barlow train shed has been completely restored and extended, and the station is now the apotheosis of 21st century travel luxury with boutique shops, restaurants, an arts venue and even a farmers' market. Not least, it contains a 90-m (300-ft) long Champagne Bar open from 8.00 am for champagne breakfasts.

You may need the champagne sparkle in your eye to soften the shock of the red-brick brutalist architecture of the British Library, opened next to St Pancras in 1997. But go through the courtyard and you enter an inner world of calm spaciousness – a soothing contrast to the vibrant bustle of St Pancras. Here, in one of the world's greatest research libraries, is a vast global collection of books, journals, music and stamps. Wander through the wonderful exhibition galleries where, among many rare and beautiful manuscripts, you can see the Magna Carta, the Lindisfarne Gospels, the Buddhist Diamond Sutra – the world's oldest printed book, and the 14th century gold-lettered Sultan Baybar's Qur'an – one of the world's most significant Islamic manuscripts.

Stroll through the back streets of Bloomsbury, passing Coram's Fields and Charles Dickens' house in Doughty Street, to Lincoln's Inn Fields, the largest public square in London. Sir John Soane lived at number 13. The son of a bricklayer, Soane became an influential architect and art collector. He left his collection to posterity and you can wander through his house, seeing an amazingly eclectic selection of paintings, drawings and objets d'art. Once relatively unfrequented, Soane's museum has grown ever more popular, so at times it can be crowded.

WHERE:
Central London
BEST TIME TO GO:
Any time
DON'T MISS:
The statues in St Pancras – Martin Jennings's charming statue of John Betjeman on the main concourse. Betjeman's one-man campaign to preserve St Pancras saved it from demolition in the 1960s and the station pub is named after him; Paul Day's controversial outsize sculpture A Meeting Place, a 9 m (30 ft) bronze statue of a pair of lovers, criticised by some for overshadowing the famous St Pancras clock at the apex of the Barlow shed.
AMOUNT OF WALKING:
Moderate, with plenty of opportunities to stop and sit down.
COST:
Reasonable but it could be expensive if you hang about at the St Pancras Champagne Bar.
YOU SHOULD KNOW:
Anyone can apply for a reader's ticket to the British Library, as you can see from the motley people poring studiously over their books in the Reading Rooms. Among the archives, you can hear recordings of authors reading from their work and music recordings from Bach to The Beatles.

Christmas lights adorn Hamleys toy shop.

Hamleys Toy Shop

CHINATOWN AND MADAME TUSSAUDS

Hamleys of Regent Street, one of London's oldest shops, is a favourite West End tourist attraction. Founded by William Hamley in 1760, the shop has grown from modest beginnings in pokey Holborn premises to become what was until recently the largest toy shop in the world, occupying an entire seven-storey Regent Street building. Hamleys stocks an incredibly impressive variety of toys and games – there is nothing you can't find here. It is a delight to watch small children go goggle-eyed over the stupendous soft toy displays at the entrance, but after touring all seven floors they may well feel glutted and it will be time for a swift change of scene.

Off Shaftesbury Avenue you will see the pagoda arches of Chinatown. The first Chinese immigrants to London were 18th century sailors working for the East India Company who settled around Limehouse docks, but today's Chinatown emerged out of World War II. Enterprising Hong Kong migrants, attracted to the West End by low property prices, opened restaurants to satisfy the demand for oriental food among soldiers returned from the Far East. An area that once had a rather seedy ambience of drugs and prostitution has gradually been transformed into the cultural heart of Chinese London, a vibrant pedestrianized zone of exotic food shops, oriental herbalists and, of course, restaurants. A dim sum (Chinese fast food) meal here is good value and great fun – pick your dishes from circulating trolleys, whizzed round the tables by speedy waiting staff.

Take the tube from Piccadilly Circus to Baker Street and Madame Tussaud's. The most famous waxwork museum in the world was founded in 1835 by Marie Tussaud, an extraordinarily enterprising Frenchwoman who initially acquired fame by making wax death masks of victims of the French Revolution. You can meet perfect replicas of your favourite historical figures and celebrities and be scared witless in the Chamber of Horrors.

WHERE:
Central London
BEST TIME TO GO:
If you can face the crowds go in November or December to see the famous Regent Street Christmas lights and spectacular shop window displays; or time your visit to coincide with one of the dozen or so Chinatown festivals. The largest is the Chinese New Year parade in late January or early February.
DON'T MISS:
The Grade II-listed Tudor-Revival building and window displays of Liberty's on the corner of Great Marlborough Street, just up the road from Hamleys. The shop was founded in 1875 and became closely associated with Art Nouveau style.
AMOUNT OF WALKING:
Moderate
COST:
Expensive
YOU SHOULD KNOW:
Madame Tussaud's is such a popular attraction, that there are inevitably quite long queues. You can fast track your way in by booking tickets in advance online.

Trafalgar Square

NATIONAL GALLERY AND NATIONAL PORTRAIT GALLERY

Sooner or later, when out and about in London, you are bound to end up in Trafalgar Square. It has been a central meeting place since the Middle Ages when it was known as Charing, and later marked by a cross, the point from which all distances from London are measured. Designed in its present form by John Nash in the 1820s, it is famous for its fountains, pigeons and of course Nelson's Column.

On the north side is the National Gallery where the nation's art collection is held on behalf of the British public. All art lovers and students of art history will be in their element here. The gallery houses outstanding works by all the important European artists, dating from 1250 to the present day. Although not a particularly large collection by international standards, it is certainly one of the most impressive in terms of the quality of its paintings.

On the north-eastern corner of the square is the 18th century St Martin-in-the-Fields church where you can attend a free lunchtime concert. There are also regular evening candlelight recitals and jazz nights in the crypt. You can just walk in and listen to some music or go down to the crypt café, an atmospheric den in the nether regions of the church where you can get good substantial food at very reasonable prices.

You can spend an entertaining couple of hours at the National Portrait Gallery in St Martin's Place. You don't come here so much for the greatness of the paintings (although there are some wonderful works) as for the fascination of seeing famous (and infamous) people recorded for posterity, both before and after the invention of the camera. All the great characters from history as well as contemporary figures can be seen here. The Tudor Galleries are among the most interesting displays and the temporary exhibitions are particularly popular.

WHERE:
Central London
BEST TIME TO GO:
Any time
DON'T MISS:
The controversial sculpture 'A Conversation with Oscar Wilde' by Maggi Hambling in Adelaide Street behind St Martin-in-the-Fields. The only public monument to Wilde, it is a bronze sculpture of his head and arm, cigarette in hand, mounted at one end of a coffin-shaped granite block.
AMOUNT OF WALKING:
Moderate
COST:
Reasonable
YOU SHOULD KNOW:
Trafalgar Square is only a short walk from Somerset House in the Strand, which houses the Courtauld Collection, and the ICA (Institute of Contemporary Arts) in The Mall, where there is a continuous programme of avant-garde art, film and events.

The National Gallery looks on while children cool off in a Trafalgar Square fountain.

British Museum and Covent Garden

WHERE:
Central London
BEST TIME TO GO:
Any time
DON'T MISS:
The Egyptian mummies, the Elgin Marbles, the Sutton Hoo treasure and the Rosetta Stone in the British Museum.
AMOUNT OF WALKING:
Moderate
COST:
Reasonable, unless you are tempted by the shops in Covent Garden in which case it could become rather expensive.
YOU SHOULD KNOW:
The ongoing programme of evening films and lectures at the British Museum are excellent value, and it is always worth having a look to see what happens to be on.

The British Museum is a place to come back to time and again. It owns more than 6 million objects – treasures and antiquities from all over the world – and although they are not all on display, it is still far too much to even contemplate looking round all ninety galleries. It is a wonderful place to while-away a rainy day, and you invariably emerge with your interest awakened in some hitherto unknown aspect of human civilizations.

From its beginnings in 1753, when it was established to house more than 70,000 curiosities from the vast private collection of Sir Hans Sloane (of Sloane Square fame), the British Museum has grown to be one of the world's great museums of history and culture. Over the years many alterations have been made to the building, the latest one being the spectacular glass-roofed Queen Elizabeth II Great Court, designed by Norman Foster and opened in 2000. At its centre is the historic circular domed Reading Room, itself a superb example of Victorian design and technology. The Great Court is the largest covered public square in Europe, nearly 1 hectare (2 acres) in size.

The walk to Covent Garden is an interesting one. In the side streets behind Charing Cross Road, you will find an arcane selection of specialist antiquarian book, art and music shops. Covent Garden was designed by Inigo Jones in the 17th century as London's first planned public square. The area gradually degenerated from the height of respectability into a notorious red light district on the fringes of 'Theatreland'. When the fruit, flower and vegetable market was relocated to Nine Elms in 1973, Covent Garden was pedestrianized and the 19th century market building was converted into an attractive arts and crafts arcade. It is a delightful place to sit and have a drink, watching the world go by and being entertained by a myriad of street performers.

A street performer in Covent Garden

Palace of Westminster

WESTMINSTER ABBEY AND TATE BRITAIN

The Palace of Westminster, better known as the Houses of Parliament, is without doubt the greatest of all London's exceptionally fine Victorian buildings. As you stand in Parliament Square, gazing up at the Clock Tower listening to the chimes of Big Ben, you cannot help but be overawed by the 'Mother of Parliaments' and everything it represents. The palace stands on the site of the original Westminster Palace where from the 11th century the monarchy had its seat until a fire forced Henry VIII to evacuate to Whitehall. Again in 1834, fire swept through the palace, this time completely gutting it. It was rebuilt as a magnificent golden-coloured Gothic-Revival edifice, designed by Charles Barry and Augustus Pugin. It contains more than 1,000 rooms and took more than thirty years to complete.

Westminster Abbey is a World Heritage Site.

Tucked away to the side of Parliament Square, small in comparison with the neo-Gothic splendour of the Palace of Westminster, is the genuinely Gothic Westminster Abbey which boasts the largest nave in England. A church has stood here since the 10th century and the present 700 year-old building is a World Heritage Site for its outstanding medieval architecture. Ever since William the Conqueror, who chose to be crowned here in 1066, all coronations and royal funerals have taken place here. The Abbey is also the nation's mausoleum, where outstanding citizens are commemorated. More than 3,000 famous corpses are buried under the flagstones, including seventeen monarchs.

A short walk along Millbank takes you to Tate Britain, an imposing building on the site of the old Millbank prison, demolished in 1890. Here you can see the story of British art unfold through a wonderful collection of paintings dating from 1500 to the present day. This is where the Turner Prize contemporary art nominees have their work displayed every winter, and there are regular temporary exhibitions and events.

WHERE:
Central London
BEST TIME TO GO:
Any time
DON'T MISS:
The tombs of Elizabeth I and Mary, Queen of Scots in Westminster Abbey.
AMOUNT OF WALKING:
Moderate
COST:
Reasonable
YOU SHOULD KNOW:
If you want a free, guided tour of the Palace of Westminster and Big Ben or if you want to watch a debate in the House of Commons, you should check www.parliament.uk for information and access times.

Kensington Palace

Kensington Gardens

SLOANE STREET AND CHELSEA PHYSIC GARDEN

As you stroll down the Broad Walk of Kensington Gardens, you can easily imagine yourself to be in another century. This elegant inner city park with its long formal avenues lined with trees, beautifully planned flower beds and masses of open green space for dogs and children exudes a sense of tranquil timelessness.

Walk past the Diana Memorial Children's Playground and see the 900 year-old Elfin Oak. Go through the sunken garden and the Orangery at the back of Kensington Palace, originally the royal home of William and Mary, then walk around the Round Pond, and cut across the park to the Serpentine, where you can linger amongst the fountains and flower displays of the Italian Garden. Stroll past the Long Water and you will see the renowned statue of Peter Pan surrounded by fairies, rabbits and mice. At the Serpentine Gallery, one of London's most idiosyncratic small galleries, there is always some avant-garde exhibition on, with free entry; every summer a different artist is invited to create a bizarre new canopy for its pavilion café. Lastly, have a look at the Albert Memorial glinting in the sunlight, dazzlingly gold after its recent restoration.

Hop on a bus from Kensington Gore to Knightsbridge, then wander down Sloane Street amusing yourself window-shopping in one of London's chicest streets, stuffed with designer shops. From Sloane Square, make your way through the back streets to the Chelsea Physic Garden, by the Embankment. Established by the Society of Apothecaries in the 17th century, it is quite unlike any other botanic garden. Surrounded by high walls, its entrance gate secreted down a narrow side street, this mysterious garden exudes an aura of exotic romance. It is an especially wonderful place for anyone seriously interested in the properties of herbs and the history of plants.

WHERE:
West London
BEST TIME TO GO:
April to July to see the Chelsea Physic Garden beds and Kensington Gardens flower borders at their best. Kensington Gardens is also really spectacular from late September to the end of October when the leaves are turning colour and you can collect conkers.
DON'T MISS:
The 400-year-old olive tree in Chelsea Physic Garden.
AMOUNT OF WALKING:
Lots
COST:
Low
YOU SHOULD KNOW:
Sir Hans Sloane gave the Society of Apothecaries the land that the Chelsea Physic Garden stands on and appointed the great botanist Philip Miller as Head Gardener, with the mission of cultivating and studying plants for their therapeutic properties, a tradition that continues today.

'Albertopolis'

THE THREE GREAT MUSEUMS OF SOUTH KENSINGTON

The Victoria and Albert, Natural History and Science Museums are a legacy from the Great Exhibition of 1851. This had proved such a success with London's populace that Prince Albert, in a grand gesture of philanthropy, used the profits to buy all the land to the south of Kensington Gardens, with a view to creating a permanent cultural quarter. Out of this vision, which he did not live to see fulfilled, emerged the Royal Albert Hall, Imperial College, the Royal Colleges of Music and Art and the three great South Kensington museums. The area was somewhat satirically labelled 'Albertopolis', a name that later fell out of use but which has recently been revived.

Each of these world-class museums vies with the British Museum for interest, but perhaps the Natural History is best of all. It was in fact originally part of the British Museum, which had run out of space to display its ever-increasing number of specimens; the present gargantuan building was purpose-built in 1881. The V&A has galleries devoted to fashion, arts and crafts, photography, and treasures from every corner of the Empire as well as Islamic, Chinese and Japanese objets d'art. It houses the largest collection of Indian art outside India and the largest collection of Renaissance sculpture outside Italy. The Science Museum has over 300,000 exhibits, covering the entire history of western science, medicine and technology.

The museums attest to the Victorian obsession with collecting. It would be impossible nowadays to even begin to imagine the enormousness of the task of gathering together the countless specimens, objects and artefacts of every size, shape and material, natural and man-made that have been gathered here. You cannot hope to cover the contents in a single day so it is best to make a beeline for specific galleries and come back for more another time.

The Diplodocus skeleton greets you at The Natural History Museum.

WHERE:
West London
BEST TIME TO GO:
Any time
DON'T MISS:
The exquisitely painted ceiling of the Central Hall in the Natural History Museum.
AMOUNT OF WALKING:
Moderate
COST:
Low, unless you want to look round any of the temporary exhibitions; these are generally well worth the quite reasonable admission fee.
YOU SHOULD KNOW:
An easily locatable central meeting place is the V&A's museum café in the exquisitely decorated Morris, Gamble and Poynter Rooms at the back of the ground floor.

The Changing of the Guard

ST JAMES'S PARK, BUCKINGHAM PALACE AND THE QUEEN'S GALLERY

WHERE:
Central London
BEST TIME TO GO:
August and September if you want to see inside the palace (Buckingham Palace is closed to the public the rest of the year).
DON'T MISS:
The Royal Mews – south of the palace on Buckingham Palace Road are the cavalry stables and royal carriages. You can peek at the horses from the entrance but it is worth paying the entry fee to go in and see the royal carriages. The golden State Coach is pretty spectacular close up.
AMOUNT OF WALKING:
Moderate
COST:
Low
YOU SHOULD KNOW:
The Changing of the Guard (the sentries outside Buckingham Palace) takes place at 11.30 am every day April-July (except when it's raining) and alternate days September-March.

The Changing of the Guard

As the capital city of one of the last and most ancient monarchies in the world, wherever you turn, London is full of reminders of the royal presence. But it is still worth setting a day aside to revel in a bit of pomp and ceremony.

You can see the Changing of the Guard outside Buckingham Palace, but a far more dramatic (and frequent) display is given at Horseguards Parade where there is a full-blown swap of a mounted troop of horse-guards every morning at 11.00 am (Sundays at 10.00). When you have watched this colourful historic ritual, stroll across St James's Park to Buckingham Palace.

St James's is the oldest of London's royal parks, transformed from a swamp into a deer park by Henry VIII. It was later made into a garden by Charles II, who had a canal dug, introduced a pair of pelicans and opened it to the public. Unfortunately Birdcage Walk soon degenerated into a notorious hangout for lowlife, and only when Nash had redesigned the park as a lakeside landscape in the early 19th century did it become respectable again. Today the brilliant flower displays and exotic waterfowl – pelicans included, make St James's a soothing central London retreat.

Buckingham Palace may be big but cannot be described as beautiful. This ungainly building was once the Duke of Buckingham's London residence, acquired for the monarchy by George III in 1762 since when substantial additions have been made. There are 660 rooms of which nineteen state-rooms are open for viewing. Inside, it is all unbelievably grand with some priceless masterpieces on the walls. It is also worth visiting the Queen's Gallery on the south side of the Palace, where a changing selection of paintings from the Royal Collection are exhibited, and the Royal Mews stables to see the royal horses and carriages.

Portobello Road Market and Holland Park

Browsing the antiques on Portobello Road.

London's most famous street market sells everything from cabbages to candlesticks. What started as a fruit and vegetable market in the 19th century had by the mid-20th become famous for its antiques, and since then has gone on expanding to swallow up the flea market in Golborne Road, a distance of more than 2 km (1.3 mi). At the Notting Hill end you will find the more up-market antiques arcades and clothes stalls. These give way to the fruit and vegetable market, until by the time you reach the area under Westway you are caught up in a chaotic swirl of ethnic and vintage clothes, old CDs and costume jewellery.

The atmosphere of the market is quintessential London – an ebullient ethnic melting pot of cultures, creeds and styles, rich and poor, all rubbing along together for the sake of a common purpose: the making and spending of money. From the urbane antiques dealer in the arcade to the old Cockney totter selling cheap tobacco, there is nothing you cannot find here.

By mid-afternoon you may want to swap a crowded bar for a bit of open space. It is only a short walk to the alleyway off Holland Park Avenue leading up into Holland Park. One of the smaller London parks, what it lacks in size it makes up for in terms of atmosphere. You walk along peaceful woodland paths leading to the formal splendour of the Japanese Garden and the brilliantly coloured ordered beds. Peacocks, supposedly fenced in, are remarkably persistent escapees and it is not at all unusual to see one strutting his stuff round the café. The café itself, in the shade of huge trees, is a lovely place to sit and watch the world go by as the day draws to a close.

WHERE:
West London
BEST TIME TO GO:
April to October
DON'T MISS:
The Moroccan and Lebanese cafés and street food vendors in the Golborne Road flea market, at the northern end of Portobello. The food here is not only delicious but excellent value, compared to the rest of the market which gets pricier the nearer you are to Notting Hill.
AMOUNT OF WALKING:
Moderate but with lots of breathing space.
COST:
Low, unless you start buying…
YOU SHOULD KNOW:
Although Portobello Road is open every day of the week, the full complement of stalls is only here on Saturdays. If you prefer a slightly less frenetic pace, Fridays gives you, in some ways, a more authentic picture of the market and it's a lot less crowded.

A Stroll Along the South Bank

WHERE:
Central London
BEST TIME TO GO:
May to September. This is an outdoor experience for a sunny day. It can feel a bit bleak in the winter months.
DON'T MISS:
Christopher Wren's house – an inconspicuous little building next to the Globe Theatre with a view across the river to St Paul's; you can imagine the master architect gazing out of his window conjuring up a vision of what he wanted his cathedral to look like, then sitting down at his drawing board to make it happen.
AMOUNT OF WALKING:
Lots
COST:
Depends on you. You can have a wonderful day costing nothing at all but you could also make it really expensive.
YOU SHOULD KNOW:
You can take a London Eye and River Cruise, a circular tour between Westminster Bridge and Tower Bridge that takes 40 minutes – it's a really easy way of seeing the famous sights on both sides of the river.

The London Eye and City Hall

The South Bank is a really satisfying urban walk. It is also a really practical one – at any point you can just cross the nearest bridge to be back in the heart of London. From Westminster Bridge to Tower Bridge most of the walking is along the riverfront, passing some of London's best-known arts venues with superb views of the city's famous bridges and buildings. The whole area is buzzing with cafés, bars, market stalls, musicians, street artists and performers. You will find your attention constantly shifting from one iconic landmark to the next and by the time you reach Tower Bridge, or even if you only make it to Tate Modern, you will have seen an awful lot of London.

Cross the river at Lambeth Bridge to visit the Garden Museum at St Mary's Church, a quirky little museum dedicated to the history of gardening, then check out Lambeth Palace on your way to the London Eye. The Eye is not cheap, but it is worth every penny.

At Waterloo, you will pass the Southbank Centre. The maze of concrete walkways was once 'Cardboard City' – where the homeless sheltered until Southbank got a facelift in the 1990s. It is now a favourite haunt for skateboarders; watch them performing hair-raising stunts.

Gabriel's Wharf, once a row of run-down garages, has been converted into trendy craft shops and cafés and the Oxo Tower, originally a power station, is now a landmark building with a free public viewing gallery. So if you missed doing the Eye, take the lift here instead.

Most people have run out of steam by the time they reach the Globe Theatre, a faithful reconstruction of Shakespeare's playhouse, but the more energetic will find a lot more to see if they carry on to Tower Bridge; or stagger heroically all the way to Greenwich.

London Aquarium and Imperial War Museum

The imposing mass of the vast County Hall building, which stands on London's South Bank, opposite the Houses of Parliament, was built between 1911 and 1922. After being the headquarters of the Greater London Council for many years, it was sold privately in the early 1990s, and today is home to a variety of attractions, including the London Aquarium.

Ranged over three floors, the aquarium contains a series of tanks covering fourteen different zones, through which you can experience the rivers, lakes and oceans of the world. The two largest tanks, the Pacific and Atlantic zones, can be seen from every level, and contain a vast array of marine life. Altogether, more than 350 species can be found here – everything from sharks, piranha and jellyfish to the brightly coloured inhabitants of tropical coral reefs.

In comparison with some existing aquaria, this one seems a little tired, but new owners have come to the rescue, determined to make it their flagship attraction. With a strong breeding and research programme, drop-in talks and feeding displays, as well as an open tank where visitors can stroke friendly rays, this is an interesting and educational place to while away an hour or three.

Further south, in Lambeth, you'll find the Imperial War Museum, a really wonderful place. Opened in its present location in 1936, it collects and displays material covering every military operation involving Britain and the Commonwealth since 1914.

Here you can see tanks and planes, permanent exhibitions such as that of the Holocaust, and special exhibitions on many different subjects that change from time to time. There are paintings here, and memorabilia, weapons and military vehicles, a pleasant restaurant and a tempting shop. Even if the subject is anathema to you, this is one of London's supreme museums, worth visiting time and again.

Can you get any closer?

WHERE:
Central and South London
BEST TIME TO GO:
Any time, except 24th, 25th and 26th December.
DON'T MISS:
Watching the sharks being fed at the London Aquarium. Check on days and times in advance.
AMOUNT OF WALKING:
Moderate
COST:
Reasonable – the London Aquarium is expensive, but the Imperial War Museum is free to enter, although there may be a charge for certain exhibitions.
YOU SHOULD KNOW:
The Imperial War Museum is housed in what was the infamous Bethlem (Bedlam) Royal Hospital. Now located near Beckenham, Bethlem Hospital, together with the Maudsley, provides the foremost portfolio of mental health services in the country.

Spitalfields Market

Columbia Road Flower Market

SPITALFIELDS AND THE CITY OF LONDON

For anyone waking up jaded early on a Sunday morning a great way of brightening your mood is to spend the day in the City of London. Columbia Road flower market, in Shoreditch, starts at 8.00 am. It opened in 1869 as a covered food market; the original building was demolished in 1958 to make space for today's flower market, which takes place in this narrow, Victorian street.

Here you will find a vivid, thriving, hive of activity, with 52 plant stalls plus garden accessory shops and cafés. Vast bunches of gorgeous flowers can be bought quite inexpensively, especially if you turn up towards the end of the day, at about 1.00 pm. The scene is a mass of colour, the scent delicious – altogether a good start to the day.

Visit Spitalfields Market, for a totally different and equally worthwhile experience. Granted a license in 1638, it was consumed by the Great Fire of London in 1666. Remade in the 19th century as a wholesale fruit and vegetable market, it became a trendy, somewhat bohemian place in the 1990s. Art is sold here, but so is organic food, clothes and knick-knacks from around the world – Spitalfields is enormous and there will be something of interest for everyone. Check out the Nicholas Hawksmoor designed church across the road at the eastern end.

After lunch, take a stroll around the City. Full of historically and architecturally interesting buildings, you can climb up to the top of the Monument and visit churches built by Sir Christopher Wren. There are various suggested walks around the area, including guided tours, but you'll find plenty of fascinating places just by wandering about.

WHERE:
In and around the City of London
BEST TIME TO GO:
Any Sunday
preferably on a pleasant day.
DON'T MISS:
Lunch in a Bangladeshi restaurant in Brick Lane.
AMOUNT OF WALKING:
Lots
COST:
It's entirely up to you!
YOU SHOULD KNOW:
Jack the Ripper's second victim, Annie Chapman, was found in a back yard in Hanbury Street, Spitalfields, in September 1888.

Attend a Top Auction Sale

If you have never been to an auction sale, why not start at the top, and go to enjoy the action at one of London's three renowned auction houses: Christie's, Sotheby's or Bonham's? Held several times a week, throughout the year, experiencing a big sale can be an adrenaline rush, whether or not you have any direct interest in the matter.

All three of these major auction houses have one or more salerooms in central London. Established in 1793, Bonham's is the world's largest fine art and antiques auctioneer, and it remains in British hands. Christie's and Sotheby's also began during the 1700s, and now they all have offices and salerooms across the world, turning over billions of pounds annually.

If you can, go to the public viewing. Held in advance, it gives you the chance to look closely at the various lots for sale. Buy a catalogue too, so you can follow the bidding. The sales themselves are well attended. Everyone is seated in front of the auctioneer, who presents the lots and asks for bids. These come from around the room – there are often representatives of clients who can't be there in person taking direction by telephone, and it is also possible to bid online.

The tension is palpable, particularly when the stakes are high, and there can be great flurries of excitement when two or more people become caught up in the race to become the owner of a famous painting, or a collector's piece that they long to acquire. Be warned – don't wave at a friend you've just spotted across the room in case you find yourself the owner of something you don't want and can't afford!

WHERE:
Central London
BEST TIME TO GO:
Any time of year
DON'T MISS:
The public view – you might see something you have always wanted and become a participant.
AMOUNT OF WALKING:
Little
COST:
Low – unless you buy something.
YOU SHOULD KNOW:
Members of the public are able to attend most auctions, although a few are restricted. Check with the auction house you are planning to visit to find out what is on and to make sure you'll get in.

Be careful not to bid accidentally – no waving!

Wembley Stadium Tour

ARSENAL MUSEUM AND THE EMIRATES STADIUM

WHERE:
North London
BEST TIME TO GO:
Any time of year, but it is dependent on fixtures and closed during some bank holidays. Check in advance.
DON'T MISS:
The Bobby Moore statue at Wembley.
AMOUNT OF WALKING:
Moderate
COST:
Expensive
YOU SHOULD KNOW:
It is possible to book a special Arsenal Legends Tour, where a footballing hero from Arsenal's past escorts you on your tour and gives you an insider's view on what it is like to play here.

The great arch above Wembley Stadium can be seen for miles.

If you and your family are football crazy, you can have a fabulous day out visiting two of London's great stadiums, as well as enjoying the exciting, modernistic, newly re-vamped Arsenal Museum.

Wembley's history goes back a long way, but the stadium we see today is very new, having been completed in 2007, when the keys were formally handed to the Football Association. With its eye-catching arch, and 90,000-seat capacity – each one under cover – Wembley is the most expensive stadium ever built. Mainly used by the England team and for domestic football finals, it also hosts other sporting events and major rock concerts. It is an integral part of London's 2012 Summer Olympics plan.

During your tour, you will follow in the footsteps of some of the world's sporting and musical superstars, and get an idea of what it must feel like if you were doing this for real. You'll see the changing rooms, the warm-up area, the VIP reception zone and the Royal Box. You even get to walk through the tunnel, from which you have, no doubt, seen many of your heroes emerge.

Your next stop is Arsenal's new ground – the superb Emirates Stadium. Opened in 2006, this also functions as a conference facility and a music venue. The first gig, played here in May 2008, was Bruce Springsteen and the E Street Band. Tour the Director's Box, the changing rooms, walk down the player's tunnel, sit in the Manager's seat and visit the Press Conference room, before entering the museum where you will discover Arsenal's impressive history. See fascinating memorabilia donated by former players, watch films at the Legends Theatre and amuse yourself with interactive sections based on Arsenal's past. If you love football, you'll love this full-on day out.

Wimbledon

Traditional whites only please!

In the minds of many, the start of the Wimbledon Lawn Tennis Championships heralds the beginning of summer. For the next two weeks, the sound of tennis balls thwacked over the net, and the sight of players, all dressed in traditional whites, dominates our media. If you love tennis, and happily sit at home watching hours of play, imagine how exciting it would be to attend in person. You may not get quite such a good view, but you will find the atmosphere of the world's leading tennis tournament absolutely thrilling.

Originally a private club, the lawn tennis championship began in 1877, for men only – the ladies singles were inaugurated in 1884. In 1922 the grounds were moved to their present location, and by the 1950s many overseas players were competing. In 1968 professional players were admitted for the first time. Over the years, the venue has been upgraded, expanded and modernized, and currently the final stages of a long-term plan to ensure Wimbledon's place in the 21st century are being completed, including the erection of a retractable roof over Centre Court, which will enable major matches to be completed without the inevitable rain breaks.

Throughout most of the year it is possible to visit Wimbledon for a guided tour of the grounds and the museum, opened by the Duke of Kent in 2006. Here you can watch a fantastic, panoramic film that introduces the viewer to the science of the game, a collection of Wimbledon tennis fashions throughout its history, play with interactive new technologies and visit the courts, terraces and studios that are the background to some of the best tennis matches in the world.

WHERE:
South West London
BEST TIME TO GO:
During the Championships in June, or at any other time of year except 24th, 25th and 26th December and 1st January.
DON'T MISS:
The cleverly projected 'ghost' of John McEnroe giving you a tour of the re-created 1980s Gentlemen's Dressing Room.
AMOUNT OF WALKING:
Moderate
COST:
Tickets to the Championships are expensive, but the tour and the museum are reasonable.
YOU SHOULD KNOW:
In 1907 Thomas St Leger Goold, from County Cork, and a semi-finalist at Wimbledon in 1879, was accused of murder. Subsequently sentenced to life imprisonment and transported to Devil's Island penal colony, off the South American coast, he died a year later.

Maritime Greenwich

A day out to Maritime Greenwich is a day that everyone in the family will enjoy. Situated on the River Thames, Greenwich is a beautiful spot: the landscape and parkland is serene, with gorgeous views in every direction, and the architecture is spectacular. It is also home to several historic landmarks, of so much significance to Britain's magnificent maritime history and royal past that it was recognized as a UNESCO World Heritage Site in 1997.

It will make the day more fun if you travel there and back on different forms of transport and by different routes. You could, for example, take the Docklands Light Railway out, and a riverboat back, so you'd see two completely different aspects of London en route.

Start with the Greenwich Maritime Museum; established by an Act of Parliament in 1934, its collection of maritime art, manuscripts, maps and navigational instruments is the last word on Britain's seafaring history. The Old Naval College, close by, is a domed, architectural gem, built by Sir Christopher Wren. Inside you can visit the Painted Hall, possibly the finest dining hall in the world, decorated with paintings by James Thornhill. This is where Nelson's body lay in state after his death at the Battle of Trafalgar.

Another 'must visit' at Greenwich is the Royal Observatory. Founded in 1675 by Charles II, it has recently been upgraded and re-developed. This is the site of the Prime Meridian, the place from which everywhere on earth is measured, to the east or west of the line. If you stand with one foot on either side, you are standing in both of the world's hemispheres. The new, state of the art Planetarium runs a number of wonderful shows: inspiring and educational, there's even one for the under fives!

From the Observatory in Greenwich Park you have a great view of the Thames and London.

Thames Barrier

VISITOR CENTRE AND THE O2

WHERE:
South East London
BEST TIME TO GO:
Any time of year
DON'T MISS:
An intimate concert by a favourite
musician at indigO2.
AMOUNT OF WALKING:
Moderate
COST:
Thames Barrier Visitor Centre: low;
O2: probably expensive, though it
depends on what you choose to do
there.
YOU SHOULD KNOW:
With increased sea levels expected,
due to global warming, fears have
been raised regarding the 'life
expectancy' of the Thames Barrier. In
2005 a suggestion was made that a
second barrier should be
considered, possibly stretching from
Sheerness, Kent to Southend, Essex.

The Thames Barrier is not only extremely impressive to look at, but it is also an amazing piece of engineering construction. The world's biggest moveable flood barrier stretches for 520 m (1,716 ft) across the Thames, at Woolwich. Although it was completed in 1982, after eight years of building, it looks extremely futuristic, and is certainly worth a visit. The best view is probably from the river – there are several tours running to the Barrier. However, if you take the boat you will have to miss the Visitor Centre, and all that it can offer.

The idea of the Thames Barrier was first mooted in 1965. There had been some serious floods over the years, and after the devastation caused by flooding in 1953, it was realized that London should be protected. Since its inauguration, the barrier has been raised about 65 times. The Visitor Centre has good exhibits on the history of the river, and about what exactly could happen if and when the capital is inundated. Those interested in its construction will be able to learn everything they want to know.

Conveniently nearby, on dry land, stands the O2 entertainment centre, formerly known as the Millennium Dome. Built for the millennium celebrations, the Dome was the centre of heated political dispute, and by the end of 2001 it began to be transformed into an entertainment venue. It now contains many bars and restaurants on Entertainment Avenue, a 20,000-seat multi-purpose arena, which opened in 2007, a music club called indigO2, a wonderful exhibition space on two floors, built in a bubble, and an eleven-screen cinema complex, all using the latest technology and practising environmentally sound policies. Its owners were deeply disappointed not to win their bid for the country's first super casino, but still hope to achieve that aim in due course.

*The futuristic domes of the
Thames Barrier*

Hampton Court Palace

A visit to Hampton Court Palace, on the River Thames, is an exploration of British history. Originally a 14th century manor house and rebuilt as a palace by Cardinal Wolsey, it was confiscated by Henry VIII, who added the Great Hall and the Royal Tennis Court. Subsequent kings of England built new wings and revamped the interior but, during the 18th century, it finally ceased to be a royal residence. Queen Victoria opened Hampton Court to the public in 1838, and it has remained a major tourist attraction ever since.

A day spent here is both educational and fun. You can join a guided tour, or take an audio tour during your visit, to enhance the experience. Admire the Great Hall, the country's grandest medieval hall. Richly decorated with Tudor tapestries, it has a magnificent hammerbeam roof. Visit the Chapel Royal, or even attend a service here: the Chapel has been in use continuously for more than 450 years. You will see Henry VIII's State Apartments, and the Queen's Apartments, created for Mary, wife of William III. A highlight of your visit will be the astonishing Tudor kitchens, which were designed to produce meals for some 800 courtiers twice a day.

The buildings alone cover about 2.4 hectares (6 acres), but there are some 24 hectares (60 acres) of lovely, riverside gardens to be discovered too. You'll see the Great Fountain Garden, with its triangular shaped yews, the Privy Garden, laid out as it was originally designed in 1702, and the Pond Gardens, which are flower-, rather than fish-filled these days. The famous Great Vine, planted by Capability Brown in 1768, is thought to be the oldest in the world. Last but not least is The Maze, created in 1702. But beware – you can easily get lost in there.

WHERE:
The Borough of Richmond upon Thames
BEST TIME TO GO:
May to September for the best of the gardens.
DON'T MISS:
The superb collection of paintings.
AMOUNT OF WALKING:
Moderate
COST:
Reasonable
YOU SHOULD KNOW:
A list dating from Elizabeth I's reign shows that, during the course of one year, 1,240 oxen, 8,200 sheep, 2,330 deer, 760 calves, 1,870 pigs and 53 wild boars were cooked and eaten!

The gardens are as impressive as the Palace.

Kew Gardens

WHERE:
South West London
BEST TIME TO GO:
Any time of year is interesting, but summer is still the best.
DON'T MISS:
The Chinese Pagoda. Built by William Chambers in 1762, the ten octagonal stories reach 50 m (163 ft) in height. It makes a good rendezvous should any of your party become lost.
AMOUNT OF WALKING:
As much or as little as you want.
COST:
Reasonable if you spend all day here. Children under 17 are free if accompanied by an adult.
YOU SHOULD KNOW:
Kew Gardens is thought to have the largest compost heap in the world. Made from the waste from the stables of the Household Cavalry, and from the gardens themselves, the compost is occasionally auctioned to raise funds for Kew Gardens, although most of it is, of course, used right here.

Should you wake up on a sunny summer's day, with no particular plan in mind, go to Kew Gardens – you'll be glad you did. Originally Lord Capel of Tewkesbury's exotic garden, Kew was extended and expanded over the years until, in 1840 it was designated a national botanical garden. Today it is much more than simply a visitor attraction; it is a leading centre of botanical research and provides training for professional horticulturalists. It became a UNESCO World Heritage Site in 2003.

Set in 121 hectares (300 acres), Kew Gardens contains a number of wonderful conservatories, including the world famous Palm House, repository of every type of palm there is, and the vast Temperate House, the largest Victorian glasshouse in the world. The Princess of Wales Conservatory contains several collections, including carnivorous plants, cacti and orchids. If you're feeling chilly, don't miss the Waterlily House: hot and humid, it contains a large pond full of many different varieties.

The collections aside, Kew Gardens is also an arboretum with a huge variety of trees. A recently opened walkway enables visitors to walk 200 m (660 ft) into a woodland canopy. There is much here to amuse children, including Britain's first interactive botanical play zone, Climbers and Creepers, which is both educational and fun. If you feel lazy, hop on an environmentally friendly road train that, for a fee, will take you around the gardens. With several stops along the way, tickets are valid all day long.

Take a picnic or have lunch at the Orangery, but make sure to leave room for tea. Not far away, in Kew Road, you'll find the renowned Maids of Honour teashop, and here you must taste the eponymous pastries. Thought to have originated in Henry VIII's kitchens at Hampton Court, their recipe is a closely guarded secret.

The Palm House

Chislehurst Caves and Eltham Palace

First recorded in 1250, Chislehurst Caves are a complex of over 32 km (20 mi) of passages and caverns that were carved out over centuries in the search for chalk and flint. Last worked during the 1830s, the coming of the railway brought visitors, and by the early 1900s, concerts took place here.

During World War I the caves became part of the Woolwich Arsenal, and during World War II they were turned into an air raid shelter for some 15,000 souls. During the 1960s, gigs were held here, featuring bands such as Jimi Hendrix, the Rolling Stones and David Bowie.

Divided into 'Roman', 'Saxon' and 'Druid' areas, take a lamp-lit tour with a knowledgeable guide who will point out many interesting features, wall carvings, and the Cave Church, which served those who sheltered here from enemy bombs.

It is a short drive on the A208 from Chislehurst to Eltham Palace. Originally a royal palace, and used thus from the 14th to the 16th century, Henry VIII grew up here. In 1933, Sir Stephen and Lady Virginia Courtauld began restoring the Great Hall and built the house beside it. While the exterior echoes the older building, the interior is a magnificent creation of Art Deco, Swedish and 1930s glamorous ocean-liner-style design.

After revelling in this amazingly exotic house, with its fabulous entrance hall, dining room and vaulted bathroom, the Great Hall with its hammerbeam roof comes as a contrast. The gardens are gorgeous, and if you bring a picnic there are many perfect settings in which to enjoy it, though there is a tearoom to visit if you just want a snack. The audio tour and the Courtauld's home movie are fascinating, as is the exhibition that recognizes the forty years during which the Royal Army Educational Corps was based here.

The moat has been turned into gardens at the amazing Eltham Palace.

WHERE:
London's southern suburbs
BEST TIME TO GO:
Any time of year. Chislehurst Caves are closed on Monday and Tuesday except during school holidays, and Eltham Palace is closed from 22nd December until the end of January.
DON'T MISS:
The cage that was home to the Courtaulds' pet lemur, Mah-Jongg, which comes complete with central heating and wall murals.
AMOUNT OF WALKING:
Moderate
COST:
Reasonable
YOU SHOULD KNOW:
The Courtaulds returned their lease to the Crown in 1944, after living there for only eight years. Sadly, the newly restored Great Hall had suffered bomb damage during this period. Many films and TV programmes have been filmed here, including *I Capture the Castle*, *The Gathering Storm* and 'Antiques Roadshow'.

Epping Forest

Autumn in Epping Forest

London is well endowed with green spaces. Some are very central, and some, like Epping Forest, lie on the periphery. With Epping to the north and Forest Gate to the south, this is a vast area (2,400 hectares, almost 6,000 acres) of ancient woodland, heathland, grassy glades, rivers and ponds. Its age and range of wildlife habitats have secured its designation as a Site of Special Scientific Interest.

Made a royal forest by Henry III, both Henry VIII and Elizabeth I hunted here. Its status enabled commoners to graze livestock, gather food and wood but not to hunt. In 1878 an act was passed that undoubtedly saved Epping Forest for future generations, and today a conservation herd of English Longhorn cattle still graze an area of heathland.

The forest is renowned for its 50,000 plus ancient trees, including hornbeam, oak and beech. These are carefully conserved, as without care the crowns would become too heavy, causing the trees to split, fall and die. These old trees provide habitats for insects, moss, lichen and fungi. Indeed, the 1,200 species of fungi here make it one of the country's richest sites, although you must apply for a licence before you pick!

It's easy to spend a day in Epping Forest. The Visitor Centre is full of guides to the forest, and you can book special activities for children, horse riding licences and even tickets to the open-air theatre. There are walks to suit all comers, mountain bike trails and two Iron Age camps to be discovered. The forest is home to many species of bird. All three species of British woodpecker live here, and herons, Great Crested grebes and swans can be found on the many lakes and ponds. Frequently seen mammals include both Muntjac and Fallow deer.

WHERE:
North East London.
BEST TIME TO GO:
Any time of year
DON'T MISS:
Queen Elizabeth's Hunting Lodge in Chingford; built by Henry VIII in 1543 and renovated for Elizabeth I in 1589, it is now a museum.
AMOUNT OF WALKING:
Moderate or lots, depending on your energy levels.
COST:
Low
YOU SHOULD KNOW:
In 1882 Queen Victoria dedicated Epping Forest thus:'for the use and enjoyment of my people for all time'. It then ceased to be a royal forest and was placed under the management of the City of London Corporation, whose responsibility it remains.

160

Hampstead Heath and Kenwood

At 320 hectares (791 acres), the Heath, as it is commonly known, is north London's largest and oldest area of public parkland. A long, sandy ridge set on a band of clay, Hampstead Heath encompasses ancient woodlands, grassy hills and valleys, lakes and ponds, formal gardens and the smallest Site of Special Scientific Interest in the capital. Londoners come here to relax, walk, picnic and play, and hold this place dear.

The Heath comprises a number of specific areas: Parliament Hill Fields, to the southeast, has a number of sporting facilities, such as tennis courts and an athletics track. The highest point, busy with kite flyers, offers panoramic views across London, including Canary Wharf, St Paul's and the London Eye. Highgate Ponds are another big draw – thousands of people come here to swim in the open air each summer, and some hardy souls swim every day of the year. There are two single sex ponds, and one that is mixed, as well as a lido at Gospel Oak, to the south of Parliament Hill. Many organized sports can be played, ranging from cricket and croquet to cross-country running and petanque, and there are special events such as guided walks, the fun fair, and various entertainments for children.

To the north stands elegant Kenwood House. Rebuilt and furnished during the 18th century by Robert Adam for the first Earl of Mansfield, it is set amongst landscaped gardens, and contains a wealth of superb paintings by Reynolds, Gainsborough, Rembrandt, Turner and other major artists. The front lawn slopes down to a small lake that, during summer, is the site of several outdoor concerts. There can be few more delightful ways of ending a happy day spent on the Heath than listening to music in this bucolic setting.

WHERE:
North London
BEST TIME TO GO:
Any time of year, but a sunny day is generally best.
DON'T MISS:
Sculptures by Henry Moore and Barbara Hepworth.
AMOUNT OF WALKING:
Moderate, but as much as you choose.
COST:
Low
YOU SHOULD KNOW:
West Heath has long been popular with the gay community. The playwright Joe Orton used to frequent the area.

Kenwood House

A Day at the Races

WHERE:
The southern and western suburbs of London
BEST TIME TO GO:
Any time of year, but a sunny day makes all the difference.
DON'T MISS:
Placing at least one bet – it really does add an edge to the experience.
AMOUNT OF WALKING:
Moderate
COST:
Reasonable and, of course, low if you win and more expensive if you lose.
YOU SHOULD KNOW:
Tickets vary in price depending on the meeting. Entry to classic race meetings is expensive. Check to find out when and where you can go.

London is within easy reach of several racecourses: Ascot, Epsom, Kempton Park and Sandown Park, all of which are accessible by rail as well as road, and all of which are in beautiful locations.

Travelling by train is fun – you find yourself alongside a gaggle of punters, some of whom are newcomers and some obviously old hands – their sharp hats giving them away. The carriages are full of people avidly reading the racing pages, meeting friends and swapping tips – you never know, you might pick up the name of a long-odds winner right here.

At Kempton Park, the train deposits you right at the course; follow the stream of people leaving the train, and you'll find the way. After buying and studying a race-card, have a look around. Visit the paddock where you'll see the horses being shown, before they canter down to the starting post – you might spot one that takes your fancy. Bets can be placed at the Tote or with individual bookies, but of course you don't have to bet, it just makes things rather more exciting. Find a good spot where you can sit or stand to watch the race itself, and listen to the crowd roar as they urge on their favourites – you'll almost certainly find yourself joining in.

There are plenty of facilities – bars, restaurants, cafés, stalls selling hats, scarves, umbrellas and souvenirs. If it's raining you can cheat and watch the race on a big screen indoors, but really, there's nothing to beat the atmosphere outside. The noise, the crowds, the horses all beautifully groomed, with shining coats and jangling stirrups, topped by brightly clad jockeys, combine to make a jolly day out, and if you win something – well, that's just the icing on the cake.

Derby Day at Epsom

Chessington World of Adventures and Zoo

Runaway Mine Train
roller coaster

If you're looking for a family day out, particularly with younger children, you could give Chessington World of Adventures a whirl. Just 19 km (12 mi) from central London, and close to both the M25 and the A3, Chessington offers a range of attractions that will keep you all amused for hours.

Originally a zoo, rides were added in 1987, since when the park has been much expanded. There are currently nine themed areas, as well as the zoo and the new, 250,000 litre Sea Life Centre. At its heart is the Market Square, where you'll find food stalls, restaurants, shops and arcades as well as the entrance to the Safari Skyrail, a monorail offering a bird's eye view of the zoo. The themed areas, such as Transylvania, Land of the Dragons, and Mystic East have a number of fun, family orientated rides on appropriately designed roller coasters, and smaller, gentler affairs for younger visitors.

The zoo, also divided into areas, is a major attraction. Trail of the Kings enables you to walk very close to enclosures holding large mammals such as lions and tigers. There is the Monkey and Bird Garden, Sealion Bay, where otters and penguins play, as well as sea lions. Small children will love the Children's Zoo, full of pygmy goats and baby rabbits, while boys will relish the Creepy Caves where they will see a large python, a hairy tarantula and much more. Throughout the day there are animal shows, and you can watch several different feeding displays.

Some of the rides at Chessington are showing their age, but each year brings something new to do. During school holidays there can be long queues, and occasional breakdowns, which can be frustrating if you've been in line for a while. In the main, however, Chessington delivers.

WHERE:
South west of London
BEST TIME TO GO:
You'll probably enjoy it more if you avoid the main school holiday periods. Check in advance that everything you want to see and do is available.
DON'T MISS:
The new aquarium, with its interactive 'rock pools' and walk-through ocean tank.
AMOUNT OF WALKING:
Reasonable
COST:
Expensive, but discounts are available if you book in advance.
YOU SHOULD KNOW:
None of the rides here are really thrilling, so older teenagers may not find it very exciting.

Elegant Ham House dates from 1610.

A Picnic in Richmond Park

HAM HOUSE

WHERE:
West London
BEST TIME TO GO:
A fine day between mid-March and the end of October.
DON'T MISS:
The first floor drawing room in Ham House.
AMOUNT OF WALKING:
As much or little as you choose.
COST:
Reasonable
YOU SHOULD KNOW:
The present owners of Ham House, the National Trust, have declared that it is 'unique in Europe as the most complete survival of 17th-century fashion and power'. The house is open from 12.00 pm to 4.00 pm but is closed on Thursdays and Fridays. The garden has different opening times.

A great way to spend a sunny day is to take a picnic lunch to Richmond Park, the largest of the Royal Parks in London, covering an area of 1,012 hectares (2,500 acres). Despite being surrounded by buildings, once you have walked into it you feel as though you have stepped back in time – the landscape here has remained much the same for centuries.

Charles I had the most influence of any monarch on this land. Escaping from the plague in town, he visited Richmond, and realized this was land he could hunt. In 1637, ignoring all complaints, he turned it into a hunting park containing some 2,000 deer, and enclosed them inside a 13-km (8-mi) long, brick wall.

The deer and the hunt changed the look of the park. Mature trees – some of which still stand today – were pollarded to protect them from being eaten. Ponds were dug to provide water. Later on, planned vistas were designed, and small woods added – fenced for protection. Today some 350 fallow deer and 300 red deer still inhabit the park and continue to shape the landscape. Whilst you relax, you might see exotic looking birds flitting from tree to tree – this is home to a large population of parakeets.

After your picnic, head west to Ham House. Built for Sir Thomas Vavasour in 1610, it has a fascinating history. Between 1626 and the end of the century the house, by this time under different ownership, was transformed into a luxuriously furnished villa, and much of its décor and contents can still be seen today. Standing on the banks of the Thames, Ham House also has magnificent gardens that include a 17th-century orangery and what is believed to be the oldest Christ's thorn bush in the United Kingdom.

Osterley House and Park

Often ignored by Londoners speeding westwards on the M4, Osterley House is a Tudor mansion restyled as a neo-classical villa by the paragon of Palladian architecture, Robert Adam. Charged in 1761 by the Child banking family to create a country house suitable for entertaining (and impressing) business associates, Adam created every detail of the superb new interiors. The Entrance Hall is a masterpiece of muted restraint and the mathematics of space, but the Tapestry Room is simply breathtaking. Adam ordered the Boucher medallion tapestries from Gobelins in Paris, incorporating their crimson and claret into his overall design that included the carpet, furniture, upholstery, and embellishments like the tripod pedestals, vases and garlands. Marvelling at his plasterwork might crick your neck but you will not complain, because the house is spectacular, and a rare complete survival of Adam's genius. Untouched during the 19th century, its state-rooms, Long Gallery, private rooms, kitchens and even the strong-room collection of silver, all bear his mark. Only some of the paintings are not original to the house – but the loans from other collections have been chosen to compare with their 18th century counterparts.

Outside, apart from Adam's colonnaded Grand Portico, Osterley House retains much of its Tudor identity, aided by the untouched 16th-century stable block to one side. Originally 144 hectares (357 acres) of woods, streams and pastureland, part of the surrounding Park was also remodeled in the 18th century – and it is these 18th-century gardens that you now see flourishing. The 18th-century Pleasure Grounds and the Tudor Garden are especially attractive, and there's a lovely woodland walk round the lakes. The meadows and much of the Park has never been ploughed, and combined with the flower gardens, they make a wonderful family playground. Even better, you often find you have Osterley to yourself.

WHERE:
Isleworth, West London
BEST TIME TO GO:
Any time of year (but the flowers in the Pleasure Grounds are at their glorious best from June to September).
DON'T MISS:
The second-floor family personal rooms, and the servants' quarters below stairs – an unusual opportunity to see beyond the grand apartments in a major house.
AMOUNT OF WALKING:
Lots (and access, though frequently restricted, is made readily available on request).
COST:
Low
YOU SHOULD KNOW:
Eight armchairs and a sofa in the Tapestry Room are upholstered in a fabric originally created in 1751-3 for Madame de Pompadour.

The Tapestry Room at Osterley House

Bluewater

THE GRAVESEND FERRY AND TILBURY FORT

WHERE:
Kent and Essex
BEST TIME TO GO:
Any time of year
DON'T MISS:
The oral history programme, part of the interpretation scheme in the north-east bastion magazine of Tilbury Fort. It includes a really good rendition of Queen Elizabeth I's Armada Speech ('I know I have the body but of a weak and feeble woman, but I have the heart and stomach of a King, and of a King of England, too....'), which she made near this very spot in 1588, when reviewing her army.
AMOUNT OF WALKING:
Lots – but at Bluewater, access is excellent and help solicitous.
COST:
Low – unless you yield to Bluewater's blandishments.
YOU SHOULD KNOW:
Bluewater's rather authoritarian house rules ban swearing, the wearing of 'hoodies' or baseball caps, and the entry of groups of more than five people 'without the intention to shop'.

Bluewater is a behemoth of a shopping centre. Built on 97 hectares (240 acres) of disused chalk quarry at Greenhithe, near Dartford on the Kentish bank of the Thames estuary, it's one of Europe's biggest 'one-stop shopping experiences' – a temple to retail pleasure, leisure and entertainment. Bluewater's statistics are staggering. Over 25 million people each year patronize some 330 shops, restaurants, cafés and department stores in three giant, two-storey malls styled like balconied streets. To reach them, guests (not 'customers') are encouraged to 'prepare' in the Welcome Halls, where they can relax over coffee, check their available credit on the cash machines, and seek advice from 'concierge desks'. You don't even have to shop. Leisure activities include rock climbing, golf, fishing, cycling, boating and the cinema. There are innumerable forms of crèche and supervised play areas. Outside, there are 20 hectares (50 acres) of landscaped gardens and parkland, and seven lakes to encourage the genuinely astonishing range of birds and wildlife. But with 7,000 employees and parking space for 13,000 cars, neither you nor your wallet will be lonely.

From Bluewater, you could cross the Thames by car via the Dartford Tunnel (and return via Dartford's magnificent Queen Elizabeth II suspension bridge) to reach Tilbury. However, a much better idea is to drive to Gravesend, park the car, and take the Gravesend-Tilbury ferryboat. The Thames narrows here to just 740 m (2,428 ft), and there's been a ferry service since before the Domesday records of 1086. The car ferry ceased in 1965 after the Dartford Tunnel opened, but the present foot ferry is still redolent of the history of its predecessors. On the Tilbury, Essex side, it's a short stroll to Tilbury Fort, the best bit of 17th-century military engineering in England, with Charles II's circuit of moats, bastions and outworks surviving even the Victorian reconstruction. It's one of London's great secrets.

The fortifications at Tilbury Fort

Darwin's Down House

DOWNE BANK NATURE RESERVE

Down House

Charles Darwin moved to Down House near Bromley in 1842, already famous but with the years of analyzing his discoveries still ahead of him. It became his sanctuary, and evolutionary and botanical laboratory, and it still is. You step out of London's traffic into a tranquil haven, where the trellises and climbing flowers on the 18th-century house make a benign statement of its calming influence on Darwin's work. That isn't fanciful: every effort has been made to return the house to the way it was when he died in 1882, and even more, as though he were still living and working there. Papers are scattered on his desk, and books and specimens create highly convincing tableaux vivants in several other rooms. Even the children's nursery and schoolroom are authentic, so you get a picture of the scientist and family man combining to underwrite the humanity that informs *The Origin of Species*. Outside, the garden recreates six of Darwin's experiments, including the weed garden, used to confirm the theory of natural selection, studies of climbing and insectivorous plants, and the test-beds for experiments in self-pollinating orchids. Just as he did, you can also walk round and round the Sandwalk, a long, tree-lined avenue he called 'my thinking track', in reflective wonder at natural processes.

Adjacent to the house and formal gardens, a much larger area under the authority of the Kent Wildlife Trust directly continues Darwin's scientific research. The Downe Bank Nature Reserve encloses fields and meadows where Darwin found and developed much of his inspiration. On the steep chalk slopes ancient woodland hides grassy clearings full of orchids and rich and unusual flora. What you see, you share directly with Darwin himself. The undisturbed biodiversity makes this beautiful place of real importance – a living experiment already over 150 years old.

WHERE:
Kent
BEST TIME TO GO:
Any time of year – especially if you enjoy the seasonal stages of botanical experiments.
DON'T MISS:
The Glasshouse at Down House. Among the rare carnivorous plants, pitcher plants, bladderwort, Venus fly-trap and orchids, honour the Comet orchid, for which Darwin predicted the pollinator 40 years before its discovery, as a result of his theory of evolution through natural selection.
AMOUNT OF WALKING:
Lots, over uneven ground and some steep slopes.
COST:
Low
YOU SHOULD KNOW:
Darwin's family called what is now Downe Bank 'Orchis Bank' because eleven species of orchid were found there. The walk around the nature reserve is roughly 5 km (3.2 mi) long.

Dulwich Picture Gallery

DULWICH PARK AND HORNIMAN MUSEUM

WHERE:
South London
BEST TIME TO GO:
Any time of year
DON'T MISS:
The 15 special Aquarium displays at the Horniman, including the Fijian reef, the tropical rainforest, the mangrove, and the UK rock pool. Or, come to that, the bone clappers shaped like human hands, made in Egypt in 1500 BC.
AMOUNT OF WALKING:
Moderate – but there's a lot of slow shuffling. Access is excellent everywhere.
COST:
Reasonable – and free at the Horniman.
YOU SHOULD KNOW:
The Dulwich Picture Gallery describes its origins as a stroke of post-French Revolutionary luck. 'In the absence (until 1824) of a British National Gallery, the obvious candidate [for the collection] was the British Museum, but [the founders] found its trustees too "arbitrary" and "aristocratic", both loaded words in the era of the French Revolution [and] ...decided to leave the collection to Dulwich College, stating clearly that the paintings should be on public display.'

Dulwich Picture Gallery was designed by Sir John Soane in 1811. Its classical proportions are considered perfect for displaying pictures – and the permanent collections include magnificent Old Masters like Raphael, Rembrandt, Rubens, Van Dyck, Poussin, Lely, Claude, Watteau and Gainsborough. If you come on a weekend, you can get a free, guided tour of this collection, which was formed between 1790-95 by two of the Gallery's founders, whose mausoleum is incorporated into the building. That quirk apart, Dulwich is celebrated for its three annual, temporary exhibitions, almost always of international importance, and for its extensive programme of public lectures and arts education. You can get lucky on any day throughout the year.

Behind the Gallery, Dulwich Park provides an elegant and historic setting. It was created in 1890 from farmland and meadows whose boundaries were established by ancient oak trees, many of which still survive. It has flower gardens, a boating lake and duck pond, and several children's play areas. The American Garden, with its huge selection of azaleas and rhododendrons shaded by beautiful silver birch, is particularly popular. Yet Dulwich Park remains a significant bird and wildlife refuge, and you can see herons, cormorants, grey wagtails and occasional kingfishers at various times.

A short bus ride away, the Horniman Museum is a dazzling temple to the genius of eccentricity. Its three principal collections are devoted to aspects of anthropology, natural history, and musical instruments, reflecting the interests of Frederick Horniman, who for forty years only wanted 'to bring the world to Forest Hill'. Though Horniman gave the museum and 6.5 hectares (16 acres) of gardens – even in 1901 a priceless oasis – to London, his gift failed until recently to get the recognition it deserves. Now, re-organized, highlighted and esteemed, it's a triumph, and the world should beat a path to its door.

Dulwich Picture Gallery

Cambridge

There are few pleasanter ways of passing a sunny summer's day than in the cerebral atmosphere of this ancient town of colleges and churches. From the sublime medieval architecture of the city centre to the wildflower meadows along the River Cam, you are surrounded by the echoes of history: there is not a single spot that does not have some story attached to it.

Look round the old university buildings in the city centre. Trinity, St John's and King's are the grandest colleges but the smaller more modest ones like Queens' are just as beautiful in their simplicity of design. Visit the Round Church, built in 1130 and St Bene't's Church, the oldest building in Cambridgeshire. The Fitzwilliam Museum, 'the finest small museum in Europe' has a superb fine and applied art collection from all over Western Europe and Asia.

Have lunch at The Eagle, the oldest pub in Cambridge, where Francis Crick made the momentous announcement that he and James Watson had discovered DNA; then hire a punt and spend the afternoon lazily drifting along one of the most beautiful stretches of river in the country.

The Cam runs along the 'backs', behind the colleges. Starting at the Mathematical Bridge (a curious construction of criss-crossed wooden joists fallaciously attributed to Isaac Newton) go past King's College and under the Bridge of Sighs to Magdalene. Follow the river further, through the country meadowland and you will get to Grantchester, immortalized by war poet Rupert Brooke. Read his poem 'The Old Vicarage, Grantchester' while drinking tea under the trees at The Orchard.

Bring your day to a glorious close by attending Evensong at King's College Chapel. Listening to the voices of one of the world's most famous choirs in one of England's most beautiful medieval buildings as the evening shadows lengthen is pretty close to heaven.

WHERE:
Cambridgeshire
BEST TIME TO GO:
May to September
DON'T MISS:
Kettle's Yard – an idiosyncratic modern art gallery that feels as though you are in somebody's house. It was the home of Jim Ede, an avant-garde collector. He knocked together several workman's cottages off Castle Street where he held open house and displayed his collection of paintings, sculptures and objets d'art; on retirement he donated the house and all its contents to the University.
AMOUNT OF WALKING:
Moderate
COST:
Reasonable
YOU SHOULD KNOW:
Driving in the city centre is a fool's errand. You can spend hours trapped in baffling one-way systems without a parking space to be found. It is a lot less stressful to leave your car out of town and use the Park and Ride facility.

Punters on the Cam in front of King's College

Duxford Aeroplanes and Thetford Flint Mines

WHERE:
Cambridgeshire/Norfolk
BEST TIME TO GO:
May to September
DON'T MISS:
The fertility shrine in Grimes Graves.
AMOUNT OF WALKING:
Lots if you want
COST:
Entrance to Duxford is expensive.
YOU SHOULD KNOW:
Duxford was used as the set for the 1969 blockbuster film *The Battle of Britain*.

The M11 carves its way through a huge agricultural plain that is not immediately enticing. But first impressions are misleading. There is more happening here than is immediately apparent.

As you approach Junction 10 of the motorway, you might be bemused by the sight of a Spitfire darting across the sky. It is not a hallucination: you have arrived at Duxford. Originally a World War I airfield, Duxford was an important air base throughout World War II. Today it is Europe's foremost aviation museum, part of the Imperial War Museum. You can see a spectacular collection of British and American warplanes as well as a terrific assortment of tanks, military vehicles and naval exhibits, and learn about the Battle of Britain, the D-Day Invasion and the 'forgotten war' in the Far East. Thrilling displays are often given here and it is not at all unusual to see vintage planes in flight.

When you've had your fill of war machines, head north-eastwards into Breckland. In less than an hour you will be in Thetford, the largest lowland pine forest in England. There are miles of walking trails, or you can hire mountain bikes – a great place to work off excess energy.

The Thetford area has been inhabited since neolithic times and in the heart of the forest you can see Stone Age industry at Grimes Graves – not a grave at all but Europe's oldest flint mine, a Site of Special Scientific Interest. It is a weird lunar plain, scarred with mounds and pits. Using only deer-antler picks and shoulder-blade bone shovels, the neolithic miners sank shafts through chalk bedrock to depths of 9 m (30 ft) and painstakingly dug out underground galleries following the course of the flint seams. Pluck up the courage to go on a guided underground tour – it's an impressive experience.

The Lancaster is one of the many aircraft on show at Duxford.

Wicken Fen and Anglesey Abbey

Once upon a time the whole region from Cambridge to The Wash was marshy wetland. Wicken Fen is a fragment between Cambridge and Ely that remains in its original state, an ancient fenland landscape that has been conserved by the National Trust since 1899. Nature lovers will have a field day here, at one of the most important wetland sites in Europe. The rich peat bog provides a habitat for thousands of species of plants, fungi and insects – Charles Darwin used to come beetle-collecting here – and you can see wild ponies, otters, cormorants and kestrels. There are walking trails of various lengths and a boardwalk for pushchairs and wheelchairs.

One of the windmills on Wicken Fen

After a morning of roughing it in the wild, you can spend a genteel afternoon in the splendid surroundings of Anglesey Abbey in the village of Lode, a fifteen-minute drive away. This Jacobean country mansion is built on the site of a 12th-century Augustinian priory, hence its name. The Priory was axed during Henry VIII's dissolution of the monasteries in 1536, passed into private hands and was substantially rebuilt over the years. Eventually, the estate was bought by Lord Fairhaven. He was careful to preserve the remnants of the original 12th-century stonework whilst making alterations to the house but his great achievement was a sublime garden created 'with patience, single minded devotion and flawless taste' (Arthur Bryant). He bequeathed the property to the National Trust in 1966.

The inside of the house is stuffed with treasures: paintings, sculpture, tapestries, clocks, furniture, rare books and even Lord Fairhaven's clothes. Outside, you can wander through 40 hectares (98 acres) of gloriously planted grounds with twenty-three distinct 'garden rooms', said to be the most imaginatively designed 20th-century garden in England with colour throughout the year.

WHERE:
Cambridgeshire
BEST TIME TO GO:
Any time, but January to February for the striking winter garden and snowdrop display at Anglesey Abbey.
DON'T MISS:
The 18th-century water mill at Lode, restored to full working order. You can watch the flour being ground and even buy a bag.
AMOUNT OF WALKING:
Lots
COST:
Reasonable
YOU SHOULD KNOW:
Use an insect repellent on Wicken Fen. The low-lying wetland is unfortunately a favoured breeding ground for mosquitoes as well as more benign insects.

Cycling through the Fens

Originally the largest swamp in England, from the 17th century onwards the fenland has been continually reclaimed for agriculture. There is a remote, even eerie feel to the apparently endless fields and distant horizon in this sparsely populated farmland, veined with waterways and dotted with historic towns and villages. As you pedal along the back roads you get a wonderfully liberating sense of space, all too rare in England.

Ely is a small atmospheric city built on what was once an island in the fens. You can see its fairytale medieval cathedral, the 'Ship of the Fens' from miles away across the fields. Once Hereward the Wake's stronghold against the forces of William the Conqueror and later the home of Oliver Cromwell, Ely is steeped in a romantic past with a charming waterfront area and many beautiful old buildings.

At Welney Wetlands Centre, 17 km (10 mi) along the Wisbech Road, you can see thousands of wild water birds. Cycle alongside the River Nene, the border of Cambridgeshire and Norfolk, through the unusual villages of Upwell and Outwell, noted for their Flemish architecture, riverside gardens and pretty country churches.

Go through Wisbech, once a prosperous market town, and you will see some exceptionally fine 18th-century architecture. Head for the ancient port of Kings Lynn, at the mouth of the River Ouse. Close your eyes to the rather grim industrial sheds of the sprawling outskirts and explore the winding streets and back alleys of one of the best-preserved old town centres in England. The market place is especially picturesque and the 15th-century Guildhall and 17th-century Customs House are architectural gems. Gaze out over The Wash, watch the boats chugging around the harbour and feel a glow of good health from your day of freedom in the fens.

A winter sunset at
Welney Washes

The Sandringham Estate

If you want a leisurely country day out in beautiful surroundings, Sandringham will not disappoint. Just 14 km (9 mi) northeast of Kings Lynn, Sandringham House is set in 24 hectares (60 acres) of glorious gardens with lakes, a stream and rhododendron walks. Beyond is an 8,000-hectare (20,000-acre) estate of which 240 hectares (600 acres) is a Country Park with free access throughout the year. This is a wonderful place for walking. After admiring the formal beauty of the house and gardens, you can wander through the broadleaf woods and heathland of Sandringham Country Park to your heart's content.

Queen Victoria bought Sandringham for the Prince of Wales in 1862. He demolished the dilapidated old house and built what has been described as the 'most comfortable house in England'. It has been used ever since as the Royal Family's country retreat. The estate plays a major part in the local economy. More than half of it is tenanted and the rich agricultural land is used for growing fruit, vegetable and grains. Rare breeds of sheep and cattle are raised here and areas of wetland, tidal mudflats and woodland are conserved as wildlife habitats.

The ground floor of the house is open to visitors and you can snoop round the saloon, drawing rooms and dining room, regularly used by the Royals. These rooms have an Edwardian character and a pleasant, lived-in air about them. You will see beautiful objets d'art and family portraits, and, in the main corridor, a fantastic collection of armoury from the East. The old stable block has been converted into a museum full of curious mementoes from royal trips abroad, and it is worth looking inside the picturesque 16th-century country church of St Mary Magdalene, where the Royal Family always attend the Christmas Service.

WHERE:
Norfolk
BEST TIME TO GO:
April to October. Go in May to catch the rhododendrons in full bloom. NB Sandringham is closed to the public from late October to late March.
DON'T MISS:
Castle Rising, 5 km (3 mi) from Sandringham — a tranquil old world village where you can see the ruins of one of the most famous Norman castles in England. Edward II's wife, Isabella, the 'She-Wolf of France' lived out the remainder of her life here after being implicated in the king's murder. It is said you can hear her ghost howling at full moon as she prowls the battlements.
AMOUNT OF WALKING:
Lots
COST:
Reasonable
YOU SHOULD KNOW:
You can buy fresh estate produce at the Sandringham shop and there is a visitor centre and restaurant. There are excellent facilities for the elderly and disabled, including tractor and trailer tours of the estate.

Sandringham House from across the lake on the Sandringham Estate

North Norfolk Coast Drive

All who love the sea will lose their heart to the North Norfolk coast. The road from the Victorian seaside town of Hunstanton to the popular tourist resort of Cromer runs along a starkly beautiful, fragmented coastline punctuated with picture-postcard fishing villages, quaint port towns, medieval churches and old windmills that harmonize with the landscape in an idyll of rural charm. On a 60-km (40-mi) drive, you will see a staggering variety of scenery – tidal mudflats, salt marshes, sand dunes and pine woods, inlets and sand bars, dramatic cliffs and golden beaches.

Titchwell Marsh is a wetland nature reserve, frequented mainly by birdwatchers. Between Brancaster and Burnham Overy Staithe there is a superb sand beach and a labyrinth of tidal creeks; known as 'Chelsea-on-Sea', this is a favourite yachting hangout for the 'green wellie' brigade. Holkham is renowned for its breathtaking stretch of pristine white sand, while Wells and Blakeney are famous for their stunningly picturesque harbours. The marshes and reedbeds between Cley and Salthouse are one of Britain's most important bird habitats. See the World War II pillboxes on Weybourne beach and sidetrack inland at Sheringham for a walk through National Trust woods to heathland hilltops for stunning views of the sea.

Cromer is a charming Edwardian seaside resort, famous for its pier, succulent crabs and tall church tower. Explore the narrow lanes then laze on the clifftops gazing out to sea or walk around Felbrigg Hall, one of the finest 17th-century country houses in Norfolk, set in a beautiful estate of woods, fields and pastureland.

Local Norfolk culture is deeply entrenched, not easily displaced by tourism: you will see plenty of battered old fishing boats and lobster pots amongst the pleasure yachts and windsurfing gear. Come for a day and you will be hooked into returning time and time again.

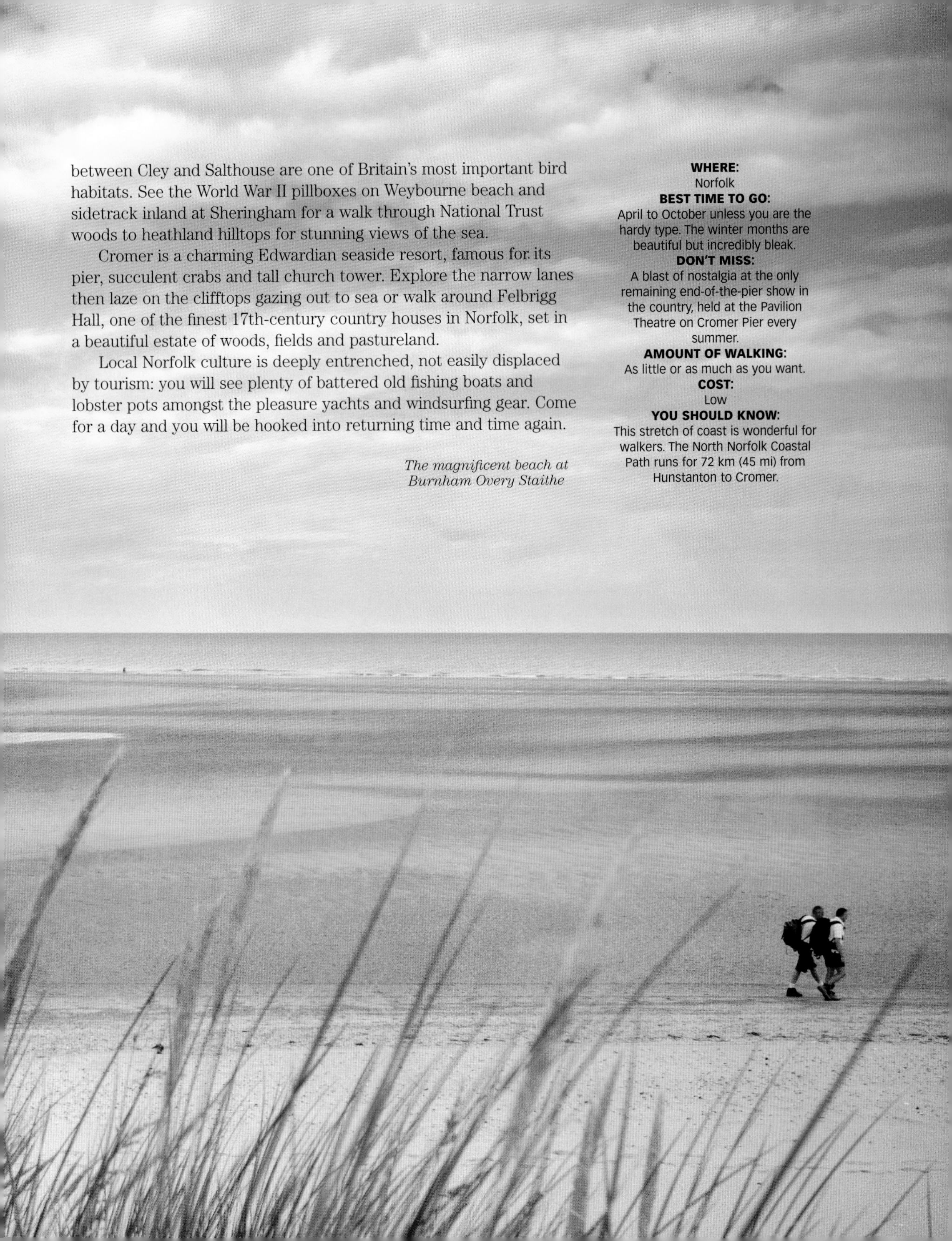

The magnificent beach at
Burnham Overy Staithe

WHERE:
Norfolk
BEST TIME TO GO:
April to October unless you are the hardy type. The winter months are beautiful but incredibly bleak.
DON'T MISS:
A blast of nostalgia at the only remaining end-of-the-pier show in the country, held at the Pavilion Theatre on Cromer Pier every summer.
AMOUNT OF WALKING:
As little or as much as you want.
COST:
Low
YOU SHOULD KNOW:
This stretch of coast is wonderful for walkers. The North Norfolk Coastal Path runs for 72 km (45 mi) from Hunstanton to Cromer.

Holt, Blickling Hall and Aylsham

WHERE:
Norfolk
BEST TIME TO GO:
April to October or December when the towns have a traditional Christmas atmosphere that shows them in their full glory.
DON'T MISS:
The Bure Valley Railway – a narrow gauge line linking Aylsham to Wroxham, on the Norfolk Broads. You can make a 30-km (18-mi) round trip in a train pulled by either steam or diesel engine. The train stops at several villages along the way and there is a cycle and foot path running alongside the line so you can take the train one way and walk or cycle the other.
AMOUNT OF WALKING:
Moderate unless you want to do lots.
COST:
Reasonable unless you go wild in Holt's gift shops.
YOU SHOULD KNOW:
Market days in Aylsham are on Mondays and Fridays and the town is well known for its Monday auctions.

East Anglia has a reputation for being boringly flat but this is far from the truth. A little way inland from the North Norfolk coast you will find yourself in a rolling landscape of verdant meadows, broadleaf spinneys and meandering streams. Picturesque towns and old rural buildings add to the charm of a region that exudes a timeless air of English country life.

Holt is an old-fashioned Georgian town of impeccable colour-washed houses, gourmet grocery stores, antique shops and picture galleries. If it seems a trifle self-satisfied, it has to be admitted that it's entitled to be. A thoroughly pleasant morning can be had browsing around the narrow back streets or watching the world from one of the cosy tea shops. The famous independent school of Gresham's, founded in the 16th century, is on the outskirts; and less than five-minutes drive, in the pretty village of Letheringsett, you can see the last working watermill in the county – an award-winning tourist attraction.

A twenty-minute drive along the Aylsham Road through glorious countryside takes you to Blickling Hall, a magnificent Jacobean house and grounds, haunted by the ghost of Anne Boleyn. Blickling is famous for its long gallery, containing one of the most important collections of rare books in England, and the gardens are a delight whatever the season, with an orangery, secret garden and woodland dell.

Aylsham is an exceptionally attractive market town of old streets, winding alleys and family-owned shops. The layout of the town centre is basically unaltered since the Middle Ages; there are 240 listed buildings, a fine Georgian market square and a beautiful 15th-century parish church. Part of the town's appeal lies in its nonchalant attitude towards tourism, which gives it an authentic country atmosphere that is increasingly rare.

Sunset at Blickling Hall

Holkham Hall and Beach

WELLS-NEXT-THE-SEA

Holkham Beach is part of a nature reserve that runs along the coast from Burnham Norton to Blakeney. It is one of the most beautiful and unspoilt stretches of sand in the whole country. Backed by pine woods and dunes, the beach is huge – almost 1 km (0.5 mi) wide at low tide and nearly 6 km (4 mi) long. The woods are criss-crossed by foot paths and are a habitat for birds, wildlife and many unusual plants. However many people there are in high season, it is so vast that it never feels overcrowded and you can always find a quiet spot.

All the land around here, including the beach, is part of the vast Holkham Estate. Have a look round Holkham Hall, 3 km (2 mi) from the picturesque port town of Wells. Thomas Coke, the 1st Earl of Leicester, famous for his pioneering farming techniques, built a magnificent Palladian mansion in the 1750s and his descendants have lived here ever since. The stunning alabaster entrance hall and twelve state rooms are open to the public and the house is set in a beautiful deer park. There is also a Bygones Museum with working steam engines and vintage cars, and an interesting History of Farming exhibition.

Wells-next-the-Sea is architecturally the loveliest town on the North Norfolk Coast. Its quaint lanes and alleyways, hidden courtyards and traditional flint houses with pantiled roofs date back to the 17th century. A spacious green, shaded by lime trees, is lined with elegant Georgian houses and the main street has an eclectic selection of small shops. Stroll along the historic quayside and see the yachts and fishing boats. Savour the nostalgic atmosphere in the small amusement arcades and end the day at a traditional country pub.

WHERE:
Norfolk
BEST TIME TO GO:
Any time. Nature lovers will appreciate the months from October to April when the coast is more or less deserted apart from the wildlife. June to September if you want to have a swim and see inside Holkham Hall.
DON'T MISS:
Burnham Thorpe, a sleepy village set back from the coast, 5 km (3 mi) from Holkham, birthplace of Nelson. Nelson's father was the parish rector and although the rectory has not survived, there is lots to see in the church, and you can still have a pint in the original pub where he drank.
AMOUNT OF WALKING:
Lots
COST:
Reasonable
YOU SHOULD KNOW:
In the summer season the road leading down to Holkham Beach can get very crowded with parked cars so it is best to get here early in the day to be sure of a space.

The beach huts on Holkham Beach

Up close and personal with the seals at Blakeney

The Seal Colonies of Blakeney

OUR LADY OF WALSINGHAM

WHERE:
Norfolk
BEST TIME TO GO:
April to October. The seals' mating season is in September.
DON'T MISS:
The Church of St Nicholas at Blakeney – a very welcoming and all too rare dog-friendly church. (It even has a water bowl in the porch). There is a stupendous 13th-century vaulted ceiling and a mysterious lighthouse tower, a miniature replica of the main church tower thought to have been used as a decoy light by Blakeney 'wreckers' to bamboozle passing ships into navigating so near the coast that they got beached. The wreckers would then send out a 'rescue' boat for the price of the goods on the vessel – the origins of the lifeboat service.
AMOUNT OF WALKING:
Moderate
COST:
Reasonable
YOU SHOULD KNOW:
The Wells & Walsingham Light Railway, a narrow gauge line, runs through scenic countryside between Wells-next-the-Sea and Little Walsingham.

Blakeney is perhaps the prettiest of all the Norfolk seaside villages: flint fishermen's cottages tumble down a steep slope to a picturesque quay with wonderful views over the salt marshes. Beyond the harbour is Blakeney Point, the tip of a 6-km (4-mi) long shingle spit, a National Trust nature reserve famous for its seals. Although you can get there on foot, it is a lot more fun, and less tiring, to be ferried in a fishing-dinghy from Morston, a small marshland village 2 km (1 mi) along the coast from Blakeney. A round trip takes a couple of hours and includes plenty of time to explore the Point where, as well as colonies of grey and common seals, you will see hundreds of birds and unusual plants. It is a brilliant place for wildlife photography.

Drive 14 km (9 mi) inland through a glorious stretch of ancient woodland to see the extraordinary village of Little Walsingham. Nearly a thousand years ago, in 1061 an influential local widow convinced the villagers that she had seen the Virgin Mary and persuaded them to build a shrine to Our Lady of Walsingham. This out-of-the-way little village became one of the most important pilgrim centres in Europe known as 'Nazareth in England', until the shrine was summarily destroyed in 1538 during the Reformation and pilgrimages were brought to an abrupt halt. Victorian religiosity led to a revival of Walsingham's fortunes, the 14th-century Slipper Chapel was restored and in 1897 pilgrimages started again. In the 1930s a new Shrine Church was built and today the pilgrimage business here is thriving, especially at Easter. The village retains its charming medieval character with timber-framed houses, an old courthouse, ruined priory and numerous historical and religious relics. It is a fascinating anachronism in the 21st century, an unlikely and unique slice of British heritage.

Cruise the Norfolk Broads

The Broads are in the largest area of protected wetland in Britain, a paradise for anyone who likes mucking around on boats and a great place for novices to learn everything from rowing to waterskiing. There are 200 km (125 mi) of waterway with thirteen navigable broads (shallow lakes) and six rivers to explore, and no awkward locks to negotiate. You can hire any sort of boat, from a luxury cruiser to a canoe, just for a day, or even an afternoon. Don't let lack of experience put you off. Most boats are pretty easy to manoeuvre and if you cruise downstream along the River Bure from Wroxham, the 'capital' of the Broads, you will be on a well-frequented stretch of water where you can easily shout for assistance.

The formation of the Broads is something of a mystery. For a long time these shallow lakes were thought to be a weird natural phenomenon, but research has more or less definitively established that they were created as a result of centuries of peat-cutting. The removal of layers of peat left holes in the ground which, as sea levels rose, filled with water, turning into giant puddles that might have been purpose-dug for boating enthusiasts.

You wend your way through lovely varied countryside, passing pretty villages, old churches, ruins and windmills. Make sure you visit Ranworth Broad, off the River Bure, said to be haunted by a 12th-century monk. From the top of the tower of Ranworth's 14th-century Church, the 'Cathedral of the Broads', you will get an amazing panoramic view from an entirely different perspective: an intricate patchwork of woods, marshes, lakes and meadows threaded with rivers spreads before you, unlike anywhere else in Britain.

WHERE:
Norfolk
BEST TIME TO GO:
April to October
DON'T MISS:
St Benets Abbey – an isolated ruin on the River Bure steeped in history and legend.
AMOUNT OF WALKING:
Little, or more if you want.
COST:
Expensive
YOU SHOULD KNOW:
If you find the idea of navigating your own boat a bit daunting, there are numerous organized cruises or if you prefer to stay on dry land you can explore the Broads by means of the many footpaths and cycling trails that run through the area.

A traditional sailing boat glides through the Broads – a rare sight these days.

Roots of Norfolk

GRESSENHALL MUSEUM AND CASTLE ACRE

WHERE:
Norfolk
BEST TIME TO GO:
March to October
DON'T MISS:
Bishop Bonner's Cottage Museum in Dereham – early 16th-century thatched cottage, the oldest house in the town.
AMOUNT OF WALKING:
Moderate
COST:
Reasonable
YOU SHOULD KNOW:
Castle Acre is an exceptionally good example of a Norman planned town, with the original village street layout still intact.

To anyone who has grown up in the inner city, rural England can seem rather remote and completely alien. Gressenhall is a gentle introduction: a sort of Norfolk in miniature, a demonstration of how ordinary rural people have lived and the changes that have taken place over the past 250 years. It is a brilliant place to bring city children who might moan at the prospect of trudging through fields but who will be instantly smitten with country life as seen at Gressenhall.

On this 20-hectare (50-acre) site near East Dereham there is a traditional functioning farm, and an 18th-century 'house of industry'. The latter has been converted into a museum where the horrors of the workhouse are vividly brought to life through re-enactments of true stories. There are collections of household objects, showing you just about everything to do with day-to-day rural life. You can also look round re-created shops, a family house, a cottage garden and a vegetable patch and see old agricultural machinery and farm implements, rare breeds of pigs and sheep and Suffolk Punch horses. Children can dress up, milk a cow, draw water with an old-fashioned hand pump and chase the chickens running around in the farmyard. There is a woodland playground and you can walk through an old orchard and have a cart ride across the fields to the riverbank.

Time passes quickly at Gressenhall but it's worth squeezing in a visit to Castle Acre, a small Norfolk village twenty-minutes drive away on Peddars Way, at one time the major trade route through Norfolk. Castle Acre was once a place of some importance, attested to by its Norman castle with massive ditched defences at one end of the village and priory at the other – one of the best-preserved monastic sites in England.

Showing children 'how it was then' at the Gressenhall Museum.

Norwich

Norwich is above all a city for shoppers – one of the top shopping destinations in the United Kingdom. But, undisguised centre of commerce though it is, there are plenty of other attractions.

In its Norman heyday the city was second only to London in importance; Norwich Castle stands imperiously on a hill overlooking the city centre as though to remind you of that fact. You can tour the dungeons and climb up to the battlements, and inside, the museum is stuffed with paintings, ceramics and other treasures. Wander through Tombland, a medieval area of narrow winding lanes lined with antique shops, bars and restaurants, and walk up Elm Hill, a picture-postcard cobbled street lined with timber-framed Tudor houses that is so quaint it hardly seems real.

Norwich Cathedral

The Norman Cathedral is breathtaking, with a spire that soars high into the sky and the largest cloisters in England. Nearby, the River Wensum flows through the city to join up with the Norfolk Broads. Stroll along the riverside or take a riverbus tour for a relaxing break before finding out more about the city's past at the Bridewell Museum, once a women's and beggars' prison. Here the city's commercial life is splendidly recreated with a replica pharmacist's shop, pawnbroker's, and smithy. Nearby is Strangers' Hall, one of the oldest buildings in Norwich, with rooms furnished according to various historical periods.

Browse among the small trendy shops in the cobbled streets of Norwich Lanes and through the largest Monday to Saturday open market in the country, in existence for nearly a thousand years. Norwich is the home of Colman's mustard and you can visit the Mustard Shop in the Royal Arcade before wending your way back towards the Cathedral to end the day at the Adam & Eve, the oldest pub in Norwich.

WHERE:
Norfolk
BEST TIME TO GO:
April to October
DON'T MISS:
Plantation Garden – 140 year-old Victorian town garden on Earlham Road, a secret oasis of tranquillity in the bustling city centre created by Henry Trevor, a Norwich businessman, on the site of an old chalk quarry.
AMOUNT OF WALKING:
Moderate but with plenty of breaks.
COST:
Reasonable; but could be expensive depending on how many museums you decide to see and whether you get carried away in the shops.
YOU SHOULD KNOW:
Norwich is said to have 'a pub for every day of the year and a church for every week', a slight exaggeration but not that far from the truth.

A Country Auction in Diss

HALES HALL GARDEN

WHERE:
Norfolk/Suffolk
BEST TIME TO GO:
April to September
DON'T MISS:
The Saints, South Elmham and
Ilketshall – an extraordinary cluster
of hamlets off the A143 on the
Suffolk side of the Waveney Valley,
each named after a saint and with
eleven medieval churches between
them. If you want a bit of an
adventure in the middle of nowhere,
set out to find St Peter's Brewery – a
traditional Real Ale brewer well
worth a tour.
AMOUNT OF WALKING:
Moderate
COST:
Low unless you want to lash out in
Diss's curio shops and auction
house.
YOU SHOULD KNOW:
Antiques and collectables auctions
are held at Gaze's on Fridays.

Diss is the embodiment of 'a historic market town'. Built beside a mere in the Waveney Valley and surrounded by farmland, it has more surviving medieval houses than any other East Anglian town of comparable size, as well as plenty of fine Georgian and Victorian architecture. The narrow winding streets and cobbled yards behind the market square are full of character and at the heart of the town stands a surprisingly grand parish church. A market has been held here for well over 500 years and the town still retains an earthy workaday atmosphere with scarcely a trace of tweeness about it. John Betjeman, poet laureate, visited Diss in 1963, fell in love with the town and wrote a poem about the train journey here.

One of the many attractions of Diss is its auction house. Gaze's started out in 1857 as a livestock and agricultural auctioneer and over the years branched out into property and chattels. There is an air of suppressed excitement in the auction room and it is riveting to see the way the auctioneer works the crowd, stirring the punters into ever-higher bids for the motley jumble of household goods and antique treasures on display.

After a morning of wheeling and dealing, have lunch in the Saracen's Head, a picturesque old pub off the market square, then head out along the Waveney Valley for a forty-minute country drive to the village of Loddon. Nearby you will find Hales Hall, the remnants of a grand Tudor house with an intact 15th-century thatched barn, the largest surviving brick-built medieval barn in Britain, and a beautifully planted walled and moated garden. There is a national collection of figs, grapes and oranges in the garden conservatories and a family-run specialist nursery centre selling all sorts of exotic plants.

St Nicholas Street, Diss

Minsmere Bird Sanctuary

ALDEBURGH AND SNAPE MALTINGS

Dawn breaks over the beach at Aldeburgh

If you're near the Suffolk coast, this is a great day out. Begin at Minsmere, the RSPB's lovely reserve, which encompasses woods, heath and reed-beds that lead down to the sea itself. In spring you'll hear well-camouflaged bitterns booming, and during summer, see rare avocets. Their distinctive black and white plumage and long, up-curved beaks provided the RSPB's emblem, and their conservation is a great success story. Marsh harriers hunt low over the reeds, while swans glide gracefully through water that ripples and glitters in the sunshine. Winter brings an abundance of waterfowl and wading birds, and this landscape is beautiful in any weather.

A few miles south – you could walk there along the beach – is the town of Aldeburgh. The attractive main street, which has shops, galleries, restaurants and even a cinema, takes you down to the marina. The beach itself, fronted mainly by Victorian houses, is shingled and shelving. Fishing huts and sheds, some selling their fresh catch, cluster together, and working boats are hauled up onto the shore. Further along stands Maggi Hambling's 'Scallop' sculpture – a powerful and moving tribute to Benjamin Britten, who lived and worked here. His efforts gave Aldeburgh the cachet that it has today.

Britten and his partner, singer Peter Piers, started the Aldeburgh Festival in 1948. During the 1960s, a nearby maltings was transformed into a concert hall, where today concerts take place all year round. However, Snape Maltings is more than a concert hall. Here you can eat, drink and visit a variety of unexpectedly tempting shops. You can admire sculpture, take gentle walks beside the tidal River Alde, or see more of the estuary on a boat trip. This is a serene part of the world, but it also has something for everyone.

WHERE:
East Suffolk
BEST TIME TO GO:
Any time of year
DON'T MISS:
The 15th-century church at Aldeburgh, where Benjamin Britten and Peter Piers are buried. Behind them lies the grave of Imogen Holst. The only child of the composer, Gustav Holst, she came to Aldeburgh in 1952 to musically assist Britten and Piers, with whom she was a close friend. She stayed for the rest of her life and was the artistic director of the Aldeburgh Festival from 1956-1977.
AMOUNT OF WALKING:
Moderate
COST:
Minsmere is free to RSPB members, but there is a reasonable fee for others. The main cost of the day will be eating and drinking, and anything you can't resist buying...
YOU SHOULD KNOW:
The site of the 'Scallop' sculpture has caused a great furore within the local community. Some say it spoils the line of the beach, and some have gone so far as to vandalize it, several times. Others find it a perfect complement to the vast Suffolk skies, the eroding coastline and the wild North Sea.

Southwold

BLYTHBURGH CHURCH, WALBERSWICK AND DUNWICH

Southwold is a charmingly old-fashioned seaside town with an atmosphere reminiscent of a more innocent age. Its pretty, pastel coloured cottages, fine Georgian houses overlooking the sea, lighthouse, delightful pier and iconic beach huts have made the town a deservedly popular holiday spot, and there are plenty of shops and restaurants too. Enjoy drinking Adnams beer, made here at the Sole Bay Brewery. Until recently, horse-drawn drays still made deliveries, but now Adnams has built a prize winning eco-friendly distribution centre, drawing inspiration from the Eden Project.

A few miles inland, but visible from afar, stands Holy Trinity, Blythburgh's self-styled 'Cathedral of the Marshes', probably Suffolk's best loved church. Built during the 15th century, it is singularly beautiful. The interior is vast, light streams in, illuminating the brick and stone floor, and angels watch from high above, their wings outstretched. If you visit only one Suffolk church, make it this one.

Drive back to the coast on the south side of the Blyth, to find Walberswick. With two pubs, a village green, a few shops, many pretty houses and surrounded by marshes and heathland, Walberswick also has a fine beach. The big skies and the quality of the light have always attracted artists and writers. Watch the boats on the river, and marvel at the quantity of crabs that small children catch, with nothing more than a piece of bacon tied onto a string.

Drive a little further south, through forest and heath, to Dunwich, a small village with a big history. Once a highly successful port, with several large churches and friaries, it is hard to imagine how important Dunwich was when you see how little remains today – most of it now lies under water. Visit the excellent museum to discover its fascinating history, then buy yourself fish and chips to eat beside the sea.

The beach huts at Southwold

WHERE:
East Suffolk
BEST TIME TO GO:
On a sunny day
DON'T MISS:
Tim Hunkin's 'Under the Pier Show' on Southwold Pier, for a highly amusing interlude for both adults and children. Take the rowing boat 'ferry' between Southwold and Walberswick, or walk across the Bailey bridge.
AMOUNT OF WALKING:
Moderate
COST:
Low, unless you have expensive meals or spend a lot in the shops.
YOU SHOULD KNOW:
Southwold and Walberswick both have a lot of 'second homes', several of which now belong to media celebrities. George Orwell lived in Southwold as a boy and Charles Rennie Macintosh lived in Walberswick for a few years from 1914. Today's celebrities include Emma Freud, Richard Curtis, Martin Bell and Julie Myerson.

Orford

UFFORD CHURCH, WOODBRIDGE AND SUTTON HOO

A quiet town, Orford lies on the picturesque River Alde, around a 12th-century castle built by Henry II. Today, only the Keep remains, but at 27 m (90 ft) high, it dominates its surroundings. From the Keep extend splendid views of Orford Ness, Europe's largest vegetated shingle spit. This extraordinary place, together with Havergate Island, is a National Nature Reserve, and fascinating walks and boat trips can be taken. For decades, Orford Ness was where the Ministry of Defence conducted secret weapons tests, and their buildings can still be seen, along with a lighthouse and a BBC transmitting station.

Some 19 km (12 mi) inland, Ufford, a pretty little village, has a wonderful church. Suffolk is known for its medieval churches, built when the area was awash with money from the wool trade. With its painted, hammerbeam roof, angels, fantastically carved 15th-century bench-ends and tall font cover, this is a hidden gem.

Next stop, Woodbridge – a thriving old town on the River Deben; it is full of handsome buildings, and boasts an attractive market place. The river is both picturesque and busy. A mass of sailing boats and dinghies zip about the water, the sound of rigging tapping against masts and seagulls' screams fill the air. The Tide Mill was, until 1957, the last working tide mill in the country. Built in 1793, a mill has stood on this spot since the 1100s. Take a tour and then enjoy a snack on the quayside, recently revamped with a Lottery grant.

Nearby, on the eastern bank of the Deben, is Sutton Hoo, the richest burial ground of East Anglia's Saxon kings ever found, and one of our most important archaeological sites. This is where an astonishing Anglo-Saxon ship, filled with treasures, was discovered. A National Trust property, Sutton Hoo deserves a visit.

WHERE:
East Suffolk
BEST TIME TO GO:
Any time, but it's best on a sunny day.
DON'T MISS:
If you like oysters, Orford is the place to go. Eat them at the Butley Orford Oysterage or buy them from the wet fish shop where there is also delicious smoked fish to be found, all from the same family business. They have their own oyster beds, fishing boats and smoke-houses too – this is a gourmet's paradise.
AMOUNT OF WALKING:
Moderate
COST:
Reasonable.
The castle is only free to English Heritage members, and entry fees are payable at the Tide Mill and at Sutton Hoo.
YOU SHOULD KNOW:
The opening times of Orford Castle and Woodbridge Tide Mill change according to season, so check before you turn up. Ufford Church is open every day until about 4.30 pm.

Face-to-face with a Saxon at Sutton Hoo

Shotley Peninsula and Constable Country

EAST BERGHOLT, FLATFORD MILL AND DEDHAM

WHERE:
South Suffolk
BEST TIME TO GO:
March to October
DON'T MISS:
The Bell Cage at the Church of St Mary the Virgin at East Bergholt. This wooden cage, erected in 1531 as a temporary home for the bells, the church having no tower, is still there, almost 500 years later.
AMOUNT OF WALKING:
As much or little as you choose.
COST:
Low
YOU SHOULD KNOW:
John Constable was not the only English painter who lived in this area – Sir Alfred Munnings, (1878-1959), the famous painter of horses, lived and worked in Dedham. His house, gardens and studio are now open to the public.

Flatford Mill on the River Stour

Situated between the rivers Orwell and Stour, the Shotley Peninsula is an area that deserves to be better known. The estuary, with its mudflats and marshes, is designated a Special Protection Area, due to the fact that it attracts internationally significant birdlife.

The peninsula is a peaceful, rural area, admired by nature lovers, bird watchers and the sailing fraternity. One road runs its length, and there are plenty of opportunities for delightful walks. A visit to Pin Mill is a must: this tiny riverside hamlet is extremely picturesque. Walk through National Trust owned woods, the path occasionally winding right down to the river, to work up an appetite for lunch. The 17th-century Butt and Oyster pub is beautifully situated, its fame established by the writer, Arthur Ransome.

From Shotley, drive to East Bergholt. Constable was born here in 1776, and you can see both the site of his birthplace and his first studio in this lovely village. There are several interesting buildings here: the church, built in the 15th century, Stour House, home to Randolph Churchill, and Old Hall, a former monastic building which houses a community of ecologically minded people living co-operatively, who are largely self-sufficient, thanks to their 28-hectare (70-acre) farm.

Both Flatford Mill, immortalized in one of Constable's most famous paintings, *The Haywain*, and Dedham, where the artist went to school, are close by. At Flatford, the Bridge Cottage complex has a permanent Constable exhibition and, during summertime, there are guided walks to the sites of some of his other paintings. Dedham, too, is a charming village, its houses reflecting its history as a successful wool town. The 40-m (131-ft) high church tower, built in 1519, is visible in several of Constable's works.

Scenic Drive

KERSEY, LAVENHAM, LONG MELFORD, CAVENDISH AND CLARE

By taking this pretty route you will not only drive through some glorious Suffolk countryside, but also visit a number of outstandingly pretty villages.

Begin with Kersey, a small village in a gently rolling landscape. The main street, bursting with attractive buildings, winds through a ford patrolled by unconcerned ducks, and at one end a handsome church stands protectively at the top of stone steps. Admire the 14th-century Bell Inn, with its timbered gable, and the marvellous Elizabethan door to River House.

Lavenham is more of a town than a village, and almost every building you see is medieval. The totality of the half-timbered cottages, the terrific 15th-century church, containing renowned late Gothic chantries and screens, the central market place and the remarkable Guildhall is visually stunning – the only downside is that Lavenham, not surprisingly, is very well known and very much visited.

Long Melford, also an ancient village, is set along a stretch of road that, like Kersey, crosses over a ford. Mentioned in the Domesday Book, the village dates back to Roman times. The church is huge, and includes a remarkable Lady Chapel, some medieval stained glass, and an alabaster 'Adoration of the Magi'. The broad main street is lined with Tudor, Georgian and Victorian buildings, and the village is known for its antique shops.

Cavendish is another lovely place: its medieval church overlooks a clutch of thatched cottages, all painted traditional Suffolk pink. Here you can visit the Sue Ryder Foundation Museum, and the Cavendish Manor vineyard.

Finally, visit Clare – another ancient wool town. Here you will find a 13th-century Augustinian priory, the remains of a Norman keep, located in the Country Park, another medieval church, and the Ancient House Museum which boasts a prime example of pargetting, the local art of decorative plasterwork, which is currently enjoying a revival.

WHERE:
South Suffolk
BEST TIME TO GO:
On a sunny day.
DON'T MISS:
Melford Hall, Long Melford. This is a magnificent brick-built, Tudor stately home, run by the National Trust. It has a splendid interior, complete with a panelled banqueting hall, and is set in lovely parkland and gardens.
AMOUNT OF WALKING:
Moderate
COST:
Low
YOU SHOULD KNOW:
In 1381, Sir John Cavendish, the Chief Justice of the King's Bench, was living near Cavendish village. The villagers rose against him because his son killed Wat Tyler, the leader of the popular Peasants' Revolt. Sir John tried to claim sanctuary in Cavendish Church, clinging desperately to the same door handles that we see today, but was dragged away to Bury St Edmunds and murdered by a mob headed by another rebel leader, Jack Straw.

Lavenham

Hadleigh to Coggeshall

VIA LAYHAM, SHELLEY, POLSTEAD, STOKE-BY-NAYLAND AND NAYLAND

Why not spend a pleasant day driving through the pretty country lanes of the Suffolk/Essex border? The landscape here is particularly lovely and you can take in some historic villages en route.

The prosperous market town of Hadleigh is a good place to begin. Lying in the River Brett valley, this was once a royal Viking town and its king, Guthrum of Denmark, died here in 890 and is said to be buried in the grounds of St Mary's Church. The attractive High Street is lined with brick and timber listed buildings, the most famous of which is the wonderful 15th-century Guildhall complex, which reflects Hadleigh's importance as a wool town. The church and the nearby Deanery tower, both built during the 1400s, deserve your attention.

Leaving Hadleigh, you can wind your way through Layham and Shelley to Polstead, where picturesque cottages are grouped around a large duck pond.

Now move on through Stoke-by-Nayland, a lovely village dominated by a spectacular church, to Nayland itself, set on the northern bank of the Stour, which here separates Suffolk from Essex. Another thriving wool town, Nayland has a wealth of Tudor and Stuart architecture, as well as a church containing a painting by Constable.

End your tour at Coggeshall – yet another medieval wool town boasting a large 15th-century church. Visit Paycockes, a spectacular 16th-century timber-framed house that is well worth seeing, as are the remaining buildings that were part of a large Cistercian Abbey, founded in 1140. Grange Barn, a very impressive National Trust property, is the oldest timber framed barn in Europe.

WHERE:
Suffolk/Essex border
BEST TIME TO GO:
Any time, but there are fabulous bluebells during spring, and you really need a sunny day to see it all at its best.
DON'T MISS:
St Mary, the church in Stoke-by-Nayland. Its fine red-brick tower was much loved by Constable, and it has possibly the best 15th-century doors in the county as well as a fascinating interior.
AMOUNT OF WALKING:
As much or as little as you choose.
COST:
Low
YOU SHOULD KNOW:
Polstead was the site of the infamous Red Barn murder of 1827, when Maria Marten was killed by her lover, William Corder. This case was absolutely sensational, and Corder's eventual conviction and execution in Bury St Edmunds was attended by thousands. Several artefacts and a copy of Corder's death mask can be found in Moyse's Hall Museum in Bury St Edmunds. Maria's home still stands, but the Red Barn, which was decimated by souvenir seekers, went up in flames long ago.

Stoke-by-Nayland village church and cottages

Castle Hedingham and Sudbury

The little village of Castle Hedingham is dominated by its castle, or rather by its castle keep, though it has attractions of its own. You'll find many medieval buildings here, and an interesting church boasting a rare double hammerbeam roof and a Norman wheel window.

The Norman keep, with its two towers, was built in 1140 by Aubrey de Vere, and at 33 m (110 ft) high, it towers over the surrounding gardens. Still owned by one of de Vere's descendants, this is all that remains of what became a great medieval castle that hosted Henry VII, Henry VIII and Elizabeth I amongst many royal guests. Walk across the handsome Tudor bridge to the castle, the grassed area is used by spectators who come to see jousting during the summer. The keep's four storeys include a Minstrel's Gallery from which a marvellous view can be had of the spectacular Banqueting Hall, itself spanned by a huge, 8-m (28-ft) Norman arch. The grounds are lovely: there are woods and a lake to walk by. This is a good spot for a picnic.

In the afternoon you can drive to nearby Sudbury, in the heart of the beautiful Stour Valley. A market town since Saxon times, Sudbury has many fine, old buildings and, unsurprisingly, a noteworthy church. The painter Thomas Gainsborough was born here, and his family house – Tudor, but with an added Georgian façade - is now a museum and gallery. If you visit on a busy market day, and want to get away from the hustle and bustle for a while, stroll down to the Quay, or wander through the riverside meadows around the town in order to appreciate the tranquillity of the landscape that Gainsborough loved to paint.

WHERE:
Essex and south Suffolk
BEST TIME TO GO:
Late March to late October if you want to visit the castle. Check their opening times – special events are sometimes held here, including Snowdrop Walks in February.
DON'T MISS:
The Sudbury Pall: a wonderful piece of 15th-century embroidery on velvet in St Peter's Church, Sudbury.
AMOUNT OF WALKING:
Little to moderate
COST:
Reasonable
YOU SHOULD KNOW:
For railway enthusiasts, the Colne Valley Railway, at Castle Hedingham, is open from early May to mid-September.

The Norman keep at Castle Hedingham

Maldon and St Peter's Chapel

BRADWELL-ON-SEA

WHERE:
East Essex
BEST TIME TO GO:
On a sunny day
DON'T MISS:
Burnham-on-Crouch, a picturesque
town of pretty, colour washed
houses on the River Crouch, known
for sailing, boat building, oysters, and
lovely walks along the sea wall.
AMOUNT OF WALKING:
Lots – especially if you walk from
Bradwell-on-Sea to St. Peter's Chapel
– even from the Chapel car park it's
a good 15-minute walk.
COST:
Low
YOU SHOULD KNOW:
Maldon Crystal Sea Salt comes from
the salt beds of the River Blackwater.
Many special events are held in the
area, such as the Maldon Mud Race,
the Maldon Regatta and the Maldon
Oyster and Seafood Festival.

*The starkly simple interior of
St Peter-on-the-Wall*

The charming hill town of Maldon slopes gently down to the Blackwater Estuary. Here you can spend a pleasant morning sauntering about and looking at all the activity around the Hythe, the town's harbour.

Maldon's history dates from Roman times. Later, the Saxons lost a major, three-day battle against the Vikings here. The Blackwater soon became a major supply route for the east coast and during the 19th century, Thames sailing barges carried cargo to and from London. There were once at least 5,000 barges – most of the few that remain today are based here. Recognizable by their tan sails, many of these splendid boats are available for charter.

Many of Maldon's buildings are 15th and 16th century, some hiding behind more recent façades. At the top of the High Street, the parish church boasts a 13th-century triangular tower with a hexagonal spire, which is unique. Further down you will find the remarkable Moot Hall, the Maldon Museum, and the library. Given to the town in 1704, this is one of the oldest public libraries in the country.

Some 11 km (7 mi) east, you will find the village of Bradwell, roughly 3 km (2 mi) from the remarkable chapel of St Peter-on-the-Wall. St Cedd built this early cathedral in 654 AD, on the remains of a Roman fort, using Roman bricks and stones in its construction. During the 11th century it belonged to a Benedictine monastery and later was used as a barn for many years.

In 1920 St Peter's was restored as a chapel, and is now a place of pilgrimage. The interior is starkly simple, with an aura of spirituality. The cross shows Christ and St Cedd, and three stones form the altar, each a gift from a community touched by St Cedd's ministry. There is one from Lastingham, one from Iona and one from Lindisfarne.

Colchester

EAST ANGLIAN RAILWAY MUSEUM

Once the capital of Roman Britain and the country's oldest recorded town, everyone should spend a day out in Colchester. In AD 43, a Roman military fortress was established here, beginning a tradition that continues to this day – at present, 16 Air Assault Brigade is based here.

The town's past is visible through its architecture: the Saxon tower of Holy Trinity Church, the medieval gateway of St John's Abbey, the Tudor era 'Dutch Quarter', where Flemish weavers lived when Colchester was a wealthy wool town, and the many Victorian buildings, including the Town Hall.

The Castle is a 'must-visit' landmark. Built in the 11th century on the ruins of the Roman temple of Claudius, it boasts the largest Norman keep ever constructed. Today it houses an award-winning museum that presents the town's history from the Stone Age to the English Civil War. Other museums in town include Tymperleys Clock Museum. The splendid 15th-century house holds an important collection of Colchester-built clocks, made between 1640 and 1840. Hollytrees Museum, another award-winner, is in an elegant Georgian house. Here you can discover the history of the family who lived here, with a particular emphasis on children, making it a good place for family visits.

Just outside Colchester, at Chappel and Wakes Colne Railway Station, is the East Anglian Railway Museum. This working museum includes the entire site, and houses the region's most comprehensive collection of rolling stock. Many special events are held here, when you can enjoy unlimited trips on steam and diesel trains, and the annual Beer and Cider Festivals are extremely popular too. The nearby viaduct is worth seeing: at 323 m (1,066 ft) long, it has 32 arches, a maximum height of 23 m (75 ft), and is a magnificent example of Victorian engineering and building skills.

Castle Park Museum

WHERE:
Essex
BEST TIME TO GO:
March to November
DON'T MISS:
The Natural History Museum: housed in the former All Saints Church, it focuses on the natural history of Essex. Its interactive exhibits are of particular interest to children.
AMOUNT OF WALKING:
Moderate
COST:
Low – the museums are free to enter.
YOU SHOULD KNOW:
In AD 61, Boudicca and her troops attacked and destroyed Colchester – then known as Camulodunum – and subsequently London became the capital of the Roman province of Britannia. Had she not been so successful, who knows – Colchester could still be Britain's capital city.

Audley End House and Gardens

Saffron Walden and Audley End

If you're in north-west Essex, you can enjoy a fine day out exploring the old market town of Saffron Walden in the morning and then the beautiful, English Heritage owned Audley End, with its magnificent gardens, in the afternoon.

There has been a settlement at what was then Chipping Walden since Roman times. By the medieval era, the wool trade was the major industry and during the 16th and 17th centuries saffron was extensively grown in the area – hence the name change to Saffron Walden. Malt and barley took over from saffron and there were several breweries here in the 19th century. Today the town still flourishes, and its success over the centuries has produced the many historic features and buildings visible today. The ruins of the 12th century castle can still be seen and the 15th-century parish church is the largest in Essex.

A short drive from town will bring you to Audley End. Given to Sir Thomas Audley by Henry VIII, the existing abbey was transformed into a palatial mansion. Over the centuries various owners added to the building, and Capability Brown re-designed the gardens. There are over thirty fabulous rooms to visit, including a superb Jacobean Great Hall, all filled with beautiful furniture and paintings by Canaletto, Holbein and other masters. There is also a unique collection of 18th-century tapestries.

Audley End's grounds are glorious. An artificial lake runs through the park, and there are temples and decorative garden buildings to admire. Walk through the Elysian Garden, a woodland grove with a bridge designed by Robert Adam, and enjoy the wonderful 19th-century kitchen garden with its 52-m (170-ft) long vinehouse. This is now an organic kitchen garden, and the produce is for sale. A well-restored formal parterre flower garden dominates the rear of the house.

WHERE:
North-west Essex
BEST TIME TO GO:
March to October, but choose a sunny day to see Audley End gardens at their best.
DON'T MISS:
The Audley End Miniature Railway, for a lovely ride through woodlands – particularly good fun for children.
AMOUNT OF WALKING:
Moderate
COST:
Reasonable – particularly if you're an English Heritage member, when it is free.
YOU SHOULD KNOW:
Check up on the summertime open-air concerts at Audley End, you might be able to stay on for the evening to enjoy one.

Hatfield Forest

THAXTED, GREAT BARDFIELD AND FINCHINGFIELD

Hatfield Forest is a unique landscape. What you see when walking here has barely changed since Henry I claimed it as a Royal Hunting Forest early in the 12th century – there are even written records to prove it.

This is a place of ancient trees, coppiced and pollarded, grassland and marsh. A stream meanders through it and there is even a lake. This Site of Special Scientific Interest and National Nature Reserve is a peaceful oasis in the midst of an area dominated by busy roads and Stansted Airport. Here you can take guided walks or wander where you like, go cycling, fishing or even horse riding. Visit the Shell House: built in 1754 and intended for summer parties for its owners; Laetitia Houblon, the daughter, decorated the entire building with exotic shells – a fashion statement at the time.

On leaving Hatfield Forest, drive through pretty countryside to visit a few delightful villages. Thaxted, mentioned in the Domesday Book, boasts some remarkable buildings, including Horham Hall, the Guildhall, St John's Church and John Webb's Windmill. Built in 1804 the mill, which includes an interesting rural museum, has been fully restored, and can be visited on weekend afternoons and Bank Holidays during the summer.

Little Bardfield, your next stop, is known for the imposing Saxon tower on its ancient parish church. Great Bardfield is a charming village -- during the 1950s it was known as the Artists' Village, so numerous were the artists who came to live and work here. It too has a noteworthy church. Finally, take a look at Finchingfield. Believed to be the most photographed village in England, it is indeed picture-postcard perfect. Its fame, however, has brought an inevitable downside in the large number of visitors it receives each year and the facilities needed to cater for them.

WHERE:
Hertfordshire and Essex
BEST TIME TO GO:
April to October
DON'T MISS:
Thaxted's annual Morris dancing festival; the Morris Ring, the national association, was founded here in1934.
AMOUNT OF WALKING:
Moderate
COST:
Low
YOU SHOULD KNOW:
The composer Gustav Holst was a resident of Thaxted, and parts of The Planets, his most famous work, were inspired by and written in the village.

Thaxted market

The Shuttleworth Collection

BIRD OF PREY CENTRE

WHERE:
Bedfordshire
BEST TIME TO GO:
April to October. The Shuttleworth
Collection and Swiss Garden are
open year round. The Swiss Garden
is particularly beautiful in spring.
Check in advance to make sure you
can see everything you want to.
DON'T MISS:
An evening display of vintage planes
in flight.
AMOUNT OF WALKING:
Moderate
COST:
Reasonable. Children up to 16 have
free entry to both the Shuttleworth
Collection and the Swiss Garden.
YOU SHOULD KNOW:
The Swiss Garden was made by Lord
Ogley for his Swiss mistress. The
wrought-iron bridges were made by
Lady Emma Hamilton's uncle, who
was a blacksmith here. The garden is
reputed to be so haunted that, in the
past, gardeners would only work
here in pairs.

The Shuttleworth Collection is actually a combination of attractions set in Shuttleworth Old Warden Park, near Biggleswade. It is centred around a large, Grade II listed Victorian mansion that lies in 202 hectares (500 acres) of parkland. The house, now the home of Shuttleworth College, but sometimes open to the public, is also available for conferences, corporate entertaining and weddings.

Shuttleworth is probably best known as an aeronautical and automotive museum. Founded by Richard Shuttleworth in 1928, an aviator himself, the Trust was set up in his memory. This is one of the country's foremost collections of historic aircraft, and it includes the oldest British plane still able to fly: a Bleriot XI, built in 1909.

There are over fifty aeroplanes in the collection, some of which are privately owned, and flying displays are put on several times each summer, allowing the public to see some of the last existing planes of their type take to the air and show off their prowess. There is also a wonderful collection of vintage cars to be seen – the oldest of these, a Panhard et Levassor, dates back to 1898. Motorbikes and tractors are also on show.

If vintage transport is not your thing, visit the Swiss Garden: a romantic, early Victorian garden surrounding a small Swiss-style cottage. Here you will walk amongst rare trees and shrubs, through a landscape full of wrought-iron bridges over small canals, pools of water, exotic structures and even a grotto.

A further treat awaits you at the Bird of Prey Centre, with its collection of about three hundred raptors from across the world. The Centre is involved in breeding and conservation programmes, particularly for rare and endangered species, and there are daily flying displays as well as the chance of learning to fly a hawk yourself.

An Avro Triplane and Avro Tutor fly the flag.

Woburn Abbey

DEER PARK AND SAFARI PARK

Nine species of deer roam free in the Deer Park.

Magnificent Woburn Abbey is one of England's treasures. The house dates back to the 12th century, when a Cistercian monastery was founded here. Gifted by Edward VI to Sir John Russell in 1547, it was transformed into the family home of the Dukes of Bedford in the early 17th century. Today it is a hugely successful visitor attraction.

The house itself contains a fabulous collection of priceless furniture and art. Visit some of the State Rooms, Queen Victoria's bedroom, and the vaults, where much of the family's gold and silver services can be seen. Explore the house alone, take an audio tour or, if you're lucky, a knowledgeable warden will escort you.

Outside, the landscaped gardens and Deer Park are also spectacular. Nine species of deer roam free, including the Pere David, rescued from extinction here. Numerous rare, old trees can be admired and the Hornbeam Maze is sometimes opened for visits. There are many old farm buildings in the grounds, used in various ways. The home of the successful Bloomsbury Stud is here, and part of the South Stable Block is now a large antiques centre.

The 13th Duke of Bedford opened Woburn Safari Park in 1970. He hoped it would improve the estate's finances and allow restoration work to be carried out on the Abbey itself, but he cannot have known what a hit it would prove to be. Here visitors can drive through large enclosures where animals roam at will. Species include lions, tigers, rhinoceros, giraffes, elephants, camels and monkeys, and the Park prides itself on its breeding programmes and conservation work. It is the largest zoo in the country, and it provides a busy programme of talks and demonstrations, while feeding times for animals such as bears and penguins are always a crowd pleaser.

WHERE:
Bedfordshire
BEST TIME TO GO:
Mid-March to late September to include visiting the Abbey. Check in advance to find out what is available.
DON'T MISS:
The Dining Room. Still in use by the family, it has a marvellous ceiling, painted by Cipriani in 1770, and a fabulous collection of paintings by Canaletto, commissioned by the 4th Duke on a visit to Venice in 1731.
AMOUNT OF WALKING:
Moderate
COST:
Expensive
YOU SHOULD KNOW:
There is so much to see and do at Woburn that you really need more than one day to do it justice. The new 'Passport' ticket enables you to do just that – check it out.

Whipsnade Zoo

No matter what age you are, whether you go on your own, with friends or family, a day spent at Whipsnade Zoo is a day that will be enjoyed by everyone.

Whipsnade began in 1926, when the Zoological Society of London bought a disused farm on the Dunstable Downs. Set in 243 hectares (600 acres) of land, the zoo opened to the public in 1931, receiving 38,000 visitors on its second day. Now, as part of the ZSL, it is deeply involved in breeding and conservation work around the world.

The face of Whipsnade has changed over the decades with the introduction of modern enclosures specially designed to emulate a variety of habitats. These enable visitors to see as much of the animals as possible, whilst allowing them their privacy. You can walk around the zoo, take a bus, drive between the enclosures, or through the Asian area where various animals roam free. If you get tired, take a trip on the steam train – it doesn't go all over the park, but you get to see elephants, rhino, Przewalski horses, and zebra, as well as wallabies, Bactrian camels and more in the barrier-free zone.

There are daily animal shows, and talks about different species – in all, several thousand animals live here. Make sure you see Cheetah Rock, an inspiring new enclosure in which Whipsnade hopes to achieve a successful breeding programme. Parts of the rock are heated, so the cheetahs can enjoy the warmth they need even on a chilly day.

There are plenty of places round the park where you can stop, have a bite to eat, and raise your energy levels for another expedition to look at the elephants, tigers, lions, the Reptile House, or whatever else takes your fancy.

WHERE:
Bedfordshire
BEST TIME TO GO:
Whipsnade is open every day, with the exception of Christmas.
DON'T MISS:
Any new arrivals – in the last year or two, not only have new species arrived here, but young have been born – a baby giraffe, African lion cubs, an Asian rhino calf and an Asian elephant calf to mention but a few.
AMOUNT OF WALKING:
As much or little as you choose.
COST:
Reasonable, considering the amount of time you can spend here. Children under 16 must be accompanied by an adult. Whipsnade and ZSL receive no government funding, but tickets are available that include a small donation.
YOU SHOULD KNOW:
In 1933, on a west-facing, chalk slope just below Whipsnade, a gigantic lion was carved. Too large to see properly close to, it is very visible from afar, and there are good vantage points on the A4146.

A family group of Asian elephants

Hatfield House and St Albans

For British history buffs, a fascinating day out can be had visiting Hatfield House and St Albans. Just 34 km (21 mi) north of London, Hatfield House is a large, Jacobean mansion standing amidst beautiful countryside. Built in 1485 by the Bishop of Ely, part of the original palace still stands to the west of the Jacobean house, itself built in the early 1600s by Robert Cecil, 1st Earl of Salisbury. It remains the home of the Cecils to this day.

Take a tour of the house: richly decorated and furnished for royal visitors, it is a fine example of the workmanship of the period. The park and gardens, too, are wonderful. Divided into sections, the West Garden was planted by John Tradescant in the early 17th century. Here you'll find a scented garden, a herb garden and the famous knot garden, near the old palace. The East Garden is more formal, with parterres and topiary, designed to be viewed from the first floor of the house.

Some twenty minutes drive away, and you'll be in St Albans, a city that goes back to the days of the Ancient Britons. The important Roman town of Verulamium followed, and later still a medieval town grew up around what was once England's principal Abbey. The first draft of Magna Carta was produced here.

Despite an initial impression of suburban housing and traffic congestion, St Albans has an historic core, dominated by the splendid cathedral. Begun in 1077, its tower includes bricks from the old Roman town. The Abbey Gateway, built in 1365, is all that remains of the original Abbey. Visit the award-winning Verulamium Museum for an eye-opening look at Roman life. Close by, you'll find the finest Roman theatre in the country, Roman shops, a shrine and the foundations of a town house.

WHERE:
Hertfordshire
BEST TIME TO GO:
Wednesdays to Sundays and Bank Holiday Mondays, from Easter to end September, if you want to visit Hatfield House and gardens. The East Garden is only open on Thursdays.
DON'T MISS:
Gorhambury House: built in 1777, this neo-Palladian house is the home of the Earls of Verulam, and contains a collection of fascinating portraits transferred from the nearby ruin of Old Gorhambury House, home of Francis Bacon (1561-1626) the philosopher and politician.
AMOUNT OF WALKING:
Moderate
COST:
Expensive
YOU SHOULD KNOW:
Elizabeth I spent much of her childhood at Hatfield Palace, where Mary, Queen of Scots kept her, almost a prisoner, after the death of Henry VIII. You can see the oak tree in the Park beneath which, in 1558, Elizabeth was sitting with a book when she received the news of her accession to the throne.

Hatfield House and Gardens

The Dove Valley

WHERE:
Derbyshire and Staffordshire
BEST TIME TO GO:
Any time
DON'T MISS:
Charles Cotton's Fishing House on
the River Dove at Hartington – he
was a great friend and fishing
companion of Isaac Walton,
contributing to Walton's classic *The
Compleat Angler* of 1653 (the
entwined initials of both men are
over the door).
AMOUNT OF WALKING:
Lots (note that some areas of the
Dove riverside are definitely not
wheelchair country).
COST:
Low
YOU SHOULD KNOW:
Viator's Bridge at Milldale is an
ancient stone bridge across the Dove
named after Isaac Walton, who called
himself Viator (Latin for 'traveller')
and described the bridge in *The
Compleat Angler*.

A good starting point from which to explore this peaceful corner of the East Midlands is Buxton, at the heart of the Peak District. Buxton has a geothermal spring of the sort Romans adored, and they duly founded the settlement of Aquae Arnemetiae here. The waters were taken throughout the Middle Ages, but it took the Fifth Duke of Devonshire to develop Buxton as an elegant and fashionable spa in the 18th century.

But this is a day for exploring scenic Dovedale and the Dove Valley south of Buxton. Leave town on the A515 road and turn right onto the B5053. The road crosses the River Dove before Longnor, with a fine walk upstream towards the source – indeed, the riverside is accessible for most of its length and walkers take full advantage.

Continue to Longnor on the River Manifold, turning left for Crowdecote back on the Dove. Popular with ramblers, the village is close to spectacular Chrome Hill, High Wheeldon and Parkhouse Hill. Go on through Pilsbury, passing the site of Pilsbury Castle en route to the delightful village of Hartington with its market hall and 13th-century parish church. Arbor Low – the finest neolithic stone circle in The Peak District – is nearby, as is the viewpoint of Wolfscote Hill.

Continue down the Dove Valley to Milldale village at the head of Dovedale – and if you haven't yet done any walking, now is the time to start. Dovedale is a fabulous stretch of river that runs for 5 km (3 mi) from Milldale to a wooded ravine near Thorpe Cloud Hill at the confluence of the Dove and Manifold Rivers. The wooded ravine contains famous stepping-stones, Dove Holes (two caves), rock pillars and a striking limestone formation like Twelve Apostles, Lovers' Leap and Reynard's Cave. It's a walk to remember.

Walking the Dovedale stepping stones across the River Dove.

Castleton Caverns

An unusual outing is provided by show caverns that encircle the Peak-District village of Castleton. It should really have been 'Caveton', because Peveril Castle above the village came much later, along with the Normans. The Castle is a picturesque ruin that has a keep complete with garderobe (medieval loo) and curtain walls.

Though there are excellent hill footpaths and walks along Peakshole Water, this is more of an underground day...with bonus boating. Speedwell Cavern is accessed through the adit (horizontal shaft) of an old lead mine, driven into the hillside to the great limestone cave within. The adit is partly flooded, so access is by boat. Thereafter, the visitor walks, seeing stalactites, stalagmites and the 'Bottomless Pit' shaft.

Treak Cliff Cavern contains traces of Blue John. This rare mineral has long been prized and the first part of Treak is a former Blue John mine. The inner caves with their fabulous array of stalactites have names – Aladdin's, Fairyland, Dream Cave and Dome of St Pauls. From the upper exit there are fine views of the Hope Valley.

Peak Cavern has an impressive entrance (exit?) portal and chamber. The aptly named River Styx formed the cavern and flows through it before emerging near Castleton, whose inhabitants once used the long cave for ropemaking (remains of the activity can still be seen).

Last up is Blue John Cavern. Castleton is the only place where this unique fluorspar is found, and this combination of mine workings and natural caves was the principal source. A mined passage descends steeply into a series of natural caverns containing absolutely stunning formations and colouring, with highlights like the Crystallised and Variegated Caverns. If you only visit one of Castleton's four caverns, make it this one.

Aladdin's Cave

WHERE:
Derbyshire
BEST TIME TO GO:
Any time
DON'T MISS:
The evidence of ancient mining activity in Blue John Cavern – an old trolley, windlass, bellows and obvious mine workings.
AMOUNT OF WALKING:
Lots (note that sadly this is not really an ideal day for wheelchair users).
COST:
Expensive (if you visit all four caverns).
YOU SHOULD KNOW:
Inevitably, the Romans were first on the scene – vases made of Blue John that must have been mined at Castleton were found during excavations at Pompeii.

199

Mature woodland surrounds Chatsworth House.

Chatsworth House

WHERE:
Derbyshire
BEST TIME TO GO:
March to October
DON'T MISS:
The amazingly deceptive trompe l'oeil of a violin and bow painted on one of Chatsworth's internal doors by Jan van der Vaart in 1723.
AMOUNT OF WALKING:
Lots
COST:
Reasonable
YOU SHOULD KNOW:
Mary, Queen of Scots was held prisoner at Chatsworth several times after 1570, living in rooms above the Great Hall now called The Queen of Scots Rooms.

Northeast of Bakewell between Pilsley and Beeley is Chatsworth House, one of Britain's most impressive stately homes. The house, completed by Bess of Hardwick in the 1560s on a wooded hillside above the River Derwent, was altered and expanded towards the end of the 17th century and a last great revamp was undertaken by the Sixth Duke of Devonshire from 1811.

These phases of development altered rather than replaced what was there, so the interiors are full of architecture and decoration from different periods. Visitors can wander at leisure through grand apartments, containing a fabulous art collection and many extraordinary objects, some going back four millennia. The First Duke's Painted Hall is magnificent; there are richly decorated State Rooms, a 19th-century library, Sculpture Gallery and Great Dining Room.

The interiors are superb and that adjective applies equally to the gardens – surrounded by a wall 2.8 km (1.75 mi) long – they have been evolving for 450 years. See the Elizabethan Garden, the First Duke's baroque formal gardens complete with assorted statuary and the famous Cascade, the Fourth Duke's garden by Capability Brown, the Sixth Duke's garden created by the great Joseph Paxton and a modern garden added since 1950 – all combining into a magnificent whole. You may need to get a guidebook and move at a brisk pace – there are around 8 km (5 mi) of paths to explore.

The huge stable block behind the house dates from 1760 and is now home to a restaurant and shop (there are actually four gift shops at Chatsworth). On the hillside above there is a working farmyard exhibit and spectacular adventure playground. Beyond the gardens, the extensive park and woodlands are freely available to walkers. The best of local produce may be purchased in the large Chatsworth Farm Shop at Pilsley.

Around Bakewell

Start the day at the Plague Village of Eyam, north of Bakewell. It is so called because the village isolated itself when the Black Death arrived in 1665 in an attempt to save others by preventing onward transmission of the deadly disease – after sixteen months the epidemic ended, but only 83 villagers out of 350 survived. There are memorials to those dark days and a fine Saxon cross in the churchyard.

Nearby Bakewell is a small but nicely formed market town that has the distinction of being the only town within the scenic Peak District National Park. The splendid All Saints Church was founded in Saxon times and there are two crosses from that period in the churchyard, where numerous Saxon fragments were found during Victorian restoration work. There is also a wonderful five-arch bridge built in the 13th century. Richard Arkwright's pioneering Lumford Mill of 1777 was here (now nothing remains).

If nearby Chatsworth House is worth a day, Haddon Hall definitely merits an afternoon. The First Duke of Rutland moved to Belvoir Castle in 1703, leaving Haddon Hall to remain virtually unchanged for two centuries. The Ninth Duke began meticulous restoration of this unspoilt gem in the 1920s, also reviving lovely terraced Elizabethan gardens beside the River Wye.

Parts of the house date back to the 11th century. The banqueting hall with minstrels' gallery, parlour and kitchens were built in the 1300s. The St Nicholas Chapel was completed in 1427 and there is a 16th-century long gallery. No work was carried out after the 17th century. The hall stands on a slope and is arranged round two courtyards. Haddon Hall has been described as 'the most perfect house to survive from the Middle Ages', and few would argue. It's open every day from May to September plus April and October weekends.

Haddon Hall dates back to the 11th century.

WHERE:
Derbyshire
BEST TIME TO GO:
Mondays, for the popular traditional market in Bakewell.
DON'T MISS:
The wonderful early tapestries to be found lining the walls of Haddon Hall.
AMOUNT OF WALKING:
Moderate
COST:
Reasonable
YOU SHOULD KNOW:
Be careful what you ask for – two shops claim the original recipe for the famous local jam-filled pastry, one insisting that the correct name is Bakewell Tart and the other claiming the true title is Bakewell Pudding.

Matlock to Wirksworth

WHERE:
Derbyshire
BEST TIME TO GO:
April to September
DON'T MISS:
A tiny carving in Wirksworth's
wonderful St Mary's Church which
shows a miner with his pick and
basket – also see the rather larger
early carved Wirksworth Stone
showing scenes from Christ's life.
AMOUNT OF WALKING:
Moderate
COST:
Low
YOU SHOULD KNOW:
D.H. Lawrence resided at Mountain
Cottage on the outskirts of
Middleton-by-Wirksworth in 1918-19,
writing 'The Wintry Peacock' there,
and George Eliot's *The Mill on the
Floss* is thought to have been based
on Arkwright's mill (her aunt lived
in Wirksworth).

Located on the edge of the Peak District, Matlock is within the area known as the Derbyshire Dales. This former spa town on the River Derwent prospered after thermal springs were discovered and became hugely popular in Victorian times, when cotton mills added to Matlock's prosperity. Hydrotherapy is a distant memory, but a distinct resort-feel remains and the place is popular with tourists. Hall Leys Park by the river is at the heart of the town. It dates from 1898 and has various attractions. The hill up to St Giles Church is the oldest area.

Matlock Bath down the A6 road has a sublime location on the River Derwent in a deep gorge beneath towering High Tor, sufficiently dramatic for Lord Byron to have described it as 'a romantic fragment of Switzerland in the heart of England' after one of his frequent visits. But these very qualities made it popular with the masses after the railways came, and it became more like a seaside resort than genteel spa. There are amusement arcades, chip shops and cafés, plus a cablecar across the gorge to the Heights of Abraham above town. Happily, the scenery remains and there are some excellent walks.

To the south of Matlock Bath is Wirksworth, a former centre of limestone quarrying and lead mining. Richard Arkwright spun cotton here from 1777, beside the rival Speedwell Mill (both mills still working). There are two heritage railways – Steeple Grange operating narrow-gauge industrial locos and rolling stock and the Ecclesbourne Valley Railway running old diesels. Wirksworth's autobiography unfolds at the Heritage Centre, a former silk mill. The Wirksworth Story is told on three floors, ranging from the ancient Woolly rhino found nearby, through Roman times to the medieval Moot Hall and development of local industries and transport. It's thoroughly entertaining.

Arkwright's Masson Mills

Hardwick Hall

When death duties fell heavily upon the new Duke of Devonshire after World War II, one of the family's finest houses was handed to the nation in part payment. His loss was the people's gain – hilltop Hardwick Hall is an awesome Elizabethan mansion speaking volumes about the power and wealth of the Duke's ancestor, formidable Bess of Hardwick.

As a secondary residence, Hardwick Hall was little altered over time — and that extends to the contents, with many items that remain in situ listed on an inventory of 1601. Each of three main storeys is higher than the one below and the message inherent in large windows ('more glass than wall') would not have been lost on Bess's contemporaries – glass was a very expensive luxury.

The grand staircase leads to an impressive suite of rooms, including a huge long gallery and vast great chamber with a spectacular plaster hunting frieze. Hardwick Hall contains much fine early furniture and outstanding tapestries. The Threads of Time exhibition ties up the story of Bess and the house's contents, whilst outside walled courtyards contain a herb garden, orchards and lawns. Ruined Hardwick Old Hall is in the grounds. It's a further tribute to Bess's ambition that she could casually consign this slightly earlier house to history to pursue her grander design. Hardwick Hall is open on Wednesdays, Thursdays, Saturdays and Sundays (weekends only in winter). The parkland is open daily. Find it between Chesterfield and Mansfield.

Speaking of Chesterfield, it's a place worth visiting if time remains. Best known for the crooked spire on St Mary and All Saints Church, much modern development has happily left The Shambles intact. This central warren of narrow medieval streets contains one of Britain's oldest pubs, The Royal Oak. There is a large open-air market around the Market Hall.

Resting in the gardens of Hardwick Hall.

WHERE:
Derbyshire
BEST TIME TO GO:
March to October
DON'T MISS:
The historic parkland at Hardwick Hall, with the Stone Centre (stonemasonry explained), rare breed animals and walking trails.
AMOUNT OF WALKING:
Moderate
COST:
Reasonable
YOU SHOULD KNOW:
Hardwick's six rooftop pavilions have Bess of Hardwick's initials E S (for Elizabeth Shrewsbury, her name after marrying her fourth husband) modestly worked into the balustrades.

Bolsover Castle

CRESSWELL CRAGS

In Bolsover may be found the eponymous castle – originally constructed in the 12th century and acquired by Sir Charles Cavendish in 1608. His mother was Bess of Hardwick, builder of Hardwick Hall, and he obviously learned a thing or two at his mother's knee. He set about rebuilding the castle, a process continued by his own son, William. The tower (known as the Little Castle) was completed in the 1620s, but Parliamentarians severely damaged Bolsover Castle in the Civil War and it again required rebuilding – a feat achieved by William Cavendish before his death in 1676, with the addition of a Terrace Range that included a long gallery, plus an incredible indoor Riding School Range (now a Discovery Centre).

Bolsover Castle is now in the care of English Heritage and, sitting on a dominant hilltop above The Vale of Scarsdale, it has far-reaching views. The fairytale Little Castle is a fabulous expression of Elizabethan romance, whilst the beautiful Venus Garden has secluded love seats, statues and an ancient fountain.

Proceed along the lanes from Bolsover via Elmton to Creswell, where nearby Creswell Crags is a limestone gorge honeycombed with caves and fissures, which have produced fascinating evidence of prehistoric life between 50,000 and 10,000 years ago. Creswell Crags hit the headlines in 2003 with the discovery of Ice-Age cave art (including figures of birds, deer, bison and horse) that is some 13,000 years old, to add to many other fascinating finds made since excavations began over a century ago.

The Museum and Education Centre proudly presents the Age of Ice, giving visitors enhanced understanding of this nationally important Ice-Age site – a scheduled Ancient Monument and Site of Special Scientific Interest. After seeing the exhibitions, it's possible to take cave tours and then enjoy a pleasant lakeside walk around the impressive gorge.

Bolsover Castle sits atop a hill overlooking the Vale of Scarsdale.

WHERE:
Derbyshire
BEST TIME TO GO:
Any time
DON'T MISS:
Magnificent wall paintings in Bolsover's Little Castle – if you can appreciate images carefully described as 'symbolic and erotic'.
AMOUNT OF WALKING:
Moderate
COST:
Reasonable
YOU SHOULD KNOW:
The importance of Creswell Crags began to emerge after a local man's wife dreamed of buried treasure in the cave now known as Mother Grundy's Parlour and sent him there to dig. The result was a hippopotamus tooth and the rest is, as they say, history.

Calke Abbey

MELBOURNE HALL AND DERBY

Today's the day to put the words 'time' and 'capsule' together and come up with Calke Abbey, an extraordinary Baroque mansion built around 1700 that has changed little since Victorian times. The need to raise death duties in the 1980s led to Calke Abbey's inevitable passing to the National Trust. The beauty of Calke is a huge variety of contents, grand and mundane, amassed over time – and, as the fortunes of the Harpur family declined, those contents were crammed in here, there and everywhere, almost burying such treasures as a wonderful 18th-century silk bed.

The National Trust rightly decided this eccentric interior should be left as found – an intriguing monument to that difficult period when traditional country houses struggled to survive. Enjoy also the surrounding park – a National Nature Reserve made for walking. Calke Abbey is off the A514 road south of Derby, at Ticknell. The house is sometimes closed on Thursdays and Fridays, but Calke Park is always open.

From Calke, go on to nearby Melbourne, a fine Georgian market town. Melbourne Hall (rebuilt in the 17th century but originally rectory to the adjacent Norman church) and Gardens should be visited if open – the Hall on August afternoons and the Gardens from April to September (afternoons on selected days). It's as well to get it right, especially for the Gardens. Thomas Coke's imaginative 18th-century work has been sensitively updated, but the real highlight is a stunning collection of garden statuary.

Find time before the day is over to plunge into the hustle and bustle of Derby city centre, to find the Museum and Art Gallery in The Strand. There's a wide range of interesting exhibits, but the unique attraction here is the internationally important collection of early English porcelain manufactured at William Duesbury's Derby factory from about 1755.

WHERE:
Derbyshire
BEST TIME TO GO:
April to September
DON'T MISS:
The cellars and extraordinary servants' tunnel at Calke Abbey, constructed so the 'great and the good' wouldn't be offended by the sight of scurrying lackeys.
AMOUNT OF WALKING:
Moderate (with wheelchair access to some parts of Calke Abbey restricted).
COST:
Reasonable
YOU SHOULD KNOW:
Yes, Melbourne in Australia was indeed named after Queen Victoria's first Prime Minister, Viscount Melbourne – who was originally a Lamb, connected with Melbourne Hall by marriage.

Calke Abbey – the embodiment of an 18th-century English country house

Lincolnshire Wolds

WHERE:
Lincolnshire
BEST TIME TO GO:
Any time
DON'T MISS:
Wolds Top – the highest point in the Lincolnshire Wolds, marked by a trig point just north of Normanby-le-Wold.
AMOUNT OF WALKING:
Lots
COST:
Low
YOU SHOULD KNOW:
Be sure to take a good map on your tour, as the maze of minor roads can be confusing and it's easy to get lost ...no matter, you'll just get to see even more of the Wonderful Wolds!

Eastern England's undiscovered pastoral gem is Lincolnshire's Wolds – an Area of Outstanding Natural Beauty. From Caistor down to Spilsby, the Wolds run roughly parallel to the North Sea. A drive through the sparsely populated landscape is not about pretty villages, but seeing unspoilt countryside. In fact, many villages have shrunk since their medieval heyday, or vanished altogether.

There are four distinct areas to see, and an ideal way to appreciate the differences is a scenic circular tour from Caistor, taking a picnic and stopping for a stroll or two along your choice of many marked footpaths ...or simply sitting in the car and admiring far-reaching views across surrounding flatland to distant landmarks like Lincoln Cathedral.

From Caistor, take the A46 and turn left at Nettleton to Normanby-le-Wold, before finding the B1225 and turning right, almost immediately going right again to Tealby. This has taken you through

the north-western scarp's dramatic slopes, wooded valleys and rough pastureland.

Rejoin the southbound B1225 and enter the southwest's complex arrangement of ridges bisected by deep combes and wide river valleys, with a patchwork of hedges and fields, woodland and rivers. Go on through this attractive area and turn right for Donington-on-Bain, wending through lanes via Goulceby, Belchford, Tetford, Hagworthingham and Partney to Gunby.

Head north on the main A1028 and A16 roads, through the heart of the wooded south-eastern claylands with their remote, isolated feel. Turn off the Louth bypass onto the A631, turning right for Kelstern, Binbrook and Rothwell, and from there back to Caister. This takes you across the chalk wolds, an extensive open plateau of rolling hills, where large arable fields contrast with the secluded valleys with their wooded slopes and lush pastures. Best of all, you won't find a single tourist trap from beginning to end!

Looking across the wheat fields onto the Lincolnshire Wolds.

Lincoln Cathedral

Lincoln

The Lincoln Imp is the city's traditional symbol. Various legends surround him, but one sure fact is that his graven image may be found within Lincoln Cathedral. Unfortunately, like the whodunit secret in Agatha Christie's *The Mousetrap*, those in the know must not reveal the Imp's location (clue – the Angel Choir is very special). Mind you, looking for him is no hardship – St Mary's Cathedral is awe-inspiring, described by influential Victorian writer John Ruskin as 'worth any two other cathedrals we have'.

Lincoln Castle is another magnificent survivor. William the Conqueror's fortress is well preserved, thanks to continued use as a prison and law court. An original copy of the Magna Carta is here and a walk round the massive 12th-century ramparts offers great views of Cathedral and city without and Castle complex within.

Lincoln has many other historic buildings, notably those around the Bailgate and down Steep Hill to High Bridge. The latter is a rare example of an early bridge bearing half-timbered housing jutting over the river. There are three splendid ancient churches – St Mary le Wigford and St Peter at Gowts (11th century), plus St Mary Magdalene (13th century).

After seeing town churches, who could resist a short trip to the small village of Stow between Lincoln and Gainsborough? There you can find one of the oldest churches in Britain, Stow Minster. Part Saxon and part Norman, it has tall Saxon arches, Viking longboat graffiti, an early English font on supports with pagan symbols and an early wall painting dedicated to martyred Thomas Becket. Complete a satisfying church-crawl at St Edith's in Coates. It's tucked away in the middle of nowhere along a lane from Stow and – in direct contrast to huge Stow Minster – is a tiny but delightful church of Norman origin with Lincolnshire's only Early English rood screen.

WHERE:
Lincolnshire
BEST TIME TO GO:
Any time
DON'T MISS:
The 19th-century prison chapel in Lincoln Castle – it was designed so that each worshipper was confined within an individual 'cell' that precluded covert conversation with his fellows.
AMOUNT OF WALKING:
Moderate (note that wheelchair access to some features of Lincoln Castle is not possible).
COST:
Low
YOU SHOULD KNOW:
Lincoln Cathedral was the world's tallest building for 250 years, until the soaring spire was blown down in 1549, never to be rebuilt...so those brilliant medieval cathedral builders didn't always get it right (indeed, the main tower collapsed in the 1230s!).

Around Rutland

England's smallest county is big enough to offer interesting contrasts. This outing in Rutland takes in a pleasant market town, a medieval maze, a church that's also a museum, England's largest reservoir, a peninsular village and a castle. Sounds interesting!

The market town is Uppingham – an old-fashioned place with a handsome school (founded 1584) and a Market Square and High Street reflecting varied architectural styles from the 17th century. There is a 14th-century church.

The maze is north of Uppingham at the picturesque village of Wing. It won't delay you for long but is great fun, being a turf-cut maze (technically a labyrinth) in which you have to follow a convoluted path to the centre.

The church that is also a museum may be found through Edith Weston at Normanton. One of Rutland's most famous landmarks stands alone on a promontory – once threatened with a watery grave, the church was saved by public outcry and now serves as a museum detailing the construction of its near nemesis, Rutland Water. Which is, of course, the vast reservoir. Drive round it via Empingham and Whitwell to enjoy lake views, or stop off and sample leisure activities ranging from waterside walks through to cruises.

The peninsular village is Hambleton, surrounded on three sides by the aforementioned Rutland Water. It has a pub and 12th-century church, plus a great view across to the great Palladian mansion at Burley.

The castle would be a few humps and bumps next to the church in Rutland's nearby county town, Oakham – were it not for the survival of the splendid Great Hall of Oakham Castle. This fine example of 12th-century domestic architecture is decorated with six sculptures of superb quality, each showing a musician playing a different instrument. There couldn't be a more satisfying way to end this varied Rutland day.

Rutland Water was opened in the 1970s, but Normanston Church Museum was built in 1826-9 and designed by Thomas Cundy, then architect to the Grosvenor Estate in Westminster.

WHERE:
Rutland
BEST TIME TO GO:
Any time
DON'T MISS:
If you can find time, the Rutland Railway Museum is north of Oakham between Cottesmore and Ashwell. It is unusual in featuring the recently active but now forgotten iron-ore industry of the East Midlands.
AMOUNT OF WALKING:
Moderate (be aware that not all the leisure activities at Rutland Water are for wheelchair users or those with small children).
COST:
Low
YOU SHOULD KNOW:
Rutland was greedily swallowed by Leicestershire in the 1970s, but soon regained its independence...and after a spirited campaign it even reclaimed its status as a postal county in 2008, severing the last official link with Leicestershire.

Burghley House

The Industrial Revolution passed Stamford by, and this quaint town on the River Welland retains many streets of timber-framed or mellow old stone buildings, with interesting shops tucked away down intriguing side alleys and numerous fine old churches. Without the street signs and traffic, parts of Stamford could still be stuck in a previous century – indeed, the town is often used as a convincing location for period film and TV dramas. It's easy to spend a couple of satisfying hours exploring this delightful place, but Stamford is just the starter.

The main course is nearby Burghley House, one of the largest and grandest Elizabethan houses in Britain. Notwithstanding its architectural magnificence and vast physical presence, the really interesting thing about Burghley is that it has never changed hands, so the interior reflects the acquisitive tastes of one family over the centuries.

And acquire they did, especially in the 17th and 18th centuries (helped by marriage to the occasional wealthy heiress). The contents of Burghley are breathtaking, and may be appreciated with the help of a guided tour (alternatively browse through the collections with the help of knowledgeable stewards). Along the way are spectacular State Rooms, including the magnificent George Rooms, together containing one of the world's most important collections of Italian 17th-century paintings. Other notable rooms are the Blue Silk Bedroom (complete with vast 18th-century bed), Heaven Room (gorgeous painted walls by Antonio Verrio) and Hell Staircase (infernal ceiling also by Verrio).

Outside, gardens and grounds by the omnipresent Capability Brown offer sweeping vistas to the spires of Stamford. There is a modern sculpture garden, lakeside walk and a new Garden of Surprises designed to confuse and delight the senses. The gardens are open daily, as is the Park. The house is closed on Fridays.

Burghley House – the grandest of the grand!

Althorp House and Rockingham Castle

Perhaps it was once one stately home among many, but now Althorp House (off the A428 road outside Northampton) forever stands out as the eternal resting place of Diana, Princess of Wales. She is buried on a peaceful island in a lake at the ancestral home of the Spencer family.

The original Tudor house was radically altered in the 18th century. It is now rather severe, but there is an impressive interior complete with important furniture, ceramics and pictures collected over five centuries. The attractive sandstone stable block has been converted into an exhibition dedicated to Diana's memory. Outside, it's possible to stroll through the park or relax in beautiful gardens. After seeing the house, visit the estate village of Great Brington to see the Church of St Mary with St John, with its Spencer Chapel full of flamboyant monuments.

An even better church awaits up the A508 at Brixworth. All Saints is a truly outstanding example of Anglo-Saxon architecture from the early 700s. This Romanesque structure actually does contain stone recycled from a Roman villa, and the oldest part of the church consists of an arcaded nave, presbytery and one of only four remaining Anglo-Saxon stair turrets in England.

Continue to Market Harborough and Corby, turning onto the A6003 Oakham road just before getting there. The destination is Rockingham Castle, built to the order of William the Conqueror. The interior has a strong Tudor flavour and includes the Great Hall (divided in the 1600s to create the additional Panel Room) and Long Gallery. Outside are extensive gardens. The Castle stands on an escarpment giving dramatic views over the Welland Valley and five counties. Rockingham Castle is open from noon on Sundays and Bank Holiday Mondays in April and June, and on Tuesdays, Sundays and Bank Holiday Mondays from July to September.

The Diana Memorial at Althorp House

WHERE:
Northamptonshire
BEST TIME TO GO:
July or August (for Althorp).
DON'T MISS:
The opportunity to take a walk along the shores of Pitsford Reservoir after visiting Brixworth Church – perhaps taking a hamper that may be unpacked and the contents consumed in the scenic picnic area.
AMOUNT OF WALKING:
Moderate
COST:
Reasonable.
YOU SHOULD KNOW:
Althorp House is always closed to the public on 31 August, the anniversary of Diana's death.

Foxton Locks

A whole way of life has evolved around Britain's waterways with its own sub-culture, traditions and folk art. At Foxton Locks you can spend a fascinating day on the Grand Union Canal exploring the world of the boat people and finding out about the history and construction of the canals.

Before the advent of the railways, the canals were vital to the economy of the Industrial Revolution: throughout the 18th and early 19th century, they were the means of transporting goods throughout the country. Foxton Locks is an important point on the Grand Union, where two branches of the Leicester arm of the canal meet, about 5 km (3 mi) west of the attractive country town of Market Harborough. Here you can watch the machinations of the narrow-boats as they negotiate a flight of ten 'staircase' locks, an intricate system of interlocking gates to enable the boats to climb uphill. Navigating these locks is a serious challenge – it takes up to an hour for a narrow-boat to get through. If you want to try your hand rather than just watching, you can hire a boat for the day; the lock-keeper is on stand-by to guide you through the finer points of lock-manoeuvring.

Foxton is surrounded by lovely countryside that has been turned into a country park. Stroll along the canalside and admire the brightly-coloured 'roses and castles' designs painted on the narrow boats, visit the museum to find out about the history of the canal and the clever technology of the locks, roam around the side ponds watching the wildlife or simply slope off to the canalside local for a quiet pint while the family go on a boat trip. If you weren't already a canal-boat enthusiast before a visit to Foxton, you certainly will be afterwards.

The top five of the ten locks that lead up to the lock-keepers cottage

The National Space Centre

SNIBSTON DISCOVERY PARK

You will notice the National Space Centre long before you get to it – its futuristic rocket tower, 42 m (140 ft) high, sprouting from the north bank of the River Soar, has become an icon on Leicester's skyline. Opened in 2001, the building was designed by Nicholas Grimshaw (architect of the Eden Project in Cornwall) and proved an immediate hit, attracting visitors in droves.

There is no other attraction anywhere in the country remotely like it. Everything to do with the universe and space travel can be discovered here. You will be introduced to all the latest developments in space travel, see a genuine Soyuz spacecraft and be transported to another galaxy in the Space Theatre – the country's largest planetarium. The themed galleries have brilliant interactive displays and simulated rides using amazing technological tricks to illustrate new concepts. Anyone with an interest in science fiction will immediately be in their element, but even if you've never really thought about Space before, you will find your imagination stirred by this mind-expanding, extra-terrestrial experience.

From exploring the mysteries of outer space, return to the wonders of planet Earth at Snibston Discovery Park in Coalville, a former mining town 22 km (14 mi) from Leicester. Here you can see how technology impacts on our everyday lives through more than 90 permanent exhibits and additional special events. Snibston is on the site of a defunct colliery, now a nature reserve and country park. The colliery was closed in 1985 but some of the industrial buildings were preserved for posterity and an indoor and outdoor museum was established dedicated to industry, technology and design, telling the story of technological progress in everything from coal-mining to fashion. There is something here to attract the interest of everyone and you will leave the museum buzzing with new ideas.

Get ready for lift off!

WHERE:
Leicestershire
BEST TIME TO GO:
Any time
DON'T MISS:
The display of historic and contemporary costumes in the Fashion Industry Gallery at Snibston.
AMOUNT OF WALKING:
Little
COST:
Expensive
YOU SHOULD KNOW:
The National Space Centre won the 2007 Visitor Attraction of the Year Award. It is advisable to book tickets in advance if you are going at peak holiday periods.

Stoke-on-Trent Potteries

WHERE:
Staffordshire
BEST TIME TO GO:
Any time of year
DON'T MISS:
Two especially good visitor centres –
Spode in Stoke, and Moorcroft
Heritage in Burslem – take you to
some of pottery's stylistic extremes.
Their astonishing displays help you
discern the fine line between
designer's artistry and commercial
imperative; and the compromises
that have worked and failed.
AMOUNT OF WALKING:
Moderate, or lots if you choose to
explore the canal towpath linking
most of the factories.
COST:
Low, if any. But the factories and
visitor centres are crammed with
pieces of exquisite charm and
timeless beauty, and it's difficult to
get out without making a purchase.
YOU SHOULD KNOW:
When you visit the Potteries Museum
& Art Gallery, you'll see that the most
prominent display by far is, strangely,
nothing directly to do with pottery. It
is a Supermarine Mk XVI Spitfire from
World War II, and it is there as a
tribute to R.J. Mitchell, the local boy
who designed it. The Museum
justifies its prominence quite simply
– 'No Mitchell, No Spitfire; No
Spitfire, No Potteries'.

The 'Six Towns' of Tunstall, Burslem, Hanley, Stoke, Fenton and Longton were famous as 'The Potteries' for 250 years before they became a federation as the City of Stoke-on-Trent in 1910. Local coal and clay supplied raw materials to make and fire earthenware on an industrial scale. Then the Trent & Mersey Canal was built to take it to market, and to bring in the special china clay that ever since has inspired some of the world's finest bone china and creamware. Household names crown the tall chimneys, bottle kilns and brick barracks of the factories lining a single 16-km (10-mi) stretch of the canal – Minton, Spode, Royal Doulton, Copeland, Royal Stafford and Wedgwood among them. Walking or cycling the towpath is a journey through a unique industrial heritage, dazzling in its architectural novelty. Most factories have guided tours; but you can also see how pottery of this excellence is (and used to be) made, and examples of the craft, at a number of very good local museums.

The Gladstone Pottery Museum at Longton is a genuine Victorian pottery, complete in every respect, and you can see traditional skills in action at the original workshops and bottle-shaped ovens. The Dudson Museum in Hanley tells the story of one company since 1800 – and it's actually located inside a giant (Grade II listed) bottle kiln. Nearby, the Etruria Industrial Museum has Britain's last steam-powered potters' mill, with working bone- and flint-grinding machinery from 1856. Burslem is home to Royal Doulton, and to Royal Stafford, where visitors to the 'ceramic café' can paint their own piece of pottery (and the company will fire it, then mail it home to you). The Wedgwood Visitor Centre at Barlaston is distinguished by the classical elegance of the displays; and Stoke's Potteries Museum & Art Gallery brings together the best pottery from them all, matching local industry to local history and geography.

The bottle-shaped ovens at the Gladstone Pottery Museum

Alton Towers

To make the most of a great day at Alton Towers, even the management agrees that you need a little cunning. The problem is popularity – it's so much fun whirling through the air, spinning in stomach-churning loops at high speed and splashing through make-believe tropical lagoons that the best rides are besieged by long queues. You can avoid them, quite legally and officially, by pre-booking or buying 'shortcut' tickets for priority. Of course, you also have to be quite stern with yourself, by deciding (as much as you can without actually seeing them first) which rides you most want to take. They vary from year to year, but you can always be sure there will be a version of the Flume, the River Rapids, the aerial cable car, the Haunted House, the Runaway Train, the Corkscrew rollercoaster, and a variety of white knuckle spectaculars, with chilling names like Oblivion and Nemesis.

If the whole family is going, you need to check what restrictions may apply to your chosen rides. It might seem a bit like kitting out an expedition – but if you know that age or height (or temperament) might be a governing factor, you can't be disappointed; and in any case, the better prepared you are with pre-bookings, vouchers, or any other kind of information or dispensation, the more time you'll have to enjoy actually doing things.

One of Alton Towers' best features is that everyone in the family gets to do their own thing. Children are cheerfully supervised on Toyland Tours or at the Farm if adults want to take a tranquil break rowing gently on the lake, or strolling in the beautiful gardens of what was once a Victorian mansion designed by Pugin. Beyond that, you can blend your own thrill of fun, fright, laughter, adventure, speed, contortion and spookiness. For a day, you can be your own daredevil and superhero.

The 'Spinball Wizard' ride

WHERE:
Staffordshire
BEST TIME TO GO:
Any time of year
DON'T MISS:
The roller coasters – Alton Towers speaks of 'taming the metal monsters…real beasts in the form of fearsome, nerve-wracking, pitch-black drops and speed-driven vertical Gs…'
AMOUNT OF WALKING:
Lots, by the end of the day – but with so much adrenaline pulsing through you, you may not notice.
COST:
Expensive – but you can make impressive savings by doing a little research and booking in advance.
YOU SHOULD KNOW:
Alton Towers will help you plan your visit (and reduce the cost) if you contact them. For example, you can get a map of the whole site before you go, and make sure in advance that you have everything you need (like knowing what to do about lost children) to banish worry.

Bridgnorth and Much Wenlock

Once a major river port, and then an important market town, Saxon Bridgnorth early on protected its strategic interests by dividing into 'Low Town', down by the Severn, and 'High Town', connected to its twin by seven ancient flights of steps and a precipitous cart track up a 34 m (111 ft) sandstone cliff. Since 1892, locals and visitors have had a third option – the Bridgnorth Cliff Railway. Two carriages (like the smartly-liveried hollow shells of 1930s buses) run in counterbalance on parallel tracks at a 33° incline, bolted deep into solid rock. The funicular is fundamental to life in Bridgnorth, turning every day into an adventure. You rise from the quayside to a fantastic panorama from Castle Walk, the view King Charles I declared 'the finest in all my kingdom' (shortly before the 12th-century castle dominating the countryside was all but destroyed by Parliamentarians). High Town is full of beautiful, half-timbered 17th- and 18th-century buildings, including the stupendous Town Hall on its arched base; and of notable Victoriana like the Costume and Childhood Museum, with toys, dolls and games collected by four generations of a single local family.

Local industrial history is served by the Severn Valley Railway, a heritage (1858-62) steam passenger service between Bridgnorth and Kidderminster; and Daniel's Mill, a restored 12-m (38-ft) iron waterwheel, owned and operated since 1771 by the same family, and still producing wholemeal flour which you can take home and bake.

To the northwest, Much Wenlock's medieval buildings appear untouched by modernity, and rival even Bridgnorth's picturesque antiquity. The magnificent timber-framed 1577 Guildhall is still used for Town Council meetings. Here, too, you can dream among the clipped topiary and smooth lawns of the ruins of St Milburga's Priory, a religious site for thirteen centuries. Sacked by 9th-century Danes, and restored by Godiva (of nude in Coventry fame), Wenlock Priory weaves you into the pageant of English history.

WHERE:
Shropshire
BEST TIME TO GO:
April to October
DON'T MISS:
The spectacular ruins of Wenlock Priory, including much of the 107-m (350-ft) long church nave and transepts.
AMOUNT OF WALKING:
Moderate; and highly accessible (though wheelchairs must be folded on Bridgnorth's funicular, and you need to be able to manage two or three unavoidable stairs).
COST:
None, except for the low funicular fare.
YOU SHOULD KNOW:
The founder of the modern Olympics, Dr William Penny-Brookes (1809-95), was born in Much Wenlock. The Wenlock Olympian Society held its first Games in 1858, and their idea was developed across the world under the supervision of Baron de Coubertin, until the first international Olympics were held in Athens in 1896. Much Wenlock arranges its own Olympic games every July.

The Bridgnorth Cliff Railway

Lichfield

NATIONAL MEMORIAL ARBORETUM AT ALREWAS

Known variously as the 'Three Maids' or 'Three Ladies of the Vale', the triple spires of Lichfield's magnificent cathedral dominate the small city. In fact the medieval Gothic building hides 7th-century Anglo-Saxon origins and Norman modifications in its stunning architecture; and despite horrific depredations during the English Civil War, still retains treasures like the 8th-century illuminated Chad Gospels and superbly carved 'Lichfield Angel', and seven huge window panels of very rare, original 16th-century Flemish stained-glass. Beyond the quiet Cathedral Close, Lichfield's prominence as an 18th-century coaching hub is pleasantly obvious. Bypassed by the mainline railways, it has the old-world charm of pre-industrial streets and buildings. Among them is the 1709 birthplace museum of Dr Johnson, the inventor of the Dictionary and some of the best aphorisms in the English language; and of the botanist and poet Dr Erasmus Darwin (grandfather of Charles), whose lovely Georgian house in Cathedral Close is also a museum. You'll enjoy strolling through Lichfield's tree-lined, waterside heart, now one of the country's most famous centres for antiques.

With history so much in the air, you'll appreciate the inspiration behind the National Memorial Arboretum, set in 61 hectares (150 acres) of the National Forest of Staffordshire at Alrewas, between Lichfield and Burton-upon-Trent on the banks of the River Tame. It's conceived as a living memorial to the 20th-century heroes and heroines who sacrificed themselves in the service of their country. Here 40,000 trees, planted to a variety of designs in some sixty plots, commemorate branches and units of the armed forces, the civil and emergency services, charities and volunteer organizations – with the circular Armed Forces Memorial, opened in 2007, at its heart. As yet, the trees are small things; but the children who see it now will show a flourishing forest to their grandchildren, and those commemorated here will not be forgotten.

The Armed Forces Memorial at Alrewas

WHERE:
Staffordshire
BEST TIME TO GO:
Any time of year
DON'T MISS:
The Lichfield Heritage Centre, at St Mary's in Market Square – besides the gleaming silverware of the Treasury, the Muniment Room with its 13th- and 16th-century charter documents, and Sylvia Everitt's award-winning Millennium Embroideries (ten astonishing tapestries telling 1,000 years of Staffordshire's history), there are excellent children's 'trails' to hold them spellbound.
AMOUNT OF WALKING:
Lots
COST:
Low, if any. Lichfield Cathedral makes no charge except for special group tours, but suggests a small donation. The Arboretum makes a small charge for car parking only.
YOU SHOULD KNOW:
The idea for the National Memorial Arboretum owes much to the influence of Group Captain Leonard Cheshire. It is the only place in the UK which observes a two-minute silence, accompanied by the Last Post and Reveille, at 11.00 am on every day of the year.

Cannock Chase and Shugborough Hall

WHERE:
Staffordshire
BEST TIME TO GO:
Any time of year – but choose a sunny day.
DON'T MISS:
Shugborough's Grade I listed riverside gardens, full of historic monuments and follies. One of the best ways to see them is in the context of the 'working estate' tour, which although it includes the kitchens, dairy, water mill, farm and brewhouse, also demonstrates why the exotic gardens were considered to be so revolutionary and technologically advanced in 1805 – the year to which they have now been 'returned'.
AMOUNT OF WALKING:
Lots – but even in Brocton Coppice, some paths are flat enough to be wheelchair accessible.
COST:
None, to walk in Cannock Chase; Shugborough is reasonable, with reductions for advance bookings.
YOU SHOULD KNOW:
The Anson family, owners of Shugborough, includes the late Lord (Patrick) Lichfield, the photographer who chronicled late 20th-century Society; and Admiral Lord (George) Anson, First Lord of the Admiralty, circumnavigator of 1740-44 in HMS *Centurion*, and captor of the biggest single prize in British naval history – one of the Manila Galleons. Anson's 'Captain's Share' (one-quarter of the total) was £400,000.

Woodland at Beaudesert Park, Cannock Chase

Bounded by Lichfield, Cannock, Stafford and Rugeley, Cannock Chase is one of England's most surprising Areas of Outstanding Natural Beauty. The unusual landscape variety is more than matched by its rich wildlife, including a herd of about 750 fallow deer. You don't expect such pleasures so close to major conurbations. The Chase is a jumbled mixture of open heath, coniferous plantations and natural deciduous woodland, with lakes, ponds and streams. Across much of it you can discern encroachments of ancient logging, mine and quarry workings, but Brocton Coppice, the northwest sector, remains almost untouched since Richard I gave the Chase to the Bishop of Lichfield as a hunting reserve in 1189. Some of Brocton's 600 sessile oak trees are 600 years old, and most are over 200. It's a truly wild, tangled place, where you really can get lost – or meet a fully-grown Red deer stag – between the woods and water of the Sherbrook Valley, or in the bracken of the heath. Now that military claims on the area have been reined in, it's one of the loveliest places to walk in the West Midlands.

Yet Cannock Chase isn't remote. Its wilderness is balanced by the highest expression of mannered civilization on its very edge – Shugborough Hall. This is a classical Georgian mansion, remodeled from 1745-8 on a 17th-century original block; and is still a family home though the National Trust manages it as a working estate. In fact, it's complete in every respect. The fabulous State Rooms, filled with paintings, silver, china and rare furnishings are staffed by actors in period costume who bring it alive with their bustle. The Servants Quarters are 'authentically' Victorian, and you can get involved in many of their highly entertaining domestic activities in the kitchens or the walled gardens and parkland, all restored to their original plans.

Ironbridge Gorge

*The famous iron bridge
at Ironbridge*

The Severn Gorge in Shropshire lies 8 km (5 mi) south of Telford. At Ironbridge, a graceful parabola arches across the river – the intricate web of iron ribs and struts welded into the world's first cast-iron bridge. From its opening on New Year's Day 1781, the bridge was a potent symbol of industrial progress and achievement. It was made from local iron ore and fired by local coal; its construction made transporting raw materials in, and finished manufactured goods out, much easier; and its design showed that iron could be aesthetically pleasing as well as strong and practical. The iron bridge quickly gave its name to the community. Now, though no longer a roadway, it is the epicentre of the World Heritage Site which recognizes both the natural beauty of Ironbridge and its fundamental importance to the industrial revolution.

The mining industries (iron, coal and clay), the foundries and the factories which flourished – and still flourish – here have an epic story of adventure and drama to tell. You can jump in headfirst at any one of the eight local museums collectively known as the Ironbridge Gorge Museum Trust. The Tollhouse Information Centre on the bridge's south side will give you details. At Blists Hill Victorian Town, the staff in the shops and householders going about their business wear Victorian costume, and you can ride a horse and cart to the fairground. At the Darby Houses, you can see how the original Quaker Ironmasters, the Darby family, lived, with grandstand views over the (restored) Furnace Pool that powered the Ironworks. The Museum of Iron is at Coalbrookdale, with exhibits including superb iron works of art and Aga cookers in all their iron forms. You can see (and make your own) Coalport China and Jackfield Tiles, and 'Enginuity' is a palace of imaginative games in design and engineering.

WHERE:
Shropshire
BEST TIME TO GO:
Any time of year
DON'T MISS:
The remains of the water-powered blast furnace in which Abraham Darby I (A. Darby III, his grandson, designed the iron bridge) refined the secret of smelting iron with coke instead of charcoal – the discovery that ensured that iron became the essential material of industrial revolution. It's at the Coalbrookdale Museum of Iron.
AMOUNT OF WALKING:
Moderate
COST:
Low
YOU SHOULD KNOW:
Ironbridge uses the slogan 'the birthplace of industry' with some justification. Within a very small area you can see how raw materials were extracted (the 200 year-old, brick Tar Tunnel next to Coalport China and the Shropshire Canal still has raw bitumen oozing from the walls), prepared in furnaces, shaped by engineers and craftsmen, and fired into their final commercial form. And at every stage, in one or other of the Ironbridge Museums, you can have a go!

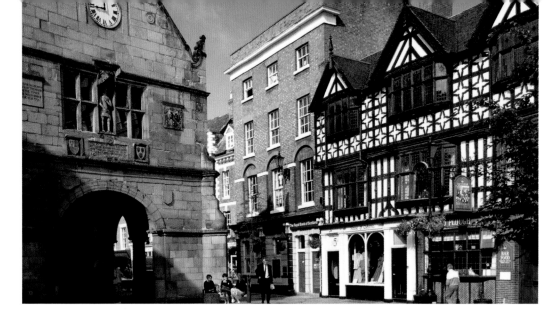

The Old Market Hall, Shrewsbury

Shrewsbury and Hodnet

Shrewsbury is almost an island. It stands in a great loop of the River Severn, where Celts, Romans, Saxons and then Normans established their castles and walled the town. An inland port which prospered in the wool trade, it was the richest prize on the Welsh marches, and the strongest. Its medieval charms were enhanced in Tudor and Jacobean times by wealthy merchants who built huge 'black-and-white' mansions like Ireland's Mansion and the Abbot's House along ancient lanes with names like Gullet Passage, Grope Lane, Dogpole and Shoplatch.

Shrewsbury's centre is a maze of streets whose entire frontages pre-date 1600 or earlier – and woven into them is a network of 'shuts', narrow alleys that squeeze through and under the buildings. Bear Steps Hall is a good example – Bear Steps 'shut' cuts right up through it. Across the English Bridge stands the impressive 11th-century Abbey, ranked second only to Canterbury as a favourite destination for pilgrims.

You can sail right around Shrewsbury on the Severn, and the river's constant proximity, with lawns, pastures and gardens sloping from it to the city's ancient frontages, makes it one of England's most serene and beautiful historic towns. It's perfect for the series of festivals, fairs and events that take place throughout the year, and it's easy to check what's happening before you go.

In any case, you need to check the opening times of Hodnet Hall Gardens, 11 km (7 mi) northeast towards Market Drayton. Their infrequent openings are horticultural red-letter days. The neo-Elizabethan style Hall was built in 1870 high above a 24-hectare (60-acre) bog. In 1922, the gardens were created around a series of ornamental lakes and ponds. Now they bring year-round colour to the terraces, the magnolia walk and stunning walled garden. The surrounding park boasts magnificent beeches, oaks and limes.

Ludlow and Stokesay Castle

Ludlow is one of England's finest surviving medieval market towns, set in a wooded bend of the River Teme, around a magnificent castle on the small hill at its centre. The Normans built it as part of the Marcher bulwark against the marauding Welsh. It grew into a huge royal palace only to be abandoned in 1689, after which it fell into the ruins Daniel Defoe described as 'the very perfection of decay'. It still is – but the damage was arrested, and now the castle is the site of a perpetual round of fairs, festivals and re-enactments that often extend to the entire town. The 'modern' shops and houses include some of Britain's best-preserved Tudor, Elizabethan and Georgian architecture, but their medieval foundations are still apparent. With some 500 listed buildings crammed into a small area, Ludlow's beauty flatters your senses. It has also become a centre of gastronomic excellence – Ludlow was the first English town to join the international Cittaslow movement which strives to preserve 'the authenticity of individuality', and demonstrate special care for its residents and visitors – so you'll find its evocative ambience especially rewarding, and welcoming. The extraordinary decorations of the 1619 half-timbered Feathers Hotel, and the Castle would on their own make Ludlow special; but in context, they are merely par for the course, and you never tire of marvelling at the historic streets.

To Ludlow's north, where the River Onny breaks the long ridge of Wenlock Edge, Stokesay Castle is a survivor of 700 years of border and civil wars. It was a rich wool merchant's 13th-century dream house; and its moat, crenellations and stern walls demonstrate that such features were considered 'romantic' long before the Victorians or modern tourism. Its buildings are complete, and breathtaking – Stokesay is the best fortified manor house, bar none, in Britain.

WHERE:
Shropshire
BEST TIME TO GO:
Any time of year
DON'T MISS:
The cruck-built timber roof and gable windows of Stokesay's open-hearthed Great Hall; or, indeed, the elaborate timber framing of the 17th-century Gatehouse, one of the finest examples of this regional style anywhere.
AMOUNT OF WALKING:
Moderate – Ludlow is quite small, but some of its narrow lanes and cobbled enclaves can be difficult for wheelchairs.
COST:
Reasonable (at least in terms of entrance charges).
YOU SHOULD KNOW:
Ludlow's astonishing beauty has brought it great fame; and since it can't be expanded, great exclusivity. Nothing in the town is particularly cheap, but if you take advantage of the many events that take place in the castle, you can often find ways to make your visit less expensive.

The Norman castle at Ludlow

Birmingham Jewellery Quarter

SOHO HOUSE AND THE BIRMINGHAM MUSEUM & ART GALLERY

WHERE:
Birmingham
BEST TIME TO GO:
April to October – the only time
The Museum of the Jewellery
Quarter is open.
DON'T MISS:
The wonderful Edwardian Tea Room
at the Birmingham Museum –
essential relaxation after so much
deep thought.
AMOUNT OF WALKING:
Lots
COST:
Low, if any.
YOU SHOULD KNOW:
Give Birmingham a chance, and it'll
knock spots off your preconceptions.

*The imposing façade of the
Birmingham Museum
& Art Gallery*

For generations, Birmingham hid its secrets beneath a pall of black factory smoke, and the rest of England undervalued one of its greatest cities. That's changed. Birmingham is still a centre of manufacturers, but it has cast off its grime, corrected the mistakes of the 1960s, and emerged like a butterfly from its chrysalis.

It's a modern shopping paradise, and some of the best is to be found in the city's oldest quarters. The Jewellery Quarter has existed for 350 years in Hockley. More than 400 jewellery businesses still cluster round the busiest gold assay office in the world. They are direct descendants of the 17th- and 18th-century toymakers who gathered to share the secrets of their craft and manufacturing capabilities – secrets which attracted other manufacturers, and the men of science and engineering who launched the industrial revolution from the area. At the Museum of the Jewellery Quarter (you have to take the guided tour) you can see an authentic workshop in action – and discover how the coming of canals and the steam engine played their part in the Quarter's evolution.

Guiding Birmingham's industrial growth – by influence of intellect and suggestion – the pioneers of science and engineering like Matthew Boulton and James Watt used to meet at Boulton's elegant early Georgian Soho House, a short (3 km/2 mi) walk from the Jewellery Quarter. The house, incidentally the first to be fitted with central heating since the Romans, attracted as many philosophers as scientists. Boulton encouraged what we now call 'blue sky' thinking, the free exchange of seemingly fantastic ideas. His meetings rapidly became known as the Lunar Society – and at Soho House you'll see how much Britain owes to its members.

The Birmingham Museum & Art Gallery's outstanding collection of pre-Raphaelite pictures explores the Brotherhood's use of art to question the social issues of industrialized Britain. With Soho House, the Museum adds incalculably to any perspective on the industrial revolution.

Cadbury World

Cadbury World is an enclave about 7 km (4 mi) from the centre of Birmingham. It comprises a museum and a series of displays that tell the story of chocolate as a commodity, and the history and social philosophy of the Cadbury family; and the factory where the chocolate is made in all its delicious forms. It is a chocoholic's dream – and yes! you do get free chocolate as you make your way round the factory, plus the opportunity at the end to buy whatever you want at factory prices (though it's perfectly all right to skip the tour and go straight to the shop!).

For health and safety reasons you can't tour the halls where real production is taking place. Instead, you follow a marked route at your own pace through otherwise disused parts of the factory, each a themed environment (like 'jungle' or 'the street') in which you discover a different aspect of chocolate. When the story demands it, you are entertained with holograms, interactive videos, and at one point, a 'sensurround' show in a theatre where the seats shake violently to emulate factory machinery. You learn that the Cadburys were one of three families of Quaker social philanthropists (with the Frys and Rowntrees) in the chocolate business who believed that looking after their employees was at least as important as making a profit. Cadbury World is in fact sited in Bournville, a community purpose-built to provide housing, shops, recreational facilities and religious worship for the chocolate workers. The Cadburys were ahead of their time with advertising, too, and there are some hilarious reminders of their successes, including a look at the mock-up chocolate set used to make the Coronation Street TV commercials. But for all you learn about Aztec origins and ways of processing cocoa beans, Cadbury World is about indulgence. You will never have seen so many happy faces.

All that chocolate and all for tasting...

WHERE:
Birmingham
BEST TIME TO GO:
Any time of year
DON'T MISS:
The chocolate jungle, with boardwalks and waterfalls; the 3-D fantasy world of the Happiness Dance Room; and the choc-bot called Flex6 (sic), a robot who 'performs' a complex (and brilliantly theatrical) process of packing and wrapping chocolate.
AMOUNT OF WALKING:
Moderate
COST:
Reasonable to expensive.
YOU SHOULD KNOW:
Over half a million people visit Cadbury World every year. Although the Visitor Centre includes 'the biggest Cadbury shop in the world', the only way to guarantee getting in is to book ahead, especially during peak periods in the summer.

223

Warwick Castle stands firm on the banks of the River Avon.

Warwick and Henley-in-Arden

Warwick lies almost at the centre of England; a steep cliff above the River Avon has always given it strategic importance and it has seen some momentous historical events. Rebuilt in the 14th century on the site of an earlier fortification, mighty Warwick Castle is, despite extensive 19th-century reconstruction, known as Britain's 'greatest medieval castle'. It is magnificent, towering above the river, and its impressive walls and towers are best seen from Castle Bridge. There are gloomy dungeons, a torture chamber and the 'Kingmaker Exhibition', the history of Richard Neville, the powerful Earl of Warwick. The Great Hall houses a collection of armour. In the sumptuous State Rooms, waxworks re-create an 1898 royal weekend party. The grounds are very extensive; medieval pursuits like jousting and archery take place on River Island; there is a lovely Rose Garden and, in the Peacock Gardens, live peacocks wander among topiary birds.

Many of Warwick's old buildings, destroyed by the 1694 fire, were replaced by elegant Queen Anne architecture. Parts of St Mary's church survived, notably the Beauchamp Chapel with its outstanding carved tombs, including that of Robert Dudley, Earl of Leicester and favourite of Elizabeth I. Dudley founded the Lord Leycester Hospital, a group of fine timbered buildings with a galleried courtyard which housed old soldiers. The town has several museums worth exploring.

Little of the Forest of Arden remains, but the countryside surrounding Henley-in-Arden, west of Warwick, is lovely, as is the town. The long High Street is a Conservation Area, with buildings from the 15th century onwards. The oldest part of Joseph Hardy House (a Heritage Centre) dates to 1345; the restored Guild Hall and market cross are 15th century.

WHERE:
Warwickshire
BEST TIME TO GO:
Any time of year
DON'T MISS:
The Mill Garden, in a superb setting beneath the walls of Warwick Castle, is a delightfully peaceful, informal riverside garden with winding paths and dramatic views.
AMOUNT OF WALKING:
Moderate
COST:
Reasonable – expensive (ticket prices for Warwick Castle vary considerably throughout the year).
YOU SHOULD KNOW:
Henley-in-Arden's Guild Hall was home to the Court Leete, an ancient manorial court whose records – covering such matters as the prevention of horses being parked in the streets – go back to the 16th century. The Leete still meets here every year.

Kenilworth Castle

PACKWOOD HOUSE AND BADDESLEY CLINTON

Kenilworth is England's largest castle ruin and its red sandstone walls still loom over the peaceful countryside. The remains of the inner court date from the 12th to 16th centuries; the Tudor gatehouse is fairly intact. The Castle's ownership changed through the years – it was the stronghold of kings and great lords, including Simon de Montfort and John of Gaunt. Elizabeth I gave it to her favourite, Robert Dudley, who made extensive alterations. (Sir Walter Scott's romance, *Kenilworth* tells of the lavish entertainments for Elizabeth, which almost ruined Dudley.) Oliver Cromwell ordered its 'sleighting': the Great Mere was filled in and the keep demolished, to prevent the castle's defensive use.

Packwood House was built in the 16th century and extended and altered over the years. Its interiors now reflect a wealthy 20th-century connoisseur's taste for the Elizabethan and Jacobean, with collections of tapestries, stained glass and textiles. The large, tranquil gardens include a famous terraced herbaceous border and a 17th-century collection of large, clipped yews, said to represent the Sermon on the Mount; the numerous sundials and clocks of the same date may also reflect a desire for the contemplative life.

Just two miles from Packwood, Baddesley Clinton is a beautifully situated 14th-century manor house, little changed since 1634. During the 1590s it became a refuge for Jesuits, and 'priests' holes' survive.

WHERE:
Warwickshire
BEST TIME TO GO:
March to November (Kenilworth Castle is open all year).
DON'T MISS:
The recently restored Tudor Gatehouse of Kenilworth Castle. Built by Robert Dudley for entertaining his Queen, this superb building now houses exhibitions covering the castle's turbulent history and documenting the relationship between Elizabeth and the Earl I of Leicester.
AMOUNT OF WALKING:
Moderate
COST:
Reasonable (family tickets available; joint tickets for Packwood and Baddesley Clinton).
YOU SHOULD KNOW:
The first potatoes grown in England are thought to have been planted in the Little Virginia area of Kenilworth after Walter Raleigh brought them back from South America.

Packwood House

Compton Verney and Burton Dasset

WHERE:
Warwickshire
BEST TIME TO GO:
May to December
DON'T MISS:
Compton Verney holds the largest collection of British Folk Art in the UK. It was purchased in its entirety to prevent it from being split up.
AMOUNT OF WALKING:
Moderate
COST:
Reasonable
YOU SHOULD KNOW:
Edward II outlawed the Templars, but Isabella of France granted them amnesty. In 1350, soon after building All Saints Church, they and the whole Burton Dasset community were wiped out by the Black Death.

The German Gallery at Compton Verney

Compton Verney is a fine 18th-century Robert Adam mansion, set in grounds landscaped by Capability Brown. In the late 19th century, its fortunes declined and decades of neglect followed. In 1993, the Peter Moores Foundation purchased the estate – by now in a state of sad decay – with the aim of transforming the house into a first-class art gallery which would allow as many people as possible to enjoy works of art and experience new art projects. The restored Grade 1 listed building opened in 2004; it consists of three floors of galleries and a purpose-built learning centre. The six excellent permanent collections include British portraits and Chinese bronzes, and are presented in different styles, to suit the works. Changing exhibitions, events, workshops and educational projects complement the collections, and family activity packs allow adults and children to enjoy art together. The lovely grounds are also open to visitors.

Southeast of Compton Verney, the tiny, ancient village of Burton Dasset lies in an area of limestone hills, now a Country Park. The strange contours of the lumpy green sheep pasture cover traces of 19th-century ironstone quarrying and older ridge and furrow field systems. The hills offer fine walking, and great views over the Warwickshire countryside. Outside All Saints Church is a Holy Well, with steps leading down to the water and a 19th-century well house. The church, which was built by the Knights Templar in the 1330s, has some interesting wall paintings, including an early Three Magi, and capitals charmingly carved with animals.

The Avoncroft Museum of Historic Buildings

HANBURY HALL

Just south of Bromsgrove, the Avoncroft Museum of Historic Buildings offers glimpses of architecture and life over the centuries. The Museum was founded in 1964 after a failed attempt to save a 16th-century Bromsgrove building from demolition. This, the Merchant's House, became the first building to be painstakingly reconstructed, restored and erected on the site, now home to more than twenty rescued buildings.

Domestic buildings include a forge cottage, an Edwardian showman's splendid living wagon and a 1940s 'Prefab'. A group including a working windmill, cider mill, and a cruck barn represents traditional farming. Utility buildings range from a tin Mission Chapel, a nail-shop, and an ice-house to an 18th-century, three-seater earth closet. Craftspeople and enactors demonstrate the working and domestic life of the buildings and their inhabitants, and summer holiday events include a Medieval Fair and a 1940s weekend.

Nearby Hanbury Hall was built in the William and Mary style for a wealthy lawyer in 1701, remaining home to the Vernon family till 1940. The handsome red brick building has a magnificent staircase and flamboyant murals; an exhibition in the Long Gallery tells the house's story. The Hall is surrounded by 160 hectares (395 acres) of fine parkland. Garden areas include a re-created early 18th-century formal garden, fruit gardens and a bowling green with pavilion. There is an orangery and a Mushroom House, and formal walks in the park.

The entrance gates of Hanbury Hall

WHERE:
Worcestershire
BEST TIME TO GO:
April to October (Avoncroft opens some winter weekends but is usually closed on Mondays; opening times at Hanbury vary throughout the year).
DON'T MISS:
The National Telephone Kiosk Collection at Avoncroft shows kiosks from the 1920s to the present.
AMOUNT OF WALKING:
Moderate (access at Avoncroft is generally good, though some of the historic buildings have difficult/restricted access).
COST:
Reasonable (Family tickets available at both attractions; admission at Avoncroft covers special events).
YOU SHOULD KNOW:
Sir James Thornhill, who was responsible for the Painted Hall at Greenwich, had a hand in the creation of the staircase at Hanbury Hall, and was also responsible for the building's superb painted ceilings.

The Malverns

Herefordshire Beacon

The Malvern Hills, a range of sharp peaks, dips and hollows, runs along the Worcester-Hereford border, rising dramatically to form a distinctive jagged skyline which is visible from miles around. Great Malvern is the main town in the Malverns. Now known for its music and drama festivals, the agricultural Three Counties Show and hand-built Morgan cars, it was an important residential spa town. Medicinal waters were found in the 17th century, and exploited in the 18th as a 'water cure'. The 19th century (and the railway) brought prosperity, the Pump Room and Baths, the Winter Gardens pavilion and many hotels. Past residents and visitors include Princess Victoria, Edward Elgar (he taught here and the Elgar Route visits some of his favourite spots) and the exiled Haile Selassie. Spa water can still be drunk at St Ann's Well, while water from the hills is bottled commercially.

Modern Great Malvern is a pretty, hilly town of Regency and Victorian buildings. The Priory Church is all that is left of the Benedictine priory around which the town originally grew; it is famous for its medieval stained glass, unique 15th century wall tiles and lively misericord carvings. The Abbey Gatehouse, another medieval building, is now the Town Museum, with displays on the history of the spa town and on the development of radar during World War II at Malvern's defence research establishment.

The Malvern Hills offer marvellous day hikes or shorter walks; among the landmarks is British Camp. The huge ramparts of this Iron Age hill fort are still clearly visible and from here the views – east over the Vale of Gloucester, north and west over rolling countryside towards the misty Welsh mountains – are magnificent.

AMOUNT OF WALKING:
Moderate or lots (Great Malvern's streets are very steep).
COST:
Low
YOU SHOULD KNOW:
When the popularity of spa treatments declined, Great Malvern became a desirable retirement town, particularly or lots (Great Malvern's India – it reminded them of the steep wooded slopes of the delightful summer hill stations.

Worcester

WHERE:
Worcestershire
BEST TIME TO GO:
February to December (though the Porcelain Museum and Cathedral are open all year).
DON'T MISS:
Of the many fine tombs in the Cathedral, that of King John (1216) is exceptional; this, the oldest royal effigy in England, lies, at the king's own request, between the shrines of Saxon Oswald and Wulstan.
AMOUNT OF WALKING:
Moderate
COST:
Reasonable
YOU SHOULD KNOW:
Worcester and its surroundings are prone to winter floods; a gate from the riverside walk into the Cathedral precincts is marked with past floodwater levels.

Worcester is beautifully situated on a broad curve of the River Severn; the racetrack and cricket ground lie over the water from the town and the Cathedral, whose pinnacled tower rises above the trees. It was started in 1084 and the Chapter House and huge crypt are Norman; the beautiful choir is 13th century, and Sir Gilbert Scott's embellishment of the exterior took place in the 19th century.

The narrow streets of this interesting, bustling town are lined with Tudor and Georgian buildings – and some unfortunate modern developments. A fine shopping and market town, Worcester has a busy canal basin, an imposing Queen Anne Guildhall and several museums, some in glorious historic buildings. Tudor House Heritage Centre and the Greyfriars, with its peaceful garden, occupy half-timbered houses. The fascinating Commandery was the Royalist headquarters during the Civil War – the first and last battles of which took place at Worcester.

For many, though, Worcester is synonymous with fine porcelain, and the Worcester Porcelain Museum houses a collection of exquisite pieces and tells the Company's story in Georgian, Victorian and 20th-century galleries. There is also a 'seconds' shop.

A red brick cottage in the village of Lower Broadheath, west of Worcester, was the birthplace of Edward Elgar, one of England's finest composers. His study houses a display of personal memorabilia, while the Elgar Centre collection illustrates his musical life, with scores, manuscripts, etc. An introductory video is available.

The Firs–birthplace of Edward Elgar

Golden Valley Drive

The Golden Valley is the name given to the beautiful, gently rolling valley of the River Dore. Heading southwest from Hereford to Pontrilis, where the valley starts, there is a rewarding detour to the little Norman church at Kilpeck. North of Pontrilis, all that remains of Ewyas, Harold's once important Norman castle, is a mound and some crumbling walls, but at Abbey Dore, the medieval Cistercian monastery, Dore Abbey, is now the village church. Founded in the 12th century, it fell into disrepair after the Dissolution and was restored in the 17th century. The fine red sandstone building, though now lacking a nave, contains fragments of sculpture and much original stonework. Nearby, the formal gardens and riverside walks of Court Gardens are a haven for plant and bird lovers. On the river bank a few miles northwest, the church of Peterchurch is a quiet, imposing 12th-century building. Outside Dorstone, Arthur's Stone, a neolithic chamber tomb, is Herefordshire's oldest man-made structure. The diarist Francis Kilvert, rector of St Andrews in the lovely village of Bredwardine to the east, lovingly described local life; he is buried in the churchyard.

Hay-on-Wye, an attractive town straddling the Welsh border, is synonymous with books. In 1961, Richard Booth (later 'King of Wye') opened his first second-hand bookshop, and now the town is full of them, from great barns to tiny specialist shops. Hay holds an annual Literature Festival.

A northwest loop from Hay towards Hereford passes through Weobley, the largest of the pretty 'Black and White Villages'. Weobley has a Norman church and a wealth of glorious medieval buildings; it is a thriving rural community with good local shops and three pubs.

Weobley is one of the prettiest 'black and white villages'.

WHERE:
Herefordshire
BEST TIME TO GO:
Any time of year
DON'T MISS:
Kilpeck Church is tiny, well preserved and lavishly decorated. The south doorway is carved with fantastic figures, and under the eaves runs a circle of remarkable corbels – birds, animals, faces and grotesques.
AMOUNT OF WALKING:
Little or moderate
COST:
Low
YOU SHOULD KNOW:
'Golden Valley' is probably a confusion of the name of the river; the Normans mistranslated the old Welsh 'dwyr', 'river' to the French 'd'or', 'of gold'.

Hereford Cathedral beside the River Wye

Hereford

BROCKHAMPTON ESTATE

Hereford, with its spacious Georgian streets and narrow lanes of half-timbered houses, is a pleasing city. The River Wye, once protection against the Welsh, provides a riverside walk between two ancient bridges, with views of the handsome red stone cathedral.

Built on a Saxon site, Hereford Cathedral contains examples of architecture from Norman times onwards – medieval cloisters, fine Early English Lady Chapel and some notable monuments. The sympathetically purpose-built New Library contains the Cathedral's great treasures – the Mappa Mundi and the Chained Library. The Mappa Mundi, drawn on vellum around 1300, shows a flat, circular world centred on Jerusalem, bordered by oceans and enlivened with historical, mythological and biblical illustrations. The Chained Library is an extensive collection of manuscripts and early printed books, housed in 17th-century book presses, with attached desks, to allow study without removal of the works. The Cathedral stands in gardens and green spaces, where there is a charming bronze of Elgar and his faithful bicycle.

Hereford has its fair share of museums and galleries, and one spotlights an age-old aspect of Herefordshire life – cider making. The Cider Museum shows the processes as well as the history of cider and perry making, and hosts an annual Cider Festival.

North-east of Hereford, near Bromyard, the Brockhampton Estate is a large area of traditionally farmed land with miles of meandering walks through park and woodland, rich in wildlife from dormice to buzzards. At the heart of the Estate, Lower Brockhampton is a beautiful 14th-century manor house. Romantically moated, it is entered through a pretty timber-framed gatehouse. As well as guided walks, the estate stages special events including Christmas fairs and bat walks.

Stratford-upon-Avon

An attractive riverside market town in the heart of England, Stratford's claim to fame is that William Shakespeare was born here in 1564. Though little is known of his time in Stratford, he is everywhere – street names, souvenirs, statues, pub signs, theatres and the 'Shakespeare Houses'. The Shakespeare Birthplace Trust administers these, undertaking continuing research and restoration and equipping the buildings with period furniture and fittings, exhibitions, and a variety of 'living history' displays.

The Birthplace and Visitor Centre can be packed. This was also the workplace of William's father John, and part of the house has been restored as a glover's workshop. Shakespeare bought New Place for his retirement, and he died there; the house no longer stands, but an Elizabethan knot garden occupies the site. His granddaughter lived in Nash House next door. Hall's Croft was occupied by his daughter Susannah and her doctor husband; it contains a reconstruction of Dr Hall's consulting room, with a display of 16th-century medical items.

Set in lovely gardens, Ann Hathaway's Cottage, childhood home of the Bard's wife, is a thatched farmhouse in Shottery, just outside town, while in Wilmcote, 5 km (3 m) away, the family home of his mother Mary Arden is once again a working '16th-century' farm, complete with dairy and rare breed animals.

Shakespeare died in 1616 and is buried in the chancel of Holy Trinity Church; his family added the well-known effigy seven years afterwards. In his lifetime, Stratford had no theatre; now, the Royal Shakespeare Theatre and the Swan Theatre (a replica Elizabethan theatre) stand on the riverside. As well as performances, the theatres offer a collection of costumes and theatre memorabilia and back-stage tours.

Gardens, riverside walks and boat hire offer respite from the crowds.

Anne Hathaway's Cottage in Shottery

WHERE:
Warwickshire
BEST TIME TO GO:
Any time of year (if possible, avoiding the tourist season and school holidays).
DON'T MISS:
Harvard House, a strikingly beautiful Elizabethan House on High Street (it now contains a Pewter Museum), was home to the mother of John Harvard, the man who sailed to the American colonies in the 17th century and founded the eponymous university. Open May – October.
AMOUNT OF WALKING:
Moderate (Stratford's centre is compact and flat; some of the houses have restricted access in parts, but there is always plenty to see).
COST:
Reasonable – expensive (while tickets for the Shakespeare Houses can be purchased individually, well-discounted tickets allow entry to the three 'in-town' houses, or all five)
YOU SHOULD KNOW:
The window panes in Shakespeare's house have suffered graffiti over the years; scratched signatures include Sir Walter Scott, Thomas Carlyle, Henry Irving and Ellen Terry.

Carlisle to Settle Railway

WHERE:
Cumbria and Yorkshire
BEST TIME TO GO:
All year round. The colours of the
landscape are sumptuous in the
autumn.
DON'T MISS:
The view of Ribblehead Viaduct from
Ribblehead Station.
AMOUNT OF WALKING:
Little. Each train can accommodate
at least one wheelchair user.
COST:
Reasonable. Group and period tickets
are available.
YOU SHOULD KNOW:
Although many of the stations are
run by volunteers, the Carlisle to
Settle Railway is a real working line,
connecting outlying communities
with shops, schools and work.

Carlisle is Cumbria's only city. Attractions include a 900 year-old castle and a museum that brings the Borders' history to life; although it's a place that can be gloomily grey on a rainy day. Settle is a busy little market town at the south-western edge of the Yorkshire Dales; it once outshone Bradford as the centre of the wool industry, but now seems a bit isolated and remote. What makes these two disparate places special though, is that they form the termini of one of the world's truly great railway journeys.

The 115-km (72-mi) journey from Carlisle to Settle takes you over breathtakingly high viaducts, through numerous tunnels, past pristine stations and along the Eden Valley – one of the most beautiful landscapes in England. On leaving Carlisle, the first stop is Armathwaite Station; thereafter the valley opens up and the views to your left of the Eden gorge are stunning.

After passing Lazonby, the line crosses the River Eden on the spectacular Eden Lacy viaduct, before taking you through two tunnels and pulling into the market town of Appleby. To your right, on a clear day, the distant fells of the Lake District appear eerily close. When passing through Helm Tunnel, you are at the halfway point of the journey, before crossing Smardale Viaduct, the highest point on the line. After leaving Kirkby Stephen, with its imposing church, the train begins its long descent into Settle. The charming stations at Dent and Garston are passed before you reach Ribblehead Viaduct, the most spectacular of them all. This amazing feat of Victorian engineering is suspended above the ground by twenty-four imperious arches.

After passing Horton-in-Ribblesdale Station, with its award-winning gardens, the distinctive peak of Pen-y-Ghent, stands out on your right. The landscape now flattens out as the river meanders this way and that, until Settle comes into view.

Steaming across Blea Moor and heading towards Ribblehead.

The barren landscape of Hartside Pass

Scenic Drive from Penrith to Alston

A thousand years ago Penrith was the capital of the semi-independent kingdom of Cumbria and this robust little town still acts as a hub for those wishing to explore the eastern lakes. Lying just outside the National Park, it has good transport links, being both close to the M6 motorway and on the West Coast mainline. Penrith is rich in history, from the imposing castle ruins to its fine arcades. A solid clock tower marks the town centre and the skyline is dominated by the square tower of St Andrew's Church, which contains some superb stained glass windows.

The 30-km (19-mi) drive from Penrith to Alston, along the snaking A686, ranks as one of the most scenic in Britain. On leaving Penrith, the first place you reach is the charming village of Langwathby with a pretty village green encircled by cottages, an inn and the cute 18th-century St Peter's Church. Further along the road you come to the picturesque hamlet of Melmerby, where red sandstone dwellings overlook a large common.

After Melmerby, the road climbs the Hartside Pass to an elevation of 580 m (1,904 ft), from where there are glorious views out over the Solway Firth and beyond to southern Scotland. The nearby 13th-century Church of St John the Baptist is worth a visit, if only to admire the view of Melmerby Fell from its east window. The road then follows the course of the Black Burn across moorland purple with heather, down into Alston, Britain's highest market town. This busy little town has a cobbled main street, lined with many 17th-century buildings. Famed for its mouth-watering local produce, especially the cheese and the mustard, Alston is a perfect place to end an idyllic journey.

WHERE:
Cumbria
BEST TIME TO GO:
All year round. However snow and ice can block the road any time between November and March.
DON'T MISS:
The wonderful stained glass windows of St Andrew's Church, Penrith.
AMOUNT OF WALKING:
Little. The steep cobbled main street in Alston is hard going for wheelchair users
COST:
Low
YOU SHOULD KNOW:
As well as giving you a thrilling drive, the combination of hills and bends on the A686 makes it an accident hotspot, especially for motorcyclists. Particular care is required when undertaking this drive and, if you don't feel confident, you can always take the bus.

Take to the water – it really is the best way to see all the sights!

Lake Windermere

WHERE:
Cumbria
BEST TIME TO GO:
The steamers run the full length of
the lake only from Easter to
September.
DON'T MISS:
The Round House, on Belle Isle.
Though damaged by fire in 1996, this
pepperpot shaped building has now
been fully restored.
AMOUNT OF WALKING:
Little
COST:
Reasonable. Combined tickets for all
the attractions mentioned are
available at good discounts.
YOU SHOULD KNOW:
Though mostly benign, very localized
storms can occur on the lake,
making the water very choppy. You
should bear this in mind, especially if
venturing out on your own in a
small boat.

Leaving Ambleside, with its triangle of delicatessens, pubs and cafés behind you, it is but a short walk to Waterhead, which offers you the first glimpse of England's largest lake, Lake Windermere. At 17 km (10.5 mi) long and 1.6 km (1 mi) at its widest, the lake has the appearance of a large river, although its calm waters belie this. Without doubt, the best way to savour all the scenic and historical wonders of Windermere is to take to the water. Steamboats have plied their trade on Windermere for over 150 years and, once you board at the jetty, the true magnificence of the lake becomes fully apparent. All eyes are immediately turned to the right as the boat takes you past Wray Castle, a building that looks as though it were made of giant chess pieces. The steamer then passes the tip of Belle Isle and pulls into Bowness, where you can disembark to explore this vibrant place and its sister town of Windermere, just a twenty-minute walk away.

Back on board, the boat takes you further south along the lake, where, to your right, you can see Hill Top, the former home of Beatrix Potter. Soon the imposing Arts and Crafts house, Blackwell, comes into view on your left. This last leg of the journey takes you through the least populated part of the lake, as you are flanked by forest on both sides, until you reach Lakeside, at Windermere's southern tip. Just a short walk from the steamboat quay lies the Aquarium of the Lakes, Britain's largest freshwater aquarium where you will find pike, sharks and otters among a variety of other aquatic life. Lakeside also serves as the terminus of the Lakeside and Haverthwaite Railway where you can extend your journey southwards along the River Leven.

Beatrix Potter Trail

It would be difficult to overstate Beatrix Potter's importance to and influence on the Lake District. She first came to this idyllic part of Britain on family holidays in the 1880s. It is here that she met one of the co-founders of the National Trust, the Vicar of Wray, Canon Rawnsley, who, while encouraging her artistic and literary talents, also ignited an interest in preserving the countryside. Throughout her life she contributed fully to Lakeland living – as well as being a most accomplished writer, she was a pig and sheep breeder, mycologist, artist and landowner.

For those who grew up with Squirrel Nutkin and Peter Rabbit, it is heartening to learn that Beatrix used the wealth gained from becoming a bestselling children's author for the common good. The Potter story goes far beyond cute animals in enchanting stories. The Monks Coniston estate is probably the jewel of this extraordinary bequest. She bought these 1,600 hectares (4,000 acres) of land between Little Langdale and Coniston in 1930, and immediately sold the beautiful Tarn Hows section to the National Trust. The rest passed to the Trust on her death in 1943 along with almost all of her property.

Many companies offer Beatrix Potter tours and several places house her drawings, most notably Hill Top Farm at Near Sawrey, The Beatrix Potter Gallery at Hawkshead and the Armitt in Ambleside. You can even stay in Yew Tree Farm, one of her former residences.

Even if you didn't grow up with her work, the Potter theme provides the perfect frame for your own tour of the southern lakes. Starting from the World of Beatrix Potter in Bowness, you can take the ferry over the lake to Near Sawrey, travel to Hawkshead and Coniston, and then back round to finish in Ambleside.

WHERE:
Cumbria
BEST TIME TO GO:
All year round. The weather is best from March to October.
DON'T MISS:
Tarn Hows – an exquisite little lake set in lush woodland, framed by the Langdale Pikes.
AMOUNT OF WALKING:
Moderate, or lots if you want to make the whole journey on foot, but that would leave little time to visit the attractions.
COST:
Reasonable
YOU SHOULD KNOW:
Tarn Hows has a circular pathway that offers superb disabled access. The route has miles without stiles and, though the path can get muddy in wet weather, it is generally well maintained.

Hill Top, the home of Beatrix Potter

Arts and Crafts

BLACKWELL AND BRANTWOOD

WHERE:
Cumbria
BEST TIME TO GO:
Both houses are open for most of
the year. Blackwell closes from
Christmas to mid-January.
DON'T MISS:
Arriving at Brantwood by boat. Both
the Coniston Launch and SY *Gondola*
call regularly at Brantwood's jetty,
offering you the best view of the
house and grounds.
AMOUNT OF WALKING:
Little. Both houses have made
strenuous efforts to accommodate
wheelchair users, but some areas
remain inaccessible due to the age
of the buildings. The grounds on the
approach to Brantwood are quite
steep (*brant* means steep in
old English).
COST:
Reasonable. Group tickets and
concessions for older adults and
children are available.
YOU SHOULD KNOW:
The roads in the Lake District can get
very busy anytime from Easter to
early September. It does have a
good, though underused, bus
network linking all the major towns
and villages.

The usual advice for someone embarking on a day out in the Lake District is to avail themselves of a good set of waterproofs and comfortable boots. However, all you will need to do for this exploration of two of the area's finest houses is put your thinking cap on. Starting from Bowness and taking a short shuttle-bus journey south, you arrive at Blackwell, one of the finest Arts and Crafts period houses in the world. Designed by M.H. Baillie Scott and completed in 1900, this magnificent house overlooking Lake Windermere was fully restored by 2000, and it now houses some of the finest work from the late-Victorian/early 20th-century movement. From the simple elegance of the White Drawing Room to the fabulous natural lighting of the Main Hall, Blackwell is a true triumph of both iconic design and modern renovation. The house has an ever-changing series of exhibitions, so it is advisable to check ahead to see what is on.

Returning to Bowness, you can now take a bus around the top of Lake Windermere and over to Lake Coniston, where you will find the former home of another pillar of the Arts and Crafts movement. As well as being a superb house in a most beautiful setting, Brantwood was the home of John Ruskin from 1872 until his death in 1900. The house became one of the foremost artistic and literary centres in the western world and the great and the good, including Mahatma Gandhi, Marcel Proust and Frank Lloyd Wright, all came to pay homage to Ruskin. The house is filled with his artwork, books, furniture and personal effects. In the spirit of Ruskin, Brantwood still serves as an education centre, as well as housing live theatre and numerous exhibitions. It truly lives up to its billing as having 'A wealth of art, a wealth of nature, a wealth of things to do'.

Blackwell, one of the finest Arts and Crafts period houses

William Wordsworth

DOVE COTTAGE AND RYDAL MOUNT

Although considered a bit dull by his more extrovert contemporaries, Shelley and Byron, William Wordsworth led a most interesting life. A true son of the Lakes, he was born in 1770 in Cockermouth into a well-to-do family and studied at Cambridge, before journeying to France. Touched greatly by the principles of the French Revolution, he returned to England in 1799 to take up residence in Dove Cottage. It is here we begin our homage to his life. This spartan dwelling, located in the hamlet of Townend, Grasmere, was home to the great poet during the most productive period of his life, but such was the poverty he, his wife and sister lived in that they used newspaper to cover the walls.

Bought by the Wordsworth Trust in 1891 and now fully restored, Dove Cottage sits alongside a magnificent museum dedicated to Wordsworth and other Lakeland poets. The museum is forward looking and encourages present day poetry through workshops and, by excellent curation, it has acquired an interesting variety of exhibits, including modern interpretations of Coleridge's Rime of the Ancient Mariner by notable artists such as Mervyn Peake and Hunt Emerson.

Wordsworth and his growing clan soon outgrew Dove Cottage, and in 1808 they moved to nearby Allen Bank, a house Wordsworth harshly condemned as an eyesore. By 1813 the poet's increasing fame brought great reward and the family were able to move to the much grander Rydal Mount, near Ambleside, where he lived until his death in 1850. Though they had never owned it, the house returned to the Wordsworth family in 1969, when the poet's great great granddaughter bought it and opened it to the public. Now filled with manuscripts, portraits and period furniture, it is still used as a summer retreat by Wordsworth's descendants and retains the atmosphere of a family home.

WHERE:
Cumbria
BEST TIME TO GO:
All year round but Dove Cottage and Museum are closed in January.
DON'T MISS:
The gardens at Rydal Mount. The house also has great views over Rydal Water and Windermere.
AMOUNT OF WALKING:
Little. The museum has good wheelchair access, however Dove Cottage and Rydal Mount cannot accommodate wheelchair users. A virtual tour of Dove Cottage is available at the museum.
COST:
Reasonable. Family and combined tickets are available.
YOU SHOULD KNOW:
The bodies of Wordsworth and his wife Mary, who outlived him by nine years, were laid to rest in St Oswald's Church in Grasmere. It is now one of the most visited shrines in Britain.

Dove Cottage

The Topiary Garden at Levens Hall

Scout Scar and Levens Hall and Gardens

WHERE:
Cumbria
BEST TIME TO GO:
Levens Hall and Gardens usually opens from Sundays to Thursdays from late March to early October, but check ahead for exact times.
DON'T MISS:
There is normally some work-in-progress going on in the Topiary Garden, so if you get the chance to observe these astounding living sculptures being created take a ringside seat and prepare to be amazed.
AMOUNT OF WALKING:
Moderate. The walk up to Scout Scar is not difficult but does require a fair level of fitness.
COST:
Reasonable; family tickets are available at Levens Hall.
YOU SHOULD KNOW:
The locally produced Morocco Ale was named by Colonel James Grahme of Levens, who was a courtier of King Charles II. It is believed that the secret recipe for this spiced ale was buried in the grounds of Levens Hall for safekeeping, during the English Civil War.

This double header starts with a circular three-hour hike up and along an inland cliff in the morning, while the afternoon is taken up with a visit to a stately home that is, whisper it low, fun. If you ask a hundred different lake lovers what their favourite vantage point is, then you will most likely get a hundred different answers. However, for maximum reward with minimum effort, the panoramic view from the ridge of Scout Scar is difficult to trump.

Kendal is a good place to begin your day. It is well served by both rail and bus and only a short distance from the M6 motorway. Starting at the tourist information centre, where maps of this walk are available, you head west along All Hallows Lane. Soon you will have the green of Serpentine Wood to your left and, after a climb up a relatively steep grassy slope, you will have a fine view over Kendal to the hills behind. Another ascent takes you on to Cunswick Scar, where you are greeted by uninterrupted views of Coniston Fells round to the Langdale Pikes. The views get even more spectacular when you reach Scout Scar. As well as most of the southern fells to the west, the expansive sands of Morecambe Bay fill the horizon to the south and, on a clear day, even Blackpool Tower is visible.

After returning to Kendal, take the 555 or 556 bus which drops you right outside the splendid Levens Hall. The building itself is essentially a fine Elizabethan manor house built around a medieval, defensive pele tower. But really it is the gardens that steal the show and provide the fun – you really have to see them to appreciate this spectacularly topiaried wonderland. Originally laid out in 1694, these award-winning gardens are, of their kind, one of Britain's oldest.

Ravenglass & Eskdale Railway

CLIMBING SCA FELL PIKE

Such is the popularity of Britain's highest mountain, that there are times when the climb to Sca Fell Pike resembles a broken down up escalator at London Bridge Station. There is however another way. It is estimated that only one in a hundred people who make the ascent do so from Eskdale. This exclusivity comes at a price, as it is the toughest route but also the most rewarding.

There is no finer way to arrive in the Esk Valley than via the magnificent Ravenglass & Eskdale Railway, known affectionately as Lil Ratty. Originally a freight line transporting iron ore to the coast, it was saved from the scrap merchants by a group of enthusiasts in the late 1950s. By the 1970s it was fully restored and turned into the popular tourist line that we enjoy today. The 11-km (7-mi) route is one of the most scenic in Britain, taking you past Muncaster Castle before following the course of the River Esk into the heart of the fells.

Leaving the train at Dalgarth (the end of the line), the path towards the mountain is about ten minutes' walk from the Woolpack Inn. After crossing the bridge over Cowcove Beck, the path then meanders around High Scarth Crag, giving you fabulous views of the River Esk. The vista gets ever more spectacular as you walk alongside the waterfalls of Cam Spout. It is from here that you can see the east buttress of Sca Fell. Though only a short distance, the final ascent to Sca Fell Pike takes you over the scree of Mickledore, as any defined pathway disappears. After savouring the amazing panoramic views, you can return the same way you came or head down to the Esk by way of Little Narrowcove. This brings you back onto the original route and returns you to the Woolpack Inn.

WHERE:
Cumbria
BEST TIME TO GO:
Such is the length of the climb, you can only really combine it with the train from June to August, when Lil Ratty runs from morning to early evening.
DON'T MISS:
Allow plenty of time to admire the views along the way, particularly from the summit.
AMOUNT OF WALKING:
Lots
COST:
Reasonable
YOU SHOULD KNOW:
The route up to Sca Fell Pike is only meant as a rough guide. You should carry a detailed map, compass or satnav, waterproofs, provisions and always be prepared for delay due to sudden bad weather. If in doubt, take advice from those who know the area.

Lil Ratty steams on up to Dalgarth!

Keswick

BORROWDALE AND BUTTERMERE

WHERE:
Cumbria
BEST TIME TO GO:
All year round. Honister Pass can be closed due to bad weather any time from November to March.
DON'T MISS:
The view over Buttermere when you start the descent into the valley at Honister Pass.
AMOUNT OF WALKING:
Moderate if you just want to walk around the lake or lots if you want to add a bit of fell climbing.
YOU SHOULD KNOW:
Though farmers in Borrowdale had long used graphite to mark their sheep, it wasn't until the reign of Queen Elizabeth I that cottage industries producing pencils were set up. When the exceptionally pure graphite was found to have a military use – it was used to line the moulds of cannon balls – armed guards were sent to escort the mineral to London.

It is the humble pencil that takes centre stage in this exploration of Keswick and its surrounding countryside. Once home to such luminaries as Southey and Coleridge, Keswick owes much of its wealth to the production of pencils and after the visit to a fine museum dedicated to this most basic of writing implements, you can take a drive along the beautiful valley where deposits of graphite were first found.

Keswick is the archetypal Lake District town. Set on the shores of Derwentwater, it has the smooth Skiddaw Hills to the north and the rugged mountains of Borrowdale to the south. Though it caters well for the tourist trade, unlike other towns in the area it isn't completely dominated by it. There are plenty of 'real' shops mixed in with the usual assortment of delis and climbing outfitters. To see Keswick at its best you should visit the 16th-century Moot Hall, which hosts a colourful market on Thursdays and Saturdays.

Next door to the magnificent Art Deco pencil factory, you will find a museum dedicated to the town's premier product. Home to the world's largest pencil, this eccentric little museum brings to life the history of the graphite pencil, first produced locally on an industrial scale in 1832.

It's only a short journey from Borrowdale over the spectacular Honister Pass into the exquisite valley containing the sister lakes of Buttermere and Crummock Water. Separated by a fertile plain, the lakes are contained within an amphitheatre of steep-sided fells with tumbling waterfalls. The walk around Buttermere is easy on the legs, but nonetheless rewarding. If you are feeling more energetic, the view from the 648-m (2,126-ft) high Fleetwith Pike is truly breathtaking. Less committed walkers can content themselves with a postcard, as this is one of the most photographed views in the Lakes.

The B5289 and Gatesgarthdale Beck winding through Honister Pass.

Museum of Lakeland Life

The Museum of Lakeland Life

ABBOT HALL, QUAKER TAPESTRY EXHIBITION, KENDAL AND KIRKBY LONSDALE

The hills are green, the rivers are rushing and the lakes are full. Yes, it rains a lot in Cumbria and it is always worth having a plan B, even if your first instinct is to enjoy the great outdoors. Centred on Kendal, this tour includes a fabulous museum, a glorious art gallery, a place of peace and harmony and ends up in as pretty a town as you could wish to see.

The Museum of Lakeland Life offers intriguing insights into the traditional rural trades of the area. Housed in a converted stable-block, it is positively crammed full of things from the Lake District's past. The permanent collections include exhibits related to the Arts and Crafts movement and to *Swallows and Amazons* author Arthur Ransome, while the centrepiece is a lovingly recreated Edwardian street scene.

Located opposite the museum is an excellent art gallery, housed in the splendid Abbot Hall. With strong links to the Tate Gallery, it has a fine collection of oils, watercolours, furniture and objets d'art. More indoor delights await you across town in the shape of the Quaker Tapestry Exhibition. Housed in an award-winning exhibition centre on New Road, it is the perfect marriage of religion and craft. The Quaker Tapestry is a celebration of centuries of Quaker thought and understanding, embroidered in storybook crewel work on 77 panels of woven wool. Even the non-spiritual will feel uplifted by its beauty.

After a day spent indoors looking at the past, it is time to head 21 km (13 mi) south-east along the A65 to Kirkby Lonsdale. This historic and well-preserved market town stands on the River Lune and has as its main attraction the Devil's Bridge, a medieval arched structure. The view from the Norman St Mary's Church over the river is one of the classic Lakeland scenes, much loved by Ruskin and J.M.W. Turner.

WHERE:
Cumbria
BEST TIME TO GO:
The museum and art gallery open all year round, but close on Sundays. The Quaker Tapestry Exhibition opens year round, from Monday to Friday.
DON'T MISS:
Don't forget to take a photograph of the view from St Mary's Church in Kirkby Lonsdale. Known as Ruskin's View, it really is breathtakingly beautiful.
AMOUNT OF WALKING:
Little. There is wheelchair access to the ground floor only at the Museum. The other two attractions have good step-free access.
COST:
Reasonable. Abbot Hall is free to those in full-time education.
YOU SHOULD KNOW:
The Devil's Bridge in Kirkby Lonsdale is a popular meeting place for motorcycle enthusiasts and the roads in and around the town can get congested, especially on Sundays.

Long Meg and Her Daughters

Eden Valley Drive

WHERE:
Cumbria
BEST TIME TO GO:
All year round. The area is particularly nice on a crisp winter's day.
DON'T MISS:
Taking a picnic and sitting out in the middle of Long Meg and Her Daughters.
AMOUNT OF WALKING:
Little. A dirt track leads to nearby Long Meg and you can park quite close.
COST:
Low
YOU SHOULD KNOW:
Of the many legends associated with the stone circle, the most enduring is that the Scottish wizard Michael Scott put a spell on a coven of witches and turned them to stone. The stones are said to be uncountable and if anyone counts the same number twice the witches will come back to life. Playing this game with any group of small children present should ensure a quiet journey home!

The River Eden is one of only a handful of large rivers in England that flows north and, starting in Appleby-in-Westmoreland we follow its path through idyllic countryside, punctuated by charming villages, and finish at one of Britain's greatest relics. Before leaving Appleby you should allow yourself good time to wander around this immaculate market town. Famous for its horse fair at the beginning of June each year, the town has a fine castle, an unusually wide high street, Boroughgate, and a delightful collection of almshouses. Taking the A66 northbound, you follow the course of the river as it widens, travelling through fertile fields. A short diversion to the right takes you to Kirkby Thore and, if you can ignore the smoke from the nearby gypsum factory, the views over the valley are wonderful. Back on the A66 the next stopping place is Temple Sowerby, a charming village of thatched buildings set around a delightful village green. For those interested in religious architecture, St Lawrence's Church, in the nearby hamlet of Morland, has the only Anglo-Saxon tower in England.

Leaving the A66 and joining the B6412, it is time to head further north towards Little Salkeld. Although it has a fully working watermill that is well worth visiting, its main attraction lies just beyond. Long Meg and Her Daughters is the second biggest stone circle in England. Standing just outside it Long Meg guards a circle of stones that were probably placed here over 3,500 years ago. Many myths and legends surround these fabulous megaliths, but they probably served the same astrological purpose as the more famous Stonehenge, and a trace of banking around the circle suggests that it may once have been similar in structure.

Blackpool and Fleetwood

The coming of the railway combined with the granting of week-long workers' holidays in the 19th century, transformed Blackpool from a sleepy fishing village to the 24/7 fun-filled town you see today. Famed for having more visitors than Portugal, Blackpool is positively crammed with amusements and attractions and is the closest thing the UK has to Atlantic City or Las Vegas.

Stretching from the North Pier to the Pleasure Beach, the Golden Mile is the best place to soak up the kiss-me-quick nature of Blackpool. The unplanned *son et lumière* show provided by the slot machines in the various arcades has to be experienced to be believed, while fortune tellers, waxworks and toffee apple stalls vie for your custom, on this most traditional of British seaside promenades. For those seeking out the quieter parts of town, a ride on Blackpool's famous tramway is a must, while any visit should also include a trip up the Blackpool Tower. A scale model of the Eiffel Tower, it has near its top the wonderfully over-the-top rococo-style Grand Theatre.

Venturing 13 km (8 mi) north along the A587 or taking the tram up the coast, you arrive at the altogether more refined town of Fleetwood. Used as a stopping point for Queen Victoria on her way to holidays in Scotland, it still retains much of its 19th-century charm. Much of the town centre was designed by Decimus Burton, who also planned London's Regent Street, and it is a perfect place to just amble and admire the architecture. Fleetwood is also home to a flourishing market (open Monday to Saturday, except Wednesdays, from May to October) and a museum dedicated to the town's now dwindling fishing industry.

WHERE:
Lancashire
BEST TIME TO GO:
All year round
DON'T MISS:
If you can visit in the autumn, the world-famous Blackpool Illuminations are quite something to behold. The great switch-on happens at the end of August and the lights stretch for 10 km (6 mi) along the seafront.
AMOUNT OF WALKING:
Moderate
COST:
Reasonable
YOU SHOULD KNOW:
Blackpool is the stag and hen party capital of England. If this is not the sort of fun you are looking for, the town centre is probably best avoided at weekends.

Clitheroe and Ribble Valley

WHERE:
Lancashire
BEST TIME TO GO:
Any time of year
DON'T MISS:
The labyrinth in the Clitheroe Castle grounds, the only one in Lancashire.
AMOUNT OF WALKING:
Lots
COST:
Low
YOU SHOULD KNOW:
If you do not feel like walking the Tolkien Trail a worthwhile alternative is the Roman Museum at Ribchester, 5 km (3 mi) down the Ribble Valley.

Think Lancashire and images of mills and industrial landscapes come to mind. Yet this diverse county also contains some of England's most striking countryside and Clitheroe is a good base for exploring it, being not only close to the Forest of Bowland Area of Outstanding Natural Beauty but also situated in the lovely Ribble Valley. Serving a large rural hinterland Clitheroe is a busy market town which has retained its distinctive character over the years. This is particularly evident in the numerous specialist shops you will find about town, including a sausage shop selling over fifty varieties and a wine merchant's that is a veritable Aladdin's Cave of underground cellars.

The town's unmistakable focal point is the Castle on its prominent limestone outcrop. Dating from Norman times, only the keep remains; with rooms just 6 m (20 ft) square, it is said to be the second smallest in England. In the castle grounds the small museum and the linked North West Sound Archive have both benefited from a recent major refurbishment of their facilities.

The attractive stone-built village of Hurst Green lies 8 km (5 mi) west of Clitheroe and is the starting-point for a 9-km (5.5-mi) round walk known as the Tolkien Trail, so called because the celebrated writer often stayed at a guest house in the grounds of nearby Stonyhurst College while he was working on *The Lord of the Rings* trilogy. This gentle walk takes you through the woods and rolling farmlands of the lower Ribble Valley. As well as Stonyhurst itself, now a famous Catholic public school, there are good views of Pendle Hill and Clitheroe Castle and you will also pass the spots where the Hodder and Calder tributaries join the Ribble.

Clitheroe Castle

Pendle Witches Trail

In the turbulent years of the early 17th century Lancashire was an important stronghold for Roman Catholic believers, who found themselves a regularly persecuted minority in King James's newly Protestant nation. It was against this background that exotic tales of witchcraft in the remoter parts of the country gained easy currency, of which the most famous is undoubtedly that of the Pendle Witches, a group of local women from the villages around Pendle Hill who were convicted of witchcraft in 1612. You can follow the route they took from their homes to their eventual trial and execution in Lancaster on this 72-km (45-mi) drive, which passes through some of Lancashire's wildest and most spectacular scenery.

The Witches Trail starts at the Pendle Heritage Centre in Barrowford where you can read up on the story of the Pendle Witches and learn about the times in which they lived. The first part of the Trail takes you on country lanes through the little villages that cluster around the base of mighty Pendle Hill and which were home to the alleged witches. The distinctive whale-backed mass of Pendle Hill is, at 557 m (1,830 ft), a landmark for miles around and was the supposed site for the covens where the witches practised their black arts. From Pendle the Trail takes you via Clitheroe and across the Forest of Bowland, a western spur of the Pennines that is not actually forest at all but an area of lonely and rugged moorland which was once a royal hunting ground. Journey's end is the forbidding bulk of Lancaster Castle where the witches were tried and hanged in August 1612. The Castle is still in use today as a prison and a court.

WHERE:
Lancashire
BEST TIME TO GO:
Any time of year (though the drive through the Trough of Bowland is particularly spectacular in August, when the heather is in bloom on the moors).
DON'T MISS:
The little stone-built village of Downham, one of Lancashire's loveliest and most unspoilt.
AMOUNT OF WALKING:
Little (though you will be hard pressed not to be tempted out of your car as you drive across the Forest of Bowland).
COST:
Low
YOU SHOULD KNOW:
Barley is the best place from which to climb Pendle Hill. The moderately demanding ascent will take you about an hour.

The unspoilt village of Downham in the Ribble Valley

Whooper swans feeding at Martin Mere.

Martin Mere and Rufford Old Hall

WHERE:
Lancashire
BEST TIME TO GO:
Any time of year (but note that Rufford is not open in the winter months when Martin Mere is often at its liveliest).
DON'T MISS:
The beavers beavering away in their natural habitat, a recent introduction at Martin Mere.
AMOUNT OF WALKING:
Moderate (Martin Mere has level access and hard-surfaced paths. All the hides are accessible to wheelchairs).
COST:
Reasonable
YOU SHOULD KNOW:
There is a legend that Martin Mere is the lake into which King Arthur's sword Excalibur was thrown, to be caught by a woman's arm rising from the water.

The area of West Lancashire lying between Preston and Liverpool consists largely of flat fertile farmland, much of which was under water in earlier times. An extensive network of drainage ditches now means that the rich soils yield a wealth of produce all year round. The two principal attractions in the area lie close together and make up this rewarding day out.

A short distance inland from Southport, Martin Mere Wetland Centre is one of nine visitor centres in the UK run by the Wildfowl and Wetlands Trust (WWT). Established in 1976 on the site of one of England's oldest and largest lakes, Martin Mere's 150 hectares (370 acres) of reclaimed marshland now provide an important refuge for thousands of wintering wildfowl. In the landscaped waterfowl garden some birds will feed straight from the hand, whilst a network of hides throughout the site makes it easier to observe many of the shyer species. Martin Mere's most spectacular sight is the winter migration of vast numbers of pink-footed geese.

Nearby Rufford Old Hall is one of the finest Tudor buildings in the North West. Its 16th-century timber-framed Great Hall is a glorious sight with its ornate hammerbeam roof and richly carved wooden screen. Legend has it that the young William Shakespeare performed here for the owner Sir Thomas Hesketh. The hall contains fine collections of oak furniture and Tudor weapons and armour. The small gardens feature some unusual displays of topiary and there is a pleasant walk along the towpath of the Leeds and Liverpool Canal, which borders the property.

Burnley

QUEEN STREET MILL AND GAWTHORPE HALL

Burnley owed its initial fame and fortune to King Cotton, growing rapidly in the 19th century to become one of the principal cotton manufacturing towns in the British Empire. Its Victorian prosperity is still evident in the many fine municipal buildings in the centre, including an imposing town hall. Opened in 1895 as a workers' co-operative, Queen Street Mill was a relatively late addition to the local industrial landscape and remained commercially active for less than ninety years. Fortunately, however, most of the original machinery has been preserved intact and in situ in what is now an excellent museum, which shows it off in daily working demonstrations. Queen Street is now the world's only surviving steam-powered cotton mill and it gives a remarkable insight into Victorian factory life. As you stand in the weaving shed and hear the deafening sound of the 300 looms in action, it is sobering to reflect that the shed was once three times this size and that in its heyday the mill boasted over 1,100 looms. It produced plain cloth for shirts and other basic clothing items for export throughout the Empire.

A very different world is conjured up at Gawthorpe Hall in the small town of Padiham just west of Burnley. This fine Elizabethan house on the banks of the River Calder was for 350 years the family seat of the Shuttleworths, whose last resident formed the internationally recognized collection of needlework and lace, which is now one of the highlights of the interior displays. Gawthorpe was extensively remodelled in the 1850s by Sir Charles Barry who created the extravagant interiors you see today. The Long Gallery houses an outstanding collection of 17th-century portraits of society figures, many on loan from the National Portrait Gallery in London.

WHERE:
Lancashire
BEST TIME TO GO:
May to September (but note that Queen Street Mill is closed on Sundays and Mondays and Gawthorpe Hall is closed on Fridays and Mondays).
DON'T MISS:
Make time for the short trip to the Singing Ringing Tree, an award-winning musical sculpture high up on the moor on the southern edge of town.
AMOUNT OF WALKING:
Moderate
COST:
Low (accompanied children get free entry at both attractions).
YOU SHOULD KNOW:
The magnificent 500 hp steam engine which powers the Queen Street looms was given its somewhat surprising name – Peace – as a mark of respect to the local soldiers who did not return home from the First World War.

The Singing Ringing Tree

Salford Quays

A run-down, unprepossessing area of redundant dockland not far from Manchester's city centre has been transformed over the past decade into one of the country's most exciting and architecturally dynamic leisure complexes. At the heart of this spectacular example of urban regeneration and overlooking the Manchester Ship Canal is The Lowry, a large arts and entertainment centre boasting no less than three performing spaces, including a 1,730-seat theatre which hosts major productions of musicals, opera and dance. The foyers and public spaces are open throughout the day and there are many cafés and bars where you can sit and enjoy the great views out over the canal and the quayside. The Lowry's art gallery houses the country's largest public collection of paintings by L.S. Lowry, the Manchester-born artist whose canvases with their distinctive stick figures are, for many people, the defining images of the factory landscapes of the north.

Crossing the footbridge over the Ship Canal brings you to the other major attraction in this area, the Imperial War Museum North, one of England's newest and most unconventional museums. The work of the controversial architect Daniel Libeskind, the Museum has a highly complex design, based on the idea of a globe torn apart by conflict and broken into three great 'shards' that symbolize earth, air and water. The disruption and disorientation of war are also evoked in the interior's sloping floors and ceilings. The state-of-the-art displays focus more on ordinary people and their experiences of war than on weapons and military artefacts.

If you need a break from history and culture The Quays also contain a multiplex cinema and a factory outlet shopping mall, where famous labels are sold at heavily discounted prices.

*The Imperial War
Museum North*

Imperial War Museum - North

Liverpool

Known affectionately as the 'Three Graces', the trio of impressive buildings that line the north bank of the River Mersey along Pierhead bear majestic witness to Liverpool's past glories as one of the world's great seaports. The pair of iconic Liver Birds atop the Royal Liver Building gaze out over the Atlantic and westwards to the world, emphasizing the fact that the city's outlook has always been international and cosmopolitan. Although its days of trading might are long gone, a visit to Liverpool today still evokes a strong sense of a world apart, reflected in its designation as a UNESCO World Heritage Site in 2004.

No day out here is complete without taking the ferry across the Mersey.

You are definitely spoiled for choice in the relatively compact city centre but no day out here, especially for the first-time visitor, is complete without taking a ferry across the Mersey. If you are of the right generation you may want to sing the famous song as you enjoy wonderful views looking back at the Pierhead waterfront. The fine Victorian brick buildings of the Albert Dock now house a wealth of leisure facilities. Here you will find the Maritime Museum and a world-class modern art collection at Tate Liverpool. In 2007, the bicentenary of the abolition of the British slave trade, Liverpool blazed another trail with the opening of the country's first museum dedicated to the history of slavery.

Everyone knows that Liverpool became a world player again in the 1960s, this time on the popular music scene, and thousands come to the city to recapture the sights and sounds of the Merseybeat era. The Beatles Story is the city's major tribute to its four most famous sons and should be on every music-lover's itinerary. And you can still visit the Cavern Club, where the Fab Four had their first regular gigs.

WHERE:
Merseyside
BEST TIME TO GO:
Any time of year (though music fans should note the Beatle Week held annually in August).
DON'T MISS:
The chance to complete your Beatles experience with a guided tour to the modest childhood homes of John Lennon and Paul McCartney.
AMOUNT OF WALKING:
Moderate
COST:
Reasonable (Liverpool's public museums all have free entry).
YOU SHOULD KNOW:
The numerous major construction projects in the city are evidence of Liverpool's most recent accolade as European Capital of Culture in 2008.

*The National Waterways
Museum at Ellesmere*

Port Sunlight

NATIONAL WATERWAYS MUSEUM

In the late 1880s the industrialist William Lever, later First Viscount Leverhulme, started looking for a new location for his soap manufacturing business. The site he chose – marshy ground on the south bank of the Mersey facing Liverpool – did not seem a promising one, but the once wild Wirral Peninsula was becoming a fashionable residential area for wealthy Liverpool commuters. Lever put his ideas of enlightened commercial and social patronage into practice when he created the model industrial village of Port Sunlight, named after his most famous soap brand. Port Sunlight was designed as a self-contained community for his factory workers and Lever financed many of the public buildings, including the church and art gallery, from his own pocket. Today it is a conservation area with strict controls on development. With its gardens and broad tree-lined roads, Port Sunlight is a pleasant place to wander around.

The village's major attraction is the Lady Lever Art Gallery, established by Lord Leverhulme in 1922 as a memorial to his wifeand to house his personal art collection. The gallery boasts an outstanding collection of British art, including the works of the pre-Raphaelites and landscapes by Turner and Constable; there are also fine porcelain and furniture collections.

At the foot of the Wirral Peninsula, the town of Ellesmere Port is home to a branch of the National Waterways Museum. The historic dock complex, built at the point where the Shropshire Union Canal joins the Mersey Estuary, has been converted into a museum devoted to the country's canals and inland waterways. An extensive collection of narrowboats and other craft and of stories about the people who worked on them give you an absorbing and entertaining insight into a vanished way of life.

WHERE:
Merseyside & Cheshire
BEST TIME TO GO:
Any time of year (but note that the daily canal-boat trips the museum offers operate only during the summer months).
DON'T MISS:
'How to Build a Boat', a touch-screen and interactive display housed in the island warehouse at Ellesmere Port Boat Museum.
AMOUNT OF WALKING:
Moderate
COST:
Low (the Lady Lever Art Gallery has free entry).
YOU SHOULD KNOW:
Lever's initial interest in art was as a means to promote his soap products. Many Sunlight Soap advertisements were based on paintings he had purchased.

Chester

The city of Chester owes its origins to the Romans who 2,000 years ago established the military settlement of Deva at this strategic site by the mouth of the River Dee. Designed as a bulwark against the fractious Welsh tribes to the west, the original Roman fortress now lies beneath the modern city but much remains above ground to remind you of Chester's importance in Roman times. Start your visit with an overview of the city from its ancient walls which, though Roman in origin, are mainly medieval. They form the most complete set of town walls in Britain. With fine views of the cathedral and the river, walking the 3-km (2-mi) circuit will take you about an hour.

The Grosvenor Museum houses the major archaeological finds from the area, including an outstanding collection of Roman tombstones. You can see the Roman amphitheatre, the largest yet found in Britain; and you can unwind in a lovely garden near the walls dotted with Roman columns and other remains. For a complete immersion in the spirit of ancient times, however, you should visit the Dewa Roman Experience. This thoroughly hands-on attraction has been designed to fire the imagination of all ages. As well as enjoying the sights, sounds and even smells of a Roman street you can try on a suit of replica armour and handle genuine Roman pottery.

Chester has all the leading stores and brands which you expect to find in any high street, but what makes shopping here so special is the presence of The Rows, a unique series of two-tiered covered galleries which radiate from the High Cross. Dating back to the 13th century The Rows are the precursor of today's shopping mall and they retain their harmonious appearance thanks to careful Victorian restoration of the half-timbered frontages.

WHERE:
Cheshire
BEST TIME TO GO:
Any time of year
DON'T MISS:
The much-photographed clock on the Eastgate Arch. If you are here at noon in the summer months look out for the Town Crier issuing his proclamations.
AMOUNT OF WALKING:
Moderate
COST:
Reasonable
YOU SHOULD KNOW:
'Dewa' is not a mis-spelling for the original Roman name of Chester but a more accurate representation of how the Romans pronounced 'Deva'.

The 13th-century buildings along High Cross

Chester Zoo and Norton Priory

Lying on the northern outskirts of the city, Chester Zoo is the largest zoo in Britain. Its justly famous collection of more than 7,000 animals from some 500 different species is displayed in 45 hectares (110 acres) of glorious landscaped gardens. Chester has long been at the forefront of conservation, becoming an early haven for many rare and endangered creatures and a pioneer of captive breeding programmes. Over the years the Zoo has built a number of magnificent new enclosures, which aim to recreate the animals' natural habitats as closely as possible. Highlights include the very rare black rhinos, the Asian Elephant House and the Spirit of the Jaguar, where the most reclusive of the big cats roams freely. The Zoo's newest exhibit is the Realm of the Red Ape, where its group of breeding orang-utans enjoy the run of a recreated Indonesian forest. If you get tired of walking, the overhead monorail will give you a bird's eye view of the animals.

A short drive up the motorway brings you to the peaceful surroundings of Norton Priory, an oasis of woodland gardens that run down to the Bridgewater Canal. Established in 1134 by an Augustinian order of black canons, the priory was comprehensively destroyed after the Dissolution of the Monasteries in the 16th century. Modern excavations have uncovered the remains of the church, chapter house and a well-preserved undercroft. There are many impressive finds in the attractive museum, including an outstanding collection of medieval floor tiles and a giant 14th-century statue of St Christopher. The grounds include a charming walled garden from Georgian times, a recreated medieval herb garden and a woodland and sculpture trail.

A child reading up on the Red-crowned Crane!

Red-crowned Crane

Red-crowned Cranes breed in remote marshland areas of east Russia and North China. They migrate southwards for the winter to parts of east China and Korea. In 1924 only 20 birds remained in northern Japan but today, as a result of protection and artificial feeding, around 600 birds can be

The main threats to these cranes are from habitat loss, pesticides and disturbance. Because of their remote habitat and migratory habits, operation involving China, Russia Japan is needed to ensure their re in the wild.

Zoo breeding programme

Chester is part of an internationally co-ordinated conservation breeding programme (EEP). Chicks were first bred here in 1991 and many chicks reared here since. The viable zoo population is a very necessary precaution should disaster strike the vulnerable wild populations.

Macclesfield's Silk Museum

LITTLE MORETON HALL

Tucked beneath the hills of the High Peak, the East Cheshire town of Macclesfield built its fame and fortune on silk. In the 18th and 19th centuries Macclesfield was the country's premier silk manufacturing town. Silk is still woven here, although in nothing like the quantities of its heyday, when as many as 120 mills and dye houses produced the fabric that has long been a byword for luxury and refinement. Macclesfield today celebrates its commercial heritage in the Silk Museum, which gives a comprehensive introduction to the textile spread over three sites. Here you can learn about the processes of silk cultivation and the development of the silk industry from its roots in ancient China. The museum's highlight is Paradise Mill, a working Victorian silk mill whose interiors re-create working conditions in the 1930s. Commercial production ceased as recently as 1981; today you can see daily demonstrations of the silk weaver's art on twenty-six restored handlooms.

Little Moreton Hall

The North West is noted in architectural history for the strikingly bold patterning of its timber-framed Tudor houses. You can visit the classic example of a Cheshire 'black-and-white' house at Little Moreton Hall, 21 km (13 mi) south west of Macclesfield. The first sight of the Hall across a defensive moat, its exterior a riot of ornate half-timbered banding, makes an unforgettable impression. With its irregular lines, overhanging gables and huge expanses of leaded windows the building seems to belong to the realm of fairytale, yet it owes its all too solid origin to Ralph Moreton who began construction in 1480. This is Tudor skill and craftsmanship at its finest and if you can tear yourself away from contemplating the marvellous exterior, well-informed guides are on hand to show you the Hall's many interior delights, including the Long Gallery with its extravagant plasterwork.

WHERE:
Cheshire
BEST TIME TO GO:
April to October (but note that the Paradise Mill section of the Silk Museum is not open on Sundays).
DON'T MISS:
The chance to buy locally made silk products in the museum shop in Macclesfield.
AMOUNT OF WALKING:
Moderate
COST:
Low (accompanied children under 16 get free entry to the Silk Museum).
YOU SHOULD KNOW:
You can see another fine example of a Tudor half-timbered manor house at Gawsworth Hall near Macclesfield.

Hadrian's Wall

WHERE:
Northumberland
BEST TIME TO GO:
Any time of year (but note that the wall tends to be very exposed, so go prepared for blustery conditions).
DON'T MISS:
The Corbridge Lion, a masterpiece of Roman-Celtic sculpture on display in the site museum.
AMOUNT OF WALKING:
Lots (but note the Hadrian's Wall Country Bus which operates between April and October as a service designed particularly for walkers).
COST:
Reasonable
YOU SHOULD KNOW:
Because of their importance and extreme fragility most of the Vindolanda writing tablets are now in the British Museum, including what is probably the world's oldest birthday party invitation. However there should always be a few tablets on display in the site museum.

When the Roman Emperor Hadrian visited the far-flung province of Britannia in 122 AD he decreed that a wall be erected on the northernmost border of his empire 'to separate the Romans from the barbarians' (as his biographer put it at the time). It took the legionaries six years to build a mighty wall extending 117 km (73 mi) from coast to coast, linking Bowness on the Solway Firth in the west with Wallsend near the mouth of the River Tyne in the east. Today Hadrian's Wall is the most prominent evidence of Britain's 400-year occupation by the Romans and one of the supreme engineering achievements of the ancient world.

You are unlikely to forget your first sight of Hadrian's Wall snaking off into the distance across some of the wildest and most dramatic countryside in northern England. Hugging the crags and ridges of the Great Whin Sill, the wall offers wonderful walking opportunities and various car parks give good access for walkers. The eastern stone-built end is the best preserved, especially the section between Hexham and Haltwhistle. A good starting-point for a wall walk is Housesteads where you can see the remains of the most complete Roman fort excavated in Britain, including the soldiers' communal latrine.

Other sites which conjure up the life of the Roman soldiers who guarded this frontier include the cavalry fort at Chesters, guarding the crossing of the River North Tyne; the major supply base at Corbridge, south of the wall; and the fort at Vindolanda, a fascinating site where you can see reconstructed sections of the wall. Annual excavations in the waterlogged soil continue to reveal rare artefacts of leather, wood and textiles. The most famous finds here are the unique wooden writing tablets, which give extraordinary insights into the daily lives of the garrison.

Part of Housesteads Roman Fort near Hexham Abbey

Farne Islands

*High density housing on the
Farne Islands!*

Mention the words 'Farne Islands' to an ornithologist and you will be greeted with a mixture of excitement and reverence as this group of islands off the lonely Northumberland coast is a veritable paradise for lovers of birdlife. There are twenty-eight islands in all, although only fifteen are visible at high tide. One of Europe's top nature reserves, the Farne Islands provide a nesting ground for more than twenty species of seabird, including terns, guillemots, razorbills and – most people's favourite – puffins with their striking multi-coloured beaks. Boats leave Seahouses harbour for the short journey out to the islands, the first of which you reach just 3 km (2 mi) offshore. You are unlikely to come often to this remote spot so, if you have your sea legs, make the most of the day by taking the all-day trip lasting some six hours, during which you visit the two islands where landings are permitted.

In the morning you go ashore at Staple Island in the outer group where the 'Pinnacles' – rock stacks rising out of the sea – are often covered in migrating or nesting seabirds. In the distance you should spot the distinctive red-and-white stripes of the Longstone lighthouse, site of Grace Darling's famous rescue of shipwreck survivors in 1838. In the afternoon you visit Inner Farne where a wooden boardwalk makes for an easy exploration of the island. If you visit during the nesting season, between April and July, you should wear a hat, as you are liable to be buzzed by Arctic terns protecting their eggs and chicks. The island also has historical associations with Celtic Christianity; it was here that St Cuthbert lived a hermit's life and where he died in 687 AD. St Cuthbert's Chapel, however, dates from the early 14th century.

WHERE:
Northumberland
BEST TIME TO GO:
April to September (but you should check with the boat company for weather and tidal conditions before setting off).
DON'T MISS:
Once on the boat watch out for a sight of Atlantic grey seals basking on the rocks.
AMOUNT OF WALKING:
Moderate (note that Staple Island is an exposed outcrop of rock so you should be prepared for more challenging conditions here).
COST:
Expensive (as well as the boat fares there are landing fees for the islands, although these are free to National Trust members).
YOU SHOULD KNOW:
You should take your own food and drink as there are no catering facilities on the Farne Islands.

Lindisfarne and Bamburgh

WHERE:
Northumberland
BEST TIME TO GO:
March to October
DON'T MISS:
The facsimile of the 7th-century
'Lindisfarne Gospels', one of the
world's most precious illuminated
manuscripts, on display in the Heritage
Centre (the original is in the British
Library in London). There is also an
electronic version where you can 'turn
the pages'.
AMOUNT OF WALKING:
Moderate (more if you decide to walk
over the causeway to Holy Island).
COST:
Reasonable
YOU SHOULD KNOW:
As the opening times of the sights on
Lindisfarne are determined by tidal
conditions you should check tide
tables (published in local newspapers
and online) before travelling.

Lindisfarne, or Holy Island as it is also known, is one of the most ancient and venerated sites of Christianity in the British Isles. Connected to the mainland by a 5-km (3-mi) causeway, Lindisfarne is only accessible at low tide, a restriction which serves to heighten the special aura surrounding the place. Irish missionaries established a monastery on the island as far back as the 7th century. The greatest of Northumbria's holy men, St Cuthbert, was bishop of Lindisfarne and was originally buried here before his bones were moved to Durham. An atmosphere of monastic calm still prevails as you wander around the ruins of the 12th-century Priory church whose pink sandstone walls look particularly appealing against a blue sky. When Henry VIII laid waste to the monasteries many of the Priory stones were incorporated into Lindisfarne Castle.

Perched on its rocky pedestal the castle was converted with considerable ingenuity in 1903 into an Edwardian country house by the young Edwin Lutyens, later to become one of England's most famous architects.

Back on the mainland the unmistakable profile of Bamburgh Castle dominates the coastline for miles around. Whilst the great stone keep dates from the castle's Norman origins in the 1150s, the castle's remarkably complete appearance today, which has made it a favoured location with film-makers, is actually due to two much later restorations. The second of these was carried out in the early years of the 20th century by Lord Armstrong, the prominent industrialist, who commissioned a series of sumptuous faux-medieval interiors. In the village the Royal National Lifeboat Institution runs a museum dedicated to Grace Darling which preserves the rowing-boat used by the young lighthouse-keeper's daughter in her heroic rescue of shipwreck survivors from treacherous seas off the Farne Islands.

Bamburgh Castle

Early morning mist rises from Kielder Water.

Kielder Water

HARESHAW LINN WATERFALL

Kielder Water was a remote, uncultivated land of marsh and bogs until 1982, when it was flooded to create the largest man-made reservoir in the UK. Surrounded by 63,000 hectares (155,000 acres) of mature spruce, larch and scots pine woods, the lake, earth-dammed at one end, already feels ancient – a haven for wildlife and for enthusiasts of nature and outdoor pursuits.

There are three visitor centres. Tower Knowe has long views over the lake from the massive dam; 17th-century Kielder Castle – once the Duke of Northumberland's hunting lodge – has the Minotaur Maze, play areas and way-marked walks; but nearby Leaplish Waterside Park is the centre for most of the activities on Kielder. Besides the pool, crazy golf and full range of water sports, there's an excellent Birds of Prey Centre with frequent flying displays set against the magnificent lake scenery, a hands-on children's pet corner, sculpture trail, ferry cruises and guided walks. Kielder's success as a natural amenity is in balancing adventure against tranquillity – it's vast enough to absorb occasional crowds.

Romantic solitude is a certainty if you stop at Bellingham on the Hexham road. Bellingham has a 12th-century church, but its prime was as a Victorian iron centre. When you follow Hareshaw Burn out of Bellingham, and through the long, wooded gorge as it deepens to a waterfall of poetic serenity, it's almost impossible to imagine Hareshaw Linn in the 1840s as the site of two blast furnaces, seventy coke ovens and a range of other iron works belching noise and smoke into such beauty. Now, Hareshaw Linn's rare ferns, lichens and 300 kinds of moss are protected as it's a Site of Special Scientific Interest, and in the pure air, woodpeckers, warblers and flycatchers dart across waterside sylvan perfection, and rare red squirrels play by the splashing falls. This lovely walk is about 4 km (2.5 mi) long, and takes ninety minutes.

WHERE:
Northumberland
BEST TIME TO GO:
Any time of year – though the deciduous woodland of Hareshaw Linn is obviously more exuberant in summer.
DON'T MISS:
The illuminating displays at Kielder Castle visitor centre about the vast forest – its history long before it was planted to become the largest man-made forest in Europe; and the flora and fauna to look out for during your visit.
AMOUNT OF WALKING:
Lots – but access on many of the Kielder paths and tracks is good.
COST:
Low – for most, but not all activities; and there are no entrance charges.
YOU SHOULD KNOW:
Kielder Water covers 6.5 sq km (4 sq mi) and has a perimeter of 43 km (27 mi). Kielder Forest, all around it, covers 243 sq km (152 sq mi).

Cragside House and Gardens

ROTHBURY

Looming out of the trees and huge rhododendrons stacked high above Debdon Burn, outside Rothbury on the edge of the Northumberland National Park, Cragside is the spectacular Victorian mansion built by one of Britain's great industrialists. William, Lord Armstrong was an inventor of genius, and his house was described as 'The Palace of a Modern Magician'. Even now, the gadgets, machines and systems he devised for the comfort of his guests and to save his staff unnecessary labour will astound you. Cragside was the first house in the world to be lit by hydro-electricity, powered by its own generators. Hot and cold running water, passenger lifts, central heating, fire alarms, telephones and dozens of smaller refinements were the wonder of Armstrong's age. Effectively, he automated a house designed to the grandest specifications by some of the greatest artists and architects of the era, including William Morris. The rooms are beautiful, always made of the finest materials and in exquisite detail – and because the original furniture and fittings are still in place, the house retains its family intimacy, which makes its magnificent eccentricities seem rather homely and appealing.

The garden will make you gasp, too. The house faces down a rocky gorge, bridged by a graceful arch, and leading to 405 hectares (1,000 acres) of thick woodland (Armstrong planted 7 million trees and bushes on the bare hillsides to get his desired effect). The estate is full of hidden corners for children (especially) to find, like Nelly's Labyrinth and the adventure play area, with its tunnels, slides and swings. Red squirrels scuttle along more than 50 km (30 mi) of paths and lakeside walks, Europe's biggest rock garden and the amazing Orchard House, which still produces mouthwatering fresh fruits and berries. Colourful, terrific fun, and full of surprises, Cragside, in its day, represented all the marvels of 'the Future'.

WHERE:
Northumberland
BEST TIME TO GO:
Any time of year, but remember the rhododendrons are at their best in May and June.
DON'T MISS:
The opportunity to see the influence of the Arts and Crafts design movement on a grand scale – whole series of rooms in which the decoration, furniture and embellishments are in unified stylistic harmony, with stained glass by William Morris.
AMOUNT OF WALKING:
Lots – and the National Trust advises stout footwear to cope with 'uneven ground, steep and slippery footpaths and distances between parts of the property'. At the house, assistance for the disabled is available on request.
COST:
Reasonably expensive
YOU SHOULD KNOW:
Cragside House is notable for its brilliant butterflies. From June to August, it attracts all the garden butterflies, plus breeding populations of several others.

Cragside House

Alnwick Castle

CRASTER AND DUNSTANBURGH

Alnwick is one of Europe's great fortress castles – so old, so huge and so magnificent that it is called 'The Windsor of the North'. It rises imperiously from the bank of the River Aln , dominating the medieval cobbled streets of Northumberland's historic county town. Its keeps, towers and crenellations inspire the most colourful chivalric fantasies. In fact, its credentials as a magic castle are impeccable: it is the location for Hogwarts School in the Harry Potter films. For visitors, the magic is real enough, because within the ancient fortifications are stupendous suites of apartments and State rooms reflecting the changing tastes and requirements of the Percy family, who have lived there since 1309. Some of the best are furnished in the Italian Renaissance style and you can see paintings by Titian, Canaletto and Van Dyck among some of England's rarest masterpieces of furniture and porcelain. There are besides, full and partial guided tours (even Harry Potter tours!), Story-Telling by the Castle Jester, Swordsmanship and Archery classes, and dozens of participatory distractions. The Gardens (separate entry) have recently been planned to match the castle's magnificence: after just a decade, they are already maturing round the spectacular cascade tumbling the length of a hillside, in grounds originally designed by Capability Brown.

Alnwick Castle

Even during Alnwick's week-long costumed fairs, there are few crowds at Craster, a 13th-century fishing village 10 km (6 mi) to the northeast. Deservedly famous for its oak-smoked kippers, Craster is also renowned as the perfect place from which to approach Dunstanburgh Castle. 14th-century Dunstanburgh once rivalled Alnwick in grandeur. Now it is a colossal, romantic ruin, dominating only sheer cliffs, the lonely grass sward of the Northumbrian shore, and the insistent sea. In typically changeable weather, that combination charges the twenty-minute walk from Craster with epic atmospheric drama: 'sic transit gloria mundi'.

Newcastle-upon-Tyne and Gateshead

Newcastle is the most fun you can have in any English city outside London. It's utterly modern, yet its distinctive 'Geordie' culture of hospitality is steeped in tradition. It is a city that values the arts in all their forms: any day you might see a poetry reading in Eldon Square, street theatre, public sculptures or an open-air concert, in addition to the treasures in Newcastle's first-class galleries and museums.

The same combination of old and new makes an architectural time machine of the city centre. From Castle Keep, built circa 1170 under Henry II, Hadrian's Wall heads east to Wallsend. From its roof (134 steps up) you get a fantastic view of the ultra-modern Quayside regeneration development, from its bars, galleries and restaurants, Sir Norman Foster's Sage Concert Hall and the Baltic Square warehouse transformation of Gateshead Quays, to Newcastle's array of famous bridges, now framed by the giant double parabola of the Gateshead Millennium Bridge, which tilts like a blinking eye to allow ships to pass up and down river. In the centre, Roman, medieval, Jacobean, Georgian and Victorian building styles sit comfortably alongside colourful Chinatown and the mammoth Eldon Square shopping and entertainment malls. The happy jumble helps make Newcastle feel especially cosmopolitan. Grainger Town is all Georgian elegance, yet the dashing modern signature of the Quayside rivals the Paris Bercy complex.

For visitors, Newcastle's quirky jigsaw of sights and activities is a glittering invitation to understand why the city is called 'the party capital of the north east'. Walk round the city, and you'll see the variety of ingenious ways Geordies turn local history and culture into something heroic – and elevate habitual good humour into world-class bonhomie.

Appropriately, Earl Grey, the great 19th century political and social reformer idolized for establishing Newcastle's prominence, is actually best remembered as a delicate kind of tea.

The Sage Centre snuggles below the Tyne Bridge.

WHERE:
Tyneside
BEST TIME TO GO:
Any time of year (and any time of day or night too).
DON'T MISS:
The 1.5-km (1-mi) circular river walk from the Swing Bridge, under the classic Tyne Bridge along Gateshead Quays to the 'art factory' Baltic Centre, over the tilting Millennium Bridge and back through the buzzing glamour of the Quayside. You'll see how successfully Newcastle integrates its history and industrial heritage into optimism for the city's future – and how highly it values public art.
AMOUNT OF WALKING:
A little to a lot – Newcastle is full of attractions that can stop you in your tracks.
COST:
Low, if any (unless you are smitten by the high-end luxury emporia of Grainger Town). Surprisingly, the hands-on exhibitions and interactive displays of museums like the Discovery Centre and the Centre for Life are free.
YOU SHOULD KNOW:
Newcastle and Gateshead's commitment to public artworks goes well beyond the 200-ton 'Angel of the North' you see on the A167 entering Gateshead. Newcastle's Quayside includes the 11-m (35-ft) steel 'River God' sculpture, the 7.6-m (25-ft) conical 'Blacksmith's Needle', and 17 river-themed carvings spread along 30 m (100 ft) of sandstone wall, among many others.

No supermarkets here!

Beamish Open Air Museum

WHERE:
County Durham
BEST TIME TO GO:
Any time of year
DON'T MISS:
The Jubilee Confectionery, where not only will the staff show you sweet-making secrets, but you can buy old fashioned delights like Cinder Toffee, Sherbet 'n' Liquorice or Victory 'V's; or choose from a selection including chewy, floral, tart, fizzy, fruity, medicated or minty traditional sweets. Gobstopping doesn't cover it.
AMOUNT OF WALKING:
Lots – and in these period buildings, much of the access is stepped. Where actual access is impossible or difficult, 'photo access' is available.
COST:
Expensive, but worth every penny.
YOU SHOULD KNOW:
Beamish is especially popular with groups of schoolchildren on course-related visits. In fact, their costumed participation and huge enthusiasm for everything from going underground down the mine to 'clippy' mat-making in the pit cottages greatly enhances any visit. It's one museum where the more children you get, the better the atmosphere. Adults always want to retire to the pub.

There is nothing traditional about Beamish. Conceived as a repository of the modern history of the entire northeast of England, it is a 'living' museum dedicated to telling the story of the fundamental changes wrought by industrial revolution on a predominantly rural society. You don't look at documents or artefacts in glass cases – at Beamish you literally join in society as it was in either 1825 or 1913.

The experience goes far beyond mere authenticity: the 121-hectare (300-acre) woodland site contains a small town, as it would have been in 1913. The streets of terraced houses come complete with shops, bank, pub, Masonic hall, printing works, dentist's, surgery, motor and cycle works, stables, solicitors, running trams and a costumed population prepared to include you in their daily round of work or business. From the same era, there's a colliery village, a railway station (with running locos) and a home farm. Every brick, rail, picture or piece of furniture has been brought here from its original location. Nothing has been 're-created' – just rebuilt, and the effect is astounding. The same goes for Pockerley Manor, presented with its gardens, farm buildings and estate management as though it were 1825, before workers left the land to go mining or into the factories. Here you can also see the third oldest railway engine in the world, built in 1822 by George Stephenson, and now housed in the period Running Shed of the 1825 Pockerley Waggonway – and you can ride a replica (Beamish's only exception to its rule) of the first train to carry passengers, the 1825 'Locomotion No 1'.

More than 200 costumed staff make Beamish tick. They'll introduce you to anything from ploughing a furrow with Shire horses to working the mineshaft lift, or making sweets. You will be engrossed and enthralled. This is one of Britain's best days out.

Durham

Durham is one of Britain's most beautiful and dramatic cities. Its heart and soul is the rocky promontory where the River Wear curls in a mighty 'U' around its base. Above its steep, wooded flanks stand both the Cathedral, and Durham Castle, dominating a tight cluster of steep narrow streets below that haven't changed much in centuries. The Cathedral is the best example of Norman architecture in England. It is indivisible from the Castle, begun by William the Conqueror in 1072, and later established as the fortified seat of the Prince Bishops who ruled the Palatinate of Durham – then a wild and turbulent place given equally to warfare and learning – from the 11th to the 19th century. The 13th-century Great Hall and everything else is now used by the oldest of Durham University's colleges, and you can only see it by taking a guided tour. Don't miss it – especially the 18-m (57-ft) high Black Staircase, one of the Castle's dramatic highlights.

The Cathedral and its side chapels embody centuries of architectural ingenuity and exquisite craftsmanship. The glories of the building include the hammerbeam oak roof of what was once the medieval monks' dormitory, the Chapter Library with its large collection of pre-Conquest manuscripts, St Cuthbert's Treasures, and the beautifully carved Neville Screen of Caen stone. But to appreciate the colossal symbolic power of the Cathedral/Castle, walk on the opposite bank of the River Wear round the bend between the Framwellgate and Elvet Bridges (or take a boat or cruise from Elvet Bridge). Looking up, as citizens, armies, pilgrims and kings have done for 1,000 years, you'll see how it sings praise to the god of believer and unbeliever alike; and backs that praise with a mailed fist challenging all comers. Durham may be bit of a history lesson, but it packs the most tremendous punch.

WHERE: Durham
BEST TIME TO GO: Any time of year (but the river walk is better in summer, with the eights rowing and the meadows in bloom).
DON'T MISS: The hunting scenes carved on the northwest column of the Norman Chapel in the Castle, built in 1080.
AMOUNT OF WALKING: Moderate
COST: Low – there's no fee other than for specific sights, but you may be asked for, or want to make, a small donation.
YOU SHOULD KNOW: St Cuthbert, a monk from Lindisfarne (d 687), is one of England's most revered early saints. He is buried in Durham Cathedral, and his shrine was one of the most lavish and wealthy until its despoliation. When he was brought to Durham in 1104, his body was inspected and found to be in a state of perfect preservation. His shrine remains one of England's sacred sites.

Durham Cathedral

The Bowes Museum

TEESDALE AND HEXHAM

WHERE:
Durham and Northumberland
BEST TIME TO GO:
Any time of year – but while winter bleakness is starkly attractive, the unclassified roads may be closed by weather conditions.
DON'T MISS:
The Silver Swan at the Bowes Museum – a 230 year-old, life-size automaton of a swan made of pure silver, with an intricate mechanism that, when wound, simulates a swan twisting, bending, and catching a fish. Ring ahead if you can to check what time of day it will be activated: it's too fragile to be demonstrated more often.
AMOUNT OF WALKING:
Moderate
COST:
Low – reasonable
YOU SHOULD KNOW:
If the outstanding natural finery of Teesdale isn't enough, you'll find (at the Middleton Centre) that Teesdale and the River Tees cater for every kind of walking or outdoor sport (on or off the water) you can think of, with the added attraction of the world's longest pedestrian rope bridge over the Tees itself.

The castle at Barnard Castle is enough to distinguish the ancient market town, but it is home to one of northern England's greatest incongruities. The Bowes Museum, built in the 19th century, looks like a huge French chateau. It was the 'marriage project' of a wealthy Scottish aristocrat, John Bowes, and his French wife, Joséphine Benoîte, who from the beginning intended to fill it with works of art to benefit people of the region, who at that time had little access to such things. They were wildly successful, and apart from the house itself, which is full of beautiful rooms, it is bursting with a stunning collection of paintings by the likes of Goya, El Greco, Tiepolo, Boucher and Canaletto among hundreds more. The furniture, china, and most everything are a tribute to the couple's very good taste and magpie instincts – and the house is big enough to hold temporary exhibitions of international standard as well as its permanent collections. Set in lovely parkland, it's a wonderful playground, which will leave you smiling with pleasure.

Teesdale runs north and west from Barnard Castle, and promises some of England's distinctively northern rural beauty. Drive up past Middleton-in-Teesdale, pausing at the splendid Eggleston Hall Gardens – four acres of informally laid out garden packed with many rare herbaceous plants and shrubs. At Bowlees you'll find the Durham Wildlife Trust discovery centre, and it's only a 45-minute return walk to the High Force, England's highest single-drop waterfall; then from Langdon Beck, you can take the unclassified and thrillingly steep lane across Chapelfell Top, and drive down Weardale to the Dales Centre at Stanhope. The fells and moors of Teesdale and Weardale – as far as Blanchland and medieval Hexham, overlooking Tynedale – were shaped by glaciers. The alpine grasslands feel raw, wild and rare. Stop anywhere and breathe in their transcendent beauty.

The Bowes Museum

The North Yorkshire Moors Railway

The North Yorkshire Moors Railway is both a living museum of full-size steam railways and a social asset highly valued as one of the best ways of introducing visitors to the beauty of the moors. The 29-km (18-mi) line runs from the historic town of Pickering, via Levisham, Newton Dale and Goathland to Grosmont. It's the middle section of the former York to Whitby line, and trains from Pickering often continue from Grosmont to Whitby using Network Rail. Because the NYMR has built up a phenomenal collection of rolling stock, it attracts a far wider spectrum of fans than just rail enthusiasts. Its locos include design classics like the super-streamlined 'Flying Scotsman' class, and many other former mainline railway princes. Passengers can experience the comfort of the old 1st Class, including the luxury of Pullman dining cars and sleepers. With a bit of forward planning, you can choose the exact composition of the train (named locos and types of carriage are part of the scheduled timetable), or enjoy one of many themed trips throughout the year.

The NYMR system fittings are a triumph of rescued authenticity, but the moors themselves are stunning. With a Rover ticket, you can explore the wildlife and magnificent scenery in easy walking distance from Levisham or Newton Dale. Goathland Moor is one of Yorkshire's wildest and most rugged – and if Goathland Station seems familiar, it's because it is famous as both Aidensfield in TV's 'Heartbeat', and Hogsmeade in the Harry Potter films. It looks like 1922, but it's hardly been touched since it was built in 1865 to haul locally quarried lead and stone. Grosmont, the old northern terminus, is a rail or mining enthusiast's paradise of active maintenance sheds, warehouses, kilns and equipment. Regular trains provide a supremely stylish way to enjoy the character of each station, and its surrounding moorland delights.

WHERE:
North Yorkshire
BEST TIME TO GO:
Any time of year. The hiss of steam and mournful whistle in the sharp winter air can greatly enhance the snug comfort of the railway experience; and in summer, the moors are endlessly lovely.
DON'T MISS:
Mallyan Spout, a waterfall just a short walk from Goathland Station, and one of the Yorkshire Moors' most attractive beauty spots.
AMOUNT OF WALKING:
Moderate
COST:
Reasonably expensive – but the transport is sensational and the scenery better.
YOU SHOULD KNOW:
If you want to stay in the North Yorkshire Moors for a few days, you can rent a NYMR 'Camping Coach' at Goathland or Levisham in the National Park. They are luxurious apartments fitted into old railway carriages. Pullman carriages of different eras are also used for special dining excursions like the 'Moorlander', which specializes in a traditional Yorkshire Sunday Lunch (whatever day of the week it runs).

Steaming up to Grosmont.

Whitby

ROBIN HOOD'S BAY

You approach Whitby via some of North Yorkshire's most exhilarating countryside and coastline. The first thing you see are the ruins of Whitby Abbey, in silhouette on the edge of precipitous cliffs. Founded in 657 by St Hilda, the home of the poet Caedmon, and for 1,000 years one of England's most illustrious centres of learning, the Abbey also features in Bram Stoker's *Dracula*; but Stoker's actual inspiration came from the churchyard of St Mary's Parish Church, 199 steep steps above Whitby's harbour.

Whitby straddles the River Esk, its steep maze of cobbled streets a testament to its ancient seafaring traditions. It's where Captain Cook learned his trade, and his 17th-century former house is one of the most fascinating small museums in the country. Just across the bridge, the Lifeboat Museum tells of more recent heroic deeds performed on this very coast; and the Whitby Museum is an engrossing magpie's miscellany, including a 'Hand of Glory' and the 'Tempest Prognosticator'.

The 13 km (8 mi) from Whitby south to Robin Hood's Bay is spectacular, and the spikes of black rock exposed by the tide below the cliffs at Saltwick Nab help to explain the drama of this coastline's history and age-old legend. The village of Robin Hood's Bay does so even better. Don't try and drive down the vertical, twisting lane running down to the harbour. Park at the top of the cliff, and explore the tiny alleys worming their way between the stone cottages crammed into the small ravine where a stream gushes out into the harbour. The village and its setting are beyond fabulous: so old and intriguing that children vow to grow up to be smugglers, and you can't blame them. At low tide, they also love exploring the rock pools, and looking for fossils along the storm-scoured cliffs.

The ruins of Whitby Abbey

Rievaulx Abbey

North Yorkshire Moors

THIRSK, RIEVAULX, HELMSLEY

WHERE:
North Yorkshire
BEST TIME TO GO:
March to October, to see it at its best
– but its winter severity also attracts
a large following.
DON'T MISS:
The 'Meandering Monks' trail at
Rievaulx Abbey – one of several
brilliant children's activities there;
and there are many more at
Duncombe Park and Helmsley Castle.
AMOUNT OF WALKING:
Little – it's more about stepping out
of the car and having a good look.
COST:
None, to enjoy the spectacular
beauty of the moors; but expensive if
you want to visit all the special
places.
YOU SHOULD KNOW:
The Ryedale Folk Museum is spread
over 1.2 hectares (3 acres), and
includes local history displays from
an Iron Age fort to a Victorian
classroom and a whole
reconstructed village to tell the story
of 19th-century moorland mining. It's
outrageous fun, especially for
children – and so is the famous
homemade ice-cream shop in
Hutton-le-Hole.

The market and racing town of Thirsk is famous as the hub of
'Herriot Country', and it's easy to see why a vet should flourish in
such delightful farmland and countryside. But Thirsk also offers one
of the most dramatic entrances to the North Yorkshire Moors
National Park.

To the east the Hambleton Hills rear up in a sheer ridge called
Sutton Bank. The moors begin at its crest, from which you can see
the White Horse of Kilburn to the south. Kilburn is the home of
Robert Thompson, the 'Mouseman', whose Arts and Crafts tradition
of oak furniture – each piece embossed with a carved mouse – is
still continued. Next to it, Coxwold is an ancient village famous for
its strange, octagonal church tower, and for Shandy Hall, the home
of Laurence Sterne, author of *Tristram Shandy*. Turn north, past
Byland Abbey, a beautiful ruin, and Ampleforth Abbey, a very much
current and prosperous Benedictine monastery and school. Behind
Ampleforth you reach the moors proper, with the wooded rills of
Rydedale cut into them.

Rievaulx Abbey, founded by Cistercians in 1132, is one of
Britain's most impressive and picturesque ruins. The tiny River Rye
leads to the Baroque grandeur of Duncombe Park, to Rievaulx
Terrace, one of Yorkshire's best 18th-century landscape gardens,
and to Helmsley, the delightful market town with a 13th-century
castle and a terrific buzz of activity. Helmsley is one terminal of the
Cleveland Way, the great North Yorkshire circular trail. It's also the
last small town for miles and miles of remote moorland of
surpassing beauty. Stick to the smallest lanes to enjoy the best of
the vast skyscapes and panoramas. Past hamlets and sturdy farms
tucked in the folds of the land, you'll reach Hutton-le-Hole and the
Ryedale Folk Museum, a truly rewarding destination for tea.

Bolton Abbey

GRASSINGTON, KETTLEWELL AND AYSGARTH

In the heart of the Yorkshire Dales, where the National Park announces itself by opening a panorama of ancient woods, clear rivers, and a distant patchwork of green pasture and gold-brown bracken cresting the hills, Bolton Abbey sits in vivid serenity on the banks of the River Wharfe. Outside the quaint village, the ruins of 12th-century Bolton Priory stand shrouded in dignified splendour, in parkland by the river's edge. It's a classic landscape. The primeval oak and broadleaf Strid Wood (bluebell heaven in season) leads to the Strid itself, where the river is channelled into a boiling torrent. Follow Wharfedale upstream via the 'Valley of Desolation' – a lovely, wooded ravine that brings you via Posforth Gill falls to Simon's Seat, a rocky promontory overlooking Appletreewick. One vista succeeds another. In the cobbled square of old Grassington, get local directions for Linton, one of the Dales' most intriguing and beautiful villages. The beck flowing through its middle has stepping stones, a clapper bridge and a packhorse bridge, each of which, like the village green, the early 18th-century almshouses, the mill buildings, and the completely outstanding 12th- and 15th-century church, speaks of its amazing history.

Upper Wharfedale brings you closer to the equally lovely purple heather and bracken of Hebden and Conistone Moors. For over 1,000 years, Kettlewell has thrived here, below 704-m (2,310-ft) high Great Whernside. It's a thoroughly traditional Dales village, a welcoming centre for walkers, cavers and potholers – but most famous for its eccentric, summer Scarecrow Festival. From Kettlewell you can see the harsher beauty of high moorland at its best by following Bishopdale Beck north to Wensleydale. The road drops steeply into the wooded gorge where the triple falls of Aysgarth make their spectacular descent in cascades covering 1.5 km (1 mi) of the River Ure. You share it only with birds, squirrels, deer and wild flowers.

WHERE:
North Yorkshire
BEST TIME TO GO:
April to October – though in fairness, the region's beauty doesn't diminish in winter. It only changes in character.
DON'T MISS:
Stopping for a while at the Wharfedale Folk Museum and/or the National Park Centre in Grassington; not least to prepare yourself with some information about Linton's extraordinary church and extremely rich history (its scenic attractions tell their own story).
AMOUNT OF WALKING:
Lots. (Or very little, but you'll certainly want to stop frequently to take in the staggering views.)
COST:
None
YOU SHOULD KNOW:
The pleasant woodland walk to the Strid at Bolton Abbey has been known to relax visitors to the foolhardy point at which they believe they can jump the 'stride-wide' chasm where the river thunders. Although at its narrowest, the Strid is 2 m (7 ft) wide, the rocks are very slippery and the water is vicious. There is no record of anybody surviving a fall here – the river sucks you into underwater caves and eroded channels hidden below the rocks.

Looking down on the village of Kettlewell and along Wharfedale.

Pickering and Castle Howard

WHERE:
North Yorkshire
BEST TIME TO GO:
Any time of year (the gardens at
Castle Howard are open all year, the
house is closed in November and
from late December till early March).
DON'T MISS:
The Grinling Gibbons frieze carved in
plain wood around the north door of
the Crimson Dining Room at Castle
Howard, and the dining table set
with a Crown Derby dessert service
of 1796 to 1801.
AMOUNT OF WALKING:
Lots (but note that a 'land train' will
transport visitors at Castle Howard
from the car park to the main house;
take it and save your feet for the
tour).
COST:
Moderate
YOU SHOULD KNOW:
Castle Howard is familiar to the
world as the setting for two
successful film productions (one a TV
series) of Evelyn Waugh's *Brideshead
Revisited*; and for the less well-
known independent film parody
Brideshead Revised.

Barely concealed by its predominant Victorian and later façades, the hallmarks of Pickering's medieval roots are a much better indication of the market town's historical importance. Just north of Pickering's Steam Railway Station, the Castle's unusually well preserved ruins are highly evocative. The classic motte and bailey design – built by William the Conqueror, and reinforced by successive medieval kings as a hunting lodge – still retains its keep, towers and most of its walls. Like the castle, the medieval church dominates the town from a small hill right in the centre. When you see the size and intricacies of the 15th-century frescoes that fill its walls (rediscovered in the 1850s after being covered by a Puritan limewash 300 years earlier) you realize how colourful churches used to be, and the ingenious lessons in moral philosophy contained in their decoration. The wealthy patronage that benefited Pickering like this, and in other eras, is best explained at the Beck Isle Museum (just by the bridge over Pickering Beck). Particularly good fun for children, the Museum houses detailed reconstructions of local trades, crafts and occupations down the centuries.

Just 18 km (11 mi) south, Castle Howard sits high in the Howardian Hills, manifesting power of a later era, and visible for miles in every direction. The biggest house in Yorkshire, designed by Vanbrugh in 1699 (before his second commission, Blenheim Palace), with Nicholas Hawksmoor as his Clerk of Works, Castle Howard is sensational. It reeks grandeur from the 22-m (70-ft) high Dome over the marble Great Hall to the superb drawing rooms, salons and galleries filled with Chippendale, Sheraton, Holbein, Gainsborough, Rubens, Van Dyck, Meissen porcelain and the inheritance of generations of magpie participants on the Grand Tour. You literally gasp at the details of Palladian harmony, and the whimsy of wealthy indulgence: get your breath back in 405 hectares (1,000 acres) of equally magnificent parkland and formal gardens.

The magnificent Castle Howard

York Day 1

YORK MINSTER AND THE CASTLE MUSEUM

Even within its ancient walls, built and rebuilt by Romans, Saxons, Vikings, Normans, Tudors, Georgians and Victorians – all of whom contributed some of their finest works to its historic fabric – York is a bustling, modern, university city. It only looks like a time machine. Though there are distinctive streets and buildings from every era, at its heart York is medieval, and York Minster is its triumph. The Normans built on earlier ruins: the Emperor Constantine worshipped here during Roman occupation. What you see represents the accretions of 250 years from 1220 – an architectural masterpiece illuminated by glorious stained glass, alive with centuries of daily worship, and redolent of its participatory history in religious and political strife. Outside, that history is manifest in The Shambles, Europe's best-preserved medieval street; in Clifford's Tower and 12th-century Micklegate Bar, the traditional royal entrance to the city, and the place where traitors' and rebels' heads were displayed on poles. If you choose to be guided, history can also be seen in a hundred vaults and undercrofts where the evidence of centuries collides.

The York Castle Museum makes the process of time-travel even easier. You'll find it in a group of 18th century former prison buildings. Besides the Jane Austen costume collection, giant dolls' houses, and riveting memorabilia of social history, the museum consists of two major reconstructions. 'Kirkgate' is a Victorian Street in every particular. You can go into the shops, visit folk in their home, and complain at the police station. 'Half Moon Court' shows street life in Edwardian York. It's built in what was the Debtors' Prison; but you can also see the original prison cells, including the cell where the Highwayman Dick Turpin spent his last night before 'dancing' on the gallows. York enjoys showing visitors its turbulent historical underbelly as much as its symbols of royal and national importance.

Tourists take a ride to York Minster.

WHERE:
Yorkshire
BEST TIME TO GO:
Any time of year
DON'T MISS:
The Great East Window at York Minster. Created between 1405-8, and covering 194 sq m (636 sq ft), this masterpiece illustrates the books of Genesis and Revelation. It is the biggest surviving medieval glasswork in the world – and certainly one of the most beautiful.
AMOUNT OF WALKING:
Lots, in short bursts.
COST:
Low to reasonable. Donations may be sought more often than fees are charged.
YOU SHOULD KNOW:
Check out the 'York Pass', which gives you access to a large number of the city's highlights for a single, reduced fee. There's a similar scheme for local buses to help you travel between them.

273

York Day 2

JORVIK VIKING CENTRE AND THE NATIONAL RAILWAY MUSEUM

More than an interpretation or even reconstruction, Jorvik Viking Centre is an archaeological super-dig that tells the tumultuous story of York when it was a Viking city. The Centre is built on the very streets that stood here circa 950. Now a long way below present ground level, they have been reconstructed as they were 'unearthed' by archaeologists. Visitors ride a 'time car' to the year 1067 when Normans sacked the Viking city at one of its cyclical heights of its prosperity. The shops, houses and workshops are filled with detailed tableaux, or actors in the roles of carpenter, coinmaker and even a Saxon nun at her loom. The realism is breathtaking – and scientific. From bones recovered on-site, you learn how York's residents 1,000 years ago cooked, ate, made love and war, recovered from footballing injuries (really!) and entertained themselves. Everything is based on actual, impeccable fieldwork, and the Finds Hut is crammed with over 800 artefacts recovered from the Coppergate excavations.

Across the Ouse down Micklegate, you can walk the city walls to the station, next to which is the National Railway Museum, a child's paradise of very grown-up toys. It's Britain's premier railway collection, of paraphernalia and memorabilia as well as some forty of the oldest, fastest, prettiest, sturdiest and most innovative locos ever built. Three huge halls hold legends like the 1829 Agenoria, the Flying Scotsman, Mallard (the world's fastest steam locomotive) and the sleek Japanese Bullet Train. There are several 'Royal' coaches among the rolling stock. Queen Victoria's Royal Saloon is a lesson in luxury, a travelling palace crammed with silks, brocades and exotic polished woods. And even if you don't coincide with one of the many special events held throughout the year, the Museum's interactive displays open up a hands-on experience of railway history, innovation and dramatic technology.

WHERE:
Yorkshire
BEST TIME TO GO:
Any time of year
DON'T MISS:
Mallard – to wonder at the most beautiful livery, sleekest streamlining, and most romantic evocation of a bygone era, of any locomotive in the world.
AMOUNT OF WALKING:
Little to moderate. Access is excellent at the Railway Museum, but restricted at Jorvik because of the nature of the displays (though staff are generous in their willingness to give assistance).
COST:
Reasonable; and at the National Railway Museum, except for some special events like 'Thomas the Tank Engine' days, free.
YOU SHOULD KNOW:
1. Jorvik's sister attraction is DIG, which offers adults and children the chance to learn and practise real archaeology in fascinating historical contexts. 2. Railway enthusiasts of every age will be besotted by the York Model Railway, sited the other side of the station from the museum. Four main oval systems have 20 trains running on 323 m (1,060 ft) of 00 gauge track – with lots of interactive buttons!

Steam locomotives at the National Railway Museum

York Day 3

YORK MAZE AND YORKSHIRE AIR MUSEUM

Each May, on the Hull road just outside York, a 12-hectare (30-acre) field is laid out with 1.5 million maize plants. In June, the growing field is cut with a complex series of pathways to a design that changes completely each year. Maize grows quickly – as much as 3 m (10 ft) in 10 weeks – so by July, it can hide a tall man. The York Maze exists only from July to September, when it is harvested normally. Until then, it's the world's biggest maze, and it's studded with clues to help visitors find their way through it, and to lead them to secret bowers, picnic areas and other surprises en route. One year, the clues took the form of giant talking wood sculptures carved with a chainsaw; but the maze designs themselves have included a Viking longship, a spider's web, Big Ben, the Statue of Liberty, Star Trek and the Flying Scotsman locomotive – all on a colossal scale. Conceived with wit, a sense of mischief, great skill and outstanding showmanship, the York Maze guarantees you have enormous fun for the 1.5 hours it usually takes to get round it.

A little further towards Hull is Elvington, a former World War II RAF Bomber Command base, now fully restored as a historic monument, and home of the Yorkshire Air Museum. It's got the lot – the original Control Tower, Ops Rooms and other buildings; the Air Gunners' Collection of turrets and weaponry; comprehensive uniform, badge and medal displays; historic military vehicles; the Barnes Wallis Collection including the revolutionary geodetic Wellington Bomber and one of his 'bouncing bombs' used in 617 Squadron's Dam Busters raid; and over forty beautiful, innovative, fantastic, and mostly battle-hardened aircraft from 1850 to the present. Though the aircraft collection is of international importance, the museum makes you feel an intimate part of the 'home squadron' – a welcome matched by the authenticity and accessibility of the exhibits.

The Starship Enterprise maize maze

WHERE:
Yorkshire
BEST TIME TO GO:
Any time of year for the Yorkshire Air Museum; necessarily, mid- to late-summer (dates vary slightly) for the Yorkshire Maze.
DON'T MISS:
Sir George Cayley's Glider, at the Yorkshire Air Museum. In 1849, the Cayley glider pioneered the first manned flight at Brompton Dale, near Scarborough, 54 years before the Wright Brothers' first powered flight took place with a pilot on board.
AMOUNT OF WALKING:
Lots – but the Maze pathways have been designed with wheelchairs in mind, and the Air Museum is readily accessible.
COST:
Reasonable
YOU SHOULD KNOW:
The Yorkshire Air Museum holds displays and special events regularly throughout the year.

The Yorkshire Dales

RICHMOND AND SWALEDALE TO HAWES

WHERE:
North Yorkshire
BEST TIME TO GO:
Any time of year, in sun, mist, rain or snow.
DON'T MISS:
1. The view from Great Shunner Fell, of Westmorland and Cumberland on one side, and the whole Swaledale valley on the other – 'a vast hill country, a wilderness of blue ridges and shadowy summits'.
2. Hardrow Force waterfall, on the Wensleydale side of Buttertubs Pass above Hawes.
AMOUNT OF WALKING:
Little to moderate
COST:
None
YOU SHOULD KNOW:
The Congregational Chapel at Low Row was for a long time the only Non-Conformist chapel in Swaledale, because it was licensed under the Five Mile Act, and Grinton and Muker were five miles to east and west, and both had churches. It was built in 1690 by the same Lord Wharton whose legacy was a trust fund for the annual purchase of 1050 Bibles, still known as Wharton Bibles.

Swaledale

If you follow the River Swale from the walls of Richmond Castle to Thwaite, you will see the very best of the northern Yorkshire Dales. Eleventh-century Richmond Castle provides a perfect metaphor for the region: like the Romans 1,000 years earlier, the Normans felt the necessity to fortify themselves against both the singularly bloody-minded local inhabitants, and the rigours of the uncompromisingly bleak uplands. The wooded hollows of Swaledale shelter a series of typical Dales stone-built villages, ancient and hard-edged communities huddled against the rugged beauty of the moors and fells rising on either side.

The Swale is one of England's fastest-flowing rivers, fed by dozens of becks, flashing silver in the patchwork of green and grey hillsides. Once they powered mines, and you can see traces of workings from Healaugh and Feetham to Gunnerside and Muker. Men shaped this landscape: Angles, Saxons and Vikings left their names in local dialect, and their culture in local history and folklore. Their stories – of Viking rapine, Jacobite escape and Non-Conformist hideout are in the remotest hamlets – like the Fairy Hole cavern at Crackpot, across the Swale from Low Row up Crackpot Gill, banked with ferns and wild flowers. A similar cave at Swinnergill was used for worship in times of religious persecution; part of Swaledale's romantic aura rests in its history of matching human indomitability to the land.

At Muker Swaledale heads north. Turn south instead at Thwaite. The rough, very steep and seldom-used road to Hawes runs between Lovely Seat (675 m/2,213 ft) and Shunner Fell (717 m/2,351 ft). At this watershed between Swaledale and Wharfedale you'll find the Buttertubs, a series of deep pits around columns of splintered limestone, carved by trickling water over millennia. The view is immense, of beauty in bleakness, and you descend to the cheerful market town bustle of Hawes with gratitude.

Keighley and Worth Valley Railway

THROUGH BRONTE COUNTRY

It's only 8 km (5 mi) long, but there's so much to do on the Keighley and Worth Valley Railway that you need a one-day 'Rover' ticket to really enjoy it.

The Brontë Parsonage Museum

It's a well-established heritage line running south from Keighley to Oxenhope, and very much part of the industrial history of the area. Each of its six stations has a distinct claim to fame, and the Railway has dressed each of them in the detailed livery of different eras. Keighley (platforms 3 and 4 are designated KWVR) recalls the 1950s. At Ingrow West you can try the comforts of Victorian and Edwardian plush at the Vintage Carriages Trust Museum. Damems, the smallest complete station in Britain (with waiting room, booking office, signal box and level crossing), is still lit by gas and heated by coal: it was the BBC's Ormston in 'Born and Bred'. The milk churns and old posters at Oakworth date it as 1910 – and bring a smile of recognition as the set for the film The Railway Children. You'll recognize lots of locations from the film along the line and in Oakworth village. And at Oxenhope, the terminus is a chance to be amazed at the collection of locos in the Exhibition Shed. Beautifully restored and maintained, they represent every period and function of steam railway power.

Between Oakworth and Oxenhope is the line's biggest attraction, the literary Mecca of Haworth. The station is dressed for the 1950s; the cobbled streets of Haworth village, though bustling with shops and activity, are understandably influenced by the Brontë Parsonage at its heart. It's about 1.4 km (1 mi) from the station, one of several delightful walks in the area relating to the Brontë family. Between trains, you can walk up to Top Withins, a farmhouse ruin believed to have inspired *Wuthering Heights*.

WHERE:
West Yorkshire
BEST TIME TO GO:
Any time of year
DON'T MISS:
The Brontë Parsonage Museum. The house is preserved as it would have been in the 1850s, and there is a wealth of intimate Brontë memorabilia, including some of the miniature books the children wrote about their imagined world of Gondal.
AMOUNT OF WALKING:
Little to moderate
COST:
Expensive – but reasonable for the enormous variety of entertainment on, and accessible from, the Keighley and Worth Valley Railway.
YOU SHOULD KNOW:
Leaving Keighley by steam train is usually quite dramatic. The Worth Valley line runs up a famously difficult gradient. Once the steep banks of the valley were lined with wool mills; now they echo to the crashing grunts and clouds of hissing steam and smoke from the labouring engine. The experience does wonders for preparing you for the atmospheric period features along the line.

Fountains Abbey

STUDLEY ROYAL WATER GARDENS AND STUMP CROSS CAVERNS

Adults and children alike are spellbound by Fountains Abbey. Britain's largest monastic ruins are set in a charming wooded river valley defined by dramatic (and highly picturesque) cliffs on either side. A quirk of ecclesiastical history brought lay brothers to the small community of Cistercians who created the Abbey from 1132. Their worldly skills made it splendid, rich and self-sufficient, and it has never lost its aura of dignified grandeur. Children love it as an adventure playground with a constant programme of medieval re-enactments, theatre, trails and introductory craft workshops. Adults are stunned not just by the elegance of the greensward setting, but by the Elizabethan mansion next to the ruins, the 12th-century watermill (still working, and you can eat the bread made from its flour), the medieval deer park, and the glorious Studley Royal Water Gardens designed specifically to incorporate Fountains into its series of ingenious perspectives.

Since the 18th century, when Studley Royal and Fountains were merged into a single estate, the Gardens – a series of demi-lune water channels and circular ponds running through woods specially planted to create surprise views towards temples and other follies – have utilized the same River Skell that runs under the Abbey itself (providing medieval 'convenience' on a grand scale) to enhance the Skell Valley's natural beauty with artful 'wilderness formality'. If you join one of the free tours, your guide will make sure you get the most out of the jaw-dropping scenic surprises planned into Studley Royal's original conception.

Save some gasps for a short afternoon drive past Pateley Bridge to Stump Cross Caverns in Nidderdale. Opened in the 1860s, there are 7 km (4 mi) of passages and halls, full of stalactites and stalagmite formations at least 150,000 years old – and beautifully lit to show the rainbow sparkle of their component minerals.

WHERE:
North Yorkshire
BEST TIME TO GO:
Any time of year
DON'T MISS:
The view from 'Anne Boleyn's Seat' – a raised bank at the base of a 'U'-shaped water course, with Fountains Abbey majestic on its lawns, glimpsed through the noble trees flanking the water; and with a simultaneous view down the other branch of the 'U' of the landscaped magnificence of Studley Royal's gracious Georgian follies.
AMOUNT OF WALKING:
Lots – and even though wheelchair access isn't great, there's so much to see, and it's so beautiful, it is worth the effort.
COST:
Reasonable.
YOU SHOULD KNOW:
Fountains Abbey and Studley Royal Water Gardens are collectively a UNESCO World Heritage Site, nominated as much for aesthetic appeal as for historic importance.

Fountains Abbey

Saltaire

SHIPLEY GLEN TRAMWAY AND BINGLEY'S FIVE-RISE LOCKS

The UNESCO World Heritage Site of Saltaire is the pre-eminent example of Victorian philanthropic paternalism in Britain. Purpose built by Sir Titus Salt in 1853 to house the 3,000 workers in his wool mill, Saltaire is a perfect time-capsule of the industrial age. Sir Titus built the mill next to the Leeds-Liverpool Canal – a palace of industry surrounded by the houses, school, library, park and recreational facilities of the factory community. It was a visionary idea, and his employees loved him for it. Now the magnificent Salts Mill is full of shops and art galleries, including a large selection of paintings, opera sets, and other works by David Hockney who was born in Bradford; and the neat arrangement of the village is the model for 'garden city' projects all over the world. At Saltaire's heart, you'll notice all the streets are charmingly named after Sir Titus' children. From here, across the canal and the River Aire, it's a short walk to the Shipley Glen Tramway.

Shipley Glen is a thickly wooded, bluebell-carpeted gorge below the immense open vistas of Baildon Moor. The Tramway was built in 1895 to ferry factory workers up the steep glen to their favourite local beauty spot. The 20-inch gauge 'toastrack' cable-hauled trams climb a gradient of 1 in 7. It's not a long ride, but it's a sheer joy of elemental pleasure amid such natural beauty. Bracken Hall Countryside Centre is at the top.

A little way north, at Bingley, you can see the Leeds-Liverpool Canal's fascinating *pièce de resistance*. The 1774 Bingley Five-Rise is a masterpiece of 18th-century engineering: a unique 'staircase' of five locks, the steepest flight in the country, with the tallest lock gates to enable the 19 m (61 ft) descent. From its heights, there's an inspirational panorama of a rural landscape re-shaped by our most productive industrial heritage.

WHERE:
West Yorkshire
BEST TIME TO GO:
Any time of year (but bluebell-time if you can).
DON'T MISS:
The superb Grade-1 listed Saltaire United Reformed Church, built in 1889 by Sir Titus Salt for the benefit of his employees. He spared no expense on its unique Italianate religious architecture, and the church also has a first-class organ.
AMOUNT OF WALKING:
Lots, and all wheelchair-accessible, including the Tramway, though there are some fairly steep, short inclines.
COST:
Low – unless you get completely captivated by the 1930s style dodgems rink at the top station of the Tramway.
YOU SHOULD KNOW:
The Bingley Five-Rise is brilliant, but quite slow. All five locks must be 'set' before use in either direction: to ascend, the bottom lock must be empty, and the others full, because each of them empties/fills directly into the next. It can take up to 90 minutes to complete the flight.

The old factory at Saltaire

Mounted Cavalry at the Royal Armouries

Leeds
Day 1

ROYAL ARMOURIES AND THACKRAY MUSEUM

Most children will agree that instruments of war, invasive surgery and torture are a terrific recipe for a fun day out – and so they are, especially if they come with 1,000 ways to dress for combat, and direct encouragement to see what it's like to draw and fire a crossbow, or wield a sword and shield. Ever since the national collection of arms and armour was moved from the Tower of London to purpose-built halls by the River Aire in the centre of Leeds, its curators keep finding new ways not just to display them, but to present them in context and bring them alive. The museum has five principal galleries called War, Self-Defence, Oriental Armour, Hunting and Tournament. It has medieval jousting outside by the river. It has machine-gun demonstrations and a torture chamber. It summons up the pitiless horror of war, notes its glamour, and invites even younger visitors to think 'Yes, but…?'. That may be worthy, but it's also responsible, and should reassure parents that the museum glorifies valour, not war.

The Thackray Museum also feels (rightly) compelled to make social history integral to its displays. An exhibit called 'Pain, Pus and Blood' illustrates a real story of an amputation in 1824, and so is driven to explain why an eleven year-old girl was even working in a mill in those days; and compares the gruesome treatment she received to the advantages of modern keyhole surgery. Adults frequently blanch at the enthusiastic displays of injury, but children's eyes gleam with new possibilities. They can walk through giant intestines to find out why their tummies rumble, or try on an 'Empathy Belly' to see what it's like to be pregnant. Like the Royal Armouries, the Thackray is a new kind of Museum – exciting, colourful, highly interactive, and profoundly illuminating in ways that inspire you for a long time afterwards.

WHERE:
West Yorkshire
BEST TIME TO GO:
Any time of year
DON'T MISS:
The Thackray Museum's eye-opening revelations about Leeds' Victorian slums. A replica street of workshops and houses tells the stories of some of the poorest families, who shared their homes with pigs and chickens, constantly exposed to the threat of crippling or fatal diseases like diphtheria and tuberculosis.
AMOUNT OF WALKING:
Low
COST:
Reasonable – at the Royal Armouries, you pay only for certain special events or temporary exhibitions.
YOU SHOULD KNOW:
The Thackray Museum is housed in some splendour, in the Grade II listed old Workhouse buildings of Leeds' St James Hospital. Don't be fooled by the handsome entrance – it was reserved for visitors, while inmates used a side door.

Leeds Day 2

HAREWOOD HOUSE AND THE YORKSHIRE SCULPTURE PARK

Harewood is a mid-18th century masterpiece by three of the era's greatest: Robert Adam and John Carr of York, who created the house and many of its fittings, and Capability Brown, who landscaped the spectacular gardens at the same time. This harmonious homogeneity is one of Harewood's most attractive features, and includes works by Chippendale, Reynolds and many other contemporaries.

The Lascelles family, who built Harewood and still live there, are unusually frank about their history. Displays at the house show how it was built on the proceeds of the 17th-century sugar trade, involving slavery (not that it was then illegal); and there's a 'Maids and Mistresses Trail' which picks out the role of women in the house (like the notorious Lady Worsley). In the exotic State and Drawing Rooms, and below-stairs too, a series of intelligent, themed tours highlight the significant details of the house and its occupants down the ages; just as in the gardens, subtle prompts guide you to the enchanting lakeside walk, the Himalayan Garden with its Stupa next to the Cascade, and to the rather incongruous Bird Garden of some 120 non-native species including Chilean flamingoes and penguins. Harewood has real style, and it's a house you can get really attached to.

Across Leeds, take exit 38 towards Huddersfield from the M1. At West Bretton you'll find the Yorkshire Sculpture Park. Inspired by Henry Moore, who constantly mentioned the influence of the West Yorkshire landscape on his own development, the park lifts sculpture out of the sterile gallery atmosphere, and turns it into an encounter and surprise. In beautiful countryside, you 'discover' works by Moore, as well as sculptures by Elisabeth Frink, Eduardo Paolozzi, and Andy Goldsworthy. There's an Access Sculpture Trail of paths, sculpture and plantings designed 'to respond to the seasons'. Like the Park as a whole, it's a revelation.

WHERE:
West Yorkshire
BEST TIME TO GO:
Any time of year
DON'T MISS:
The Chinese hand-painted wallpaper in the East Bedroom at Harewood. In 1988, some 20 rolls of it were discovered in an outbuilding, and it is considered to be the finest of its kind in existence.
AMOUNT OF WALKING:
Lots, and access is good, even at the Yorkshire Sculpture Park.
COST:
Expensive
YOU SHOULD KNOW:
The 7th Earl and Countess of Harewood were, on the quiet, great patrons of modern art. During 40 years of collecting out of personal commitment, they created a brilliant collection of 20th-century paintings, drawings and sculpture.

Harewood House was built with the proceeds from the sugar trade.

Leeds Day 3

TEMPLE NEWSAM HOUSE AND HENRY MOORE INSTITUTE

WHERE:
West Yorkshire
BEST TIME TO GO:
Any time of year
DON'T MISS:
The 'scent of history' at Temple Newsam House. Since the restoration of the Tudor 'still room', where cooks made jam, cordials and perfumes, you can sample the authentic smells of bygone eras. There's evidence that the room's equipment was also used to make potions for illnesses like 'mad dog bite'.
AMOUNT OF WALKING:
Moderate
COST:
Low
YOU SHOULD KNOW:
Children really are welcome at Temple Newsam's home farm. You get a free bag of grassnuts to feed the rare pigs (Tamworth, Middle White, Saddleback and Large Black), and they are all approachable. So are horses, ducks and a host of others; and daily farm activities include bottle-feeding lambs and calves.

Sometimes compared to Hampton Court, Temple Newsam House is a palatial Tudor and Jacobean mansion set in 607 hectares (1,500 acres) of parkland, woods, farms and lakes. As the city of Leeds expanded around the estate, Temple Newsam passed straight to Leeds Council after 300 years in the same family. Keen to preserve the ambience of long continuity, the city has managed both to develop the estate as a civic amenity, and to transform the house into a living museum of the lives of its actual former residents. It's brilliant. You can visit forty spectacular staterooms, halls, libraries and bedrooms on three floors – lavishly furnished and crammed with outstanding pictures, furniture, porcelain, silver and decorative objects. Their history is that of (among others) Lord Darnley, husband of Mary, Queen of Scots, who was born here; and the Marchioness of Hertford, the Prince Regent's mistress circa 1800; and of course, the legion of staff whose quarters you can tour through the underground passages and enormous cellars of this fascinating, endlessly grand house.

Discovering how the upstairs-downstairs Temple Newsam communities lived gets even more interesting in the Park. The home farm includes one of Britain's best collections of rare breeds of sheep, pigs, cattle and poultry, and there are re-enactments of agricultural and dairy crafts and skills. Children are encouraged to get hands-on, and the undulating parkland by Capability Brown is an invitation to walking, cycling or just playing games.

Leeds' civic collections of art are particularly rich in sculpture, thanks to the Henry Moore Institute. Though it hosts its own, temporary exhibitions, the Institute curates the sculpture holdings of other civic galleries. Its own collection (including work by Henry Moore, Jacob Epstein, Barbara Hepworth and Auguste Rodin) is actually on display in the Leeds City Art Gallery next door. But go to the Henry Moore Institute if you want to see how exciting, dramatic and beautiful modern sculpture can be.

Henry Moore's 'Reclining Woman' outside the Leeds City Art Gallery

Harrogate

The sleek, well-bred elegance of Harrogate comes from its history as one of Europe's great spa towns. Its oldest medicinal spring, Tewit Well, was discovered in 1571, but it was the Georgians who popularized the town and built the Royal Pump Room in 1824 over the Old Sulphur Well. It's now a museum, and the best place to go to find out about Harrogate, as well as to taste the water. The town's fortunes have never really waned. The Georgian legacy of beautiful terraces and elegant classical porticos was enhanced by wealthy Victorians. Royalty came too – and though the present town is dominated by the big, ultra-modern International Centre (catering to the political and business conventions on which Harrogate depends), you still feel a much stronger influence of more gracious eras. In the centre of town, this feeling is strengthened by the Stray, an 81-hectare (200-acre) strip of open parkland running down the middle; and by the existence of a special treasure called Bettys Café Tea Rooms.

More than a landmark or institution, Bettys embodies the quintessential ethos of Yorkshire, and Harrogate in particular. Opened in 1919, Bettys glass-fronted Verandah Café overlooks the green slope of the Stray (opposite the Cenotaph), and you can ogle the astonishingly delicious things they bake there in the displays underneath the wrought-iron canopy. Inside, all is tranquil gentility; and the civilized aura increases downstairs where you can see the Art Nouveau décor commissioned from Alsace by Bettys founder in the 1930s.

A perfect day out in Harrogate means pampering yourself – and it's a balancing act between working up an appetite strolling round the Royal Hall and other public landmarks, indulging yourself at Betty's, and enjoying a Turkish Bath at the exotic Royal Baths, first opened in 1897.

Bettys Café Tea Rooms in Parliament Street – not to be missed!

WHERE:
North Yorkshire
BEST TIME TO GO:
Any time of year
DON'T MISS:
The pleasure of actually using the opulent Turkish Baths, the only remaining treatment of more than a dozen at the Royal Baths. The glazed brickworks and amazing painted ceilings are redolent of the late 19th century; and the plunge pool, three interconnecting heat rooms, and languid relaxation areas have all been fully restored.
AMOUNT OF WALKING:
Moderate
COST:
None to look; expensive, but worth it, if you treat yourself to a Turkish Bath or indulge a lot at Betty's.
YOU SHOULD KNOW:
About that 'Yorkshire ethos' of Betty's – continuing a long tradition of offering an unpretentious and genuine welcome, good service, and first-class things to eat, made on the premises from the best ingredients, with love. It sounds very old-fashioned, but it does your soul good.

SCOTLAND

Great Border Abbeys

If you're impressed by medieval religious architecture hurry to the Scottish Borders, where it's possible to visit four great abbeys in one day – an effort that will be rewarded on earth.

Melrose Abbey was founded in 1136 by Cistercians and built in the form of a St John's Cross. Enough remains to show what a spectacular place this once was – notably some splendid carvings of saints, dragons, gargoyles and plants. It is said that the heart of Robert the Bruce is interred in the Abbey's grounds. A surviving 16th-century building serves as a museum.

Close by is wonderfully secluded Dryburgh Abbey beside the River Tweed. This has fared less well than Melrose over the years, having faced constant financial difficulties and being abandoned by 1600. Though the Abbey Church has all but vanished, well-preserved domestic offices – especially the Chapter House – make it easy to imagine the everyday lives of the monks. The most famous burial is that of Sir Walter Scott.

Hurry on to Jedburgh, the truly splendid ruined Abbey above the Jed Water – complete with Visitor Centre that explains all. Founded as a priory, this soon became an Abbey populated by Black Canons (Augustinians). The magnificent buildings proved an irresistible goad to the English, and Jedburgh Abbey was frequently attacked, even serving as a fortification for the invading English and defending French in the 1540s.

Last but not least is Kelso, once the grandest of the Border Abbeys.

Jedburgh Abbey

Sadly, its proximity to England again led to trouble – and the Abbey's partial destruction in the 1540s. Though a segment was restored as a parish church, most of the ruins were cleared in 1805, leaving the sections of the West Tower and its transepts that remain today. Even so, these are impressive enough to hint at the magnificence of Kelso Abbey in its prime.

Kelso and Floors Castle

Floors Castle – a fairytale confection of turrets, pinnacles and cuplolas

After admiring the remains of once-mighty Kelso Abbey, the town itself deserves lengthy exploration. Kelso is the most attractive of the Border market towns, with impressive architecture and one of the best settings. It sits in a loop of the River Tweed, opposite its confluence with the River Teviot. In the centre of town lies the largest market square in Scotland, a vast expanse of cobbles surrounded by handsome Georgian buildings. Off the square are interesting streets full of appealing buildings and good shops.

The big attraction after exhausting the town's offerings is an extended visit to nearby Floors Castle, which may be reached along the pretty Cobby Riverside Walk from the town centre, passing the point where Tweed and Teviot merge. Floors is actually a rather splendid house rather than a castle, completed in 1726 by William Adam, architect father of the renowned Robert Adam.

This ultra-grand stately home remains the ancestral seat of the Dukes of Roxburgh and is the largest inhabited castle in Scotland. It began life as an older tower house extended by William Adam into a classic Georgian country mansion, but was then extensively remodelled by Edinburgh architect William Playfair in the 1840s. The result is today's fairytale confection of turrets, pinnacles and cupolas – an awesome place in scale and appearance.

Wander through fabulous staterooms filled with the finest tapestries, furnishings and European paintings to see how the Scottish nobility once lived. Floors Castle is set in extensive grounds that greatly enhance the visitor experience. Highlights include a woodland and river walk, the Star Plantation, Millennium Parterre and Walled Garden. The latter provides a stunning riot of summer colour, and Queen Victoria took tea there in 1867. There is also an adventure playground, picnic and play area, restaurant, café, gift shop and garden centre.

WHERE:
Scottish Borders (formerly Roxburghshire).
BEST TIME TO GO:
April to September
DON'T MISS:
The bridge at Kelso, which may seem familiar – it was designed by John Rennie, who was just getting his hand in for more famous later creations...the London's Waterloo, Southwark and London Bridges.
AMOUNT OF WALKING:
Moderate
COST:
Reasonable
YOU SHOULD KNOW:
Floors Castle featured in the 1984 movie *Greystoke: The Legend of Tarzan, Lord of the Apes* as the ancestral seat of the Earls of Greystoke.

Smailholm Tower near Kelso

From Coldstream to Melrose

WHERE:
Scottish Borders (formerly Berwickshire and Roxburghshire).
BEST TIME TO GO:
April to September
DON'T MISS:
At Smailholm Tower – the history of Smailholm and the stories of Sir Walter Scott, brought to life through an extensive array of model people crafted by local artists.
AMOUNT OF WALKING:
Lots
COST:
Reasonable
YOU SHOULD KNOW:
The Scotts of Harden obtained Smailholm Tower in the 17th century and carried out rebuilding work before abandoning the place in the 1700s and moving to adjacent Sandyknowe Farm – they were ancestors of Sir Walter Scott, who spent time there with his grandparents as a child.

Across the River Tweed from England lies Coldstream, from whence marched the eponymous regiment under General Monck that forced the restoration of King Charles II in 1660. Here too is The Hirsel, family seat of the Earls of Home. Visitors can enjoy Hirsel Country Park on the western outskirts of town, with lovely walks by river, lake and through woodland in Hirsel Estate grounds. There is an interesting Visitor Centre with a small museum of rural life.

Proceed to Kelso and take the A6089 Gordon road, turning left onto the B6397. Drive to the village of Smailholm and follow the signs for Smailholm Tower. This 15th-century peel tower stands in a dominant position upon a rocky outcrop atop Lady Hill. It was built for self-defence in the lawless Borders and was indeed attacked several times in the 1500s – also defended successfully against the English in 1640. As well as being a wonderfully romantic building in a superb setting, Smailholm operates as a museum and there are magnificent countryside views from lofty wall-walks. If you only manage to see one peel tower in the Borders, make sure it's this one.

From the Tower, turn right and right again onto the B6404. After a short distance you will find the Mertoun House Gardens – an extensive and long-established garden with wonderful herbaceous borders, fine mature trees, an arboretum, walled garden and ancient dovecote. It's a wonderful location for a relaxing stroll (but note that the house isn't open to the public).

After leaving Mertoun take the B6356 towards Earlston and find the impressive sandstone statue of Braveheart, William Wallace, after a short walk along a forest road. Finish the day at Priorwood Gardens in Melrose, a specialist centre for dried flower arranging run by the National Trust for Scotland.

Around Jedburgh

If you decide against the Border Abbeys tour, you should at least visit Jedburgh Abbey. There couldn't be a more atmospheric ruin and the Visitor Centre is fascinating. If you've already seen the Abbey, Jedburgh and the local area can still deliver a great day out.

This charming border town has been ravaged by Anglo-Scots conflicts down the centuries but always bounces back, remaining a welcoming place geared to the needs of the surrounding countryside and travellers on the Edinburgh road. Do seek out Jedburgh Castle Jail and Museum. It may look like a castle, but isn't – built on the site of a destroyed Royal Castle, this splendid building is in fact a Victorian jail. Now a local history interpretation centre, it makes for an interesting visit. The other 'must see' is the Mary, Queen of Scots House. She stayed at this enchanting tower near the Abbey in 1566 and exceptional displays within bring this tragic figure to life – nowhere is her story more thoroughly explored.

Moving on, take the northbound A68. Off the road near Ancrum you'll find the Harestanes Countryside Visitor Centre, offering events, exhibitions and a terrific children's play park. It's an ideal spot for a splendid walk – perhaps up to the soaring hilltop Waterloo Monument, built to commemorate Wellington's victory over Napoleon.

After the pastoral pleasures of Harestanes, try something completely different. Drive back down the A68 and turn left onto the A698. Past Eckford is the Teviot Smokery and Water Gardens. This not only offers a selection of fine smoked foods, but also a restaurant, gift shop, aquatic and garden centres. The beautiful and tranquil Water Gardens and Riverside Walk are a huge bonus, offering an oasis of peace and quiet in an area of outstanding natural beauty. End the day laden with smoked delicacies!

WHERE:
Scottish Borders (formerly Roxburghshire).
BEST TIME TO GO:
April to September
DON'T MISS:
A quick 'cuppa' at the café in the last shop in Scotland...and another in the first shop in Scotland – of course it's one and the same Jedburgh Emporium, depending on your direction of travel.
AMOUNT OF WALKING:
Lots
COST:
Reasonable
YOU SHOULD KNOW:
The local delicacy is the Jethart Snail, a mint-flavoured brown boiled sweet. Why 'snail'? It's said that the recipe was brought to Jedburgh by French prisoners in the Napoleonic Wars, so you may draw your own conclusions.

Jedburgh Castle is a jail and a museum.

Melrose and Abbotsford

WHERE:
Scottish Borders (formerly Roxburghshire).
BEST TIME TO GO:
April to September
DON'T MISS:
The gun, broadsword and dirk that belonged to the legendary (and actual!) folk hero Rob Roy MacGregor – they're in the armoury at Abbotsford.
AMOUNT OF WALKING:
Moderate
COST:
Reasonable
YOU SHOULD KNOW:
Of more than 1,500 visitors to Abbotsford in 1887, quite a few were from the USA – nothing new there, then!

The pretty town of Melrose on the River Tweed dates back to the time when the Iron Age Votadini tribe built a fort atop the adjacent Eildon Hills, with their three distinctive peaks. The Romans followed, with a large settlement – Trimontium (Place of the Three Hills) at Newstead just east of Melrose, and it's the Roman connection that launches the day.

You'll find that the Three Hills Roman Heritage Centre in the Market Square is packed with artefacts and information on the Roman garrison at the Trimontium Fort occupied during the 1st and 2nd centuries. On certain days it is possible to take a circular guided walk of Melrose and the Roman site, conducted by knowledgeable local volunteers.

Then it's time to head for the day's main attraction – as interested visitors have done for a century and a half (Queen Victoria beat you to it by over 140 years). Nearby Abbotsford was the home of Scottish icon Sir Walter Scott, who died there in 1832. The literary superstar of his day had rekindled national belief in a distinctive Scottish identity, and almost immediately his home became an object of interest to admirers.

Amazingly, he created the magnificent house that set the trend for Scottish Baronial architecture from a humble farmhouse. Touring the splendid public rooms is like taking a journey back in time, for they are almost exactly as Sir Walter left them. He might have been in his study yesterday (a modest description for a grand room), the library contains thousands of his books, the armoury his collection of Scottish weaponry. Other special rooms are the drawing room, dining room (where he died), entrance hall and chapel. Outside, it's possible to explore parts of the gardens with their lovely views. Believe it – Abbotsford is an un-missable experience!

The magnificent Abbotsford

Hawick

Worth a day of anyone's time? You bet! There's a load to see and do in Hawick, the largest town in the Scottish Borders. It is beautifully situated on the River Teviot where it is joined by Slitrig Water – both having played a significant part in the town's industrial development.

But first came Angles (in the 600s) and Normans (in the 1100s), the latter building a large motte (still there) upon which they perched a wooden castle (long gone). Hawick inevitably suffered in vicious border wars from the 14th to the 16th centuries, losing most of its able-bodied menfolk in the disastrous Battle of Flodden in 1513. But after the dust settled on conflict, Hawick set about generating prosperity through textile work – first by hand, then by water-driven machinery as the town's rivers were harnessed using a complex arrangement of sluices and culverts. By the late 1800s thousands of men, women and children were employed in Hawick's mills and the scale of the industry was vast.

This industrial background may sound ominous, but in fact Hawick is an attractive and interesting town with a splendid High Street, amazing Town Hall in soaring Scottish Baronial style and a selection of lanes and alleyways that cry out for exploration. One essential visit is to the Border Textiles Tower at the west end of the High Street, where the former peel tower (Drumlanrig's Tower) has recently been redeveloped to showcase the Borders' rich textile heritage and to display many fine contemporary designs. The Hawick Museum and Scott Gallery detail the town's fascinating history and host visiting exhibitions.

After exploring the town, relax by enjoying the tranquil riverside and tree-lined walks in Wilton Park, beside the Teviot. Here, too, you will find the spectacular Hawick Walled Gardens, responsible for the town's repeated victories in the Scotland in Bloom competition.

Hawick Town Hall

WHERE:
Scottish Borders (formerly Roxburghshire).
BEST TIME TO GO:
April to September
DON'T MISS:
Various factory shops offering great deals on textiles – including some of the very best names like Peter Scott (Buccleuch Street) and Hawick Cashmere (Trinity Mill, flagship store in Arthur Street).
AMOUNT OF WALKING:
Moderate
COST:
Low
YOU SHOULD KNOW:
After its fighting men were decimated at Flodden, Hawick's boys fought off English raiders the following year and captured their standard – a triumph remembered each year in early June by the 'Common Riding', in which hundreds of horse riders patrol the burgh's boundaries.

The ruins of Hermitage Castle

Hawick Moorland Drive

For a scenic tour of the southern uplands, start from Hawick and drive down the B6399. After passing Berry Fell Hill and forested Windburgh Hill, you reach Hermitage Castle.

This uncompromising fortress was built around 1390, replacing an earlier structure. It sits beside beautiful Hermitage Water, surrounded by moorland, and is one of the most sinister and atmospheric castles in Scotland – in 1320 an early owner was accused of witchcraft and boiled to death by oppressed tenants. The place eventually passed to the Douglas family who had it rebuilt by master mason John Lewin of Durham Cathedral. Hermitage Castle looks massively complete and it's easy to imagine how threatening it looked to those who sought to take it by force. In the 1800s it merely appeared romantic – Sir Walter Scott had himself painted before the place.

Continue down the Liddesdale valley, turning right at Newcastleton and proceeding across the moors to Langholm. Along the way, spot the modernistic memorial to poet Hugh MacDiarmid. Note also the hilltop obelisk of the Malcolm Monument, in memory of Sir John Malcolm who died in 1833.

Stop and explore Langholm. This pleasing town in its attractive setting is the first in Scotland on the road from Carlisle to Edinburgh, but for all the through traffic it seems rather remote. Langholm lies at the confluence of the River Esk and Ewes Water, and the remains of the castle around which it grew may be found in the angle formed by the two.

Take the B709 road out through New Langholm and follow it across the moors back towards Hawick. At remote Eskdalemuir, much to your surprise, you will find the Kagyu Samye Ling Monastery and Tibetan Centre, the largest Buddhist monastery in the Western World – visitors to the temple and grounds are welcome.

WHERE:
Scottish Borders (formerly Roxburghshire) and Dumfries and Galloway (formerly Dumfries).
BEST TIME TO GO:
April to September (to see the interior of Hermitage Castle).
DON'T MISS:
The ancient stone circle of Nine Stane Rig, just northeast of Hermitage Castle – standing in a forest clearing aligned with the major southern moonset, it has become sadly neglected despite its historical importance.
AMOUNT OF WALKING:
Moderate
COST:
Reasonable
YOU SHOULD KNOW:
In 1566 Mary, Queen of Scots (still married to another) made a marathon journey on horseback to see her lover (the Earl of Bothwell) at Hermitage Castle after he was wounded in a skirmish with border reivers.

Innerleithen

Hard by Peebles is Innerleithen which – together with nearby Traquair – provides a surprisingly varied day out for such a small place. It stands at the confluence of the Rivers Tweed and Leithen, surrounded by hills (many topped with Iron Age forts). There was once an extensive textile industry here but most mills have been demolished – though the first, built by pioneer Alexander Brodie in the 1780s, still stands in Damside.

One call that must be made in the sloping High Street is to Robert Smail's Printing Works, a preserved example of that now-vanished essential of commercial life – the local letterpress printer. Powered by an undershot waterwheel until 1930, this wonderful time capsule with its record of everything printed from 1866 until 1951 speaks volumes about Scottish provincial life.

See also St Ronan's Well Interpretive Centre – a spa built in 1828 where the (allegedly) health-giving waters were bathed in and imbibed. It now houses displays explaining the site's history and exploring links with Sir Walter Scott and local literary figure James Hogg. There's a sampling pavilion, so you can decide on the efficacy of the waters for yourself.

Move on to fabulous Traquair House, the country's oldest continually inhabited dwelling. Dating from around 1100 with various later additions, it has been essentially unchanged since 1695. In all that time it has naturally featured large in Scottish history – King William I signed a charter here that led to the founding of Glasgow, Kings Edward I and II of England stayed here, King James III owned it, Mary, Queen of Scots stayed...and so on. Much of the fabulous interior is on view, including an informative museum. Outside there's a brewery, restaurant, craft workshops and a wonderful maze that should absorb any time that remains (perhaps more!).

WHERE:
Scottish Borders (formerly Selkirkshire).
BEST TIME TO GO:
April to September
DON'T MISS:
The Runic Cross – found in the Leithen Valley, this carved Celtic stone of considerable antiquity may be seen in the courtyard of Innerleithen Parish Church.
AMOUNT OF WALKING:
Moderate
COST:
Reasonable
YOU SHOULD KNOW:
The St Ronan's Borders Games held annually at Innerleithen in early July are the oldest such event in the Scottish Borders, dating back to 1827.

Traquair House

The historic town of Peebles

Peebles

Should there ever be a contest for the most genteel burgh in Scotland, Peebles would hope to win by a refined street. This historic town stands at the confluence of the River Tweed and Eddleston Water. It has been a popular spot for a long time – there are Iron Age and Roman remains close by and (several times) the English thought it much too pleasant to leave undestroyed.

The heart of Peebles is its main shopping area, consisting of Eastgate and the High Street. Where they meet stands the Mercat Cross, dating back in part to the 1600s. The grand Old (actually, it's not that old – built in 1887) Parish Church stands at the end of the High Street, close to the splendid Tweed Bridge. The River Tweed with its grassy banks runs parallel to the High Street. There are other fine churches in town, notably Leckie Memorial Church and St Peter's Episcopal Church. The ancient tower of St Andrew's survives along with the ruined Cross Kirk (founded in 1261).

Visit the Tweeddale Museum and Gallery in its lovely courtyard setting, then take a walk in Hay Lodge Park for excellent views of Niedpath Castle, a splendidly uncompromising tower house just outside Peebles dating back to the 14th and 15th centuries. It's romantic, but sadly not open to the public.

Perhaps that's just as well, because it leaves time to drive out of Peebles to see the Dawyck Botanic Garden at Stobo, surely one of the best arboreta in Britain. It benefits from the cooler environment in the heart of the Borders, and specimen trees have been planted there for over 300 years. There are dazzling displays of colour throughout the season, from the Azalea Terrace in late spring to the Beech Walk's sensational autumn foliage.

WHERE:
Scottish Borders (formerly Peeblesshire).
BEST TIME TO GO:
February to November (for Dawyck Botanic Garden).
DON'T MISS:
The oldest street in Peebles – the unassuming but charming Biggiesknowe, once at the centre of the town's hand-weaving cottage industry.
AMOUNT OF WALKING:
Moderate
COST:
Reasonable
YOU SHOULD KNOW:
Author John Buchan, of *The Thirty-Nine Steps* fame, practised law in Peebles around 1900 – there is a commemorative plaque on his house opposite the old Sheriff Court.

Grey Mare's Tail Nature Reserve

This is a day for fit walkers only, for the magnificent upland Nature Reserve begins where the Grey Mare's Tail Waterfall cascades into the Moffat Valley, continuing up steep slopes to Loch Skene and its corries beyond. The high point is the summit of White Combe at 821 m (2,693 ft), by which time event the fittest tramper will be breathing heavily.

The Reserve contains the richest, most varied collection of alpine and mountain plants in Southern Scotland and has consequently been declared a Special Area of Conservation. To appreciate just how special, go to the Visitor Centre with its panoramic view of hillside features. For those who want to know more, there is a programme of guided walks throughout the summer, where participants will not only be shown rare flora but may also expect to see upland birds that include black grouse, peregrine falcons and ring ouzel.

Those who prefer driving to serious perambulating will find that it's still well worth spending a few not-too-strenuous hours in and around the Visitor Centre. But for non-hikers the day could begin with a wander around Moffat. Travelling from the English border, this is the first town in Scotland that you reach, and it gives a great impression – it's one of the most attractive towns in the country. Its strategic position on the route from England to Central Scotland ensured that the High Street has many fine coaching inns and hotels including Britain's narrowest hotel, the Star. The spectacular Moffat House, built for the Earl of Hopetoun by architect John Adam in 1767, is now also a hotel. Other notable buildings are the Town Hall (built as a spa in 1827) and the splendid St Andrew's Church that shows Victorian craftsmanship at its very best.

WHERE:
Dumfries and Galloway (formerly Dumfriesshire).
BEST TIME TO GO:
June to August (when the Visitor Centre is open).
DON'T MISS:
The internationally important geological and fossil site at Dob's Linn, site of pioneering work by Charles Lapworth in the 19th century.
AMOUNT OF WALKING:
Lots
COST:
Low
YOU SHOULD KNOW:
In the Visitor Centre at the Nature Reserve it is possible to see fascinating TV pictures produced by a live feed from a peregrine falcon's nest.

The Moffat Hills

Bowhill House near Selkirk

Bowhill House and Country Park

WHERE:
Scottish Borders (formerly Selkirkshire).
BEST TIME TO GO:
July (for Bowhill House) or April to August (Country Park only).
DON'T MISS:
The 20-minute film entitled *The Quest for Bowhill,* shown at regular intervals in the Bowhill Little Theatre.
AMOUNT OF WALKING:
Moderate to lots
COST:
Reasonable
YOU SHOULD KNOW:
The Duke of Buccleuch and Queensbury K.T. may not be at home when you visit – he also owns Drumlanrig Castle near Thornhill, Dalkeith Palace and Boughton House in England. Sadly, the Douglas family's various grand mansions in London are long gone.

Here's a day out to remember, in a very special place – and you won't be the first to be smitten.

'When summer smiled on sweet Bowhill,
And July's eve, with balmy breath,
...The aged Harper's soul awoke.'

was the way one admirer put it – Sir Walter Scott. In fact, the Duke of Buccleuch was busy rebuilding Bowhill House at about the same time that Sir Walter was constructing his beloved Abbotsford, though the Duke was rather more ambitious – well, much more ambitious, actually. However, at least they are both beside the River Tweed.

This most stately of homes is just west of Selkirk, and has a truly fabulous art collection, with works by the likes of Canaletto, Claude, Raeburn, Reynolds, Gainsborough, Ruysdael, Van Dyck and Wilkie. In addition, the State Rooms have wonderful displays of tapestries, outstanding French furniture, silver and continental porcelain. Successive Duchesses of Buccleuch served as Queen Victoria's Mistress of the Robes, and the grateful Monarch's letters and gifts are on display at Bowhill. By way of belated tribute to all those unsung heroes who kept the fires burning, the restored Victorian kitchen provides interesting insight into life below-stairs.

Outside may be found a James Hogg Exhibition, the Courtyard Tea Room, Little Theatre, Gift Shop and Visitor Centre. The latter gives estate information, and provides a perfect introduction to the Country Park that surrounds Bowhill House. There are miles of paths that meander through parkland, beautiful woods and beside rivers and lochs. The whole place is a haven for a variety wildlife and it's easy to spend hours wandering through this wonderful landscape – though for those who prefer to be shown the highlights, guided ranger walks can be booked. For full-of-beans youngsters there's an adventure playground.

Around Gordon

Mellerstain House, just south of Gordon, is extraordinary. This grand stately home was a long time in the making (1725 to 1778) and it's easy to understand why. Mellerstain must surely be one of Scotland's finest Georgian country houses, showing the classical work of the renowned Adam family of architects and designers at its very best.

Splendid Robert Adam interiors with intricate plasterwork and vibrant colours have survived, giving a wonderful impression of the house just as it would have appeared over two centuries ago. The picture is completed by fabulous paintings, exceptional furniture, embroidery and china collections. Outside, the Italian terraced garden offers stunning views to the distant Cheviots. The estate has lakeside and woodland walks, with a wide variety of wildlife to see and appreciate.

At the nearby village of Gordon find Greenknowe Tower beside the A6105 road – park carefully and take the path. This classic tower house was built in 1581, more as a residence than stronghold, and is a fine example of the classic L-plan tower that still retains its original *yett* (iron gate). It's a ruin, but a splendid one.

Return to Gordon and head to Lauder, and Thirlestane Castle. Built on the site of an earlier fortress for the influential Maitland family in 1590, with additions in the 1600s and 1800s, the house has sumptuous interiors. Self-guided tours not only include the fine rooms, but also the nursery wing and service areas. The Castle is set in extensive parkland overlooking the Lammermuir Hills and there is a peaceful picnic area and good woodland walk.

At the end of this particular day it's impossible not to reflect that – far from being the claymore-wielding warriors of legend – much of the Scottish nobility lived in the grandest of houses with the finest of contents.

WHERE:
Scottish Borders (formerly Berwickshire).
BEST TIME TO GO:
May to September (to see the houses).
DON'T MISS:
The fascinating and ever-changing Border Country Life Exhibitions at Thirlestane Castle – find these informative displays in the South Wing.
AMOUNT OF WALKING:
Moderate
COST:
Reasonable
YOU SHOULD KNOW:
There's supposed to be a secret corridor at Thirlestane, and those who walk down it never return. Is it true? Sadly, nobody could be found to answer that question...

Thirlestane Castle

Paxton House

WHERE:
Scottish Borders (formerly
Berwickshire).
BEST TIME TO GO:
April to September
DON'T MISS:
The Union Bridge (sometimes called
The Chain Bridge) just upstream from
Paxton – connecting Fishwick with
Horncliffe in England, it is the oldest
suspension bridge in the world that
still carries road traffic (opened in
1820).
AMOUNT OF WALKING:
Moderate (lots if you do Paxton's
grounds thoroughly).
COST:
Reasonable
YOU SHOULD KNOW:
Ellem Fishing Club (the world's
oldest, founded 1829) has a
permanent exhibition of historic
equipment and angling dress off the
courtyard at Paxton.

Situated on the (Scottish) bank of the River Tweed, Paxton House must be one of the finest 18th-century Palladian country houses in Britain. This splendid Adam building (design by James and possibly John Adam, interiors by Robert Adam) was completed in 1766, as part of an unsuccessful plan by one Patrick Home of Billie to woo a Prussian heiress.

Whatever the reason, the result is an unqualified architectural triumph. In the early 1800s a sympathetic new wing was added to contain a library and gallery for pictures brought back from an extended Grand Tour. The house has magnificent interiors with fine Chippendale and Trotter furniture, plus over seventy wonderful paintings from the National Galleries of Scotland hang in the picture gallery. The old kitchen has been restored and a charming child's nursery re-created.

But that's just the start of the day's entertainment. Outside the gardens, parkland, woodland and a long stretch of riverbank are just waiting to be discovered. The grounds are alive with birds (viewing hides provided) and red squirrels may be seen, along with Highland cattle. Beside the River Tweed is an interesting Net Fishing Museum. After exploring there's plenty more to do, with picnic areas, adventure playgrounds, croquet, putting greens, tearoom and the shop.

Should time remain after Paxton's delights, cross the border to Berwick-upon-Tweed. This interesting town ('too far north for England, too far south for Scotland') changed hands many times before the English prevailed. If it's any consolation to the Scots, Berwick was originally the county town of their very own Berwickshire and retains strong cultural links with Scotland...and of course Berwick Rangers FC plays in the Scottish Football League. Though a traditional market town at heart, it retains some impressive military features like defensive ramparts and accompanying barrack buildings.

Paxton House

Dumfries

There's more to Dumfries than Robert Burns. Like its football club Dumfries is known as 'Queen of the South', serving as the administrative centre of Dumfries and Galloway and capital of a large rural area.

Dumfries had historical low points – frequently sacked by the English, scene of witchcraft trials and burnings in the 1650s and Scotland's last public hanging in 1868. Oh, and Robert the Bruce was excommunicated in 1306 for killing his rival Red Comyn in Greyfriars Church (not the splendid Victorian one we see today, but a now-demolished church across the street).

However this charming old country town survived and prospered. Perhaps its most notable landmarks are the Midsteeple in the High Street, built as a jail in 1707, and one of Britain's oldest standing bridges – the Devorgilla Bridge, constructed in 1432. The town offers much more to see and do, too.

A review of the area's history may be found in Dumfries Museum. Its most unusual asset is a camera obscura, built into the top floor of an old windmill in 1836, offering panoramic views of Dumfries and the surrounding countryside. The Old Bridge House Museum built into Devorgilla Bridge is the oldest house in Dumfries and a museum of everyday life.

For culture-vultures, the Gracefields Arts Centre on Edinburgh Road presents contemporary arts and crafts, plus Scottish paintings. The Crichton Grounds on Bankend Road to the south of town consist of parkland, with the Rock Garden and neighbouring Arboretum being special points of interest.

Aviation buffs (and others!) will find the Dumfries and Galloway Aircraft Museum compelling. Based around the control tower of the former RAF Dumfries, the star exhibit is a Spitfire recovered from Loch Doon. There's also an extensive collection of artefacts, memorabilia, flying clothing and items retrieved from crash sites.

*The Camera Obscura
in Dumfries*

WHERE:
Dumfries and Galloway (formerly Dumfriesshire).
BEST TIME TO GO:
Any time
DON'T MISS:
The ruined Lincluden Collegiate Church just beyond the northern bypass, a church and living accommodation for canons founded by Archibald the Grim in 1389 – the splendid chapel was added by his son and contains the wonderful monumental tomb of his wife Margaret.
AMOUNT OF WALKING:
Moderate
COST:
Reasonable
YOU SHOULD KNOW:
Robert Burns is not the only Scottish literary celebrity to have lived in Dumfries – *Peter Pan* author J M Barrie was sent to Dumfries Academy at the age of 13.

Berwickshire Coast

St Abbs is an attractive fishing village.

Start the day in Eyemouth, a delightful little fishing port with narrow streets and vennels, the narrow cross passages between buildings beloved by smugglers. After a quick stroll, stock up with a picnic and head north for St Abbs and St Abb's.

What's the difference between St Abbs and St Abb's? St Abbs is another attractive fishing village and St Abb's Head is a rocky promontory that juts out into the North Sea. This National Nature Reserve is home to tens of thousands of assorted seabirds – herring gulls, fulmars, guillemots, kittiwakes, puffins, razorbills, shags – that nest on rugged cliffs. All that activity makes for dramatic viewing and the cliff-top walks are spectacular. There's plenty of other wildlife to be spotted by the eagle-eyed, and a visit to the Nature Centre will tell you what to look for. Or ranger-guided walks are available – along with a café, textiles shop and art gallery.

Return to the A1117 and turn right, soon reaching the minor road on the right that leads towards the ruins of Fast Castle – then walk across the moorland to Fast Castle Head for more splendid views. Not much remains of the castle, but it's possible to see the last remains and appreciate that it was a typical coastal fortress

built on an easily defended rocky spur jutting out into the sea.

Continue to Cockburnspath with its unusual round-towered church, and also find the atmospheric medieval Dunglass Collegiate Church within the parish. If there's any time (and/or energy) left, explore the small-but-perfectly-formed Pease Dean Nature Reserve above Pease Bay. The area nearest the sea is an open valley with grassland, gorse and alder. Further inland it becomes wooded.

Robert Burns Trail

Rabbie Burns, the Ploughman's Poet, Scotland's Favourite Son, the Bard of Ayrshire or simply The Bard – call him what you will, Robert Burns is a Scottish literary institution and national poet. Born in 1759, he died aged 37, but not before writing poems and songs that endeared him to a nation (and provided its unofficial anthem in Auld Lang Syne).

He was born near Ayr in a house that is now the Burns Cottage Museum. After indulging in his passion for wine, women and song (especially women – eight illegitimate children by five different women, plus nine more with his wife) – Burns took a post as an excise officer in Dumfries and it is here we pick up his trail.

His fine statue is overlooked by Greyfriars Church. Along the High Street is Rabbie's favorite haunt, the Globe Inn. The tavern is full of character – and Burns memorabilia. His chair remains by the fire and a window etched with his diamond ring survives. Next is the great man's town house in (you guessed it) Burns Street – it's now a comprehensive shrine to the poet. Proceed to St Michael's kirkyard where the Burns Mausoleum may be found – he lies there with wife Jean and five family members. Stroll on to the Robert Burns Centre in an old mill beside the River Nith for a fine display of Burns items and a meticulous model of Dumfries, as he would have known it.

North of Dumfries at Auldgirth is Ellisland Farm, where the poet lived with his wife from 1788 to 1791 and wrote some of his finest work. You can see Jean Armour's kitchen and the music room. There's a riverside walk, farming exhibits and a heritage trail. The Hermitage – a tiny stone building where Burns sometimes slept and wrote – is nearby.

The birthplace of Robert Burns, in Alloway, is now a museum.

WHERE: Dumfries and Galloway (formerly Dumfriesshire).
BEST TIME TO GO: April to September
DON'T MISS: The Theatre Royal in Dumfries – one of the oldest theatres in Britain, Burns was a regular patron and some of his work was performed there. It's still in use today.
AMOUNT OF WALKING: Moderate
COST: Low
YOU SHOULD KNOW: Rabbie's given name was Robert Burness – he was one of seven children of farmer William Burness and only changed his surname in 1786 when he was in his late 20s.

301

Drumlanrig Castle is set in glorious parkland.

Drumlanrig Castle

North of Dumfries near Thornhill is Drumlanrig Castle, set amid the Queensberry Estate. It's the home (well, one of the homes) of the Duke of Buccleuch and Queensberry, Britain's largest landowner.

Drumlanrig Castle – one of Scotland's first Renaissance buildings in the grand manner – was completed in 1691. Built of local pink sandstone, it is set on a hill (drum) at the end of a long (lang) ridge (rig) with fabulous views. Today's visitor can enjoy a tour of the grand interior that reveals treasures beyond price.

Principal rooms are the Front Hall (arches to the courtyard added at the suggestion of Sir Walter Scott), Morning Room (wonderful garden views), Staircase Hall (outstanding paintings), Dining Room (carvings by Grinling Gibbons), Bonnie Prince Charlie's Room (a bed to die for), the Ante-room (exceptional furnishings including clocks and a tapestry), the Drawing Room (royal and family portraits), the Boudoir (early French furniture) and finally the White Bedroom.

Outside, spend at least half a day exploring the Victorian glasshouse, rose garden, Long Terrace Walk, Great Avenue, the Shawl (colourful planting includes the family crest), Low Sand Garden, Low Garden (a wonderful view of the Castle), Arboretum, Wilderness (an old woodland garden), Rock Garden, historic Cascade, a wonderful rhododendron collection and more. You are spoilt for choice!

If there's time after all those delights, go north in search of Morton Castle. It's not quite in the same league as Drumlanrig, but well worth seeing. Start up the A752 from Carronbridge and take the first right turn. Follow the narrow road to the junction with a forest track, park and walk to the castle. It's a substantial ruin in a breathtaking setting on a bluff above Morton Loch, with far-reaching views.

Around Caerlaverock

The scenic coastal area south of Dumfries makes for a great day out. Start by finding one of the most attractive ruined castles you'll ever see (just off the B725, close to the point where the River Nith flows into the Solway Firth). Can there be anything more pleasing than Caerlaverock Castle in Britain? Perhaps, but it is certainly everything an old castle should be – broad moat, sturdy towers, huge gatehouse and the unique Nithsdale Lodging of 1634, in effect a newer house within the older castle. There's a very good visitor centre, reconstructions of the sort of medieval siege engines used to take Caerlaverock in 1300 and a castle-themed play park.

Close to Caerlaverock Castle you will find the Wildlife and Wetlands Trust Centre. This is a place where the modern world fades into insignificance, compared with coastal splendour and big skies, filled with the sights and sounds of wild nature from dawn to dusk. The most famous visitors are barnacle geese that return each October from the Arctic and stay until April – representing a conservation success story, with numbers recovering from around 500 to over 25,000. In spring and summer you can see the action in osprey and barn owl nests via CCTV, spot Britain's rarest amphibian (the Natterjack Toad), use Salcot Merse Observatory to look out over the Solway's vast salt marshes to the distant English Lake District and take a wildlife safari.

To round off the day, drive the short distance to Ruthwell, where the internationally significant Ruthwell Cross may be seen in the church. It was carved by Northumbrian craftsmen in the 8th century and is incredibly beautiful. In the village is a rather unusual attraction – the Savings Bank Museum, in the very building where the world's first savings bank operated.

WHERE:
Dumfries and Galloway (formerly Dumfriesshire).
BEST TIME TO GO:
All year round (winter's best for migrating wildfowl at the Wetland Centre).
DON'T MISS:
If you visit the Wetland Centre in the winter months you will not only see tens of thousands of migrating wildfowl, but also hundreds of wild Icelandic Whooper swans being fed each morning – watch from the Peter Scott Observatory.
AMOUNT OF WALKING:
Moderate
COST:
Reasonable
YOU SHOULD KNOW:
There's a bonus at Caerlaverock Castle for those who care to look – the remains of an older castle to be found at the end of a nature trail to the south of the present fortress.

Caerlaverock Castle with the Solway Firth and the Lake District in the distance

Stranraer Castle

Around Stranraer

The lively harbour town of Stranraer faces Loch Ryan, on the neck of land that makes the Rhins of Galloway a peninsula rather than an island. Stranraer's starting point may still be seen – built behind the broad beach at the head of Loch Ryan in 1511, the Castle of St John now stands in the town centre and is a museum that tells the Castle's tale – featuring medieval landowners, Government troops who were headquartered here during the 17th-century 'Killing Times' and those imprisoned over the centuries.

After Stranraer, head north up the Rhins of Galloway to Leswalt, where the Tor of Craigoch is topped by the Agnew Monument, built in 1850. Climb the stepped footpath to the Monument, if only for far-reaching views over Loch Ryan to Aisla Craig and Arran. Be aware that scattered stones amongst the gorse bushes are the remains of an Iron Age hill fort.

From Leswalt go on to Kirkcolm and see the fascinating 10th-century Viking carved stones in the church and churchyard that combine Christian and pagan mythology. Drive back down the scenic West Coast to Portpatrick, taking the minor road through Cairngarroch to Kirkmadrine Burial Chapel, which displays some of the oldest Christian monument stones in Scotland – find them in the glass-fronted porch.

Further south, close by the fishing village of Port Logan, is a special way to end the day, with two wonderful gardens to enjoy. Logan House Gardens are full of exotic tropical plants and shrubs, plus a variety of rhododendrons, all set around a fine Queen Anne House. Almost next-door is the renowned Logan Botanic Gardens, also home to many rare and exotic specimens. It has a walled garden, bog garden, woodland walks, discovery centre, café and botanical shop...not to mention sensational views.

WHERE:
Dumfries and Galloway (formerly Wigtownshire).
BEST TIME TO GO:
April to September
DON'T MISS:
Stranraer Museum in the Old Town Hall, with its displays of 19th-century Wigtownshire life and tributes to the town's polar explorers, Sir John Ross and his nephew James Clark Ross.
AMOUNT OF WALKING:
Moderate
COST:
Reasonable
YOU SHOULD KNOW:
Port Logan attracts visitors curious to see the fishing village that featured in the TV series 'Two Thousand Acres of Sky'.

Castle Douglas

Between Dumfries and Stranraer lies Castle Douglas – once called Carlingwark, it was renamed in 1792 after Sir William Douglas flattened the old village and built a new one to a neat street plan. This was not altogether altruistic – he hoped to establish a centre for spinning cotton, but the plan soon failed when water-powered industrial mills replaced his hand-workers.

But Castle Douglas thrived as the market town for a large rural hinterland and an important stopping point for traffic passing through Southwest Scotland. It's a pleasing place that sits beside Carlingwark Lock (which Sir William didn't bother to rename) – dotted with islands, it calls for a boat trip or a picnic in the park beside the water. From there, a scenic path along the south shore – known as Lovers Walk – will eventually take you on to Kelton Hill and Threave Garden.

The latter is a teaching centre of the National Trust for Scotland, with the Victorian mansion serving as the Trust's School of Practical Gardening. The public rooms have been restored to 1930s appearance, the Maxwelton collection of local bygones may be found in the servants' quarters and there is a Countryside Centre in the old stables. Outside there are walks through an important wetland that is home to breeding waders and wintering wildfowl.

Last but not least is Threave Castle – it's not easy to get there but worth the effort. This massive tower was built in the late 1300s by Archibald the Grim, Lord of Galloway. He chose a superb defensive site – an island in the River Dee. Park at Kelton Mains Farm and walk down through fields to the river, where a small jetty and brass bell await. Ring it vigorously and a boatman will come from the island and convey you to the castle. Romantic indeed!

WHERE:
Dumfries and Galloway (formerly Kirkcudbrightshire).
BEST TIME TO GO:
April to September (for Threave Castle).
DON'T MISS:
The Buchan – a group of old cottages by the Carlingwark Loch on the western approach to Castle Douglas, dating from the time when the loch was used as a source of marl (lime-rich mud once used as a soil conditioner).
AMOUNT OF WALKING:
Lots
COST:
Reasonable
YOU SHOULD KNOW:
Threave Castle was abandoned after a long siege in 1640, though it was used for a time to house French prisoners during the Napoleonic Wars.

The ruins of Threave Castle reflected in the River Dee.

Castle Kennedy Gardens

Castle Kennedy Gardens

Nobody should leave the Stranraer area without seeing the amazing Castle Kennedy Gardens, dramatically located just outside the town on an isthmus between ruined Castle Kennedy and Lochinch, its ambitious 19th-century replacement. Sea in three directions combined with the influence of the Gulf Stream creates a benign micro-climate that allows all sorts of unexpected plants to thrive, and these famous gardens were originally laid out by the second Earl of Stair in the 1700s. The present earl still resides here and continues the long-standing family interest in horticulture.

The landscape has been shaped by man between two natural lochs, and is internationally known for the great selection of rhododendrons, including many species brought back by Victorian plant hunter Sir Joseph Hooker after his first Himalayan expedition. These are complemented by azaleas, magnolias and embrothriums that provide a riot of colour in late May and early June. Castle Kennedy Gardens also contain a variety of tender trees, Victorian pinetum, monkey puzzle avenue, walled garden, huge circular lily pond and specialist plant shop. Spectacular!

If Castle Kennedy Gardens have been two centuries and more in the making, that makes Glenwhan Gardens down the road at Dunragit all the more praiseworthy. Only two decades ago there was nothing here but rough ground, gorse and bog – where today a beautiful garden centred on two lakes is full of tender plants from the Southern Hemisphere. There are great views across Luce Bay to the Mull of Galloway, too.

Round off the day with a quick visit to the ruins of Glenluce Abbey, just along the A75. This Cistercian abbey was founded in 1192 and there are substantial remains set in a tranquil valley, including a handsome chapter house dating from the early 1500s. A small museum displays objects found at the abbey.

WHERE:
Dumfries and Galloway (formerly Wigtownshire).
BEST TIME TO GO:
June (to see the gardens at their best).
DON'T MISS:
The perky red squirrels that may be seen in the Glenwhan Gardens.
AMOUNT OF WALKING:
Lots
COST:
Reasonable
YOU SHOULD KNOW:
When the Castle Kennedy Gardens were laid out by the second Earl of Stair, he was the Army's Commander-in-Chief and a lot of work was carried out by soldiers of the Royal Scots Greys and Inniskilling Fusiliers – as a valuable training exercise, no doubt.

Whithorn

The village of Whithorn seems attractive but unremarkable – yet first impressions can be deceptive, for this was the cradle of Scottish Christianity. Here the mysterious British holy man St Ninian arrived around 390 AD and established his mission, and here he lies buried.

Learn all about it at the Whithorn Story Visitor Centre, which provides an amazing encounter with history, going right back to the dawn of Scottish life. There is an Audiovisual Theatre, Discovery Centre, Museum and explanation of the Whithorn Dig, an investigation of the settlement's ancient origins. You will also see the ruined nave of 12th-century Whithorn Cathedral-Priory, plus a well-preserved crypt and the presumed site of St Ninian's Candida Casa (White House) – Scotland's first church and a renowned Christian foundation that became a place of pilgrimage.

At nearby Isle of Whithorn (no longer an island, just a pretty harbour village) is St Ninian's ruined chapel, built near the point where the Saint first landed for the many pilgrims who followed in his footsteps. If you return to Whithorn and turn left along the main road, you will soon see the signs for St Ninian's Cave – a small sea cave at the end of a delightful walk down the wooded Physgill Glen.

If further confirmation of the area's long history is needed, it may be found near Port William, just up the coast, where Drumtroddan Cup and Ring are three groups of carved bedrock dating from the Bronze Age in an important prehistoric landscape that also includes standing stones.

But if the family has had enough ancient history for one day, forget Drumtroddan and go straight from St Ninian's Cave to Monreith, where the Animal World Shore Centre and Museum presents all sorts of happy animals in large enclosures plus birds, reptiles and cuddly rodents.

WHERE:
Dumfries and Galloway (formerly Wigtownshire).
BEST TIME TO GO:
April to October
DON'T MISS:
The impressive display of early Christian cross slabs in the Whithorn Cathedral-Priory Visitor Centre.
AMOUNT OF WALKING:
Moderate
COST:
Low
YOU SHOULD KNOW:
The Drumtroddan standing stones appear to be aligned towards sunrise at the Summer Solstice and sunset at the Winter Solstice.

Whithorn Priory

Rhins of Galloway

WHERE:
Dumfries and Galloway (formerly Wigtownshire).
BEST TIME TO GO:
April to September (for the Mull of Galloway Lighthouse).
DON'T MISS:
The fabulous stretch of sand between Ardwell and Milton along the west and north Shores of Luce Bay.
AMOUNT OF WALKING:
Lots
COST:
Low
YOU SHOULD KNOW:
The view marker near the Mull of Galloway Lighthouse isn't fibbing – Skiddaw in the English Lake District really does lie due east.

Scotland's most southerly point

This hammerhead peninsula juts out from Scotland's West Coast, separated from the mainland by Loch Ryan to the north and Luce Bay to the south. Drive across from Stranraer and make a stop at Portpatrick on the west shore, facing the Irish Sea's North Channel. This little town is set around a small bay, with pretty pastel-coloured houses along the sea front. Take a short cliff walk to see dramatic Dunskey Castle, perched on a rocky outcrop above the sea.

Cross over to Sandhead on the opposite shore, using the B7042, and make leisurely progress down scenic Luce Bay to Drummore, the largest settlement in the narrow southern half of the Rhins. This pretty village huddles round its own bay and has a harbour that once served a local lime-making industry.

This part of the Rhins of Galloway has a remote but charming island feel. From Drummore take the dead-end road to the tiny settlement of Maryport with its broad beach, before returning and going on to find the Mull of Galloway Lighthouse and Visitor Centre at the most southerly point in Scotland. High on 75-m (250-ft) cliffs, this attractive white tower was constructed by Robert Stevenson in 1830 and still works for a living.

The Visitor Centre was once the accommodation used by workmen who built the lighthouse and it houses impressive audio-visual displays on the local scenery and wildlife. The surrounding area is an important bird reserve, and the warden from the Royal Society for the Protection of Birds is usually on hand to answer questions or lead an occasional tour. Even if he isn't, a long walk along the cliffs will not only produce sightings of numerous seabirds, but also sensational views across to the Isle of Man and Ireland in one direction and to England in the other.

Around Gretna Green

The destination of choice for many eloping couples since 1753!

You don't need to be eloping to appreciate Gretna Green nowadays, though once this village was a magnet for runaway lovers from England desperate to marry without parental consent. It all happened at The World Famous Old Blacksmith's Shop, where marriages were performed over the anvil from 1753. The shrewd owner opened it as one of Scotland's first visitor attractions in 1887 and now it draws huge numbers. But there are plenty of other attractions in Gretna Green and adjacent Greta reflecting the area's self-proclaimed status as Britain's marriage capital.

Move on to King Robert the Bruce's Cave, where the great warrior hid in the winter of 1307 after suffering defeat by Edward I. Here depressed Robert saw a persistent spider continuing until it had spun its web, despite frequent reverses, reputedly causing him to coin the phrase 'if at first you don't succeed, try, try and try again' before sallying forth to begin the campaign that ended with his rousing victory at Bannockburn. See the site of his inspiration at Kirkpatrick Fleming, north of Gretna.

Suitably inspired, hurry on – for there's more to see today. Who could resist The Devil's Porridge Exhibition at Eastriggs west of Gretna? Actually, Devil's Porridge was the term used to describe explosives manufactured at the world's greatest munitions plant, built near Gretna in 1915. The Exhibition tells the fascinating story of this vast secret city that employed and housed 30,000 workers, and covers Britain's worst rail disaster at Quintinshill.

After all that death and destruction there should just be time for some counter-balancing culture – a visit to the birthplace of the great Victorian essayist and historian Thomas Carlyle at the delightfully named Ecclefechan. The Arched House today is a small museum full of Carlyle memorabilia, first opened in 1883 and largely unchanged since then.

WHERE:
Dumfries and Galloway (formerly Dumfriesshire).
BEST TIME TO GO:
June to September (for Thomas Carlyle's birthplace).
DON'T MISS:
Thomas Carlyle's grave in the village cemetery at Ecclefechan – along with that of Archibald Arnott, Napoleon's doctor on St Helena.
AMOUNT OF WALKING:
Moderate
COST:
Reasonable
YOU SHOULD KNOW:
If you're thinking of tying the knot, over a thousand romantic weddings are still held in the original blacksmith's shop at Gretna Green each year.

Culzean Castle

Maybole and Culzean Castle

WHERE:
South Ayrshire
BEST TIME TO GO:
From 21 March to 31 October for the Castle and the Walled Garden, but the Country Park can be visited all year round.
DON'T MISS:
The magnificent Oval Staircase, a design masterpiece.
AMOUNT OF WALKING:
As much or little as you please.
COST:
Reasonable – but it's expensive to stay here.
YOU SHOULD KNOW:
William Burnes and Agnes Broun met and married in Maybole. Their famous son, Robert Burns, was born in nearby Alloway.

During the 12th century, Maybole, then known as Miniboll, was the capital of the kingdom of Carrick. Today, this small town is part of south Ayrshire, located some 8 km (5 mi) east of the Firth of Clyde and 14 km (9 mi) south of Ayr. Situated on a hillside, it provides the visitor with splendid views of the southern uplands.

Stretching from the Town Hall, built in 1887, and the impressive 16th century Maybole Castle, the main street has many interesting buildings. Standing on a corner, the castle – originally the town house of the Earls of Cassillis, the region's dominant family – is an unexpected sight.

Just 6 km (4 mi) to the west of town, on the cliffs, stands Culzean Castle and Country Park. Owned by the National Trust for Scotland, it is set in 243 hectares (600 acres) of terraced gardens, woodland and sandy beaches. Visitors can enjoy the swan pond, wildlife garden, walled garden, vineyard, deer park and the children's adventure playground, and free guided walks and other events take place regularly.

The castle itself is 18th century, designed by Robert Adam for the 10th Earl of Cassillis. The tour is fascinating – the armoury is the largest in the UK apart from that held at Windsor Castle – and rooms such as the State Apartments, the Blue Drawing Room and the Saloon are testament to Adam's talents. The castle's top floor, once an apartment used exclusively by General Eisenhower and his family, now serves as a small hotel available to both private and corporate clients.

Culzean Castle is a worthwhile experience for everyone. Multiple amenities make it easy to spend hours here, and you will love the superb views across the water to Arran and Ailsa Craig. Even on a misty day they add to the charm and romance of the place.

Mauchline

Situated in the east of Ayrshire, some 18 km (11 mi) northeast of Ayr, is Mauchline, a small town resting on a gentle slope that rises up from the River Ayr. First mentioned in 681 BC, it has a long history. Picts and Scots battled on Mauchline Moor; Cistercian monks built an abbey here in the 12th century, and in the 15th century Mauchline Castle was built, as a monastic residence.

The town also has a history of trade, beginning with the quarrying of sandstone from nearby quarries. At its height, sixty wagons of stone were leaving Mauchline every day, some even being shipped to America. At the same time, the town gained a reputation for clock-making, and the grave of one of the leading exponents, John 'Clockie' Brown, can be found in the kirkyard. Curling stones were also made here, and still are – although the industry has declined, the Mauchline factory is the only one in the world. Popular Maughlineware boxes, produced up until 1933, were made of local wood and decorated with local scenes. They were hugely successful souvenirs at a time when the railway had just opened up the country for tourism.

However, the town's main claim to fame is its Robert Burns connection. Burns lived at Mossgeil Farm from 1784 to 1788, during a period of great creativity, which saw the writing of famous works such as 'Holy Willie's Prayer' and 'The Holy Fair'. His great friend and mentor, Gavin Hamilton, lived in Mauchline Castle, and Burns is believed to have married Jean Armour in the castle dining room. Take a look at the bronze statue of Jean Armour, unveiled in 2002 at Mauchline Cross. Burns' former home is now a museum filled with fascinating original manuscripts, poems, letters and items that he used.

WHERE:
Ayrshire
BEST TIME TO GO:
Any time of year
DON'T MISS:
15th-century Sorn Castle, just 6 km (4 mi) from the town of Ayr. Essentially a family home, visits can be arranged by appointment.
AMOUNT OF WALKING:
Little
COST:
Low
YOU SHOULD KNOW:
Jean Armour had nine children with Robert Burns. The last was born on the day of his funeral.

The Burns Memorial

Girvan

Girvan is situated on the coast 34 km (21 mi) south of Ayr. This picturesque, unspoilt town is a popular spot, not only because of its proximity to many good walking trails, but also for its harbour, which is often busy with boats arriving and departing. While this part of the coast is rather dramatic, the beach at Girvan is child friendly – safe, sandy and long.

People have lived in this region for at least 5,000 years. In 1668, King Charles II granted Thomas Boyd a charter to build a seaport with a harbour and a fort. Architecturally, Girvan's streets boast many an imposing building, probably the best known being Stumpy Tower, built as the town jail in 1827. Fishing was always a major occupation here, right up until the middle of the 20th century, but today the harbour sees more pleasure boats than working vessels.

Nearby Kennedy's Pass is a geological site of some importance. Here you can explore extraordinary rock formations that are over 450 million years old. Access to the beach is, of course, on foot, but there are various convenient lay-bys in which to park. And, from all along this coast, wonderful views of Arran can be enjoyed.

At Bennane Head, 17 km (11 mi) south of Girvan, the land thrusts into the Firth of Clyde, forming the north of Ballantrae Bay. The soaring cliff faces contain many caves, which attract experienced climbers. From a lay-by on the A77, a steep and tricky footpath drops to the infamous Sawney Bean's cave. Legend has it that during the 15th century, Sawney Bean and his wife, together with their children and grandchildren, murdered and ate more than a thousand people!

Ballantrae Bay, Strathclyde

Loch Lomond

PADDLE STEAMERS AND BIRDS OF PREY

Maid of the Loch *moored on the shore of Loch Lomond with snow capped Ben Lomond in the background.*

For centuries, Loch Lomond has been a metaphor for the romance of Scotland. Geographically, it traces the transition from the gentle southern glens of limpid lochs and forested hills to the wilder, rugged beauty of the Highlands. It's easy to reach – a 40-minute train ride from Glasgow, or by car or bus; and Balloch, on its southwestern shore, is the gateway to the Loch Lomond and Trossachs National Park. Balloch's crowded marinas offer every kind of cruise on the Loch, but nothing spurs your imagination more than the old paddle steamer at its slipway mooring – gleaming in its red, black and white livery, and pulsing a thin trickle of smoke from its re-born copper and brass engineering. The *Maid of the Loch* is the last paddle steamer ever built in Britain, and it was commissioned in 1953 especially for Loch Lomond. Now restored, the *Maid*'s every detail proclaims its direct descent from the first Loch Lomond paddle steamer of 1818. Its antique grandeur captivates children and adults, and makes the perfect introduction to the spirit pervading the Loch.

After a long lunch on board, drinking in the gorgeous views, take the opportunity to visit the Loch Lomond Bird of Prey Centre, close by at Ballagan. You'd be lucky to see these magnificent birds in the wild: getting close to them, and seeing highly-trained handlers put them through their hunting paces, makes your throat tighten with awe. The soaring specks that hurtle straight at you, talons raking as they swoop over your head, are nature's masterpieces. The centre offers regular flying displays, 'hawk walks' and training demonstrations that explain why these resolutely wild creatures can show loyalty to humans. In its Loch-side setting, the Centre shows the skills of traditional wildlife husbandry at their most moving, spectacular and illuminating.

WHERE:
Strathclyde/Central (Dunbartonshire).
BEST TIME TO GO:
Any time of year (Bird of Prey centre); April to October, and Saturdays & Sundays during winter (*Maid of the Loch*).
DON'T MISS:
The gundog and ferret racing team at the Bird of Prey Centre.
AMOUNT OF WALKING:
Little (wheelchair access is good at the Bird of Prey Centre, and limited on board the paddle steamer).
COST:
Low (unless you go overboard in the *Maid of the Loch*'s restaurant).
YOU SHOULD KNOW:
The *Maid of the Loch*'s importance is recognized by the paddle steamer's inclusion since 2004 on the National Register of Historic Vessels.

A typical bedroom in Hill House

The Hill House

HELENSBURGH AND GEILSTON GARDEN, CARDROSS

When you see the 'Welcome to Helensburgh' sign on the A818, turn right for Charles Rennie Mackintosh's masterpiece of domestic architecture, The Hill House. Commissioned to design a country house by the Glasgow publisher Walter Blackie in 1902, Mackintosh was already well established locally for his many public buildings in Glasgow. The Hill House, to be built on the edge of Helensburgh, on a high hill with long views over the Clyde, posed a new set of challenges. Since the National Trust for Scotland restored it in the minute detail originally specified by the architect (and his equally talented wife, Margaret), you can once again marvel at the triumph of light and shadow, of dark wood and elegant friezes, and of numerous 'Arts & Crafts' features now considered characteristic of Mackintosh rather than the movement. The hallway, drawing room and master bedroom are superb – so stunning and complete that you regret the absence of original furniture in most of the rest of the house. Now, we are amazed by its apparent modernity – but its design is timeless, and an unmissable treat.

Just down the road at Cardross, the National Trust for Scotland maintains a different kind of magic at Geilston House. The 18th-century stone house isn't open, but the ten acres of gardens include a sensational combination of woodland wilderness, walled formality, botanical 'secret surprises', and a fantastic kitchen garden that provides mouthwatering produce you can take away and eat. The tranquillity of the 200 year-old woodland is enhanced by Geilston Burn bubbling through it, and the waterfall, bridges and mossy trackways. The walled garden opens to reveal an enormous giant Wellingtonia tree, surrounded by plantings maintained according to early 19th century fashions. Best of all, the plantings are rich without fanfare: you feel you could live here, too.

WHERE:
Dunbartonshire & Argyll
BEST TIME TO GO:
April to October (the blazing, scented allure of May and June at Geilston is glorious).
DON'T MISS:
Having a picnic by Geilston Burn in one of the mossy woodland dells.
AMOUNT OF WALKING:
Lots. Hill House only has limited wheelchair access. Geilston Gardens is limited by occasional steep gradients, a few steps, and moss-covered paths, but much of the best is accessible, and help is at hand.
COST:
Reasonable to expensive (by the time you leave the kitchen garden shop!).
YOU SHOULD KNOW:
You can't take photographs at The Hill House. You are allowed to play the piano in the drawing room but not to touch anything else.

The Trossachs

DISCOVERY CENTRE, GLENS, LOCHS AND ADVENTURES

The Trossachs National Park is where the Lowlands meet the Highlands, and the Trossachs Discovery Centre in the little town of Aberfoyle will provide you with the key to the region's secrets. Don't be put off by the crowds milling about. They are a measure of the Centre's successful exhibitions and displays about the Trossachs' flora and fauna, geology, history, and activities for all seasons, all interests and all age groups. With a children's play area as an on-site diversion, it transforms the often querulous task of planning into a fascinating kind of trivial pursuit about competing local attractions.

Tear yourself away in good time. Aberfoyle is just the gate to the playground filled with dramatic gorges, sweeping glens – where woodland trails lead you from broadleaf groves and stilled pine forests to the rocky open ground of bracken ferns and purple heather – and the lochs and silver streams of some of Scotland's most classically beautiful scenery. There are dozens of discreetly signed trails for walkers and cyclists based on Aberfoyle. The best of them take you deep into the sublime Loch Ard Forest, lost to the world between the magnificent backdrop of Ben Lomond, and the Strathyre Forest stretching far to the north. Loch Ard is beautiful, and the oaks, beeches, pines and birches around it quite obviously belong to the Gaelic kingdom of faerie. If you're skeptical, make sure you find the trail called Doon Hill Fairy Knowe.

Come back via the Queen Elizabeth Forest Visitors' Centre on Duke's Pass, just north of Aberfoyle. There are lovely views over Lochs Drunkie and Venacher; and you can end the day on the Go Ape High Wire Forest Adventure, zapping from tree to tree 12 m (40 ft) above the forest floor. After the magic of Loch Ard, it's like Tarzan meets Tinkerbelle – weird but energetically wonderful.

WHERE:
Stirlingshire
BEST TIME TO GO:
March to October (keep in mind Aberfoyle's April 'Tramping Through the Trossachs', and late September's Mushroom Festival).
DON'T MISS:
The tranquility of the southwestern Trossachs' natural landscape. It's incredible that such an outstanding wilderness of red deer, capercaillie, blackcock and red squirrel could remain so pristine and seemingly remote, within an hour's drive of both Edinburgh and Glasgow.
AMOUNT OF WALKING:
Potentially, lots – it really is up to you.
COST:
Low (but the Go Ape thrill ride is expensive).
YOU SHOULD KNOW:
From April to October in Aberfoyle, 'Fame Academy for Sheepdogs' is performed three times a day at the Scottish Wool Centre on Main Street.

Loch Ard near Aberfoyle

Callander

THE FALLS OF LENY AND KILMAHOG WOOLLEN MILL

WHERE:
Stirlingshire
BEST TIME TO GO:
Any time of year. The footpath/cycle track through the Pass to the Falls of Leny can be dangerously slippery after heavy rain, and may be closed in extreme conditions.
DON'T MISS:
The daily tastings at the Whisky Shop attached to Kilmahog Woollen Mill.
AMOUNT OF WALKING:
Lots, some of it moderately difficult.
COST:
Free. It only gets expensive if you absolutely must have full Highland Dress, made to measure at Kilmahog.
YOU SHOULD KNOW:
Rob Roy MacGregor (1671-1734) was born at Glengyle near Loch Katrine, and buried at Balquhidder Glen by Loch Voil.

The outstanding natural beauty of the Trossachs is encapsulated by the short walk (or bike ride) from Callander through the Pass of Leny, one of the ancient routes to the Highlands. Callander itself is a pretty town, the biggest community in the Trossachs, and a showcase for every form of Scottish culture. It holds a Highland Games of distinction every July, and daily kilt demonstrations. It is particularly proud to claim Rob Roy as a native son: the historic association is genuine, even if Callander's overt sympathies were pragmatically with the Duke of Montrose (who paid for all kinds of civic improvements), Rob Roy's sworn enemy.

As you walk through the broad meadows by the River Teith, looking across the forests of oak, chestnut and beech to the gently rising contours of Ben Ledi, purple heather and blue shadow on the skyline, you are literally tracing Rob Roy's steps. At Kilmahog, the river turns northwest between two mountain spurs. The banks become steep and densely forested, and the constricted river races white-water angry, a boulder-strewn torrent. This is the Pass of Leny, and the enchanting Falls at its northern end mark the entrance to Rob Roy MacGregor's ancestral lands, close to his birthplace, his farm, and his present grave. It's also the geographical beginning of the Highlands, and what could be more romantic than that?

You might pause at Kilmahog, for more than the fabulous scenery. Close to the bridge where the deep water still runs fast, a 250 year-old woollen mill, complete with its original water wheel, still produces authentic textiles on old looms. Attached is a shop which brings together the best Scottish tweeds, tartans and woollens still made by hand in cottages and workshops across the Highlands. In such a picturesque and historic setting, you feel grateful that every rug and garment is the real thing.

The Falls of Leny

Dumbarton Castle

AND THE CLYDEBANK TITAN

Dumbarton Castle sits atop Dumbarton Rock.

Dun Breatann ('fortress of the Britons') was a vital strategic fortification long before St Patrick wrote about it in 450. Set on a volcanic rock high above the Clyde at the mouth of the River Leven, Dumbarton Castle was the almost impregnable capital of the ancient Kingdom of Strathclyde until the Vikings pillaged it in the 9th century (and they needed 200 longships to carry off their spoils). When you climb the 547 steps to the peak of the rock, you work your way up a narrow defile through the 14th century Portcullis Arch, a ruin built on the ruinous exploits of Edward I, William Wallace and Robert the Bruce from 1296-1328. You pass the buildings and fortification walls from which Mary, Queen of Scots, sailed to France in 1548 on her betrothal to the Dauphin; and from which subsequent English rulers squeezed western Scotland in their mailed fists. Dumbarton Castle is an intimate feature of the milestones in Scotland's rich history. From its summit you sense its ghosts and its grandeur. Spread before you, the Clyde's north bank is itself synonymous with Scottish power in all its forms – dynastic, royal, (English) colonial, and most recently, industrial.

At Clydebank, nearby on the same road, there's a symbol of that industrial power every bit as potent and fascinating as Dumbarton Castle. The Clydebank Titan Crane is a 94-m (150-ft), 150-ton behemoth rearing high above what used to be the colossal Clydebank shipyards. One hundred years old, its massive intricacies are a marvel of engineering and one of the wonders of Scotland's – and the world's – industrial heritage. You can visit its workings and wheelhouse controls; and at the top, where its awesome power feels strongest, you sense the same historical magnitude that emanates from Dumbarton Castle.

WHERE:
Dunbartonshire & Strathclyde
BEST TIME TO GO:
May to October, Friday to Monday only – the Clydebank Titan Crane (but check: opening times vary annually); any time of year – Dumbarton Castle.
DON'T MISS:
The 45-minute Clydebank Titan Crane tour: a shuttle bus takes you across the former John Brown shipyards in the shadow of the Titan. The panorama from the giant gantry eastwards towards the Erskine Bridge and the smudge of Glasgow beyond is a revelation of the significance of the Clyde in the seesaw of Scotland's fortunes.
AMOUNT OF WALKING:
Lots, up and down the steps at Dumbarton Castle; very little at the Titan, where there is good wheelchair access to the shuttle and the gantry.
COST:
Low (and the Titan tour has reduced rates for families and groups).
YOU SHOULD KNOW:
Dumbarton Castle is built so that the two rocky peaks ('The Beak' and 'White Tower Crag') comprising Dumbarton Rock are actually grassy, open ground. In the years since the Castle was properly inhabited, the Rock has attracted rare and unusual flora and fauna. Now, it is a designated SSSI (Site of Special Scientific Interest).

Stirling Castle

Stirling Day 1

STIRLING CASTLE AND CHURCH OF THE HOLY RUDE

WHERE:
Stirlingshire
BEST TIME TO GO:
Any time – even if you can't see one of the colourful pageants or re-enactments, there's so much else to get your hands on. The Church of the Holy Rude is open from Easter to the end of September.
DON'T MISS:
The Regimental Museum of the Argyll & Sutherland Highlanders, in the King's Old Buildings.
AMOUNT OF WALKING:
Lots, by the time you've gone up and down and in and out of the buildings and fortifications. Wheelchair access is widespread but not complete.
COST:
Reasonable
YOU SHOULD KNOW:
The Church of the Holy Rude is the only active church in the United Kingdom, other than Westminster Abbey, which has held a coronation – on 29 July 1567 when the infant James VI was crowned King of Scotland, following the forced abdication of his mother, Mary, Queen of Scots.

Stirling Castle is the strategic key to central Scotland. Standing on a 72-m (250-ft) high plug of volcanic rock at the head of Stirling's Old Town, it commands the plain in every direction, and controls the easiest ford across the River Forth. It bears the scars of 600 years of bloody history, its importance growing as it became first a refuge, then a palace for generations of royalty. It's huge, more grand and at least as strong as Edinburgh Castle, and no other castle can offer such close, hands-on access to its inner workings.

Watch the A/V introduction to the castle when you arrive (follow the sign to the 1714 fortifications alongside the Queen Anne Gardens). Then follow one of the tours to help you decide what to look at more closely. The Great Hall has a medieval hammer beam roof; the Royal Palace is considered the finest Renaissance building in Scotland; the Chapel Royal is magnificent; and in the working kitchens, armouries, workshops and Royal apartments, you can see re-enactments of domestic life to match the pageantry and military swashbuckling taking place in the castle's outside baileys and jousting-grounds. Throughout the summer, Stirling Castle bustles with activities demonstrating the scope of its self-reliance and military importance. Spending a day here is worth a gap year anywhere else!

By teatime you'll be ready for something equally glamorous, ancient and historically significant – but more tranquil. If for no other reason, visit the neighbouring Church of the Holy Rude ('Holy Cross') for its magnificent stained glass. Medieval and modern, the intricate traceries of bold colour add to the extreme eccentricity of other architectural accretions to the Church; and like them, provide marvellous opportunities for reflective contemplation on the theme '*sic transit gloria*'. Since the 1130s, Holy Rude has provided somewhere to wind down from thoroughly worldly Stirling Castle.

Stirling Day 2

ARGYLL'S LODGING AND THE OLD TOWN JAIL

Reclaimed from service as a 19th-century military hospital, and then a youth hostel, Argyll's Lodging is the most complete example of a 17th-century town house to survive in Scotland. It sits behind a screen wall along the road below the esplanade of Stirling Castle, its glory hidden until you step through the gateway arch at the front. It's like stepping on stage – you find yourself in a courtyard enclosed on three sides by a very grand building that looks like a typical French *hôtel particulier* of the period. Turrets topped by conical grey slate roofs overlook the courtyard from each corner, and ahead is an elaborately dressed stone doorway beneath the carved arms of the 9th Earl of Argyll. He acquired the house from the Earl of Stirling, and enlarged it to its roughly present state in the 1670s.

You can only visit Argyll's Lodging on a guided tour, which starts with static and multimedia presentations on the history of the house. They make essential viewing, but far better are the actors who frequently appear in costume to play out scenes that reveal the stories behind the historical occupants. Among the tapestries, intricately-carved furniture and hangings, you feel you're eavesdropping on conversations with people like Charles II in 1651, or 'Butcher' Cumberland on his way to Culloden in 1746.

Stirling's Victorian past will come to even greater life for you, back in the Old Town, at the Old Town Jail. As you explore its grim dungeon cells and dank corridors, you may be confronted by an escaping prisoner, chased by truncheon-wielding guards. One of the Victorian Wardens will tell you what to do. You may have to be locked in a cell, briefly; and you're sure to meet the hangman checking his noose. You'll be enthralled, perhaps as much as the children.

WHERE:
Stirlingshire
BEST TIME TO GO:
Any time of year, but at the Old Town Jail the actors perform daily from April to October. From November to March, they only perform at weekends.
DON'T MISS:
The Prison Beastie Hunt, just for children.
AMOUNT OF WALKING:
Moderate, but at Argyll's Lodgings, wheelchairs will need assistance to negotiate narrow corridors and doorways (and the most elaborately-decorated rooms are on the first floor at the top of a flight of stairs).
COST:
Low to reasonable, depending on whether you qualify for concessionary tickets.
YOU SHOULD KNOW:
Although Warders at the Old Town Jail re-create the prison as it was in Victorian times, they will also use its oldest rooms to show you what medieval prison conditions were like on the same site – even harsher!

Argyll's Lodging

319

Inveraray

THE TOWN, THE CASTLE AND THE JAIL

Inveraray is a gem of untouched 18th-century Georgian architecture set on the shores of Loch Fyne. The town was planned as a whole by the 3rd Duke of Argyll in 1743-6, both as a commercial and legal centre for the region, and (more importantly) as an elegant match to his own new castle a short distance away. Inveraray Castle is a fairytale blend of neo-Medieval French chateau and crenellated Scottish baronial styles. Set in beautiful gardens, its thickets of spires and turrets reflect quite different architectural eras. So do the magnificent state and family rooms. Their furnishings, including weaponry and clothing displays, recall every period back to the 15th century Campbell Barony – but much of the castle's romantic charm derives from its continuous role as the family home (500 years on the same site) of the Chief of Clan Campbell. The tour guides weave Campbell family anecdotes into their expertise on many generations-worth of family collections, adding humour to what is already a thoroughly entertaining morning.

Afterwards, Inveraray town's homogenous grandeur seems perfectly natural and ducal. Dominated by a neo-classical church built in two parts (to separate Gaelic and English speakers), the whitewashed terraces of cafés, pubs and shops on Main Street make you feel you've stepped into a time warp. You'll enjoy your own double take on the staff of Inveraray Jail, who walk the streets in full period costume, amiably searching for 'victims' to act out roles as criminals, juries, witnesses and warders in the actual jail and the original courtroom. You can experience being locked in a cell, 'punishment' at the Crank Wheel or Whipping Table, and all the sounds, smells and misery of prison conditions long ago. Children love the lurid tales, and the whole family will be irresistibly drawn into the fun and games.

Inveraray Castle

WHERE:
Argyllshire
BEST TIME TO GO:
Any time of year (Inveraray town & Jail); April to October (Inveraray Castle).
DON'T MISS:
Inveraray Maritime Museum (at the town pier), including the 1911, 3-masted Schooner *Arctic Penguin*, and Scotland's last working Clyde Puffer, *Vital Spark*, featured in the TV version of the *Para Handy* stories – and now moored a few yards from the birthplace of Neil Munro, the author of *Para Handy*.
AMOUNT OF WALKING:
Lots, particularly if you explore the 6.5 hectares (16 acres) of gardens and nature trails at the Castle.
COST:
Reasonable – and there are all kinds of discounts for families and groups at Inveraray Castle, Jail and Maritime Museum. The castle gardens can be visited free of charge.
YOU SHOULD KNOW:
The current Duke of Argyll maintains a family tradition – as the captain of an Elephant Polo team.

Bannockburn

HERITAGE CENTRE AND THE NATIONAL WALLACE MONUMENT

Everyone who cares about Scotland wants to see the place where, against heavy odds, King Robert the Bruce defeated King Edward II in 1314. The victory meant that England lost its last Scottish stronghold – Stirling Castle – and Scotland finally secured its independence. Though the exact site of the battle isn't certain, the Bannockburn Heritage Centre, 3.5 km (2 mi) south of Stirling towards Glasgow, stands where tradition says Bruce had his frontline command post. The noble statue of Bruce in full armour astride his caparisoned charger is even supposed to mark the spot where, the day before the main battle, the Scottish King slew the arrogant English knight Sir Henry de Bohun in single combat, cleaving his helmeted skull with a single axe blow. The Centre brings to life every detail of the battle, and explains the struggle for freedom of which it was the culmination. The Rotunda, the audio-visual displays and chivalric exhibitions help you envisage the clash of armed columns, the brightly coloured heraldry of the cavalry sweeping forward, and the awesome surge of untrained Scottish citizens whose appearance at the battle's height churned English bowels to water, and whose fury routed the English army.

Massively appealing to children, the Centre also strikes a deep chord in adult hearts. After witnessing the glories of Bannockburn, there's time to pay tribute to William Wallace, greatest of all Scottish heroes. The National Wallace Monument towers 67 m (220 ft) above Abbey Craig, looking 3.5 km (2 mi) south to Stirling Castle across the scene of Wallace's finest victory, the Battle of Stirling Bridge in 1297. 246 steps and four floors, on which enthralling displays (including Wallace's 1.6m (5 ft 4 in), 700 year-old sword!) describe his inspirational history, eventually leading to Scotland's most emotional panorama. Before you are both Highlands and Lowlands – the Scotland Wallace died to set free.

WHERE:
Stirlingshire
BEST TIME TO GO:
Any time of year
DON'T MISS:
The panorama from 'the Crown' (the highest floor) of the National Wallace Monument.
AMOUNT OF WALKING:
Little (apart from the 246 steps) at the Monument; moderate at Bannockburn. Both are accessible to wheelchairs, again apart from the actual Wallace Tower. In 2009, a new Visitor Pavilion by the car park at the foot of Abbey Craig greatly improved disabled access and facilities – and for everyone who does not want to walk up the hill, a mini-bus shuttles between the car park and the foot of the Monument throughout the day.
COST:
Reasonable, even low if you qualify for one of the family/group/school concessionary tickets available.
YOU SHOULD KNOW:
'Scots Wha Hae', the stirring song exhorting Scotsmen to seek their birthright, was conceived by Robert Burns as a fictional address by Robert the Bruce to boost the morale of his outnumbered army on the eve of Bannockburn.

Robert the Bruce statue and The National Wallace Monument

The Falkirk Wheel and Callendar House

WHERE:
Falkirkshire

BEST TIME TO GO:
Any time of year; but there are more open-air facilities at Callendar House Park and the Falkirk Wheel Visitor Centre from April to September. There are three times as many daily boat trips, too.

DON'T MISS:
The magnificent, oak-panelled, Victorian Library at Callendar House holds the archive of Falkirk District's History Research Centre. Ring before you go, and you can see amazing documents of the area's heritage.

AMOUNT OF WALKING:
Moderate, and both the Visitor Centre and boat trips at the Falkirk Wheel are fully accessible to wheelchairs. At Callendar House and park, wheelchair restrictions are few, but they do exist.

COST:
Reasonable. The only charge at the Falkirk Wheel is for boat trips; and at Callendar House access to the Park is free.

YOU SHOULD KNOW:
The Falkirk Wheel operates on Archimedes' principle of displacement. That is: 'The mass of the boat sailing into the gondola will displace an exactly proportional volume of water so that the final combination of 'boat plus water' balances the original total mass.' It is deeply satisfying to watch.

This is a day to combine the romance of Scottish history with an exciting promise for Scotland's future. It begins at the colossal baronial mansion and park of Callendar House, for more than 600 years one of the nerve centres of Scottish power and political intrigue. Only three families have owned it since the 11th century. It looks now like a French chateau, and its warren of grand rooms bears witness to the fashions of passing centuries – but its ghosts are everywhere. Mary, Queen of Scots lived here with her guardian. Kings like Alexander II in 1239, the murdered James I in 1436, Charles II in 1660 and Bonnie Prince Charlie before Culloden were all intimately associated with the house. Now, 'costumed interpreters' re-create the domestic routines of the past, upstairs and down. The authentic Georgian kitchen is fully functional (and you can eat the results). In the morning room or library, the staff may be Victorian. In the workshops, a printer and clockmaker will show you the Regency way of doing things. Callendar House is a hive of interactive activities, re-telling history for you to have fun with.

Around mid-afternoon, it's a very short drive to the Falkirk Wheel for the day's finale. The Wheel replaces a ladder of eleven locks, and links the Union with the Forth and Clyde Canal in a single, sheer, 35 m (115 ft) drop. Its technology is breathtakingly simple, and poetry in motion to observe. You'll appreciate it even more by taking the one-hour boat ride that includes being lifted between the canals. Often described as 'reminiscent of a Celtic double-headed axe', the Wheel has the elegant beauty that belongs only to the perfect marriage of form and function. Book the last ride of the day: afterwards you'll be too awestruck for anything but reflection.

The Visitors' Centre and the amazing Falkirk Wheel

Kilmartin and the Ancient Stone Sites

Less than an hour's drive south from Oban, the tiny village of Kilmartin stands in the centre of Scotland's greatest concentration of Neolithic and Bronze Age sites. The whole of Kilmartin Glen, overlooking the Sound of Jura, is filled with mounds, standing stones, rock carvings and cairns – 150 prehistoric sites and 300 other ancient monuments within 10 km (6 mi). What is now a sparsely populated, remote farming community was once bursting with life; and the record of some 5,000 years of pre- and post-Christian community history is now being preserved, researched and further developed at Kilmartin House Museum. Discreetly housed in what used to be the Old Manse, the Museum has won awards for everything from landscape interpretation to its café. It is in fact a radically modern research centre with an excellent Visitors' Centre, and the best way to start your day is to see 'The Valley of Ghosts', an A/V presentation of sublime beauty and fascinating suggestion. The Museum will furnish you not only with names and places, but also with a social-historical context into which you can fit them. For example, the largest cup and ring marked site in Europe is at Achnabreck in Kilmartin Glen. The Museum can tell how and why that's significant, and show you the artefacts found in immediately related sites.

Christianity came to Argyll at roughly the same time the fortress of Dunadd was established in circa 500 as the centre of power and coronation site of Scotland's earliest kings, further down Kilmartin Glen. Across from the Museum, Cille a Mhartainn ('Church of Martin') has a unique, linear cemetery much older than the current church building. It's full of crosses and medieval grave-slabs only slightly less than contemporary to that period. Wander Kilmartin Glen – use the Museum and Church as focal points for an amazing insight into Scotland's oldest recorded history.

The Ballymeanoch standing stones in Kilmartin Glen

WHERE:
Argyllshire
BEST TIME TO GO:
Any time of year (remember that Argyll is washed by the Gulf Stream, so even in winter's depths it can be warmer than elsewhere).
DON'T MISS:
Dunadd, built on a much older site by the Dal Riata people from Ireland, and the place where Scotland came into being. Look out for the rock carvings, and artefacts taken from the many excavations.
AMOUNT OF WALKING:
Little to moderate, depending on your willingness to examine the sites first-hand up and down the Glen.
COST:
Low (just your petrol, food and drink).
YOU SHOULD KNOW:
At the fort of Dunadd, look for the carving of a wild boar. Nearby you'll see a carved footprint: try your foot for size, because it used to be part of the coronation ceremonies of the Scotti tribe.

Killin and the Breadalbane Folklore Centre

WHERE:
Perthshire
BEST TIME TO GO:
April to October (Breadalbane
Folklore Centre); May to September
(Moirlanich). If you're lucky, you'll find
the Falls of Dochart in spate after
rain in the surrounding hills.
DON'T MISS:
The beheading pit on the north side
of Finlarig Castle, 0.6 km (0.4 mi) E of
Killin. Built in 1620 by Black Duncan
of the Cowl – quite the nastiest of
the acquisitive Clan Campbell
chieftains – the Keep is an evocative
ruin. The beheading stone was still
there until recently; but is now
believed to have a new home
somewhere in Killin.
AMOUNT OF WALKING:
Little to moderate
COST:
Low
YOU SHOULD KNOW:
Replicas of St Fillan's Quigrich (the
head of his crozier) and bell are kept
at the Breadalbane Folklore Centre
(the originals are in the National
Museum in Edinburgh). They are
used each year in the traditional
ceremony of bedding St Fillan's
stones in fresh river wrack and straw
to preserve their healing potency.
Believers still use the stones to cure
a variety of ailments.

Killin is an attractive village straddling the main road for over half a mile close to the western end of Loch Tay. Spending the day there is like being pampered in a physical and cultural wellness centre: you get total sensory immersion in all forms of 'Scottishness', and feel purified and energized as a result. Even as you arrive you notice how stunningly beautiful the area is. Killin is framed by wild, mixed woods and forests, the tranquil Loch Tay and rivers rushing down from Breadalbane (the 'high country'). The village begins where the road crosses the river on an ancient, very narrow, stone bridge. Below, the Falls of Dochart rumble and crash in a series of white water cascades fiuming round the striations and massive boulders of the bedrock for hundreds of metres behind the village.

By the bridge is a lovely old mill, its wheel restored. It's where the Irish prince-monk St Fillan performed his legendary contemplation of beauty, and afterwards honed his magical powers. These days St Fillan's Mill also houses the Breadalbane Folklore Centre. It's crammed with imaginative ways to tell you about mystical giants, local legends, histories of the clans and the traditional natural folklore of the Celtic high country. After a fascinating hour or two, you'll have no trouble at all believing in the redemptive power of St Fillan's 1,300 year-old 'healing stones', which you can see at the Centre.

Be careful not to overload yourself with information and history. Take a picnic and wander between the woods and water. It's only a 1.5-km (1-mi) stroll (or drive) north-west to the National Trust's Moirlanich Longhouse, a traditional mid-19th-century cruck frame cottage and byre that was fully functional until 1968. In such spectacular landscapes, riven with Celtic mysticism, Moirlanich is a gentle reminder of the virtues of simplicity.

The Falls of Dochart

Campbeltown

ST KIERAN, SINGLE MALTS AND OWLS

A day out and around Campbeltown, one of Argyll's biggest and most remote towns, is a perfect introduction to the generally eccentric delights of southern Kintyre. The town (still called Kinlochkilkerran locally) was renamed in the 1600s, and the many fine buildings you can see demonstrate its economic success as a fishing port, and a centre for shipbuilding and whisky distilling. It's still one of only a handful of designated whisky producing regions in the whole of Scotland, though only three of thirty-four distilleries remain of the famous 'Campbeltown Single Malts'.

Campbeltown harbour on the Kintyre Peninsula

You can tour the Springbank Distillery in Well Close – neither its buildings nor methods have changed much since 1828, and you do get to taste the product. In Hall Street look out for the 'Wee Picture House' – a fabulous modernist rotunda which is Britain's oldest working cinema, opened in 1913. A few yards away, where Main Street (with its 'ice-cream tower' on one of Scotland's best Town Halls) meets the quayside, Campbeltown Cross is a 14th-century giant stone of exceptionally intricate carvings of saints, animals, and interlaced foliage. You have time to visit the Heritage Centre (called the 'tartan kirk' because of its brickwork and former function) to learn about St Kieran, who established Christianity in 6th-century Scotland. Further up Witchburn Road is the Scottish Owl Centre. Time your visit for early afternoon when you can meet the largest collection of owls in Scotland during the interactive flying displays.

Afterwards, if the tide is right, you can cross the causeway to Davaar Island, which shelters Campbeltown Loch from the worst weather. It's an opportunity to admire the birds and wildlife along Kintyre's dramatic coastline, and to visit St Kieran's cave and the extraordinary painting of the crucifixion in another cave nearby.

WHERE:
Mull of Kintyre
BEST TIME TO GO:
April to October
DON'T MISS:
The tide at Davaar Island. The island is perfectly lovely, but you can be marooned when the causeway is covered even by shallow water.
AMOUNT OF WALKING:
Moderate
COST:
Low – unless you take a fancy to some of the very old single malts.
YOU SHOULD KNOW:
The well-known folk song entitled 'Campbeltown Loch, I Wish You Were Whisky' was inspired by the town's heyday as 'the world capital of whisky' around 1900.

Benmore Botanic Garden

WHERE:
Argyllshire
BEST TIME TO GO:
March to October (but if you have a special seasonal interest, Benmore is happy for you to call them to check what is flowering).
DON'T MISS:
The Glen Massan Arboretum, which includes a massive, 55-m (180-ft) Douglas fir among some of Scotland's tallest trees.
AMOUNT OF WALKING:
Lots, because you won't be able to resist – and Benmore will supply a wheelchair and assistance for the less able.
COST:
Low, especially with family and other concessions.
YOU SHOULD KNOW:
Benmore, in the lee of the Firth of Clyde, gets the full advantage of the mild climate, caused by the tail end of the Gulf Stream in those waters.

A great day gets better if you take the A815 north out of Dunoon, across from Gourock on the Cowal Peninsula. The road rises for 11 km (7 mi) into the glens, and at the edge of the Argyll Forest you come to Benmore Botanic Gardens, one of Scotland's greatest horticultural glories. Magnificently set among the mountains, Benmore's 61 hectares (150 acres) are by turns dramatic, enchanting, grand, intimate and formal. In any season, their beauty will make you gulp.

The entrance is through a spectacular avenue of Giant redwoods, planted in 1863 and over 40 m (130 ft) tall. It's just a teaser: throughout the displays, you find plantings from Bhutan, Chile, New Zealand, Africa, Iberia, China, Japan and the Himalayas whose presence is as much a proclamation of historic exploration as of supreme botanical taste. In spring vast showings of azaleas combine with 300 different species of rhododendrons in an explosion of vibrant colour. In summer you get the Eucryphias at their best. Autumn brings a richness of depth that defies exaggeration – and always, every flower, shrub and tree along the many way-marked walks is shown to its best advantage, past a beautiful reflecting pool, trailing down the hillside, or in suitably formal formations. There's even one walk which entices you gradually up to a 130-m (450-ft) high clearing for one of the finest views you'll see in your life. Truly heart-stopping.

In the middle of this splendour you'll find the Courtyard Gallery, which holds exhibitions and events throughout the year. Next to it the Benmore Café is independently listed (in food guides) for its home baking and other sustenance; and expert advice is available at the shop, along with cuttings from the Gardens and an excellent selection of relevant books and other plants. Enjoy your day.

The spectacular avenue of Giant redwoods at Benmore

Bute and Rothesay Castle

Grand Victorian houses line the seafront at Rothesay.

Just 24 km (15 mi) long and 8 km (5 mi) wide, the Isle of Bute is full of extraordinary surprises and diversity. You feel it on the ferry from Wemyss. The 35-minute trip transforms your mental map, not just because it is famously beautiful, but also because it makes you feel you are approaching a new country instead of a Scottish island in the Firth of Clyde. As soon as you land in the heart of Rothesay, Bute asserts its amazing 'apartness'.

The 13th-century, circular castle in the centre of town is a reminder that Bute was virtually a kingdom when the Norse Empire fought over it with Scottish kings who lived here. Its more recent heyday as a Victorian resort town revived its reputation for elegant eccentricity, but Rothesay is no faded rose. Victorian is still a style choice that takes its cue from the Victorian Gothic masterpiece of Mount Stuart, home of the Marquess of Bute. The enormous house is a glory of marble and stained glass, even if its 121-hectare (300-acre) garden was laid out long before in the 1700s.

Bute's greatest attractions are either ancient, like the stone circles, cairns and cup markings, Iron Age fort and 6th-century Christian ruins at Kingarth and Kinagoil; or natural, either domesticated like Ardencraig Gardens, the Ascog Hall Fernery and Garden, or wild like Scalpay Bay and the island's wildlife as described (especially for children) in the Bute Museum; or Victorian, like Rothesay's palatial public lavatories (view only!), the Winter Garden (site of the visitor centre), and most of what still makes Rothesay such a vibrant resort to visit.

Provided you visit Rothesay Castle and Mount Stuart, Bute is a constant cornucopia all of which is within easy driving reach. Follow your whims on the day.

WHERE:
Bute

BEST TIME TO GO:
April to October. Remember Bute holds its own traditional Highland Games on the last weekend of August; a Jazz Festival in May, and a Folk Festival in late July. All are of exceptional quality – but you'll discover that so is the general standard of entertainment.

DON'T MISS:
The magnificent marble Hall and the blindingly white marble Chapel at Mount Stuart. When the sun shines through stained glass onto the marble…

AMOUNT OF WALKING:
Moderate. But if the essential romance of Bute gets you, you can walk a long way on deserted strands, or along Rothesay's sea front.

COST:
Reasonable to expensive, even though Bute's wild beauty is free.

YOU SHOULD KNOW:
The Highland/Lowland divide passes straight through the middle of Bute, at the point where fresh water Loch Fad all but cuts it in two. The south and east is gentle green farmland and leafy hollows; the west and north is barely inhabited, isolated, bleak and serenely beautiful.

Clackmannan

THE TOWER TRAIL AND THE FRUITS OF INDUSTRY

Across the River Forth from Stirling, the 'wee county' (Scotland's smallest) of Clackmannan punches well above its size for outstanding places to see and things to do. Take the A91 along the southern edge of the majestic Ochil Hills. The 'Hillfoot' villages – Blairlogie, Menstrie, Alva, Tillicoultry and Dollar – all stand at the end of one of the beautiful Ochil glens cut into the escarpment. This is where Scotland's cottage weaving became an industrial process. Past each village swept the water that powered the mills that later expanded when local coal was exploited to fire the huge new machines. But the story of the textile industry is woven into much older regional history. The Dollar Museum explains what happened, here in the Devon Valley. You'll be inspired to walk up the romantic, thickly-wooded gorge called Dollar Glen to 15th-century Castle Campbell. It's one of several magnificent towers on the Tower Trail (another is at Menstrie), on the day's agenda.

It's a lovely drive on the back roads between Dollar and Clackmannan. Early 14th-century Clackmannan Tower is the awesome remnant of a mansion complex, but the interior isn't open for viewing. Instead, just look around at Clackmannan itself: the Tolbooth, Mercat Cross, Church, Co-op Society chimney stones and buildings speak of centuries of Scottish change. Fascinating though they are, drive the extra couple of miles to Alloa Tower for lunch. Here you can contemplate what was once one of Scotland's most impressive palaces; and see inside its 3.4-m (11-ft) thick walls to period restorations ranging from the 13th-18th centuries. Children will enjoy the quizzes, costumes and historical games on offer.

The whole family will enjoy completing the Clackmannan tour at Gartmorn Dam Country Park. Built in 1713 to power local coalmine airpumps, it's now a wildlife paradise with lakeside walks and a visitor centre.

WHERE:
Clackmannanshire
BEST TIME TO GO:
April to October, when Visitor Centres at Alloa Tower and Menstrie Castle are open. Note that Castle Campbell is actually open year-round, while Clackmannan and Sauchie Towers are only open by special arrangement at any time. Gartmorn's status as a Site of Special Scientific Interest depends in part on its spectacular waterfowl being publicly accessible year-round.
DON'T MISS:
The domed Italianate staircase leading to the Great Hall of Alloa Tower – its 1712 gentility in marked contrast to the pit dungeon, internal well and medieval groin vaulting down below.
AMOUNT OF WALKING:
Lots, if you walk right around the 4-km (2.5-mi) perimeter of Gartmorn Dam and the whole of Dollar Glen. But the day is designed as much for driving and stopping to look round, so you can choose how much you want to walk.
COST:
Low to reasonable
YOU SHOULD KNOW:
Next to the belfry tower, all that remains of Clackmannan's 1592 Tolbooth, stands a rough-hewn column of whinstone cut from the outcrop on which the Wallace Monument is built near Stirling. Since 1833, the column has supported an ancient boulder, the standing stone or 'Clack' of Mannan, the Celtic god of the sea (aka Manau).

Castle Campbell near Dollar is also known as Castle Gloom.

Bo'ness & Kinneil Railway

SCOTTISH RAILWAY EXHIBITION

Since settling on its permanent site at Bo'ness in 1979, the Scottish Railway Preservation Society (SRPS) has achieved spectacular success. It has established the Scottish Railway Exhibition on redundant industrial land on the shores of the Forth, and created the Bo'ness and Kinneil Railway to allow new generations to experience the special thrill of steam locomotion.

When you arrive, you automatically suppose that the SRPS took over and adapted working railyards and equipment. But Bo'ness (short for Borrowstounness) Station, the signal boxes, range of workshops, marshalling areas and display sheds full of working engines and various goods wagons and coaches, were all built from scratch, or acquired from far afield.

The scale of the achievement is remarkable, and you can appreciate it best by taking the short trip to Kinneil and Birkhill on one of the 'scheduled' services. This line was specially built, and though it connects to the main railway network, it has to be further upgraded beyond Birkhill for public use that will eventually run trips anywhere in Britain. Take the trip, and visit the fireclay mine at Birkhill before returning (mine visits are coordinated with the train timetable). The authenticity of the train journey – the hooting and hissing as much as the railway artefacts that contribute to your visual pleasure – makes a subsequent tour round the Exhibition much more exciting, because you've seen it all in action. There is 3,159 sq m (34,000 sq ft) of space in which display tracks show off all manner of passenger and freight vehicles, including a brake van, a Saxa Salt wagon, a 1909 wooden-bodied passenger coach, and Scotland's only Royal Saloon, built in 1897. Clambering among the gleaming pipe-work of the locomotives, you'll get deep satisfaction from rediscovering the glory of steam heritage. Start early, to make sure you get a full day of hands-on fun.

WHERE:
Falkirk
BEST TIME TO GO:
Any time of year. Look out for regular 'Days out with Thomas the Tank Engine®' with at least one of the TV stories' mechanical stars. Other special trips for children include 'Steam'n'Scream' Halloween fancy dress rail journeys, and Christmas 'Santa Specials' with presents for children (and 'seasonal refreshments' for adults).
DON'T MISS:
The section of original branch line after Kinneil station. The train climbs through woods: watch out for a waterfall on the left, and high above, Kinneil House, where James Watt experimented with steam. As the train leaves the woods, it turns inland across the route of the Roman Antonine Wall.
AMOUNT OF WALKING:
Moderate, around the Exhibition area.
COST:
Reasonable, especially with family discounts.
YOU SHOULD KNOW:
Bo'ness station is a fascinating compilation: the station building came from Wormit; the train shed is from Haymarket; the signal box from Garnqueen South Junction, and the footbridge from Murthly. The signal box and signals won the Westinghouse Signalling Award.

The steam train runs along the specially built track.

Dunblane and Blair Drummond Safari Park

WHERE:
Fife and Stirling
BEST TIME TO GO:
Any time of year – and it's worth checking if there are any special events. The Park often holds special parties associated with the animals, like celebrating a new lion cub or baby rhino.
DON'T MISS:
The Giant Astraglide at Blair Drummond Safari Park.
AMOUNT OF WALKING:
Moderate, but there's lots of standing and looking.
COST:
Expensive, unless you qualify as part of a group of at least 15 people, and book (and pay) a minimum of 2 weeks ahead. On the other hand, the Safari Park will arrange your child's birthday party.
YOU SHOULD KNOW:
Technically, the Church of Scotland has no cathedrals. Dunblane Cathedral is just the active parish church for the town – but it retains its title in recognition of its long Roman Catholic history and general ecclesiastical significance.

Dunblane is only 8 km (5 mi) north of Stirling. It's a busy, prosperous town, with all the hallmarks of having been at the heart of events for generations – and with no through traffic, it's a magnet for commuters to Edinburgh and Glasgow. It's old and thoroughly charming, characteristics epitomized by its Cathedral, one of the most interesting yet least pretentious in all Scotland. None of its sections seems to fit with the others, and you can see some preposterous joins in the fabric. The tower is aligned differently from the rest, and the inside walls of the nave are as weathered as the exterior. There was a church here (on the 'Old Dun') circa 600, established by St Blane, and the original stone building of 1150 was successively remodeled from 1233 to 1560. The choir survived the Reformation, but the nave was an open-air ruin until 1893. Now, the church has a human-scale air of tranquillity and piety. The magnificent woodwork of the choir and screen, and the splendour of the huge stained-glass windows beaming colour on the stone celebrate a house of – clearly – living worship. That's worth stopping for.

Gather your breath for the children's treat. From Dunblane it's a short drive southwest to Blair Drummond Safari & Adventure Park, and you should aim to get there before lunchtime. Start with the drive-through. Lions, giraffes, rhinos, deer, ostrich, chimps and monkeys are among the many creatures to set your imagination (and pulse) racing. Then, on foot, you can explore various wild animal 'adventure areas' for close-ups, take the boat safari to Chimpanzee Island, watch the Sea Lions Show, visit the Pets' Centre, take out a family-size pedal boat and see the Birds of Prey display. Besides the animals, there's a funfair, a huge wooden castle and a pirate ship. You can't go wrong.

*A giraffe at Blair Drummond
Safari Park*

House of the Binns and Blackness Castle

Although the National Trust for Scotland now owns the House of the Binns, off the A904 near Old Philpstoun, the house is and has been occupied by the same family since 1612. Binns is the historic family home of the Dalyells, and their continuous presence there has helped to preserve the evidence of the transition from late 16th-century fortified house to much larger and more elegant 17th- and 18th-century country mansion. The furniture and fittings (mainly late 18th and early 19th century) fit into the feeling of organic continuum that pervades the house above and below stairs. There's a secret passage, a lovely collection of blue porcelain (especially Delft), and besides the grand rooms, you can see the 17th-century 'General's Kitchen', including the former bake-house, in the ovens of which (according to legend and the house guide), the most notorious member of the family, General Tam Dalyell ('the Muscovy Brute'), roasted his enemies. He also introduced thumbscrews to Scotland, and raised the original Royal Scots Greys regiment. Outside, the 19th-century crenellated towers look over 81 hectares (200 acres) of beautiful woodland walks, with panoramic views across the Forth to the Highlands.

After a morning at Binns, take the B9109 to the foreshore at Blackness. From the village – once an important port in Scotland's medieval Baltic trade – the shore curves out to a promontory. There, in bleak, fortified swagger and surrounded on three sides by water, stands Blackness Castle. Once one of Scotland's strongest forts, a medieval and Napoleonic era prison, and labyrinthine defensive maze, it's the definitive castle 'playground' for visitors. You can climb the towers, shiver in the dungeons, walk the walls, lording it over the Forth Rail and Road bridges in the distance, and fantasize in the forbidding keeps. With a shop and a small café on site, let yourself get carried away.

House of the Binns

WHERE:
Linlithgow
BEST TIME TO GO:
Any time of year (Blackness Castle, and the grounds of House of the Binns, which feature spectacular displays of snowdrops and bluebells in season). The House of the Binns itself is only open between June and September.
DON'T MISS:
The ceiling and cornice mouldings in the principal downstairs rooms – among the earliest (1630) made in Scotland.
AMOUNT OF WALKING:
Lots, and scrambling too, about the crannies of Blackness. The Castle's cobbles and hewn-rock floors make wheelchair access very difficult. At Binns, everything except two first floor rooms is accessible – and for those unable to get upstairs, there's an 'armchair photographic tour' of the bits they're missing.
COST:
Reasonable (except that at Binns, you have to pay extra, per hour, to park).
YOU SHOULD KNOW:
Blackness Castle is so totally fulfilling as a medieval fortification, it has featured in movies like *The Bruce*, Franco Zeffirelli's *Hamlet*, *Macbeth*, and the BBC-TV series of 'Ivanhoe' (in which special effects moved the castle from its riverside location on the Forth to anonymous moorland).

Linlithgow Palace and the Canal Centre

In the centre of Linlithgow, on a smooth grassy hill by the side of Linlithgow Loch, stands one of the most majestic, and saddest ruins in all Scotland. Enough details remain to show how Linlithgow Palace grew from the fortified Royal manor of King David I, sprouting complex ramparts, beautifully carved fountains and decorative motifs during 550 years as a primary royal residence of Scottish monarchs and English invaders. You can still look down on the Great Hall of 1500, and wander the corridors and lesser halls emblazoned with the coats of arms of the Scots, French, Norwegian and English royal families who called it home.

Mary of Guise, when she married James V (who was born there in 1512) compared Linlithgow's palatial splendour to the noblest chateaux of France – but all you can see now is what was left after its roofs and interiors were burned out by the Duke of Cumberland ('Butcher') in 1746. The North Range, where you gaze at the full height of six stories of sumptuous apartments, now a chequer-board of gaping window-spaces, is especially poignant. Take a picnic, and after exploring the Palace, sit by the loch and reflect on the ghosts that people its illustrious history.

It's a short walk from Linlithgow Palace to the Canal Centre on Manse Road. It only opens in the afternoon, and the best boat trip it offers, along the Union Canal to the Avon Aqueduct, departs at 2.00 pm, returning at 4.30 pm. It's a miracle that such a leafy, tranquil highway can still wind through the heart of urbanized Scotland. Just as you're appreciating the wildlife, the canal banks disappear and you find yourself 26 m (86 ft) up on the 247-m (810-ft) long Avon Aqueduct, the grandest on the Union Canal. There's no better place to spend a summer afternoon.

WHERE:
Linlithgow

BEST TIME TO GO:
Easter Saturday to the first weekend in October. The Avon Aqueduct trip takes place only on Saturdays and Sundays; but shorter canal trips are available on weekdays for small groups. Check in advance for special events – on one September weekend, the Linlithgow Folk Festival inspires musical canal cruises in the afternoon and evening; occasionally, there are cruises all the way to the ingenious Falkirk Wheel.

DON'T MISS:
The best view of Linlithgow Palace and the surrounding countryside, from the top of the northwest tower: it's called 'Queen Margaret's Bower', because this is where Margaret Tudor, Henry VIII's sister, watched in vain for the return of her husband, James IV. He was killed on Flodden's Field.

AMOUNT OF WALKING:
Little. Linlithgow Palace offers very limited wheelchair access, but its surfaces are cobbled or of broken stone. The Canal Centre is fully accessible (museum, picnic area and outside seating).

COST:
Reasonable to expensive, but family tickets help.

YOU SHOULD KNOW:
The Union Canal between Edinburgh and Falkirk is 51 km (31.5 mi) long, and is Scotland's only contour canal. Known at the time of its building as 'the Mathematical River', the canal followed the 73-m (240-ft) contour throughout its length, making locks unnecessary. With 62 fixed bridges, the canal's traffic flow was much faster than usual.

Linlithgow Palace

East Neuk Fishing Villages

CRAIL TO EARLSFERRY

The East Neuk, or 'corner', of Fife defines the series of ravishingly beautiful fishing villages on the roughly 18 km (12 mi) of coastline between Crail and Earlsferry. In any weather, at any season, it is one of Scotland's loveliest regions – and though you'll spend a magical day there, you'll wish you had a week or a month to know it better. Start at Crail, the oldest. Already important to Scotland's medieval trade with Europe in the 9th century, Crail was created a Royal Burgh by Robert the Bruce in 1310. Typically of all the East Neuk villages, its whitewashed houses feature outside staircases, red pantiled roofs and crow-stepped gables in the Dutch style they adapted after years of trading; and it is best discovered on foot through the 'wynds' and alleyways of its ancient harbour-side centre.

Each village is distinct in character, but shares the regional distinction of preserving the look and feel of authentic working communities. You'll pass castles and great public buildings, but East Neuk is about the industriousness which made Scotland a medieval European player. Pittenweem is picture-perfect, and full of art galleries – but it still has a proper fishing fleet. At St Monans, look out for the network of sturdy fishermen's terraces around 'The Pend', an architectural study in centuries of self-reliant community spirit. St Monan's Kirk, right by the shore, retains the same palpable feeling of antique eccentricity. At Earlsferry, the 'Chain Walk' is another example worth visiting.

If one place helps illuminate East Neuk it's the unlikely-sounding Scottish Fisheries Museum back at Anstruther, the biggest village. Set round a 14th-century courtyard – even then used to sell fish and store fishermen's equipment – it's much bigger than it looks, historic in its own right, and full of riveting displays about herring fishing, fishermen and fishing boats. It reeks of ozone and tar, and it's brilliant.

Anstruther Harbour

WHERE:
Fife
BEST TIME TO GO:
Any time of year. You will never be disappointed.
DON'T MISS:
The 16th-century Abbot's Lodging, the 1724 Merchant's House, the 19 historic boats (including the sailing flagship *Reaper* featured on BBC TV's 'Coast'), and above all the sensational photo archive of the Scottish Fisheries Museum.
AMOUNT OF WALKING:
Moderate, unless you choose to walk sections of the Fife Coastal Path, which includes the East Neuk villages.
COST:
Low – it costs nothing to enjoy the beauty of East Neuk, and the Fisheries Museum is free to accompanied children under 16.
YOU SHOULD KNOW:
Crail is associated with famous Scotsmen including John Knox, the Protestant reformist zealot who delivered one of his most violent sermons in the parish kirk; and Robert Louis Stevenson, whose grandfather designed Crail's west pier in 1826-28.

St Andrews

These days, St Andrews is known chiefly as the HQ of golf, and as home to Scotland's oldest and most prestigious University. The minute you see it, it's obvious why history ranks it even more highly. The modern city beats with a medieval heart. Its central street plan was established in the 12th century, and though the Cathedral and Castle are now spectacular ruins (thanks to a combination of weak stone joinery, brutal weather and the Scottish Reformation), the many walls, buildings, monuments and remnant fortifications still extant are enough to retain its medieval character. Walk round it, starting from the harbour. You cross the tranquil Cathedral grounds, full of fascinating tombstones of the great and good of several centuries, through the 13th-century arches of The Pends, to the Castle, perched over the sea. Then zig-zag your way through the 'wynds' (narrow alleyways) connecting North and South Streets. You'll see outstanding Georgian and Victorian buildings alongside 16th- and 17th-century architecture, where they have replaced medieval shops and merchant houses. The drama of St Andrews' history as one of Europe's most important religious sites, in an era when religion was also politics, is barely hidden by its incarnation as a lively undergraduate city and golf Mecca.

One big surprise is that the Royal & Ancient Golf Club, and the Old Course itself, are actually in the city, north of the Martyrs Monument on The Scores, the shoreline area occupied by St Salvator's, the University's oldest collegiate complex. Next to it is the Golf Museum, reinforcing this as the focus of modern pilgrimages to St Andrews. It is just one of several good museums – the St Andrews Preservation Trust by the Cathedral, and the St Andrews Museum by the North Haugh are worth a visit if you can tear yourself away from the authentic historical gems of Market Street.

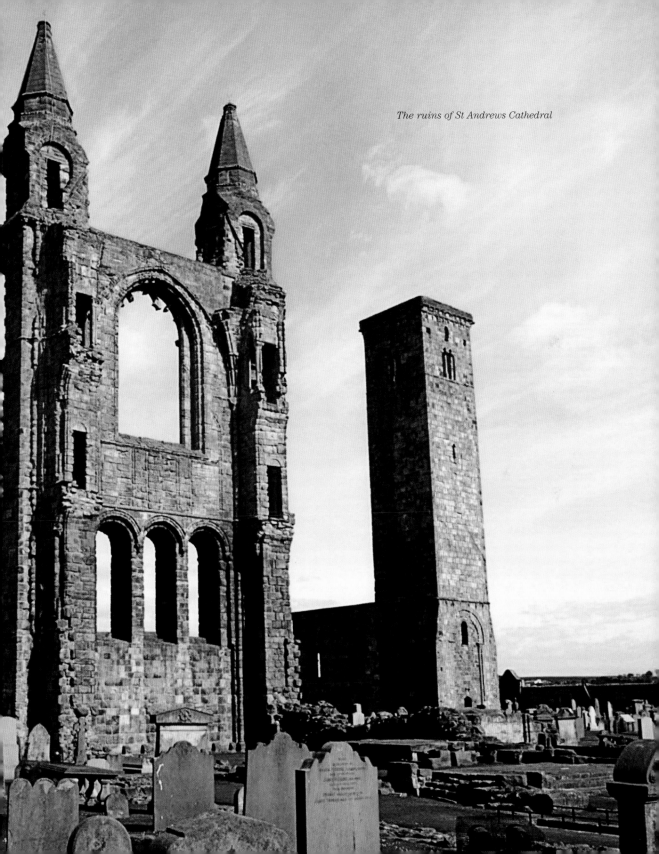

The ruins of St Andrews Cathedral

Edinburgh Day 1

EDINBURGH CASTLE AND GLADSTONE'S LAND

WHERE:
Edinburgh
BEST TIME TO GO:
Any time of year (Edinburgh Castle);
March to October (Gladstone's Land)
DON'T MISS:
The 'Honours of Scotland' at the
Royal Palace in the Castle's Crown
Square – the Crown, the Sceptre and
the Sword of State (broken in two
when being smuggled out of
Dunnottar Castle in 1652), together
with the 'Stone of Destiny' (formerly
the Stone of Scone), restored to
Scotland, from England, in 1996.
AMOUNT OF WALKING:
Lots, and while access is generally
very good at the Castle, the 17th-
century layout makes it very difficult,
and partial at best, at
Gladstone's Land.
COST:
Reasonable to expensive
YOU SHOULD KNOW:
At the top of the Castle, by St
Margaret's Church, stands Mons
Meg, a 6-ton siege gun given to King
James II in 1457. When fired to
celebrate the marriage of Mary,
Queen of Scots in 1558, it hurled a
stone projectile over two miles.

Like an organic extension of the 80-m (260-ft) high volcanic rock on
which it sits, Edinburgh Castle commands both the city and Scotland
itself. Fortified since 900 BC, it was developed between 1124-53 by King
David I and subsequent Scottish monarchs as a palatial bolt-hole in times
of military strife. It's a vast, uncompromising complex, picturesque
(thanks mainly to Victorian additions like the Gatehouse and the Argyll
Tower) but not at all romantic. In fact, attempts to separate its continuing
military functions from its ceremonial use as Scotland's foremost
attraction give you an intriguing, spooky sensation of being manipulated.

If so, the Castle is a glorious sleight-of-hand. You travel through
history, from the Esplanade (site of the annual Military Tattoo) and Lower
Ward, through the Portcullis Gate to the cobbled Middle Ward, where the
One O'Clock Gun is fired every day except Sundays (set your watch!).
Here you are guided to regimental museums, ordnance storehouses and
crannies of historic functional significance; but the Governor's House, and
much more, is closed to the public. Instead, climb onwards via Foog's Gate
to Crown Square in the Upper Ward. You'll immediately notice the
difference: the spectacular Royal Palace, the Great Hall of 1511, and St
Margaret's Chapel (built on the highest crag in 1120 by David I to honour
his mother) share a sense of soul and human scale that transcends
centuries, but is integral only to the Upper Ward. It's Edinburgh Castle's
most extraordinary surprise.

Leaving the Castle, spend an hour at Gladstone's Land in Lawnmarket.
Built in 1620, its six stories preserve the cramped tenement conditions
once considered prestigious in that location. One 17th-century painted
ceiling is original – and so are many of the 17th- and 18th-century
furnishings. The Castle folk governed, but the inhabitants of Gladstone's
Land made Edinburgh tick.

Edinburgh Castle

Edinburgh Day 2

THE NATIONAL GALLERY COMPLEX AND ROYAL YACHT BRITANNIA

Artfully sited between East and West Princes Gardens in the very centre of Edinburgh, the National Gallery Complex makes a perfect destination for a stroll, coffee, and a couple of hours contemplating some of the world's greatest painters. The Complex joins the National Gallery of Scotland and the Royal Scottish Academy via the Weston Link, which adds facilities like a lecture theatre, IT gallery, information desk, restaurant and cafés to the stunning art on either side. Scotland's national collections include works by Raphael, Titian, Velazquez, Rembrandt and Rubens, as well as Monet, Cezanne, Van Gogh, Degas and Gauguin. Scottish painters include Ramsay, Raeburn and Wilkie. The underground passage of the Weston Link takes you to the Academy, re-opened in 2003 as a venue for major national, and touring, temporary exhibitions. The arrangement of the permanent rooms and the three buildings makes it a treat to alternate your favourite artists with browsing in the Weston's shops and stargazing over Princes Street Gardens.

From Princes Street, you can get a bus or taxi for the short drive to the port of Leith. If you've booked ahead during the morning, you can walk straight aboard the Royal Yacht *Britannia*, now permanently berthed at the Ocean Terminal. As trim and elegant as ever, *Britannia* shows few obvious scars from 968 official voyages covering over a million miles at sea. She's been maintained just as if the Royal Family were on their way – and the state of readiness emphasizes the distinctions of space and grandeur of fittings that divide State from private staterooms, passengers from crew, Admiral from officers, officers from other naval ranks, and, in the triple-tier bunks, the rest of the 280-strong crew facilitating the comfort, food and laundry of them all. Your eyes will pop. You'll ogle. You'll gossip. You'll love it!

The National Gallery

WHERE:
Edinburgh
BEST TIME TO GO:
Any time of year.
DON'T MISS:
Raeburn's famous and much-loved painting of The Reverend Robert Walker Skating on Duddingston Loch (often called 'The Skating Minister').
AMOUNT OF WALKING:
Lots. There's full access at the National Gallery Complex; at *Britannia*, a clever lift system in a glass tower gives access at four levels. Access to the lift itself is from the Visitor Centre on the second floor of the quayside Ocean Terminal (where you can see the interpretive exhibitions before you board).
COST:
Free, at the National Gallery Complex; expensive at *Britannia*.
YOU SHOULD KNOW:
Often described as a 'floating stately home', *Britannia* is certainly a very big 'yacht'. At 125 m (410 ft), she is the same length as the biggest ferries in Scottish waters, the *Hrossey* and the *Hjaltland* Shetland ferries.

Edinburgh Day 3

MURRAYFIELD STADIUM AND EDINBURGH ZOO

You need to book it 48 hours in advance, but it would be inhuman not to pause to tour Murrayfield Stadium on your way to Edinburgh Zoo. Book the 11.00 am tour (the alternative is 2.30 pm), any day of the week, but not during the week before, or the two days after a home international game, when the Stadium is full of people setting or clearing up. Murrayfield is the home of Scottish rugby, and like Hampden Park for soccer, famous for the quality of its enthusiastic crowds. You can hear them even in the empty vastness of the stadium's 67,500-seat capacity – especially when, fresh from Scotland's dedicated dressing rooms, where each locker is emblazoned with the names of those players who have previously used it, you step through the unusually short Tunnel, out across the encircling running track, onto the pitch itself. The roar thrums and fills your head: this is an Ultimate Fantasy fulfilled, and it affects men, women and children alike. Not even the steps up to and into the Royal Box compare. Being on the pitch is It.

A short walk or bus-ride along Corstorphine Road will take you to the Zoo by 1.00 pm. Edinburgh Zoo occupies 33 well-hidden hectares (82 acres) on Corstorphine Hill, but there's a free 'Hilltop Safari' shuttle to take you to the top. Seeing the lions, tigers and other big cats in their naturalistic enclosures, and the 'plains' full of zebra, gazelles and giraffes, you understand why the Zoo's educational reputation is so high. At 'Rainbow Landings', fabulous Rainbow lorikeets sip special nectar from your hand; the 'Budongo Trail' (named after a field programme in Uganda) lets you get close to some forty chimpanzees in their natural environment. So, with penguins, flamingos, rhinos and Steller's sea eagles and much more to admire, you'll have a surprisingly busy day.

Edinburgh Zoo is very interactive.

WHERE:
Edinburgh
BEST TIME TO GO:
Any time of year, 365 days a year. Special Events are arranged to celebrate animal anniversaries, births, and new displays as circumstances dictate.
DON'T MISS:
'Close Encounters', a free 45-minute hands-on session (2.30/3.15/4.00 pm) with lots of different animals – even snakes, bearded dragons and armadillos. It's in the building next to the Education Centre.
AMOUNT OF WALKING:
Lots, if you resolutely visit all the Zoo's fascinating corners; but it's more likely you'll get absorbed in some of the many interactive attractions.
COST:
Reasonable
YOU SHOULD KNOW:
The focal point of Edinburgh Zoo is the Scots Baronial pile called the Mansion House, originally built in 1793. Now it's owned by the Royal Zoological Society of Scotland and is flanked by the Educational and Discovery Centres, and two good cafeterias. The turreted Manse, within earshot of a variety of animals, is a popular venue for weddings.

Edinburgh Day 4

EDINBURGH DUNGEON AND THE REAL MARY KING'S CLOSE

Forever embalmed in the past, a whole warren of streets on the slopes of Edinburgh's Royal Mile still exist, the upper stories of their houses decapitated in the 1750s, and the rest paved over to form the foundations of newer buildings. All but forgotten until the latter part of the 20th century, they harbour the ghosts of their former residents, and resound to the echo of past howls of deprivation. Wear stout shoes, and make the family hold hands: the Edinburgh Dungeon is a horror thrills attraction that squeezes the maximum fright fun out of this jagged rent in Edinburgh's ancient fabric. Live actors involve you in harsh courtroom dramas and the grisly punishments of bloodied victims. Melodrama of the highest order pulls you this way and that in the shadowed vaults. Witches, grave robbers, executioners and plague-burners torment your imagination, and interactive special effects raise hackles of terror and make the strongest heart beat faster. The thrills are all based on real people and events. Coming thick and fast, they make Edinburgh's seamy history into a very entertaining – sometimes even scary – theme ride.

Follow it up around the corner. An archway opposite the High Kirk of St Giles is the entrance to a much larger section of Edinburgh's undercroft. The Real Mary King's Close uses the same techniques to greater purpose. Guided by an actor who remains in period character, you share and sometimes participate in specific episodes relating to the streets and their history. In and out of real houses, 'untouched' since the 17th and 18th centuries, the tours weave a great deal of authenticity and emotional involvement into their prepared improvisations. Slower paced than the high jinks of the Dungeon, ultimately the Real Mary King's Close experience is more genuinely participatory, serious in its preparation, and so more fun and more rewarding. At its best, it's a thrilling revelation.

WHERE:
Edinburgh
BEST TIME TO GO:
Any time of year, any day except Christmas Day.
DON'T MISS:
Looking out of a real window in a real 17th century merchant's house, into a real street that happens to be 10 m (32 ft) under Edinburgh's 21st century traffic.
AMOUNT OF WALKING:
Lots, much of it over uneven ground (though for safety reasons, some original rough floors and flat ceilings have had to be covered). The nature of the Dungeon and Mary King Close, and restrictions on altering historic buildings, mean that wheelchair and pushchair access is not possible.
COST:
Expensive, by the end of the day.
YOU SHOULD KNOW:
What with grisly surprises, sudden shocks, screams, flashing lights and howls of pain, the day's attractions may not be for everybody. Children under 16 must be accompanied, and you should inform your guide if you suffer from epilepsy or asthma (the guide carries a walkie-talkie just in case).

Spooky and scary times in the Dungeon

Edinburgh Day 5

MUSEUM OF CHILDHOOD, HUNTLY HOUSE MUSEUM AND THE PEOPLE'S STORY

WHERE:
Edinburgh
BEST TIME TO GO:
Any time of year
DON'T MISS:
The collar and feeding bowl of 'Greyfriars Bobby', along with the original maquette for the bronze statue in Candlemaker Row, at the Museum of Edinburgh.
AMOUNT OF WALKING:
Surprisingly little. All three museums are close neighbours, and you'll only be wandering from room to room.
COST:
Low
YOU SHOULD KNOW:
At The People's Story, the outstanding collections of Trade Union banners and Friendly Society regalia look increasingly poignant, as the principles which brought their adherents together become increasingly unfashionable – but what goes around, comes around.

This is a leisurely day for a stroll along Edinburgh High Street and Canongate, picking out some of Scotland's more unusual collections. While you're fresh and full of energy, the Museum of Childhood at 42, High Street, is four floors of sheer delight for every age group. There are toys and games from all over the world in the shape of dolls, teddy bears, train sets (some dazzling in operation), pedal cars and tricycles. Watching new generations getting excited about them, it's hard to not be nostalgic, even about the antiques. In any case, the museum brings the past alive: you can watch Edinburgh children of the 1950s playing street games; hear 1930s children chanting their multiplication tables in class; and discover the different ways children used to be brought up, taught and dressed. With the video presentations and activity areas and games, the museum's reputation as 'the noisiest in town' is not a surprise.

At 142 Canongate, Huntly House (now the Museum of Edinburgh) is typical of 16th-century buildings in the street, with triple gables hanging over two lower stories. Appropriately for the variety of its aristocratic, merchant and latterly artisan residents, it specializes in collections relating to Edinburgh itself, including Edinburgh silver and glass, shop signs, pottery and long-case clocks. Its greatest treasure is the National Covenant for Scottish Presbyterianism, signed by its leadership in 1638.

Opposite, the late 16th-century Canongate Tolbooth at number 163 tells the People's Story in a different way. Oral reminiscence and written materials recount ordinary lives at work and play in Edinburgh during the last 300 years. The reconstructions use the realia of the mundane to bring to life the sights, sounds and even smells of the wash-house, pub, tea-room and 1940s kitchen, and the people who used them. It's vivid and often extremely moving. You'll want to linger.

The charming Museum of Childhood

Edinburgh Day 6

THE PALACE OF HOLYROODHOUSE

Holyrood Palace, as it's usually known, is the official residence in Scotland of HM the Queen, as it has been for Scottish monarchs since the 15th century. It stands at the east end of the Royal Mile, facing Edinburgh Castle, on the edge of Holyrood Park and against the dramatic backdrop of Arthur's Seat. Except when the Queen is in residence for State occasions (she uses Balmoral on private visits to the country), a remarkable number of the apartments and Rooms of State are open to visitors. Try to make it among your first ports of call in Edinburgh, because its history makes sense of everything else you will see.

The present Palace is built on the site of the 1128 monastery founded by David I, and the ruined Abbey still stands at one side. The original 14th-century guesthouse was incorporated into the north range of the elegant quadrangle added to it in 1501. It houses the Chapel Royal, Gallery, Royal Apartments and Great Hall – and you can hire an audio guide which points out how different monarchs imposed their changing tastes on the spectacular decorations and furnishings. The highlight of the older buildings is the apartments of Mary, Queen of Scots. Aside from the magnificent Tudor wooden ceilings and fabulous embroidered hangings, you can see the secret staircase linking Mary's bedroom with her husband's, Lord Darnley, and the northern turret room, Mary's intimate retreat, where David Rizzio was infamously murdered in her presence in 1565.

The stories associated with Holyrood are legion. Charles II remodeled it after Cromwell's depredations; Bonnie Prince Charlie held court there during the 1745 Jacobite Rising; and Louis XVI's brother the Comte d'Artois lived there following the French Revolution. Still very much in use, its glittering Royal history is alive and accessible. It is wonderful.

WHERE:
Edinburgh
BEST TIME TO GO:
Any time of year
DON'T MISS:
The Throne Room; and the Great Gallery, full of the portraits of Scotland's monarchs by Jacob de Wet – some of the earliest of whom he had to imagine!
AMOUNT OF WALKING:
Lots, but wheelchair access is excellent.
COST:
Reasonable
YOU SHOULD KNOW:
A new display opened in 2008 to show the history and significance of the Order of the Thistle – Scotland's equivalent of England's legendary Order of the Garter. It includes the dazzling insignia and mantle of the Order, which are worn by its members at the Thistle Ceremony held each July at Edinburgh's St Giles' Cathedral.

The Changing of the Guard at Holyrood Palace

The Museum of Flight and Myerton Motor Museum

WHERE:
East Lothian
BEST TIME TO GO:
Any time of year – but from November
to March, both museums are only
open at weekends. Check with both
museums before you go for the
special events (including fly-pasts,
backstage restoration projects, the
'radar room', and 'teddy-bears picnic')
that are held throughout the year.
DON'T MISS:
1. The Concorde Experience hangar,
where (for an extra, pre-booked
'Boarding Pass' fee) you can clamber
aboard the actual Concorde Alpha-
Alpha, even into the truly space-age
cockpit. 2. The BMW Bubble Car; the
extraordinary display of children's
pedal-powered and motorized cars.
AMOUNT OF WALKING:
Little. Both museums have good
wheelchair access.
COST:
Expensive, but worth it.
YOU SHOULD KNOW:
The Me 163B-1a Komet at the
Museum of Flight carries the serial
number and insignia in which it was
captured at Husum, Schleswig-
Holstein in 1945. This rocket/aircraft
shot down RAF Lancasters and USAF
B17s during the war.

*The famous Concorde
Experience hangar at the
Museum of Flight*

Where the Lammermuir Hills flatten out by the North Berwick foreland, Scotland hides some of the best of its 'boys' toys'. The Museum of Flight rivals far bigger aeronautical collections, not least because it is sited at East Fortune Airfield, an operational base since 1916 when its aircraft defended Edinburgh from Zeppelin attack, and – virtually unchanged since 1945 – now scheduled as an Ancient Monument. Even its civilian pedigree is longstanding: it was the 1919 launch site for the first east-west Atlantic crossing by an airship, R34. Like a Spitfire's glycol, it exudes authenticity. Now its four hangars and other buildings house some fifty complete aircraft, and numerous nose-cones, cockpit interiors and other parts, military and civilian. There are staggering rarities, like the Fieseler Fi 156 Storch; the only flying prototype of the 1935 Kay Gyroplane; and the plug-ugly pod of the world's first and only operational rocket-powered interceptor, the Messerschmitt Me 163 Komet of 1944. It's aviation paradise, its displays fashioned from intelligence, taste, and hard-won experience. Its intimacy brings aviation history very much alive.

Incredibly, a twenty-minute drive away at Aberlady, the Myreton Motor Museum achieves the same effect for similar reasons. It tells the story of motoring in a series of genuine workshops set up by the Museum's founder on his farm. His hobby evolved into the current collection of thirty cars and other vehicles, some on loan but all superbly maintained. The oldest car, an 1899 General Electric that really does look like a horseless carriage, was driven into the museum under its own power in 1994. The walls and spaces are crammed with 100 years' worth of motor advertising, road signs, petrol pumpheads, signposts and other automobilia. Fascinating for the young, perhaps nostalgic for others, Myreton is a model of quirky inspiration.

Inchcolm Island and Abbey

Hopetoun House and Inchcolm Island

Hopetoun House easily justifies its description as 'Scotland's finest stately home'. Built between 1699 and 1707 on the southern shore of the River Forth in wooded parkland, what you see is predominantly the later work of William Adam, who made a splendid house even grander around 1748, and whose sons John and Robert enlarged it still further and completed the interiors. Follow the tour. The succession of Drawing Rooms, Halls, Libraries, Bedchambers, Galleries and Staircases earn their capital letters as masterpieces of the Adam family's legendary talents. Everything is on an epic scale, almost to the point of superfluity. The vast Ballroom, for example, was conceived as yet another Library, designed for dancing, but used as an indoor riding school until later generations remembered it was there. The furnishings are equally spectacular, especially the tapestries and paintings; and the Adams' attention to detail extended below stairs (don't miss the Butler's Pantry) and to the Stable Block, where you can now have a much-needed cup of tea.

From Hopetoun, the road leads back to South Queensferry, in the shadow of the mighty Forth Bridges. Get there for the early afternoon to catch the ferry to Inchcolm, one of several islands in the Firth. The trip takes 3 hours, with 1.5 hours to wander Scotland's best-preserved group of monastic buildings. Originally a hermitage (its oldest relic is a 10th-century hogback tombstone), Inchcolm gained an Abbey after 1123, when Alexander I took refuge there. The 13th-century octagonal Chapter House is one of many rooms that survive, roofed; and three covered cloister walks indicate the community's former size and significance. With gannets, guillemots, shags, skuas, puffins and cormorants (perhaps even the rare roseate tern) wheeling about you, and seals, ducks and even dolphins cavorting in the water, Inchcolm is a memorable contrast to the magnificence of the morning.

WHERE:
West Lothian
BEST TIME TO GO:
March to September
DON'T MISS:
The Front Stairs at Hopetoun House – the staircase is contained within an octagonal structure set with beautiful and intricately designed decorative panels.
AMOUNT OF WALKING:
Lots – but Hopetoun has installed ramps and a lift to make sure there is as much wheelchair access as possible on the ground and first floors. Inchcolm is a little more difficult, but willing assistance is at hand.
COST:
Expensive, even with family tickets – but both places are the best of their ilk.
YOU SHOULD KNOW:
Given the amazing state of preservation of the Abbey, it should be no surprise to see the medieval inscription on its doorway: 'Stet domus haec donec fluctus formica marinos ebibat, et totum testudo permabet orbem' – meaning, 'May this house stand until an ant drains the flowing sea, and a tortoise walks around the whole world'.

343

Dalmeny House and the Queensferry Museum

Should you be in the area during July and August, make a special effort to visit Dalmeny House, set in broad, wooded acres to the east of the great Forth Bridges, it commands a huge panorama of the Firth. Dalmeny remains very much a private house (it belongs to the Earl of Rosebery), but it opens briefly in the summer. It looks much older than it is: its crenellations and highly ornamented chimneys, and the formalized grandeur of its principal elevations, remind you of the great 16th century English mansions like Hampton Court or Hatfield House. It was the first of the Tudor Gothic revivals, and it was designed by the same architect (William Wilkins) who afterwards built London's National Gallery and most of King's College, Cambridge. Inside, though the apartments are decorated in the then 'modern' Regency style, their size and relationships are consistent with the Gothic style. As you walk round, their arrangement makes sense of the various collections on display. These include a jaw-dropping assembly of French furniture in the Drawing Room, which came (by marriage) from the Rothschild's Mentmore Towers, and the most important collection of Napoleonic art and memorabilia outside France, in the Napoleon Room. Yet even though the splendid rooms are stripped down for corporate functions throughout the year, and summer visitors, the house still feels lived-in.

The Dalmeny Estate abuts Queensferry itself. It is a fascinating town in its own right, and its Museum, sited on the High Street between the Road and Rail Bridges, is a blast of fresh air in its approach to local history – which in Queensferry's case, is of national significance. It also has telescopes for studying the bridges, and the wildlife thronging the Firth.

WHERE:
Lothian
BEST TIME TO GO:
July and August (Sunday, Monday and Tuesday only). Throughout the year, there is provision for guided group tours, by prior arrangement with the Dalmeny Estate.
DON'T MISS:
Dalmeny's two-storey high Entrance Hall with a hammer-beam ceiling – directly comparable to that of King's College, Cambridge – and the Library (considered to be the birthplace of the Edinburgh Festival).
AMOUNT OF WALKING:
Moderate
COST:
Reasonable – and the Queensferry Museum is free.
YOU SHOULD KNOW:
On a Friday in early August, for nine hours, Queensferry is patrolled by the 'Burry Man'. His head-to-toe costume is entirely covered with the burrs of the burdock plant (see the life-size model in the museum), and he is garlanded with flowers. The annual ceremony has been taking place for so many centuries, its origins and meaning are actually lost; but being chased by the Burry Man (whose assistants feed him whisky through a straw) is a lot of fun.

Dalmeny House

The Scottish Parliament Building and Rosslyn Chapel

The realities of political devolution in Scotland found a novel solution in the siting and architecture of the country's new Parliament. Scotland has never had an assembly comparable to Westminster. It was important that the new building bridged the divide between Scotland's own Royal history and its independent democratic future within the constitutional monarchy. So placing it in the shadow of Holyroodhouse Palace, historically the home of Scottish monarchs, and now the Queen's official Scottish residence, was inspired. It's worth a close look just to see how its extraordinary modern fusion of glass, steel, oak and granite fulfils its essential functions, yet symbolizes Scotland in a dozen different ways. It's certainly extreme. Enormous fingers probe between existing buildings, challenging their historic elegance with frankly brutal modernity. But their form drew on Charles Rennie Mackintosh's flower paintings, and upturned boats on the seashore. The design claimed to be 'growing out of the land', and to blend with neighbouring Holyrood Park and Salisbury Crags. The excellent guided tour will at least give you the details of what the building is trying to do. Only you can decide if the mixture of shapes, materials, and decorative additions actually adds to the city called the 'Athens of the North' for its architectural beauties. You could even listen to a debate while you ponder.

When politics makes your head swim, take the bus to Roslin, just outside Edinburgh's centre. Since 1446, Rosslyn Chapel has resisted categorization, but its lavish and intricate stonework never fails to delight and amaze visitors. It's always had an aura of mystery, and tenuous links to Freemasonry and the Knights Templar (exploited in the book *The Da Vinci Code*) have multiplied the legends associated with it. Judge it on what you see: it will simultaneously excite your appreciation of beauty, and soothe your soul.

Rosslyn Chapel features in the bestselling novel The Da Vinci Code.

WHERE:
Edinburgh
BEST TIME TO GO:
Any time of year – but parliamentary business means that guided tours aren't always available on every day.
DON'T MISS:
The astonishing intricacies of the 'Apprentice Pillar', where the South Aisle meets the Lady Chapel at Rosslyn.
AMOUNT OF WALKING:
Moderate, and both the Parliament buildings and Rosslyn Chapel have good wheelchair access.
COST:
Low. In fact you can visit the Scottish Parliament at no cost whatever – you only pay for the professional guide, and s/he's worth it. At Rosslyn Chapel, under 18s don't pay.
YOU SHOULD KNOW:
Some buildings at the Scottish Parliament are externally covered with 'trigger panels', made out of wood or granite. Extremely controversial, they have been described as looking like anvils, hairdryers, question marks or guns. The architect hoped the panels' shape would evoke Henry Raeburn's painting of 'The Skating Minister', an icon of Scottish culture; but his widow said the design was simply a representation of a window curtain pulled back.

Glasgow Day 1

KELVINGROVE

WHERE:
West End, City of Glasgow
BEST TIME TO GO:
Any time
DON'T MISS:
Surrealist Salvador Dali's world-famous painting *Christ of St John of the Cross* – see it on the first floor of the West Gallery.
AMOUNT OF WALKING:
Lots (by the time you've seen everything).
COST:
Low
YOU SHOULD KNOW:
The Museum shows its imposing front elevation not to Argyle Street but Kelvingrove Park – it was in part built with profits from an 1888 international exhibition in the Park and symmetrically became the main focus of a repeat international exhibition there, held in 1901.

Before beginning an exploration of this great city's many and varied delights, take a trip on the Glasgow Underground. This circular rail service is nicknamed the Clockwork Orange after the colour of its schematic map and is a convenient link between the city centre and West End venues, also servicing several attractions south of the River Clyde. It was opened in 1896 but was modernized in the 1980s after a century of sterling service.

Get off at Kelvinhall to spend a delightful day with another old-timer that received a sensational facelift after a hundred years – the Kelvingrove Art Gallery and Museum. This magnificent red sandstone edifice reflects the city's enormous civic pride – and wealth – in the Victorian era, whilst its recent refurbishment reflects the city's recent (and continuing) regeneration as it reinvents itself for the 21st century.

Kelvingrove quickly displaced Edinburgh Castle in top spot as 'Scotland's most visited attraction' and once inside it's easy to understand why. There is one of the world's finest collections of arms and armour (including a rare Supermarine Spitfire fighter aircraft), a vast natural history collection and a world-class display of paintings by many schools, including Old Masters, Dutch Renaissance, French Impressionists, Glasgow School and Scottish Colourists (among others!). There are Discovery Centres where visitors (of all ages) can find out more about the collections, children are well catered for and there is a café and gift shop. Is one day enough? Decide for yourself!

But after enjoying the rather special Museum and Art Gallery experience, take a stroll in Kelvingrove Park and just look at the building – could there be a better statement of self-confident Victorian pride in the progress made in industry, science and art? And it confirms that self-confidence is swiftly returning to Glasgow after years of stagnation.

Kelvingrove Art Gallery and Museum

Glasgow Day 2

POLLOK COUNTRY PARK

When in Glasgow, there's no ignoring a star attraction that has been named 'Best Park in Britain'. That a wonderful open space so close to the city centre has survived unspoilt is miraculous, and explained by the fact that Pollok Country Park was preserved by the Maxwell family as part of their estates until they presented it to Glasgow in the 1960s. The River Cart flows through the Park and it is home to a drove of Highland Cattle – the closest many Scots ever get to their famous native breed!

The Maxwell's former home, Pollok House, is also open to the public. This splendid house was designed by renowned Scottish architect Robert Adam and built in 1752. It sits within delightful gardens, whilst the house itself contains the finest collection of Spanish paintings in Britain, plus antiques and a wonderful 'upstairs downstairs' contrast between lavish family rooms and servants' quarters.

But that's just the start of the day. Glasgow's role as a 19th-century industrial powerhouse made many men rich. One of the richest was shipping magnate Sir William Burrell, who donated his vast collection of antiquities and antiques to the city in 1944, specifying that it should be housed in a rural setting – a condition that could not be fulfilled until Pollok Country Park was acquired. The museum simply known as the Burrell Collection was built there and opened in 1983.

Burrell collected a diverse range of objects and this splendid L-shaped building contains a fabulous selection of artefacts from ancient China and Egypt, medieval weapons and art including stained glass and tapestries, Islamic art, impressionist paintings and modern sculpture. Romanesque doorways from the collection are built into the structure and there's a recreation of three important rooms from the Burrell family home, Hutton Castle.

WHERE:
Pollok, City of Glasgow
BEST TIME TO GO:
April to September
DON'T MISS:
The Spanish paintings at Pollok House – they are all exceptional, but one of the very best is El Greco's famous *Lady in a Fur Wrap*.
AMOUNT OF WALKING:
Moderate
COST:
Reasonable
YOU SHOULD KNOW:
In 1877 a ship belonging to the Burrell family fleet salvaged Cleopatra's Needle – the famous obelisk that stands on the Thames Embankment in London – after it was lost at sea in the Bay of Biscay.

Pollock House and gardens

British cars in the Museum of Transport

Glasgow Day 3

HAMPDEN PARK

In truth, this is something of a boys' day out – it's all top sport, trains and vintage cars. The top sport is soccer, beginning with a tour of the Scottish National Stadium at Hampden Park. Start in the underground walkway as players do on match days and proceed via the warm-up area (test the speed of your shot!) to the changing rooms. Walk down the players' tunnel and emerge to the famous Hampden roar (sadly a mere recording!), before climbing the steps to the presentation area and Royal Box.

That's just the start of the day's soccer 'fix'. Scotland was in the forefront of soccer's development, and the Scottish Football Museum at Hampden Park reflects that fact. There are over two thousand exhibits in one of the world's most impressive collections of football memorabilia, dating from the dawn of the organized game in the 1860s right through to the present day, including many souvenirs of epic matches against the Auld Enemy (that's England, in case you are unaware of the ancient rivalry).

After the soccerfest, catch the Glasgow Museum of Transport at Kelvin Hall – a favourite for generations of Scottish parents and their children. The Museum uses its extensive collection of vehicles and models to tell the tale of transport by land and sea – albeit with a slight Glasgow bias! All forms of transport are featured, including assorted horse-drawn vehicles, cycles, motorcycles and cars. The Clyde Room has 250 wonderful models of ships celebrating Glasgow's great shipbuilding heritage. Locomotive manufacture was also an important local industry and there is an impressive collection of steam engines. A popular feature consists of the trams, Underground station and Kelvin Street re-creation that captures the atmosphere of old Glasgow. It's a terrific half-day out...for boys and girls!

WHERE:
Southside (Hampden Park) and West End (Kelvin Hall), City of Glasgow.
BEST TIME TO GO:
Any time
DON'T MISS:
The world's oldest surviving pedal cycle in the Museum of Transport – based on the 1839 invention by Kirkpatrick MacMillan, a blacksmith who was fined five shillings for speeding when demonstrating his new-fangled invention in Glasgow.
AMOUNT OF WALKING:
Moderate
COST:
Reasonable
YOU SHOULD KNOW:
The first World Cup was won by Renton in 1888. Renton who? That would be Renton of Dumbartonshire (Scottish Cup Holders), who beat English FA Cup Winners West Bromwich Albion 4-1 in a match dubbed 'The Championship of the United Kingdom and the World'.
Oh happy days!

Glasgow Day 4

HERITAGE

Glasgow has many fine and interesting buildings, and three of the best will provide an interesting day out and real insight into the city's heritage.

Start with Glasgow Cathedral. The patron saint of Glasgow, St Mungo, built his church where the Cathedral stands today. Technically this is a Church of Scotland kirk but the grander term is appropriate – it is one of the few medieval churches in Scotland to have survived the Reformation unscathed and is a superb example of Gothic architecture. After inspecting the magnificent interior, make an atmospheric journey into the past by walking through the Glasgow Necropolis, on the hill above the Cathedral, full of impressive monuments to the dear departed.

The next stop should be Provand's Lordship in the Cathedral's shadow. This is one of few medieval structures remaining from Glasgow's distant past, built by Bishop Muirhead in 1471 as part of St Nicholas's Hospital (where Glasgow Royal Infirmary now stands). This house is furnished in period, thanks to a donation of early Scottish furniture by philanthropist Sir William Burrell, and a first-floor room contains a display about a 16th-century priest who lived in the house, Cuthbert Simson. Those with ecclesiastical interests can visit the adjacent St Mungo Museum of Religious Life and Art.

The day's final call should be to The Tenement House, to appreciate the way of life lived by ordinary people in Glasgow during the 19th and early 20th centuries, where most occupied tenements tailored to the appropriate social class. This preserved example in a typical city-centre sandstone tenement building was the home of Miss Agnes Toward, and it has hardly changed in over a century of occupation. Those interested in the life of ordinary Glaswegians should also visit the People's Palace and Winter Gardens in the East End, the city's museum of local history.

Glasgow Cathedral

WHERE:
Centre, City of Glasgow
BEST TIME TO GO:
Any time
DON'T MISS:
The 15th-century Quire Screen in the Cathedral, hiding Quire from Nave – it's the only one of its kind left in any non-monastic Scottish church that dates back to pre-Reformation times.
AMOUNT OF WALKING:
Moderate
COST:
Reasonable
YOU SHOULD KNOW:
The physic garden at Provand's Lordship contains herbs and medicinal plants that were used in the 15th century, thus reflecting the house's original purpose.

Glasgow Day 5

RIVER CLYDE

WHERE:
West Dunbartonshire (Clydebank), Renfrewshire (Braehead), City of Glasgow.

BEST TIME TO GO:
May to October

DON'T MISS:
Experiencing the reality of shipbuilding in the giant MV *Rangitane* stage set at Clydebuilt – see all the construction elements familiar to the 'black squads' of skilled workmen who made Clyde shipbuilding famous the world over.

AMOUNT OF WALKING:
Moderate

COST:
Reasonable

YOU SHOULD KNOW:
When the expensive and difficult Clyde Tunnel was finally completed in 1963-64, the reason that caused it to be built (that a bridge would prevent vital shipping movements) had been negated by the decline of Glasgow's port – and two bridges (Kingston and Erskine) opened a few years later.

Glasgow prospered through industry and commerce – benefiting from maritime trade and becoming the world's greatest shipbuilding centre. A river made it all possible and – whilst shipbuilding has long been blown away by winds of change from the East – the River Clyde provides fascinating contrasts between vanishing industrial heritage and the gleaming symbols of regeneration.

Spend a day exploring the Clyde's banks, starting with the Titan Crane at John Brown's former shipyard in Clydebank, now a visitor attraction offering great views from the top. Upstream on the south bank at Braehead is the Scottish Maritime Museum's Clydebuilt, bringing to life the interlinked story of Glasgow and the Clyde from 1700. There's so much to see at Clydebuilt that your day may end there, but it doesn't have to. Nearer the city centre is the Clyde Tunnel – cross to the north bank to find the Finnieston Crane, once used for lifting locomotives for export. It stands close to the handsome North Rotunda, entrance to the now-defunct Clyde Harbour Tunnel (its twin is on the opposite bank).

Another reminder of glories past is the tall ship in nearby Glasgow Harbour – *Glenlee* is a three-masted steel barque built here in 1896, rescued from Spain as a hulk and fully rebuilt – now a major tourist attraction. Close by is obvious evidence of the dramatic development of the modern riverside, with the extraordinary Scottish Exhibition and Conference Centre (built on reclaimed docklands) – nicknamed The Armadillo for reasons that will be obvious the moment you set eyes on it – that stages a concert of some sort practically every night. Right across the river is the equally impressive three-structure Glasgow Science Centre. Looking at these ultra-modern buildings, it's apparent that – not for the first time – the River Clyde is busy reinventing itself for the benefit of Glasgow.

The Scottish Exhibition and Conference Centre – nicknamed The Armadillo!

Glasgow
Day 6

CHARLES RENNIE MACKINTOSH TRAIL

No visit to Glasgow could be completed without admiring the works of local boy Charles Rennie Mackintosh, a designer in the Arts and Crafts movement and the main exponent of Art Nouveau in Britain. This great architect, designer and watercolourist had a relatively short career, but nonetheless greatly influenced European design.

The mahogany interior of the Glasgow School of Art

And Glasgow is the place to see why, with a ticket for the Charles Rennie Mackintosh Trail providing access both to prime examples of his work and the public transport that connects them. This allows you to see as many classic Mackintosh sites as can be crammed into a day, and mighty impressive they are.

Attractions on offer demonstrate the full range of a design virtuoso's talents. Most famous is the Glasgow School of Art building (often called the Mackintosh Building) – a masterpiece with breathtaking interiors. The Lighthouse is Scotland's centre for architecture and design and contains exhibitions, the Mackintosh Centre and a viewing platform with sensational city views. His Church at Queen's Cross is a treasure, with wonderful carvings and deceptively simple use of light and space. Nothing is more intimate than Mackintosh House where he lived with wife Margaret from 1906 to 1914, with interiors and furniture by the man himself.

The Scotland Street School Museum is in an impressive Mackintosh school. The façade of the Daily Record Building shows skilful use of colour. The Martyrs' School of 1897 is an early Mackintosh building. Ruchill Church Hall is a well planned though minor work. The House for an Art Lover was completed in 1996 to a Mackintosh design. The iconic Hill House is out of town at Helensburgh. But the day must surely end with a cup of tea in the exquisite Willow Tea Rooms, a re-created Mackintosh masterwork on Sauchiehall Street (or perhaps those in nearby Buchanan Street).

WHERE:
Around the City of Glasgow, Argyll and Bute (Hill House).
BEST TIME TO GO:
April to October
DON'T MISS:
The Glasgow Style Gallery at Kelvingrove Art Gallery and Museum for paintings, furniture and decorative objects that put the work of Mackintosh in the context of turn-of-the-century Glasgow.
AMOUNT OF WALKING:
Moderate
COST:
Reasonable
YOU SHOULD KNOW:
After moving to the Suffolk village of Walberswick, Mackintosh was arrested in 1915 as a spy – suspicious locals saw him walking the shore at night with a lantern (to signal German ships, obviously)...and the army unit that questioned him mistook his strong Glasgow accent for a German one, thus costing Mackintosh a week in jail.

Glasgow Science Centre

Glasgow
Day 7

GLASGOW SCIENCE CENTRE

Here's a challenge – try and do everything at the Glasgow Science Centre in a single day. It can't be done, but there's lots of fun to be had giving it a serious go. GSC is justifiably one of Scotland's most popular attractions. Located at Pacific Quay beside the River Clyde, this futuristic complex has three titanium-clad buildings. Within the Science Mall are more than 300 interactive exhibits, workshops, shows and laboratories. Then there's the sense-surround IMAX cinema and soaring Glasgow Tower.

Floor 1 of the Science Mall has loads of hands-on exhibits, including an illusions section and creepie-crawlies. It also houses a Climate Change Theatre, Science Show Theatre and Planetarium. Floor 2 bulges with more hands-on science stuff like face morphing, 3-D face modelling and thermal imaging. Science in the Dock allows the posting of views and images on the interactive voting wall and it's possible to decide which characters explore space in the Blast Off exhibit. Floor 3 has hair-raising exhibits like the Indoor Tornado, Bernoulli Blower and Whirlpool, plus the amazing Bubble Wall and giant Plasma Globe, where indoor lighting can be created.

The IMAX Cinema will be a revelation to those who have never experienced this extraordinary technology – and renewed delight for those who have. With a huge screen and digital sound system, dramatically increased image resolution seems to fill the vision and create a weird sense of being part of the action – some have even suffered from motion sickness during performances, which can be either 2-D or 3-D, the latter a piece of optical trickery that is entirely convincing. See and believe!

The revolving Glasgow Tower offers a short tour of its unique machinery, followed by a slow ride skywards to the cabin, with its unrivalled views over the city and surrounding countryside.

WHERE:
Centre, City of Glasgow
BEST TIME TO GO:
Any time
DON'T MISS:
Workshops in the stage area (Floor 2 of the Science Mall) that include practical activities like stilt walking, building hot air balloons or finding the culprit in DIY Detectives.
AMOUNT OF WALKING:
Moderate
COST:
Expensive (if you visit all three attractions).
YOU SHOULD KNOW:
The Glasgow Tower is closed in winter, and during adverse weather conditions (such as high winds) at other times of year.

Glasgow Day 8

XSCAPE

Does it ever rain in Glasgow? The answer seems obvious when you arrive at Xscape at Braehead, because this extraordinary 21st-century complex offers all the indoor entertainment anyone could want – including activities normally reserved for the great outdoors – beneath the protection of a very large roof. Find it near Junction 26 on the M6 motorway (plenty of parking or go by bus) – and prepare for an inside day out like no other!

The Soccer Circus offers testing fun on a fully automated football shooting range, culminating in an incredible final game. Those who prefer more relaxed action can play mini-golf at the Paradise Island Adventure Golf Course, putting through palm trees, huts and ancient ruins before tackling the demanding final hole (non-players in the family can watch from the Clubhouse Bar's balcony). There's 10-pin bowling, too.

Winter-sporters will be in heaven, because even in summer it snows on the 200-m (650-ft) SNO!zone slope every day, with skiing, snowboarding, tobogganing and a daring ice slide on offer to young and old. People with a head for heights will be pretty satisfied when they come across the Climbzone. It has various challenges, including one of Britain's largest freestanding climbing walls. With auto-belays, and routes to suit all standards, it is the vertical challenge par excellence. If rock climbing seems, well, a little boring there's always the Skypark – an aerial adventure course 15 m (50 ft) above ground – or freefall fan jumping. Then there's the Robocoaster, the UK's only robotic arm ride. All activities are fully supervised.

If none of that appeals (it will, it will!) there's always the last refuge of any rainy day – a state-of-the-art cinema. And of course there are numerous choices when it comes to lifestyle shops, food and drink. Just remember to take a spare credit card!

WHERE:
Renfrewshire
BEST TIME TO GO:
Any time
DON'T MISS:
If you haven't dropped after all that action, why not shop? The adjacent Braehead Shopping Centre and Retail Park has the small matter of 100+ major stores to choose from.
AMOUNT OF WALKING:
Moderate
COST:
Expensive
YOU SHOULD KNOW:
There's no charge for entry to Xscape, though there is obviously a fee for organized activities – but those who just want to look will find plenty of free entertainment, workshops and performances in the school holidays.

Climbzone at Xscape

New Lanark

Situated in lovely countryside where southern highlands meet Scotland's central belt, historic Lanark is a small country town that repays a stroll around its fine parks and buildings. But the jewel in its crown is the nearby mill complex, built from the end of the 18th century.

New Lanark was the visionary creation of entrepreneurs who appreciated that a wild and rugged gorge on the River Clyde was the ideal site for water-powered cotton mills, and they proceeded to build three, complete with a wide range of ancillary buildings needed to support both manufacturing and the workers who made it possible. The scale of their undertaking is breathtaking today, but must have seemed awesome at the end of the 1700s. What's more, owner Robert Owen was a social visionary – although the workers lived in conditions that seem impossibly primitive today, they were almost luxurious by contemporary standards. Childcare, schooling, healthcare and co-operative shopping were all ideas pioneered at New Lanark.

The mills continued to operate until the late 1960s, by which time many buildings on the site had become derelict. Demolition loomed, until intervention by the New Lanark Conservation Trust saw restoration work begin. This successful process was eventually rewarded with well-earned UNESCO World Heritage Site status.

Park at the edge of the village and walk down into another world, with not a telephone wire or TV aerial to be seen. You'll want to simply wander around for ages, taking it all in. But then it's time to go inside – find the main Visitor Centre, housed in New Lanark's 'Institute for the Formation of Character' (don't ask!) and buy a passport ticket that gives access to New Lanark's specific attractions: New Millennium Experience; Robert Owen's School; Robert Owen's House; Millworkers' House; Village Shop; working textile machinery; People and Cotton. Extraordinary!

Millworkers' House

Paisley

Though to all intents a suburb of Glasgow, Paisley retains (and takes pride in) a distinctive identity, though the town's best-known product – eponymous patterned cloth based on Indian designs – is better known throughout the world than the place from which it originated.

Paisley's eminence in the textile field predates the development of its famous cloth – the town boomed throughout the 1700s by producing fine lawn, muslin, silk gauze and (latterly) cotton. After 1800 a major thread industry developed with the Clarks, owners of the Anchor mill, battling for supremacy with chief rival Sir Peter Coats. As is often the case where commercial rivalry and textile wealth came together, the result can be magnificent buildings, and Paisley certainly has plenty of those. The Clarks funded that imposing Town Hall, and Sir Peter countered with the Museum and Library.

Thomas Coats Memorial Church

Though Paisley fell on hard times with the decline of traditional industries, the large selection of splendid Victorian buildings, pedestrianised town centre and old street network behind the main shopping areas cry out to be explored.

Then there's the Abbey – close to the Town Hall, it dates back to the 12th century. After falling (literally!) into decay in the 1500s after the tower collapsed, it was restored from the mid-1800s and both exterior and interior can only be described as magnificent. Other worthwhile churches include the Gothic Revival Thomas Coats Memorial Church, St Mirin's Cathedral and the Art Nouveau St Matthew's Church.

The rest of the day can easily be absorbed by the Museum and Art Gallery with its comprehensive range of exhibits and activities – including a definitive collection of Paisley shawls, fine pictures, contemporary craft pottery and a selection of child-orientated displays. But should an hour remain it could enjoyably be spent close by at the more-than-interesting Victorian Coats Observatory (thread money again!).

WHERE:
Renfrewshire
BEST TIME TO GO:
April to September
DON'T MISS:
The marble tomb of King Robert III (1337-1406) in Paisley Abbey, also commemorating many Royal Stewarts buried in the Abbey – it was donated by Queen Victoria after her visit in 1888.
AMOUNT OF WALKING:
Moderate
COST:
Low
YOU SHOULD KNOW:
The concrete Piazza Shopping Centre and Gilmour House which spans the River Cart are typical 1960s brutalist edifices that replaced the Victorian County Buildings, police station and town jail.

Calderglen and Craignethan Castle

WHERE:
South Lanarkshire
BEST TIME TO GO:
April to September
DON'T MISS:
A descent down the rustic trail path from Craignethan Castle into the deep glen of the Nethan Water (and the rather more energetic return climb).
AMOUNT OF WALKING:
Moderate (lots if you tramp the trails at Calderglen and Craignethan!).
COST:
Low
YOU SHOULD KNOW:
Craignethan's great tower was thought to be the inspiration for Tillietudlem Castle in Sir Walter Scott's novel *Old Mortality* – despite the eminent writer's denial, the Caledonian Railway Company named the nearest station Tillietudlem and a local hamlet also adopted the name.

Sally forth from Glasgow and be surprised at the beautiful open spaces that can be found close to the city. Refresh your lungs by visiting Calderglen Country Park in East Kilbride. It really does fulfill the classic boast of 'something for everyone', with a superb visitor centre, play area, children's zoo, ornamental garden, conservatory and extensive nature trails beside the river or through the woods. Don't spend more than a morning here, though, because something fascinating awaits.

Drive to Hamilton and take the A72 towards Lanark, turning right into the lanes at Crossford and following the brown signs to Craignethan Castle. It is located in splendid countryside and it hardly seems possible that such a peaceful spot is within hailing distance of Glasgow. Craignethan stands high above the River Nethan and was the last purpose-built fortress constructed in Scotland, employing the latest in early 16th-century military design to make it impregnable, even to attackers with new-fangled artillery.

Built around 1530, formidable defences were never tested, though Craignethan changed hands frequently as political winds shifted. Its demise came in 1579 when the then owners fled to France after championing the losing cause of Mary, Queen of Scots. The Castle was quickly 'slighted' – rendered defenceless by the demolition of its massive West Wall, once high enough to protect all the Castle buildings from cannon fire. Ironically, this ultimate fortress never saw any serious action, though it surrendered more than once.

The substantial remains are full of surprises and there's a lot to explore – domestic buildings around an outer courtyard, a deep ditch, tower house and further range of buildings. One unusual feature is a caponier at the bottom of the ditch, allowing well-protected defenders to fire on attackers attempting to cross. As ruined castles go, this really is a hidden gem!

Craignethan Castle

Hamilton

Hamilton, too, almost seems to have been sucked into Glasgow, but has a history and identity all its own. The Hamiltons were once Scotland's second family, after only the Royal Stewarts, and the bustling town that bears their name (they changed it from Cadzow in 1455) offers a rewarding day out.

Evidence of their heavyweight presence remains, the most obvious reminder being the Hamilton Mausoleum. Looking like a massive pepper-pot towering above the nearby motorway, it was constructed in the 1850s as an ambitious chapel of rest. The place has extraordinary acoustics, including the longest echo in the world (as demonstrated by slamming the entrance doors) and the ability of two people on opposite sides to hold an eerie whispered conversation whilst facing away from each other.

The adjacent Low Parks Museum offers a vivid celebration of local life, plus the Regimental Museum of the Cameronians (Scottish Rifles). The Hamilton connection persists – the Museum is in the family's former stables near the site of now-demolished Hamilton Palace, their grand residence, and Low Parks was its surrounding grounds.

The Palace was built on the site of an earlier castle in 1695 and revamped in the 1840s. It was said to be the western world's largest non-Royal residence but running costs became ruinous and the place was sadly demolished in 1921. How the mighty are fallen – municipal sports facilities, a health club and supermarket now occupy its former site.

Complete the day by visiting Chatelherault Park with its charming Adam hunting lodge, completed in 1734 – with a hunting lodge this big, the Palace must indeed have been vast. There's an interesting interior and informative visitor centre at the back but the real joy of Chatelherault (another Hamilton title!) lies in exploring the dramatic Avon gorge with its impressive bridge and woodland walks.

WHERE:
South Lanarkshire
BEST TIME TO GO:
April to September
DON'T MISS:
A rare breed indeed – the herd of long-horned white Cadzow cattle that live in fields overlooked by Chatelherault Hunting Lodge.
AMOUNT OF WALKING:
Lots
COST:
Low
YOU SHOULD KNOW:
After all that it's worth mentioning that the Hamiltons no longer live in Hamilton – the 14th Duke decamped to Lennoxlove near Edinburgh in 1946, taking what remained of the fabulous Hamilton Palace collection of furniture and paintings with him.

Chatelherault Hunting Lodge and formal garden

Ferry from Largs to the Isle of Great Cumbrae

WHERE:
Ayrshire
BEST TIME TO GO:
May to September, on a sunny day.
DON'T MISS:
The Wedge: a private house in Millport that boasts the smallest frontage in the UK.
AMOUNT OF WALKING:
As little or as much as you choose.
COST:
Reasonable
YOU SHOULD KNOW:
In 1263, the people of Largs defeated a Viking force of 160 longships after they were caught in a storm. A Viking Festival is held here each September in commemoration.

Take the ferry from Largs across the Firth of Clyde to Great Cumbrae for a splendid day out. The crossing, taking ten minutes, is especially beautiful on a fine day, providing views of both the mainland and the island across the placid waters.

The ferry is always met by a bus, which takes you to Millport, Great Cumbrae's main settlement, and the best starting point for exploring the island. En route you'll see two of Millport's famous rocks: Lion Rock, which certainly lives up to its name, and Queen Victoria Rock, which is more difficult to spot. Once in town, you can rent bikes if you like, but as the island is just 6 km (4 mi) long and 3 km (2 mi) wide, you can see much of it on foot.

Millport, a rather old-fashioned town, has been a Clyde coast favourite for decades. Pleasures to be enjoyed include a safe beach and crazy golf for children, and an 18-hole golf course for adults. Here too is the National Watersports Centre, where lessons can be taken in kayaking, power-boating, dinghy sailing and windsurfing. Don't forget to take a look at what is probably Europe's smallest cathedral. Designed by William Butterfield in Gothic Revival style and set amongst gardens and woodland, it opened in 1851.

Walk to the island's highest point for panoramic views towards Ben Lomond in the north, Bute, Arran and the Kintyre peninsula to the west, and south to Paddy's Milestone, the halfway mark to Northern Ireland, and beyond. Nature lovers will find a large and diverse seabird population here as well as occasional sightings of both Sea and Golden eagles, while marine life includes seals, dolphins and Basking sharks. Before you leave Millport, visit the 1960s style Ritz Café for a homemade ice cream.

The ferry leaving Largs.

Kelburn Castle and Country Centre, Largs

If you fancy a day out from Glasgow with the family, Kelburn Castle and Country Centre might be your ideal getaway. Situated about 51 km (32 mi) west of the city, Kelburn Castle with its spectacular view across the island-dotted Firth of Clyde, stands in magnificent grounds.

This is the home of the Earl of Glasgow, Patrick Boyle, and having been in the family for over 850 years, it's probably the oldest Scottish castle to have been continuously inhabited by the same family. The original 'de Boyvilles' arrived with William the Conqueror in 1066, and settled in Kelburn in 1140. Since that time, the building has seen many additions – a Mansion House was added in 1700 and a Victorian wing, complete with original William Morris wallpapers, was built in 1879.

The Castle itself is often open for afternoon tours, well worth joining as not only will you see the different decorative styles within, but also enjoy the intimate atmosphere of a place that is lived in. However, for many visitors it is the Country Centre and the grounds that prove irresistible, including as they do a dramatically romantic glen, through which trails lead up to wonderful viewpoints, past deep gorges and tumbling waterfalls.

The gardens here are famous: the walled garden encloses two 1,000-year-old yews and a Weeping Larch that have been designated as some of Scotland's most important heritage trees by the Forestry Commission. There's a wonderful 'Secret Forest' to discover. Overhead walkways and trails lead through a dense wood that is full of fantasy features, such as a Ginger Bread House, a Crocodile Swamp and even a Pagoda, which you can climb. For the young there is an excellent Adventure Course, indoor and outdoor play areas, activities that vary day by day, and a Falconry Centre.

The drawing room at Kelburn Castle

WHERE:
Ayrshire
BEST TIME TO GO:
July, August and the first week of September if you'd like a guided tour of the Castle. The Country Centre is open from Easter to October.
DON'T MISS:
The Robert Adam designed memorial to the 3rd Earl, and the renowned sundial, built by the 1st Earl in 1707.
AMOUNT OF WALKING:
Moderate
COST:
Reasonable, although there is an extra charge for the indoor play area.
YOU SHOULD KNOW:
Kelburn Castle is available for all sorts of functions, both private, such as weddings, and corporate. If you wish to visit the Castle, check in advance that the tours are not all fully booked up.

Oban Day 1 FERRY TO MULL & IONA

WHERE:
Argyll & Inner Hebrides
BEST TIME TO GO:
April to October
DON'T MISS:
Relig Odhrain and St Oran's Chapel, on your right as you approach Iona Abbey. It's the oldest religious building on Iona, and stands in a pre-medieval graveyard full of the graves of Scottish and Norwegian Kings. Many of the exquisitely wrought stone Celtic crosses broken during the Reformation are on display in the Infirmary Museum behind Iona Abbey.

Duart Castle on Mull

Stay on deck for the 45-minute ferry crossing from Oban to Mull. Behind you, the natural amphitheatre of its setting shows Oban at its best; ahead lie markers of 1,500 years of Scottish history, and some of its most historic and beautiful marine landscapes. Guarding what was once a vital marine crossroads, 13th-century Duart Castle still stands in implacable magnificence on a sheer rocky promontory. Framed by Atlantic skies and the purple, green-gold and misty blue hills of Mull, it's one of the most haunting and evocative images in all Scotland. The ferryport is 3.5 km (2 mi) north, at Craignure. Turn right, and follow the narrow Sound of Mull to Tobermory at the island's northern tip. Children recognize the 'prettiest village in the Hebrides' as TV's 'Balamory' – and identifying some of the Balamory locations is one of the 22 challenges posed by 'The Quest', a children's adventure created by the people of Mull. The Quest encourages children to identify wildlife, find historic curiosities, and discover Gaelic culture, wherever they go on Mull and Iona; and they can participate from a car, bus, bicycle or out walking.

You're sure to see plenty of wildlife between Craignure and Fionnphort. The rugged beauty of the hills shelters red deer, golden eagles and otters. The 61-km (38-mi) drive to the Iona ferry runs in part along the sea loch. There, or elsewhere on Mull's 480-km (300-mi) coastline of 300-m (1,000-ft) sea cliffs and pristine white sand coves, you regularly see whales, dolphins, basking sharks, seals, puffins and sea-eagles.

Just 10 minutes from Fionnphort, Iona's timeless tranquility will make your day. Sea, sky and land combine in elemental harmony; and you realize that the ancient Abbey, surrounded by generations of Scottish kings at peace, houses the soul of Celtic culture.

AMOUNT OF WALKING:
Moderate
COST:
Low. Some of the children's challenges on the Quest involve a small charge – like the Isle of Mull railway from Craignure to Torosay Castle and Gardens, or the entrance fee to Duart Castle.
YOU SHOULD KNOW:
Duart Castle's grandeur includes its own ferry service direct from/to Oban.

Oban Day 2

SEA LIFE SANCTUARY AND THE HOLLOW MOUNTAIN

WHERE:
Argyll & South Highlands
BEST TIME TO GO:
Mid-April to early November
DON'T MISS:
1.The 'Loch Creran Experience' – a touch-pool, where you stand in the middle of a shoaling ring while salmon, rays, or any of the many species found in the loch's margins swim round you, dizzyingly face-to-face.
2. The Visitor Centre at the outflow to Loch Awe – it explains the genius of the system.
AMOUNT OF WALKING:
Moderate (lots, only if you go for the Loch Creran nature trails).
COST:
Reasonable to expensive
YOU SHOULD KNOW:
Very few Scottish people realize that without Cruachan's capacity to generate a huge amount of power in a few seconds – and keep it coming for 22 hours – the unprecedented surge of demand on the grid would have meant that hardly anyone in England would have been able to watch the 1966 Football World Cup Final all the way through extra time.

North of Oban, a 20-minute drive takes you to one of the South Highlands' loveliest sea-lochs. Protected from Atlantic weather by Loch Linnhe and by the Isle of Lismore across its mouth, Loch Creran is the perfect, remote site for the Scottish Sea Life Sanctuary. Here you can wander in the spruce forests along the shore, where special observation areas enable you to watch native species like the European otter diving and swimming in the wild. There are over thirty marine habitats to discover and learn about, with feeding displays and demonstrations by staff generously willing to spend time with entranced children. One multi-dimensional sea aquarium shows you how creatures like starfish, shrimps and stingrays interact in their own environment. But the sanctuary's most fascinating 'open-door' feature is its SOS seal rescue facility. Every year, it receives large numbers of stray, sickly or injured seal pups – and you're encouraged to watch every stage of their recovery and growth. If you're really lucky, you might see some of them being released back to the wild.

After a morning at the Sanctuary, it's a short detour along the A85 to the dark, steep confines of the Pass of Brander (where Robert the Bruce crushed Edward II's allies in 1309). It opens onto the north end of Loch Awe, and the staggeringly beautiful view of Kilchurn Castle reflected in the water. Above you is the 'hollow mountain', 1,126m (3,694 ft) Ben Cruachan, highest of the Cruachan Horseshoe surrounding a reservoir enclosed by a dam. This water is pumped up from Loch Awe. When there's a sudden demand for power on the national grid, its release crashes 1,000 m (3,280 ft) down into turbines housed deep inside the mountain, generating full output from standby in two minutes flat. You can tour the dark tunnels of this witchy, engineering masterpiece.

The seal rescue facility, Loch Creran

The Orkneys

The charming port of Stromness on West Mainland and the island of Hoy in the background

This group of islands off Scotland's northeastern tip offers a 'ferry' special day out. The shortest route (60 minutes) to the Orkneys is from Gill's Bay west of John o'Groats. By taking the morning ferry and returning on the evening boat, it's possible to spend eight hours driving around these beguiling islands. The route from Scrabster, near Thurso, is more scenic but longer (90 minutes), allowing under six hours in Orkney. The recommended option is to book a different carrier each way.

Take the outbound Scrabster ferry, which gives a great view of a famous waterside stack known as the Old Man of Hoy before arrival at the charming port of Stromness on West Mainland. You'll be spoilt for choice, even though the day out will take in only five of seventy islands. Mainland alone could occupy a week, with wonderful hill scenery, spectacular cliffs and secluded sandy bays. And there is much evidence of human activity from time immemorial, including notable prehistoric tombs, remains of ancient houses, stone circles, standing stones, old churches, mills and farm museums. A good road network circles the coast of West Mainland and criss-crosses the interior.

After finally arriving at Kirkwall (itself well worth exploring), check out the smaller East Mainland. There may be time to seek out its many attractions, but if not head south across the Churchill Barriers (built in World War II to protect the British Navy in Scapa Flow) connecting the southern islands of Lamb Holm, Glimps Holm, Burray and South Ronaldsay. Each has points of interest and the return ferry to Gill's Bay runs from picturesque St Margaret's Hope at the top of South Ronaldsay. It will mark the end of a long but rewarding day.

WHERE:
Orkney
BEST TIME TO GO:
April to October (a visit in spring or autumn can be relatively tourist free and the driest months are April, May and June).
DON'T MISS:
St Magnus Cathedral in Kirkwall, begun in 1137 by Earl Rognvald – a striking reminder of Orkney's Norse heritage.
AMOUNT OF WALKING:
Moderate
COST:
Expensive
YOU SHOULD KNOW:
For those who do not wish to take the car there is a short passenger ferry crossing from John o'Groats to Burwick on South Ronaldsay in summer, with various guided tours of Orkney offered as part of the package.

Dunvegan Castle

Isle of Skye

'Speed bonnie boat like a bird on the wing...over the sea to Skye' – the haunting Skye Boat Song tells of Bonnie Prince Charlie's escape after his defeat at Culloden in 1746, serving as a reminder that the Highlands are steeped in history, much of it bloody. It is still possible to take a boat from Mallaig or Galltair to Skye, but, since 1995, most people use the short but controversial road bridge over Lochalsh (an expensive toll was resisted by locals, who succeeded in getting it abolished).

The largest and most northerly of the Inner Hebrides – unlike many other Scottish islands – is thriving, with an increasing population and strong tourist industry based on superb landscapes, abundant wildlife, fascinating heritage and vibrant local culture (with Gaelic widely spoken).

Whilst enjoying the sheer pleasure of driving through some of Scotland's finest scenery, that bloody heritage cannot be escaped – numerous castles, often ruined, testify to bitter clan battles that once raged. None of these magnificent strongholds is more impressive than Dunvegan Castle, seat for nearly 800 years of the MacLeod of MacLeod, chief of Clan MacLeod. This romantic waterside castle with formal gardens should not be missed.

There's another tradition that has definite appeal – the creation of fine Scotch whisky at the traditional waterside Talisker Distillery in the village of Carbost. Notable for its peaty taste, Talisker specializes in single malt whiskies matured for long periods (up to thirty years). The result isn't cheap, but standard and connoisseurs' distillery tours are quite reasonable.

If neither of these highlights is to your taste, Skye offers plenty of alternatives. Indeed, many visitors happily spend a week or more on this delightful island, so anyone coming for but a single day has far too many choices to make!

WHERE:
Highland (formerly Inverness-shire).
BEST TIME TO GO:
May to September
DON'T MISS:
Portree – the island's capital and largest settlement, with its famously picturesque harbour plus the Skye Heritage Centre and associated Aros Experience that bring the island's history and character to life.
AMOUNT OF WALKING:
Moderate
COST:
Reasonable
YOU SHOULD KNOW:
Flora MacDonald, famous for assisting Bonnie Prince Charlie's escape to Skye, was actually from South Uist – but she is forever associated with Skye and her grave may be seen on the island at Kilmuir in Trotternish.

Caithness

This distinctive area has wilderness charm, and a day exploring the unique delights of Caithness will be well spent. Unlike most of the Highlands, Scotland's northeastern tip is flat country, with numerous rivers, burns and lochs. Recent conifer plantings have changed the face of a previously treeless landscape, but it remains a place of dramatic coastal scenery with numerous seabird colonies, blanket bog, rolling moors, farmland and scattered settlements – all combining to create a very distinctive atmosphere.

Perhaps this is coloured by ample reminders of those who went before. There are rich remains of prehistoric occupation and many ruined castles with origins in the Norse era. There are few enough roads, though a coast road links Latheron in the south via Wick to Thurso, from where it's a straight inland run back to Latheron. That said, some of the lonely side roads that serve the empty interior should definitely be explored.

Along the way, an essential landmark is John o'Groats at the 'top of the country' (an honour actually held by nearby Dunnet Head, a short but worthwhile diversion from the main road). Close to John o'Groats is another highlight – the 16th-century Castle of Mey. Rescued from dereliction by Queen Elizabeth the Queen Mother in the 1950s it became her much-loved holiday home and she created a wonderful garden there.

This imposing castle stands on rising ground above the shores of the Pentland Firth, with views to Orkney. In 1996 the Queen Mother gifted the castle to a trust charged with the preservation of Scottish heritage in the form of buildings and animals (notably Aberdeen Angus cattle and Cheviot sheep). The Castle of Mey regularly wins awards as a top-quality visitor attraction with the castle, gardens, animal centre, gift shop and tearoom contributing to a memorable visit.

WHERE:
Highland (Caithness).
BEST TIME TO GO:
May to September (to visit the Castle of Mey).
DON'T MISS:
The Neolithic Grey Cairns of Camster, along a minor road to the southwest of Wick – notably the Long Cairn and Round Cairn with their atmospheric interior chambers.
AMOUNT OF WALKING:
Moderate
COST:
Reasonable
YOU SHOULD KNOW:
The Castle of Mey is closed for ten days at the end of July and beginning of August for an annual visit by the Duke and Duchess of Rothesay (HRH Prince Charles and the Duchess of Cornwall if you prefer to be formal).

Sitting on the cliffs of Dunnet Head above Pentland Firth.

Ben Nevis towers over Loch Linnhe at Lochaber.

Fort William

WHERE:
Highland (formerly Inverness-shire).
BEST TIME TO GO:
May to October
DON'T MISS:
Be sure to snatch a quick visit to 13th-century Inverlochy Castle just outside town en route to the Nevis Range gondola – it's a classic ruined castle.
AMOUNT OF WALKING:
Moderate
COST:
Reasonable
YOU SHOULD KNOW:
Should it rain (it sometimes does in Scotland!), Fort William has two leisure centres – the Lochaber (swimming pool with water slides, sauna, solarium and bouldering climbing wall) and the Nevis (children's play area, tenpin bowling, games hall).

When Inverness attained city status, the West Coast's Fort William became the largest town in the Highlands. It lies at the foot of the Great Glen on the shores of Loch Linnhe, Scotland's longest sea loch. It is the commercial centre of Lochaber, an area renowned for natural beauty and historical importance. As Fort William has a strategic location on the Road to the Isles and the Great Glen Way, in close proximity to popular destinations such as Ben Nevis, Glen Coe and Glenfinnan, it has become a popular tourist base – but before sallying forth to explore enjoy a day in and around the town.

Fort William has a pedestrianized High Street and there are pleasing squares to explore – all against the magnificent backdrop of Ben Nevis. A visit to the small but quirky West Highland Museum in a former bank building will reveal a wonderful collection of pictures, photographs, archives and artefacts that throw light on Lochaber life since prehistoric times.

After that, a visit to the Ben Nevis Distillery at Lochy Bridge is bound to raise the spirits – it's one of the oldest licensed distilleries in Scotland and offers a Visitor Centre where the legendary giant Hector McDram lurks, plus a distillery tour and complementary tasting. Then it's time for some very fresh air, with a ride up nearby Aonach Mor on the Nevis Range gondola – find it 11 km (7 mi) out of Fort William on the Inverness Road. In winter the gondolas carry skiers, in summer mountain-bikers or para-gliders – and also those who merely want to enjoy a scenic fifteen-minute ride that delivers sensational views of the Great Glen, Ben Nevis and the Inner Hebrides followed by a bracing walk. It's an awe-inspiring way to end a busy but rewarding day.

Glenfinnan and Loch Shiel

Those who pass through Glenfinnan Station on the West Highland Line without disembarking miss a trick – it's well worth taking an extra day out to explore Glenfinnan, which is rich in history. For here Charles Edward Stuart – Bonnie Prince Charlie – began the Jacobite Rebellion destined to end in disaster at the Battle of Culloden. Then, as he fled vengeful Hannoverian troops, the Prince boarded a French frigate and left his beloved Scotland for ever from Loch nan Uamh, just west of Glenfinnan, at the very point where he had arrived with such high hopes eight months earlier.

Reminders of those turbulent times remain – there is a tower at the head of Loch Shiel surmounted by a kilted highlander, built in 1815 to commemorate the raising of Bonnie Prince Charlie's standard. Owned by the National Trust for Scotland, it has a visitor centre that includes a 'Glenfinnan and the '45' exhibition, shop and café. A pleasant walk leads to the Prince's Cairn on the shore of Loch nan Uamh, the Bonnie One's ignominious departure point.

But Glenfinnan has more than Jacobite memories to offer. This beautiful little village lies within a stunning valley that has Loch Shiel at its centre. Its isolation was first broken with the arrival of Thomas Telford's Fort William to Arisaig road in 1812, compounded in the early 1900s by construction of the West Highland Railway. Construction of the latter included the amazing 21-arch Glenfinnan Viaduct, which famously features in the much-loved 'flying car' sequence in *Harry Potter and the Chamber of Secrets*. There is also a charming restored station complete with museum and a wonderful church in a spectacular location. After seeing the sights and strolling around the village and its environs, a cruise on Loch Shiel can provide a perfect end to the day.

WHERE:
Highland (formerly Inverness-shire).
BEST TIME TO GO:
May to October
DON'T MISS:
A meal in the Glenfinnan Dining Car – a restored 1950s carriage that offers refreshments, lunches, cream teas and dinner, with breathtaking views of Loch Shiel and the mountains (open June to early October, booking for dinner essential).
AMOUNT OF WALKING:
Moderate
COST:
Reasonable
YOU SHOULD KNOW:
The traditional burial island of Eilean Fhionnain in Loch Shiel has a wonderful Celtic cross, many old funerary monuments and the ruined St Finan's Chapel – also historic associations with St Columba.

The Glenfinnan Monument

Caledonian Canal Scenic Drive

WHERE:
Highland (formerly Inverness-shire).
BEST TIME TO GO:
April to October
DON'T MISS:
The substantial remains of one of three forts built in 1718 to subdue the Highlands after the Jacobite Rising of 1715 – see it in the grounds of the Lovat Arms Hotel at Fort Augustus.
AMOUNT OF WALKING:
Moderate
COST:
Low
YOU SHOULD KNOW:
Ruined Invergarry Castle on the shores of Loch Oich – once a stronghold of Clan Donald – was sacked by 'Butcher' Cumberland after the Battle of Culloden because Bonnie Prince Charlie rested there. A MacDonald descendent who lived nearby strenuously opposed the construction of the Caledonian Canal.

The Caledonian Canal was a heroic failure. Built by Thomas Telford in the early 1800s, it connects the West and East Coasts, following the 100-km (62-mi) Great Glen. The Canal was not required to cover the full distance, as two-thirds of the length is made up of Lochs Lochy, Oich, Ness and Dochfour. Even so, it was twenty years in the making and soon had to be deepened, though the arrival of the railway ensured that it was never a commercial success.

It was still a masterpiece of canal engineering with four aqueducts, ten bridges and twenty-nine locks. Leave Fort William on the A830, immediately arriving at Banavie to view one of the Canal's most spectacular features – the eight-lock Neptune's Staircase. Continue to Corpach Sea Lock to see the Canal's beginning, noting two locks and two swing bridges on the way, before retracing your steps and turning left onto the B8004 to follow the Canal to Gairlochy.

Cross the Canal and turn left onto the A82, following Lochs Lochy and Oich – meeting the Canal at various points as you go – up to Fort Augustus, where there is a dramatic flight of five locks. Beside them is the Caledonian Canal Heritage Centre, telling the story of the history and current operation of this fascinating waterway. The strategic importance of Great Glen was recognized by three forts – Fort William, Fort Augustus and Fort George near Inverness, built to control those troublesome Highlanders who defied the all-conquering Hanoverians. The original Fort Augustus became an Abbey that closed in the 1990s.

From Fort Augustus take the scenic drive to Invermoriston alongside Loch Ness, turn left onto the A887 along Glenmoriston, and left again onto the A87 to follow the shores of Lochs Loyne and Garry to Invergarry, where the A82 will return you to Fort William.

The famous eight-lock Neptune's Staircase at Banavie

Fort George and Cawdor Castle

Cawdor Castle and gardens

Stand by to be wowed by two of Britain's best-preserved monuments to military ambition, situated close together some 18 km (11 mi) northeast of Inverness.

Built at Ardersier on a spit jutting into the Moray Firth, the massive Fort George complex was constructed after the 1745 Jacobite Rising as the 'final solution' to the threat posed by Highlanders in general and Jacobites in particular. Ironically, the danger had passed by the time Fort George was completed, perhaps explaining why this extraordinary fortification has remained largely unaltered.

The Visitor Centre and shop are in the outlying guardhouse and the main entrance is reached via a raised walkway with drawbridge. Once inside, range after range of beautiful stone buildings stretch away, surrounded by wide grass-topped walls that contain casemates (bunkers) capable of protecting the garrison from artillery attack.

The facilities of a small town are here so there's plenty to see: barracks, officers' quarters, bake-house, brew-house, chapel, provisions and munitions stores – plus great views from the battlements. There are reconstructions of early life at Fort George, the Seafield Collection of Arms and the Regimental Museum of the Queen's Own Highlanders. Indeed, the problem is leaving before the entire day evaporates.

That would be unfortunate, because Cawdor Castle – with a keep built in 1454 that is a superb example of medieval defensive architecture – is a 'must see'. If Central Casting sent for the perfect Scottish castle they would be ecstatic when Cawdor turned up – it really is that impressive (the Shakespeare connection via Macbeth is a bonus!). Still privately occupied, the Castle tour is fascinating and this magnificent building is set amidst stunning gardens, and there's also the ancient Big Wood to see. A word of warning – don't start the day here, or there won't be time left to see Fort George!

WHERE:
Highland (formerly Nairn).
BEST TIME TO GO:
May to September (when Cawdor Castle is open).
DON'T MISS:
The Grand Magazine at Fort George – fitted out as it would have been in the 1700s, it now serves as a stage for actors who re-create stories about soldiers of the period.
AMOUNT OF WALKING:
Moderate
COST:
Reasonable
YOU SHOULD KNOW:
Cawdor Castle was built around a holly tree, the remains of which can still be seen in the vaulted cellar of the keep – and there are resident ghosts (a mysterious lady in a blue velvet dress and John Campbell, the first Lord Cawdor).

Jacobite Steam Train

Crossing the Glenfinnan Viaduct near Fort William.

Those who appreciate dramatic Highland scenery will love the final 65-km (42-mi) section of the West Highland Line (WHL) from Fort William to Mallaig, romantically titled Rathad Iarainn nan Eilean in the Gaelic – the Iron Road to the Isles. This is surely one of the great scenic railway journeys, starting near Britain's highest mountain (Ben Nevis), crossing Britain's longest inland waterway (Caledonian Canal plus lochs), visiting Britain's most westerly mainland station (Arisaig), passing Britain's deepest freshwater loch (Loch Morar), Britain's shortest river (River Morar) and Europe's deepest sea loch (Loch Nevis) before arriving at the fishing port of Mallaig.

Although it's possible to take one of the scheduled trains that leave Fort William every couple of hours, a truly rewarding day out awaits those taking a trip from Fort William to Mallaig and back on The Jacobite. There's undoubtedly something magical about combining the romance of steam with timeless Highland scenery, and this special heritage steam train service runs on weekdays between late spring and early autumn, with added weekend services in July and August. It leaves Fort William at 10.20 and reaches Mallaig at 12.25, departing on the return journey at 14.10 to arrive at Fort William at 16.00.

The trip along the single track passes through the pretty little stations of Banavie, Corpach, Loch Eil Outward Bound, Locheilside, Glenfinnan, Lochailort, Beasdale, Arisaig and Morar before arriving at Mallaig. The Jacobite makes a twenty-minute stop at Glenfinnan to justify its name – for here the second Jacobite Rebellion began in 1745. Legs can be stretched and a quick turn taken around the interesting Station Museum before re-boarding the train for the onward journey to Mallaig. There's time to explore this charming town with its bustling harbour, busy with fishing boats and ferries to the Small Isles and Skye.

Loch Ness

WEST SHORE

WHERE:
Highland (formerly Inverness-shire).
BEST TIME TO GO:
April to October
DON'T MISS:
The five 'staircase' locks on the impressive Caledonian Canal at Fort Augustus.
AMOUNT OF WALKING:
Moderate
COST:
Reasonable
YOU SHOULD KNOW:
Loch Ness contains more fresh water than all the lakes in England and Wales combined.

Beware monsters (not!). Well, maybe you'll be the first to get a pin-sharp picture of Nessie, the mythical Loch Ness Monster that has been hunted for many a long year. Even if that memorable feat eludes you, exploration of this magnificent loch's West Shore will provide a delightful day out.

The A82 hugs the shore, giving views across water to the hills beyond. Loch Ness stretches for 37 km (23 mi) to the southwest of Inverness, making it Scotland's second largest (after Loch Lomond). From Inverness, the first stop after Lochend is Drumnadrochit, with good facilities and various 'Nessie' displays (no, they haven't actually found the beast either).

The 'daddy' of them all is the Loch Ness Exhibition Centre. Making use of lasers, digital projection and special effects, this modern facility takes visitors through themed areas, progressing from the dawn of time to the present. Needless to say, the Loch Ness Monster takes the limelight, with a voluminous record of sightings real, imagined or downright hoaxes plus serious analysis of the ecology of this unique Scottish loch. Might Nessie really exist? After a couple of hours you can decide for yourself.

Then something that indubitably does exist awaits you nearby. Urquhart Castle is the ultimate romantic ruin. Abandoned in the 1690s, it stands in a dramatic location on a headland overlooking Loch Ness. There's a new visitor centre with shop, café, audio-visual displays and a superb model of the castle in days gone by. But it's the ruin and view that count – most Nessie sightings have been from hereabouts, but even without mysterious ripples it's a view to die for.

Complete the day by driving down through Fort Augustus and taking the scenic loop from Invergarry back to the shores of Loch Ness at Invermoriston, before returning to Inverness.

The ultimate romantic ruin – Urquhart Castle

Loch Ness Scenic Drive

Breathtaking scenery surrounds Loch Ness.

The West Shore of Loch Ness with its busy main road and top attractions is one of Scotland's most popular destinations, but the East Shore is a relatively well-kept secret. A leisurely day's drive will take you through breathtaking scenery, allowing time to stop and explore as the fancy dictates.

Leave Inverness on the A9 and head south to Tomatin. If it's not too early for a very wee dram, you can drop by the Tomatin Whisky Distillery Visitor Centre and gift shop – if you're tempted to linger there will be a distillery tour at 11.00. There endeth formal tourist activities! Leave Tomatin on the minor road across Findhorn Bridge to Dalmigavie, taking the first right turn (just before Dalmigavie Lodge) and wind through the hills until reaching the B851. Turn left and go on to East Croachy, where a right turn will take you to the RSPB's Loch Ruthven Bird Sanctuary.

Continue along the road between Lochs Ruthven and Duntelchaig, before turning left onto the B862 and drive through Torness to Errogie at the head of Loch Mhor. Follow the lochside and go through Glebe Village, before almost doubling back at the B852 and driving to the substantial settlement of Foyers. Once the site of a major aluminium plant powered by a hydroelectric plant, this now merely generates electricity for the National Grid.

Park outside the Post Office and take the steep but well-maintained path down forested slopes to a viewing area overlooking the Falls of Foyers, where the river makes a heart-stopping plunge into a gorge leading to Loch Ness. From Foyers, the B852 runs along the shore of Loch Ness, giving a great view of Urquhart Castle on the opposite shore. From Dores the B862 will return you to Inverness alongside the Caledonian Canal.

WHERE:
Highland (formerly Inverness-shire).
BEST TIME TO GO:
April to October
DON'T MISS:
The splendid Findhorn Viaduct at Tomatin, an impressive curved structure just to the east of the village that carries the Perth-Inverness railway line high above the valley of the River Findhorn.
AMOUNT OF WALKING:
Moderate
COST:
Low
YOU SHOULD KNOW:
The B852 alongside Loch Ness follows the road built by General George Wade in the aftermath of the 1715 Jacobite Rebellion – it was aimed at suppressing Highland resistance, but ironically Wade's roads proved to be of more value to Jacobite rebels than the Government in the Jacobite Rising of 1745.

Inverness Castle overlooks the River Ness.

Inverness and Culloden Moor

The capital of the Highlands is on the Moray Firth. Its location at the head of the Great Glen and status as a transport hub makes Inverness an excellent base for wider exploration. But this lively city full of leisure opportunities, good shops, pubs, restaurants and late-night venues deserves a day of anyone's time.

There's plenty to see, though few ancient buildings remain – Inverness has a violent past, with Clan Donald frequently torching the town. Inverness Castle in its commanding location overlooking the River Ness is a 19th-century building on the site of an earlier castle. It serves as the Sheriff Court but is also the setting for the Castle Garrison Encounter, a costume re-enactment of an 18th-century soldier's life. A piper plays on Castle Hill every evening from 19.00 to 19.30 (June to September).

A 'must' is the Inverness Museum and Art Gallery. Its collection focuses on geology, wildlife, history, craftwork and fine art, with everything having a Highland connection. It also stages exhibitions with a wider remit. Another essential experience is the Holm Woollen Mill. James Pringle Weavers have combined a working factory with their 'Story of Tartan' Exhibition – and a more-than-tempting mill shop.

Any Inverness day must include a visit to nearby Culloden – site of the last battle fought on British soil. It became a place of Victorian pilgrimage and there is a memorial cairn, simple stones marking mass clan graves, the desolate Field of the English, the Well of the Dead and one of the battle's few survivors – Old Leanach Cottage with its heather-thatched roof. There's also a spanking new Visitor Centre that tells the whole Culloden story in an innovative and interactive way. The old one was actually on the battlefield site, which the National Trust for Scotland is restoring to its original state.

Culbin Forest

After the heritage feast of Fort George and Cawdor Castle, a very different experience awaits nearby – a walk on the wild side (of Moray Firth, that is). Coastal Culbin is a fabulous 14-km (9-mi) stretch of shore consisting of sand dunes that once moved inexorably, engulfing everything in their path. They were eventually stabilised by tree planting, a process completed in the 1960s.

From Inverness, take scenic minor roads (B9006 and B9091) to the resort of Nairn. The ancient fishing port and market town is still evident around Thomas Telford's harbour, whilst genteel Victorian villas occupy the West End. Continue along the A96 to the main entrance to Culbin Forest at Wellhill, near Forres. Park and explore along an excellent network of paths and tracks (cycling permitted). The Forest and its ever-changing coastline offer an almost limitless variety of natural wonders to be discovered.

A good circular walk is the Hill 99 Viewpoint Trail, which should take two or three hours. It winds through the forest to Gravel Pit Ponds, an ideal spot to picnic or bird-watch. From there the route takes in forest tracks, shingle ridges and lichen beds before ascending Hill 99 – Culbin's highest dune at a mighty 30 m (99 ft). A viewpoint above the tree canopy provides squirrel's-eye views of Culbin and gives an idea of how extensive this natural wonderland actually is. Descending through Hill 99's mossy glades, the Trail passes an attractive woodland pool known as Dragonfly Pond, before returning to the start point.

After all that exercise there's an optional helping of heritage – a visit to Spynie Palace between Lossiemouth and Elgin could round off the day nicely. Home of the Bishops of Moray from the 14th century, it is dominated by a massive tower with great views over Loch Spynie.

WHERE:
Highland (formerly Nairn and Moray).
BEST TIME TO GO:
April to October (though the forest is open all year).
DON'T MISS:
Findhorn Bay – you may see seals or ospreys fishing in the river mouth . . . but if not it's a delightful spot for a picnic with a wonderful view across to the village of Findhorn.
AMOUNT OF WALKING:
Lots
COST:
Low
YOU SHOULD KNOW:
Culbin Forest sits atop dunes that cover former fields and old croft houses – finally swallowed by sand in 1694 after the last of a series of great storms that finally drove out the residents for good.

Walking the sand dunes at Findhorn.

Glencoe

For a date with one of Highland history's most notorious occurrences – and some splendid scenery – drive south from Fort William along Loch Linnhe, against the backdrop of Ben Nevis and the Grampians. At North Ballachulish, turn left onto the B863 and drive beside Loch Leven to Kinlochleven. Stop awhile, taking in a Visitor Centre that reveals the village's unusual history before strolling to the impressive Grey Mare's Tail waterfall. Then continue along the south shore of Loch Leven until you reach the village at the foot of Glencoe – and that date with history.

In 1692 the authorities ordered a massacre of the MacDonalds of Glencoe, who had been a few days late in swearing allegiance to newly enthroned King William. Worse still, the killers of thirty-eight people were welcome guests of the clan and forty women and children died of exposure after their homes were burned. This infamous act has never been forgotten and it's easy to imagine that ghosts of the slain still haunt the forbidding heights above Glencoe.

Nowadays Glencoe is not the lonely place it was then. The A82 road runs through it and many visitors are drawn to one of Scotland's most striking glens to walk, climb or simply admire. But for all its austere beauty Glencoe has a melancholy air, engendered by wild and precipitous mountains that enclose it on all sides. It runs up to desolate Rannoch Moor and narrows halfway at the Pass of Glencoe, where there is a spectacular waterfall – park, view and take a scenic wander. After reaching the Moor and enjoying a drink at the isolated 17th-century Kings House Hotel, return to the Visitor Centre east of Glencoe village, where informative state-of-the-art displays put the landscape, wildlife and history of this atmospheric place into context.

The Pass of Glencoe

Cairngorms Railway Day

A railway day in the Cairngorms? It sounds unlikely, but that's just what awaits when you arrive at Aviemore Station for a journey on the Strathspey Steam Railway from Aviemore to Broomhill and back, with a five-minute stop at Boat-of-Garten beside the River Spey en route. This delightful outing combines the nostalgia of steam travel with some wonderful scenery.

After a morning journey back in time a thoroughly modern experience awaits, though it's one that highlights an eternal dilemma – people are drawn to wild places by unspoilt natural beauty, but the facilities created to serve their needs impact on the very thing that attracted visitors in the first place.

However tourism is a vital part of the Highland economy, and a chairlift to take skiers (winter) and sightseers (summer) up the northern flank of Cairngorm was built in 1961. By the 21st century this was outdated, being replaced by the 2-km (1.25-mi) funicular Cairngorm Mountain Railway that climbs to Ptarmigan Station 150 m (490 ft) below the summit (the top section runs within a concealing tunnel). So drive from Aviemore along the dead-end road to the Cairngorm Ski Area and decide for yourself if the railway has a negative impact.

Even if it does, there's no denying that the experience is amazing. In winter the trains hurry up in five minutes, packed with skiers who can't wait to speed back down, but the summer approach is different. A slow ride allows maximum viewing from panoramic windows, and Ptarmigan offers a complete visitor experience with a superb viewing area, an impressive Mountain Exhibition, restaurant and shop. As an eco-compromise, access to the fragile Cairngorm plateau is not allowed, but those who fancy a mountain stroll can take a way-marked walk from the car park at base station.

WHERE:
Highland (formerly Inverness-shire).
BEST TIME TO GO:
April to October (limited Strathspey Railway service in April, May and October).
DON'T MISS:
Check out the Rothiemurchus Visitor Centre on the way back to Aviemore from the CairnGorm Mountain Railway – it'll tell you all about the open-air options that might be tomorrow's day out!
AMOUNT OF WALKING:
Moderate
COST:
Reasonable
YOU SHOULD KNOW:
Broomhill Station may seem familiar as it became Glenbogle Station for the popular BBC TV series 'Monarch of the Glen' – Glenbogle House was actually nearby Ardverike House on the shores of Loch Laggan, one of Scotland's finest private houses, whilst Laggan doubled as Glenbogle village.

The Funicular railway

Highland Wildlife Park

Just to the west of the mighty Cairngorms, within the National Park of the same name, is the Highland Wildlife Park near Kingussie. This safari park and zoo is run by the Royal Zoological Society of Scotland and certainly makes for a great day out from a base in Aviemore or one of the nearby villages.

Until recently the Wildlife Park offered the chance to see Scottish birds and animals in a wonderful natural setting (there is a splendid enclosure with raised boardwalk for the wolf

A majestic Red deer stag looks over his domain.

pack), but the remit has been expanded to include international animals of mountains and tundra that are endangered, fulfilling the modern requirement that such establishments should have an active programme contributing to the conservation of rare animals.

A drive through the various enclosures and habitats of the Main Reserve offers the opportunity to see herds of reindeer, red deer, European bison, yaks, Tibetan wild ass...plus one of the world's rarest animals, the Przewalski horse. A number of trails can then be explored on foot, revealing further favourites at every turn – beavers, wolves, red squirrels, otters, pine martens, wildcats, snow monkeys, lynx, red pandas and even Amur tigers. Feeding talks take place in the walking area twice daily, and knowledgeable keepers are always on hand to answer questions.

The drive towards more exotic animals aimed at increasing visitor appeal and fulfilling conservation objectives is likely to see a further reduction in the presentation of native species – a fact that is not to everyone's liking, especially locals who argue that animals like Highland cattle, Soay sheep, red foxes, badgers and polecats may not be endangered but are very much part of the Highland scene, though visitors may find it hard to actually see them in the wild.

WHERE:
Highland (formerly Inverness-shire).
BEST TIME TO GO:
April to October (though the Wildlife Park is open all year).
DON'T MISS:
A quick visit to the Highland Folk Museum's living history site at nearby Newtonmore brings the domestic and working conditions of earlier Highland dwellers to life.
AMOUNT OF WALKING:
Moderate
COST:
Reasonable
YOU SHOULD KNOW:
Informative guided tours of the Highland Wildlife Park offer terrific insight into the wildlife and Scottish natural history, but advance booking is required.

Aberdeen

Depending on the weather, Aberdeen is the austere 'Granite City' (raining) or the sparkling 'Silver City with the Golden Beaches' (sunny). It stands on a sandy coastline and is largely built of granite shot through with mica that glitters in the sun. A third alternative always applies – 'The Oil Capital of Europe'. Aberdeen's economy was transformed by North Sea Oil, with 'black gold' replacing declining industries like fishing and shipbuilding. It might even acquire a fourth nickname as 'The Floral City', having won the Britain in Bloom contest a record number of times.

This plethora of names reflects the city's many faces. Aberdeen received Royal Burgh status from Robert the Bruce in 1319 and has been important ever since. It's easy to while away a day wandering round this lively port city, appreciating splendid early 19th-century buildings (don't miss St Andrew's Cathedral, the Town and Country Bank, the Music Hall, Trinity Hall and the Town House) and many fine gardens and parks. But that would be to miss highlights that should make any 'must see' list.

Old Aberdeen – a separate burgh until 1891 – is north of the city centre. It is rich in historic buildings, including St Machar's Cathedral, King's College Chapel and the Brig o' Balgownie, possibly Scotland's oldest bridge. The University occupies much of Old Aberdeen, a reminder of Aberdeen's long tradition of educational excellence. Another great tradition is represented by the Maritime Museum at Shiprow, which is also the location of the splendid Provost Ross House of 1593. The Aberdeen Art Gallery has excellent pictures, silver and glass whilst the University's Marischal Museum focuses on fine arts and archaeology. Indeed, the problem in Aberdeen is not what to do, but fitting a fraction of what's on offer into a single day.

WHERE:
City of Aberdeen (formerly Aberdeenshire).
BEST TIME TO GO:
April to October
DON'T MISS:
Footdee – the delightful area known locally as 'The Fittie', a picturesque former fishing village at the north end of the harbour.
AMOUNT OF WALKING:
Moderate
COST:
Low
YOU SHOULD KNOW:
The imposing Marischal College on Broad Street (opened by King Edward VII in 1906) is the world's second-largest granite building (Madrid's Escorial being the biggest) – after years of neglect, it is being redeveloped as the new HQ of Aberdeen City Council.

Aberdeen is Scotland's third largest city.

The Queen's home in Scotland

Balmoral Castle

WHERE:
Aberdeenshire
BEST TIME TO GO:
April to July (Balmoral's opening months).
DON'T MISS:
The largest room in Balmoral Castle – the great ballroom, the only part of the building itself that is open to the public.
AMOUNT OF WALKING:
Moderate
COST:
Reasonable
YOU SHOULD KNOW:
Queen Victoria's beloved Highland retainer John Brown is buried in Crathie churchyard.

Amidst the magnificent scenery of Royal Deeside in the shadow of towering Lochnagar is the Balmoral Estate. One of the most beautiful estates in Scotland, it was acquired by Queen Victoria in 1848 and described by the diminutive monarch as 'my dear paradise in the Highlands'. The Scottish home of the Royal Family stands at the heart of a vast area that has been carefully tended to preserve its architecture, scenery and wildlife for successive generations of locals and visitors to enjoy.

It is possible to make a summer visit to Balmoral Castle, where at least two hours are needed to explore the grounds, formal gardens, vegetable garden, gift shop and coffee shop. Interesting exhibitions are mounted each year to round out the experience. But don't expect to run into the Royal Family, as Balmoral is closed prior to their annual arrival in August.

When the Family is in residence, the traditional method of Royal-watching is to be outside Crathie Kirk when Balmoral's residents walk to the Sunday service. The church was built in the late 19th century with Queen Victoria laying the foundation stone (she also donated two stained glass windows). There are various items of Royal memorabilia within the church, where the south transept is reserved for Royal use. The church is well worth a visit, and also offers a grand viewpoint overlooking the River Dee.

The wee town of Crathie also merits exploration. And there another sort of spiritual experience may be found – a tour of the Royal Lochnagar Distillery, sole producer of exclusive Deeside single malt whisky, on the south side of the River Dee close to Balmoral Castle. A one-hour tour shows how this traditional elixir is produced – and it ends with a bracing dram of Royal Lochnagar Single Malt.

Banchory and Crathes Castle

Drive west from Aberdeen and find Banchory, the 'Gateway to Royal Deeside'. This fine town is surrounded by gentle rural countryside and beautiful hills, and its attractions can easily cause you to linger for a pleasant day before proceeding to the delights of Deeside.

Banchory is an excellent base for visiting surrounding areas, but is interesting in its own right. One essential sight is the Falls of Feugh – stand on the footbridge in season (spring and summer) and watch determined salmon battling white water. The Banchory Museum concentrates on local celebrity J Scott Skinner, the great Scottish dancing master, violinist and fiddler. And it's a crime to explore Banchory without visiting the famous landmark of Scolty Tower, 3 km (2 mi) from town. Walk from Banchory, or drive to the car park in Scolty Woodland Park and go from there. Views from the top of the 19th-century tower are far-reaching.

Tired? The day isn't over by a long way. Drive back towards Aberdeen, shortly approaching the village of Crathes. Don't turn into the Castle (yet!) – instead park in the Milton Arts & Crafts Village opposite. After checking out the shops, art gallery and restaurant, see if the adjacent Visitor Centre of the Royal Deeside Railway is open. Located in two vintage carriages, it explains how local enthusiasts are trying to bring a section of this scenic line back to life.

After that it is time to visit the splendid 16th-century Crathes Castle across the road. Allow plenty of time. Not only does the Castle have interesting interiors, including Jacobean painted ceilings, but there is also a vast walled garden – divided into sections by ancient topiary hedges, it has fabulous herbaceous borders separated by gravel paths. There is also an informative visitor centre and teashop.

Crathes Castle

WHERE:
Aberdeenshire
BEST TIME TO GO:
April to October
DON'T MISS:
Drum Castle on the way back to Aberdeen, one of the oldest tower houses in Scotland (and the least altered) – it's a terrific sight, even if you don't have time to look round. If you do, it's open during the summer months.
AMOUNT OF WALKING:
Lots
COST:
Reasonable
YOU SHOULD KNOW:
Crathes Castle was the ancestral home of the Burnetts of Leys, and the jeweled Horn of Leys displayed over the fireplace in the Great Hall is said to have been a gift from Robert the Bruce to a Burnett ancestor in 1323, though some doubt the claim.

Braemar

WHERE:
Aberdeenshire
BEST TIME TO GO:
The first Saturday in September, for
the annual Highland Games – or at
any time between April and October
for a quieter visit.
DON'T MISS:
The abundant wildlife – red deer, roe
deer, red squirrels, hares, golden
eagles, buzzards, game birds . . .
there's always something to see.
AMOUNT OF WALKING:
Lots
COST:
Low
YOU SHOULD KNOW:
Robert Louis Stevenson began
writing his much-loved classic
Treasure Island whilst on holiday in
Braemar – there is a display of
material about the author in an
upper hallway of Braemar Castle.

Nothing could be more 'Highland' in character than the highest parish in Britain, surrounded by mountains and glens. If the attractive village of Braemar's status were doubted, that is swiftly dispelled by the fact that it holds the most prestigious Highland Games in Scotland – often known simply as 'The Games', The Braemar Gathering is attended by members of the Royal Family who travel from nearby Balmoral.

The Highland Heritage Centre is the place to start. There is an audio-visual presentation on the history, geography and ecology of the area, together with an exhibition focusing on The Games and Royal patronage plus a specialist clan and tartan shop. The parish church – one of four in Braemar – is right by the Heritage Centre and this bustling village has a good variety of shops.

Just outside the village stands Braemar Castle, a fine tower house now run as a visitor attraction by the local community. There's no missing Braemar Castle, but remnants of an earlier, more important castle may be found on the east bank of Clunie Water. Kindrochit Castle was built by King Malcolm III in the 11th century, but is now no more than grassy mounds and truncated stonewalls near the main car park.

The village is well worth exploring, and the easy climb from the village centre to the summit of the rounded hill of Morrone adds a rewarding excursion. The lower slopes are covered with a unique survivor, the Morrone Birkwood – Britain's only sub-alpine birch-juniper wood. The view from the summit is extensive, and the day can be rounded off nicely (after refreshments in the village) with another splendid walk. Drive along the unclassified road west from Braemar to the Linn of Dee – a delightful feature where the River Dee rushes through a narrow gorge.

A highland dancing competition at the annual Braemar Gathering

Pennan and Aberdour Bay

West of Fraserburgh on the Moray Firth lie villages that are picture-postcard perfect when the sun shines, but the most inhospitable of places when an arctic gale blows. Since visitors rarely arrive in winter, the happy face is the one they see. One such place sprang to fame by appearing in the film *Local Hero*, with a quayside red telephone box featuring prominently. Pennan lies down a hazardous hill just off the coast road, a single row of white cottages squeezing into the space between cliff and sea.

Delightful though a stroll through this pretty hamlet may be, it hardly makes for a full day out. But there's plenty of interest nearby. A footpath leads to Aberdour Church – one of the oldest in Scotland, founded by St Columba and St Drostan (St Drostan's Well marks the point where he landed in Aberdour Bay). Bold explorers can find the remains of Dundarg Castle on a clifftop. For those who prefer organized attractions, Northfield Farm Museum near New Aberdour should be just the ticket.

Cullykhan Bay to the west of Pennan is a popular sandy beach. On a promontory above is Fort Fiddes, a Bronze Age site offering superb views over the Lion's Head cliff face and the gash of Hell's Lum, that leads to a sea tunnel through solid rock – a path from Cullykhan leads to Hell's Lum. Overlooking the Bay is Troop Head, reached on foot, with panoramic coastal views and a vast seabird colony. Beyond Troop Head are two more delightful fishing villages – Crovie and Gardenstown, connected by a footpath beneath the cliffs. The Tore of Troop is a wooded ravine that runs inland – a haven for wildlife with wild paths to explore.

Not enough to fill a day? You'll never get it all done!

WHERE:
Aberdeenshire
BEST TIME TO GO:
April to September
DON'T MISS:
The Jane Whyte memorial fixed to the ruins of an old woollen mill in Aberdour Bay – during a great storm in 1883, she struggled through raging seas to carry a line to the grounded steamer *William Hope*, thus saving the lives of fifteen sailors.
AMOUNT OF WALKING:
Lots
COST:
Low
YOU SHOULD KNOW:
The famous red telephone box in Pennan was actually a film prop created for *Local Hero*, but a real one was subsequently installed by popular demand and it swiftly became a listed structure that cannot be removed.

The delightful fishing village of Crovie

Castle Fraser at Kintore

Around Inverurie

WHERE:
Aberdeenshire
BEST TIME TO GO:
April to September
DON'T MISS:
The atmospheric ruins of medieval Kinkell Church, close to the east bank of the River Don just south of Inverurie – there is some superb early stone carving somewhat at odds with the huge paper-mill across the river!
AMOUNT OF WALKING:
Moderate
COST:
Reasonable
YOU SHOULD KNOW:
The splendid Castle Fraser is open daily in July and August (Friday to Tuesday only in April, May, June and September).

The inland town of Inverurie has played its part in history, with three major battles fought locally: the first in 1308 during the Wars of Scottish Independence; the second a bloody land dispute in 1411; the third during the Jacobite Rising of 1745.

Today's thriving market town is worth visiting, and makes an ideal base from which to explore the historic surroundings. Start at the beginning by heading west from Inverurie, following signs for Easter Aquhorthies Stone Circle. This is a fine example of the many 4,000-year-old stone circles that survive in Aberdeenshire. Another find is the Brandsbutt Pictish Stone – signs at the north end of Inverurie unexpectedly lead through a housing estate to the mysteriously inscribed stone.

On the south side, a cemetery beside the B993 is adjacent to a line of Pictish stones. Here it's possible also to move forward in time, with the two great mounds known as the Bass of Inverurie forming the site of a 12th-century motte and bailey castle. There is a cairn commemorating the battle of 1745. The next battlefield to explore is Harlaw, fought northwest of Inverurie and marked by a splendid stone monument. This is also close to the site of the first battle, fought at nearby Hill of Barra.

But by far the most impressive tribute to Aberdeenshire's violent past may be found at Castle Fraser – one of the very best tower houses in Scotland, that has evolved from a 15th-century tower that remains at the heart of the Castle, extended during succeeding centuries whilst entirely retaining its dramatic character. Allow at least half a day – there is a fabulous tour of the building, a superb walled garden, the usual shop and tearoom...and hundreds of acres of surrounding estate to explore.

Portsoy, Sandend and Fordyce

The north coast of Aberdeenshire is an engaging area that offers splendid coastal scenery combined with beguiling towns and villages – and unspoilt Portsoy is one of the most interesting places there. Situated midway between Cullen and Banff, Portsoy was established as a burgh in 1550 by charter signed by Mary, Queen of Scots. The Old Harbour was built in 1692 and – surrounded by many fine buildings dating to the early 18th century – is largely unchanged to this day. The New Harbour was constructed in 1825, farther round the bay, to serve prosperous Portsoy's booming trade and the herring fleet. Although both trade and fishing declined through the 20th century, this delightful town has a most attractive centre with quaint streets winding down towards that splendid Old Harbour.

The next stop should be a visit to the characterful village of Sandend. Appropriately titled (it is built on sandy land around the Scattery burn and has a fabulous beach), this is one of the smallest but most attractive fishing villages along this coast, huddling around a sturdy harbour built in the early 1800s.

But there's more to this part of the world than picturesque coastal towns. Just inland from Portsoy and Sandend is one of the most magical villages in Scotland – Fordyce. This ancient place has a warren of narrow medieval streets, with Fordyce Castle making a magnificent centerpiece that sits comfortably cheek-by-jowl with the village's stone houses. Fordyce Old Church dates back to the 13th century on the site of an earlier church established by the Pictish St Tarquin and – together with its kirkyard – is a fascinating place. Today Fordyce – once a roistering market village renowned for its Fairs – is a tranquil backwater with colossal charm. A visit is the perfect way to end a satisfyingly inexpensive day.

WHERE:
Aberdeenshire (formerly Banffshire).
BEST TIME TO GO:
April to September
DON'T MISS:
The romantic ruins of Findlater Castle on a cliff overlooking the Moray Firth near Sandend – the first castle was built in the 1200s, though that which remains today dates from a 14th-century rebuilding (don't miss the 16th-century dovecote near the parking area).
AMOUNT OF WALKING:
Lots
COST:
Low
YOU SHOULD KNOW:
Ruined Boyne Castle just to the east of Portsoy was home to the Lairds of Boyne who created the Old Harbour and profited by its success – until they supported the Jacobite cause in the mid-1700s (foolishly as it turned out), losing their estates as a result.

The charming village of Fordyce

Stonehaven

South of Aberdeen is Stonehaven, a town with distinctive character and charm, despite an influx of oil-industry activity. It lies behind crescent-shaped Stonehaven Bay and over the ages has prospered as a result of having the only harbour along this coast that offered safe haven in a northeasterly gale.

Approach from the south and stop before descending into Stonehaven for an excellent overview of the harbour and adjacent town. Continue on and park in the Market Square on Allerdyce Street, the main thoroughfare, overlooked by imposing Market Buildings with their slender spire. The harbour and old town behind it are full of interest and character, encouraging exploration.

The morning can be rounded off with a trip to the RSPB's Fowlsheugh Nature Reserve, where high cliffs support prolific seabird nesting colonies. Keen walkers will reach there by using a public clifftop trail, whilst the less energetic can go by boat from Stonehaven harbour.

The afternoon must be taken up with a visit to the extraordinary Dunnottar Castle, back along the road to the south. Scotland's most impregnable fortress sits on a flat-topped rock surrounded by the sea (it was once connected to the mainland by a narrow spur, but this was carved away to increase defensive capability). The only remaining ways in were through the strongly defended main gate or via a steep cliff path from a cave and rocky creek.

Although a fortified site from time immemorial, the extensive remains of Dunnottar date from the 1300s to the mid-1600s. It was the last place in Britain to hold out for Charles I against Cromwell's forces, and when the final surrender came after an eight-month siege the Parliamentary forces were disappointed to discover that the King's papers and Scottish Crown Jewels had been spirited away (they were hidden in nearby Kinneff Church until the Restoration).

Dunnottar Castle

Around Tomintoul

Corgarff Castle

The highest Highland village is Tomintoul, on the northern slopes of the Cairngorms. It was built by the Duke of Gordon in the aftermath of the 1745 Jacobite Rising to re-house displaced tenants and to help control endemic cattle rustling and whisky smuggling. Today, the old Duke would still recognize his handsome stone-built village with its wide main street and spacious central square.

Illegal distilling may have been controlled, but the legal version thrived then as now. There are many distilleries in the Tomintoul area, and the famous Glenlivet Distillery north of the village offers an interesting tour (with the modest cost redeemable against a purchase!).

Farther up the B9008 is Ballindalloch Castle, known as 'the Pearl of the North'. The Macpherson-Grants have resided here since 1546, and their renowned home is one of Scotland's most beautiful castles. The tour includes rooms packed with family memorabilia and there is a fine collection of Spanish paintings. Outside are magnificent grounds set between the Rivers Spey and Avon, and the estate has a famous herd of Aberdeen Angus cattle.

For those with a great taste for Scotch whisky, a short run along the A95 in the direction of Aberlour will take you to the long-established Glenfarclas Distillery – bought by the Grants in 1805 for £511 and still run by the family today.

If you haven't had enough of castles, retrace your steps to Tomintoul and drive south to Cock Bridge. There stands Corgarff Castle in a wild and lonely spot at the head of Strathdon. Finished in striking white harling (rendering, using small stone chips), this 16th-century castle was converted to a Government barracks in the aftermath of the 1745 Rising as part of the attempt to pacify the Highlands, and has been restored to represent its character at that time.

WHERE:
Moray (formerly Banffshire).
BEST TIME TO GO:
April to September (for Ballindalloch Castle).
DON'T MISS:
At Ballindalloch Castle – the superb rock garden with its tumbling spring, laid out by the 7th Baronet in 1937, and the peaceful Walled Garden redesigned in 1996 to celebrate the Castle's 450th anniversary.
AMOUNT OF WALKING:
Moderate
COST:
Low
YOU SHOULD KNOW:
Captain W E Johns was the author of the hugely successful Biggles novels about a World War I fighter pilot (and many more books besides) – he lived at Pitlochry Lodge on the Ballindalloch Estate from 1947 to 1953, where he wrote furiously and indulged his passion for salmon fishing in the River Spey.

Forfar and Glamis Castle

WHERE:
Angus (formerly Forfarshire).
BEST TIME TO GO:
April to September (though Glamis
Castle is open from mid-March to
December).
DON'T MISS:
The Angus Folk Museum in Glamis
village – six 18th-century cottages
housing exhibitions that give vivid
insight into bygone life on the land.
AMOUNT OF WALKING:
Moderate
COST:
Reasonable
YOU SHOULD KNOW:
Glamis is said to be Britain's most
haunted castle, full of ghosts and
dark secrets – including tales of a
soul lost gambling with the Devil and
regular visitations by the 'Grey Lady'
(said to be the spirit of Lady Janet
Douglas, burned at the stake in 1537
for plotting against the King).

The former Royal Burgh of Forfar is a market town serving the farms of surrounding Strathmore. The town's history goes back to Pictish times, when chiefs met at a stronghold by Forfar Loch to discuss how invading Romans might best be repelled from their ancient kingdom.

Sited between two lochs, Forfar remains a traditional country town with many small shops selling local produce – including the famous Forfar Bridie, a meat-filled pastry that used to be a staple for farm workers. After strolling around the town a visit to the Meffan Gallery and Museum brings Forfar's history to life. Another essential outing is to Pitmuies Gardens with its roses and herbaceous borders, plus a woodland walk.

After exploring the town, the rest of the day should be spent at nearby Glamis Castle – legendary setting for Shakespeare's *Macbeth*, ancestral home of the Earls of Strathmore and Kinghorne and childhood home of Elizabeth Bowes-Lyon, later Queen Elizabeth and then Queen Mother (her second daughter Margaret was born at Glamis). This magnificent red-stone pile stands amidst fabulous gardens at the end of a long tree-lined drive, at the centre of a vast estate set in the fertile valley of Strathmore.

A visit should start with a guided tour of the house. It has wonderful interiors, including some of the finest plaster ceilings in Scotland. An original 14th-century tower house remains at the heart of a building that looks more classic French chateau than medieval stronghold, following extensive alterations in the 17th and 18th centuries. After the house tour, there's plenty to explore in the surrounding grounds, including the walled kitchen garden, the fabulous Italian Garden, a nearby nature trail and the Pinetum beside the Glamis Burn – an arboretum that contains a wide variety of exotic tress, including many from North America.

King Charles II watches over Glamis Castle.

Arbroath

The extensive remains of Arbroath Abbey seem incongruous – what are they doing in the middle of town, when they should be in some remote coastal spot? But of course when the Abbey was constructed in the 12th century that's precisely the sort of location it occupied. A port soon grew around the religious foundation, eventually eclipsing it. The old 14th-century harbour was swept away in 1706 but its replacement ensured that Arbroath remained an important fishing and trading port.

Today, Arbroath attracts visitors drawn by the great Abbey. The Abbey Church is ruined, but parts such as the Abbot's House have survived. This green oasis amidst the town now has a visitor centre, a striking glass and red-stone structure topped with a moss-covered roof that complements the ancient Abbey.

Other attractions include the Signal Tower Museum, built in 1813 as the shore station for the Bell Rock Lighthouse erected by Robert Stevenson southeast of town. The Library and Art Gallery are worth a look and the High Street and town centre contain a range of fine civic buildings and good shops. Kerr's Miniature Railway, which was established in 1935 as a private venture, is now operated by volunteers. And of course no visit is complete without sampling an Arbroath Smokie – a pair of haddock smoked over slow-burning hardwood chips. Get a Smokie from a local fishmonger or any number of small smoke-houses around the harbour.

Round off the day with a walk on Whiting Ness, an atypical stretch of cliffs north of Arbroath that stands out on the largely sandy Tayside coast. Go all the way or simply enjoy a stroll next to Victoria Park in town. But if you do venture farther along the Arbroath Cliffs you will be impressed by eye-catching red sandstone formations like the infamous Devils Head.

WHERE:
Angus (formerly Forfarshire).
BEST TIME TO GO:
April to September
DON'T MISS:
Make time for a swift visit to Barry Mill, just south of Arbroath near Carnoustie – a working example of a traditional water-powered oatmeal mill.
AMOUNT OF WALKING:
Moderate
COST:
Low
YOU SHOULD KNOW:
In 1320 the Abbot penned The Declaration of Arbroath – deemed the most important document in Scottish history, it was signed by the Scottish nobility and begged Pope John XXII to declare Robert the Bruce King of Scotland and nullify his excommunication (imposed after Robert murdered Red Comyn in Greyfriars Church, Dumfries).

The fishing fleet at Arbroath

Dundee

WHERE:
City of Dundee (formerly Forfarshire).
BEST TIME TO GO:
All year
DON'T MISS:
City Quay on the Dundee waterfront, where factory outlets offer a huge range of designer goods at reduced prices.
AMOUNT OF WALKING:
Moderate
COST:
Reasonable
YOU SHOULD KNOW:
Generations of small boys should have Dundee as their spiritual home – for it is here that publisher D C Thomson has produced the long-running *Dandy* and *Beano* comics since their launch in the 1930s.

Scotland's fourth-largest city was frequently destroyed, damaged or pillaged in earlier years, before Dundee became a Victorian powerhouse complete with whaling fleet, flax mills, a vast output of sailcloth and sacks...and sordid slums. But the city was transformed in the 1870s, acquiring impressive buildings that largely survive and the first Tay Bridge (which unfortunately soon collapsed).

Dundee has reinvented itself for the 21st century, becoming a cosmopolitan place with a lively cultural quarter. There is fine Victorian architecture, an excellent variety of shops and a wide choice of museums and galleries.

Maritime heritage is celebrated at Discovery Point Visitor Centre, where Captain Scott's Antarctic expedition ship RRS *Discovery* has returned to her roots. In Victoria Dock is the frigate *Unicorn*, launched in 1824 and preserved 'in ordinary' (as the mast-less depot ship she was for most of her long life).

One of the best visitor attractions in Scotland is the Verdant Works, a restored jute mill where original machinery runs and a realistic time-capsule that transports you back a century has been created – admittedly with a little help from actors, film and multimedia computers.

On the scientific front, the Mills Observatory offers free entry and displays, with a small charge for public planetarium shows. If you can be there to study the night sky, it's an awesome experience. The Sensation Science Centre in the West End is devoted to the five senses, offering stimulating hands-on opportunities to experience the magic of science.

Time left? Then choose from the wonderful Claypotts Castle tower house, the University Botanic Garden, nearby Camperdown Wildlife Centre, Broughty Beach and Castle Museum, the McManus Galleries and Museum's insight into Dundee's history...come to think of it, why not spend two days here?

RRS Discovery

Montrose

Dukes of Montrose have played a huge part in unfolding Scottish history, and the seaport and market town whose name they bear is between Arbroath and Aberdeen. The illustrious family's seat is actually at Auchmar, near Loch Lomond, but the first Marquis of Montrose was born here and this Royal Burgh has history enough of its own, having attracted the attention of various passing armies over the centuries.

Montrose lies between the North and South Esk Rivers, beside a large tidal lagoon known as the Montrose Basin, an important nature reserve. This attractive town has the widest High Street in Scotland, with fine buildings and intriguing closes leading to secluded gardens. The centre is dominated by the soaring spire of Montrose Old Church and to the south of the High Street is the busy harbour area, whilst to the east is greensward, dunes and a splendid beach with the usual resort facilities.

Those who prefer more secluded seashore should head further south to rugged Boddin Point at the northern end of Lunan Bay, one of Scotland's finest beaches and ruined Red Castle. Beyond the Bay is Ethie Haven – beginning a run of low cliffs that leads to Arbroath, providing a scenic three-hour walk for those who go all the way. Or head north to the village of St Cyrus and enjoy the National Nature Reserve centred on the cliffs and dunes there.

Outside Montrose is the magnificent House of Dun, a classic Georgian house and policies (outbuildings) overlooking the Montrose Basin, built in the 18th century to a design by influential Scottish architect Robert Adam. Visitors can enjoy a guided tour and the superb Victorian grounds contain the Lady Augusta Walk, a walled garden, terraced gardens, woodland dog walk...and an adventure playground – there's something for all the family.

WHERE:
Angus (formerly Forfarshire).
BEST TIME TO GO:
April to September
DON'T MISS:
The Montrose Basin Wildlife Centre with binoculars, telescopes, hides and remote-control video cameras – it's heaven for bird-watchers.
AMOUNT OF WALKING:
Moderate (unless you do the cliff walk to Arbroath!).
COST:
Reasonable
YOU SHOULD KNOW:
The Montrose Air Station Heritage Centre to the north of town tells the story of Britain's first operational military air base – established here by the Royal Flying Corps in 1913, it again saw service in World War II as an active fighter airfield and major training base.

Lunan Bay

The Spittal of Glenshee

Glenshee

The mighty Grampian Mountains certainly have presence – and one of the most spectacular ways of appreciating their rugged grandeur is to drive up Glenshee. This is not a heritage expedition, or even an outing that will contain much contact with the works of man. Instead, prepare to experience the natural glory of the remote and empty Scottish Highlands at their most awesome.

But start the day in a gentler way – with a stroll around the pleasant town of Blairgowrie – there are plenty of fine buildings, good shops and excellent riverside walks. After packing a picnic, follow the rushing River Ericht north along the A93 road to Bridge of Cally. Here beginneth Glenshee!

Before long, rich farmland gives way to rolling hills and you begin to appreciate that the A93 through Glenshee to Royal Deeside is the highest main road in Britain – once feared for the Devil's Elbow that must have seemed almost vertical to toiling travellers. Modern road building has done for the Devil, but the further north you go the more dramatic the landscape becomes, until at the head of the Glen some of the highest and most impressive mountains in the Grampians crowd the road. The Glenshee Ski Centre, Scotland's largest and oldest ski resort, stands here, with its somewhat antiquated assortment of lifts.

This is a day that demands some strenuous open-air activity – especially as there's nothing else to do in Glenshee but admire the scenery. One option is to pause along the road and take short walks at any spots that appeal. Alternatively, stop at the Spittal of Glenshee halfway up the Glen and take a section of the way-marked Cateran Trail up to Lairig Gate, the Trail's high point at 650 m (2,130 ft) – so it's downhill all the way back!

Kirriemuir

Question –– where was *Peter Pan* author J M Barrie born? Answer – Kirriemuir. But there's more to this interesting town than one famous former inhabitant. Indeed, its main claim to fame – and prosperity – long depended on women's corsets. In the mid-1700s a local weaver developed a double-thickness cloth that was ideal for constructing the constraining garments, and by 1860 there were 2,000 hand-loom weavers in prosperous Kirriemuir and surrounds.

The fashion for corsets died in World War I, and with it Kirriemuir's textile industry – though Britain's last jute mill, Marywell Works, did survive into the 21st century. The town centre is charming, a place of narrow streets, interesting nooks and crannies. There's a small museum in the Old Town House and Kirriemuir Aviation Museum houses an extensive collection of World War II memorabilia and artefacts assembled by a veteran of that conflict.

But J M Barrie inevitably grabs the headlines and his birthplace may still be seen. This humble cottage houses a re-created kitchen and bedroom, plus Barrie's writing desk. It's extraordinary to think that a family with ten children lived in these cramped quarters. There are two Peter Pan statues in town (plus Hook's Hotel) and Barrie himself lies in a simple grave in the local cemetery.

After exploring Kirriemuir a scenic walk up the Kirrie Hill will lead to Barrie's unusual gift to the town – at first sight looking like any old bungalow but in fact a fascinating camera obscura, which projects an inverted image of its surroundings. Don't weaken, as there's one more walk to round off the day. Drive west along the A926 to Alyth and turn north onto the B954. Park and walk to the rushing Reekie Linn Falls on the River Isla, so named because spray hangs in the air like smoke after heavy rain. Magical!

9 Brechin Road is the birthplace of J M Barrie.

WHERE:
Angus (formerly Forfarshire).
BEST TIME TO GO:
April to September
DON'T MISS:
An ice cream from Visocchi's enticing shop in Kirriemuir's main square, opposite the Old Town House Museum.
AMOUNT OF WALKING:
Lots
COST:
Reasonable
YOU SHOULD KNOW:
Local hero J M Barrie co-authored an opera called *Jane Annie, or The Good Conduct Prize* with Sherlock Holmes creator Sir Arthur Conan Doyle – first performed in 1893 at the Savoy Theatre, it flopped and has rarely been seen since.

Blair Castle

The village of Blair Atholl is pleasant but unremarkable, but the great house that may be found nearby is another matter. Blair Castle stands proudly above its estate village, picked out in brilliant white against the dark pines and heather-covered hills beyond. The historic seat of the Dukes and Earls of Atholl began life as a 13th-century tower, with additions in the 1500s, 1700s and 1800s that created the magnificent house we see today.

Strategically placed to dominate access to the Grampians and Inverness, it was besieged by Cromwell's army and – a hundred years later – Jacobites. Around thirty of the Castle's finest rooms are open to the public, who may wander at their own pace or join an informative guided tour. These great rooms have stunning contents – furniture, pictures, arms and armour, ceramics and costumes, all complemented by unique Jacobite relics. Of particular note are the imposing entrance hall, vast ballroom and a dining room created from the original 16th-century Great Hall.

Outside, the extensive gardens, grounds and huge estate offer numerous leisure opportunities. For the energetic there are signed trails and cycle paths, pony trekking and horse trails. Nor will garden lovers be disappointed. The recently restored Hercules Garden is over 250 years old and other highlights include Diana's Grove (named after the Roman Goddess of Hunting), St Bride's Kirk and Hercules Walk.

If there's any time left after visiting this magnificent stately home, pause in Blair Atholl to visit the stone-built working watermill – dating from the early 17th century, it's a delightful building and a super spot to pause for refreshments. Then drive to the northwest of the village, where the old road meets the new – there you will find the so-called 'Harrods of the North'. The House of Bruar is, somewhat unexpectedly, a luxury and quality goods outlet.

Blair Castle – a magnificent stately home

Pass of Killiecrankie

Once upon a time every traveller dreaded the Pass of Killiecrankie, north of Pitlochry – the narrow wooded gorge served as a mountain pass between Ben Vrackie and Tenandry Hill and was notoriously dangerous, with an ever-present risk of attack. Happily, times have changed, and it's now part of the Tummel's National Scenic Area and one of Perthshire's most delightful beauty spots – beloved of naturalists and walkers alike.

Killiecrankie Visitor Centre above the gorge is an excellent starting point. It looks at the area's superb natural features, has some excellent paintings, describes a bloody Jacobite battle fought near here in 1689...and has remote cameras showing nesting woodland birds in spring and early summer. By the Visitor Centre is Soldier's Leap, where Donald MacBean jumped for his life and escaped pursuing Highlanders after the 1689 battle. Was it possible? Decide for yourself – there's a stone-walled rotunda in the car park that shows the distance claimed, and if it seems considerable just imagine the impetus provided by a pursuing pack of bloodthirsty, claymore-wielding Highlanders.

Then it's a case of getting down into the gorge and walking along the deep fissure carved over many millennia by the River Garry. There are a number of trails beside the water and through fine oak and deciduous woodland, where walkers may not only enjoy the wonderful surroundings but also expect to see a variety of wild life including roe deer, red squirrels, many different woodland birds and various butterflies.

After enjoying the Pass of Killiecrankie, complete an invigorating open-air day by visiting the nearby Linn of Tummel at the confluence of the Rivers Garry and Tummel, where the two rivers flow into the head of beautiful Loch Tummel. Watch for leaping salmon in autumn before taking a scenic drive along the loch-side.

The River Garry in the Pass of Killiecrankie

WHERE:
Perth and Kinross (formerly Perthshire).
BEST TIME TO GO:
April to October (when the Killiecrankie Visitor Centre is open) – September or October are the months for spectacular autumn leaves.
DON'T MISS:
The wonderful view of the Pass from the high Garry Bridge – bring your camera and take some super pictures!
AMOUNT OF WALKING:
Lots
COST:
Low
YOU SHOULD KNOW:
Killiecrankie is derived from the Gaelic for 'The Aspen Wood'...but don't spend too much time looking for all those aspen trees, as very few now remain in the Pass.

Scone Palace and the surrounding countryside

Around Perth

WHERE:
Perth and Kinross (formerly Perthshire).
BEST TIME TO GO:
April to September
DON'T MISS:
If there's any time left, finish the castle tour by driving south to Glenfarg and walk up to Balvaird Castle in its commanding hilltop position overlooking the A912 road (it's only open to the public on summer weekends, though).
AMOUNT OF WALKING:
Moderate
COST:
Reasonable
YOU SHOULD KNOW:
The Stone of Scone (also known as the Stone of Destiny) resided in Westminster Abbey for seven centuries after Edward I confiscated it – 'kidnapped' by Scottish students in 1950, it was formally returned to Scotland in 1996 whilst a replica sits on Moot Hill at Scone Palace, where Scottish Kings of old were crowned.

Historic Perth has been an important settlement since Roman times. Strategically located at the lowest bridging point on the River Tay, it thrived as a trading centre and remains a significant regional focal point – as evidenced by its grand buildings and bustling atmosphere. There's plenty to see in town – including St John's Kirk behind City Hall, Balhousie Castle (HQ and museum of the Black Watch regiment), Caithness Glass Visitor Centre and the Perth Mart Centre that explores the area's farming heritage.

Perth has a lot to offer but it's best not to linger too long – there's much to see in the surrounding area. First port of call must be Scone, just to the north, where Scottish monarchs were invested from 838 AD upon the ceremonial Stone of Scone – until Edward I took it in 1296. Scone Palace dates from 1580 and was built in the grounds of the now-vanished abbey where Kings were crowned. It sits in parkland with rare trees and the state rooms have impressive collections of furniture, ceramics, ivories and clocks. The grounds are extensive and include a maze.

Don't stop there. Hurry back to Perth and find Huntingtower Castle on the western fringe of town. Standing in well-tended grounds, it's a time capsule that transports anyone with imagination straight back to the medieval era – though in fact it was not abandoned as a residence until the 1700s.

On the opposite side of Perth, on the south bank of the River Tay, stands Elcho Castle. It may not be the most famous in Scotland, but is one of the best. The main structure is well preserved, though extensive outbuildings are gone. Here, too, it is easy to imagine 16th-century castle life. There is a restored dovecote by the nearby mill stream and a quarry garden.

Pitlochry

Three very different happenings decided Pitlochry's rise from remote settlement to thriving town. General Wade drove one of his military roads north through the place in the 1700s. Queen Victoria sparked interest in Pitlochry after commenting favourably during a stay at nearby Blair Castle in the 1840s. And the railway's arrival in the 1860s allowed curious tourists to come and see what the fuss was about.

Today's visitor will quickly appreciate the enduring appeal of Pitlochry, discovering a vibrant town full of sturdy stone Victorian buildings in a superb mountain setting that offers a splendid choice of hotels, pubs, restaurants and shops ranging from the normal to the up-market. And Scotch whisky lovers will find that the Blair Atholl Distillery welcomes them with a wee dram – it is one of Scotland's oldest, founded in 1798.

Pitlochry has its very own dam to generate hydroelectric power, plus an amazing salmon ladder with 34 chambers, allowing the fish to reach Loch Faskally above as they complete a 9,500-km (5,900-mi) annual journey to their spawning grounds. The chances of actually seeing a salmon making the supreme effort to swim up the ladder are not great but the glass-walled viewing chamber is certainly impressive, as is the Visitor Centre at the neighbouring power station.

After enjoying the Pitlochry main course, there's a choice of open-air desserts. Nearby Ben Vrackie can be climbed from the village of Moulin on the northeastern outskirts of town for bracing exercise and great views. Or take the way-marked Edradour Walk through Black Spout Wood, to enjoy the quiet woodland and impressive Black Spout waterfall, before proceeding up the Edradour Burn. There, the Edradour Distillery offers home baking and a grand dram – it's Scotland's smallest distillery and a survivor of the great Highland tradition of (once illegal) farmhouse stills.

WHERE:
Perth and Kinross (formerly Perthshire).
BEST TIME TO GO:
March to November
DON'T MISS:
Pitlochry's cultural highlight -- its Festival Theatre, reached on foot by a suspension bridge across the River Tummel...theatre addicts should note that should they stay around for a week they could see eight different plays.
AMOUNT OF WALKING:
Lots
COST:
Low
YOU SHOULD KNOW:
Those who prefer beer to Scotch need not despair – in addition to its distilleries, Pitlochry has a working brewery at the Moulin Inn in the village square of Moulin.

Pitlochry

WALES

Cardiff

WHERE:
South Glamorgan
BEST TIME TO GO:
All year round. The covered arcades
provide good shelter in wet weather.
DON'T MISS:
The Animal Wall in Bute Park – an
extraordinary collection of stone
animals created by William Burges,
the architect who in the 1860s made
the castle the Gothic masterpiece
that you see today.
AMOUNT OF WALKING:
Moderate
COST:
Reasonable (entrance fees are
charged to the castle and the
museum.)
YOU SHOULD KNOW:
Rugby is almost a religion in Wales
and if you are near Cardiff's
Millennium Stadium on a match day,
the sound of the crowd singing can
be awesome.

Although settled for over 2,000 years, the Welsh capital has really blossomed since the end of the last millennium, finally swapping coal for cool to become a truly modern European city.

The best way to start a tour of Cardiff is to lose yourself in the city's iconic arcades; just a short walk from Cardiff Central Station, they provide a labyrinth of delightful shops, stalls and cafés. Castle Arcade is the perfect place to sit, enjoy brunch – café latte and some Welsh cakes would be the most apt – and people watch. If you leave the arcade via the Duke Street exit, the imposing walls of Cardiff Castle will be just ahead of you. This former ancestral home of the Bute family takes you on a journey through time from its excavated Roman walls through to the 12th-century Norman keep, up to the Gothic fancy you see today.

Leaving the castle by the side exit takes you into the wonderfully compact Bute Park and, if the weather is kind, the banks of the rejuvenated River Taff provide the perfect place for a picnic. A 3.2-km (2-mi) walk along the Taff brings you to the gem that is Llandaff Cathedral, a fully restored masterpiece of Reformation architecture, with stained glass windows by Edward Burne-Jones and Dante Gabriel Rossetti.

For a quick way back into town, take a southbound bus along Cathedral Road and walk across Bute Park behind the castle. Here the polished Portland stone of the Civic Centre lies directly ahead. Its wonderfully manicured lawns and baroque-style buildings are perfect for ambling. At its centre is the superbly eclectic Museum of Wales where portraits by Renoir and Van Gogh sit alongside models of mammoths. The day can be rounded off with a boat trip around the newly developed Bay area or if you like the performing arts, try the Sherman Theatre on Senghennydd Road.

The Millennium Stadium alongside the River Taff

Castell Coch and St Fagans National History Museum

Just fifteen minutes drive from the centre of Cardiff, lie the twin delights of Castell Coch and St Fagans National History Museum. The first is a folly to trump all follies, a fantasy dwelling created for the then richest man in the world (the 3rd Marquis of Bute), the latter a lovingly restored collection of Welsh life throughout the ages.

Perched high on a green hillside overlooking the River Taff, Castell Coch – literally the Red Castle – is a spectacular piece of Bavarian-style kitsch transported to the South Wales countryside. Built in the 1870s on the site of a dilapidated Norman fortress, this striking structure stands as a testimonial to the curious tastes of the Marquis of Bute, the man who profited most from South Wales' economic rise in the late 19th century. Once inside you are greeted by the most outlandish examples of Victorian medievalist design. Beneath all of this it is however possible to see the original structure of the towers and, if each room is seen in isolation, there are some gems to be discovered.

St Fagans National History Museum (formerly the Museum of Welsh Life) is a superb outdoor exhibition of dwellings taking you from Celtic Wales up to the present day. Set in 40 hectares (100 acres) of the grounds of St Fagans Castle, it has grown to become the most visited attraction in Wales. Over 40 buildings have been transported to the museum, piece by piece, from all over the country to create a faithful record of the nation's life. Traditional crafts and farming methods are practised, making this a most dynamic, living museum. It is a place where children can learn about the past in an exciting, interactive way and where adults can get nostalgic as they peer inside the homes of the recent past.

Castell Coch

WHERE:
Near Cardiff, South Glamorgan
BEST TIME TO GO:
Any time of year, but the weather is better from March to September.
DON'T MISS:
Lady Bute's bedroom in Castell Coch – a delightfully shocking clash of cultural influences.
AMOUNT OF WALKING:
Moderate
COST:
Low (entrance to St Fagans National History Museum is free).
YOU SHOULD KNOW:
If you are driving on the M4 at night, the sight of Castell Coch, lit up against the dark hillside, is the most spectacular of sights.

Coity Castle

Coity Castle and Llangynwyd Village

WHERE:
Mid Glamorgan
BEST TIME TO GO:
All year round
DON'T MISS:
Allow plenty of time to walk around Llangynwyd. It has several hidden gems, including the 18th-century Bethesda Chapel and the wonderfully proportioned Corner House.
AMOUNT OF WALKING:
Moderate, but be prepared for some steep inclines.
COST:
Low. Coity Castle is free to enter.
YOU SHOULD KNOW:
Buried in the Llangynwyd graveyard are Wales's most famous star-crossed lovers, the thatcher and poet Wil Hopcyn and the daughter of nobility, Ann Thomas. Their ultimately tragic story formed the basis of the Welsh folk tale 'The Maid of Cefn Ydfa'.

To the casual visitor it may seem that South Wales is an area that sprang into life only during the industrial revolution of the 19th century. This was a time when most of its valleys turned to the exploitation of coal and its ports grew into bland conurbations. But if you look hard enough, you can find reminders of the region's pre-industrial past.

Just to the northeast of Bridgend lie the ruins of Coity Castle. Whilst now little more than a collection of eerie grey walls sitting astride a hill-top, they have the history of Wales etched in them. The castle was originally built around 1100 but most of the fortification dates from the 14th century. It proved its worth during a siege of 1404-5, when the armies of Owain Glyn Dwr almost pounded it into submission. Gradually though, like most other castles, Coity became redundant with the increasing power of the cannon. It was finally used as a family home by the wealthy Gamage family, before falling into disrepair in the 17th century.

Heading north from Bridgend on the A4063, you will find a more vibrant reminder of the region's past in the form of Llangynwyd Village. Once again you find yourself on the top of a hill, but this time at as well preserved a place as you could ever wish to find. Built on the site of a 6th-century Celtic settlement, Llangynwyd Village is a place left virtually untouched by the last 200 years of development. At its centre there is a commanding tall-towered church and at its cultural hub is the wonderful Yr Hen Dy (Old House), possibly the oldest surviving thatched inn in South Wales. It is a perfect place to wander, and at almost every turn you will find something of historic or architectural interest.

Rhondda Heritage Park and Big Pit Mining Museum at Blaenavon

Heritage is an extremely difficult thing to describe. At its best it is a distillation of positive things from the past, and at its worst it is what you are left with when all else has gone. Separated by the Heads of the Valleys road, the two attractions of the Rhondda Heritage Park and the Blaenavon Big Pit Mining Museum make a valiant attempt to bring the recent past to life, without glossing over the undoubted hardships endured by those engaged in the coalmining industry.

Although coal had been mined in the region since Roman times, the Victorian demand for iron led to an explosive growth in the industry that changed the landscape and demographics of the area forever. In 1860 the population of the Rhondda Valleys was around 3,000, within fifty years it had grown to over 160,000. The last pit closed in 1990, leaving a void that is yet to be filled.

The Rhondda Heritage Park, located on the site of the former Lewis Merthyr Colliery at Trehafod, is one of the top visitor attractions in South Wales and it offers an inspirational and pleasurable day out for young and old alike. The entrance is through the visitor centre with its art gallery, gift shop and café. Once inside there is plenty to do and see. The highlight of the day is probably the Black Gold Tour, a simulated journey down a mine shaft, escorted by a former pitman. The clammy atmosphere, smells and renovated machinery give you a small inkling of what it must have been like to toil at great depths. The Big Pit Mining Museum stands on the edge of Blaenafon, a town that played a pivotal role in the Industrial Revolution. Now a UNESCO World Heritage Site, it also offers guided underground tours and access to renovated colliery buildings.

WHERE:
Mid Glamorgan
BEST TIME TO GO:
Anytime, though Rhondda Heritage Park is closed during December. The Big Pit Mining Museum has restricted opening hours in December and January.
DON'T MISS:
The art gallery, housed in a former colliery building at the Rhondda Heritage Park. It contains a fine permanent exhibition as well as showing new local art.
AMOUNT OF WALKING:
Little. Both attractions have good wheelchair access, but you have to notify them in advance.
COST:
Low. The Rhondda Museum charges a small fee for a full tour (under 5's get in free). The Big Pit Museum is free to enter.
YOU SHOULD KNOW:
Nowhere is the human cost of the unregulated drive for coal more apparent than in the history of the Rhondda. In 1896 more than seventy miners were killed in an underground explosion at Rhondda's Tylorstown Colliery. The subsequent enquiry revealed that the pit had not been inspected for nearly a year and a half.

The old pit head in Rhondda Heritage Park illuminated at night

Brecon Mountain Railway and the National Showcaves Centre for Wales

WHERE:
Powys
BEST TIME TO GO:
Both attractions are open only from March to October, although the caves open for the Christmas holidays.
DON'T MISS:
The dome at the end of Cathedral Cave – well worth the walk.
AMOUNT OF WALKING:
Moderate. The train has full wheelchair access, but those with disabilities will find a visit to the caves difficult.
COST:
Expensive. Both attractions charge but family tickets are available.
YOU SHOULD KNOW:
Cathedral Cave has a licence to hold weddings and civil partnership ceremonies. So if you can't afford St Paul's in London, here is a cheaper way to tie the knot under a magnificent dome!

Without wanting to deter over half the population, the double delights of the Brecon Mountain Railway and the Dan yr Ogof caves, have 'father-and-son day out' stamped all over them. It is possible to marvel at a magnificently masculine steam engine in the morning and after lunch sample the subterranean splendour of Wales's most accessible cave system.

Located just to the north of Merthyr Tydfil, the Brecon Mountain Railway takes you on a steam-filled adventure, passing along the shores of the magnificent Taf Fechan Reservoir and into the heart of the Brecon Beacons. Get there early and you can look at locomotives being serviced in the repair workshop, before watching the engine being stoked up. On leaving the station at Pant, the views are immediately stunning, with the calm waters of the reservoir to your left and the Brecon Beacons all around. The round trip takes just over an hour, including a twenty-minute stop at Pontsticill.

From Merthyr, take the A465, Head of the Valleys road, towards Neath. Leave it at Glynneath and head towards Abercraf in the Swansea Valley. It is here that you will find one of Wales's true natural wonders. There are three caves to explore at the National Showcaves Centre. Dan yr Ogof stretches for over 16 km (10 mi) and is a veritable wonderland of stalactites and stalagmites. Bone Cave is not for the fainthearted, as more than forty skeletal remains of former human and animal inhabitants have been found there. Finally there is the serpentine Cathedral Cave, the most fantastic of them all. Faithful reconstructions of cave dwellers past greet you near the entrance, but it is the surreal beauty of the walls that catches the eye. The cave finally opens up into the most amazing domed structure with water pouring down from all sides.

Life-size dinosaurs at Dan yr Ogof National Showcaves

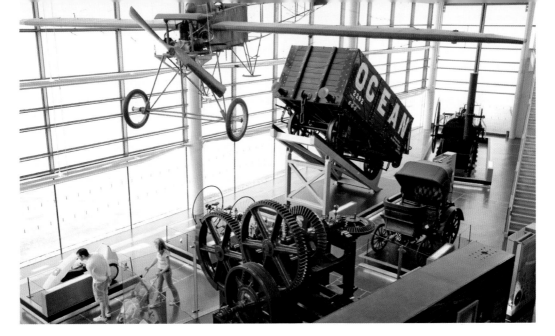

National Waterfront Museum

Swansea

Framed by seven hills and nestled in a sheltered bay, Swansea is Wales's second city. Starting in the Maritime Quarter, you can marvel at the new Swansea while still learning about its past. Then it is off to find out about the city's most famous son and finally the day can be rounded off with a walk along the golden sands of the world-renowned Mumbles.

At the heart of the maritime quarter is the fabulous glass and slate structure that houses the National Waterfront Museum. This award-winning building is worth viewing on its own, but there is much inside to satisfy the enquiring mind. The museum is divided into fifteen areas, each with a different slant. You can learn about such diverse things as coal, family trees and the history of money.

Lunch can be taken in any one of the increasingly smart eateries on Wind Street, before an afternoon devoted to Dylan Thomas, Wales's greatest poet. For those who would like to make the pilgrimage, fifteen minutes' walk through the old town takes you to 5 Cwmdonkin Drive, the great man's birthplace. From here, head back towards the waterfront where you will find the Dylan Thomas Centre, tucked behind Swansea Museum. Inside you will find extensive displays of Thomas's life and works. The centre also hosts several special literary events throughout the year, so it is worth checking their programme of events before you visit.

From Oystermouth Road you can catch a bus through the town centre and out towards The Mumbles. No visit to the area would be complete without strolling along the sands of this wonderful stretch of coastline. If you time it right, the sunsets viewed from Mumbles Head can be stunning.

WHERE:
West Glamorgan
BEST TIME TO GO:
All year round. Its sheltered position means that Swansea can be most pleasant even on a winter's day if the weather is set fair.
DON'T MISS:
The view across the marina from the Dylan Thomas Centre.
AMOUNT OF WALKING:
Little. There is step-free access to both the Museum and the Centre.
COST:
Low. Entry to both buildings mentioned is free.
YOU SHOULD KNOW:
The stretch of the seafront known as the Mumbles Mile is lined with pubs and is best avoided at weekends, as it plays host to numerous hen and stag parties.

Plantasia tropical rainforest

Plantasia and the Gower Heritage Centre

For those with children whose curiosity extends beyond the colour of candyfloss or the speed of a fairground ride, these two attractions near Swansea make for a perfect day out. Plantasia and Maze World offer countless opportunities for the inquisitive mind to interact with and find out about our natural surroundings in a wonderfully informal setting. The Gower Heritage Centre is the place to learn about our pre-industrial past and to watch traditional craftspeople at work.

Plantasia's gentle moulding of the local landscape is designed to delight and inform. The woodland gallery is a mature forest where wind chimes create an ever-changing symphony and the trees produce a wonderful bouquet. Those with a head for heights and a greater need for excitement will want to sample the views from the treetop trail, before taking a rest in the beautifully proportioned orchard. As well as plants, the area has been populated with a range of animals – real life versions of those any toy farm-set would be proud to house. Cute miniature pigs, goats, Shetland ponies and even alpacas live happily within the park. There is also a splendid barbecue and picnic area.

As an extra treat, the adjoining Maze World has six themed mazes, each offering glimpses into the far flung corners of the globe. As a reward for those clever enough to complete all six there is even a prize.

The Gower Heritage Centre at nearby Parkmill is built around a renovated 12th-century water-powered saw-and-corn-mill and serves to keep traditional crafts alive. Look out in particular for the puppet makers who offer workshops during most summer weekends. There are also opportunities to buy locally produced stained glass, wooden gifts and cloth.

WHERE:
Near Swansea, West Glamorgan
BEST TIME TO GO:
Open all year round but best March to October. The orchard is great in blossom (April) or in fruit (September).
DON'T MISS:
Feeding time in the 'meet the animals' area (Plantasia).
AMOUNT OF WALKING:
Moderate (although for small children it may seem like lots).
COST:
Reasonable – family and season tickets are available.
YOU SHOULD KNOW:
Plantasia makes a wonderful place for a children's birthday party and if the staff are given advance notice they will lay on an unforgettable day.

Tredegar House and Park

Located 3 km (1.9 mi) west of Newport (Casnewydd), Tredegar House is one of the architectural marvels of Wales and indeed one of the most important 17th-century structures in the whole of the UK. It served as the ancestral home of the wealthy Morgan family until 1951, when it became home to St Joseph's R.C. Girls' School. Newport Borough Council bought the – by then run down – building in 1974 and funded an ambitious programme of restoration that is still ongoing.

The house is now open to the public from April to September, giving you the chance to savour one of the region's hidden gems. Three centuries of changing fashions in interior design – from the 1600s to the early 1930s – are represented in different rooms of the house. A guided tour is recommended to help interpret the incredible array of bits and pieces on show. The guides also give interesting insight into the often eccentric previous inhabitants of the upstairs of the house, whilst not glossing over the privations of those who worked below.

The surrounding 36 hectares (90 acres) belonging to the house are also worthy of a visit in themselves, with the park and woodland walks open all year round. Pre-eminent among many buildings of note in the grounds are the magnificent Orangery, approached through a walled garden, and the handsome Great Stables. The house also has a visitor centre where you can purchase a memento or glean further information.

WHERE:
Near Newport, Gwent
BEST TIME TO GO:
Fully open to the public from April to September, but open for special events throughout the year.
DON'T MISS:
Sitting in the Orangery during blossom time (May).
AMOUNT OF WALKING:
Moderate. There is good wheelchair access to the house and grounds.
COST:
Low (accompanied children under 15 get in free).
YOU SHOULD KNOW:
Of all the former residents of Tredegar House, Catherine Morgan was perhaps the most eccentric. Believing herself to be a bird, she would build nests around the grounds and roost on them.

Tradegar House with its magnificent ornamental gates

Tintern Abbey, Monmouth and the Nelson Museum

WHERE:
Gwent
BEST TIME TO GO:
All year round
DON'T MISS:
Agincourt Square, situated at the heart of Monmouth – a most handsome quadrant and a good place to get your bearings.
AMOUNT OF WALKING:
Moderate
COST:
Low. There is a small fee to enter the museum and admission to Tintern Abbey is free.
YOU SHOULD KNOW:
For a good view of Monmouth and the Wye Valley, head a short way east and follow the steep road that rises to Kymin Hill until you reach a magnificent vantage point crowned by a white tower.

Located just to the north of Chepstow on the Wales-England border, the wooded Wye Valley reaches from Tintern to Monmouth and makes for a perfect day's expedition of historical discovery. Founded by Cistercian monks in 1131, Tintern Abbey is tucked away in a remote corner of this sumptuous valley. It was the first Cistercian abbey in Wales, and despite its missing roof, it is otherwise well preserved. The cruciform structure is divided in the classic Cistercian way, with segregated chapels and a mightily impressive aisled nave.

Following the winding A466 northwards along the course of the Wye, more remnants of times past await you, in the form of the spectacularly pretty market town of Monmouth. Its Roman and Medieval beginnings have been overlaid with the best architecture from the Georgian and Victorian eras. It is a vibrant market town and this, coupled with the fact that the original medieval street plan is still in place, gives Monmouth the feel of a place out of time.

Nelson has strong connections with Monmouth through his mistress Lady Hamilton, who lived here, and the town boasts the finest collection of Nelson memorabilia in the world. Britain's greatest seafaring warlord is reputed to have planned the Battle of Trafalgar in the round tower of what is now Monmouth's Nelson Museum. The museum is home to a wonderfully diverse range of material, from naval artefacts to letters to his wife and mistress. It even houses several fakes, such as something purporting to be Nelson's glass eye.

The ruins of Tintern Abbey

Exploring the Gower Peninsula

Three Cliffs Bay

Residents of the breathtakingly beautiful and diverse landscape that forms the Gower Peninsula (Penrhyn Gwyr) are rightly proud that their region was the first in the UK to be declared an 'Area of Outstanding Natural Beauty'. Over half a century has passed since the bestowing of this accolade and, whilst much has changed in the outside world, this very special area of South Wales has retained all of its old world charm.

A good, reliable bus service from nearby Swansea takes you swiftly to this tranquil haven. Once there it is possible to reach most points on the peninsula by local buses. The Gower's isolation has made it a significant area for wildlife conservation, and a wide array of creatures can be seen. Badgers, otters, rare bats and a multitude of seabirds all thrive in this unique ecosystem. The Gower is filled with historic reminders of the past, from ancient standing stones, through Iron Age hill forts, to medieval castles. All this is set amongst a superb natural landcape of hills, valleys, beaches, dunes, cliffs and caves.

The Parkmill Heritage Centre is the ideal place to make your first stop – it's a good place to pick up a guidebook and get advice on where to go. From there it is a short hike to the hauntingly impressive Three Cliffs Bay – a trident-shaped outcrop perforated by a natural arch. Travelling westward there are many bays to discover, but the two that stand out are Oxwich, framed by dunes and ash forest, and Rhossili at the western end of the Gower. Rhossili Bay has a wonderful edge-of-the-world feel, with wild windswept beaches that are popular with surfers and paragliders. At the northern edge of the bay lies the picturesque chilled-out village of Llangennith – a perfect place to wander for a while before heading back.

WHERE:
Near Swansea, West Glamorgan.
BEST TIME TO GO:
All year round (the best weather is from April to October, although winters are usually mild).
DON'T MISS:
Oxwich Castle, an extraordinary Tudor mansion.
AMOUNT OF WALKING:
Moderate. Reaching some of the more secluded spots on the peninsula requires some walking.
COST:
Low – cheap daily bus passes are available.
YOU SHOULD KNOW:
The area was once a centre of smuggling and pillaging of shipwrecks, and at low tide a few of those wrecks are still visible, most notably the skeletal remains of the *Helvetica* in Rhossili Bay.

409

A boat trip around Ramsey Island

Ramsey and Skomer Islands and surrounding waters

WHERE:
Dyfed
BEST TIME TO GO:
The trip around Ramsey Island operates all year round. The trip to Skomer runs from March to October.
DON'T MISS:
Such is the unpredictable nature of wildlife watching, the highlight of your day could happen at almost any time, from the spotting of a whale or school of dolphins to the mass flocking of birds.
AMOUNT OF WALKING:
Little
COST:
Reasonable
YOU SHOULD KNOW:
Flexibility in planning is required to complete both trips. Your plans are at the mercy of the tides and the weather. The voyage around Ramsey is less susceptible to cancellation because of inclement weather, but its course may alter substantially.

The islands of Skomer and Ramsey sit like bookends at either end of the spectacularly pretty St Brides Bay. This area of the Pembrokeshire coast is home to great colonies of sea birds and the nutrient-rich waters provide good feeding grounds for a host of sea mammals.

When the weather is good, it is possible to enjoy watching whale and dolphins around Ramsey Island in the morning and, after lunch, take a boat trip across to the impressive Skomer Island for bird watching. From St Justinian, 3 km (2 mi) outside St David's, you can embark on the most memorable 'sea safari'. This journey, in thrillingly bumpy zodiac-style boats, takes you around the southern tip of Ramsey Island, into open waters and out towards Grassholm Island. It is here that you are most likely to see schools of bottlenose and white-sided dolphins and, if you are lucky, orcas and pilot whales. Grassholm Island sits isolated, like a giant Belgian bun, the 'icing' that you see being made of huge groups of gannets. Then you spin round and head back towards Ramsey and the mainland, on the way navigating around imposing cliffs and through gorges and sea caves.

Taking the coastal road south around the bay you arrive at the scenic village of Dale and from there you can cross over to Skomer. Cut off from the mainland by the narrow and treacherous Jack Sound, Skomer's isolation offers protection from predators, making it one of the most important bird breeding grounds in Britain. To avoid too much disturbance, the number of visitors is strictly limited. If you are fortunate enough to be included in the quota, you will witness one of the most spectacular wildlife scenes to be found in our coastal waters.

The Stackpole Estate and Barafundle Bay

Set in the midst of the Pembrokeshire Coast National Park, the Stackpole Estate is an area of extraordinary beauty and much charm. Its relative seclusion and varying habitats provide a haven for wildlife and the well-marked trails make it perfect for exploration. This classic 16-km (10-mi) circular walk starts and finishes at the Stackpole Centre and takes you along a lake, over dunes and onto two of the finest beaches you could wish to find anywhere.

Following the path with the lake to your left, you soon come to a spectacular expanse of lily ponds, which provide a perfect home for innumerable creatures – from dragonflies to otters. From here it is but a short step across a low stone bridge onto the dunes of Stackpole Warren – a unique ecosystem that has proved vital in stemming coastal erosion. To your right lies the secluded Mere Pool Valley and ahead the amber sands of Broad Haven beach, a perfect place to rest for a while or even have a swim.

The remainder of the coastal part of the walk takes you along the tops of cliffs and out onto Stackpole Head, where, on a clear day, you can see as far as Lundy Island. The path then guides you down to the pristine golden sands of Barafundle Bay. Framed by dunes and woodland this secluded spot, often voted 'Best Beach in Britain', is an ideal place to roll out a picnic, build sandcastles or just stroll around with the sand between your toes.

A long flight of stone steps then leads you across the cliff tops and on to the petite and picturesque Stackpole Quay, an 18th-century fishing village. It is then a 1-km (0.6-mi) walk across pretty countryside to return to the Stackpole Centre.

WHERE:
Dyfed
BEST TIME TO GO:
March to September
DON'T MISS:
The tranquil beauty of Barafundle Bay.
AMOUNT OF WALKING:
Lots – though, apart from the climb up from Barafundle Bay, the walk is relatively flat. A bus service (April to September) connects with parts of the walk.
COST:
Low
YOU SHOULD KNOW:
Don't waste too much time looking for otters; they are very secretive creatures with acute senses. It is very probable that they will have spotted you first and disappeared from view.

The golden sands of Barafundle Bay

Coastal walk from Stack Rocks to St Govan's Chapel

WHERE:
Dyfed
BEST TIME TO GO:
April to September. There is usually no firing at weekends, but you should check all the same.
DON'T MISS:
The view of Stack Rocks in the Bristol Channel.
AMOUNT OF WALKING:
Moderate. You do have to retrace your footsteps if you have arrived by car. It is possible to complete the journey one-way using a combination of buses.
COST:
Low
YOU SHOULD KNOW:
The waters from the well at St Govan's Chapel were said to have great healing powers. Unfortunately you can no longer test the validity of that claim, as the waters have long since dried up.

The Green Bridge

It is not every day that one would recommend a firing range as a day out. However, the fact that the stretch of coast between Stack Rocks and St Govan's Chapel is used by the Ministry of Defence for shell firing practice has kept this part of the Pembrokeshire coast relatively free from the type of human erosion suffered by much of Britain's coastal footpath. This area of imposing limestone cliffs is home to a wide variety of birds, which it would seem have got used to the intermittent disturbance.

Having checked with the MoD that they are not shooting that day, it is time to head out along this splendid section of coastline. On leaving the car park at Stack Rocks you are immediately greeted by the two erect pillars of limestone that give the area its name. In June and July they are covered in nesting guillemots. From here you can also see the magnificent Green Bridge, a natural arch carved over millennia by wind and sea.

To your right you have the sound of the sea crashing on the cliffs and to your left is rich grassland, home to rare reptiles and mammals. A spectacular stone staircase down to St Govan's Chapel, a 13th-century single-roomed building, marks the end of the walk. Although relatively short (5 km/3 mi), this hike takes you across some of the most spectacular coastal scenery to be found anywhere in Britain.

Exploring Tenby and a Ferry Trip to Caldey Island

Tenby Harbour

If you leave the A40 at St Clears and take the A477 and then the A478, you will reach the picture-postcard perfect seaside town of Tenby. This gem of the Pembrokeshire coastline has a charm that harks back to the golden age of the British seaside. As well as having over 4 km (2.5 mi) of sandy beaches, the town is rich in historical buildings, most notably the 15th-century St Mary's Church and the imposing Tudor Merchant's House. Both are open to the public and are well worth visiting.

Although Tenby's narrow streets are full of delightful shops, pubs and restaurants, most people are drawn to the harbour. The sight of the sun twinkling on the deep blue sea of Carmarthen Bay can be quite magical. Tenby's beauty can also be its Achilles heel, as it can get maddeningly busy at almost any time of year, if the weather is good. However, respite is near at hand in the form of the handsome monastic island of Caldey. Reachable by ferry, just 5 km (3 mi) across the tranquil waters of Caldey Sound, the island has been home to religious orders for over 1,500 years. It is currently owned by the Reformed Cistercian Order, whose monks, aside from devoting their lives to God, make the most scrumptious chocolate and wild flower perfume.

On landing on Caldey, a short woodland walk takes you to the island's hub where the magnificent Chapel of St David's and the 12th-century St Illtud's Church will both reward a visit. Caldey has a gentle charm that makes it feel far removed from the hustle and bustle of the mainland. For a last outstanding view from the island, head towards the pristinely white lighthouse. The sparkling light of the sea will linger long in the memory.

WHERE:
Dyfed
BEST TIME TO GO:
Caldey Island is open to visitors only from April to October. Tenby is lovely all year round if the weather is good.
DON'T MISS:
The view of Caldey Island across the water from Tenby harbour.
AMOUNT OF WALKING:
Moderate
COST:
Reasonable
YOU SHOULD KNOW:
Women are barred from touring the monastery on Caldey, but they can stand outside and listen to an introduction!

St David's Cathedral

St David's Cathedral, Bishop's Palace and St Brides Bay

As well as having the distinction of being Britain's smallest city, St David's is also the birthplace of the patron saint of Wales, from whom the city takes its name. Dominated by an imposing 12th-century cathedral, St David's is rich in history, myth and legend. The cathedral is one of the most significant religious places in Britain and, throughout its history, it has drawn the finest craftspeople and the highest nobility. The west wing was redesigned by Nash in 1773, while George Gilbert Scott embarked on extensive work on this vast structure in the mid 19th century.

The true enormity of the building can only be fully appreciated by entering it. You are immediately greeted by two original giant columns. The ornate decorations and detailed carvings of the interior are extraordinary, and in every corner there is something to delight in. From the magnificent oak ceiling above the nave, to the gloriously impressive organ, it is a building to lose yourself in for hours on end. Save some of your capacity for wonder, though, as just across the way from the Cathedral lies the 13th-century Bishop's Palace, a roofless ruin with a wonderful Great Hall and superb wheel window.

The drive out of St David's takes you along the north shore of St Brides Bay to the picturesque fishing village of Solva and then on to the golden sands of Newgate Beach. Solva is a wonderfully compact little place that begs to be explored and, while tourism has replaced fishery as its main source of income, it has lost none of its charm. The stretch of coast between Solva and Newgate has a well-maintained footpath and those who feel the need to stretch their legs, will find the 5-km (3-mi) walk most rewarding.

WHERE:
Dyfed
BEST TIME TO GO:
All year round
DON'T MISS:
If you can visit in May, the St David's Festival is a celebration of classical music that brings this magnificent monument fully to life.
AMOUNT OF WALKING:
Moderate, although the entire trip can be undertaken by car.
COST:
Low. Both the Cathedral and the Palace are free to enter (donations are welcomed).
YOU SHOULD KNOW:
Much of the charm of St David's is that it is little larger than a village. This makes it ill equipped to cater for the large numbers of visitors who flock there in high season (Easter to September). It is advisable to bring your own lunch, or be prepared to drive a little way out of town to find a place to eat.

Kenfig National Nature Reserve

Lovers of nature at its truest should head for the Kenfig National Nature Reserve. This precious piece of the Glamorgan coastline – a Site of Special Scientific Interest – can be reached by leaving the M4 motorway at junction 37 and following the signs. Kenfig is a mystical, magical place of sand, lake and sea. Its rolling dunes and wetlands make it one of the most important breeding grounds for birds in Wales. It is also home to a large array of plant and insect life.

Kenfig is a Glamorgan birding hotspot with a wide diversity of birds on view all year round. Just a short walk from the car park and visitor centre, Kenfig Pool is the best place to start a tour of the area. The largest natural lake in South Wales, it is flanked by reed beds and willow scrub on three sides and is an ideal habitat for waterfowl.

Between the lake and the dunes lies a stunning succession of meadows, which are home to a whole host of wild flowers, most notably orchids. When in flower the pungent smell and vibrant colours generated can be almost overpowering. A walk along the nearby beach provides ample opportunity for spotting wading birds such as greenshank and plover. Even if the birds hold no fascination for you, this sometimes bracing walk has great charm of its own and the views over Swansea Bay are dramatic.

With the aid of volunteers, the reserve is managed so that the fragile equilibrium of habitats is maintained and visitors have the chance to enjoy this most lovely coastal ecosystem. If you have the time or the inclination, you can enquire about helping out at the visitor centre.

WHERE:
Mid Glamorgan
BEST TIME TO GO:
All year round. Most of the orchids are in flower by June/July.
DON'T MISS:
The interactive exhibition for children, in the visitor centre.
AMOUNT OF WALKING:
Moderate. There is wheelchair access to the visitor centre, but access to the dunes is difficult for the less mobile.
COST:
Low. There is no charge for entry and there are plenty of free parking spaces.
YOU SHOULD KNOW:
The best bird watching is to be had in the winter when several rare species are often blown off their usual migratory trails by strong winds.

The reedbeds at Kenfig

Rhayader and the Elan Valley

WHERE:
Powys
BEST TIME TO GO:
Any time of year (though the Visitor
Centre is closed in winter)
DON'T MISS:
Red Kites gather for afternoon
feeding at Gigrin Farm near Rhyader
and, along with buzzards and ravens,
they give a wonderful aerial display.
AMOUNT OF WALKING:
Little or moderate (depending on
activities)
COST:
Low
YOU SHOULD KNOW:
Rhyader is reputed to enjoy the
largest number of pubs per capita in
the UK.

The ancient market town of Rhayader owed its prosperity to its position on the River Wye, a crossroads for drovers heading for the English market towns and a staging post on the Aberystwyth to London coaching route. Lying in a loop of the Wye, it is surrounded by the unspoilt Cambrian hills and, to the east, the Elan Valley with its spectacular reservoirs and protected wildlife. It is still an important agricultural centre as well as a popular base for walkers, cyclists, naturalists and anglers. The handsome town has an interesting folk museum and a lovely riverside walk. It is remembered for the 'Rebecca Riots' which took place between 1839 and 1844, when the hard-pressed poor disguised themselves as women and tore down tollgates. Mountain bikes can be hired here – the countryside is criss-crossed by quiet lanes and bridleways and the Elan Trail is suitable for all, from cyclist to wheelchair-user. North of the town, Gilfach Farm Nature Reserve covers forest, moorland and river habitats, and there's a restored Welsh longhouse which holds exhibitions.

The chain of four reservoirs in the Elan Valley was constructed in the late 19th century to supply water to Birmingham. Farms and homes were flooded but now careful monitoring of the catchment area preserves the rare flora and fauna which flourish in this Site of Special Scientific Interest – including the Red kite. At Caban Coch dam there is a Visitor Centre; from Garreg Ddu viaduct, the road skirts the water and loops back to Pen-y-garreg dam, a huge wall of falling water when the lake overflows. Craig Goch dam is a curving wall of graceful arches. From Claerwen Reservoir, to the west – built in the 1950s – several hill walks begin.

Garreg Ddu viaduct

Snowdon

The highest British mountain south of the Scottish Highlands, Snowdon is a massif, a star of ridges rising to four peaks, the tallest reaching 1,085 m (3,560 ft). The mountain figures large in the history and legend of Wales and this – its Welsh name, Yr Wyddfa, means 'The Burial Place' – is the site of an ancient tumulus. Snowdon has been a popular climb since the 18th century naturalist Thomas Pennant published a lyrical account of dawn on the summit. Most chose, as they do now, the long (8 km/5 mi) shallow path from the town of Llanberis, and in 1896 the Snowdon Mountain Railway was opened. It runs alongside the path, and makes the top of Snowdon accessible to non-walkers.

The train pushes up Snowdon.

The north and east faces are steep and rocky, with shallower, grassy slopes to the south and west. Marked and named paths join and cross, allowing a combination of routes. Even the longer, easier paths – Llanberis, Watkin and Snowdon Ranger (named for an early mountain guide) – involve steep sections and rough terrain, and walkers in unsuitable footwear and clothing (it is often sunny in Llanberis but cold and wet at the summit) frequently have to be rescued from the mountainside. The shorter paths involve painstaking ridges, knife-edge traverses and, in the long winters, ice, and they are demanding enough to provide training for ascents of the world's great peaks.

The train (Britain's only rack and pinion line) can be over-subscribed at weekends and in summer; it is wise to book ahead. The round trip allows half an hour at the summit, though many choose to walk down and take time to enjoy the views.

WHERE:
Gwynedd
BEST TIME TO GO:
Any time of year (though the train runs to the summit only between May and October, and only experienced climbers should attempt the steeper paths in winter).
DON'T MISS:
The views. If the weather allows, the panorama from the summit can reach as far as England, Scotland and Ireland.
AMOUNT OF WALKING:
Little or lots (even one way is a tough walk).
COST:
Low or expensive (though the train fare is worth it!).
YOU SHOULD KNOW:
Railway enthusiasts should note that many of the engines in service are diesel; the ticket office has daily information on the use of steam.

The mirror-like surface of Lake Vyrnwy

Lake Vyrnwy

WHERE:
Powys
BEST TIME TO GO:
Any time of year (in winter, peace replaces the activities and the dolphin sculptures appear to be leaping from the high water).
DON'T MISS:
The beauty and tranquillity of this place, with sheep, cattle and ponies grazing in the heather and butterflies, dragonflies and birds on the wing.
AMOUNT OF WALKING:
Little to moderate
COST:
Low to reasonable
YOU SHOULD KNOW:
Lake Vyrnwy is the water source for Bombay Sapphire Gin.

In a lovely valley in north Powys, with a backdrop of the magnificent mountains of Snowdonia, Lake Vyrnwy, like many Welsh reservoirs, was constructed in the late 19th century – drowning a village in the process – to provide water for a rapidly growing English city, in this case Liverpool. Long and narrow and surrounded by countryside rich in wildlife, Lake Vyrnwy, with its impressive dam and fairytale tower rising from the waters (actually functional, a straining tower) is very picturesque. Above the lake, a grand hotel built to accommodate those who came to see what was then Europe's biggest dam, offers, as it did then, a variety of field sports and fishing.

A road runs around the lake, but this is a marvellous place for outdoor activities. The whole area is a nature reserve, with marked trails, and the RSPB has hides around the lake. The heather moorland is being restored and broadleaf trees planted to replace conifers as habitat for the many species found here.

Since the late 1990s, in the valley below the dam, Lake Vyrnwy's exciting sculpture park has been evolving. Using local timber and on-site materials, artists from Wales, Eastern Europe and Australia have been working on the themes of the diversity of nature and the interaction of man in the environment.

For the more energetic there are walking and cycle trails – bikes can be hired. On the water, tuition in sailing, kayaking and white-water rafting is offered, and boats may be rented.

Scenic drive from Llanidloes to Machynlleth

Llanidloes is a lively, attractive town on the Severn, once a stronghold of the Chartists. Its architecture ranges from imposing 19th- century chapels to a black-and-white stilted Market Hall (unique in Wales) built in the early 17th century. The local history museum is quirkily fascinating and regular events in town include an annual Fancy Dress Night.

From here, the road runs north-west through a landscape of sparse grandeur. Llyn Clywedog reservoir lies harmoniously in the glorious Clywedog Valley; a circular drive allows views of the towering concrete dam and dense Hafren Forest on the bleak slopes of Plynlimon, the source of several rivers including the Severn and the Wye. A walk leads down to the Bryn Tail lead-mine workings in the Clywedog Gorge and the lake offers boating and fishing. This is a great bird-watching spot; residents include Red kites and buzzards.

A narrow mountain road climbs past the spectacular ravine of Dylife Gorge. From the tiny, isolated village of Dylife – a flourishing lead-mining town in the 19th century – good walks lead to the old mine-works and the lovely hills. West of the village, a memorial to the broadcaster Wynford Vaughan-Thomas overlooks a marvellous panorama of valleys and mountains.

In 1404, Owain Glyndwr set up parliament in Machynlleth; now the Parliament House has a display on the Welsh hero's life. Machynlleth is a handsome, agreeable place; still a busy market town, it is now very much a centre for the arts. Plas Machynlleth, an 18th-century mansion, is a centre for Celtic studies, and just north of the town is the fascinating Centre for Alternative Technology.

WHERE:
Powys
BEST TIME TO GO:
March to November
DON'T MISS:
The Centre for Alternative Technology occupies a lovely site (once a disused slate quarry); its interactive displays and activities appeal to all ages.
AMOUNT OF WALKING:
Moderate
COST:
Low or reasonable (depending on activities on the way).
YOU SHOULD KNOW:
Llyn Clywedog Reservoir is regularly stocked with trout and is the venue for the annual European Open angling competition.

Clywedog Reservoir and Dam

Aberystwyth

Aberystwyth lies on the long sweep of Cardigan Bay. With its curving promenade, seafront Regency terraces, fine hotels and two beaches, it was a popular and elegant resort in the 19th century and remains an attractive and interesting seaside town. There is a pier, breezy walks around the castle ruins on the headland, pleasure boats and fishing trips from the old harbour, and the longest cliff railway in Britain. This was opened in 1896, and originally water balanced. It climbs to the top of Constitution Hill at the northern end of the seafront where, as well as cafés and telescopes to look at the fine panorama, there is a Camera Obscura. The present building is a recreation of the popular Victorian attraction; using revolving balanced mirrors and lenses it projects detailed close-up and long-shot views of the town and its surroundings.

Aberystwyth's relative isolation has given it a strong Welsh cultural identity. It is home to part of the University of Wales, and to the National Library of Wales, which is open to the public and houses, as well as a huge collection of Welsh volumes – including some rare and ancient manuscripts – permanent and changing exhibitions.

The original settlement from which Aberystwyth grew, Llanbadarn Fawr (now almost joined to the town) was the spot where Breton St Padarn set up a monastery in the 6th century. St Padarn parish church was built in the 13th century; the impressive building with its steep churchyard has an exhibition on the monastic foundation. North of Aberystwyth, the wide sands of Borth attract windsurfers; the expanse of sand dunes on the Dyfi estuary forms the excellent Ynyslas Nature Reserve.

The beach and colourful Victorian seafront buildings by Constitution Hill, Aberystwyth

Portmeirion

A fantasy village on the seashore, where buildings and ornaments from many lands and periods rub shoulders, Portmeirion is best known as 'The Village' in the 1960s cult TV series, 'The Prisoner', though it has provided exotic locations for many other television programmes and films.

Architect Clough Williams-Ellis dreamed of building 'a light-hearted live exhibition of architecture, décor and landscaping', and in the 1920s he found a wilderness he could fill with endangered buildings and architectural salvage from Britain and abroad. His work continued for about fifty years, and the project was self-financing from the start – he used profits from the waterside Victorian hotel for on-going works. His guiding principle in creating this 'tribute to the Mediterranean' was that natural beauty and profitable development could exist together. In 1973 Portmeirion was scheduled as of architectural and historical importance and later designated a Conservation Area. Today it is owned by a registered charity and many of its buildings, including the recently converted, castellated Victorian mansion Castell Deudraeth, are part of the extended hotel.

Portmeirion is one of Wales's top tourist destinations; day visitors wander around the enchanting dream world where portico and campanile, oriental statue and brewery clock, town hall and pastel-washed cottages cluster round an Italian piazza. There are shops (including a seconds outlet for the popular pottery) and on-site catering, or visitors can picnic on the shore or in the extensive sub-tropical woodlands, which are planted with thousands of self-sustaining plant species.

WHERE:
Gwynedd
BEST TIME TO GO:
Any time of year (in spring the rhododendrons and camellias are in bloom; summer can be very crowded, winter eerie and mysterious).
DON'T MISS:
The surreal and theatrical juxtaposition of buildings and styles, the oddities of scale and perspective.
AMOUNT OF WALKING:
Moderate (although this is a steep site with lots of steps, there are also long sloping paths to all areas).
COST:
Reasonable
YOU SHOULD KNOW:
Portmeirion hosts an annual 'Prisoner' fan convention and there is a year-round 'Prisoner' souvenir shop.

Relaxing in the gardens of Portmeirion.

The picturesque village of Beddgelert

A Walk from Beddgelert to Gelert's Grave

The lovely grey stone village of Beddgelert is surrounded by the glorious scenery of the southern slopes of Snowdon – woods, lakes, deep valleys, tumbling streams and a dramatic skyline of peaks. It lies at the confluence of the Colwyn and Glaslyn, just before the rivers plunge into the Aberglaslyn Gorge. Beddgelert means 'burial place of Gelert' and though this probably refers to Celert, a 6th-century saint, those who take the pleasant walk along the Glaslyn come to visit a fenced-off stone, Gelert's Grave, the grave of a legendary dog. The tale of faithful Gelert, mistakenly slain by his master Prince Llywelyn – the blood the horrified prince saw was not that of his baby son but of the wolf Gelert had killed to save the boy – may be an 18th century invention but it has become lore, and this is the village's most famous attraction.

Further along the path, a reddish stain on the hillside marks the position of the copper mine. The Romans were the first to extract ore here and in the 19th century the mines brought great prosperity. They were deserted in 1903, but have been successfully restored, and now offer self-guided audio tours of the multiple layers of tunnels and galleries. Hard-hatted visitors wander at their own pace past interpretive displays explaining the mining process, along dank, dripping passages where seams of ore still gleam, and through chambers bristling with stalactites and stalagmites. The mine is lit, though visitors may want to carry a torch in the dim chill of the tunnels. An adventure playground and various activities, including gold-panning, are available. From the end of the tour there is a fine view towards the rocky outcrop of Dinas Emry, the legendary birthplace of the Red Dragon of Wales.

WHERE:
Powys
BEST TIME TO GO:
March to October (the mine is open for restricted hours in winter but the riverside walk gets rather wet).
DON'T MISS:
The remarkable stalagmites and stalactites have formed since the closure of the mine; unlike the usual slow-growing limestone formations these are of ferrous oxide.
AMOUNT OF WALKING:
Moderate (there are several flights of steps in the mine).
COST:
Reasonable
YOU SHOULD KNOW:
In 1958 the mountainside around Sygun was transformed into a Chinese village when *The Inn of the Sixth Happiness* was filmed here.

Llechwedd Slate Caverns

Though little is now produced, slate remains a potent symbol of north Wales. Quarried or mined, it splits readily into thin sheets and has been used since Roman times for roofing. During the Industrial Revolution, as working towns mushroomed, the Welsh slate industry flourished. Blaenau Ffestiniog, huddled in a landscape of heaped, shattered grey slate on the southern outcrops of Snowdonia, was a prosperous town in the 19th century when the fine blue slate mined in the Ffestiniog Valley was loaded here for rail transport to the coast. Now tourists travel on the narrow-gauge railway and visit the slate caverns at nearby Llechwedd.

In the 1970s, parts of the abandoned mine were re-opened to make a tourist attraction which gives insights into the skills and appalling working conditions of the Victorian miners. It is set in a Victorian mining village, complete with forge, a working pub and various shops, including a sweet shop where visitors can use the 'Victorian' coins exchanged in the bank to buy old-fashioned sweets.

Two tours are available: The Miners' Tramway uses a little train to dive into the mountainside using a tunnel that dates from 1846. This trip incorporates son et lumiere tableaux and the opportunity to alight and learn more of the slate mining processes. It passes caverns of awe-inspiring scale. Those who chose the Deep Mine tour descend (clad in helmets and waterproofs) in Britain's steepest funicular railway to a walk through a series of ten impressive caverns with sequences of tableaux on the life and work of the miners.

WHERE:
Gwynedd
WHEN TO GO:
Any time of year (the Caverns remain open in winter and the landscape has a harsh dramatic beauty).
DON'T MISS:
The Miners' Tramway passes Chough's Cavern, where these rare, crow-like birds are re-establishing a nesting colony.
AMOUNT OF WALKING:
Little (the walk in the Deep Mine tour is about 25 minutes)
COST:
Reasonable (there is a good discount for taking both tours; above ground is free).
YOU SHOULD KNOW:
Welsh slate can be found in an array of small souvenirs, but is best seen in the roadside fences of thin broken slabs and the carved fireplaces still found in pubs.

Splitting the slate for roof tiles.

The Great Little Trains of Wales

WHERE:
Gwynedd
BEST TIME TO GO:
March to October (only the Ffestiniog line runs all year).
DON'T MISS:
The scenery on the Ffestiniog line is glorious – the silvery estuary at Porthmadog, the lush green valley and the slow steep gradients through the blue-grey slate hills.
AMOUNT OF WALKING:
Little (unless you get off to walk; some of the rolling stock is adapted for wheelchairs).
COST:
Reasonable to expensive (depending on the lines and number of trips – buying a Discount Card reduces fares on all Great Little Trains by 20 per cent).
YOU SHOULD KNOW:
The Ffestiniog and Caernarfon lines organize special events – dining trains, jazz trains, Real Ale trails, etc.

Some of the world's first railways were built in Wales – at first, hauled by horses – to carry coal and slate from pits and quarries in the mountains to the coast. The lines fell into disuse with the decline of the industries, but many have been restored by volunteer enthusiasts who now run vintage trains, mostly steam-hauled, on some wonderfully scenic routes. These are united as The Great Little Trains of Wales, and North Wales in particular is heaven for steam buffs as well as for those who enjoy dramatic and unspoilt landscapes.

Llanberis Lake Railway with its hour-long round trip offers a taste of narrow-gauge travel, running along the shore of Lake Padarn between Gilfach Ddu and Llanberis, with superb views of the mountains and the picturesque ruins of Dolbadarn Castle. The two sections of the Welsh Highland Railway will soon join to run from Porthmadog to Caernarfon; at the time of writing, it offers two separate trips – a short run from Porthmadog's fine station and a visit to the engine sheds, and an exciting climb from Caernarfon and its magnificent castle to Rhyd Ddu, in the foothills of Snowdon. The train runs along 19 km (12 mi) of snaking track behind the most powerful 2' gauge steam locomotives in the world.

The Ffestiniog Railway is the best-known line, and since its beginnings in 1832 as a gravity and horse-drawn line it has provided instruction and inspiration to the world's railway engineers. The ride is outstanding, twisting and looping, climbing steadily. Halts en route (and the timetabling) allow walks – on to the next stop to rejoin a train, or just to a local pub for lunch.

The Ffestiniog Railway runs from Porthmadog to Blaenau Ffestiniog.

Rhyl

One of the north coast towns which, in the heyday of the British seaside holiday, catered for the huge influx of workers from the cities of north-west England, Rhyl remains popular (witness the battalions of caravans along the coast roads!). For a brash and breezy day out it has the lot – miles of sandy beaches for swimming, sandcastles, donkey rides and a two-mile promenade scattered with traditional and state-of-the-art attractions. The Prom throbs with music from the rides, the flashing and beeping of arcade games, the smell of chips.

Amusement park and boats in mouth of the River Clwyd in Rhyl

At the eastern end, the Sun Centre is an undercover complex of pools, slides and flumes (one of the pools offers a Tropical Rain Storm). The Sea Life Centre contains various marine habitats including the Sea at Night, where fish lurk in the dim ocean depths, but the star attraction is the walk-through underwater tunnel where sharks and other big fish swirl and circle around the visitors. In Drift Park, a wooded walkway linking a children's playground, crazy golf, a skateboard park and the Events Arena, stands the 72-m (240-ft) Sky Tower. Here, an observation tower rotates and climbs around a central column, providing views and commentary. The Knights' Cavern shows a remarkable animatronic version of the 'splendour and tragedy of Ancient Wales'. The Ocean Beach Amusement Park, at the western end of the Prom, provides a range of white-knuckle rides and traditional funfair amusements.

Relative peace can be found in the Botanical Gardens or the Museum, or at Marine Lake. This large man-made lake, used in the 19th century for bathing and now for water-sports, is circled by a mile-long track where a 15' gauge railway train chugs slowly round as it has since 1911.

WHERE:
Denbighshire
BEST TIME TO GO:
May to September (all year for those not taking children, and who enjoy an out-of-season atmosphere).
DON'T MISS:
Shark feeding time at Sea Life is a pleasantly scary experience.
AMOUNT OF WALKING:
Moderate
COST:
Reasonable to expensive (depending on the number of rides and games you can avoid!).
YOU SHOULD KNOW:
The Sky Tower rises and rotates quite fast; it's not for the faint hearted.

The tram travels up the Great Orme.

Llandudno

The premier resort on the North Wales coast, Llandudno came to fashionable prominence in the Victorian era, an origin amply reflected in the elegant streets, crescents and squares of its compact town centre. Although the town has no shortage of modern attractions, this period appearance has helped it to retain the relaxed charms of a traditional British seaside resort more successfully than most. The gentler activities of bygone years, such as donkey rides, boat trips and Punch and Judy shows, can all be enjoyed still on the main North Shore beach, while for a quieter experience of sea and sand you should head for the less developed beach on the West Shore.

Llandudno faces out to the Irish Sea between the Great Orme and Little Orme headlands. Built by the Victorians as a carriage drive the 6.5-km (4-mi) Marine Drive winds its way around the Great Orme headland, linking North and West Shores. In no time at all from the town centre the Drive brings you to coastal scenery of rugged, isolated grandeur. The Drive is mostly one-way with plenty of stopping places, but for the best experience leave the car behind and walk or cycle the route.

Another popular excursion is to the summit of Great Orme itself, where you are rewarded with views of Anglesey, Snowdonia and the Isle of Man. A modern cable car whisks you to the summit but the more atmospheric way to reach it is by the hundred-year-old tramway, the only remaining cable-hauled tramway operating on a public highway in Britain (and one of only three surviving in the world, the others being Lisbon and San Francisco). As the beautifully restored historic tramcar carries you uphill, look out for the wild Kashmiri goats that roam the headland.

WHERE:
Conwy
BEST TIME TO GO:
Any time of year (but note that many attractions, including the tramway, are only open during the summer season (March to October).
DON'T MISS:
Stop off half way up the tramway for an excursion to the fascinating Great Orme Copper Mines, thought to be the largest known prehistoric mine in the world.
AMOUNT OF WALKING:
Moderate. Marine Drive involves a very gentle ascent and descent.
COST:
Reasonable. There is a car toll payable for Marine Drive.
YOU SHOULD KNOW:
Llandudno was where Alice Liddell, the real-life Alice in Wonderland, spent her childhood summers. You can savour something of her adventures down the rabbit hole at the Alice in Wonderland Centre.

Conwy

For a town of its size Conwy is unusually rich in historic sites and associations. With an attractive location at the mouth of a river bearing the same name, Conwy contains some rare survivors from past eras of urban design, including Aberconwy House, a 14th-century merchant's house that is one of the oldest in the country, and 16th-century Plas Mawr (Welsh for 'Great Mansion'). With its prominent stepped gables and an interior boasting ornate plaster ceilings and wooden screens, Plas Mawr is the best-preserved town house of its kind in Britain and a vivid reminder of the wealth and ostentation of the first Elizabethan age.

Binding all together are the town walls, another remarkable survivor from medieval times. You can walk along a section of the 1.2-km (0.75-mi) circuit, which includes no fewer than twenty-one towers. Wherever you are in the town, be it on the walls or down by the river, you cannot escape the presiding guardian of the place, Edward I's sternly imposing castle, perched high on a rocky outcrop. You can spend a good couple of hours exploring the castle's intriguing design and taking in the outstanding views from the battlements, not only of the valley and surrounding countryside but also down into the enormous roofless expanse of the Great Hall.

Younger family members will certainly be intrigued by a visit to the quayside where they can enter the smallest house in Britain. This former fisherman's cottage measures a mere 1.8 m (6 ft) wide by 3 m (9.75 ft) high; incredibly, its last occupant stood 1.9 m (6.25 ft) tall! And the spirit of the early industrial age is evoked in Thomas Telford's handsome suspension bridge over the river, dating along with its tollhouse from 1826.

WHERE:
Conwy
BEST TIME TO GO:
Any time of year (but note that some buildings, such as Plas Mawr and Aberconwy House, are closed during the winter months (November to March).
DON'T MISS:
The stunning views from the castle battlements.
AMOUNT OF WALKING:
Moderate
COST:
Reasonable
YOU SHOULD KNOW:
If the views entice you to explore the surrounding countryside, a trip up the Conwy Valley to the Trefriw Woollen Mills is a recommended excursion.

Conwy Castle

The Castles of Edward I

WHERE:
Gwynedd and Conwy
BEST TIME TO GO:
Any time of year (but Harlech in particular can be exposed to chilly sea winds in the winter).
DON'T MISS:
The distinctive coloured bands in much of the stonework at Caernarfon.
AMOUNT OF WALKING:
Moderate. A reasonable level of stamina is required to climb up towers and scale battlements, especially for three castles in a day!

Harlech Castle

The rebellious Welsh caused the English king Edward I considerable trouble in the first years of his reign. Once he had finally subdued them in the early 1280s, Edward proceeded to stamp his authority on this remote part of his realm, building an 'iron ring' of castles to keep a stern eye on the native population. As a consequence Wales boasts some of the world's supreme achievements in military architecture, a fact recognized when UNESCO World Heritage status was awarded in 1986.

If you plan carefully you can visit three of these majestic edifices, at Conwy, Caernarfon and Harlech, in a single day; comparing their differing structures is definitely a worthwhile experience. All three are situated on the north-west coastline surrounding Snowdonia, so should you tire of fortifications there are always views of the distant hills to soothe the eyes. Start your day early at either Conwy or Harlech; the journey to the other via Caernarfon, which is roughly half-way, is some 80 km (50 mi). Building began in 1283 but whereas work at Conwy and Harlech was complete by the end of the decade, it continued at Caernarfon, the mightiest of them all, until well into the following century; parts of the structure, indeed, have never been finished.

Harlech, high on a crag above the Irish Sea, is a superb example of the concentric model of castle design, with an outer line of walls encompassing a massive inner ward. Conwy and Caernarfon, by contrast, are linear structures, their irregular and elongated shapes determined by their respective geographic sites. Caernarfon, built to be a royal residence as well as a military stronghold, is famed for its unusual polygonal towers and for being the site of the investiture of Prince Charles as Prince of Wales in 1969.

COST:
Reasonable. As the castles are all in the care of Cadw (the historic environment service of the Welsh Assembly), it is worth considering buying an annual membership, especially if you are a family with more than one child under 16 (this gives you free admission to Welsh sites and half-price admission to many sites in England and Scotland).
YOU SHOULD KNOW:
Edward earned his nickname, 'Longshanks', on account of his stature: at 1.9 m (6ft 2in) he was unusually tall for his time.

Bodnant Garden & Penrhyn Castle

Two grandiose creations of the 19th century combine for this day out in the lovely coastal hinterland of North Wales. A few kilometres south of Conwy town, Bodnant Garden offers a spectacular setting overlooking the Conwy Valley together with the stunning backdrop of the Snowdonia range away to the west. The garden was begun in 1875 and is the work of successive generations of the Aberconway family who wanted it to be a true garden for all seasons. You are guaranteed colourful displays whenever you visit, although the azaleas and rhododendrons in spring, the laburnum arch which flowers in late May, and the autumn blaze are particular highlights. The upper level features formal lawns, wide terraces and terrific views, whereas you can indulge in your own explorations in the wilder areas of the wooded valley and stream below.

Just 30 km (20 mi) west of Bodnant on a site close to the Menai Strait separating the Welsh mainland from Anglesey, stands Penrhyn Castle. Now run, like Bodnant, by the National Trust, Penrhyn is one family's fantasy of a medieval castle, built in the first half of the 19th century in mock-Norman style. The family in question were the Pennants who had become rich from harvesting Jamaican sugar and mining Welsh slate. The castle contains a striking collection of original furniture, specially designed for its setting, and an unexpectedly good family art collection. Life below stairs is imaginatively evoked in the extensive Victorian kitchens, while for the younger visitor there are fine displays of dolls and model railways in the stable block.

WHERE:
Conwy and Gwynedd
BEST TIME TO GO:
March to October (both places are closed over the winter months).
DON'T MISS:
The extraordinary slate bed at Penrhyn, made for Queen Victoria and weighing in at one tonne.
AMOUNT OF WALKING:
Moderate.
There is good wheelchair access to the ground floor and stable block at Penrhyn. There is a special accessible route at Bodnant, where there are many steep slopes and steps.
COST:
Reasonable –
RHS (Royal Horticultural Society) members get free admission to Bodnant Garden.
YOU SHOULD KNOW:
Penrhyn Castle offers a good audio-guide (adult's and child's versions) for which there is a small extra charge.

The laburnum arch is at its best in late May.

Rheidol Power Station & Red Kite Feeding Centre

Rheidol Power Station lies in the Rheidol Valley 13 km (8 mi) east of Aberystwyth. It is the largest conventional hydro-electric scheme in England and Wales and has been supplying power to the national grid for nearly fifty years. Through the construction of dams and reservoirs this clean, renewable energy source harnesses the power of flowing water to generate electricity. A visitor centre at the Power Station features exhibits and interactive displays explaining the process; free guided tours of the site are offered during the summer months. Information is also available about the adjacent wind farm, which opened ten years ago.

Rheidol takes its relationship with the local environment very seriously. There is careful management of the landscape to encourage biodiversity; on your tour you will learn about the rich variety of birdlife on the site, about its bat colonies and the steps that have been taken to conserve the spawning grounds for the river's salmon and trout. The most spectacular example of this harmonious co-existence with nature can be seen at the nearby Bwlch Nant yr Arian Forest Visitor Centre, where wild red kites are fed every afternoon. These graceful birds are among the largest of the country's birds of prey, although they are mainly scavengers rather than active predators. As you watch them wheeling and soaring ever higher on the thermal currents over the valley, before swooping suddenly to grasp a morsel in their talons it is hard to believe that they were once regarded as vermin and were almost extinct 200 years ago. Now, thanks to a number of breeding programmes, Red kite numbers are once again relatively healthy, with over 300 pairs in Wales alone.

WHERE:
Ceredigion
BEST TIME TO GO:
Any time of year for the kite feeding; power station tours May to September only.
DON'T MISS:
The gentle 1-km (0.6 mi) walk around the lake at the Forest Centre for the chance to see Red kites in their element, as well as herons, buzzards and kestrels.
AMOUNT OF WALKING:
Little (although there are some excellent walking trails from the Forest Centre if you want to see more of the landscape).
COST:
Low
YOU SHOULD KNOW:
Listen out for the distinctive call of the Red kite: a high-pitched, insistent mewing that has been likened to a shepherd's whistle.

A Red kite swoops down on its prey.

WHERE:
Ceredigion
BEST TIME TO GO:
March to October
DON'T MISS:
The experience of going underground at Llywernog (warm clothing and good footwear advised).
AMOUNT OF WALKING:
Moderate (but note the steep descent down to the river at Devil's Bridge).
COST:
Reasonable
YOU SHOULD KNOW:
If you're only visiting Devil's Bridge consider leaving the car at home and taking the delightful Vale of Rheidol narrow-gauge steam railway, which chugs up the valley from Aberystwyth.

Llywernog Silver-Lead Mine & Devil's Bridge

These two attractions are a short drive inland from Aberystwyth. The Silver-Lead Mine at Llywernog is an award-winning mining museum created on the site of a real mine first worked in the mid-18th century. In its heyday more than sixty miners laboured to extract the silver-lead ore, and strong links were forged with the Cornish mining industry. By the end of the 19th century rich new deposits in Australia and the USA had spelled the end of the mine as a viable enterprise; the mighty waterwheel, built in 1874, stands as a poignant reminder of a final desperate effort to keep it going. Much of the original equipment and machinery can now be seen on a tour of the site, which also takes you down into the underground workings. You can even try some panning yourself; the museum offers the inducement that you keep anything you find!

A short distance down the Rheidol Valley brings you to Devil's Bridge, a famous beauty spot. Local legend has it that the devil, disguised as a monk, built the bridge at the behest of Megan, an old lady whose cow was stranded on the other side of the steep gorge. The devil's part of the bargain was to take the first living creature across the bridge, but wily Megan proved more than his match, contriving to send her dog over first. In fact, three bridges, built one on top of the other, are to be seen, as well as a series of spectacular waterfalls dropping 100 m (300 ft). If you have the time and energy you should take the informative nature trail, which descends the 100 steps of Jacob's Ladder down into the gorge and over the Mynach River to the Robber's Cave on the far side.

Rhaeadr Mynach waterfall

Powis Castle and Garden

With its dramatic location surmounting a rock above the Severn Valley, there is no mistaking the origins of Powis Castle as a fortress for the medieval Welsh princes to guard the border against the old enemy England. Although the stern exterior with its crenellations and turrets still evokes these more unsettled times, we owe it to the

Powis Castle

enterprise and imagination of successive generations of the Herbert family that the castle as we see it today has become one of the great houses of Britain. Regular modifications to the interior in response to changing tastes have resulted in a remarkable history lesson illustrating the main styles of British interior design over the centuries, from the 14th to the 20th. Highlights include the Elizabethan Long Gallery with its splendid plasterwork ceiling and the sumptuously decorated State Bedroom and Blue Drawing-room, from the 17th and 18th centuries respectively.

When you have marvelled at the castle interiors and their fine collections of furniture and paintings, an altogether different pleasure awaits you outside. The justly famous garden was the vision of one man, the first Marquess of Powis who in the late 17th century transformed an unprepossessing slope on the south-eastern side of the castle into a series of formal terraces in the fashionable Italian style; four survive today from the original six. Take your time on these terraces to appreciate the profusion of planting in the borders and the splendid views over the Severn Valley to England. Particularly delightful are the charming (and original) lead statues of shepherds and shepherdesses on the balustrade of the third terrace.

WHERE:
Powys
BEST TIME TO GO:
March to October (only the Garden is open in November).
DON'T MISS:
The small but outstanding collection of treasures from India which celebrates the Powis family's association with Clive of India, one of the great military figures of the early British Empire.
AMOUNT OF WALKING:
Little (but bear in mind that there are a lot of steps and slopes within a compact area).
COST:
Low
YOU SHOULD KNOW:
The Castle is built from the same ruddy-coloured rock on which it stands, giving it a particularly striking appearance in the morning sun.

433

Offa's Dyke is now a long-distance footpath.

Offa's Dyke Centre & Walk

The origins of the earthwork known as Offa's Dyke may be shrouded in mystery but there is no denying the sheer scale and ambition of this unusual survivor from the period preceding the Norman Conquest. Offa was an 8th-century King of Mercia who ruled over a large area of central England. An uncompromising ruler and effective administrator, Offa used every opportunity to consolidate his territory, in this case by constructing a huge rampart and ditch to delineate his kingdom from the lands of the Welsh princes to the west. The Dyke was probably built as a defensive boundary and may have run the entire length of the border between England and Wales, from the mouth of the Severn to the Dee estuary, although today it can be traced for just 130 km (80 mi), somewhat less than half its total length, principally in the central area between the Wye Valley and Wrexham.

The course of the Dyke is remembered today through the Offa's Dyke National Trail, a long-distance footpath which runs for 285 km (177 mi) from Chepstow on the banks of the Severn to Prestatyn on the North Wales coast. The small village of Knighton in Powys is situated at the half-way point on the Trail; here you will find the Offa's Dyke Centre which houses an excellent interactive exhibition about the history of the Dyke and of the Marches, as the border area is known. If after visiting the Centre you want to see the Dyke for yourself you can head out on the section of the National Trail that runs south from Knighton, where you will encounter both well-preserved sections and splendid views.

Abbey-Cwm-Hir & The National Cycle Collection

When the Cistercian order of monks set about establishing their great abbeys in Britain during the 12th century they chose remote rural locations, the better to enhance the spiritual tranquillity of the monastic life. Few places in Wales are as remote as the Abbey-Cwm-Hir, which translates as the "Abbey in the Long Valley". This lovely, secluded spot 16 km (10 mi) north of Llandrindod Wells was the site of the largest Cistercian foundation in Wales, though you need to exercise your imagination to summon up past glories from the modest ruins visible today.

As with so many of the great monasteries following their dissolution by Henry VIII, Abbey-Cwm-Hir fell victim to subsequent generations of builders who looted the site for its high-quality materials. Traces of medieval masonry can be found in several buildings in the village, including the Hall at Abbey-Cwm-Hir, an imposing mansion built in 1834 by Thomas Wilson in the fashionable Gothic Revival style. The Hall's fifty-two rooms and grounds have been restored with great care and affection by its present owners, who are often on hand to conduct you around personally. The interior boasts outstanding examples of craftsmanship, most of it original, including fine plasterwork ceilings, a rare stained-glass lantern roof, and no fewer than fourteen marble fireplaces.

Back in Llandrindod Wells, a pleasant couple of hours can be spent in the National Cycle Collection. Even if you are not in thrall to the delights of pedal power, this remarkable assemblage of bicycles and artefacts associated with the history of cycling will have something to capture your interest. As you gaze on the early penny-farthings and boneshakers it is sobering to reflect on the rigours and perils to which our ancestors so willingly subjected themselves in the name of progress.

WHERE:
Powys
BEST TIME TO GO:
Any time of year (but note that from November to February the National Cycle Collection is only open Tuesdays, Thursdays and Sundays).
DON'T MISS:
The modern memorial slab in the Abbey ruins to commemorate the supposed burial place of Llywelyn ap Gruffydd, the last of the native princes of Wales.
AMOUNT OF WALKING:
Moderate
COST:
Reasonable
YOU SHOULD KNOW:
You can only visit the Hall at Abbey-Cwm-Hir on a pre-booked tour, but these are available throughout the year.

The drawing room at Abbey-Cwm-Hir

Crickhowell

WHERE:
Powys
BEST TIME TO GO:
April to September, when Tretower
Castle and Court are open.
DON'T MISS:
The views from Table Mountain and
the remains of an Iron-Age hill fort
on the summit.
AMOUNT OF WALKING:
Lots (if you want to take full
advantage of your surroundings).
COST:
Low
YOU SHOULD KNOW:
For the more energetic and
adventurous there are plenty of
other outdoor activities on offer,
including riding, white-water rafting
and hang-gliding.

The busy little market town of Crickhowell lies on the A40 trunk road between Abergavenny and Brecon. Nestling in the picturesque Usk Valley, Crickhowell is surrounded by hills: the Black Mountains to the north and east and the Brecon Beacons to the west. The town itself more than warrants a morning or afternoon's exploration; wandering around its compact little streets you will discover several historic gems, including a 12th-century parish church and the Bear Hotel, an old coaching inn dating from the early 15th century, which still has its cobblestone courtyard. Crickhowell's most memorable sight is the 16th-century bridge spanning the River Usk, notable for having either twelve or thirteen arches, depending on your vantage point!

The town is an excellent base for exploring the glorious countryside. Details of the many local walks are available from the tourist information office, housed in the new Resource and Information Centre which also displays the work of local artists and craftspeople. One of the most popular walks is the climb up Table Mountain, whose distinctive profile north of the town sends out a challenge that is hard to resist. Although steep in places the views from the top are worth the effort; the whole ascent and descent should take you around 2.5 hours.

Among the numerous excursions from Crickhowell, Tretower Castle and Court is one of the easiest. Just 5 km (3 mi) north west of the town, Tretower has a fine old courtyard house, which dates from the 15th century and has some outstanding original timberwork; there is also a restored formal garden of the period. Next to the house are the ruins of the Norman castle which first occupied the site, its most striking feature is a round tower added in the early 13th century.

*The many-arched bridge
into Crickhowell*

Beaumaris Castle and Anglesey Sea Zoo

Beaumaris Castle

Lying just off the north-west coast of Wales the Isle of Anglesey is separated from the mainland by the narrow Menai Strait. This day out highlights one of the Isle's attractions that is solidly land-based and one that reveals hidden treasures beneath the waves. You start your day by taking a right turn after crossing the Menai Bridge and driving the short distance to Beaumaris, where you will find the last and largest of Edward I's great Welsh castles. Designed by Master James of St George, the mason-architect Edward brought over from the continent to oversee his castle-building programme, Beaumaris was begun in 1295; it remained unfinished, however, as Edward's military concerns moved to Scotland. Consequently, these sophisticated fortifications were never put to the test, apart from some minor Civil War action in the 17th century.

The Castle is considered a perfect example of the concentric design, with a lower outer circuit of walls encompassing an inner defensive ring featuring six mighty towers. The whole is surrounded by a partly restored moat; the calm, atmospheric scene which greets you today, complete with swans and ducks, is a far cry from its warlike origins.

A 16 km (10 mi) drive south of Beaumaris brings you to the Anglesey Sea Zoo at Brynsiencyn. Lying close to the Menai Strait shoreline, Wales's largest marine aquarium recreates a range of local marine habitats around Anglesey and the North Wales coastline to showcase over 150 species of sea-life. Highlights include the Shark Pool, the Shipwreck and the Big Fish Forest. Fish feeding takes place daily and there are regular talks and diving demonstrations. If all this leaves younger visitors still unsatisfied, there is an impressive choice of outdoor entertainment too, including bouncy castle, crazy golf and model boats.

WHERE:
Isle of Anglesey
BEST TIME TO GO:
April to October (though Beaumaris Castle is open all year round).
DON'T MISS:
The delightful little chapel at Beaumaris and the breathtaking views of the Snowdonia range from the castle wall walks.
AMOUNT OF WALKING:
Moderate
COST:
Reasonable (a family ticket for the Sea Zoo is valid for 7 consecutive days).
YOU SHOULD KNOW:
Beaumaris Castle was designed, like Caernarfon, to be a royal residence as well as a fortress. You can still see something of the grandeur of the planned but unfinished state apartments in today's ruins.

The Brecon Beacons

WHERE:
Powys
BEST TIME TO GO:
March to October (winter walking
has its special attractions, too, but
make sure you are well equipped
and prepared for sudden changes in
the weather).
DON'T MISS:
The information display at Llangorse
Lake describing the Crannog found
there. Crannogs were small man-
made islands used as refuges in
prehistoric times; the one at
Llangorse is unique in Wales.

*The Beacons sit below a
brooding sky.*

Brecon Beacons National Park protects some of the finest upland
landscapes the country has to offer. It is a paradise for lovers of the
great outdoors and for anyone wanting to escape the crowds and
traffic of urban life. Covering 1,344 sq km (519 sq mi), the Park falls
into three main sections. The best starting-point for exploring the
central Beacons is the National Park Visitor Centre at Libanus,
10 km (6 mi) south of Brecon, which has displays on the Park's flora
and fauna and the people who make a living in it. The large picnic
area offers extensive views of the distinctive flat summit of Pen y
Fan, at 886 m (2,907 ft) the highest point in southern Britain.

This is superb walking country and the Visitor Centre has any
number of suggestions for day walks to suit a wide range of abilities.
The Park authority publishes a booklet describing twelve Wildlife

Walks, none longer than two hours, which are particularly popular with families. You could comfortably tackle one of these walks, Mynydd Illtyd, as it leaves from the Centre itself and crosses open ground to the site of an Iron Age hill fort.

Llangorse Lake, just 13 km (8 mi) east of Brecon and still within the Park boundary, provides a dramatic contrast to the landscape around the Visitor Centre. South Wales's largest natural lake is a haven for birdlife and another of the Wildlife Walks takes you on a 5-km (3-mi) stroll through water meadows and beside reedbeds along its southern and western edges. Along the way you will come across a bird hide from where you should be able to spot reed warblers, Canada geese, herons and – if you are very lucky – the shy water rail.

AMOUNT OF WALKING:
Lots (whilst this area attracts the serious walker, the Park authority also publishes an excellent Easier Access Guide with details of places that are accessible to those with more limited mobility).
COST:
Low
YOU SHOULD KNOW:
In the summer months (June to September) Beacons Bus operates around the Park, providing a network of very useful bus routes designed to service walkers on one-way hikes.

*Home for the Ladies
of Llangollen*

Plas Newydd & Valle Crucis Abbey

WHERE:
Denbighshire
BEST TIME TO GO:
April to October
DON'T MISS:
The two medieval stone fonts in the grounds at Plas Newydd, rumoured to have come from Valle Crucis Abbey.
AMOUNT OF WALKING:
Moderate
COST:
Low (during the winter months you can visit the Valle Crucis site for free).
YOU SHOULD KNOW:
Plas Newydd is not to be confused with the other 'New Hall' of the same name, James Wyatt's great house on the shore of the Menai Strait built for the Marquess of Anglesey.

The lively little market town of Llangollen is famous throughout the world for its Eisteddfod, an international music festival held each July, which celebrates at its core the rich tradition of song in Welsh culture. But there is plenty to interest the visitor at other times of the year, and this day out features two of the area's more intriguing sights. On a hill above the town stands Plas Newydd, home to the renowned Ladies of Llangollen from 1780 to 1829. Lady Eleanor Butler and Miss Sarah Ponsonby were members of the Irish gentry who made a pact as young women to flee their many suitors and their native country for a new life in Wales. Still possessing most of the original features which the Ladies introduced, the house today is a remarkable evocation of the tastes and fashions of two well-bred women of the Regency period. The Ladies had a particular penchant for ornamental wood and the house is filled, both inside and out, with fine examples of the woodcarver's art, mostly acquired from old churches and other buildings in the area.

Only 3 km (2 mi) up the valley from Llangollen, the well-preserved ruins of the great Cistercian Abbey of Valle Crucis stand in a characteristically tranquil setting of green fields ringed about by steep-sided hills. You can sense some of the splendour of the original foundation from 1201 in the walls of the abbey church, many standing close to their full height. The west front with its richly carved doorway and lovely rose window is of particular note, as is the fine rib-vaulted roof of the chapter house. Rumours still circulate of an earlier building on the site that had associations with King Arthur and the legend of the Holy Grail.

Llangollen Canal & Motor Museum

There are few more effective ways to escape the stresses and strains of modern life than a gentle excursion on water through beautiful countryside, and a trip on the Llangollen Canal is one of the best. Running for 65 km (41 mi) from Nantwich in Cheshire to Llangollen in the North Wales hills, the Canal was built in the first part of the 19th century as a vital transport artery for the early Industrial Revolution, providing a link between the English canal system and the inland waterways of North Wales.

Nowadays its traffic is purely recreational but the scenery remains as stunning as ever. You can enjoy a two-hour trip from Llangollen Wharf in a motorized narrow boat, complete with on-board commentary. Travelling east from the town there are views of the lovely Dee Valley and surrounding hills. The highlight of your journey comes just short of your destination at Froncysyllte (from where a coach whisks you back to Llangollen) when you cross one of the wonders of canal engineering, the aqueduct at Pontcysyllte. Built 200 years ago by Thomas Telford, this is the country's largest navigable aqueduct, its eighteen stone piers carrying the canal in an iron trough a dizzying 38 m (126 ft) above the River Dee.

Back on dry land you can continue the theme of transport in ages past with a visit to the Llangollen Motor Museum. This is a private museum run by its enthusiastic owners, who are a mine of information on anything connected to motor transport, both two- and four-wheeled. A collection of over sixty vehicles, mainly from the 1920s to the 1970s, includes all the classic British brands. The museum also features a small display on the development of the local canal network.

A narrow boat crossing the Pontcysyllte aqueduct.

WHERE:
Denbighshire
BEST TIME TO GO:
March to October (however, if you are willing to risk the less predictable weather conditions in the winter months for the sake of fewer crowds, the heated canal boats operate throughout the year).
DON'T MISS:
Provided you have a head for heights, the view as you cross the aqueduct straight down to the valley floor.
AMOUNT OF WALKING:
Little
COST:
Reasonable
YOU SHOULD KNOW:
For an even more peaceful experience consider taking a canal trip by horse-drawn boat, when the only sounds you are likely to hear will be the occasional plod of a hoof or swish of a tail.

NORTHERN IRELAND

Belfast Day 1

TITANIC QUARTER, GOLDEN MILE AND QUEEN'S QUARTER

WHERE:
County Antrim
BEST TIME TO GO:
April to September
DON'T MISS:
The Victorian glasshouses at the Botanic Gardens – the birdcage-domed Palm House is one of the earliest examples of a curvilinear cast iron glasshouse, pre-dating the one at Kew Gardens. The Tropical Ravine House has a waterfall and gully full of exotic climbers viewed from above.
AMOUNT OF WALKING:
Lots
COST:
Reasonable (but expensive if you pay for a guided tour of the Titanic Quarter or splash out on lunch).
YOU SHOULD KNOW:
Don't try to get to Queen's and the Botanic Gardens by car – parking is impossible. You can take a bus if you don't want to walk down the Golden Mile. Check that the Ulster Museum is open again following its major refurbishment.

After years of unremitting bleakness, Belfast has emerged triumphantly from the Troubles as a rejuvenated city, full of character and upbeat optimism. An exuberant post-modern ambience in a splendid setting of Edwardian maritime grandeur makes it a great place for a city break.

Whatever else you do (and there's a lot going on in this heritage city) don't miss the Titanic Quarter. Belfast docks are undergoing a massive regeneration and you can happily spend a morning at Queen's Island, where the ill-fated leviathan was built. Everything here is on an outlandish scale. Walking the length of Thompson Dock, you will be awestruck by just how large the *Titanic* was; Belfast's iconic landmark, a pair of towering yellow cranes, known affectionately as Samson & Goliath, hang over the largest dry dock in the world; and the Victorian pumphouse is one of Belfast's finest historic buildings.

Back in Donegall Square at the city centre, stroll through the grounds of City Hall. This magnificent belle époque pile of Portland stone, is an extravaganza of turrets and domes. You can see a bust of William Pirrie, Lord Mayor of Belfast and chairman of the shipbuilding company that built the *Titanic*, as well as a memorial statue to the ship's passengers and crew.

Walk along the famous Golden Mile where you will find most of the city's entertainment, bars and restaurants. You might stop at the historic Crown Liquor Saloon, Northern Ireland's best-known pub, before reaching Queen's Quarter, the vibrant university area where you can spend the afternoon soaking up the atmosphere around the impressive university buildings, see some of the splendid exhibits in the Ulster Museum and explore the Botanic Gardens – a spectacular example of Victorian horticultural heritage with incredible glasshouses, one of the longest herbaceous borders in the British Isles and the world's largest water lily.

Belfast City Hall, Donegall Square

Belfast Day 2

Belfast Castle on Cave Hill

CAVE HILL, CLIFTON HOUSE AND THE ZOO

To the north, Cave Hill dominates the Belfast skyline. Within spitting distance of the city centre, it rises to almost 370 m (1,200 ft) with Belfast Castle standing proudly on its south-eastern slope overlooking the city. This magnificent edifice, built in 1870 by the Marquis of Donegal as a family residence, was modelled on Balmoral. It is set in 80 hectares (200 acres) of beautifully landscaped grounds in Cave Hill Country Park with spectacular panoramic views over Belfast Lough – on a clear day you can see as far as Mull in Scotland.

With a bit of forethought and if the weather is fine you can avoid buying lunch at the Castle restaurant by taking a picnic to eat in the idyllic surroundings of Cave Hill Country Park – a 300-hectare (750-acre) haven of woods and moorland. You can see the caves that give the hill its name and stroll through the woods to the foot of the promontory known as Napoleon's Nose, or even brave the steep moorland climb to McArt's Fort – an Iron Age earthwork at the summit. It is all too easy to while away the afternoon but do try to fit in a visit to Belfast Zoo, one of the most pleasant zoos in the British Isles – not least because of its unusual hillside setting. It is run on ethical principles to protect endangered species as naturally as possible.

Heading back into the city centre, spare a minute to admire Clifton House. Built in 1774 as the Poor House, it is one of Belfast's oldest and finest buildings. Nearby is the Clifton Street Graveyard, where thousands of victims of the 1840s great famine were buried as well as Henry Joy McCracken, ringleader of the 1798 Uprising. Round off your day with a drink at one of Belfast's oldest pubs, Kelly's Cellars, where McCracken's men planned their rebellion.

WHERE:
County Antrim
BEST TIME TO GO:
April to September
DON'T MISS:
The white tiger at Belfast Zoo.
AMOUNT OF WALKING:
Lots
COST:
Reasonable (entry to the zoo is free for over 60s, under 4s and disabled and there is a reduced family rate).
YOU SHOULD KNOW:
Cave Hill was supposedly the source of inspiration for Jonathon Swift's novel, *Gulliver's Travels*.

Ards Peninsula

GREY ABBEY AND MOUNT STEWART HOUSE

East of Belfast, the Ards Peninsula is a finger of land separating Strangford Lough from the sea. The Lough itself is a designated area of special scientific interest with extensive areas of mudflats and salt marsh – a haven for migratory birds and a popular rural playground for inhabitants of Belfast. For a memorable jaunt, drive along the lough shore to Grey Abbey and then round off your trip with an afternoon at Mount Stewart.

Grey Abbey was a 12th-century Cistercian monastery and its ruins are the finest example of Anglo-Norman ecclesiastical architecture in Northern Ireland. Although surrounded by private parkland, there is complete freedom of access to the Abbey grounds and you can picnic among the ruins whilst admiring the spectacular Gothic stonework and enjoying the peaceful atmosphere. The monks were renowned practitioners of herbal medicine and their physic garden has been lovingly reconstructed. The nearby village of Grey Abbey is worth exploring too for its antique shops and traditional coaching inn.

A few kilometres up the road is Mount Stewart, the 40-hectare (98-acre) estate of the Londonderry family. The opulent 18th-century house has a magnificent collection of artefacts and works of art, but it is the World Heritage garden that will grab your attention. Planted by Edith, Lady Londonderry as a 'green fairyland' in the 1920s, it is one of the great European gardens. Included in the intricate design of themed parterres and terraces is a Temple of the Winds and the family burial ground, as well as 6 hectares (15 acres) of rhododendron woods and a picturesque lake. An amazing array of tender plants thrives here in the protection of the mild microclimate of the Ards Peninsula and the entire garden is an idiosyncratic delight that is truly unforgettable.

Mount Stewart House and garden

WHERE:
County Down
BEST TIME TO GO:
April for the best of the rhododendron flowering; May to July to see the garden in full bloom.
DON'T MISS:
At Mount Stewart Garden: The Dodo Terrace -- an extraordinary statuary; The Sunken Garden, designed by Gertrude Jekyll; The Mairi Garden of 'silverbells and cockle shells'.
AMOUNT OF WALKING:
Moderate
COST:
Reasonable
YOU SHOULD KNOW:
Mount Stewart House has an impressive history. Many leading political figures were entertained here and you can see the embroidered chairs used at the 1815 Congress of Vienna as well as George Stubbs's famous painting, *Hambletonian*.

446

Bellaghy Bawn

LOUGH BEG NATURE RESERVE

A trip to Bellaghy Bawn draws back the veil on England's murky colonial past. Right in the centre of Northern Ireland, at the mouth of the marshes to the north west of Lough Neagh, Bellaghy village was built as part of the 17th-century Ulster Plantation and the Bawn erected to defend the settlement against the wrath of the dispossessed Irish. Bawns – 'cow-forts'–– were the traditional means of protecting home and livestock against marauders and the Bawn of Bellaghy is a classic example of these fortified buildings – a walled courtyard, with brick corner towers, enclosing the landowner's house. Here you can find out about the Ulster Plantation, the 1641 rebellion and the history of English colonial rule. A bonus is the library devoted to the great Irish poet Seamus Heaney, who grew up in Bellaghy. You can take a look at Hill Head Forge, the subject of one of his poems, before spending a wild afternoon in the marshes of Lough Beg.

The great attraction of Lough Beg Nature Reserve is its beautiful expansive views and complete absence of tourism. It is an untamed fringe wetland, a haven for a huge variety of wildlife and rare plants. You will find yourself in an unbelievably tranquil landscape, the only sound being the mews and cries of the birds. The only landmark for miles around is a church spire rising mysteriously from the marshes. It is on an islet in the middle of the lough; but walk along the causeway to reach it and you will find there is no church. Known as Hervey's Folly, the spire is purely for show. The islet was once the site of an early Christian monastery and there are traces of an ancient church dating from St Patrick's time.

WHERE:
County Londonderry
BEST TIME TO GO:
June to September. August is the peak time for birds. The marshland is inundated in the winter months.
DON'T MISS:
The Bullaun Stone on Church Island, said to have healing powers.
AMOUNT OF WALKING:
Lots
COST:
Low
YOU SHOULD KNOW:
The natural beauty of the landscape around Lough Beg has inspired poets and songwriters. It is one of the best ornithological sites of the British Isles with 171 species.

The Bawn of Bellaghy

Around Lough Neagh

ANTRIM TOWN AND RAM'S ISLAND

A thoroughly soul-stirring day can be had around the wilderness shores of Lough Neagh, the largest freshwater lake in the British Isles. Renowned for its bird colonies, historic towns and villages, monastic icons and monuments, Lough Neagh is steeped in the heritage of ancient Ireland. According to one of many legendary tales, the lake was created by the famous giant, Finn McCool – he tore up a clod of earth to hurl at a Scottish rival on the Giants' Causeway, leaving a gaping hole in the ground; but he aimed so badly that the clod flew into the sea to become the Isle of Man.

Start the day with a morning stroll through the atmospheric riverside town of Antrim, a little way from Lough Neagh. Besides the obviously impressive heritage buildings – the splendid Market Square and Old Courthouse, the early 19th-century twin-towered Barbican Gate, the 17th-century Artillery Fort – make sure you discover the architectural gems tucked away in the back streets of the old industrial quarter, and visit the Castle Garden. Antrim Castle burned down in 1922 and all that remains is a solitary free-standing tower but the wonderful 17th-century water garden is intact, with a delightful walk along a canal path lined with lime and hornbeam.

Drive southwards to Crumlin Glen and Sandy Bay marina on the eastern shore of the lough, and get ferried out to the romantic wilderness of Ram's Island, a timeless oasis of tranquillity where you wander along dappled paths through the woods to suddenly stumble upon the 19th-century ruins of a summerhouse, and an ancient round tower in the middle of nowhere. You may well feel unaccountably sad when the time comes to depart, and be left wondering where legend ends and reality begins.

Antrim Castle and beautiful walled garden

ECOS Millennium Environmental Centre and Glenariff Forest Park

You can crack the intractable problem of a cheap and cheerful family day out with a visit to the ECOS Millennium Centre at Ballymena followed by the woods and waterfalls of Glenariff Forest Park.

Home of Northern Ireland's Environmental Information Centre, the ECOS Centre may not sound promising, but you're in for an incredible surprise. Set in idyllic surroundings, this innovative high-tech building has won awards for its design and construction based on sustainability. The public galleries are stuffed with entertaining interactive displays where you can calculate your carbon footprint, find out how green technology works and learn about wildlife – a really stimulating way of educating yourselves and the next generation, exploring man's relationship with the natural world and opening your eyes to the ecological challenges facing the planet.

Outside, you would never guess that the Nature Park was formerly derelict farmland. There are 8 km (5 mi) of footpaths through 60 hectares (150 acres) of woodland, with ponds and meadows chockful with wildflowers and colourful butterflies. If the kids turn up their noses at pond-dipping, duck-feeding and the willow tunnel, then they can ride toy tractors or simply be dumped in the play-park while you watch for the otters in the river.

Half an hour later you can be at the 'gateway to the Glens'. Glenariff Forest Park is in perhaps the most beautiful of all nine Antrim glens. It is bisected by two small fast-flowing rivers and there are steep gorges, waterfalls and spectacular views as far as the sea. This is a brilliant place to introduce town kids to the joys of the countryside, with four marked trails of varying lengths, a visitor centre and a café.

The Waterfalls Walkway in Glenariff Forest

WHERE:
County Antrim
BEST TIME TO GO:
April to September
DON'T MISS:
The Waterfall Walkway in Glenariff Forest Park.
AMOUNT OF WALKING:
Moderate
COST:
Low
YOU SHOULD KNOW:
The ECOS Centre is wheelchair friendly both inside and out and electric bicycles are available for hire to explore the grounds.

Rathlin Island Boat Trip

Rathlin Island

Rathlin is a wild, windswept island 10 km (6 mi) off the north coast of Antrim and only 25 km (15 mi) from Scotland. With its towering basalt cliffs and limestone heathland, it is a wonderful place for walkers, cyclists and nature lovers as well as being of considerable historical interest. For such a small place – only 7 km (4 mi) across – Rathlin has a remarkably turbulent past, inextricably entwined with the history of both Ireland and Scotland. It was for a long time disputed territory and not until 1617 was it officially declared Irish. In the past, the island supported a population of 1,200 but today fewer than one hundred people live here permanently.

The half-hour ferry journey from the seaside town of Ballycastle is an exhilarating start to the day, breathing the salt air as you cut across the choppy waters of the North Atlantic, watching the mainland recede into the distance. The currents are fierce here and the Rathlin coast is the site of numerous shipwrecks. It was also a smuggler's haunt and myths and legends abound, the most famous one being that one of the sea-caves on the island's north coast was Robert the Bruce's hideout, where he had his renowned encounter with the spider that inspired him to continue his battle for the Scottish Crown.

When you land at the picturesque shoreline of Church Bay, where almost all the islanders live, you are immediately struck by a pervasive sense of isolation and tranquillity. A day is quickly passed exploring this wildly beautiful island – roaming over the heath among the standing stones, cairns, ancient churches and ruins, wandering along cliff-top paths with wonderful views, and taking the island bus to the dramatic western headland to see the largest seabird colony in Northern Ireland.

WHERE:
County Antrim
BEST TIME TO GO:
May to AuguSt May and June is the best time for the birds.
DON'T MISS:
The 'upside-down' lighthouse
AMOUNT OF WALKING:
As little or as much as you want.
COST:
Reasonable
YOU SHOULD KNOW:
There are very few cars on Rathlin and you can only take your car over with special permission. You can take guided bus or walking tours round the island.

Causeway Coastal Drive

Here is one of the world's great scenic drives – you cannot go to Northern Ireland and miss doing it. If you push it, you can cover the 120 km (75 mi) in half a day but far better to linger along the way, gaze at the coastal views and look round the historical sights. The rugged coastal scenery is spectacular from beginning to end: romantic glens, castle ruins, charming villages, picturesque towns, and the oldest distillery in the world. The high point is of course the Giants Causeway, but round every bend of the road there is some amazing sight to awaken even the most jaded eye.

Look around the Norman castle and 12th-century church at Carrickfergus, then hit the road. Northwards from Larne, you will drive through some of Europe's most mind-blowing coastal scenery, passing the foot of each of the nine glens of Antrim with views across the sea to the Scottish coast. Each village you go through has its own unique character – the castle of Glenarm, the harbour at Carnlough, the Cushendall curfew tower (built in 1809 to confine 'idlers and rioters') and the picturesque cottages of Cushendun.

As you turn the corner to the North Antrim coast, there is a breathtaking view of Rathlin Island from Torr Head. You must stop to tread the hexagonal basalt stepping stones of the Giants Causeway, one of the world's great natural wonders, supposedly created by Finn McCool, Ireland's legendary giant hero. The coastal villages of Portbradden, Ballintoy and Portballintrae are particularly beautiful spots and, just before you reach the popular beach resort of Portrush, you will catch sight of Dunluce Castle perched on the headland – the most romantic ruin in the whole of Ireland, a stunning grand finale to a spectacular drive.

WHERE:
County Antrim
BEST TIME TO GO:
April to September
DON'T MISS:
The Giants Causeway
AMOUNT OF WALKING:
Little
COST:
Reasonable
YOU SHOULD KNOW:
You can make it all the way to Londonderry in a single day by taking the coastal route, as long as you don't dawdle on the way.

The Giants Causeway

The Walled City of Derry

WHERE:
County Londonderry
BEST TIME TO GO:
May to September
DON'T MISS:
The sign at Free Derry Corner and the Bloody Sunday memorial.
AMOUNT OF WALKING:
Moderate
COST:
Reasonable
YOU SHOULD KNOW:
Londonderry is known locally as Derry. The name is derived from the Gaelic *daire* meaning 'oak grove'. St Columba built a monastery here in the 6th century from which the medieval town of Derry developed. The 'London' was prefixed in 1618, in honour of the City of London Guilds which funded the building of the walls for a new planned city that was to be the 'jewel in the crown' of the English settlers' Ulster Plantation.

The lively city of Derry, or Londonderry, is one of the oldest inhabited places in Ireland, and one of the most exciting. The finest example of a walled city in the British Isles, Derry has a poignant past that makes for a fascinating day of historical discovery among its winding streets.

The 17th-century city walls, complete with cannons, gates and bastions, are an irresistible draw. Clamber onto the ramparts for a birds' eye views of the city skyline, Bogside and the River Foyle. You can walk all the way around – about 1.5 km (1 mi) – stopping on the way to look at some of the great historic buildings built alongside the walls. Admire the arches of St Colomba's Cathedral, built in 1633; be dazzled by the famed stained glass of the neo-Gothic Guildhall; look towards the quay and conjure up thousands of 19th-century emigrants setting sail for the New World. End your circuit at the Tower Museum where you can see the award-winning exhibition, The Story of Derry, and learn about the great siege. Afterwards stroll down Shipquay Street to the picturesque Craft Village, in the heart of the old city. Here you can wander down cobble-stoned streets in a historically accurate reconstruction of artisans' workshops, specialist craft shops and a traditional Irish cottage.

Down in Bogside, just outside the walls, you will see the most outstanding political murals in the world: The People's Gallery, painted as a homage to the people of Derry. Find out more about the artists at the Bogside Artists' Studio then visit the Museum of Free Derry to learn about the city's troubled years of sectarian strife and the Bloody Sunday massacre. You will find yourself touched by the vibrant optimism on the streets of Derry today in the light of the brutal pathos of the city's past.

The Runner mural is part of the Peoples Gallery Mural in Rossville Street in the Bogside area of Derry.

Old Bushmills Distillery and Hezlett House

An advertising poster from the 1900s

The Antrim Coast, apart from being staggeringly beautiful, is stuffed with historic sites. Just five minutes drive from the Giants Causeway is the village of Bushmills. Here you will find the oldest legal whiskey distillery in the world – one of only three left in the whole of Ireland. King James I first granted an official licence in 1608 when Bushmills Distillery had already been in operation for years and it has been producing whiskey continuously ever since.

You can spend a fascinating morning here watching whiskey being made and discovering how a single malt gets its distinctive taste. The art of distilling is a complex one, and Bushmills is exceptional in maintaining the entire production and bottling process under one roof. Spring water from nearby St Columb's Rill is mixed with malted barley mash in copper stills and laid down to mature in old sherry casks infused with flavour. Naturally there is plenty of opportunity to sample the end product, so make sure that somebody is willing to take on the responsibility for driving you away again.

From Bushmills, head for Coleraine then take the coast road and turn off towards Castlerock to see one of the oldest buildings in Ireland. Hezlett House is a picture-book thatched cottage dating from 1690. It is remarkable that it is still standing, given that it has no foundations. It is what is known as a 'cruck' structure: oak timbers trussed together with earth and rubble walls. The tiny interior has 19th-century furnishings and there is a museum of traditional farm instruments, all exceptionally well maintained by the National Trust. The atmosphere of everyday rural Irish life is vividly conjured up at an open peat hearthside through the story of the experiences of the people who lived here – a thought-provoking glimpse into Ireland's social history.

WHERE:
County Antrim and County Londonderry
BEST TIME TO GO:
May to September
DON'T MISS:
The attractive pedestrianized town centre of Coleraine.
AMOUNT OF WALKING:
Little
COST:
Expensive (although you can get family tickets at a reduced rate for both attractions).
YOU SHOULD KNOW:
There is a restaurant attached to Old Bushmills Distillery and refreshments are available at Hezlett House.

The library at Prehen House

Ballygroll Prehistoric Complex and Prehen House

Derry is situated in a beautiful landscape of undulating countryside (great for cycling) and there is plenty of interest beyond the city walls. Cross the River Foyle to Waterside and spend a day visiting some of the out-of-town historic sights.

Stone circles invariably have an enigmatic charm about them – the mysterious marks left by our ancestors, standing since the dawn of history. The Irish ones are all in wonderful settings and are a reminder of just how ancient this legendary land is. Only 9 km (6 mi) from Derry, off the main Belfast road, you will find the Ballygroll Prehistoric Complex – a remarkable assortment of ancient stones. You can go on a 2.5-km (1.5-mi) circular walk through hillside farmland, enjoy the view and contemplate the meaning behind the system of prehistoric field walls, scattered cairns, tombs and stone circles dating from 4,000-1,500 BC.

Head back towards the city by cross-country minor routes to join the main Strabane Road. Just 3 km (2 mi) from Waterside is Prehen House, an early Georgian family home built in 1740, one of Derry's most significant architectural heirlooms. The house is privately owned but is an arts centre and gallery open to the public for guided tours. An afternoon here is a real treat. You can find out about the Knox family and the terrible tale of Half-Hanged McNaughton – a very Irish story of seduction, gambling and the gallows. Go for a walk in nearby Prehen Wood, 7 hectares (18 acres) of ancient oak and beech trees, a haven for red squirrels and wild flowers – all that remains of the 16th-century woodland that was once part of the Prehen Estate. From both house and wood, there are superb views of Derry and the hills beyond the River Foyle.

WHERE:
County Londonderry
BEST TIME TO GO:
May, for the carpet of bluebells in Prehen Wood; September to October for wonderful autumn colour.
DON'T MISS:
The wooden sculptures in Prehen Wood.
AMOUNT OF WALKING:
Moderate
COST:
Reasonable
YOU SHOULD KNOW:
If you don't have access to a car, there is a regular bus service to Prehen House from Waterside, Derry.

The North Antrim Coast around Portrush

The old fishing village of Portrush, built on a promontory jutting out into the ocean, is a popular seaside resort town with pristine sandy beaches, a world famous golf course and loads of places of interest in the immediate vicinity. You can spend a heavenly day in the open air exploring the sensational North Antrim coastline.

East of the town, walk among the dunes of Curran Strand to the limestone cliffs of White Rocks – a spectacularly beautiful part of the coast where the thundering waves and fierce tides of the Atlantic Ocean have caused countless shipwrecks and beaten the soft limestone of the cliffs into a natural sculpture of fantastic arches, huge caves and contorted shapes. About 5 km (3 mi) along the coast, you will see the medieval ruins of Dunluce Castle perched on a desolate headland with sheer drops on all sides. It is said to be haunted, and it certainly feels it. It is well worth summoning the energy to climb up and wander round it.

After an energetic morning's walking, drive or cycle westwards from Portrush to the Downhill Demesne, just past Castlerock. Originally the estate of Earl Hervey, Bishop of Derry, Downhill is now run by the National Trust. There is a wonderful ruined mansion, beautiful landscaped gardens and a clifftop walk leading to the 18th-century Mussenden Temple. Hervey built this exotic folly in honour of a female married cousin, modelling it on the Roman Temple of Vesta. Rather sadly, she died before the temple was completed. This eccentric landmark has only been prevented from toppling into the sea by the drastic measure of reinforcing the base of the cliff. How long this will last is anybody's guess. No doubt the ocean will win in the end and Mussenden Temple will vanish into the waves.

WHERE:
County Antrim and County Londonderry
BEST TIME TO GO:
May to September
DON'T MISS:
The limestone arch with a 15 m (50 ft) high opening on the beach at White Rocks.
AMOUNT OF WALKING:
Lots
COST:
Low
YOU SHOULD KNOW:
The currents at White Rocks are dangerously strong so, however tempting it may seem, it would be exceptionally foolhardy to attempt to swim here.

White Rocks with Portrush town in the distance

The Sperrins

The Sperrins are the wild romantic heartland of Northern Ireland. The remote glaciated landscape of heather-clad hills, wooded glens and watery peat bogland has been designated an area of outstanding natural beauty and is steeped in countless ancient tales of hidden gold, ghosts and moonshine. Stretching for 65 km (40 mi) east to west between Cookstown and Omagh and 110 km (70 mi) from north to south, this is a wonderfully isolated area in which to spend a day getting away from it all. The narrow, virtually traffic free country roads snake their way through the rolling hills and glens – perfect for a leisurely scenic drive; and there are marked cycling routes varying in distance from 17-66 km (11-41 mi).

You can take a circular 100-km (63-mi) scenic drive from Cookstown, going across the top of Slieve Gallion, a steep flat-topped mountain at the eastern edge of the Sperrins, descending to the wild peat bog lowland around Lough Fea, going through Davagh Forest and past the archaeological site of Broughderg, from where there are wonderful views over the surrounding country. Make sure you stop at the mysterious prehistoric Beaghmore Stone Circles and see the Dragon's Teeth – more than 800 small stones contained within a 21-m (69-ft) stone circle. And pause at Wellbrook Beetling Mill, a startlingly picturesque functioning linen mill nestling in an idyllic little glen which makes you feel you have just stepped back in time a couple of hundred years.

You will return to the historic streets of Cookstown at the end of the day, inspired by the exhilarating sense of freedom and space that is to be found in the wild open countryside of the Sperrins, yearning to go back for more.

Beaghmore Stone Circles

Ulster American Folk Park and Florence Court

For an entertaining day of 'living history', there are two great attractions within 65 km (40 mi) of each other. After gaining a vivid insight into Irish emigration, you can move on to be treated to a slice of early 20th century upper-crust daily life.

At Castletown on the A5 road a few minutes drive from Omagh, you will come across a fantastic open-air museum that tells the story of 18th- and 19th-century Irish emigration. The Ulster American Folk Park was established in 1976 to celebrate the United States Bicentennial. It was initially constructed around the original showpiece homestead of a small boy, Thomas Mellon, whose family emigrated to Pennsylvania. Over the years the museum has been painstakingly and extensively developed with all sorts of exhibits to show what everyday life must have been like for migrants on both sides of the Atlantic. There are authentically furnished thatched cottages and log cabins, original shopfronts and fittings, agricultural tools, workshop implements, and an incredibly impressive full-scale replica ship and quay. Museum guides, dressed in period costume, demonstrate a number of traditional crafts and skills. A trip here is a wonderfully entertaining and informative way of finding out about the Irish diaspora.

An hour's drive southward, 13 km (8 mi) past Enniskillen, and you will find Florence Court – a magnificent 18th-century mansion, once the home of the Earls of Enniskillen. It is one of the most important grand houses in Ulster, with an interior renowned for its exquisite rococo plasterwork and antique furnishings. The house is in a beautiful setting, surrounded by gardens and parkland with a sawmill and icehouse and wonderful views of the Cuilcagh Mountains. Take the themed tour with a 1920s governess or housekeeper for an amusing insight into daily life here between the wars.

A reconstruction of a Pennsylvania log farmhouse

WHERE:
County Tyrone and County Fermanagh
BEST TIME TO GO:
April to September
DON'T MISS:
The Florence Court Yew – supposedly the forebear of every yew tree in Ireland.
AMOUNT OF WALKING:
Little
COST:
Expensive
YOU SHOULD KNOW:
The award-winning Appalachian and Bluegrass Music Festival is held annually on the first weekend in September at the Ulster American Folk Park – the largest event of its kind outside the USA.

Enigmatic stone figures on White Island

Castle Archdale Country Park

County Fermanagh is a rural wetland paradise dominated by the extensive waters of Lough Erne, dotted with islands and ancient sacred sites and renowned for its scenic beauty. About 16 km (10 mi) north west of Enniskillen on the road to Kesh, you will find Castle Archdale Country Park, 90 hectares (230 acres) of woods, meadows and ponds along the shores of Lower Lough Erne. There is loads to do here for both adults and children and you can happily while away a day in the fresh air exploring it all. There are wildfowl ponds and wildflower meadows, a deer enclosure, a butterfly garden, woods and medieval ruins. You can go pony-trekking, hire a bike or take a boat out onto the lough to explore the islands, many of which are nature reserves.

Castle Archdale has an interesting history. In World War II it was the main westerly base for the flying boats which protected the North Atlantic allied convoys from Nazi U-boat attacks. You can still see the remains of ammunition dumps, slit trenches and the flying-boat docks.

At some point during the day, take the hourly ferry from the marina to White Island, one of the best known of the many islands of Lough Erne. It is famous for its 12th-century ecclesiastical remains with a splendid Romanesque doorway. There is a row of enigmatic stone figures set in a wall which predate the church by a couple of hundred years and show evidence of pre-Christian influences. They are all carved in some detail except for one that is incomplete, as though the work had been interrupted. This just adds to the mystery. Nobody is sure who or what the figures are meant to represent, although of course theories abound.

WHERE:
County Fermanagh
BEST TIME TO GO:
April to September
DON'T MISS:
The Archdale Centre at the corner of the main courtyard, where there are informative exhibitions and displays so that you can make the most of your day here.
AMOUNT OF WALKING:
As much as you want.
COST:
Reasonable
YOU SHOULD KNOW:
It is best to visit on a weekday as the park can get quite busy at summer weekends.

Belleek Pottery and the Monastic Remains of Devenish Island

You must not miss a trip to Belleek Pottery, world famous for its delicate hand-finished Parian chinaware – a superb reflection of Ireland's heritage of skilled craftsmanship. Established in 1857, it is one of Northern Ireland's top five visitor attractions. From Enniskillen, take the main road along the west side of Lower Lough Erne to the charming village of Belleek, beautifully situated on the banks of the River Erne, straddling the border with the Republic, where you can watch the entire china-making process, from the initial moulding and casting stages through to glazing and decorating. After you have toured the pottery, have a look round the museum to see wonderful examples of Period china. And if you allow yourself a peek round the showroom, you are going to need an exceptionally strong will to depart empty-handed.

A completely different aspect of the Irish tradition can be found on Devenish Island, a short ferry ride from Trory Point just outside Enniskillen. Although Lough Erne may seem a remote rural backwater today, it was once an important centre of learning, attested to by the monastery ruins scattered throughout its islands. On Devenish, the largest island of Lower Lough Erne, you will find a wealth of ecclesiastical remains. There are two churches, an oratory, graveyards, a Celtic cross, a 15th-century priory, and one of the finest round towers in Ireland. Saint Molaise established a monastery here in the 6th century. It grew to be the most famous centre of religious scholarship in Ulster and it lasted, incredibly, for a thousand years, despite two Viking invasions. As you wander around this haven of tranquillity, you cannot help being struck by the spiritual atmosphere, an almost mystical sense of stillness that hangs in the air.

WHERE:
County Fermanagh
BEST TIME TO GO:
April to September
DON'T MISS:
Climbing up the inside of the 12th-century round tower on Devenish Island.
AMOUNT OF WALKING:
Moderate
COST:
Reasonable
YOU SHOULD KNOW:
There are lovely waterway walks beside Lower Lough Erne between Belleek and Enniskillen.

A craftsman finishing off a piece at Belleek Pottery.

Enniskillen Town Centre and Castle Coole

WHERE:
County Fermanagh
BEST TIME TO GO:
April to September
AMOUNT OF WALKING:
Moderate
COST:
Reasonable
YOU SHOULD KNOW:
Oscar Wilde and Samuel Beckett both went to school at Portora Royal School, just outside the town centre on the River Erne.

A day goes quickly in Enniskillen. Picturesquely situated on an island between Upper and Lower Lough Erne, this characterful town is full of things to do. It has a stirring military history. Many battles were fought here and a garrison of English troops was permanently stationed in the Castle, originally built as the family seat of the Maguires, the chieftains of Fermanagh. They held sway over the county and established a private navy to control the waters of Lough Erne until they were finally defeated by the English in the 17th century. Today the Castle houses two museums.

See the oak doors and statues of the Town Hall, and the bells of 19th-century St Macartin's Cathedral (one of which was cast from a Battle of the Boyne cannon). Go for a walk in Forthill Park and summon the energy to climb the 108 steps that spiral to the top of the memorial column for a superb view over town and lough. As you stroll down the main street, you will be struck by the air of individuality – small family-run shops, bars and restaurants that make an incredibly welcome change from the predictable uniformity of the average high street.

Make sure you visit Castle Coole on the outskirts of town. This stunning 18th-century neo-classical mansion with Portland stone façade was built for the Earl of Belmore. You cannot fail to be impressed by the interior carving and plaster frieze-work as well as the sumptuously appointed accommodation, particularly the magnificent State Bedroom with its original Regency furnishings. You can also see the more workaday aspects of the estate – the stables, servants' tunnel and laundry house, and roam in a 285-hectare (700-acre) estate of woodlands and landscaped park containing its own lough.

Enniskillen Castle on the banks of Lough Erne

Marble Arch Caves and Cuilcagh Mountain Park

Taking the A4 and the A32 from Enniskillen, the Marble Arch Caves and Cuilcagh Mountain Park are located on the lower slopes of Cuilcagh Mountain, at 665 m (2,200 ft) the highest point in County Fermanagh. Enniskillen is not only a lively county town set on an island between the upper and lower sections of Lough Erne, but it also makes an excellent base from which to visit several other attractions nearby. Some 330 million years ago, County Fermanagh was lying under a tropical ocean. Gradually, the ocean floor formed limestone that, after millennia of erosion by ice and water, was scoured and carved into the wonderful Marble Arch Caves.

Both the caves and the mountain park were designated a UNESCO Global Geopark in 2004. First explored by Edouard Alfred Martel in 1895, they were opened to the public in 1985, and have become a major tourist attraction. The 75-minute tour begins with a flight of 150 steps down into the caves, and a fascinating boat trip through caverns full of gleaming stalactites, lofty chambers and waterfalls. The knowledgeable and amusing guides escort you along spectacular walkways, beautifully lit to reveal this magnificent underground world.

On leaving the caves, take a walk in the Cuilcagh Mountain Park. If you started out early, you might have time to reach the summit, where you will enjoy some of the most spectacular views to be found in Ireland. Even if you don't get that far, you'll walk through a splendid landscape of blanket bog and peatland, rich with sphagnum moss, heather, sundew and rare species such as starry saxifrage and dwarf willow. The park is good for bird-watchers – you may see Golden plover, which breed here, as well as ring ouzel, dunlin and merlin.

Tourists in the Marble Arch caves

WHERE:
County Fermanagh
BEST TIME TO GO:
June to September, but come well prepared as the weather can change both dramatically and very faSt
DON'T MISS:
Florence Court, an important 18th-century National Trust house.
AMOUNT OF WALKING:
Lots – you need plenty of stamina to undertake the difficult Legnabrocky Trail to the summit of Cuilcagh. Allow at least six hours.
COST:
Reasonable
YOU SHOULD KNOW:
The district council is restoring the park's peatland and blanket bog after damage was caused by mechanized peat removal. The area is an ESA, an ASSI and a Ramsar site.

The Mill is still in working order.

Wellbrook Beetling Mill and Springhill House

Less than an hour's drive from Belfast and 10 km (6 mi) west of Cookstown, Wellbrook Beetling Mill, with its water wheel and adjacent traditional cottage, can be found in a tranquil wooded valley. The 18th-century, whitewashed stone mill, beside the Ballinderry River, is the last working beetling mill in Northern Ireland. Its wheel, almost 5 m (16.5 ft) in diameter, is powered by the river.

Beetling is the final stage in the linen production process, which was a major industry during the 18th and 19th centuries. The dampened cloth is hammered by heavy, wooden mallets to produce a flat, hard surface with high lustre. Flax, with its lovely blue flowers, is an ancient crop but although it is still cultivated around the mill, most Irish linen today is made from European flax. Taken over by the National Trust in 1961, two of the seven original milling machines are still operating, and costumed guides give hands-on demonstrations. There are several delightful walks to take nearby, or bring a picnic to enjoy by the river.

In the afternoon you can visit the pretty 17th-century Plantation house of Springhill, just a short drive away. Another National Trust property, the Springhill Estate belonged to the Conyngham Family from about 1630 until 1957. It is a remarkable example of 300 years of the life of one family, and contains one of Ireland's most important libraries of 17th- and 18th- century books. The largest costume collection in Northern Ireland is displayed in the old laundry, and the house is proud to be haunted by the well-documented ghost of Olivia Lennox-Conyngham. There's a lovely circular walk around the estate and gardens, taking you through the coach yard and past the tower, and finally leading back to the house itself.

Armagh

Dominated by two cathedrals located on opposing hilltops, the city of Armagh has the smallest population of any city on the island of Ireland. It has a lengthy and important history however, having been a religious centre since the 5th century, when St Patrick built Ireland's first stone church on the site of what is now the Anglican Cathedral. The city suffered badly during the Troubles, but today it promotes itself as the ecclesiastical capital of both Northern Ireland and Eire.

Armagh has some fine Georgian architecture to admire, and there are several attractions to visit apart from the two Cathedrals. The Public Library is a gem – founded by Archbishop Robinson in 1771, the Greek inscription over the entrance means 'the healing place of the soul'. The Library contains many rare books, including Archbishop Robinson's personal collection. One of the most treasured is a first edition of *Gulliver's Travels*, annotated by Jonathan Swift himself, a frequent visitor to the city. The Library, which has museum status, also contains Robinson's wonderful collection of engravings, by the likes of Piranesi and Hogarth.

The Archbishop also founded the Observatory in 1790, still Ireland's foremost astronomical research institute. Nearby, in the attractive grounds, you can find the Planetarium and catch one of the superb shows screened on the great, domed ceiling. Visit the Astropark too, if you can – a fascinating scale model of the universe in a natural setting.

There are a couple of interesting museums to see – the Armagh County Museum and that of the Royal Fusiliers. In the former you can see the grim cast-iron skull that once sat atop the Armagh gallows. Wind up your city tour with a trip to St Patrick's Trian. This heritage centre has three interesting exhibitions, including one on Gulliver's adventures that is very popular with children.

St Patrick's Cathedral

WHERE:
County Armagh
BEST TIME TO GO:
Any time, although it should be warmer during summer!
DON'T MISS:
The fine collection of books at Armagh's Public Library.
COST:
Reasonable
YOU SHOULD KNOW:
The name Armagh comes from the Irish name Ard Macha, meaning 'the heights of Macha', after the mythical goddess Macha of ancient Ireland, who is linked to both Armagh and Navan Fort.

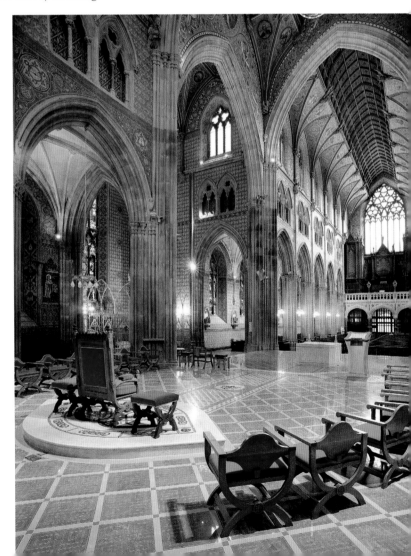

Navan Fort and Palace Stables Heritage Centre

WHERE:
County Armagh
BEST TIME TO GO:
Any time of year, though the Navan Centre is only open from April to September.
DON'T MISS:
The ruined 13th century Franciscan friary in the grounds of the Primate's Palace.
AMOUNT OF WALKING:
Moderate – but Navan Fort is unsuitable for wheelchair users and those with walking difficulties.
COST:
Navan Fort is free, and the Palace Stables are reasonable.
YOU SHOULD KNOW:
The game of road bowling is a local speciality. Contestants throw small, heavy metal bowls along quiet roads with the aim of crossing the finishing line with the fewest throws. The Ulster Finals are held in late June.

Navan Fort can be found some 3 km (2mi) west of the city of Armagh, by taking the A28 and following the signs. One of Ireland's most significant archaeological sites, Navan Fort is a large, circular earthwork on the summit of a hill set in a gentle landscape of rolling fields. It is believed to have been a ceremonial site rather than an actual fort, and traces of a large Celtic temple have been discovered here.

The site, at 240 m (792 ft) in its internal diameter, encloses a ring barrow, or Iron Age burial site, and a large mound found to have been built in 95 BC. Excavations show that the main enclosure was also built around this period. Navan Fort (or Emain Macha) is named after the pagan goddess Macha, renowned in Irish mythology, particularly in the stories known as the Ulster Cycle. Visit the Interpretative Centre and learn all about the fascinating history and legends of the area.

From the centre there is a woodland path to the base of the hill, the crest of which is reached by walking up the grassy slope. Not far away you can find two more ancient sites – the King's Stables, a man-made pool from the Bronze Age, and Haughey's Fort, a Bronze Age hill fort, thought to have been home to a highly ranked individual.

Back in Armagh you can visit the Palace Stables Heritage Centre. Once the stables of the Primate's Palace, built for Archbishop Robinson in the 18th century, the centre provides the visitor with excellent tours of this beautifully restored stable block, hosted by costumed guides. Here you will see re-enactments of life as lived in 1786, and walk through the coachman's kitchen and other areas of intereSt There's even a themed playground for children.

Navan Fort

Downpatrick and Dundrum Castle

Just 35 km (22 mi) south of Belfast lies historic Downpatrick, the place where St Patrick's efforts to bring Christianity to Ireland began and, indeed, ended – he is believed to have been buried in the grounds of Down Cathedral in 461 AD, and his grave is a pilgrimage site.

This is not only an interesting but also an attractive town, with some fine Georgian architecture in the town centre. The cathedral stands on a site first occupied by a church in the 12th century. It has been ruined and restored many times over the centuries, with additions such as an octagonal vestibule and a perpendicular Gothic tower built in the early 19th century. Another major restoration took place in the 1980s. The granite font is 11th century, and the cross on the east end of the cathedral is even older. The St Patrick Centre includes an interactive exhibition exploring the saint's life and legacy, as well as an art gallery, craft shop and restaurant.

The Down County Museum also deserves a visit, not least because it is situated in the restored 18th-century jail. Between its opening in 1796 and closure in 1830, the jail held thousands of prisoners – minor offenders, rebels captured after the battles of Saintfield and Ballynahinch and hundreds of convicts awaiting transport to New South Wales. The museum's prisoner database enables prisoner details to be researched. The Mound of Down, an Iron Age defensive earthwork, is just a walk away.

Some 11 km (7 mi) south of Downpatrick, overlooking Dundrum Bay and the Mourne Mountains, stands Dundrum Castle, one of Northern Ireland's most splendid Norman fortresses. Built by John de Courcy after his invasion of Ulster in the 12th century, its circular keep and vast, defensive walls are extremely impressive.

Down Cathedral

WHERE:
County Down
BEST TIME TO GO:
Any time of year, but between May and October is probably beSt
DON'T MISS:
The Ballynoe Stone Circle. Consisting of fifty stones, it is only 4 km (2.5 mi) south of Downpatrick.
AMOUNT OF WALKING:
Little
COST:
Low
YOU SHOULD KNOW:
Just outside Downpatrick is a beautiful racecourse which has been in use for the past 200 years.

465

The ferry sails past Castle Ward.

Exploris Aquarium and Castle Ward by Car Ferry

If you are interested in the natural world, you'll enjoy a trip to Exploris, the excellent aquarium at Portaferry, on the shore of the Marine Nature Reserve at Strangford Lough, the largest inlet in the British Isles. These usually calm waters open to the Irish Sea via a long, narrow, fast- flowing, tidal inlet. Within the Lough are seventy islands, hundreds of rocky outcrops, marshes, mudflats, headlands and small bays, providing perfect habitats for many species of flora and fauna.

Exploris, first opened in 1987 and expanded and up-graded in 1997 and 2000, gives visitors the opportunity to see, touch and learn about the marine life of the Lough and the Irish Sea. Different marine communities have been re-created in a variety of tanks, the most popular, and largest, of which is the Open Sea Tank. Containing conger eels and shark as well as well-known species such as cod and bass, the tank can be viewed either from a bridge above, or a cave beneath. The Discovery Pools enable the visitor to touch creatures such as starfish and rays, but the highlight is a visit to the Seal Rehabilitation Unit, where injured or orphaned seals are brought back to health and then released.

Take your car on the ferry to Strangford – a delightful trip of some eight minutes. A short drive on the A25 to the west of town will bring you to Castle Ward, a fine, 18th-century house with both a Classical and a Gothic façade, set in splendid, walled grounds. Take a guided tour of the house, or explore the grounds and the Wildlife Centre. Visit the farmyard, the Victorian laundry, the cornmill and the sawmill. Bring a picnic, take one of the many walks and find a gorgeous view to enjoy in peace.

WHERE:
County Down
BEST TIME TO GO:
April to October if you'd like to have a tour of Castle Ward. Exploris is open throughout the year, and ferries run very frequently throughout the year, with the exception of Christmas Day or if prevented from sailing by extreme weather conditions.
DON'T MISS:
Kilclief Castle, the oldest tower house in the county, just south of Strangford. Open in July and August, from Tuesday to Sunday, admission is free.
AMOUNT OF WALKING:
Little, unless you decide to take long walks in the Castle Ward Estate.
COST:
Reasonable
YOU SHOULD KNOW:
Strangford Lough Narrows became the world's first commercial tidal power station in 2007, generating power for 1,000 homes. The turbine is almost completely submerged and poses no threat to the environment.

Downpatrick & County Down Railway Trip

The Downpatrick & County Down Steam Railway is a joy for both steam train addicts and visitors alike. The ticket price includes a tour of the engine shed and the signal cabin as well as the return trip. Running for some 3 km (2 mi) along a section of the former main line, the steam train, whistle tooting, chunters along through the lovely Downpatrick Marshes. The trip provides fabulous views of Downpatrick Cathedral, set on the crest of a hill that has been settled for at least 2,000 years, and of the River Quoile, en route to the spectacular ruins of Inch Abbey.

Steam engines from the 1920s and 1930s, or diesel engines from the 1960s pull carriages ranging from fifty to one hundred years old. Enthusiasts can book a special trip during which they can fire up and drive a steam locomotive, or a diesel engine, and experience life on the footplate. The buffet car that stands at the station is open for snacks, and the station itself contains a small shop. A photographic exhibition and a model railway set up for younger visitors can be found upstairs.

The line runs through what is the lowest lying part of Ireland – the marshes are 0.4 m (1.3 ft) below sea level. During winter, flooding often occurs and the view at sunset, across the reflective, watery landscape to the distant Mountains of Mourne, is magical. Good views of the River Quoile may also be had – the Vikings sailed their long-ships up here on their way inland.

Leaving the train at Inch, the line's northern terminus, passengers walk to the nearby abbey. Operational since 800 AD, the ruins you see today are of a Cistercian abbey, founded in 1180. After dissolution, in 1541, it gradually crumbled away before being excavated and repaired in 1914.

WHERE:
County Down
BEST TIME TO GO:
The trains run between the last week of June and mid-September, at weekends. There are also special days and weekend trips on selected occasions such as Easter and Halloween – look up their complete calendar of events.
DON'T MISS:
The best views of Downpatrick Cathedral.
AMOUNT OF WALKING:
Little
COST:
Reasonable
YOU SHOULD KNOW:
John de Courcy, founder of Inch Abbey and Dundrum Castle, was the 12th century conqueror of East Ulster. Imprisoned by King John in 1205, he was subsequently released to go on a pilgrimage to the Holy Land.

Still steaming – the Downpatrick & County Down Railway.

REPUBLIC
OF IRELAND

Donegal Coast and Mountains

WHERE:
County Donegal
BEST TIME TO GO:
March to October
DON'T MISS:
The Donegal Railway Heritage Centre at The Old Station House, Ballyshannon – featuring the once-vital narrow-gauge railways of County Donegal.
AMOUNT OF WALKING:
Moderate
COST:
Low
YOU SHOULD KNOW:
Letterkenny is the largest town in Donegal but not the county town – neither is eponymous Donegal town because the honour goes to the smaller Lifford, connected to Strabane in Northern Ireland by a bridge across the River Foyle.

Ireland is blessed with an abundance of dramatic scenery but some of the very best may be found in Donegal. Spend a day exploring the coast, returning through mountains, and you will be treated to a variety of wild landscapes with a breathtaking view at every turn (of which there are many).

Start at the seaside town of Bundoran and drive north to Ballyshannon. There, follow the minor R231 coast road above fabulous beaches to Ballintra before making the day's first detour, to Lough Derg via the border village of Pettigoe. St Patrick's Purgatory is a tranquil religious sanctuary on an islet in the Lough that has been a place of Christian pilgrimage since the 6th century.

Retrace your steps and drive to Donegal town, beneath the Bluestack Mountains at the head of Donegal Bay. Go west through Mount Charles to Dunkineely, where a second detour takes you down the lovely St John's Peninsula and back. Next stop is Killybegs, Ireland's main fishing port. From there, follow the coast road to Carrick (pause to look at St Columba's Church) then on to Malin More and Rossan Point.

After soaking up the seascape, head for Ardara. The road takes you through the Glengesh Pass, with superb elevated views across Loughros Beg Bay. As you approach the heritage town of Ardara, Maghera Caves are on the left (access from the north side of Loughros Beg Bay at low tide, where you can also see Essaranks Waterfall). Continue along the spectacular coast road through Clooney, Dunglow, Kincaslough and Crolly.

Turn inland at Gweedore, driving through the Derryveagh Mountains and Glenveagh National Park to Letterkenny. From there, head south to Ballyboley, after which the main N15 road takes you back to Donegal Town through the Barnsmore Gap, with impressive mountains on either side.

The bay at St John's Peninsula

Inishowen Peninsula Drive

The largest of Donegal's peninsulas is also the most northerly and the sign-posted Inis Eoghain 100 (that's the distance in miles, which sounds much neater than 161 kilometres) is a circular route connecting the historical and scenic gems that Inishowen (Inis Eoghain) offers. This wonderful outing is Donegal's answer to the Ring of Kerry and it starts at Bridge End, northeast of Letterkenny. Don't hurry – part of the pleasure is stopping and simply enjoying the view or exploring an interesting ruin that catches the eye.

From Bridge End go to nearby Burnfoot and on to Buncrana, a seaside resort popular with the inhabitants of Derry. Continuing north, the road runs through Dunree and up the Gap of Mamore, one of Ireland's highest mountain passes. A stop near the next two villages, Clonmany and Ballyliffin, allows appreciation of the bogs, loughs, hills and seashores that typify Inishowen.

Carndonagh is the town that serves the northern part of the Inishowen Peninsula, and from there the road runs through Malin and Ballygorman to Malin Head, Ireland's most northerly point – with sensational views. Continue down the coast via Culdaff, Carrowmenagh and Greencastle to Moville. From there, it's a straight run beside Lough Foyle to Muff and back to your starting point.

Towards the end of the drive, be sure to visit the Grianan of Aileach, an impressive stone ring fort atop Greenan Mountain. It was restored in the 1800s, but remains one of the most significant historic sites in Ireland (which is saying something). Other heritage sites to choose from along the way include three Napoleonic War forts on Lough Swilly (Fort Dunree houses a military museum), Buncrana Castle (a ruined tower house), Burt Castle, Inch Castle, Cloncha Old Church, the Friar's Cell at Ballelaghan and Cooley churchyard with its cross and skull house.

Leenan Head from the Gap of Mamore

WHERE:
County Donegal
BEST TIME TO GO:
April to October
DON'T MISS:
Donagh Cross outside Carndonagh, the oldest standing cross in Ireland, and Gullanduff Old Bridge near Moville with strong claims to being Ireland's oldest standing bridge.
AMOUNT OF WALKING:
Lots (and there is poor wheelchair access at the Grianan of Aileach).
COST:
Low
YOU SHOULD KNOW:
Turks who take pride in inventing Turkish Baths will be devastated, because the Irish were there before them – west of Moville is Lisnalecky Sweat House, a stone beehive of the type used in Ireland from time immemorial right into the 19th century to 'sweat out' rheumatism.

Glenveagh National Park and Castle

This can be a day out for walkers with sturdy shoes and a love of the widest of open spaces, with some heritage thrown in. The heritage is a (mighty substantial) Victorian whimsy – Glenveagh Castle and gardens – the creation of 19th-century Irishman Captain John Adair, who made a fortune in America and bought up vast tracts of Donegal. He then followed the fashion for building romantic mountain retreats – indeed, his ambition was to create something grander than Queen Victoria's Balmoral.

The castle is a grand mansion house built in Scottish Baronial style (completed in 1873). It sits at the heart of Glenveagh National Park (its former estate), located west of Letterkenny (from town follow the R250 then R251 through Churchill). Surrounded by extensive gardens, the Castle is in a valley above Lough Veagh, dramatically overlooked by the Derryveagh Mountains.

Glenveagh's gardens are fabulous – perhaps best in April and May when the rhododendrons are in bloom but with lots of interest at other times, including many unusual and exotic specimens. There are woodland gardens and pleasure grounds, terraces with antique sculptures, Belgian and Italian gardens.

The castle's most striking feature is a rectangular granite keep. The interior is entrancing. Glenveagh Estate was purchased in 1938 by American socialite and art connoisseur Henry Plumer McIlhenny, who furnished it with the finest of contents and meticulous attention to detail. Admission is by guided tour only – and what a tour!

It's possible to spend the day seeing the Castle and wandering round the gardens, absorbing Visitor Centre displays, having a picnic beside the lake and taking a leisurely stroll in the immediate environs. However, serious walkers will be delighted to find they have unfettered access to a vast (165 sq km/64 sq mi) and lonely area of wild and unspoiled Donegal countryside.

Glenveagh Castle

WHERE:
County Donegal
BEST TIME TO GO:
April to October (for the Castle – the gardens and the National Park are open all year).
DON'T MISS:
Red deer – the Park is said to contain Europe's largest herd of these fine beasts, but if you should miss the deer there is an abundance of other wildlife to be spotted.
AMOUNT OF WALKING:
Lots (and good wheelchair access is restricted to the Castle and surroundings rather than the distant parkland).
COST:
Low
YOU SHOULD KNOW:
Henry Plumer McIlhenny's summer house parties at the Castle were legendary – with guests that included Hollywood greats like Charlie Chaplin, Clark Gable, Greta Garbo and Marilyn Monroe, plus leading cultural figures like Yehudi Menuhin.

Donegal History Day

This is a day to seek out something of a vanished Ireland where life was hard and grinding poverty was the norm. Start at Donegal's county town of Lifford with a visit to the handsome Old Courthouse, built in 1746. Behind its elegant façade Donegal's history comes alive with the help of models, audio-visual presentations, talking heads and a wide range of artefacts. Famous trials are recreated and the speciality of the house is treating visitors to the full 'dungeon experience' in basement cells, serving as a powerful reminder that the law was often used as an instrument of repression by the ruling classes. After that hard prison experience, you can escape to lunch in the thoroughly civilized restaurant at the Courthouse.

For those lucky enough to even have a job, work was hard in days gone by – as a tour of the Newmills Corn and Flax Mills at Milltown on the R250 Churchill Road beyond Letterkenny will confirm. It obviously required sustained physical effort to operate the machinery of this fascinating complex, even with the help of two waterwheels. This authentic reminder of bygone Ireland is on the south bank of the River Swilly. Established in the early 1800s, Newmills ground oats and barley, processed flax and also served as a public house and shop – truly a centre of the rural community. See one of Ireland's largest waterwheels in action as it drives the corn mill.

Return to Letterkenny and catch up on Donegal history at the County Museum on the High Road, a former workhouse. Speaking of which, a short drive up to the coast will take you to Dunfanaghy Workhouse, which tells the day's last story – of the Great Famine of 1845-50, and the unfortunates who had no option but to commit themselves to the workhouse, where they were subjected to horrific treatment.

WHERE:
County Donegal
BEST TIME TO GO:
March to October (for Dunfanaghy Workhouse).
DON'T MISS:
Find time to visit Biddy and Joe's Cottage in Lower Galwolie, Cloghan (southwest of Letterkenny) – there postman Michael Gallagher has created a traditional interior, full of everyday artefacts to show just how the ordinary folk of Donegal once lived (not that long ago, actually!).
AMOUNT OF WALKING:
Little
COST:
Reasonable
YOU SHOULD KNOW:
In times past, if a jury failed to reach a verdict at Lifford Courthouse they were marched to the centre of Lifford Bridge (the parish boundary) and there discharged from duty.

One of the largest waterwheels in Ireland at Newmills Mill

Donegal Castles

WHERE:
County Donegal
BEST TIME TO GO:
Mid-June to October (for Donegal
Castle).
DON'T MISS:
The Church of Ireland Cathedral (and
its atmospheric graveyard) in Raphoe
– built on the site of a monastery
founded by Adomnan, who wrote the
Life of Columba in the late 7th
century.
AMOUNT OF WALKING:
Moderate (be aware that wheelchair
access is not possible at some of the
ruined castles on Inishowen, though
just looking may be enough for most
people anyway).
COST:
Low
YOU SHOULD KNOW:
If you arrive at Carrickabraghey
Castle around high tide you can see
the spectacular 'hissing rock' that
spurts seawater driven by the rolling
Atlantic waves.

If you love castles, head for Donegal and be spoilt for choice – you'll have around forty to choose from, mostly in ruins. Here's your starter for four – a selection which guarantees an interesting day out that includes some scenic touring.

Start with Donegal Castle in Donegal Town: it, too, should be a ruin but has recently been restored to its original appearance, using traditional materials and methods. The building consists of a wonderful 15th-century rectangular keep (mirrored in the small gatehouse) and later Jacobean wing. The castle stands within a 17th-century wall on the River Eske near Donegal Bay.

Drive north from Donegal on the N15, turn left at Killygordon and traverse lonely countryside to Raphoe, where you will find the magnificent Raphoe Castle (sometimes called The Bishop's Palace). This 17th-century stronghold has impressive corner towers but fell into disrepair after falling to Cromwell's troops in 1650 and being damaged by supporters of James II in 1689. Even as standing walls only it is one of the most impressive buildings in the county.

Continue along the R236 to the A14, turning left for Letterkenny and the N56 to Creeslough. There you will see Doe Castle on Sheephaven Bay, one of Ireland's best fortresses. Built by the powerful MacSweeney family in the 16th century, the uncompromising central tower is surrounded by massive walls with marvellous sea views on three sides.

Inishowen is the northern peninsula of County Donegal, an area steeped in history. Castle lovers can enjoy several romantic ruins. These include Green Castle, Inch Castle, Buncrana Castle and Elagh Castle. If you choose only one, make it Carrickabraghey Castle. Drive up the west side of Inishowen and follow the Isle of Doagh road just outside Ballyliffin, where you will find a wonderful seashore ruin in the most dramatic setting imaginable.

Doe Castle on Cresslough

Donegal Adventure Day

The best way to appreciate the famous coastal scenery of Ireland's wild west is from the water, and one of the most rewarding methods of doing just that is by taking the Donegal Bay Waterbus from the pier in Donegal town. This luxurious jet-powered cruiser takes up to 160 passengers around Donegal Bay, offering stunning views of ocean, coastline and mountains as a dramatic journey unfolds.

Highlights include views of Donegal and Magherabeg Abbeys, Hassans (an embarkation point for passenger ships to America until the early 19th century) and St Eunan's famine causeway. Along the way abundant wildlife will include a huge variety of seabirds, whilst porpoises, seals, dolphins and even whales may sometimes be spotted. This is an outing not to be missed!

To extend the day's nautical-themed activities visit the Killybegs Maritime and Heritage Centre. This provides interesting insight into the great fishing tradition in these parts – there has long been a fishing fleet in Killybegs and this historic town remains Ireland's largest fishing port. An audio-visual journey into the past includes the memories of local fishermen and hands-on types can experience the virtual reality of challenging the Atlantic Ocean from a trawler's wheelhouse. There is also the opportunity to learn the craft of hand-knotting carpets at the Heritage Centre, a former carpet factory – also to see the world's largest hand-knotted loom, with traditional weavers explaining how carpets are individually designed and produced.

Complete this active day out with some adrenaline-fuelled driving at the Letterkenny Karting Centre. It's possible to enjoy exciting practice sessions, streaking around a 900-m (2,950-ft) track to get the feel of the flying go-karts, and racing against up to twenty other karters. If a party of twelve can be made up, a Grand Prix session with practice, qualifying races and finals can be booked.

The best way to appreciate Donegal's stunning coastal scenery is from the water.

WHERE:
County Donegal
BEST TIME TO GO:
April to September
DON'T MISS:
Those in search of some adventurous action could find a visit to Bundoran very satisfying – it has two of Ireland's finest surfing locations in Main Beach and Tullan Strand.
AMOUNT OF WALKING:
Little
COST:
Expensive
YOU SHOULD KNOW:
Every summer there is a street festival in Killybegs that celebrates the year's fish catch and incorporates the traditional ceremony of 'blessing the boats'.

Isle of Innisfree

The island of Innisfree in Lough Gill inspired W. B. Yeats to write his lyric poem 'The Lake Isle of Innisfree' – about a place where he had once romantically dreamed of living rough. Today it's possible to visit this wooded isle (in summer) by taking a waterborne excursion from Sligo Town that includes the Garavogue River. There are other options, including a waterbus from Dromahair, or it's possible to drive round Lough Gill in an hour and view Innisfree from afar. The Lough's natural splendour is enhanced by the impressive works of man – stunning Parke's Castle on the Leitrim shore.

To appreciate fully the classic Irish countryside that Yeats found so inspiring, take the pleasant hillside walk through Slish Wood beside Lough Gill. Find it some 6 km (4 mi) outside Sligo Town on the R287 road west of Dromahair. A good track from a well-signed car park offers a pleasant 3.5-km (2-mi) tramp with easy gradients and wonderful views of the lake and its tiny green islands glimpsed through trees along the way. Allow an hour. There is abundant flora and fauna to enjoy and a picnic site with a wonderfully scenic outlook offers a perfect location for a relaxing al fresco lunch.

From Lough Gill, enjoy a scenic drive from Dromahair to Drumkeeran and on beside Lough Allen to Drumshanbo, from whence the R208 takes you to Ballinamore. Here, the Glenview Folk Museum presents a display of items from pre-famine Ireland. This huge collection includes an impressive array of early farming equipment, together with a reconstructed street that contains various shops and a pub. Thousands of hand tools, household items and other memorabilia provide a flavour of rural life in the West of Ireland during the 19th century.

Lough Gill

Leitrim Heritage Day

A good way to appreciate the beautiful county of Leitrim is to mix heritage and scenic driving. Carrick-on-Shannon is an ideal starting point – you can see the mighty River Shannon in all its glory and also visit the Costello Memorial Chapel on Bridge Street. A testament to one man's love for his wife, this impressive chapel is the smallest in Ireland – dedicated in 1879 to the memory of Mary Costello, built by her grieving husband Edward. They lie side by side in glass-covered vaults.

Parke's Castle sits beside Lough Gill.

Leave Carrick and drive the short distance to Mohill, where you will find ruined Cloonmorris Church, built around 1200 as an auxiliary to the Mohill Augustinian Priory. It has plain but pleasing lancet windows and an Ogham Stone in the churchyard – the only one in Leitrim (Ogham was an early Celtic alphabet).

From Mohill, make the short trip to visit Fenagh Abbey close to Ballinamore. This ruined medieval church was built on the site of an early monastery founded by St Caillin and used by the Church of Ireland until new premises were built in 1798.

Continuing the religious theme, make the scenic cross-country journey via Drumshanbo and Drumkeeran to see Creevelea Friary near Dromahair. It dates from 1508 and the well-preserved ruins stand in a romantic setting beside the River Bonet. Note particularly two bas-reliefs of St Francis on a pillar in the cloister – in one he is preaching to those birds.

Hopefully you haven't lingered too long in getting this far, as a highlight ends the day – Parke's Castle on the Dromahair-Sligo road, standing in a truly stunning setting beside Lough Gill. This remarkably complete structure is an early 17th-century manor house built within the walls of an earlier fortress, and now has exhibitions and audio-visual presentations to complement the recently restored interior.

WHERE:
County Leitrim
BEST TIME TO GO:
April to October
DON'T MISS:
The splendid 19th-century bridge and quayside at Carrick-on-Shannon, which was opened up for commercial river traffic in the 1840s and became a major depot for timber, cement, hardware...and Guinness (spot the old barrel store!).
AMOUNT OF WALKING:
Moderate
COST:
Low
YOU SHOULD KNOW:
Leitrim does have a coastline – but it's just a rather insignificant 3-km (2-mi) stretch of Atlantic shore wedged between Donegal and Sligo.

Lough Outer Castle

Cavan Heritage Day

This day celebrates Cavan's rich history as well as outstanding natural attributes. Head north on the N3 from Cavan Town and turn left at Belturbet, to find the Ballyhugh Arts and Cultural Centre. After enjoying the extensive collection of artefacts and local photographs, drive south to Milltown. Just outside the village is Drumlane Monastery. This ruin, in a wonderful lakeside setting, consists of a round tower, church and graveyard. Spot the birds carved on the external wall of the tower and some fine stone heads.

Drumlane stands on one of Lough Oughter's arms. This complicated lake has two notable island sites. The 12th-century Lough Oughter Castle was once the stronghold of the O'Reilly family – today a ruined round tower rises defiantly from encircling trees close to Carratraw Bridge. Near Killashandra is the medieval Holy Trinity Abbey on Trinity Island, with an extant west gable and graveyard full of tumbled stones.

Leaving Lakeland, head south via Bellananagh to Ballyjamesduff and the Cavan County Museum. This magnificent Victorian building in extensive grounds houses an impressive collection devoted to the life and culture of County Cavan from the Stone Age, with a wide selection of galleries and exhibitions (closed on Mondays).

The quest continues with a drive to Mullagh, via Virginia, to visit St Kilian's Heritage Centre, celebrating the life and times of said St Kilian, born in Mullagh and martyred at Wurzburg. He was but one of Ireland's early missionaries to Europe, and their story is brought to life here. The Centre has Ogham Stones found in Cavan.

There should be time to drive up the R191 road to Cootehill, ending the tour on a high note – a quick visit to the Maudabawn Cultural Centre in its stone-walled, thatched-roofed building, a centre of excellence for the appreciation of Irish cultural heritage.

Monaghan Scenic Drive

County Monaghan – one of three counties in the Province of Ulster that is in the Irish Republic rather than Northern Ireland – has a name derived from the Irish phrase 'Land of Little Hills', referring to Monaghan's characteristic drumlin landscape formed during the last Ice Age.

This may be explored by taking a scenic tour from Monaghan Town, itself an interesting place with a centre consisting of interconnected squares. The Georgian Market House is an art gallery and the award-winning County Museum is nearby. It's also the place to purchase provisions, in anticipation of eating al fresco.

From Monaghan, take the Newbliss Road to Rossmore Forest Park. This offers woodland and lakeside walks, a nature trail and excellent viewpoints – one of which is formed by the last remnants of Rossmore Castle. The walled garden contains a Yew Walk plus water feature and there are prehistoric tombs within the park.

Continue through County Cavan via Cootehill and Shercock to Kingscourt. Take the Carrickmacross road and find Dún Na Rí Forest Park. The River Cabra's 'Romantic Glen' is full of wildlife and offers wonderful walks – all quite short but also sweet. The Park contains interesting features like Sarah's Bridge, a holy well, Cromwell's Bridge, the Lady's Lake, an old flax mill, ice house and the remains of Fleming's Castle. This is the place to have that leisurely picnic.

Continue to Carrickmacross (a renowned lace-making centre) and take the R180 road to Lough Egish, a pretty lake and surrounding rural area that played an important part in the establishment of the Irish Cooperative Movement. From there, it's a short hop to Castleblaney, the starting point for a stroll along the scenic shores of Lough Muckno, Monaghan's largest and an area of 'primary amenity value' in council-speak. From Castleblaney it's a straight run back to Monaghan Town.

WHERE:
Counties Monaghan and Cavan
BEST TIME TO GO:
April to October
DON'T MISS:
The impressive Rossmore Memorial in Monaghan town – it commemorates the Fourth Baron Rossmore, who died after a hunting accident at Windsor Castle in 1874.
AMOUNT OF WALKING:
Lots
COST:
Low
YOU SHOULD KNOW:
Castle Leslie – scene of Sir Paul McCartney's ill-fated wedding to Heather Mills – is in County Monaghan, close by the picturesque stone-built village of Glaslough.

Lady's Lake in Dún Na Rí Forest Park

Roslee Castle

Sligo Castles

WHERE:
County Sligo
BEST TIME TO GO:
April to September
DON'T MISS:
The atmospheric Abbey cemetery
and grounds at Easkey, wherein may
be found some splendid monuments
– get the key from Forde's shop in
the village.
AMOUNT OF WALKING:
Moderate
COST:
Low
YOU SHOULD KNOW:
Ballymote Castle well illustrates the
turbulence of Irish history. Built
around 1300 by Richard de Burgo,
the infamous Red Earl of Ulster, it
was soon lost to O'Connors. For the
next 250 years it regularly alternated
between them and MacDonaghs,
before being taken as an English
base, retaken by Red Hugh O'Donnell
in 1598 before...you get the
general idea!

Much like Scotland, its Celtic neighbour, Ireland was a hotbed of clan rivalry and the scene of ferocious political activity in centuries past. The result is a legacy of fine early castles, each built by a player of the day to defend his territory from ambitious rivals, even as he plotted their downfall.

An outing by car will combine the opportunity to see some fine Sligo castles with wonderful landscapes. The tour begins at the popular seaside village of Easkey, facing Donegal Bay west of Sligo Town. There, beside the pier, is Roslee Castle, a prominent landmark in West Sligo; built by the powerful O'Dowd Clan in the early 1200s, substantial remains survive.

Return to Sligo and – just south of town – find Enniscrone Castle at Inishcrone, a 17th-century fortified house, once the pride and joy of the Nolans but now somewhat distressed. Continue down the N4 and turn right for Ballymote – and find the last and mightiest of Connaught's Norman castles.

Go back to the N4 road at Castlebaldwin, where the 'castle' is actually another rather fine fortified 17th-century house. From there, continue down Lough Arrow to the next classic ruin, Ballinafad Castle by Lough Key. Known as 'The Castle of the Curlews', this sturdy military stronghold defended an important pass through the Curlew Mountains. It met its Waterloo in 1642 when sacked by insurgent Irish after running out of water and was soon abandoned.

Round off the day by driving southwest from Ballinafad via Boyle almost to Roscommon, where Clogher Castle may be found near Monasteraden and Lough Gara. Situated on a rounded ridge with the ground sloping away on all sides, this is an exceptional and well-preserved example of a Cashel fortress with massive walls, set in sublime landscape.

480

W.B. Yeats Day

No visit to Sligo could be complete without acknowledging the county's favourite literary son, poet and dramatist William Butler Yeats. Though born in Dublin, much of Yeats' childhood was spent in Sligo where his mother's prosperous family lived – he considered the area to be his spiritual home. Begin the pilgrimage with the Yeats Memorial Building on Hyde Bridge in Sligo Town, an upstanding former bank that houses a WBY Exhibition and Sligo Art Gallery. It's also a centre for various Yeats-related activities such as an International Summer School.

On the North Shore of Sligo Bay is Lissadell – a mansion built in the 1830s frequented by the aristocratically inclined Yeats in his youth. This grand house has recently been restored and has magnificent interiors – including the Yeats Bedroom (decorated with paintings by his brother Jack), the Yeats Study (full of works by Yeats and his contemporaries) and the Bow Room made famous by Yeats ('Great windows open to the south'). Outside, the gardens are returning to their former splendour and there is a tearoom and heritage shop in the former coach house.

You may wish to linger at Lissadell, but WBY is calling again. On the way back to Sligo Town stop at Drumcliff Church, built on the site of an ancient monastery of which the only evidence is a round tower and ornate High Cross. Yeats died in France in 1939 and was interred there. But in 1948 following his own specific wish ('When the newspapers have forgotten me, dig me up and plant me in Sligo'), his coffin returned home and was reburied in the peaceful graveyard at Drumcliff, where his great-grandfather had been Rector. His wife Georgie is buried beside him in the shadow of the splendid mountain of Ben Bulben.

WHERE:
County Sligo
BEST TIME TO GO:
April to September
DON'T MISS:
Abandoning Yeats for an hour, visit Sligo Abbey. This grand ruin has a wealth of carvings, tomb sculptures, a well-preserved cloister and the sole surviving sculpted 15th-century high altar in any Irish monastic church.
AMOUNT OF WALKING:
Moderate
COST:
Reasonable
YOU SHOULD KNOW:
Irish heritage comes in all shapes and sizes – a highlight of the fabulous walled kitchen garden at Lissadell is a collection of some 170 different varieties of traditional potato.

The unusual statue of the great man stands outside the Ulster Bank.

Around North Mayo

WHERE:
County Mayo
BEST TIME TO GO:
April to November
DON'T MISS:
The view of the striking view of St Muredach's Cathedral from the bridge over the River Moy in Ballina town centre – then cross the road and (in season) watch the anglers immersed to the waist in the famous Ridge Pool as they cast for running salmon.
AMOUNT OF WALKING:
Moderate (with limited wheelchair access beyond the Visitor Centre at Céide Fields).
COST:
Reasonable
YOU SHOULD KNOW:
There shouldn't be a problem communicating with inhabitants of the Gaeltacht – Irish may be the first language of many, but they do speak English too.

From Mayo's largest town of Ballina – an excellent base for exploring the region – take the Killala road and watch for signs to Moyne Abbey. Park at the third (pointing to a farm gate) and, bravely ignoring a BEWARE OF THE BULL sign (take a good look around first), walk down the lane to substantial remains of this 15th-century religious foundation, with a splendid cloister and fine mullioned windows. Turn left out of the Moyne entrance and find Rosserk Friary in a tranquil location on the western shore of Killala Bay. The ruin is substantial and interesting features remain.

Proceed to the village of Ballycastle with its colour-washed houses, situated close to the rugged coast of North Mayo. Nearby Céide Fields is the oldest known field system in the world (over 5,000 years old), and includes remains of stone field walls, houses and megalithic tombs. There is a modern Visitor Centre that explains the site with exhibitions and an audio-visual presentation; guided tours are available and there's a tearoom.

After learning how climate change devastated the lives of the local Stone Age farmers, head towards Belmullet and deeper into the Mayo Gaeltacht (Irish-speaking region). This is an area of wild natural beauty with stunning coastal vistas – take the detour from Belderg via Porturlin and Ross Port back to the main road and see for yourself! At Barnatra, turn sharp left and drive along Carrowmore Lake, an important bird habitat.

Turn right for the village of Belmullet, from whence it's possible to explore the beautiful coastline beyond – north to Erris Head or south to Blacksod – for wonderful distant views. After returning to Belmullet, drive to Bunnahowen and turn right, following the coast (a couple of side roads lead down to the sea) to Gweesalia before heading for Bangor and on to Ballina.

The Céide Fields Visitor Centre

Lakes Drive

The Salmon Festival in Ballina

Starting from bustling Ballina, there's a great scenic drive to the south that includes two wonderful lakes – Loughs Conn and Cullin. But first visit the riverside St Muredach's Cathedral, built in the 19th century.

Take the westbound N59 out of town to the shores of Lough Conn, a vast expanse of water that covers 57 sq km (22 sq mi). Stop and explore the lakeshore then continue to Knockmore, passing through some of Ireland's most beautiful and unspoiled scenery. As you reach the southern end of Lough Conn, ignore the temptation to take the road between the two lakes and continue beside Lough Cullin to Foxford.

This small town situated on the River Moy between the Nephin and Ox Mountains grew up around its woollen mills (makers of the Foxford Blanket since 1892). The Foxford Woollen Mills Visitor Centre is a premier tourist attraction. A one-hour historical tour recreates life in the 1890s, when the original mill was founded by Mother Agnes Morrogh Bernard, an Irish Sister of Charity. It also includes the opportunity to see skilled craftspeople producing Foxford's famous rugs, blankets and tweeds. The restaurant is an ideal place to have lunch or grab a snack, and there's a well-stocked mill shop, jewellery workshops and art galleries with local works for sale.

After lunch, carry on towards Mayo's county town, Castlebar, stopping en route at the picturesque village of Straide with its fine church, well-preserved Dominican Abbey and museum dedicated to Irish hero Michael Davitt, the local-born founder of the Land League. After looking round Castlebar, take the R310 and up the west shores of Loughs Cullin and Conn via Pontoon and Lahardaun to Crossmolina, then back to Ballina.

WHERE:
County Mayo
BEST TIME TO GO:
Any time
DON'T MISS:
The Salmon Festival in Ballina – held for a week in mid-July, it includes a Heritage Day when the town centre is closed to traffic and numerous arts and crafts stalls appear, plus a Mardi-Gras-style finale, culminating in a grand display of fireworks.
AMOUNT OF WALKING:
Moderate (impromptu wheelchair access to the actual shore of Lough Conn can be awkward).
COST:
Low
YOU SHOULD KNOW:
Loughs Conn and Cullin are prolific fisheries, which means there are numerous operators offering boats for hire (with or without outboard motors) if you should fancy some waterborne exploration.

Achill Island

WHERE:
County Mayo
BEST TIME TO GO:
June to August (for Westport House).
DON'T MISS:
The extraordinary collection of
waxwork figures at Westport House
that pay tribute to great literary,
artistic and musical traditions of the
West of Ireland.
AMOUNT OF WALKING:
Lots (on Achill island)
COST:
Reasonable
YOU SHOULD KNOW:
The old British observation post on
Achill Island's Moytoge Head was
built to watch for Germans
attempting to smuggle arms to the
Irish Republican Army in World War I.

Ireland's largest island (148 sq km/57 sq mi) is reached by a bridge across Achill Sound north of Westport and is well worth investigating, despite some unsympathetic modern development. Achill Island has a number of small settlements and – apart from the R313 that runs through the Island's spine to the village of Keel – a network of (very) minor roads.

Slievemore mountain dominates the centre, with an interesting abandoned village on the slopes – now not much more than standing walls and piles of stones. Just to the west is a Martello Tower built during the Napoleonic Wars. Achill also has some wonderful natural features, including the cliffs at Croaghaun at the western end – they're the highest sea cliffs in Europe, but you have to walk to see them as there's no road access. Near Achill Head, the westernmost point, is popular Keem Bay with the dramatic Moytoge Head plunging into the sea to the south.

Serious walkers could spend the day exploring Achill, but those who want more should make their way to Westport House and

Country Park. This is one of Ireland's finest 18th-century historic homes, magnificently situated overlooking Clew Bay. There are some stunning rooms in the house with splendid paintings, silver, glass and books. Actually, if history and culture aren't your thing, attractions in the grounds can provide hours of fun. They include an Animal and Bird Park, Log Flume water ride, train ride, Jungle World play area, pitch and putt golf and the Ships Galleon.

If you still have time you should head for the Granuaile Visitor Centre at Louisburgh, along the coast beyond Westport and Croagh Patrick. This small museum in an old Anglican church tells of the legendary maritime exploits of the O'Malleys and O'Flahertys in the 16th century – including the most famous of them all, Grace O'Malley, the Pirate Queen.

The lovely beach at Keem Bay

Croagh Patrick Pilgrimage

West of Westport, above Murrisk and Lecanvey, stands Croagh Patrick. It's County Mayo's third-highest mountain at 764 m (2,510 ft) but undoubtedly the most important. On Reek Sunday (the last in July), thousands of pilgrims climb the conical mountain known colloquially as The Reek, often in their bare feet.

This summer-solstice pilgrimage predates Celtic Christianity, though the mountain is named after St Patrick. He is said to have fasted at the summit for forty days in 441 AD after which he threw a silver bell, knocking she-devil Corra from the sky and banishing snakes from Ireland. The Black Bell of St Patrick, once silver but now dark with age, is a venerated relic first documented in 1098, now in the National Museum of Ireland.

There are three traditional stations on the pilgrimage. First is Leacht Benain, at the base of the cone. Here the faithful walk seven times around the mound of stones saying seven Our Fathers, seven Hail Marys and one Creed. Second is the summit, where the pilgrim kneels and repeats the prayers said at the base, prays near the Chapel (built in 1905) for the Pope's intentions then makes fifteen circuits round the Chapel saying fifteen Our Fathers and fifteen Hail Marys before walking seven times round Leaba Phadraig (Patrick's Bed) saying seven Our Fathers, seven Hail Marys and one Creed. The third station is Roilig Mhuire (Virgin's Cemetery) down the western slope. Here the pilgrim walks seven times round each mound of stones saying seven Our Fathers, seven Hail Marys and one Creed at each, finally going round the whole enclosure seven times, praying privately.

But you don't have to join the pilgrimage or be religious to enjoy the climb up Croagh Patrick – it will be an atmospheric and rewarding day whenever you go.

WHERE:
County Mayo
BEST TIME TO GO:
Last Sunday in July for mass pilgrimage, or go alone any time.
DON'T MISS:
St Patrick's statue, erected in 1928 – although not one of the three traditional Stations of the Reek it has become a place of prayer for pilgrims and an attainable objective for those who are unable to make the entire climb.
AMOUNT OF WALKING:
Lots (sadly not suitable for wheelchairs...and also pushchair unfriendly for all but the most determined).
COST:
Low
YOU SHOULD KNOW:
A potentially rich gold seam was discovered on Croagh Patrick in the 1980s but mining permission was denied by the local authorities, which declared 'the gold is just fine where it is'.

Pilgrims climb Croagh Patrick

Cong Abbey

Around South Mayo

WHERE:
County Mayo
BEST TIME TO GO:
April to October (July and August for Partry House).
DON'T MISS:
The bizarre Cong Canal connecting Loughs Corrib and Mask, complete with bridges and ruined locks – it was a failure, because it didn't hold water.
AMOUNT OF WALKING:
Moderate
COST:
Reasonable
YOU SHOULD KNOW:
Film star Pierce Brosnan was married at Ballintubber Abbey – which was once the start of an ancient pilgrimage route to Croagh Patrick (now re-opened as a cross-country trail).

Today's drive delivers some wonderful sights. Start at Castlebar, with Christchurch on the Mall. Completed in 1739, the interior of this important monument provides a record of the town between late 16th and early 20th centuries.

Take the N60 to Balla and turn for the village of Mayo – one of the most important monastic sites in Western Europe, founded by St Colman for Saxon rather than Celtic monks in 668 AD. Mayo Abbey Visitor Centre tells the story. The village also contains the 19th-century Famine Church, beside the Abbey ruins.

Continue to Clanmorris and find Partry House. The 17th-century house (open on summer afternoons) is at the heart of a delightful estate on the shores of Lough Carra. The farm and gardens are run on organic principles and the grounds contain parkland, woodland, bog and pasture.

Near Clanmorris is Knock – where locals saw 'The Apparition' in 1879 as the Virgin Mary, St Joseph and St John appeared. Knock is a major shrine on a par with Lourdes and Fatima that really hit its stride with the erection of a massive new basilica – Our Lady of Knock – in the 1960s, and subsequent construction of an international airport.

After visiting Knock Shrine and Museum, drive back to Clanmorris and visit Ballintubber, the Royal Abbey founded in 1216 and in use ever since, subject to continuing restoration. There is a small museum, plus several modern outdoor attractions like an abstract Way of the Cross, an underground crib and a Rosary Way.

End the day by driving down through Ballinrobe to Cong on the shore of Lough Corrib. There is a fine ruined medieval abbey in Cong, but its main claim to fame is as the location for the 1952 Oscar-winning film *The Quiet Man* starring John Wayne and Maureen O'Hara.

Lough Key

The bustling market town of Boyle sits at the foot of the Curlew Mountains, close to Lough Key – a place significant in Irish legend and medieval literature. This circular lake has 32 wooded islands (one for each Irish county) and is the jewel in the crown of Lough Key Forest Park. Together, they make for a day out to remember which can contain surprising contrasts.

The Park – once part of the Rockingham Estate – was acquired by the state in the 1950s and occupies an area of outstanding natural beauty. It contains extensive woodlands, gardens, nature walks, abundant wildlife and important archaeological remains, plus a viewing tower that offers sensational lake and countryside views.

It's possible to hire a dinghy with outboard at the Park's harbour to explore intriguing islands with their medieval remains. Key islands include Castle, Trinity and Church. There's a lake tour with commentary in a luxury cruise boat available, or a speedy powerboat trip with driver-guide. Castle Island was owned in succession by two powerful families, McGreevy and MacDermot. Their castle played a significant role in Irish history, but the present structure is an early 19th-century folly erected to adorn the Rockingham Estate and used as a summerhouse until gutted by fire. Lough Key's two priories were on Trinity and Church Islands.

It's perfectly possible to spend a leisurely day simply exploring the countryside and Lough – but there is an alternative. The Park has recently sought to develop as a 'family fun resource', with attractions like a lakeside Visitor Centre (information, shop and restaurant), Lough Key Experience (audio trail on the Park's history, including underground tunnels, viewing tower and treetop canopy walk), Boda Borg (a building full of imaginative puzzles, tasks and tests of ingenuity) and the Adventure Play Kingdom (outdoor activities for kids). You choose!

WHERE:
County Roscommon
BEST TIME TO GO:
April to September (July or August for the lake cruise).
DON'T MISS:
The terrific view of Lough Key from the N4 road as it ascends the mountains after passing Boyle – enhanced by a modern stainless steel sculpture of an ancient Irish chieftain.
AMOUNT OF WALKING:
Lots (but note that not all areas of the park are suitable for wheelchair users).
COST:
Expensive (if using all the attractions plus boat hire/cruise).
YOU SHOULD KNOW:
The Annals of Boyle and its successor, the Annals of Loch Key, were compiled on Trinity Island and form a priceless historical record of medieval life in these parts from around 1000 to 1590.

Castle Island – one of the 32 islands in Lough Key

North Roscommon Heritage Day

WHERE:
County Roscommon
BEST TIME TO GO:
April to September (for King House).
DON'T MISS:
The Boyle Civic Collection in King House, considered to be one of the finest collections of contemporary Irish painting and sculpture.
AMOUNT OF WALKING:
Moderate
COST:
Reasonable
YOU SHOULD KNOW:
When Roscommon County Council acquired magnificent but near-derelict King House in the 1980s the intention was to demolish the place and create a brand new...car park.

Welcome to the Irish equivalent of the South Wales Valleys – for whilst County Roscommon's coal industry may not quite have measured up to Welsh standards, it's very much part of the county's history and is remembered with pride. The Arigna Mining Experience, just off the R280 road along the shores of Lough Allen north of Carrick-on-Shannon, has an exhibition explaining the area's mining heritage and a fascinating underground tour of the old mine, complete with light and sound effects – marvel at how hard it must have been to work those oh-so-narrow coal seams.

The next eye-opener is Boyle Cistercian Abbey, just down the road from Arigna. This 12th-century Abbey is one of the best preserved in all Ireland, though some of the buildings are actually 16th or 17th century. The cloister is gone, partly as a result of destruction wrought by Cromwell's Ironsides in the 1650s, but much else of substance remains, especially the tower. In the two-storey gatehouse is a visitor centre that reveals all, serving as a reminder (if one is needed) of just how impressive this place must have seemed when fulfilling its original function.

Desire to impress certainly hadn't slackened when modestly named King House was built around 1730 to the order of influential Sir Henry King. This Georgian mansion was built on a grand scale but eventually became the barracks of the legendary Connaught Rangers, one of the British Army's Irish regiments disbanded with the formation of the Irish Free State in 1922. Fully refurbished, King House in Main Street, Boyle now consists of interpretive galleries and a museum. Wander through splendid rooms enjoying interactive displays featuring the ancient Kingdom of Connaught, the restoration of this wonderful building, the history of the King family and the Connaught Rangers. Very enjoyable!

Boyle Abbey dates from the 12th century.

Roscommon and Strokestown

Roscommon (town and county) is named after St Coman. Forest near the Dominican Friary he founded became known as Coman's Wood – *Ros Comáin* in Irish. Start the day with a visit to the Friary ruins, south of town. Remains include tracery windows and a chancel with effigies, notably that of founder Felim O'Connor and another representing eight gallowglasses in armour (medieval professional soldiers, in case you were wondering).

No doubt there were gallowglasses aplenty at Roscommon Castle in its heyday. The impressive ruin sprawls massively across fields north of the town. This large 13th-century Anglo-Norman fortress played its part in turbulent Irish history, changing hands several times between English incomers and local chieftains. There are more than enough impressive remains to show what a dominant structure this must have been in centuries past, before being partially destroyed by Cromwell's Ironsides in the 1650s.

From Roscommon it's but a short drive to Strokestown, which has some of the widest roads in Ireland – apparently because Lord Hartland wanted his estate village to have wider streets than Vienna's Ringstrasse! His former home is Strokestown Park House, a beautifully restored 18th-century Palladian mansion. A guided tour takes you through rooms furnished with their original fittings and furniture. Outside, a walled pleasure garden contains the longest herbaceous border in the British Isles, whilst the walled Georgian kitchen garden has 18th-century glasshouses and a gazebo tower. There is a restaurant and shop.

In the stable yards may be found a fascinating Famine Museum, detailing the horrors of 1845 to 1850 when two million Irish people either starved to death or emigrated after the potato crops repeatedly failed. It was Europe's greatest 19th-century social disaster but – because of the abject poverty of those most affected – few records remain, which makes the detailed Strokestown papers both rare and fascinating.

Strokestown Famine Museum with Sayer's ceramic Soup Pot

WHERE:
County Roscommon
BEST TIME TO GO:
Mid-March to October (for Strokestown House).
DON'T MISS:
Make time to visit the Mill Cottage Agricultural Museum at Elphin, north of Strokestown – a highlight is the restored windmill with thatched revolving roof.
AMOUNT OF WALKING:
Moderate
COST:
Reasonable
YOU SHOULD KNOW:
Roscommon Town had a fearsome hangwoman called Lady Betty from 1780 to 1810, who had a room in the gaol (now a shopping centre!) and left each of her unfortunate victims dangling until she had made a charcoal sketch.

The ancient Celtic stone fort of Dun Duchathair

Aran Islands

After becoming a refuge for people forced to flee Cromwell's troops in the 1650s, the Aran Islands in Galway Bay developed a subsistence economy that included unique currach fishing boats designed to cope with the temperamental Atlantic and a technique of mixing sand and seaweed on rocky ground to create fertile land that could grow crops and sustain livestock (the latter providing the wool and yarn to make hand-woven and knitted clothing), all retained within a network of stone walls.

There are three isles – in decreasing order of size Inishmore, Inishmaan and Inisheer. Irish is widely spoken, though less exclusively than before the arrival of electricity, television and ever-increasing tourist numbers in the 1970s. The Aran Islands have some of the finest scenery on Ireland's West Coast, for which read 'breathtaking', and they have an old-fashioned atmosphere (especially on the two smaller islands) that allows visitors to glimpse a way of life that has long since vanished elsewhere.

There are ferries from Galway, the fishing village of Ros an Mhil (Rossaveal) in Connemara and Doolin in County Clare – the latter also offering an Aran trip, combined with a cruise beneath the towering Cliffs of Moher. Those who are cash rich but time poor can fly in from Indreabhán Airport. Inter-island transfers are possible in the summer months.

Once there, visitors can enjoy those wonderful views, bracing Atlantic air, unique flora and fauna, prehistoric forts, ecclesiastical remains from the early dawn of Irish Christianity, castles, cliffs, sandy beaches and rich folklore that islanders are proud to recount. It's possible to explore on foot or by hiring a bicycle, though a mini-bus tour will ensure that you see everything in one day and have the informed services of a local guide. There are even pony traps for those who prefer four legs to two.

WHERE:
County Galway
BEST TIME TO GO:
July and August
DON'T MISS:
Kilurvey Craft Village – and the chance to buy one of those world-famous hand-knitted Aran sweaters from the source rather than some exclusive city shop.
AMOUNT OF WALKING:
Lots
COST:
Reasonable – expensive
YOU SHOULD KNOW:
The Aran islanders are generally friendly (and appreciate that tourism is a mainstay of their economy) but can sometimes seem distant in the manner of small, closed societies the world over when they are opened up to an influx of visitors and the scrutiny that brings.

Connemara

Galway is Ireland's second-largest county (Cork is the biggest), and one of its most romantic regions is Connemara – the broad peninsula separated from the rest of Galway by the Invermore River.

This delightful area cries out to be explored – though with all that stop-and-marvel scenery you'll be hard-pressed to visit all the attractions on offer. Take the coast road out of Galway (at Spiddle Craft Centre find artisans at work beside a blue flag beach). Continue to Costelloe (optional detour to Carraroe – 'coral' beach and Galway hookers, as in boats).

Follow the rugged coastline through Kinvarra, Glencoh, Kilkieran, Roundstone and Ballyconneely (side trip – Slyne Head) to Clifden, Connemara's principal town. If you're interested in The Connemara Heritage Centre at Lettershea make a quick detour down the N59 – the Centre is a great place to pause for refreshment and enjoy a history presentation, reconstructions of a crannog and ring fort plus the Dan O'Hara Homestead (he of the popular ballad) and pre-famine farm.

North of Clifden follow the sea along minor roads to Claddaghduff and Cleggan, before returning to the main N59 and driving through scenic Connemara National Park to Leenaun on scenic Killary Harbour (Leenaun Cultural Centre focuses on the local wool industry – with live sheep).

Head for home via Maum, Maam Cross and Oughterard. From there, a short run up the Clifden Road will take you to the Glengowla Mine, a restored silver and lead mine with a Visitor Centre and underground guided tours. Just south of Oughterard is mighty Aughnanure Castle, home of the O'Flaherty clan, ferocious medieval masters of West Connacht. This splendid tower house should not be missed. Last potential stop of the day is at the Connemara Marble Quarry Visitor Centre at Moycullen, just before Galway, home of one of Ireland's finest natural products.

WHERE:
County Galway
BEST TIME TO GO:
April to October (mid-June to mid-September for Aughnanure Castle).
DON'T MISS:
The famous Twelve Bens – a small but impressive range of snaggle-tooth mountains near Roundstone.
AMOUNT OF WALKING:
Moderate
COST:
Low (reasonable if you sample a few visitor attractions).
YOU SHOULD KNOW:
Two monuments south of Clifden are near the spot where the first non-stop Transatlantic flight (by British aviators Alcock and Brown) ended in 1919 – they thought they were landing their Vickers Vimy on a nice green field, but it turned out to be a bog and the aircraft was badly damaged.

Roundstone harbour

Longford Tour

WHERE:
County Longford
BEST TIME TO GO:
May to September
DON'T MISS:
The Ballykenny-Fishertown Raised Bog – an important wetland area typical of the Irish Midlands, on the southeastern shores of Lough Forbes near Newtown Forbes.
AMOUNT OF WALKING:
Moderate
COST:
Low
YOU SHOULD KNOW:
The French invasion of 1798 ended at the Battle of Ballinamuck in Longford, when General Humbert surrendered after defeat by superior British forces under Cornwallis – the surviving French were taken prisoner but accompanying Irish rebels were massacred (now remembered by a monument in Ballinamuck).

One of the smallest counties, Longford's principal activities are growing oats and potatoes, plus cattle and sheep raising. Much of Longford lies in the Shannon basin or upper catchment of the River Erne, with Lough Ree forming the western boundary. The northern part of Longford is hilly drumlin country and the rest consists of wetland, bog and pastureland.

For all that Ireland has modernized dramatically, Longford with its unspoiled countryside and slow pace of life retains an echo of the old way. To appreciate this delightfully old-fashioned county, start in Longford Town at St Mel's – typical of many magnificent Catholic Cathedrals in Ireland started in early Victorian times, delayed by the Famine and completed later in the 19th century.

Then drive south to Keenagh and Corlea Trackway Visitor Centre. This interprets a wooden Iron Age bog road built in 148 BC (carbon dating and tree rings explain that precise date). Continue along back roads towards Lough Ree, through a land that time seems to have forgotten. The Lough's Inchcleraun Island has the remains of an early monastery, five churches and other buildings. To actually get there you have to go down to Athlone and take a boat cruise, or round through Lanesborough to Gailey Bay on the Roscommon shore.

Continue to Cloondara (Clonra), where restoration of the ill-fated Royal Canal near its entry point to the Shannon is well advanced. From there, spend the rest of the day enjoying the scenic delights of northern Longford – drive up through Newtown Forbes and Drumlish to Arvagh, before returning to Longford via Aghnacliff and Ballinalee. Drop in on Carrigglas Manor with its wonderful stable yard just before reaching Longford. This romantic house's builder is said to be the model for Mr Darcy in Jane Austen's *Pride and Prejudice*.

Richmond Harbour on the Royal Canal in Cloondara

Lake County Tour

Westmeath is 'The Lake County' and water has always been important in the county's history – the main east-west route from Dublin passed through, and two canals (Royal and Grand) brought commercial prosperity to Athlone on the Shannon (just south of Lough Ree) which has a major inland harbour.

The day begins with a quick visit to Athlone Castle, situated at the strategic fording point (bridged long ago) on the Middle Shannon. The Castle's violent history, Athlone's military tradition and the Shannon's ecology are brought to life through exhibitions and audio-visual presentations.

Just east of Athlone along the N6 road is Moate, where Westmeath's agricultural tradition is celebrated at the Folk Park. From there, continue along the N6 before taking the N52 towards Mullingar, situated between Loughs Ennell and Owel. This busy town is the administrative centre of Westmeath, but the attraction is Belvedere House and Gardens – find it on the shores of Lough Ennell before you reach town.

Belvedere offers parkland, lakeside and woodland walks, romantic follies, rare specimen plants, an animal sanctuary, children's play area and Belvedere House itself, a former hunting lodge with original features and wonderful lake views. The Visitor Centre in the stable block has a multi-media show, exhibitions and a café.

Hurry through Mullingar and past Lough Derravaragh to Castlepollard, where Tullynally Castle and Gardens will be found. Home to the Earls of Longford, this fortified house was first remodelled as a Georgian mansion, then as a vast Gothic revival pile. The inside tour reveals a fine collection of furniture and pictures, also covering the Victorian kitchens and laundry. The Gardens are simply fabulous, encompassing woodland pleasure grounds, walled gardens, flower gardens, themed national gardens, ponds and an Adventure Trail to the lower lake. If you haven't allowed a leisurely afternoon to explore, you'll be sorry!

Belvedere has splendid original features and wonderful lake views.

WHERE:
County Westmeath
BEST TIME TO GO:
May to September
DON'T MISS:
The Kitchen Garden at Tullynally – one of the largest in Ireland, with a splendid central avenue of yews, linked by an unusual 'tapestry' hedge of holly, box, yew and magnolia.
AMOUNT OF WALKING:
Moderate
COST:
Reasonable
YOU SHOULD KNOW:
One of Ireland's most famous follies, The Jealous Wall at Belvedere, was erected by the first Earl Belvedere to hide the nearby mansion of a brother suspected of dallying with the Earl's pretty young wife, who was locked up at the age of 20 for suspected adultery and only released after the death of her tyrannical husband.

Around Louth

Start this interesting journey through County Louth at the port and industrial town of Drogheda. The attraction here is Beaulieu House, just to the north of town near Baltray – take the river road and find Beaulieu beside the River Boyne. This magical place has been home to the same family since the 1660s and today's visitor can enjoy a guided tour of the grand interior, an extensive walled garden, restored church and small but speedy-looking collection of racing cars.

From Drogheda, take the northbound M1 motorway, exiting for Ardee. From there, follow the R171 road to Louth and find Knockabbey Castle and Gardens. The house was started in the 1300s and subject to alteration, extension and refurbishment right up to the present day, notably after being torched by the Irish Republican Army in 1923. The Visitor Centre recounts the history of the house and grounds. The gardens are the crowning glory and are in the process of being restored to their historic splendour. There's a self-guided trail to ensure that nothing is missed.

After Knockabbey, take the R171 to Dundalk, then the R173 along Dundalk Bay and across to Carlingford. This picturesque coastal village was once important but fell on hard times – which meant that it has retained much of its medieval character. Look out for the Tholsel (town gate), Taaffe's Castle (a fortified town house), fragments of town wall, a ruined Dominican Friary (nave and chancel divided by a tower), the Mint (a fortified town house with exquisite windows), Market Square (now the main street), harbour and King John's Castle (great viewpoint but no access). It's all pulled together at the Holy Trinity Heritage Centre, a restored medieval church with fabulous stained glass, an informative video and displays on Carlingford from Viking times. A great way to end the day!

*The ruined Dominican Friary
at Carlingford*

The Monastic Way

An innovative journey dubbed The Monastic Way allows visitors to follow the ancient *Eiscir Riada* (Kings Highway) from Dublin to Galway, taking in places of interest on or near the route, with the Offaly section providing a stimulating day out that begins at Tullamore.

Start at Tullamore Dew Heritage Centre with an experience that's hardly monastic, but very stimulating. Housed in a former whiskey distillery, it not only covers the manufacture of the amber nectar but also explores life in a small Irish town from the early 1800s. Nearby Charleville, (just outside Tullamore on the N52 Birr road) is Ireland's finest Gothic-Revival castle. After years of neglect this magnificent structure is coming back to life in its dramatic setting amidst ancient oak woodland.

From there, head north to Rahan on the banks of the Grand Canal. Here St Carthage (also called St Mochuda) founded a monastery. The outline of this large settlement is visible and three churches remain above ground, including one taken over by the Church of Ireland. On the other side of the Grand Canal is the monastic settlement of Lynally – all that remains is a ruined church and graveyard, near a 12th-century motte and bailey.

Up the road from Rahan is the Clara Bog Nature Reserve – those early travellers must have been familiar with raised bogland, which covers a third of Offaly. Today's visitor has it easy with the help of a walkway. Proceed down the R436 from Clara to Ballycumber and St Manchan's early church with a Holy Well and Oratory connected by a causeway, before continuing to The Monastic Way's exit point from Offaly – Clonmacnoise at the Shannon crossing. Built by St Ciarán from 545, it consists of a fabulous grouping of early monastic buildings and monuments, accessed through a Heritage Centre.

WHERE:
County Offaly
BEST TIME TO GO:
May to September
DON'T MISS:
The Cross of the Scriptures in the Clonmacnoise Interpretative Centre (with a replica in its original location) – undoubtedly one of the finest surviving carved High Crosses in all Ireland.
AMOUNT OF WALKING:
Moderate
COST:
Reasonable
YOU SHOULD KNOW:
Charleville Castle is said to be one of the most haunted places in Ireland, and it has been the subject of numerous paranormal investigations – though despite these determined efforts nothing substantial has emerged.

Charleville is Ireland's finest Gothic-Revival castle.

Entrance to a prehistoric stone burial chamber at Newgrange

Boyne Valley Drive

A rewarding day's exploration of Irish history begins at Donore, west of Drogheda, where the Brú na Bóinne Visitor Centre describes the Boyne Valley's rich archaeological heritage. This is the starting point for a guided tour of Newgrange and Knowth – amazing passage tombs over 5,000 years old. Together with Dowth and satellite tombs, they form an internationally famous prehistoric site.

The next stop is the nearby battlefield where Protestant William III and his Catholic father-in-law James II came to blows at the Battle of the Boyne in 1690. William's victory cemented Protestant control of Ireland, stoking majority Irish Catholic resentment that persists to this day.

Cross the Boyne to the charming estate village of Slane, with its medieval bridge and 18th-century mill. Walk up The Hill of Slane and find numerous historic sites, including an ancient Friary. Follow the R163 road to Kells with its ruined Abbey (from whence originated the famous Book of Kells), Celtic crosses, Oratory, St Columba's Church and Heritage Centre. Take the R163 towards Oldcastle and find the Spire of Lloyd, a 1791 memorial folly in the form of a lighthouse with wonderful views from the top that now stands in a community park.

Before Oldcastle, visit the megalithic cemetery at Loughcrew with mounds, passage tombs and rock carvings equal to those at Newgrange and Knowth (it's a steep walk!). Continue through Oldcastle to Virginia on Lough Ramor, then follow the N3 road down through Kells and Navan to the day's spectacular climax – Hill of Tara, legendary seat of the High Kings of Ireland. It's just off the main road south of Navan and – while there's a visitor centre in an old church that explains all – this is essentially a peaceful place steeped in history, with wonderful distant views said to encompass a quarter of Ireland.

WHERE:
County Meath
BEST TIME TO GO:
Any time
DON'T MISS:
The Francis Ledwidge Cottage Museum near Slane on the Drogheda road, a monument to the brilliant poet who was born there in 1887.
AMOUNT OF WALKING:
Lots (though wheelchair access to all passage tombs is not possible).
COST:
Reasonable
YOU SHOULD KNOW:
Should you touch the Lia Fáil standing stone on the Hill of Tara where Kings of Ireland were crowned until 500 AD and hear it cry out, legend insists that you too are a Monarch of Ireland.

A Day at the Races

The Irish and horses go together like Guinness and the *Craic*. The country has a natural affinity with the horse and today's vibrant bloodstock industry seems to produce a never-ending stream of winners, whilst Irish jockeys are renowned the world over. There's nothing local trainers like better than overseas raids to carry off top prizes, often to the accompaniment of wild celebrations by travelling fans, but it's at home meetings that the country's love affair with horseracing may best be appreciated amidst an outpouring of passion and spontaneous excitement.

These colourful occasions are worth seeking out and Dublin provides an excellent base. There are a number of nearby courses and the jewel in the crown of Irish racing is undoubtedly The Curragh – the sole flat-only racecourse. The home to five prestigious Classic races is on the Curragh plains south of Dublin, at the epicentre of Ireland's highly successful training and breeding operations.

The Curragh may be the place to see the best thoroughbreds in action (and the cream of Irish society at work and play), but Leopardstown is Dublin's local course and stages jump racing in winter and flat races throughout the rest of the year. Some of the country's biggest races are here and there's usually extra entertainment, like evening meetings in summer followed by live music.

Though Ireland is hugely influential in the high-octane world of international flat racing, it's probably fair to say that the locals are even more passionate about National Hunt racing. Fairyhouse is the place to see the most important jump races, including the Irish Grand National on Easter Monday. Find it northwest of Dublin. To enjoy the experience of a typical everyday meeting – the real lifeblood of Irish racing – try courses like Naas, Punchestown, Bellewstown and Navan, all within easy reach of Dublin.

WHERE:
County Kildare (Curragh, Naas, Punchestown), Dublin region (Leopardstown), County Meath (Fairyhouse, Bellewstown, Navan).

BEST TIME TO GO:
Any time

DON'T MISS:
If you can possibly make it, take in the unique Laytown Races in County Meath – held just once a year (around the beginning of September). Thoroughbreds race on a beach course created for the day on the broad expanse of Laytown strand.

AMOUNT OF WALKING:
Little

COST:
Reasonable, but expensive if you bet and lose.

YOU SHOULD KNOW:
Ireland has 27 racecourses – more per head of population than any other country in the world – most offering both flat and jump race meetings, so it shouldn't be hard to find that day at the races wherever you are!

The Curragh races

The Slieve Blooms

WHERE:
Counties Laois and Offaly
BEST TIME TO GO:
Any time
DON'T MISS:
The Leviathan of Parsontown, a giant telescope in the grounds of Birr Castle – from its construction in 1845 until 1917, the Leviathan was the world's largest telescope.
AMOUNT OF WALKING:
Lots (wheelchair users should not attempt the full Knockbarron Eco-walk, though pushchairs are feasible).
COST:
Low
YOU SHOULD KNOW:
If the recommended walks are not enough, look out for four other well-signed Eco-walks in the Slieve Blooms (Glenbarrow, Glenafelly, Silver River and Gorteenameale), or assorted loop walks from trailheads at Kinnitty, Lough Boora, Cadamstown village and Clonaslee.

The Slieve Bloom Mountains do not rise to a great height. Even so, they are extensive and make a pleasant change from the largely flat bogland of Ireland's central plain. To add variety to heather-covered hillsides and upland bog the once-treeless mountains have been forested in parts. The Slieve Blooms are delightful, offering historic sites, rivers, waterfalls, mysterious glens and remote villages. They are regarded as a walkers' paradise, so take stout shoes and be prepared to let your feet take the strain.

Begin at Mountrath just west of Portlaoise. Drive along the back road to Birr, via Clareen. This passes the high point in the Slieve Blooms – Mount Arderin (526m/1,725 ft). Stop and walk to the summit, known as 'The Top of Ireland'. From there it's possible to see the highest point in each of the country's ancient provinces (Leinster, Munster, Connacht and Ulster).

Continue to Birr, with its fine Georgian architecture. Be sure to see the beautiful early 19th-century Catholic church and one of Ireland's oldest coaching inns – Dooly's Hotel. Here, also, is Birr Castle. The house is not open but the grounds are and should be visited – they contain fine specimen shrubs and trees set in a landscaped park with a river, lake and waterfalls.

Take the R440 road out of Birr to Kinnitty in the heart of the Slieve Blooms. Before reaching the village, you'll find the Knockbarron Eco-walk, a gentle 90-minute loop through woodland that takes in one of Ireland's best-preserved Ice-Age esker landforms.

After tramping the trail, turn left at Kinnitty for Cadamstown and Clonashee. Just after the village make a right turn and take 'The Cut', a spectacular mountain road beside the Ridge of Capard that rejoins the R440 for a return to the starting point at Mountrath.

The beautifully landscaped grounds at Birr Castle

Around Laois

The Rock of Dunamase and the ruins of Dunamase Castle

Heard the one about builders who start a job and then vanish, sometimes for weeks or even months? Emo Court makes them pale into insignificance, for this neo-classical mansion was begun in 1790 and only completed in 1860. Was the wait worthwhile? Probably not – it served the purpose for which it was intended for just half a century, before aristocratic occupation ended in 1914. Was the effort worthwhile? Definitely – the fine house and beautiful surroundings make for a very satisfying visit. Find Emo Court off the M7 past Kildare and view the interior by guided tour, enjoying the outside space at leisure. Extensive gardens and parkland contain statuary, lawns, a lake and woodland walks.

To continue the 'splendid garden' theme, go down the M7/N8 past Portalaoise to Abbeyleix, proceeding on the Ballinakill road and viewing (free-entry) Heywood Gardens in the grounds of Heywood Community School. This garden is associated with famous names – designed by Sir Edwyn Lutyens to complement a now-vanished house and planted by Gertrude Jekyll. There are architectural features, formal gardens, lakes and woodland.

From Ballinakill drive via Swan to Timahoe; here stands an impressively tall 12th-century round tower in a tranquil setting across a river footbridge. The doorway is elaborately carved and it stands beside the remains of a church-cum-castle. Timahoe Tower is the finest of these early monastic structures to remain in Ireland, though their actual purpose remains a subject for scholarly debate. Continue the journey back in time by ending the day at the Rock of Dunamase – a striking vantage point standing above the flat plain that was once a monastic settlement pillaged by Vikings and subsequently the site of Dunamase Castle, now no more than romantic ruins. The views are spectacular and the climb worthwhile. Find it at The Heath just outside Portlaoise.

WHERE:
County Laois
BEST TIME TO GO:
April to October
DON'T MISS:
The impressive avenue of Wellingtonias (Giant Sequoia trees) that form a long-abandoned approach to Emo Court.
AMOUNT OF WALKING:
Moderate (but users of wheelchairs will have to admire Dunamase Castle from afar).
COST:
Low
YOU SHOULD KNOW:
Bring a pair of binoculars to fully appreciate the Timahoe Round Tower, as much of the interesting detailing is high off the ground.

Whites Castle at Athy

Gordon Bennett Route

In 1903, American newspaper tycoon Gordon Bennett's annual trophy race between the new-fangled automobiles of the day took place on a road course in the depths of rural Ireland. Today, the route is signed as a tourist trail that goes through country towns, picturesque villages and wonderful countryside. It makes for a different day out, following Gorden Bennett Route (GBR) signs along the 166-km (104-mi) figure-of-eight course, stopping as the mood dictates at some of the many attractions and sights along the way.

The GBR starts at Ballyshannon crossroads (at the end of the M7/M9 motorway from Dublin) and runs via Old Kilcullen, Moone and Castledermot to Carlow, from whence it returns to the starting point through Athy. The upper loop of the figure eight continues through Kildare, Monasterevin, Stradbally back to Athy, and from there to the start-finish point (for the third time).

If that sounds like retracing too many steps, the variety lies in the choice of stops. Potential highlights on the agenda (from the beginning) include: Old Kilcullen village; Kilgowan Long Stone; Ballitore Quaker Museum; the Irish Pewter Mill at Timolin; Moone High Cross; Castledermot Abbey, round tower and high cross; bustling Carlow town, Cathedral, Castle, Military Museum and river walk; Whites Castle and bridge at Athy; the Ardscull Moat (a huge Norman earthworks where a memorial to the 1903 race is sited – perfect for a picnic); historic Kilcullen; Curragh plains and racecourse; Kildare Heritage Centre, St Brigid's Cathedral and round tower, Irish National Stud and Japanese Gardens; Monasterevin town and bridges; Moore Abbey Wood; Coolbanagher Church; Maryborough Heath Iron Age site; Morette Castle ruins; Stradbally Steam Museum and heritage railway; Windy Gap viewpoint...and so (having been spoiled for choice all the way) back to Athy.

WHERE:
Counties Kildare, Carlow and Laois
BEST TIME TO GO:
April to October
DON'T MISS:
Athy Heritage Centre, with (amongst other things) contemporary film and artefacts from the original 1903 Gordon Bennett Trophy Race.
AMOUNT OF WALKING:
Little
COST:
Low
YOU SHOULD KNOW:
You do want to know, don't you? Okay, the 1903 Gordon Bennett Trophy was contested by Britain, France, Germany and the USA won by...'The Red Devil', Belgium's very own wild man Camille Jenatzy, driving a Mercedes for the German team.

Castletown House

No argument – Ireland's finest Palladian country house is Castletown, at Celbridge west of Dublin town (direct vehicle access from the M4 motorway or bus from Dublin to Celbridge). It was built from 1722 for wealthy William Conolly and his family remained there until the 1960s. The house was then restored and a guided tour now reveals sumptuous interiors and supporting domestic offices. Outside may be found the Wonderful Barn, an extraordinary corkscrew-shaped building for corn storage completed in 1743.

Just north of Celbridge is 13th-century Maynooth Castle. Maynooth became a centre of culture and power when Garret Mór (Great Earl of Kildare) governed Ireland from the castle on behalf of the English King from 1487 to 1513. But its fortunes declined steadily thereafter, and by the 17th century it had become derelict. Today, only the ruined keep and gatehouse survive, but these are sufficiently solid to convey a real impression of the once-great whole. This is augmented by an exhibition in the keep on the castle's long history. Access involves finding the key-keeper but it's worth the effort.

Hurry along the R148/158 roads via Kilcock to Trim in order to have as much time as possible at Trim Castle on the banks of the River Boyne. Here you will find the atmospheric remains of Ireland's largest castle – indeed the largest Norman castle in all Europe. The central keep has a unique cruciform design. Extensive associated structures include curtain walls, a three-towered fore work defending the keep entrance that housed stables, a huge Great Hall with undercroft and water gate, a solar tower, aisled hall, mint building and lime kilns. The grounds offer great views of the castle and there is a pedestrian bridge across the River Boyne giving access to outlying remains. Don't miss this one!

WHERE:
Counties Kildare and Meath
BEST TIME TO GO:
April to October
DON'T MISS:
The Hill of Tara, near Trim – this archaeological complex contains many ancient sites and is the legendary seat of the High King of Ireland. There are extensive Iron Age enclosures, one of which contains the historic Stone of Destiny (Lia Fáil).
AMOUNT OF WALKING:
Moderate
COST:
Reasonable
YOU SHOULD KNOW:
Castletown House's first owner, William Conolly, was Speaker of the Irish House of Commons and said to be the country's richest man – but he declined a title and was proud to describe himself as 'Ireland's richest commoner.

Ireland's finest Palladian country house – Castletown

East Coast Tour

NORTH

WHERE:
Dublin Region, Counties Meath, Monaghan, Armagh and Louth
BEST TIME TO GO:
April to September
DON'T MISS:
The recently refurbished pier at Clogherhead, one of the finest in Ireland.
AMOUNT OF WALKING:
Little
COST:
Low
YOU SHOULD KNOW:
Navan is one of the few place names that is a palindrome. Can you think of others that spell the same forwards and backwards? Your starter for three is Eye in Suffolk, England.

This East Coast day out from Dublin begins by driving inland – there's no point in covering the same ground twice, so the sea has to await the pleasure of your company while you journey through scenic drumlin and lake countryside. Follow the N3 from Dublin to Navan, then the back road (R162) to Kingscourt. Take the R162 to Shercock beside Lough Sillan, one of several hereabouts, and go on to Castleblaney.

Cross into Northern Ireland on the R182/A25, driving to Newtownhamilton through attractive hill country known as The Fews after copses that dot hillsides. Continue to Carnlough and Newry before turning south on the B79 to Omeath on the Carlingford Peninsula – water at last and now it's coastal action all the way.

The village of Carlingford – full of medieval interest – is a mandatory stop. Thereafter minor roads hug Carlingford Lough, taking you to Greenore and Cooley Point before rejoining the main road for the run into Dundalk. Drive through this bustling industrial town to Blackrock and pick up the coast road. In quick succession you will pass through Castlebellingham (the Castle is now a hotel) and Annagassan (famous for crab salad).

Take the loop to Dunany Point and the fishing village of Clogherhead, close to...Clogherhead. The attractive harbour is Port Oriel and there is a great beach. From there, the route goes through Termonfeckin (Castle and high cross) and Baltray (standing stones). Resist the temptation to visit Drogheda and finish the seaside run to Dublin via Balbriggan (beach and Martello Tower), Skerries (resort town with pretty harbour), Rush (more Martello Towers), Lusk, Donabate, Swords (Castle and Abbey), Malahide and journey's end. Unfortunately, these towns and villages have seen intensive commuter housing development in recent years, but this has not altogether destroyed their original charm.

Clogher Beach

East Coast Tour

SOUTH

The Wicklow Mountains near Sally Gap

Out from Dublin and back in a day through wonderful mountains and coastal scenery – that's the main course on today's tempting menu, which has some tasty heritage side dishes. Take the southbound N81 before turning onto the R759 road up the Liffey Valley to the moorlands of the Sally Gap plateau in the Wicklow Mountains. At the high point, where the R759 crosses the old military road (R115), you have a choice. Turn right to drive down through the Wicklow National Park to Laragh, or go straight on past Lough Tay to Roundwood and from there to Laragh. Either way, the scenery is spectacular.

Three roads through the Wicklow Mountains meet at picturesque Laragh. Here may be found the day's heritage highlight – Glendalough, on the R756 through the Wicklow Gap. St Kevin's lonely retreat is now one of Ireland's most popular monastic sites, with lakeside ruins, a wonderful round tower and Celtic High Cross.

From Glendalough, ignore the temptation of going to Hollywood along the R756 and go back through Laragh to Rathdrum on the flank of the beautiful Avonmore Valley, with its majestic views. Another helping of heritage is served here – Avondale House, home of the great Irish political leader Charles Stewart Parnell.

Television addicts will think that the next stop is Ballykissangel and pause for a drink with familiar faces in Fitzgerald's, but everyone else will know it's the pretty village of Avoca with its copper mining and weaving heritage.

From there, drive down to historic Arklow at the mouth of the River Avoca and follow the R772 via Mizen Head, Brittas Bay and Wicklow Head to Wicklow town – like most places within easy reach of Dublin recently subjected to extensive housing development. From Wicklow, the R761 takes you through Newcastle, Kilcoole, Greystones and Bray back to Dublin's urban sprawl.

WHERE:
Dublin Region, County Wicklow
BEST TIME TO GO:
March to October
DON'T MISS:
Avoca Handweavers – operating at Ireland's oldest working woollen mill – is said to be the country's oldest surviving business (founded in 1723).
AMOUNT OF WALKING:
Moderate
COST:
Low
YOU SHOULD KNOW:
There's more to 'Ballykissangel' than met the eye – one thing that viewers never saw on screen was Avoca Station on the Dublin-Rosslare railway line – now closed, but the subject of spirited lobbying for the reintroduction of a passenger service.

Malahide Castle

Just north of Dublin is Malahide Castle, sitting in the Malahide Demesne National Park – a green oasis amidst encroaching urban sprawl. The oldest parts of the castle date back to the 12th century and it remained in the Talbot family from 1185 until 1976. Now a major tourist attraction, it offers a variety of attractions that easily justify a day-long visit.

The castle itself may only be visited on a guided-tour basis – highlights of the interior are the impressive Oak Room and the famously Gothic Great Hall. The house contains period furniture, a great collection of Irish portraits and a display on Talbot family history.

Tara's Palace and Childhood Museum in the castle courtyard is an extraordinary large doll's house that has been under construction since 1980, reflecting various elements of classical Irish architecture and containing meticulously detailed contents. The palace is complemented by a large collection of dolls, toys and smaller doll's houses, including one dating back to 1700.

Behind the castle, the Talbot Botanic Gardens cover several hectares including lawns, a walled garden, glasshouses and a Victorian conservatory. The main interest is the number of exotic plants featured, including many from the Southern Hemisphere.

The above each require payment of a fee, but the demesne may be freely explored. It is a rare surviving example of a landscaped 18th-century Irish park, with wide lawns surrounded by an enclosing belt of trees. There are woodland walks and a marked exercise trail, plus various features that are distinctly non-18th century in character, including a children's playground, golf course, pitch-and-putt course and sports pitches.

Malahide Castle

Dublin Day 1

BUS TOUR

With its long history and friendly populace, Dublin is undoubtedly a Fair City – if there is a problem, it's that there's too much to see in one day. However, if you only have one day to spare, the ideal solution is the Dublin Tour bus, complete with informative guide (who has naturally kissed the Blarney Stone). Actually, it's also a good idea even if you intend to have an extended visit, as it will provide an overview of the city's many attractions before allocating the rest of your time.

If you want to do the full circuit in one go, start at Cathal Bruga Street. Otherwise catch the Tour Bus at any one of twenty-three distinctive cream-and-green bus stops, each conveniently placed near one of Dublin's highlights. The full tour takes around ninety minutes but it's a hop-on-hop-off service and the day soon passes if you take advantage of the opportunity to explore places (like traditional Dublin pubs, to name but 500) that grab your attention along the way. A ticket also entitles you to discounts at some of the paid attractions on the route.

After boarding, you'll see O'Connell Street (where the Post Office building was at the heart of the 1916 Easter Rising), Trinity College, Nassau Street (hop off and shop for quality Irish wares, including clothes), the National Gallery, impressive Government Buildings, St Stephen's Green, the Tourist Office in a beautiful former church, Temple Bar (the vibrant Cultural Quarter), Dublin Castle, Christ Church Place, St Patrick's Cathedral, the Guinness Storehouse, Museum of Modern Art, Old Kilmainham Jail, Heuston Station, Dublin Zoo in Phoenix Park, Ryan's Victorian Bar, the National Museum, Old Jameson Distillery, O'Connell Bridge (for River Liffey cruises), Dublin Bus HQ (with Visitor Centre) and finally the Writers' Museum. Phew!

A tour bus passes Trinity College.

WHERE:
Dublin Region
BEST TIME TO GO:
Any time
DON'T MISS:
Be sure to spend an hour or two in Temple Bar – this vibrant pedestrianized area was developed in the 19th century with narrow cobbled streets, close to the River Liffey, and is alive with cultural activities, restaurants and bars.
AMOUNT OF WALKING:
Moderate
COST:
Reasonable
YOU SHOULD KNOW:
If you haven't had enough of buses for one day try the after-dark Ghost Bus Tour from outside Dublin Bus HQ on O'Connell Street – it spookily claims 'to introduce you to the dark romance of a city of gaslight ghosts and chilling legends'.

Dublin Day 2

DUBLINA AND DUBLIN ZOO

WHERE:
Dublin Region
BEST TIME TO GO:
April to October
DON'T MISS:
The wonderful herd of wild fallow deer that has been in the walled Phoenix Park since the 17th century.
AMOUNT OF WALKING:
Lots
COST:
Reasonable
YOU SHOULD KNOW:
It's possible to look a 900-year-old Dublin woman straight in the eye at Dublina – her face was forensically reconstructed from an excavated skeleton.

Start at the beginning – well, perhaps not with Dublin's earliest inhabitants, but certainly going back a long way. Dublina on St Michael's Hill is a popular multi-media presentation of the city's past, housed in a beautiful Victorian Gothic building. It offers an amazing audio-visual tour that features reconstructed life-sized medieval scenes. Upstairs is a 16th-century model of the city, together with archaeological finds. Taking you further back still is the accompanying Viking World, acknowledging the vital role those buccaneering Norsemen played in Ireland's development.

Spend the rest of the day with the living – animals, that is. Dublin Zoo in Phoenix Park was opened in 1830 and its purpose then was to show people as many different animals as possible. Today the approach is very different – the idea is to present animals in surroundings that mimic their natural habitats. The objectives of a modern zoo are conservation, study and education – with particular emphasis on conservation, working together with zoos worldwide to sustain endangered species.

That worthy aim doesn't stop Dublin Zoo presenting some hundreds of different animals, tropical birds and reptiles with themed features like the World of Cats, Fringes of the Arctic, Primate World, African Plains, Kaziranga Forest Trail, the Roberts House Aviary, Reptile House, South American House, City Farm, Pets' Corner, Discovery Centre...plus the ever-popular Meercat Restaurant. As zoos go, this is one of the very best.

A huge bonus after visiting Dublin Zoo is the opportunity to enjoy Phoenix Park, the largest enclosed urban park in Europe. Be sure to go to the informative Visitor Centre (beside Ashdown Castle, a restored medieval tower house) before enjoying the wide green spaces – it has some wonderful interpretative displays on five millennia of Dublin history. So in the end we did get right back to the beginning!

Fallow deer in Pheonix Park

Dublin Day 3

GUINNESS STOREHOUSE

Ah, the black stuff – Irish stout, that is, with its dark body and creamy head. And of course the most famous stout of all is Guinness, brewed in Dublin since 1759. And naturally one essential visit in Dublin is to the Guinness Storehouse.

Built in 1904, this extraordinary building was constructed with massive steel beams. Its core now represents a giant pint glass, with varying contents all the way up to the 'head' – the glass-sided Gravity Bar in the sky. The ground floor demonstrates the ingredients of a perfect pint – barley, hops, yeast and water. There's also the Guinness Shop. The first floor has a step-by-step guide to the brewing process, a Tasting Laboratory (test the day's brew for yourself!) and exhibits on keg transport and barrel making. The second floor is devoted to world-famous Guinness advertising. The third floor challenges visitors to examine their own drinking habits in the Choice Zone and the fourth floor is dedicated to the building itself. On the fifth you learn to pour a pint of Guinness (with a certificate to prove it), and can enjoy a meal. Then – at last – it's the top floor Gravity Bar, a complimentary pint of Guinness – and sensational views of Dublin.

After all that Guinness (only kidding), stagger on to nearby Kilmainham Gaol – not because like many a former inmate you're drunk and disorderly, but because it's a fascinating time capsule. One of the largest unoccupied prisons in Europe, it has witnessed some heroic and tragic events. There is an exhibition describing the penal and political history of the prison – including Irish Nationalism – and detailing its restoration. There's also a gallery showing the work of current inmates of the Irish prison system. Guided tours of the prison, which take about an hour, must be booked.

BARLEY PROVIDES THE BASIC RAW INGREDIENT FOR FERMENTATION, CONTRIBUTING TO THE BALANCED FLAVOUR AND UNIQUENESS OF GUINNESS BEER. THE ROASTED BARLEY GIVES GUINNESS BEER ITS CHARACTERISTIC DEEP RUBY RED COLOUR.

BARLEY

You don't have to read about it to enjoy it!

WHERE:
Dublin Region
BEST TIME TO GO:
All year
DON'T MISS:
The commemorative display of John Gilroy's work on the fifth floor of the Guinness Storehouse – My Goodness My Gilroy shows a wide selection of the artist's original work and airs the first Guinness commercials from 1955 that brought some of his wonderful animal characters to life.
AMOUNT OF WALKING:
Moderate
COST:
Expensive
YOU SHOULD KNOW:
The leaders of the ill-fated Easter Rising were held and executed at Kilmainham Jail – which perhaps explains why it was closed in 1924, soon after the formation of the new Irish Free State.

Ha'penny Bridge is particularly pretty at night.

Dublin Day 4

HISTORIC LANDMARKS

Spend a fascinating day seeing some of Dublin's best historic landmarks. Begin by setting foot on one. But don't ask the way to the Liffey Bridge (its official name) because everyone still knows this pedestrian crossing as Ha'penny Bridge, after the toll that used to be charged for using it. This splendid iron bridge – built in 1816 – was financed by the owner of ferries that previously plied the River Liffey. In return, he was granted a halfpenny toll for one hundred years.

Cross from north to south and find one of Dublin's most impressive buildings, behind City Hall in Dame Street. Originally constructed in the 13th-century on a site previously settled by Vikings, Dublin Castle operated for over seven centuries as a fortress, treasury, law courts, prison...and the seat of English administration in Ireland. Today it is used by the Irish Government for State occasions, but it's possible to view the wonderful State Apartments, Chapel Royal and Undercroft. There is also an award-winning gallery in the Chester Beatty Library, the Garda Museum in a Norman tower, a Heritage Centre, craft shop and restaurant.

From the castle, a brisk walk down Aungier Street, into Cuffe Street and across St Stephen's Green will take you to Merrion Row and then Lower Fitzwilliam Street. This walk will let you explore the heart of Georgian Dublin, and remind you forcibly that this was once Great Britain's finest Georgian City. The jewel in the crown is Number Twenty Nine, Dublin's Georgian House Museum. First occupied in 1794, the house has been returned to its original state, so visitors may take a tour from basement to attic and understand exactly what it was like for the fortunate inhabitants of these elegant town houses (and the less fortunate mortals who worked for them).

Dublin Day 5

ART AND HISTORY

You could spend the day at any one of these splendid Dublin institutions, and may decide to do so, but it's possible to cover the field by rationing your time at each.

Start at the National Gallery of Ireland on Merrion Square beside Leinster House, the Irish Parliament building. Here you will find the vast national collection of European and Irish art – over 14,000 works of art displayed in various galleries, including the spectacular new Millennium Wing. Best of all, access to this cultural treasure house is absolutely free.

You have to get your skates on to zip round three Dublin sites of the National Museum of Ireland. Begin with the Natural History Museum, close to the National Gallery. It's a classic Victorian museum in an imposing Victorian building that has hardly changed since Victorian times – often described as 'a museum of a museum'. On Kildare Street, the Archaeology and History section has displays on prehistoric Ireland, early goldwork, Viking and medieval exhibits, Church treasures and ever-changing exhibitions. The third facility is Collins Barracks, which features Decorative Arts and History – a star exhibit is the Great Seal of the Irish Free State.

If you haven't already visited the Chester Beatty Library during a tour of Dublin Castle, catch up now. It houses the collection of mining magnate Sir Alfred Chester Beatty and contains two superb collections entitled 'Sacred Traditions' and 'Artistic Traditions'. Displays include sacred texts, manuscripts, art on paper and miniature paintings from the world's great religions, plus many secular items.

The Hugh Lane (founded by a benefactor of that name) was the world's first dedicated gallery of modern art. Now officially Dublin City Gallery The Hugh Lane, it's located at Charlemont House in Parnell Street. It has a fabulous permanent collection, plus specific exhibitions.

Didn't get halfway round? There's always tomorrow...

National Gallery of Ireland

WHERE:
Dublin Region
BEST TIME TO GO:
Any time
DON'T MISS:
Famous Irish finds on display at Kildare Street, including the Tara Brooch, Ardagh Chalice and Derrynaflan Hoard.
AMOUNT OF WALKING:
Lots (unless you take buses or taxis).
COST:
Reasonable
YOU SHOULD KNOW:
In 2001, artist Francis Bacon's chaotic studio was recreated at The Hugh Lane, piece by piece, exactly as Bacon left it when he died.

Dublin Day 6

LITERARY DUBLIN

WHERE:
Dublin Region
BEST TIME TO GO:
May to September (for literary houses).
DON'T MISS:
Try and find time to visit Trinity College Library in College Street, Ireland's largest and a major facility for the university, international research and information source – a fabulous place.
AMOUNT OF WALKING:
Lots (if you do it all on foot – a great way of seeing the city).
COST:
Reasonable
YOU SHOULD KNOW:
Bloomsday on 16 June each year celebrates the life of James Joyce – and sees recreations of events in *Ulysses*, which was set on one day in the Dublin of 1904 (named after the novel's hero, Leopold Bloom, with the date being that of Joyce's first outing with wife-to-be Nora Barnacle).

There's a great literary tradition in Ireland in general and Dublin in particular, which is celebrated at the Dublin Writers Museum at 18 Parnell Square, a splendid Georgian mansion worth a visit on its own merit. The house contains museum rooms, a library and gallery, with a bookshop and café. The focus is on Irish writers who have made an important contribution to national or international literature and/or that of Dublin – they're brought to life through books, letters, portraits and personal effects. That Irish literary tradition is in safe hands – next door at 19 Parnell Square is the Irish Writers' Union, the Society of Irish Playwrights and the Irish Children's Book Trust.

If the Dublin Writers Museum represents all, there are dedicated focal points for famous individuals. The James Joyce Centre is in another fine Georgian house at 35 North Great George's Street, dedicated to promoting and understanding the writer's life and works. Fans will also want to visit the James Joyce Tower and Museum, a Martello Tower at Sandy Cove, Dublin, where he spent six nights in 1904 – leaving when his host fired a gun in his direction.

Oscar Wilde House at 1 Merrion Square was the Victorian wit and playwright's childhood home. It's an elaborate and imposing corner property. Summer tours are offered. Another great Irish playwright who went to England to find fame was George Bernard Shaw. His family's first home at 33 Synge Street has been restored to its Victorian elegance, and it's easy to believe that the Shaws have just popped out for a few moments. The Shaw Birthplace is as interesting for recreating everyday Victorian middle-class life in Dublin as it is for those literary connections.

The magnificent Library at Trinity College

Wicklow Gardens

Ireland is famous for fabulous gardens and Wicklow makes a notable contribution. To visit three of the best, go from Dublin on the southbound M50/N11 to Bray. Here you will find Killruddery, a fine early (1820) example of a Tudor-Revival country house that offers interior guided tours. But today's focus is on the superb gardens, surviving in their original 17th-century style with some later additions. These are quite simply breathtaking, consisting of the Angles (a series of walks flanked by hedges), the Long Ponds, wooded wilderness area, Beech Hedge Pond, rose and lavender gardens and a Sylvan Theatre with terraced banks for spectators. Idyllic!

From Bray, take the R117 road (known locally as 'Twenty-One Bends') to Enniskerry in the foothills of the Wicklow Mountains – and the Powerscourt Estate. This former castle was reworked into a magnificent mansion between 1731 and 1741 but it was badly damaged by fire in the 1970s and not renovated until the 1990s. Two rooms within the house may be visited, restored to their original state, but the rest has been converted into shops and a hotel. No matter, the real attraction are the gardens created over two decades in Victorian times. Highlights include the Pepperpot Tower, Tower Valley, winged horse statues, Triton Lake, Dolphin Pond, Japanese Gardens, walled gardens, Bambergh Gate and the Italian Garden. Impressive!

Proceed down through the Wicklow Mountains on the R760/R755 to Roundwood, turning left on the R764 that takes you past the Devil's Glen to Ashford. The attraction here is Mount Usher Gardens, laid out along the banks of the River Vartry. This great garden has trees, herbaceous plants and shrubs that have been introduced from all parts of the world. As with most Irish gardens, this naturalistic paradise has something visually different to offer in spring, summer and autumn. Relaxing!

WHERE:
County Wicklow
BEST TIME TO GO:
May to September
DON'T MISS:
The pets' cemetery at Powerscourt, with headstones bearing personal inscriptions that make it obvious how much the family adored their favourite animals.
AMOUNT OF WALKING:
Lots
COST:
Reasonable
YOU SHOULD KNOW:
Mount Usher is known as a Robinsonian Garden after William Robinson, the influential 19th-century Irish garden designer who tore up the rule book that required gardens to be formal and promoted a much more natural look (albeit a carefully planned one).

Powerscourt Gardens and Sugarloaf Mountain

Tipperary Tour

Actually, despite that famous claim in the popular World War I song, it's not an especially long way to Tipperary or even around Tipperary – though a day is not enough to see and do everything this splendidly Irish county offers. But have fun trying!

The day starts in the beautiful Suir Valley, at Thurles in Northern Tipperary. The Victorian Cathedral is magnificent and St Mary's Famine Church and Military Museum are worth a look. Historic Farney Castle is the only round tower in Ireland occupied as a home, by designer

Cyril Cullen. His shop is here and castle tours are offered.

Next stop is Cashel. It has a Heritage Centre, Museum of Rural Life and the GPA Bolton Library full of rare books, but the main attraction is The Rock of Cashel, rising above the surrounding countryside like a miniature Mont St Michel. This extraordinary walled complex of medieval buildings atop a limestone outcrop includes an early round tower, Cormac's Chapel of 1134 and the great Cathedral.

Tipperary town deserves to be part of the tour itinerary. This bustling market town has wide streets radiating from Main Street and a couple of important historical monuments. From here continue to Cahir, where the magnificent 12th-century Cahir Castle sits imposingly on a river island. This is one of Ireland's largest and best-preserved early fortresses and is a seriously irresistible attraction.

The tour finishes at Clonmel on the River Suir, with its attractive quays. There are many reminders of the town's medieval heritage to be found, especially St Mary's Old Church that was fortified in the 13th century, whilst impressive West Gate is a 19th-century reworking of an earlier structure. South Tipperary County Museum in Mick Delahunty Square deals with local history from the Stone Age and mounts regular exhibitions.

WHERE:
County Tipperary
BEST TIME TO GO:
April to October
DON'T MISS:
The impressive ruins of Athassel Augustinian Priory on the western bank of the River Suir, reached via a bridge and gatehouse – located near Golden between Cashel and Tipperary town.
AMOUNT OF WALKING:
Moderate
COST:
Low
YOU SHOULD KNOW:
Oliver Cromwell was so impressed by the spirited defence put up by Clonmel's people when he laid siege to the place that he presented his sword as a mark of respect – it can still be seen in the Town Hall.

The Rock of Cashel

Suir Valley Drive

WHERE:
Counties Tipperary and Waterford
BEST TIME TO GO:
April to September
DON'T MISS:
Ireland's earliest group of ringed High Crosses in a peaceful location beside the Ahenny church, a few kilometres up the R697 road from Carrick-on-Shannon.
AMOUNT OF WALKING:
Lots
COST:
Reasonable
YOU SHOULD KNOW:
It is said that the bridge across the River Clodagh at Curraghmore was built ahead of King John's visit in the early 1200s, to ensure that the tetchy monarch didn't get wet feet.

The River Suir is a vital artery that has played a significant role in the history of Tipperary and Waterford, and its beautiful lower valley merits leisurely exploration. Begin just west of Carrick-on-Suir, at the Blarney Woollen Mills in thatched cottages beside the Suir, opposite the picturesque ruin of Dove Hill Castle, an early tower.

In Carrick there is a Heritage Centre that tells the town's story by means of displays and artefacts. Also see the Old Bridge (built in 1447), three interesting Catholic Churches, an 18th-century Town Clock and Ormond Castle – a graceful Elizabethan manor (Ireland's finest) with earlier origins in parkland to the east of town. The Long Gallery is superb and there is some wonderful plasterwork.

From Carrick, take the scenic R680 Waterford road along the Suir Valley and find the Quaker village of Portlaw, a planned settlement that was expanded to support the local cotton mill. The big attraction here is Curraghmore House and Gardens. Home of the Marquis of Waterford and his ancestors since 1170, the interior is notable for exceptional plasterwork whilst the grounds contain a wonderful arboretum, 18th-century shell grotto and round tower of 1785.

Continue along the R680 to Mount Congreve Gardens where there is a fabulous plant collection that includes rhododendrons, camellias, Japanese maple, herbaceous borders, iris beds and the largest Clematis armandii in Ireland. There is also a famous pinetum, walled garden and bog garden. Everything is linked by a network of paths with a total length of around 26 km (16 mi), so it's easy to spend lots of quality time here.

Turn right when you reach the N25 and visit Fairbrook House Gardens – a romantic walled garden with a gallery and delightful millpond – before turning around and ending the drive beside the Suir on the quays of Waterford town.

Mount Congreve Gardens has the most wonderful collection of plants.

Historic Lismore

The heritage town of Lismore was founded by St Carthage (sometimes called Mochuda). His monastery was established in 635 AD and in its day was the most celebrated in Southern Ireland. However, its day is long gone along with the monastery – the site is now occupied by Lismore Castle, dominating the town from its lofty position above the River Blackwater. Is this the most spectacular castle in Ireland? Few would dispute the claim, though it's worth pointing out that most of what we see today is a fanciful Victorian confection.

It is the private Irish residence of the Dukes of Devonshire, but the Castle Gardens are open and should be the starting point for a tour of Lismore. The Upper Garden was laid out in 1605. Original terraces and outer walls remain, though planting has evolved over time to reflect contemporary taste. The informal Lower Garden dates from the castle's 19th-century makeover but the stately avenue of yews is older. Modern sculptures adorn the gardens, which offer superb views of castle and countryside.

The next stop should be the Heritage Centre, which traces the town's long history with the help of an award-winning audio-visual display. This is supported by galleries that feature historic figures reflecting Lismore life through the ages, including Robert Boyle, 'The Father of Modern Chemistry'.

From the Heritage Centre there are daily guided walking tours (or follow the route unguided). High points are Lismore Bridge and Castle, the Spout (a natural well), Millennium Park, Carnegie Library, Gallows Hill (topped by a former monastery, now Council offices), New Street (houses built in 1820 for Devonshire tenants), Lismore Workhouse and Famine Graveyard, the fine Lombardo-Romanesque St Carthage's Parish Church and St Carthage's Cathedral. The latter is superb, dating from 1620 with later additions. All in all a most satisfying day's perambulation!

Lismore Castle

WHERE:
County Waterford
BEST TIME TO GO:
Mid-March to September (for the Castle Gardens).
DON'T MISS:
Amongst other special features of the Cathedral – ancient monastic grave slabs, interesting stone carvings, the McGrath table tomb, a fine font and stained glass by Sir Edward Byrne-Jones.
AMOUNT OF WALKING:
Lots
COST:
Reasonable
YOU SHOULD KNOW:
Lismore Castle was once owned by Elizabethan adventurer Sir Walter Raleigh, but he was forced to sell it after he fell from Elizabeth I's favour and was imprisoned in the Tower of London. In those days you could get a castle and 42,000 acres for £1,500.

Copper Coast Drive

There's one UNESCO European Geopark in the Irish Republic – the Copper Coast, where lead, silver and copper were extracted from sea cliffs in the 18th and 19th centuries. But before undertaking one of Ireland's most spectacular coastal drives it's worth lapping up the ice-cream 'n' beach resort atmosphere of Tramore, south of Waterford town.

Once on the R675 road stunning views of wild cliffs, beaches, coves and caves unfold to one side, all overlooked by the brooding Comeragh Mountains. Magnificent scenery is complemented by a succession of charming villages and there are plenty of interesting sights and things to do as you go.

Fenor has a fine beach, lakeside and forest walks plus the Fenor Bog. Annestown overlooks an enticing valley and bay with beach and rock pools. Inland, find Dunhill's Stone Age dolmens and ruined castle – or simply enjoy a leisurely stop at the traditional village

The Old Copper Mine at Bunmahon

shop-cum-pub. The picturesque harbour village of Boatstrand has a path to imposing Dunabrattin Head, with its fabulous outlook over beaches and stacks to Sheep Island and distant Helvick Head.

The mineral wealth of Bunmahon gave this coast its name, and ample reminders of mining activity dot the cliffs flanking the beach. Here, also, is a ruined monastery and pleasing geological garden. Make the effort to find Ballydwane Cove near Bunmahon – it's one of the very best. The last village before the Copper Coast ends at Dungarvan is Stradbally, with three beaches and a medieval church and tower.

If you haven't dallied too long with delights along the way, Dungarvan will provide a satisfying end to the day. This harbour town is divided by the Colligan River, with the two halves connected by a causeway and bridge. There's a Town Trail that includes the quayside castle built by King John.

Waterford

Ireland's oldest city was founded in 914 AD by Vikings and it's easy to spend a rewarding day here. The River Suir flows through Waterford town and its quays were once the hub of a thousand-year-old port, though this activity has now relocated downstream to Belview.

Start at the beginning – the Viking Triangle is surrounded by original 10th-century fortifications with Reginald's Tower at its apex. The Tower (now a museum) is Ireland's oldest civic building and used to be part of the thriving Viking town, though this has become a quiet area of narrow streets, medieval buildings and open space.

Onward and upwards – Waterford expanded in the 15th century and retains more original town walls than anywhere in Ireland, with the exception of Derry. Daily tours are conducted and this fascinating walk should definitely form part of the itinerary. Another essential experience is Waterford Quay – fully 1.5 km (1 mi) long, this once-thriving port area is now a commercial and social focal point.

Notable architecture may be found in the Mall, dating from Waterford's prosperous Georgian era. The city centre has fine squares and many buildings of note, including the 18th-century City Hall, Chamber of Commerce Building and two magnificent Cathedrals – Christchurch and Most Holy Trinity.

Various museums provide insight into the city and its history. The Waterford Heritage Museum near Reginald's Tower has a reconstruction of the early settlement, together with Viking and medieval artefacts. It also houses a great collection of Royal Charters and civic regalia. In the Granary on the Quay, Waterford Museum of Treasures brings together rare and beautiful local artefacts.

No day in Waterford could be complete without a visit to the Waterford Crystal Visitor Centre, that operates a tour showing the factory's fine wares in production, from molten crystal glass to finished masterpieces.

Reginald's Tower

Kilkenny Drive

Kilkenny Castle

County Kilkenny may not have the highest profile but has lots to offer the interested visitor. Take a circular tour that includes many outstanding attractions, beginning at medieval Kilkenny town. Situated on the River Nore, it has many good buildings. Look out for St Candice's Cathedral and round tower, St Mary's Cathedral, the Town Hall, 16th-century Rothe House and Kilkenny Castle.

Head out of town on the N76 road to Callan, where a ruined Augustinian Friary may be found beside the King's River, northeast of town. Next comes Kells – and if you should decide to give anything a miss make sure it isn't Kells Priory, one of the most awesome medieval monuments in Ireland. The Priory also sits beside the King's River and from afar it looks more like a castle than a religious foundation, with square towers rising above walls that enclose the large monastic precinct. Continue to Stonyford and across country to Thomastown, where you will find substantial remains of Jerpoint Cistercian Abbey dating from 1180.

To make a change from impressive medieval ruins, head down the R700 to Inistioge and the Woodstock Estate beside the River Nore. The house is a shell, but the gardens have numerous walks and many unusual plants. Return to Thomastown, proceeding to Graiguenamanagh and finding the Catholic church into which elements of a Cistercian Monastery founded in 1204 have been incorporated. Head north along the country road to historic Gowran, where another incorporation has taken place – this time a 12th-century collegiate church into 19th-century St Mary's.

To end the day head back to Kilkenny, finding Clara Castle on the way, just off the N10 road east of town. It's a fine tower house with many original features, including a secret room reached through an opening disguised as a lavatory seat.

WHERE:
County Kilkenny
BEST TIME TO GO:
April to September
DON'T MISS:
Dunmore Cave, north of Kilkenny town close to the N78 – a smallish cave with spectacular calcite formations, where Vikings massacred a number of unfortunate locals who thought they'd found a safe hiding place.
AMOUNT OF WALKING:
Moderate
COST:
Low
YOU SHOULD KNOW:
It is said of County Kilkenny 'Ground without bog, fire without smoke, land without sea' in reference to the county's absence of bogland, smokeless anthracite coal extracted at Castlecomer's Deerpark Mines and the lack of any coastline.

Carlow and Wexford Tour

Carlow town is an appealing place that should be explored on foot. Take the official guided tour or go alone, in which case be sure to see the main features – one of Ireland's finest courthouses, 18th-century St Patrick's College, Carlow Cathedral, pedestrianized Tullow Street, St Mary's Church, Carlow Castle beside the River Barrow, ancient Graiguecullen Bridge, St Clare's Church, the Croppies Grave (a mass grave of United Irish rebels slaughtered in 1798), Haymarket, a grand Town Hall and the Millennium Bridge.

Then take the N80 road down towards Bunclody and turn left for Huntingdon Castle and Gardens near Clonegall. This fine tower house has a huge vine in the conservatory and, surprisingly, a temple to the goddess Isis in the basement.

At Bunclody visit Newtownbarry House. This Victorian mansion has the richest of interiors, a modern art gallery and excellent gardens that pre-date the house. Here you will find a splendid pond, sunken garden and rose garden. The River Slaney flows through the grounds and there are shady woodland walks and excellent views of the Blackstairs Mountains.

Continue down to New Ross on the River Barrow and find an unusual attraction at South Quay – the Famine Ship. The *Dunbrody* is a reconstruction of the three-masted barque, built in 1845, that was used to transport emigrants to the New World during the Great Famine and beyond (emigrants included now-famous families like those of Henry Ford and John F. Kennedy).

Drive south to Kilmokea, a splendid Georgian mansion near Campile, now a luxury hotel. But you don't have to stay there to enjoy the extensive gardens – consisting of formal walled gardens around the house and a lower woodland garden. Lunch and tea are served in the conservatory and there is a high-quality Irish pottery, arts and crafts shop.

The Famine Ship
Dunbrody *at New Ross*

WHERE:
Counties Carlow and Wexford
BEST TIME TO GO:
June to August (for Huntingdon Castle).
DON'T MISS:
The Cigar Divan in Dublin Street, Carlow – a wonderful Victorian shop front with elaborate iron panels and engraved glass, dating from the time when Turkish cigarettes were all the rage.
AMOUNT OF WALKING:
Moderate
COST:
Reasonable
YOU SHOULD KNOW:
It is said that the magnificent Carlow Courthouse was built here by mistake – it was originally intended for Cork, but the plans got mixed up and the rest is, as they say, history.

Around Wexford

Wexford town was founded by Vikings, seized by Norman-Irish forces, sacked and burned by Cromwell's troops and the scene of a massacre during the Irish Rebellion. The latter loomed large in these parts and is not forgotten – of which more anon.

From Wexford, drive south to Tagoat and visit Yola Farmstead Folk Park, a restored 18th-century farmstead. Take the R236 westwards and find scenic Bannow Drive – it's well signed through Duncormick, Cullenstown, Bannow and Wellingtonbridge – enjoying fabulous views of Bannow Bay as you go. Continue along the R733 and turn left for Saltmills, where the substantial ruin of Tintern Abbey sits in a lovely setting with woodland walks.

Explore the wild Hook Peninsula next – from Saltmills to Fethard and Hook Head with its lighthouse. Relax at Duncannon Blue Flag Beach on Waterford Harbour before inspecting star-shaped Duncannon Fort on its promontory. Go north to Campile and find Dunbrody Abbey – a splendid Cistercian monastery with magnificent buildings.

Take the cross-country route via Newbaun to Enniscorthy and the National 1798 Visitor Centre. This new facility beside the River Slaney imaginatively brings the Irish Rebellion to life, dramatically charting an event that is regarded as the beginning of Ireland's road to independence. Drive north on the N11 and see ruined Norman Ferns Castle, before proceeding to Ballymore Historic Features, an open-air rural museum off to the right.

Combining rebellion and traditional rural life, the Father Murphy Centre at Boolavogue (due south of Ballymore) is another restored farmstead that tells the tale of Father Murphy, who led his parishioners as they fought in the Rebellion of 1798 – and joined them in swinging from the gallows when it failed. From Boolavogue it's a pleasant return drive through back lanes to Wexford town and the end of a full but satisfying day.

WHERE:
County Wexford
BEST TIME TO GO:
May to August (for Dunbrody Abbey).
DON'T MISS:
The Westgate Heritage Centre in Wexford – located in the last remaining gate tower of seven in the medieval town walls, it brings Wexford's history to life through exhibitions and an audio-visual show (also providing access to Selskar Abbey ruins).
AMOUNT OF WALKING:
Moderate
COST:
Reasonable
YOU SHOULD KNOW:
Duncannon Fort was built in 1586 to repel a Spanish Armada that never came – though many of its storm-tossed galleons were wrecked on rocky Irish shores two years later.

Tintern Abbey

The Burren

Burren is the English translation of the Irish Boireann, meaning 'Great Rock'. Never was a name more appropriate, though the Burren is not so much large rock as extensive rocks – covering a roughly circular area of some 250 sq km (95 sq mi) bounded by the Atlantic Ocean and Galway Bay, loosely defined inland by the villages of Ballyvaughan, Kinvara, Tubber, Corofin, Kilfenora and Lisdoonvarna.

The unique karst landscape consists of rolling hills made up of limestone pavements crisscrossed with grikes (cracks) that leave isolated rocks called clints. This unusual environment encourages lush vegetation to erupt from the grikes with Arctic, Alpine and Mediterranean plants growing together.

This is ultimately a day for walking – there are roads through the Burren that let you get a feel for the place, but the best way to appreciate this very special landscape is to set foot on it, so be prepared for frequent stops at eye-catching spots.

Start the adventure in the busy regional centre of Ennis (assemble a picnic before leaving) and take the R476 to Corofin. From there, continue to Killinaboy and turn right, then left. This road takes you right through the heart of the Burren National Park. Turn left again past Lough Bunny to Carren and go up Bealaclugga on the coast. From here take the spectacular coast road (N67/R477) to Lisdoonvarna.

End the day down the R478 road at the spectacular Cliffs of Moher near Liscannor. They tower above the ocean at Hag's Head, reaching a maximum height of 214 m (702 ft) at O'Brien's Tower, built in 1835 as an observation point for visitors who – even then – were drawn to these magical cliffs. Today, there is a Visitor Centre, but the real attraction is one of the world's best cliff-top walks, offering some of Ireland's finest coastal views.

*The Cliffs of Moher offer some of
Ireland's finest coastal views.*

Around Ennis

Ennis is an old market town on the River Fergus, with a centre full of narrow streets and lanes dating back to medieval times and containing many characterful buildings. Ennis has a grand 19th-century Cathedral church, quirky St Columba's and ruins of a Franciscan Friary, established in 1240, around which the town grew up. Ennis Friary was renowned throughout Europe as a centre of learning, and even today it's possible to see what an impressive complex existed here with superb statues, carvings and tombs serving as a reminder of the Friary's heyday.

After exploring Ennis, a short trip down the R469 road towards Limerick delivers a double hit of Irish heritage. Strike One is Craggaunowen – The Living Past Experience, a recreation of life in Ireland after the Celts arrived, that shows how they lived, hunted, farmed and died. There is a recreated *crannóg* (lake dwelling), Iron Age roadway and a ring fort – plus more modern essentials such as a picnic area, restaurant and shop.

Right next-door is Strike Two – Knappogue Castle and Garden. This wonderful tower house dates back to 1467. It was sensitively restored in the 19th century and again in the 1960s, returning the castle to its former splendour whilst retaining later additions that physically chronicle its history as a dwelling. There is a magnificent and extensive walled garden dating from 1817.

The journey into Ireland's past isn't quite over. Just down the road (on the N18 between Shannon and Limerick) is Bunratty Castle and Folk Park. The Castle is the most complete medieval castle in Ireland, containing furniture and tapestries that recapture the atmosphere of the time. The Folk Park in the grounds recreates 19th-century rural and village life, with traditional crafts being carried out and (in summer only) period animators who bring the village to life.

Donkey cart at Bunratty Folk Park

WHERE:
County Clare
BEST TIME TO GO:
Mid-April to September (for Craggaunowen).
DON'T MISS:
The 'Brendan Boat' at Craggaunowen Living Past Experience – it was sailed from Ireland to Greenland to re-enact the voyage of St Brendan, who is said to have visited America long before Columbus arrived.
AMOUNT OF WALKING:
Moderate
COST:
Reasonable
YOU SHOULD KNOW:
If you're a gourmet bone-chucker, be aware that both Knappogue Castle and Bunratty Castle stage medieval banquets in summer.

Limerick

This fine city has much of interest to offer. It sits astride the River Shannon with three major crossings in the city centre. It's a major retail centre for the surrounding area – but there's heritage aplenty too. Beside the ancient Thomond Bridge is King John's imposing Castle at the heart of Limerick's medieval core, the old English town on King's Island. Limerick Museum adjoins the castle, with displays on the city's history and commercial life. St Mary's Anglican Cathedral is also close by. Founded in the 12th century, it is one of Ireland's most important medieval buildings. The city's second Cathedral is Catholic St John's, completed in 1861.

The Hunt Museum in the Old Custom House by the Shannon holds a fascinating assortment of pieces collected by local antiquarian John Hunt and his wife. There are some 2,000 items starting with artefacts from Ancient Egypt and the Stone Age and going right through to a Picasso sketch. For those who want to explore Limerick more thoroughly, there are guided walking tours and Shannon boat tours.

Close to Limerick city on the N18, just across in County Clare, an unusual survivor may be found at Cratloe – the only Irish long house still lived in as a home...and by direct descendents of the owner in 1702. Admittedly, Cratloe Woods House is somewhat longer than the conventional long house, but it still fulfils the requirement of being but one room deep. Guided tours are offered and the farmyard contains an array of vintage machinery.

Complete the day's itinerary by returning through Limerick and taking the R512 to scenic Lough Gur. Here, it's possible to explore the delightful lakeshore rich in historic sites. Alternatively you could visit the Interpretative Centre that explains how the pre-Celtic farmers lived and worked here.

King John's Castle, Limerick

Limerick Heritage Trail

Going out and about here is to take a trip through Irish history. Follow the N20 out of Limerick and bear right onto the N21 road, stopping at Adare, an ancient crossing point on the River Maigue renowned as one of Ireland's prettiest villages. There is a Heritage Centre that tells Adare's tale from 1233 to the present, and tours of riverside Adare Castle may be booked. There were once three great medieval religious establishments here, two of which have been recycled – the Augustinian Priory is the Church of Ireland parish church, the Trinitarian Abbey is the Catholic parish church and only the Franciscan Abbey is a ruin.

Continuing down the N21, the Irish Palatine Heritage Centre in the former station at Rathkeale covers the little-known story of non-conformist Palatine settlers from Germany who were introduced to this area in the early 1700s to dilute the Catholic population.

Go down the N21 to Newcastle West and find Plunkett Heritage Centre at Drumcollogher to the southeast. This restored creamery of 1889 with a working steam engine and mechanical cream separator is where the important Irish co-operative movement started.

No-one looms much larger in modern Irish history than American-born Eamon de Valera, the canny politician who was influential in the drive for Irish independence, holding office from 1917 until shortly before his death in 1975, serving both as Taoiseach (Prime Minister) and President. Take the R520 to Bruree (ancestral home of his mother, where he spent his childhood with grandparents) and visit the De Valera Museum and Bruree Heritage Centre. It recounts his life story through personal memorabilia, audio-visual displays and graphic panels, whilst the local history of Bruree is also covered. The cottage where de Valera grew up is preserved and open to visitors.

WHERE:
County Limerick
BEST TIME TO GO:
April to September
DON'T MISS:
Adare Gallery Craft Shop – specializing in colourful designer knitwear, it also offers the work of local artists and hand-crafted silver jewellery inspired by Celtic motifs.
AMOUNT OF WALKING:
Moderate
COST:
Reasonable
YOU SHOULD KNOW:
Eamon de Valera was sentenced to hang as a leader of the 1916 Easter Rising, but unlike other Republican leaders who did suffer that fate, his sentence was commuted to life imprisonment.

The Franciscan Abbey, Adare

The Skellig Ring

WHERE:
County Kerry
BEST TIME TO GO:
April to September
DON'T MISS:
The Skellig Chocolate Factory (true!)
and Siopa Cill Rialaig (an unusual art
gallery), both located in Ballinskelligs.
AMOUNT OF WALKING:
Lots
COST:
Reasonable (veering towards
expensive if the Skelligs cruise
is included).
YOU SHOULD KNOW:
Only four Tetrapod Trackways have
been found – the one on Valentia
Island, one in Scotland and two in
Australia.

If the Ring of Kerry has proved inspiring it's tempting to spend more time exploring its extension – the Skellig Ring, a scenic route around the dramatic western tip of the Iveragh Peninsula. The coastal views are awesome, and although the Ring is not long, it definitely merits a day-long outing.

Start from Cahersiveen and take the Renard ferry to Valentia Island. The sights to see (apart from wonderful views) are the Tetrapod Trackway and the gardens at Glanleam. Contrary to expectations, the former has nothing to do with racing in any shape or form – but fossilized footprints from the Devonian period (roughly 416 to 360 million years ago, long before dinosaurs). On a more modern note, Glanleam Gardens – Ireland's most westerly – are a wild subtropical paradise that is sure to enchant.

Next, take the coast road to Portmagee and there visit the Skellig Experience Centre, on the seafront right beside Valentia Island bridge. It explains all about this unique area and the Skellig Islands – Skellig Michael with its extraordinary monastic history and lighthouses, Small Skellig occupied by one of the world's great gannet colonies. Together they form the Skelligs UNESCO World Heritage Site and this is the place to book and take a boat trip (subject to weather conditions).

Cross the bridge back to the mainland and proceed over the Coomanaspig Pass. This is the place to stop, breathe bracing Atlantic air and enjoy sensational views of Puffin Island, Skellig Rocks and St Finian's Bay. Suitably invigorated, continue on to Ballinskelligs. From there, stop off at the picturesque village of Waterville (Ballinskelligs Bay one side, Lough Currane the other). If you're not interested in golf, ignore the famous links course and seek out Loher Stone Fort before returning to Cahersiveen on the main road to complete your personal Ring cycle.

Skellig Michael

Ring of Kerry

Stand by to experience stunning coastal landscapes by driving the Ring of Kerry – a 170-km (105-mi) circular route from Killarney around the Iveragh Peninsula. It may be possible to complete the journey in less than three hours, but plan on making it a long day – there are endless wonderful places and spectacular sights to detain you along the way.

Take the N71 road south from Killarney – going this way round for two reasons. Firstly because there are attractions to visit on the Ring close to Killarney, and time may have run out before getting there if travelling in an anti-clockwise direction. These include Ladies View with its fabulous lake panorama, the Blue Pool and Torc Waterfall in Killarney National Park. Secondly, the roads are narrow and coach tours go in a clockwise direction...and the only thing worse than being stuck behind a crawling caravan is being held up by a slow-moving tourist coach.

Continue along the N71 to Kenmare, before taking the coast road (N70) to Sneem. The majestic Macgillycuddy's Reek mountains are to the right, the broad waters of the Kenmare River to the left. Follow the main road through Castle Cove, Caherdaniel and Waterville to Cahersiveen, where the N70 turns east through Kells, continuing along Dingle Bay to Glenbeigh and Killorglin. Here, take the R563 that loops up to Milltown before returning to Killarney – job done!

It's impossible to list everything to see and do, but highlights include traditional Kenmare lace shops, Moll's Gap viewpoint, Sneem Church and cemetery, Staigue Stone Fort west of Sneem, Derrynane House at Caherdaniel (ancestral home of leading historical figure Daniel O'Connell), Cahersiveen Heritage Centre, Kells Beach, Rossbeigh Beach by Glenbeigh and Kerry Bog Village between Glenbeigh and Killorglin. Lots to choose from, then!

Rossbeigh Beach

WHERE:
County Kerry
BEST TIME TO GO:
April to September
DON'T MISS:
Leacanabuaile Fort at Cahersiveen – one of the best of its type in Ireland, this early round stone fort contains beehive houses, a souterrain (place of storage and refuge) and remains of a quern for grinding corn.
AMOUNT OF WALKING:
Lots (not all attractions around The Ring are suitable for wheelchair users but plenty are, so the day can still contain more than spectacular scenery!)
COST:
Low
YOU SHOULD KNOW:
Waterville was one of Charlie Chaplin's favourite holiday spots, and a statue now commemorates his frequent visits.

Ring of Beara

Glengarriff on the Beara Penninsula

WHERE:
Counties Kerry and Cork
BEST TIME TO GO:
April to September
DON'T MISS:
The boat trip from Glengarriff across
Bantry Bay to Garnish Island with its
renowned Italianate gardens.
AMOUNT OF WALKING:
Moderate
COST:
Low
YOU SHOULD KNOW:
The Ring of Beara's copper industry
was immortalized by novelist Daphne
du Maurier in *Hungry Hill*, an early
work featuring five generations of an
Anglo-Irish mine-owning family – the
real Hungry Hill is near
Rossmackowen.

Ready for another Ring? Kerry has three and they're all compelling...though in truth the Ring of Beara is shared with County Cork. This is more lonely than the Ring of Kerry, but the landscape is equally beautiful with a rugged charm all its own. This 195-km (120-mi) route links Kenmare with Glengarriff. The centre of the Beara Peninsula is occupied by the Caha and Slieve Mishkish mountains and it's bordered by the wide Kenmare River and Bantry Bay.

From Kenmare, the R571 road follows the coast past Cloonee Lough to Tuosist. Turn right onto the R573, hugging the water before returning to the R571 at Laragh. Here, make a side trip to the summit of Healey Pass, offering one of the best panoramic views you'll ever see. Don't be tempted to go on to Adrigole or you'll miss most of the Ring.

From Lauragh drive along the R571 to Ardgroom, Eyeries (where it turns into the R575), Urhin, Allihies and Cahermore, where the final metamorphosis to the R572 takes place. This road along the shores of Bantry Bay continues through Castletownbere, Ireland's largest white-fish port, Rossmackowen, Adrigole (got there in the end!) and Trafrask to Glengarriff. From Glengarriff, return to Kenmare along a precariously winding road that includes a tunnel through living rock. It's a satisfying way to close the loop.

Compared to the Ring of Kerry there's more driving and less time to stop, but this is more about compelling scenery than attractions along the way. Even so, there are colourful hamlets such as Eyeries to enjoy, characterful Castletownbere is worth a visit (see the nearby ruins of Dunboy Castle), as is the quaint former copper-mining town of Allihies with its Cornish feel and mining museum. Both Kenmare and Glengarriff are also worth a look.

Dingle Peninsula

Ballyferriter Bay

The centuries-long struggle between English conquerors and indigenous Irish ultimately gave the English but one lasting victory… of the tongue. Irish as a spoken language – for all that it appears on road signs and maps – has been driven into the Gaeltacht – isolated pockets of native Irish speakers, mostly in the far west.

Kerry's Irish-speaking population is mainly concentrated in the north of the Dingle Peninsula, once described by National Geographic as 'the most beautiful place on earth'. You will agree. This untamed land begins with steep Slieve Mish Mountain and falls away to the west, breaking up into spectacular cliffs and islands. Narrow roads often terminate in dead ends, making for a slow voyage of discovery.

Leave Tralee on the N86 road, turning right onto the R560 before Camp, soon taking the loop road to the left via Lough Slat back to the R560. Before Stradbally turn right for Castlegregory and Kilshannig, with its fabulous outlook over Tralee and Ballyheige Bays to the Magharee Islands (Seven Hogs) and Kerry Head. Return to Stradbally and head for Dingle, almost immediately turning right for Cloghane and Brandon. The road ends at Brandon Point, but the main attraction is Brandon Mountain – climb it to reach the point where St Brendan 'saw' America before setting off to sail there. This requires time and exertion but is worth the effort.

Time for a break – drive to Dingle with its natural harbour and (especially in summer) find some Irish music and refreshment in this lively town of pubs and cafés. From Dingle, take the R549/559 loop road to Feohanagh, Murreagh, Ballyferriter, Dunquin, Ventry and back to Dingle. This stunning coastal drive takes you past the most westerly point in Ireland (and Europe). From Dingle, it's a straight run back to Tralee along the N86.

WHERE:
County Kerry
BEST TIME TO GO:
April to September
DON'T MISS:
Great views of the Blasket Islands from Slea Head – now abandoned, they were occupied until the 1950s when the Irish Government evacuated the residents.
AMOUNT OF WALKING:
Lots (although those using wheelchairs should be prepared to enjoy the scenery without attempting countryside excursions like the climb up Brandon Mountain).
COST:
Low
YOU SHOULD KNOW:
Road signs in the Dingle Peninsula now give place names and directions in Irish only, so it's helpful to have a local map with which to follow a pre-planned route, explore as you go or correct wrong turns.

Around Killarney

WHERE:
County Kerry
BEST TIME TO GO:
March to October
DON'T MISS:
The Cool Wood Wildlife Park on the outskirts of Killarney, a 20-hectare (49-acre) complex consisting of a wildlife park with a wide variety of appealing animals and birds, plus a wooded wildlife sanctuary where red squirrels and golden eagles may be seen.
AMOUNT OF WALKING:
Moderate (transferring to a jaunting cart may require effort for anyone in a wheelchair).
COST:
Expensive (but the 'jaunt' through the Gap of Dunloe is worth it).
YOU SHOULD KNOW:
Killarney's tourist industry was already well established in the early 19th century, but a visit by Queen Victoria in 1861 really boosted the town's reputation as a desirable destination – and the place has never looked back, now having more hotel rooms than anywhere in the country bar Dublin.

This busy town is the major centre for tourism on Ireland's West Coast, lying as it does on the edge of stunningly beautiful Killarney National Park. Killarney is a visitor-orientated place, but it does contain some fine buildings. St Mary's Cathedral was designed by Augustus Pugin – said to be his favourite work, it has a rugged exterior and light-filled interior. Opposite the Cathedral is Deenagh Lodge Gate, the entrance to Knockreer House and Gardens, offering pastoral scenery and fine views of lakes and mountains.

The 'must do' experience hereabouts is a ride in one of Killarney's famous horse-drawn jaunting cars, driven by Blarney-powered jarvies who offer a talkative tour of the town. But a more ambitious (and rewarding) trip is taking a jaunting cart through the sensational Gap of Dunloe, beginning at Kate Kearney's Cottage and descending into the Black Valley. The narrow road crosses the Wishing Bridge and passes five lakes connected by the River Loe. Unforgettable!

Complete the day with a visit to Muckross, just south of Killarney on the edge of the National Park. Here, Muckross House is an excellent example of a Victorian country house in the Tudor-Revival style, with interiors illustrating the elegant lifestyle enjoyed by 19th-century Irish landowners – and the hard graft put in by servants to make it that way. Muckross Traditional Farms are three working farms (small, medium and large) that maintain the old traditions, providing insight into (and preserving knowledge of) Kerry's farming way of life, before electricity and tractors arrived to change it for ever.

Close by is Muckross Abbey, a Franciscan Friary founded in 1448. Although roofless, this impressive medieval structure is in a generally good state of preservation, with a large tower and near-perfect cloister surrounding a central courtyard that contains an ancient yew tree.

Muckross House

Killarney National Park

One of many jewels in Kerry's sparkling crown is Killarney National Park. Ireland's first, it was created when the Muckross Estate was donated to the state in 1932 and has since been expanded to 10,300 hectares (24,450 acres). It is a UNESCO World Biosphere Reserve for attributes that include mountains, the Lakes of Killarney, oak and yew woods, the most extensive native forest remaining in Ireland and a diversity of flora and fauna.

Put simply, this is a great place to spend a day (more if you can find the time). In addition to Muckross House, Gardens and Traditional Farms (worth a separate visit in their own right), the Park has a network of paths indicated by blue-and-white signs and many other attractions. The most impressive is undoubtedly Ross Castle beside Lough Leane. This massive stronghold was built in the 15th century, and was one of the last castles in Ireland to resist Cromwell's advance in the early 1650s.

From the castle it is possible to hire a boat and row to Innisfallen Island. Here may be found impressive remains of Innisfallen Abbey, founded in the early Christian period by St Finian the Leper. Energetic rowers can continue to the next island and cross to shore beneath O'Sullivan's Cascade. Longer lake cruises encompass all three lakes (Lough Leane, Muckross Lake and Upper Lake) and usually include a visit to Lord Brandon's Cottage, a former hunting lodge operating as a restaurant.

One beautiful spot is Dinis Cottage (now a tearoom) by the Old Weir Bridge and Meeting of the Waters, reached after a walk from the main road through oak woods adjoining Muckross Lake. Torc Waterfall is also accessed from the main road near Muckross. But wherever you go in the Park, one thing is guaranteed – the views are to die for.

A boat ride through Killarney National Park

WHERE:
County Kerry
BEST TIME TO GO:
March to October
DON'T MISS:
Old Kenmare Road and the track around Tomies Oakwood, for the breathtaking views over Lough Leane and Killarney.
AMOUNT OF WALKING:
Lots
COST:
Low
YOU SHOULD KNOW:
Ross Castle has been extensively restored – albeit in a sensitive manner that used entirely original materials and building techniques.

North Kerry

A tour of this sparsely populated but beautiful area begins where lots of people do live – Tralee, the county town. Founded by Normans, Tralee was burned in 1580 and remodelled in the early 19th century. It has become a tourist centre with indoor attractions like the Tralee Aqua Dome for those inevitable rainy days. For those of less athletic bent, Kerry County Museum can fulfil a similar role. It features archaeology and history, with an entertaining recreation of medieval Tralee and an Antarctica Exhibition built around the exploits of local man Tom Crean during Captain Scott's polar adventures. Before leaving, find Blennerville just outside the town and visit the large working windmill on the shore of Tralee Bay, a striking landmark.

From Tralee, drive north on the R551 past sandy Banna Strand and do the circular loop of Kerry Head from Ballyheige, before continuing along the scenic coast road to Ballyduff, where you will find Rattoo Tower – Kerry's only complete round tower. Continue to the cheerful resort village of Ballybunion and on up the Shannon Estuary to Ballylongford. Here, the ruins of Carrigafoyle Castle offer fantastic views for those willing to climb the long spiral staircase, and the remains of Lislaughtin Abbey are located within the town cemetery.

Go south to the market town of Listowel on the River Feale. At the heart of the town is a magnificent square, spreading beneath the towering presence of Listowel Castle, which is now open to the public. Here too, in a former Georgian residence next to the Castle, is Seanchaí, Kerry's Literary and Cultural Centre, which celebrates both the achievements of North Kerry's famous writers and the historical landscape and society that inspired them.

Leave town on the R555 before turning right at Duagh and returning to Tralee through the Glanaruddery Mountains, via Lyracrumpane.

The Lartigue Monorailway

WHERE:
County Kerry
BEST TIME TO GO:
April to September
DON'T MISS:
The extraordinary Lartigue Monorailway at Listowel that has been reconstructed to illustrate a unique piece of railway history – the original ran to Ballybunion between 1888 and 1924, using purpose-built engines and rolling stock riding on a single elevated rail.
AMOUNT OF WALKING:
Moderate (with wheelchair and pushchair access at Carrigafoyle Castle strictly limited).
COST:
Low
YOU SHOULD KNOW:
The Gaelic Athletic Association promotes and organizes the traditional sports of Gaelic football, hurling, handball and rounders. Of these, Gaelic football has been dominated by the Kerry team, by far the most successful in Irish history.

Cork City

The Republic of Ireland's second city is on the River Lee, with most of the city centre on a river island, and this major seaport has extensive quays and docks. A good way to get a feel for this vibrant city is by taking the open-top bus tour with a day-ticket that allows you to hop off and hop on as the mood dictates.

Architecturally interesting central streets are St Patrick's Street, Grand Parade and South Mall. Major buildings include St Finbarre's Cathedral, a triple-spired edifice in Gothic-Revival style. The Cathedral of St Mary and St Anne is also Victorian, but with a single square tower. Cork's oldest building is Red Abbey, a medieval tower. Cork Courthouse has a magnificent classic entrance on Washington Street and Blackrock Castle guards the river entrance to Cork – it now hosts the Cosmos at the Castle interactive exhibition exploring extreme life in space and on earth. Elizabeth Fort offers exceptional views.

The famous Church of St Anne Shandon allows you to play the bells and enjoy a stunning panorama from the viewing balcony. Why famous? Two sides of the tower are faced in white limestone and two in red sandstone, whilst the clock tower is known as 'The Four-faced Liar' because each clock face appears to show a different time.

Specific attractions include Cork Heritage Park (conservation activities in an old church), Fitzgerald Park (a great open space, with Cork Public Museum in a Georgian mansion), Crawford Municipal Art Gallery (an important collection of works by Irish artists), the Lifetime Lab (an unusual Visitor Centre created in an old Victorian waterworks building) and the rather odd combination of Cork City Gaol (the full audio-visual experience) and Radio Museum (does just what is says on the tin!).

WHERE:
County Cork
BEST TIME TO GO:
Any time
DON'T MISS
The English Covered Market in a building dating back to 1786, offering meat, fish, fruit and luxury foods.
AMOUNT OF WALKING:
Lots
COST:
Reasonable
YOU SHOULD KNOW:
Cork has the world's second-largest natural harbour, deferring only to that of Sydney in Australia.

The colourful quayside houses of Cork

Around North Cork

WHERE:
County Cork
BEST TIME TO GO:
March to October
DON'T MISS:
At Castletownroche – the
extraordinary Dinosaur Exhibition
featuring life-sized dinosaur models
created by leading sculptors (this
indoor attraction can be an
alternative to Annes Grove Gardens if
it's raining!).
AMOUNT OF WALKING:
Lots
COST:
Reasonable
YOU SHOULD KNOW:
Kanturk Castle was the only property
in the Republic of Ireland owned by
the English National Trust – who
handed it over to An Taisce (its Irish
equivalent) in 1998.

There's so much to see in Cork – Ireland's largest county – that several days are needed for thorough exploration. But the voyage of discovery can only start at one place – world-famous Blarney Castle north of Cork City. Those with a head for heights (whilst hanging upside-down) will doubtless kiss the Stone of Eloquence (Blarney Stone to you), but the place is also worth visiting for exquisite gardens and the Victorian mansion that is Blarney House.

Drive across country on the R579, turn left for Rylane and take back roads through the Boggeragh Mountains via Ballinagree to Carriganimmy. Here, go north to Millstreet Country Park, a large eco-park with Visitor Centre, gardens, walking trails, lake, wetlands, bogland and a deer farm. They even provide transport for those who want to see everything without walking.

From the Park, proceed to Millstreet and continue to the market town of Kanturk. Here, the main attraction is Kanturk Castle just south of town, built around 1610. It's an imposing rectangular building with massive towers at each corner that (although roofless) appears remarkably complete.

A short distance from Kanturk is Liscarroll, with two differing experiences to offer. An imposing 13th-century fortress towers over the village and dominates the surrounding countryside, whilst the Donkey Sanctuary has a Visitor Centre and hundreds of donkeys rescued from all over Ireland after hard lives pulling carts or carrying peat – it also has a fine view of Liscarroll Castle.

From Liscarroll take the R522 through to Doneraile. Doneraile Park is home to the Saint Leger family's former residence, Doneraile Court. The park itself is a classical 18th-century landscaped park in the style made popular by Capability Brown. There are groves of trees, water features and deer. At the next village, Castletownroche, Annes Grove Gardens is a supremely romantic place to end the North Cork day.

You need a supple body to kiss the Blarney Stone!

Around East Cork

From Cork City it's a short drive to Cobh, on Great Island in Cork Harbour. This former British naval base became a major port for shipping convicts to Australia and emigrants to America – records may be found in Cobh Museum and at the Heritage Centre. The dominant St Colman's Cathedral is a striking feature of the town.

From Cobh, follow the water through Ballymore and Belvelly to Carrigtwohill, where the main attractions are 16th-century Barryscourt Castle – with impressive halls, an Arts in Ireland Exhibition, orchard and herb garden – and Fota House. The latter not only offers elegant Regency interiors, but is also accompanied by a Wildlife Park with free-ranging animals plus an arboretum and gardens, with ornamental pond, fernery, walled garden and orangery.

At nearby Midleton make an essential salute to Irish culture – visit the Old Distillery on the banks of the Dungourney River, where the Jameson Experience recreates times past with delightful insight into the traditional process of making Irish whiskey. Bottoms up!

Go south on the R630 through Ballynacorra to Aghada and continue via Churchtown to the famous fishing village of Ballycotton, set on a rocky ledge overlooking Ballycotton Bay, with its wonderful beach that stretches away to Knockadoon Head. There is a lighthouse on Ballycotton Island and the village has a lifeboat station.

After unwinding at Ballycotton, follow the coast to Youghal on the Blackwater Estuary. This picturesque seaport has numerous historic monuments and buildings within ancient town walls and exploring the well-preserved centre is a delight. Look especially for the Clock Gate, the medieval St Mary's Collegiate Church, Tynte's Castle, almshouses, a medieval water gate and the lighthouse.

From Youghal, get a flavour of rural East Cork by returning to Cork City via Fermoy on the River Blackwater, in its scenic location beneath the Galtee Mountains.

St Colman's Cathedral and the harbour at Cobh

WHERE:
County Cork
BEST TIME TO GO:
Any time
DON'T MISS:
Find time to visit the Labbacallee Wedge Tomb, just to the northwest of Fermoy on the Glanworth road – it's one of the biggest prehistoric wedge tombs in Cork.
AMOUNT OF WALKING:
Moderate
COST:
Reasonable
YOU SHOULD KNOW:
The ill-fated Titanic's last port of call was Queenstown (now Cobh) – and amongst the most sought-after memorabilia are postcards of the ship posted by passengers from Queenstown.

535

Around West Cork

WHERE:
County Cork
BEST TIME TO GO:
Mid-April to October
DON'T MISS:
The Michael Collins Centre between
Timoleague and Clonakilty –
dedicated to the life, times and death
of this famous participant in the
struggle for Irish independence, who
was killed near here in 1922.
AMOUNT OF WALKING:
Moderate
COST:
Reasonable
YOU SHOULD KNOW:
In 1918 Whiddy Island in Bantry Bay
served as a seaplane base for the US
Navy. In 1979 the prominent oil
terminal was severely damaged
when the tanker *Betelgeuse*
exploded, killing 42 crew members.

West Cork seems to have a special character that's all its own, as an expedition to this wild and beautiful area will confirm. Start by driving from Cork City to Kinsale, which has quaint narrow streets and a reputation for entertaining visitors in style. Interesting buildings include the Courthouse, Desmond Castle (an urban tower housing the International Museum of Wine), James Fort overlooking the harbour and Charles Fort, one of Ireland's largest historical military installations.

Despite temptation, don't linger – the road is long (and winding). Proceed via the Old Head of Kinsale to Courtmacsherry, a charming one-street seashore village beneath wooded hills. The next stop is the remains of Abbeymahon Abbey on the road to Timoleague, where extensive ruins of Timoleague Abbey may be seen. Here, too, the splendid Castle Gardens may be visited (June to August only).

Nearby Clonakilty has an attractive centre and West Cork Railway Village – the four towns of Clonakilty, Kinsale, Bandon and Dunmanway in miniature as they were in the 1940s, connected by a model railway. If that's not your thing, try Inchydoney Blue Flag Beach!

Along the coast at the old-fashioned town of Skibbereen, find Liss Ard Gardens and an interesting Heritage Centre in the restored gasworks. From here, a loop diversion takes in the delightful harbour village of Castletownshend, Lough Hyne and Baltimore with its castle and famous beacon.

From Skibbereen, make for Bantry. Here, Bantry House and Gardens offer sensational views over Bantry Bay and there is also a fascinating French Armada Exhibition in the grounds, detailing the planned invasion of 1796.

The return run to Cork City through the atmospheric West Cork landscape takes you through Dunmanway (make a detour to ruined Ballynacarriga Castle if there's time to spare), Bandon (West Cork Heritage Centre) and Innishannon (two fine churches).

Desmond Castle now houses the International Museum of Wine.

Dolphin Day

Kilrush is the self-styled 'Dolphin Capital of Ireland', and the voyage of dolphin discovery begins at the Dolphin Information board in Market Square. From there, the marked Kilrush Dolphin Trail leads to a wonderful sculpture of a dolphin mother and calf in Millennium Park, before passing replica cetaceans floating in the Marina (are they dolphins, porpoises or whales?). There are also dolphin-watching trips on offer here. Just opposite is the Shannon Dolphin and Wildlife Centre that examines every aspect of these fascinating creatures (with plenty of 'dol-fun' activities for kids!). A walk along the picturesque coast road leads to Aylevaroo Point that not only offers fantastic sea views, but also every possibility of seeing dolphins at play.

The Dolphin and Wildlife Centre, Kilrush

At Carrigholt, south of Kilkee, it's possible to take an alternative boat trip to explore the rich marine environment at the mouth of the Shannon River. Although the spectacular cliffs are home to a fascinating variety of birdlife – including numerous seabirds, choughs, ravens and peregrine falcons – the real attraction is the resident group of bottlenose dolphins. They feast on fish shoals drawn into the river mouth by strong currents and breed successfully every year. Though never pursued, they often approach the boat of their own accord and the calves tend to be especially curious and playful. When conditions are right, a hydrophone makes it possible to hear dolphins chattering among themselves.

To round off the day, visit Lahinch Seaworld and Leisure Centre, situated on the seafront of this popular seaside village, overlooking the beach and Liscannor Bay up the coast from Kilkee. The Atlantic Aquarium features the marine life of Ireland's West Coast, including sharks, rays, giant conger eels, lobsters and flatfish. There's a swimming pool, sauna, Jacuzzi and steam room, together with a children's pool and play area.

WHERE:
County Clare
BEST TIME TO GO:
April to October
DON'T MISS:
The Vandeleur Walled Garden near Kilrush – once the forgotten and overgrown walled garden of Kilrush House, it has now been restored and features many unusual and tender plants along with water features and a maze.
AMOUNT OF WALKING:
Moderate
COST:
Expensive
YOU SHOULD KNOW:
An added bonus on the dolphin boat trip may be the sight of grey seals – and wild goats nimbly skipping around the clifftops.

Bere and Dursey Islands

WHERE:
County Cork
BEST TIME TO GO:
April to September
DON'T MISS:
A delightfully old-fashioned Irish classic – McCarthy's Bar in Castletownbere, fulfilling the traditional role of grocery store in one half and licensed bar in the other.
AMOUNT OF WALKING:
Lots (wheelchair access to the islands is possible, but there will be some limitation to further exploration).
COST:
Reasonable
YOU SHOULD KNOW:
Before The Great Famine of 1845-50, the population of Bere Island was over 2,000, but today it's around 200.

Even if you've done the Ring of Beara come back to see these islands, which get a big tick in the 'must see' column. But first there's terminology to sort out. Is it Bere or Bear Island, does the ferry leave from Castletownbere, Castletown Berehaven or Castletown Bearhaven and does it cross the natural harbour of Berehaven or Bearhaven? It depends which map you look at and is all very confusing. For the sake of argument, let's call them Bere Island, Castletownbere and Berehaven.

Berehaven is a large natural harbour protected from pounding Atlantic rollers by Bere Island. There are two ferry services from this important fishing port to the island, which could easily absorb the day in its own right – and may end up doing so. The islanders offer a warm welcome and there's much to see.

It's possible to take light vehicles over but the place isn't large – just 11 km (7 mi) by 5 km (3 mi) – so many prefer to explore on foot, perhaps following the way-marked Beara Way. Alternatively, bicycle hire gives access to a cycle route that guarantees exceptional views of the island, Bantry Bay and the Slieve Miskish Mountains. Bere has been fortified at various times and notable sights include the Martello Tower on Ardagh Hill and the Batteries (gun emplacements). There is also the Old Lighthouse and new Visitor Centre in the former school at Ballinakilla.

If you manage to tear yourself away from Bere, Dursey Island awaits, just down the road from Castletownbere at the tip of the Beara Peninsula. The attraction here is the cable-car (the only one in Ireland) that carries you across narrow Dursey Sound. This most westerly of Cork's inhabited islands has no facilities, but offers abandoned villages, solitude, wonderful views and a large seabird colony.

The cable-car carries you across Dursey Sound.

Sherkin and Cape Clear Islands

The enchanting Sherkin Island in Roaring Water Bay southwest of Skibbereen should not be missed. It's only 5 km (3 mi) long by 3 km (1.5 mi) wide, but this special place has become a haven for creative types with craftwork, painting and writing significant activities for islanders and incomers alike. Sherkin can be reached by ferry from Schull or Baltimore on the mainland.

It doesn't take long to explore Sherkin – there's an old medieval Franciscan Friary known as the Abbey just up from the pier, an old castle site, wonderful sandy beaches and sensational views from the top of the island. But the visitor will also find various arts and crafts exhibitions down narrow lanes and can enjoy a leisurely drink at various watering holes. Sherkin is – in modern parlance – an ideal place to 'chill'.

From Sherkin, it's but a short distance to Cape Clear Island with Ireland's most southerly point at the tip but unless you can find a helpful islander with a boat it's a case of back to Baltimore or Schull for a second ferry trip. Cape Clear Island has an altogether different feel from Sherkin. It shares natural attributes like romantic scenery, rugged hills and cliffs with its near neighbour, but Cape Clear is part of the Gaeltacht (Irish-speaking area) and in summer fills with people and activities associated with traditional language and culture (which make it pretty lively).

But there are activities and places of general appeal, too – like a famous manned bird observatory, an old lighthouse and signal tower, museum, ruined Dunanore Castle, St Kieran's Church and Churchyard, Lough Erral, two busy harbours, craft shops and galleries. You could stay for a week, but don't bother to try – all the available accommodation is booked months in advance.

WHERE:
County Cork
BEST TIME TO GO:
April to September
DON'T MISS:
The Sherkin Regatta in the third week of July – sea rowers and their followers crowd in to enjoy the races and the whole place takes on a decidedly festive atmosphere. As an alternative for the more cerebrally inclined, Cape Clear Island hosts its International Storytelling Festival over the first weekend in September.
AMOUNT OF WALKING:
Lots (wheelchair users should be aware that some specific attractions on the islands have awkward access).
COST:
Reasonable
YOU SHOULD KNOW:
Mainland road traffic regulations don't apply on these islands, so be prepared to encounter an extraordinary collection of ramshackle vehicles – and the rusting corpses of those that have died of old age.

Dunamore Castle on Cape Clear Island

Places

PICTURE CREDITS

Cover Photography:

Alamy/Chris Andrews/Oxford Picture Library; /David Ball; /Jason Baxter; /Adam Burton; /Dennis Cox; /Kasch/F1online digitale Bildagentur GmbH; /John McKenna; /nagelestock.com; /Chris Selby; /Skyscan Photolibrary; /Richard Wayman

Inside Photography:

Abbey Cwm Hir Hall 435

Alamy/AA World Travel Library 202, 459, 503; /Peter Adams Photography 42; /Malcolm Aird/Robert Estall Photo Agency 72; /Pierino Algieri/The Photolibrary Wales 432; /Chris Andrews/Oxford Picture Library 78; /David Angel 2 left, 399 inset 2, 403; /Jon Arnold Images Ltd. 181, 187, 197, 421; /Phil Arnold 47; /Bryan Attewell 265; /Steve Austin/Worldwide Picture Library 373; /Jonathan Ayres 65; /Bill Bachmann 369; /Krys Bailey 14; /Christopher Baines 149; /David Ball 114, 255; /Quentin Bargate 182; /Howard Barlow 426; /Peter Barritt 5 centre top, 10; /Dave Bartruff/Danita Delimont 509; /Jason Baxter 352; /BCS 344; /Andrew Bell 234; /Robert Bird 97; /BL Images Ltd. 70, 284, 290, 350, 430, 535; /Doug Blane (www.DougBlane.com) 195; /Jean Du Boisberranger/hemis.fr 64; /Michael Booth 319; /Mike Booth 170, 346, 348; /Mark Boulton 22, 34; /Charles Bowman/Robert Harding Picture Library Ltd. 8 inset 1, 16; /BristolK 51; /Kevin Britland 62; /Richard Bryant/Arcaid 115, 139, 226; /Adam Burton 60; /David Burton 178; /Gareth Byrne 501, 504; /Nick Cable 52; /David Cairns 345; /Piers Cavendish/Imagestate Media Partners Limited - Impact Photos 147; /David Chapman 66; /Adrian Chinery 93; /Carolyn Clarke 160; /Neale Clarke/Robert Harding Picture Library Ltd. 208; /Coaster 159; /colinspics 358; /Ashley Cooper 248; /Alan Copson/Jon Arnold Images Ltd. 81, 135; /Tony Cortazzi 438; /Roger Coulam 260, 266; /Rob Cousins/Robert Harding Picture Library Ltd. 39; /Dennis Cox 469 inset 2, 523; /David Crossland 35; /Derek Croucher 7 centre, 85, 427; /Bob Croxford/Atmosphere Picture Library 50; /Stuart Crump 3 right, 79; /Richard Cummins 518, 537; /CW Images 253, 412, 415, 422; /Martin Dalton 368; /Sigrid Dauth (Travel UK 2005) 223; /Deco 372; /Danita Delimont 469 inset 1, 481; /James Derrick 524; /Kathy deWitt 100; /Michael Diggin 531, 532; /Thomas Dobner 2008 40; /doughoughton 390; /Mark Dyball 289; /Patrick Eden 130; /Guy Edwardes Photography 36, 55, 58; /Rod Edwards 113, 183, 186, 189; /Andreas von Einsiedel/The National Trust Photolibrary 118; /Elmtree Images 132; /James Emmerson/Robert Harding Picture Library Ltd. 244, 256; /EPH/Isifa Image Service s.r.o. 467; /Robert Estall Photo Agency 424; /Greg Balfour Evans 82; /Lynne Evans 271; /Ron Evans 218; /Malcolm Fairman 107; /D.G. Farquhar 296; /Findlay 349; /Tracey Foster 378; /Joe Fox Murals 452; /Joe Fox 480; /Kevin Foy 141; /Ian Fraser 53; /Jason Friend 235; /Steve Frost 493; /Funky Switzerland - Paul Williams 268; /Derek Gale 263; /Alain Le Garsmeur 466; /Les Gibbon 275; /Gistimages 342; /John Glover 123, 239; /Jinny Goodman 124; /David Gowans 45, 257, 377, 384, 385, 387, 389, 394; /Tim Graham 158; /Jeff Greenberg 277, 283; /Greenshoots Communications 20; /Dmitry Guskov 291; /Nicola Hajduk 88; /Angela Hampton Picture Library 120; /Andrew Harris 71; /Tom Hanley 119; /David Hansford 49; /Mike Harrington 37, 185; /Brian Harris 180; /terry harris just greece photo library 150; /Ian Hay/London Aerial Photo Agency 77; /Andrew Hayes 54; /Mike Hayward/photoshropshire.com 219; /Huntley Hedworth 343; /Gavin Hellier/Robert Harding Picture Library Ltd. 67, 475; /John Henshall 5 centre, 83; /Chris Herring 6 centre, 9 inset 2, 179; /Christopher Hill Photographic/scenicireland.com 6 top, 443 inset 4, 446, 448, 450, 456, 473, 474, 478, 485, 486, 495, 499, 515, 520; /Marc Hill 28, 69; /Lynn Hilton 61; /Neil Holmes/Holmes Garden Photos 5 centre bottom, 86, 192, 205, 261, 312, 374, 477, 496; /Horizon International Images Limited 209; /Scott Hortop Travel 507; /Michael Howell 8, 117; /David Hughes/Robert Harding Picture Library Ltd. 236; /David Martyn Hughes 29, 198, 216, 225; /David Martyn Hughes/ImagesEurope 106; /ICP-Pano 27; /ICP-UK 206; /International Photobank 73, 325; /The Irish Image Collection/Design Pics Inc. 458, 476, 479, 482, 484, 488, 492, 516, 527, 528; /irishphoto.com 521; /John James 32; /Michael Jenner 462; /JLImages 491; /JMS 214; /Craig Joiner Photography 48; /David Jones 230; /Kasch/F1online digitale Bildagentur GmbH 284 inset 2, 286; /R. Kiedrowski/Arco Images GmbH 143; /David Kilpatrick 338; /Shirley Kilpatrick 298; /Mike Kipling Photography 270; /Warren Kovach 6 centre top, 9 inset 1, 148; /Kuttig - Travel 3 centre, 468, 505, 508; /Alistair Laming 171; /David Langan 383; /Peter Lewis 398 inset 3, 428; /LifeStyle 201; /Paul Lindsay 468 inset 2, 483; /Liquid Light 13, 402, 406, 414; /LondonPhotos/Homer Sykes 168; /Peter T Lovatt 418; /David Lyons 2 centre, 43, 274, 281, 365, 376, 382, 442 inset 1, 453, 455, 487, 490, 522, 539; /Tom Mackie 240; /Scott MacQuarrie

360, 362; /Manu 90; /Alan Mather 267; /Terry Mathews 6 centre bottom, 46; /Duncan Maxwell/Robert Harding Picture Library Ltd. 222, 425; /Ed Maynard 174; /Neil McAllister 471; /Andrew McConnell 526; /Andrew McConnell/Robert Harding Picture Library Ltd. 460; /Gareth McCormack 442 inset 3, 464, 502; /Tom McGahan 190; /John McKenna 5 bottom, 317, 321, 323, 355, 366; /Kirsty McLaren 445; /Ian Mears 380; /Stuart Melvin 44; /Michael Milton/ImageState 57; /Navin Mistry 333, 386; /Ball Miwako 146; /MOB Images 487; /Jeremy Moore/The Photolibrary Wales 419; /Geoffrey Morgan 336; /Jeff Morgan Tourism and Leisure 413; /Graham Morley 232; /John Morris 231; /Keith Morris 399 inset 1, 404; /Robert Morris 31, 200; /Ashley Morrison 463; /John Morrison 238; /Julie Mowbray 176; /Joanne Moyes 249; /James Murdoch/ Sylvia Cordaiy Photo Library Ltd 339; /Richard Murphy 506; /nagelestock.com 19, 94, 184, 285 inset 1, 306, 364, 511, 529; /Natrow Images 18; /Frank Naylor 304, 311; /Christopher Nicholson 15; /David Noble Photography 7 centre top, 23; /Kate Noble/David Noble Photography 177; /David Noton Photography 341, 468 inset 3, 530; /Alan Novelli 251, 252; /Bernard O'Kane 442 inset 2, 444, 465; /Richard Osbourne/Blue Pearl Photographic 326; /James Osmond 12, 228; /Peter Packer 212; /Colin Palmer Photography 56, 233, 334; /Paul Panayiotou 138; /Adam Parker 152; /Andrew Paterson 8 inset 2, 133; /Dave Pattison 327; /Doug Pearson/Jon Arnold Images Ltd. 512; /Lee Pengelly 41; /John Peter Photography 313, 370; /The Photolibrary Wales 408, 415; /Christopher Nicholson 15; /David Robertson 285 inset 2, 287, 293, 294, 310, 328, 331, 357, 381, 388, 391, 395; /Robography 330; /Mick Rock/Cephas Picture Library 26, 87; /Rough Guides 409, 440; /David Rowland 136; /Ruby 215; /Stephen Saks Photography 489, 498, 536; /samc 7 bottom, 24; /Clive Sawyer 112; /Howard Sayer 163; /T. Schaeffer/Arco Images 367; /Scottish Viewpoint 288, 301, 302, 324, 332, 359, 393; /Phil Seale 328; /Alex Segre 80, 142, 145, 161; /Chris Selby 468 inset 1, 534; /Shenval 284 inset 1, 392; /Michael Short/Robet Harding Picture Library Ltd. 510; /Skyscan Photolibrary 3, 109, 204, 224, 320, 398 inset 1, 401, 441; /Alan Slater 7 centre bottom, 84; /Allan Smith 299; /Helena Smith/Rough Guides 337; /Mal Smith 436; /Trevor Smithers ARPS 122; /Horst Sollinger/imagebroker 472; /South West Images Scotland 292, 295, 303, 305, 308, 354; /Richard Sowersby 129; /Jon Sparks 241, 246; /Paul Springett 154; /Robert Stainforth 134; /Steppenwolf 494, 533; /Billy Stock/The Photolibrary Wales 400; /Gary Stones 247; /Homer Sykes Archive 211; /Paul Tavener 193; /Alison Thompson 307; /Paul Thompson Images 245; /Peter Titmuss 77; /T.M.O.Travel 173; /TNT Magazine 140; /Charles Tomalin 196; /tommytucker 449; /travelib europe 11; /travelibUK 104, 199, 203, 203; /Trip 151; /Troy GB Images 258; /Jeff Tucker/The Photolibrary Wales 398, 411; /Nick Turner 30; /UK Alan King 280; /Frank Vetere 144; /Simon Vine 282; /Graeme Wallace/Worldwide Picture Library 397; /Victor Watts 21; /Richard Wayman 33; /way out west photography 63; /R. West/Skyscan Photolibrary 396; /Robin Weaver 128, 217; /Andrew Wheeler 169; /Nik Wheeler 101; /Paul White 375, PCL 116; /Cliff Whittem 315; /Rob Wilkinson 127; /Simon Wilkinson 156; /David Williams/The Photolibrary Wales 7 top, 405, 407; /Michael Willis 242; /willridge images 431; /D. Wolf 284 inset 3, 297; /John Woodworth 276; /World Pictures/Photoshot 102, 103 Blackgang Chine 131

Britain on View 220, 279, 316, 347; /Bill Batten/NTPL 165; /Daniel Bosworth/Kent Tourism Alliance 91, 98; /Joe Cornish 2; /Joe Cornish/NTPL 237; /Rod Edwards/Kent Tourism Alliance 96; /David Hunter 309; /Leicester Shire Promotions 213; /Nick Meers/NTPL 227; /Graeme Peacock 300; /Dave Porter 76, 210; /Craig Roberts 121; /Ian Shaw 167; /Tony West 243

Emma Beare 59

Ron Callow 110-111

Collections/Thomas Ennis 447

Corbis/Vassil Donev/epa 153; /Mark Fiennes/Arcaid 314; /Hoberman Collection 157; /Angelo Hornak 272; /Dave G. Houser 423; /The Irish Image Collection 461, 470, 514, 519, 538; /Barry Lewis 351; /Benedict Luxmoore/Arcaid 322; /Garry Penny/epa 6 bottom, 162; /Ellen

Rooney/Robert Harding World Imagery 164; /Skyscan 166; /Sandro Vannini 264, 318; /Adam Woolfitt 17, 278; /Bo Zaunders 105

Getty Images/Jamie McDonald 497

Historic Scotland Images 356

Photolibrary Wales/Chris Warren 410

Prehen House 454

Scenicireland.com/Chris Hill 500, 525

Gemma Seddon 89

Xscape Centre (www.xscape.co.uk) 353

544